Death and Salvation in Ancient Egypt

Death and Salvation in Ancient Egypt

by JAN ASSMANN

Translated from the German by
DAVID LORTON
Abridged and updated by the author

CORNELL UNIVERSITY PRESS

Ithaca and London

Library of Congress Cataloging-in-Publication Data

Assmann, Jan.
  [Tod und Jenseits im Alten Ägypten. English]
  Death and salvation in ancient Egypt / by Jan Assmann ; translated
from the German by David Lorton.
    p.   cm.
  Includes bibliographical references and indexes.
  ISBN-13: 978-0-8014-4241-4 (cloth : alk. paper)
  ISBN-10: 0-8014-4241-9 (cloth : alk. paper)
  1. Eschatology, Egyptian.   2. Egypt—Religion.   3. Death—Religious
aspects.   I. Title.
  BL2450.E8A8813   2005
  299´.3123—dc22

                                                        2005002783

Cornell University Press strives to use environmentally responsible
suppliers and materials to the fullest extent possible in the publishing
of its books. Such materials include vegetable-based, low-VOC inks and
acid-free papers that are recycled, totally chlorine-free, or partly
composed of nonwood fibers. For further information, visit our website
at www.cornellpress.cornell.edu.

Cloth printing   10   9   8   7   6   5   4   3   2   1

Permit me, permit me, my good engineer, to tell you something, to lay it upon your heart. The only healthy and noble and indeed, let me expressly point out, the only *religious* way in which to regard death is to perceive and feel it as a constituent part of life, as life's holy prerequisite, and *not* to separate it intellectually, to set it up in opposition to life, or, worse, to play it off against life in some disgusting fashion—for that is indeed the antithesis of a healthy, noble, reasonable, and religious view. . . . Death is to be honored as the cradle of life, the womb of renewal. Once separated from life, it becomes grotesque, a wraith—or even worse.

Thomas Mann, *The Magic Mountain*, translated by John E. Woods (New York, 1997), p. 197.

Contents

vii

Contents

Translator's Note

In this book, the following conventions have been followed in the citations from ancient texts:

Parentheses ( ) enclose words or brief explanations that have been added for clarity.

Square brackets [ ] enclose words that have been restored in a lacuna.

An ellipsis . . . indicates that a word or words in the original text have been omitted in the citation.

An ellipsis in square brackets [. . .] indicates the presence of a lacuna for which no restoration has been attempted.

A question mark in parentheses (?) indicates that the translation of a word or phrase is uncertain.

English-speaking Egyptologists have no single set of conventions for the rendering of ancient Egyptian and modern Arabic personal and place names. Most of the names mentioned in this book occur in a standard reference work, John Baines and Jaromír Málek, *Atlas of Ancient Egypt* (New York, 1980), and the renderings here follow those in that volume. The principal exception is the omission of the typographical sign for *ayin*; this consonant does not exist in English, and it was felt that its inclusion would serve only as a distraction to the reader.

In this volume, biblical passages are cited from the New Revised Standard Version.

D.L.

Death and Salvation in Ancient Egypt

Death and Culture

The thesis that underlies this book can be reduced to an extremely simple formula: death is the origin and the center of culture. My aim is to illustrate this thesis employing ancient Egyptian culture as my example. When it comes to the importance of death, this culture is admittedly an extreme example. But this has largely to do with the fact that we view ancient Egypt from the standpoint of a culture that is equally extreme, but in the opposite direction. From the point of view of comparative anthropology, it is we, not the ancient Egyptians, who are the exception. Few cultures in this world exclude death and the dead from their reality as radically as we do. Living with the dead and with death is one of the most normal manifestations of human culture, and it presumably lies at the heart of the stuff of human existence.

In this book, I thus pursue three matters of concern. One, and this is the most important, is to supply an introduction to the conceptual world of ancient Egyptian mortuary religion, to which the unusually large number of preserved texts afford us a privileged entrée. In ancient Egypt, mortuary religion was not simply one area of cultural praxis among others, such as the cult of the gods, economy, law, politics, literature, and so forth. Rather, in this case, we are dealing with a center of cultural consciousness, one that radiated out into many—we might almost say, into all—other areas of ancient Egyptian culture. A comprehensive treatment of the theme of death can thus constitute an introduction to the essence of all of ancient Egyptian culture. And this is indeed the second matter of concern that I associate with my intention here. I want to reach beyond the world of tombs, funerary rituals, and funerary texts and into other areas of Egyptian thought, action, and conduct, such as ethics, historical consciousness, cosmology, conceptions of the divine, and so forth and inquire to what extent these areas were stamped by the typically Egyptian preoccupation with the theme of death.

This task leads to the third area of concern: the question of the extent to which ancient Egypt offers us insights into the relationship between death and culture. My interest here lies not in ancient Egypt for its own sake, but rather in what we can learn about the essence of culture more generally through the study of this extremely early, long lived, and richly documented culture, one linked to our own through various avenues of transmission. I feel that one—and not the least important—task of Egyptology is to contribute to general cultural theory. I thus pose, in the sense of a working hypothesis, the question of whether and in what sense death and the way a culture articulates it, treats it, and copes with it might perhaps not constitute the center of the consciousness of that culture and thus of culture generally speaking. In what follows, I intend further to substantiate this third area of concern.

1. Death as Culture Generator

Culture, it is said, is man's second nature, which he needs because his first nature insufficiently provides him with the competencies and instincts he requires to survive as a living being. This negative anthropology, which defines man, along with other living beings, as defective, needing to compensate for his natural defect through cultural achievements, goes back to classical antiquity, for instance, Plato's *Protagoras*; in the eighteenth century of our own era, it was represented especially by Herder, was taken up in the nineteenth by Nietzsche, and then in the twentieth constituted the fundamental principle of various thinkers and researchers, such as Martin Heidegger, Helmuth Plessner, and Arnold Gehlen. Anyone who defines man as defective understands the function of culture as a project of supplementary and compensatory amendment. Man lacks the instinctive, assured reactions of animals; instead, he has the freedom to invent himself through culture. Thus, from necessity springs virtue, and from lack comes advantage. In place of the integration into the order of nature that he lacks, man attains a freedom that is withheld from other living beings. Instead of the optimal environmental adaptation that plants and animals enjoy, he has the freedom to shape the world and himself.

In some ancient Near Eastern myths, we encounter another picture of man. Here, too, it is a matter of knowledge and freedom. They are not, however, compensation for a lack; rather, they represent a human surplus that stems from the world of the gods and alienates man from the world of living beings. Here, man is seen not as the being capable of too little, but rather the one who knows too much.

At the center of this surplus, divine, alienating, and thus problematic knowledge stands death. Death and the necessity of dying is the common heritage of all earthly beings, shared by man with animals and plants. But animals and plants know nothing of this destiny. They make no advance provisions, they know no mortuary cult. They live for the day, they react only to actual stimuli and dangers, and they do not trouble themselves with overarching intellectual cares. This is the ideal amount of knowledge for beings that must make do with a limited lifetime. The immortal gods, however, need much more, they must know everything. Indeed, they must not die. Thus, they know the great intellectual correlations, which are summarized in the biblical myth as "the knowledge of good and evil," as well as cosmic correlations, which are summarized in the Babylonian myth as "the secrets of sky and earth."

The Babylonian myth is a story about Adapa, the son of Ea, god of wisdom.[1] Ea could bequeath wisdom, but not immortality, to his son. One day, the south wind snatched the net from Adapa while he was fishing. Adapa cursed the south wind, and since he possessed divine knowledge, his curse was so mighty that it broke the wings of the wind god. The situation was obviously intolerable: a mortal being possessed the knowledge of the gods but was no god. Adapa was summoned before the throne of Anu, king of the gods. On the way, Ea advised him not to touch any nourishment that the gods offered him, for it could be the food of death. Adapa thus refused the food that was offered to him. But in truth, it was the nourishment of life, for the gods wished to end the intolerable situation by making Adapa into a god. And so, for all time, there remained this precarious relationship between knowledge and death. It must be noted that in this myth, it is not the case that Adapa knew about his own mortality and could not live with this knowledge, but rather that he had the knowledge of the gods, which was not fitting for a man.

It is another Babylonian myth, the famous Epic of Gilgamesh,[2] that centers on knowledge of the necessity of death and the unbearable nature of this knowledge. Gilgamesh, king of Uruk, acquired this surplus knowledge that throws man off course and out of balance because he loved his friend Enkidu too much. He thus reacted to his death too intensely, with the result that the natural boundaries of his knowledge gave way in the

3

face of this truly traumatic experience, and he became conscious of his own mortality. The story goes on to depict the path of learning and suffering he had to travel to overcome this shock and cope with this knowledge.

> Gilgamesh for Enkidu, his friend,
> Weeps bitterly and roams over the desert.
> "When I die, shall I not be like unto Enkidu?
> Sorrow has entered my heart.
> I am afraid of death and roam over the desert.[3]

His fear in the face of death and his search for immortality finally lead Gilgamesh to the mountain range at the edge of the world, where the sun rises and sets. There he meets Siduri, the divine barmaid. He tells her his troubles and pleads, "May I not see death, which I dread."

Siduri then sings him a song like those sung by Egyptian harpers at banquets and by the Preacher in the biblical book of Ecclesiastes:

> Gilgamesh, whither runnest thou?
> The life which thou seekest thou wilt not find;
> (For) when the gods created mankind,
> They allotted death to mankind,
> (But) life they retained in their keeping.
>
> Thou, O Gilgamesh, let thy belly be full;
> Day and night be thou merry;
> Make every day (a day of) rejoicing.
> Day and night do thou dance and play.
>
> Let thy raiment be clean,
> Thy head be washed, (and) thyself be bathed in water.
> Cherish the little one holding thy hand,
> (And) let thy wife rejoice in thy bosom!
> This is the lot of [mankind . . .].[4]

Here, Siduri acts as spokesperson for a point of view that was widespread throughout the ancient world, one that closely linked death and merriment. In the Bible, we hear these notes in the book of Ecclesiastes,[5] as we do also in the harpers' songs from Egypt:

> Gladden your heart, let your heart forget!
> it is good for you to follow your heart as long as you exist.
>
> Put myrrh on your head,
> clothe yourself in white linen,
> anoint yourself with genuine oil of the divine cult,
> increase your happiness, let your heart not weary of it!

Follow your heart in the company of your beauty,
do your things on earth, do not upset your heart,
until that day of mourning comes to you.
The "weary of heart" does not hear their cries,
and their mourning does not bring the heart of a man back from the
netherworld.[6]

These are songs that were sung in Egypt during festive banquets. Nor was
the goddess Siduri a barmaid by chance. In the Jewish religion, the book
of Ecclesiastes is read during the Feast of Tabernacles, which furnishes a
similarly festive framework in which the convivial drinking of wine plays
a role.[7] Wine, woman, and song are means of diverting man from care
about death and restoring his inner balance. The advice and the admo-
nition of these festive songs aim at forgetting. Man's surplus knowledge
does him no good. He must find his happiness in what is granted him,
not in what is forever withheld from him. Gilgamesh is unable to accept
this advice to resign himself to his fate, and eventually, he finds Utnapishtim, the Mesopotamian Noah, the only man who survived the Flood, and
not only that, who was also accepted into the circle of the immortals. From
Utnapishtim, Gilgamesh receives a rejuvenating plant, which is stolen
from him by a serpent on his journey home. Thus, even here, there
remained the human dilemma of knowing too much and living too
briefly.

The biblical myth of the Fall has Adam and Eve eat from the tree of
knowledge, thereby becoming knowing, "like God." Here, just as in the
Adapa myth, the surplus knowledge not provided by nature is expressly
designated as divine knowledge. It was withheld from man, like all other
mortal beings for good reason: it was not, as Nietzsche put it, "knowledge
useful to life." It did little good for man to become "like God." They would
then have had to eat of the tree of life, whose fruit would have provided
them with immortality, which belonged necessarily to this knowledge, and
which stood not far from the tree of knowledge. They did not, however,
have the opportunity. Before they could eat of this tree, they were
expelled from Paradise.

All these myths deal with the theme of too much knowledge and too
little life. In the Adapa myth, it is a matter of cosmic-magical knowledge,
the secrets of sky and earth, while in the Bible, it is one of practical dis-
cernment, the knowledge of good and evil, that is, of the useful and the
harmful, of the beneficial and the injurious;[8] but in both cases, it is a
knowledge that makes the knower godlike, *sicut Deus*. But over and above
this, be it the secrets of sky and earth or of good and evil, man, and only
man, knows that he must die.[9] The gods do not know it, for they are
immortal, and animals do not know it, for they have not eaten from the

tree of knowledge. But this knowledge threatens to drive man off course. This knowledge creates an intolerable situation. He who has it should not have to die. He who is mortal should not have this knowledge, for it is the knowledge of the gods. Man thus stands between god and animal. He is a defective being only in relation to the gods, but he is a superior being in relation to animals.

The fifteenth-century Florentine philosopher Marsilio Ficino characterized man in precisely this sense, as an intermediate, hybrid being. "Blissful, heavenly ones," he exclaimed in a letter, "who know everything in the light! Securely protected beasts, who live in darkness and have no understanding of the future! Unhappy, frightened men, who wander in between, as it were, in a fog!"[10] Too much knowledge and too little life results in an imbalance that, like the "noise" of a clock, keeps man in inner turmoil. Ficino calls this condition a disquietude of the soul, *inquietudo animi*. In doing so, he takes up a concept of Saint Augustine, who spoke in his *Confessions* of a disquietude of the heart, *inquietudo cordis*: *inquietum est cor nostrum, donec requiescat in te,* "disquiet is our heart, until it rests in thee."[11] This disquietude distinguishes man; animals do not feel it. This disquietude, thought Augustine, comes from God, who created man in his image, with the result that he can find no satisfaction in what is earthly, while Ficino astutely related it to death and explained it as a longing for immortality.

This is the disquietude that drove Gilgamesh along, with the result that he rejected the well-intentioned advice of Siduri, the divine barmaid, to enjoy the brief lifetime allotted to him as best he could, and instead pressed on to the end of the world in search of immortality. Yet the word "immortality" is absent from the Sumerian and Babylonian text; we read only "life." Once Gilgamesh became aware that his earthly existence was subject to the decay of death, it was no longer "life" to him; it could seem like "life" only to one whose eyes were veiled, or who could accept the advice of Siduri. Anyone who could tear away this veil either was seized by despair or set off on a tireless search for life. This search is the theme of the Epic of Gilgamesh.

These ancient Near Eastern myths characterize the problem of human existence as a "too much" rather than a "too little." This "too much," this surplus causes man to fall outside the restrictions that characterize the animal world. But both traditions, that of a lack and that of a surplus, agree that man is characterized by a disquietude that leads him to strive for something better or higher. In both cases, it is a matter of compensating for a defect. But this defect is explained in fundamentally different ways. In the one case, it has to do with a lack of adaptation to the environment and keenness of instinct, while in the other, it has to do with a lack of immortality or life. In each case, man, who has fallen outside the order of nature either through his lack of a set of instincts or through a superabundance of knowledge, must create an artificial world in which he can live—and that is culture.

Of course, both anthropological traditions are correct, and they are in no way mutually exclusive. The one sheds light on the essence of culture from the standpoint of the problem of survival, and the other from the standpoint of the problem of death. According to the latter tradition, culture arises from knowledge of death and mortality. Culture represents the attempt to create a space and a time in which man can think his way out of the bounded horizon of his life and project the features of his action, experience, and plans out into broader horizons and dimensions of fulfillment, in which the needs of his mind can find gratification, and the painful, even unbearable consciousness of existential boundedness and fragmentation can find rest. Man cannot live without fantasies of immortality, or at least of a certain continuation beyond the all too narrow horizon of our existence on earth: such fantasies create a horizon rearranged by illusions, in which human activity can be experienced as meaningful, that "Hamlet doctrine," as Nietzsche characterized it in the seventh chapter of his *Birth of Tragedy*:

> Understanding kills action, for in order to act we require the veil of illusion; such is Hamlet's doctrine, not to be confused with the cheap wisdom of John-a-Dreams, who through too much reflection, as it were a surplus of possibilities, never arrives at action. What, both in the case of Hamlet and of Dionysiac man, overbalances any motive leading to action, is not reflection but understanding, the apprehension of truth and its terror.[12]

To this veiled condition belongs one of the culture-creating gifts that Prometheus granted to humankind:

> *Prometheus*
> I caused mortals to cease foreseeing doom.
> *Chorus*
> What cure did you provide them with against that sickness?
> *Prometheus*
> I placed in them blind hopes.[13]

The "doom" whose precise anticipation was beneficently veiled by Prometheus was man's future suffering, and especially the means and the hour of his death. Only when veiled in this manner is knowledge about death bearable. These "blind hopes" are the opposite of the despair resulting from Cassandra's visions. Blind hope creates the "veil of illusion" indispensable to the human condition. In his early Ptolemaic Period tomb, which he constructed and decorated in Hellenizing style, Petosiris, who was friendly toward the Greeks, endorsed this pearl of Greek wisdom:

God's art is to cause the heart to forget to recognize the day.[14]

One Egyptian text, though, counts knowledge of the necessity of death as one of the great beneficent deeds of the creator god:

I caused that their hearts cease forgetting the West,
so that offerings would be made to the gods of the nomes.
That is one of the deeds.[15]

Here, it is the gods who profit from this knowledge. Without recollection of the "West," that is, of tombs and death as the final goal of life, men would bring them no offerings. The thought of death leads them to think of the gods, from whom they expect help and salvation—not from death, but, as will be shown in the following chapters, from the realm of death.

The Ninetieth Psalm prays, "Teach us to count our days, that we may gain a wise heart."[16] "To count our days" means to hold each day dear, knowing that life is finite. The days derive their value from their end; since we must die, we "count" our days. Death gives life its value, and wisdom consists in being aware of this value.

My purpose here is to consider this ancient Near Eastern tradition of thought, which was much older and more widespread than the Greek and the Enlightenment myth of man as a defective being, and to make it productive for cultural theory. Culture does not seem to be a compensation for man's lack of instincts and environmental adaptability, but rather as a space in which man, with his surplus of knowledge and his troubled spirit, can devise himself, exceed himself, and for a certain time, at least, bring himself into equilibrium.

Culture both opens up and delimits a horizon of meaning beyond the boundaries of our earthly life. This horizon has an individual and a cultural aspect. The individual aspect consists in a sort of sense of immortality, without which man would fall into deep depression. The cultural aspect consists in the construction of a cultural memory that stamps our individual recollections, experiences, and expectations, integrating them into horizons and perspectives that embrace not only millennia but also possibly next-worldly spheres. Even someone who does not believe in the afterlife and immortality involves himself in activities whose consequences outlast him and whose planning exceeds the horizon of his existence, both in the social dimension of synchronic integration and in the temporal dimension of diachronic embedding. Death—or better, knowledge of our mortality—is a first-rate culture generator. An important part of our activity, and especially the culturally relevant part—art, science, philosophy, and charity—arises from the drive for immortality, the drive to transcend the boundaries of the "I" and its lifetime.[17] George Steiner, the noted literary scholar and cultural critic, wrote to this effect in his *In Bluebeard's Castle: Some Notes Towards the Redefinition of Culture*:

> What is central to a true culture is a certain view of the relations between time and individual death. The thrust of will which engenders art and disinterested thought, the engaged response which alone can ensure its transmission to other human beings, to the future, are rooted in a gamble on transcendence. The writer or thinker means the words of the poem, the sinews of the argument, the personae of the drama, to outlast his own life, to take on the mystery of autonomous presence and presentness. The sculptor commits to the stone the vitalities against and across time which will soon drain from his own living hand. Art and mind address those who are not yet, even at the risk, deliberately incurred, of being unnoticed by the living.[18]

Here, Steiner is considering only a narrow elite: artists, writers, and thinkers. This "search" is an elite undertaking, a borderline situation in the realm of human possibilities. Culture—and there can be no doubt about this fact—has first of all a normative, demanding aspect that aims far beyond everyday needs and has driven men on, not forever, but for a determined period of five or perhaps ten thousand years in the past, to ever new heights of cultural achievement. This aspect—what Steiner calls the "center" of a "true culture"—has something to do with death. My thesis is that behind this Faustian searching and restlessness stands not a lack of natural endowments, but rather a surplus of self-awareness and knowledge that can no longer be brought into balance with nature. This restlessness, this disquietude, is felt by all, but only few succeed in either finding a wisdom that brings peace or in advancing to conscious projects of self transcendence and thus into that "center" of "true culture" of which Steiner wrote. Death makes all equal, but in the matter of attitude toward death, there unfolds a huge spectrum of cultural and individual differences.

2. *Principal Distinctions in the Relationship between Death and Culture*

The following distinctions in the relationship between culture and death might serve to locate ancient Egyptian culture within the spectrum just noted.

a) This Life and the Next Life as Lifetime-Encompassing Horizons of Accomplishment

In constructing a horizon of accomplishment that encompasses a lifetime, there are two possibilities. One is located in another world, where the dead go to prolong their existence. The other denies the existence of such a world, which in any case is conceived of as a realm of shadows in which the dead do not continue to live, but rather, spend their death, and which in no way functions as a horizon of meaning or fulfillment in this life, for no comfort or orientation emerges from this concept. In my opinion, this is an important distinction. All "afterlifes" are not created equal. The distinction lies in whether I conceive of the "afterlife" as a realm in which the dead are dead, that is, in which they lead an existence characterized by the absence of what any culture whatsoever would recognize as "life," or whether I think of it as a realm of everlasting life, in which one is saved, delivered, and possibly even raised up from the condition of death. The Babylonian netherworld, the biblical Sheol, the Greek Hades, and the Roman Orcus are "realms of the dead" in which the dead are nothing other than dead. The Egyptians, too, were acquainted with the concept of such a realm of the dead, which they depicted in rather somber hues. But they also knew a third, an Elysium, in which a person was saved from death. Societies that do not recognize such an Elysian afterlife seek a horizon of accomplishment in history, in the succession of generations, in a posterity in which the horizon of meaning of this-worldly life is prolonged. Christianity and the Gnostic movements represent the first type; in them, life on earth and posterity count for little, while the soul, immortality, and the afterlife are valorized. Ancient Israel, Mesopotamia, and Greece are examples of the second type; in them, the realm of the dead was nothing more than a shadowy realm far from meaning and from the divine, and prolonged existence was accomplished either by means of the succession of generations, by children and grandchildren (Mesopotamia and Israel) or by means of the recollection of posterity (Greece).[19] Egypt, of course, belongs unconditionally to the first type, to the cultures with positive concepts of the afterlife, in which next-worldly existence is an intensified one, far from death and near to the divine. Yet it is also striking that the Egyptians apparently staked all on remaining present here, on earth, in the recollection of posterity. Why else would they have built such lavish tombs? So far as we can tell, the Egyptians combined both possibilities. And not only that, but both possibilities were culturally elaborated in a way that was entirely unique. We find not only a strong belief in immortality and an afterlife, but also an equally elaborated concept of, and hope in, a continued existence through the succession of children and grandchildren, and above all, in the recollection of posterity.

Already in the seventeenth century, Spinoza drew this very distinction between Egypt and Israel. He showed not only that the ancient Israelites and the Mosaic writings lacked the idea of immortality but also that they set something else in its stead: the concept that a man lived on in his children and grandchildren. Debts that remained unsettled in this lifetime were discharged in history, in the succession of generations. Spinoza was thus the first to note the diametric opposition between Egypt and Israel in regard to this question. As is well known, Simone Weil has also praised Egypt for its belief in immortality and criticized Israel for the materialism of its solution, which set history in the place of the afterlife and immortality.[20] In fact, not only was there no meaningful afterlife in the Old Testament world, but also no sacred space of duration in this world, such as the Egyptians achieved by means of stony monumentality. The divine and death were kept as far apart as possible, man was close to the divine only during his earthly existence, and all the accounts of righteousness had to be settled in this life; there could be no talk of immortality, yet the life of the individual was surrounded by a mighty horizon of recollection and by a promise that extended not into the afterlife, but into the chain of generations. In this chain lay the *historia sacra* (sacred history) in whose horizon the drive for immortality satisfied its need for meaning—an idea that was entirely foreign to Egypt. With this brilliant discovery, Spinoza also furnished a splendid proof for our thesis that without the basic assumption of continued life in some form, human life cannot succeed, and that the cultural solutions to this problem can be extremely diverse.

b) Death Pieced-on to Life and Life Permeated by Death

Closely related to the distinction between this-worldly and next-worldly oriented forms of self transcendence is the distinction between two concepts of the relationship between death and life. One sees death as something other than life. Life and death are mutually exclusive: where there is life, death has no business, and vice versa. Death seems to be something unrelated that is added on to life. This theory has traditionally been connected primarily with the name of Epicurus, whose aim was to ban the cares of Gilgamesh from the human realm. Man's thoughts are not to be concerned with death, for so long as he lives, death is not there, and when death is there, man is no longer alive; life and death have nothing to do with one another. Life displaces death, just as death annihilates life. Epicurus' teachings seem extreme in their rationalistic formulations, but behind them stands a widespread, basic attitude that to a large extent characterizes our own time and its relationship with death, and which Martin Heidegger generalized, in the well-known chapter on death in his *Being and Time*, as "everyday Being-towards-death." In this connection, Heidegger also makes use of the concept of "piecing-on." Dasein, which unfolds into time, always possesses a "not yet," which is not "continually pieced-on," but rather always already constitutively belongs to it. "Any Dasein always exists in just such a manner that its 'not-yet' *belongs* to it."[21] This belongingness of the not-yet to Dasein is postulated by Heidegger also for death. It is not "pieced-on" to Dasein, but rather "always already" belongs to it.

What philosophical reflection portrays as the opposition of "everyday" and "genuine" forms of a "Being-towards-death" is conceived of by the student of culture as different cultural constructions of death. The concept that Heidegger classifies as "everyday" would presumably have seemed rather foreign to the ancient Egyptians and to many other cultures and epochs. The other, opposite concept, which sees life and death as closely related to and interwoven with one another, has been at least as widespread in the history of civilization. As the German hymn has it, "in the midst of life, we are surrounded by death." Life is based on the knowledge of our finitude, and at its end, death acts in our life in a way that gives it meaning and direction, but also in a way that destroys meaning, dissolving it and making us sick. This is the stance of Gilgamesh, who set out in search of "life" because life seemed to him like an illness, like a trek toward death, precisely in the sense of Kierkegaard and Heidegger, who rediscovered this relationship to death in modern times and elaborated on it in their writings.

In light of this distinction, we must, of course, assign the ancient Egyptians to the second type. They did not repress death, but rather devoted a massive amount of care and attention to it. In particular, death played a role in their lives in two ways: first, as a source of motivation for a host of cultural efforts, and second, as an always present possibility of diminishing life, especially through the dissolution of social relationships. The Egyptians did not define life and death as we do. For them, life and death were quantifiable entities: one could be more or less alive and also more or less dead or subject to death. Death was always viewed as something at the end of life, and also as a subjection to death that permeated life, that was always present to the Egyptians and spurred them to investments that were supposed to increase the share of life and diminish that of death. Above all, these investments included the preparation of a tomb and the indissoluble integration of the self into the constellations of society. Even the tomb was a medium of such "constellative embedding," one intended to secure for the individual, for all time, a place in the social, geographical, and cultural space of the group. The tomb served life, not death, as we already read in the earliest Egyptian wisdom text, the Instruction of Djedefhor:

> Build your house for your son;
> then a place will be created for you, in which you will be.
> Richly equip your house in the realm of the dead,
> and effectively outfit your place in the West.
> Heed: death counts little for us;
> heed: life counts much for us.
> The house of death counts for life.[22]

This maxim was remembered in Egypt for millennia, and it was still cited in texts of the Roman imperial era.[23] But in all the rich tradition of Egyptian wisdom literature, it is the Instruction of Any, from the Ramesside Period, that is unique in treating this theme in detail and in words of its own:

> Do not leave your house
> without knowing where you can rest.[24]
> Let one know the place you have chosen,
> so that you will be remembered for as long as you are known.
> Place it before you as the path to take,
> while you are mentioned in what you have found.
> Furnish your place in the valley of the dead
> and the "netherworld" (i.e., sarcophagus chamber) that will shelter your
>   corpse.
> Place this before you as one of your concerns.
> Also, as concerns great old age:
> may you rest in your tomb chamber.
> No reproach befalls the one who acts thus;
> it is well with the one who is thus prepared.
> When your envoy (of death) comes to fetch you,
> Let him find you ready.
> Truly, he waits not for you.
> Say, "Here comes one who has prepared himself for you,"
> and do not say, "I am too young for you to take me."
> Indeed, you do not know your death!
> Death comes, it steals the child from the arms of its mother,
> just like the one who has reached old age.[25]

The timely construction of a tomb was a goal in life, one that afforded the certainty of not slipping, at death, out of the context of the life of the land as a social, geographical, and cultural space, but rather of having a place where one remained present after death, integrated into the community of the living.

For the Egyptians, integration into society was the most important and the most effective way of enhancing their life and denying their subjection to death. They had a saying, "One lives, if another guides him"[26]: one thus "lived," in the full sense of the word, when another gave him guidance. As the Egyptians conceived it, there was a crucial aspect of human personality that did not develop from the inside to the outside, but in the opposite direction, from the outside to the inside. They made the essential distinction within the totality of a person not that between the body and the soul, but that between the individual self and the social self (see especially chapter 4 of this volume). The "souls" of this individual, or bodily, self included the *ba* and the shadow, while the social self was comprised of the *ka* and the name. The intactness and the vividness of the social self was as important to life as the intactness and health of the individual self. At birth, life was just a possibility, one that was actualized only when the social self was developed through a process of socialization. "Life" was thus more a matter of culture than of nature. It was in this respect that the Egyptians viewed the possibility of prolonging life beyond its biological limitations through cultural effort.

c) World of the Living, World of the Dead: Border Traffic and Exclusion

Closely related to the opposition between cultures that repress death and cultures that care about death is the distinction in the forms in which cultures conceive of the relationships between the world of the living and that of the dead. A glance at the history of cultures shows that our own has taken an extreme stance on this question. This stance is connected with the expatriation of the dead, as Jean Baudrillard has impressively described in *L'Échange symbolique et la mort*.[27] Our society has developed a culture in which the realm of the dead is excluded, denied, suppressed, and unacknowledged. Like most of the traditional societies of our own time, earlier periods were convinced that there was something like a "realm of the dead," and that it was important for the living to establish a culturally formed and ordered relationship with it. The concept of a realm of the dead as an opposite to the realm of the living is the most general and widespread concept, quite independently of the question of whether this realm of the dead is conceived of as a shadowy realm devoid of life and meaning, or whether as a sphere of enhanced life, as a hell, a purgatory, or a paradise. There is probably no culture in the world that does not stand in some kind of relationship with its dead, and even in our own "enlightened" culture, such concepts still survive in countless ways, from photographs on the wall or desk to religious holidays like All Souls' Day or the secular Halloween, when children enact the irruption of the souls of the dead into the world of the living. In Japan, the souls of the dead are invited to return to this world for a day on August 15. Each family prepares itself to receive its dead and then accompanies them back to the cemetery.

In Mesopotamia, fear of revenants played an important role: the ghost of the dead (*etemmu*) would haunt this world if he had not been properly buried or had died a terrible death. Such fears are widespread; there are societies for which the "border traffic" between the world of the living and the world of the dead can never be entirely managed, and for which there are broad areas of "wilderness" that are closed to culture. In Egypt, such fears played a rather small role. In the Instruction of Any, one maxim is devoted to the *akh*, a word that we otherwise translate as "transfigured spirit," but which in this context unequivocally has the meaning "ghost," in the sense of the Mesopotamian *etemmu*.[28] A Late Egyptian story that is unfortunately preserved to us only fragmentarily tells of the appearance of such a ghost. But these are exceptions that only confirm the rule, late texts that point to Babylonian influence. In Egypt, the rule was that crossings between the realm of the living and the realm of the dead were subject to strict cultural control.

The distinction between two realms, a realm of the living and a realm of the dead, which in Egypt was also the realm of the gods, was radically challenged in the context of the Amarna Period, the religious revolution undertaken by King Amenophis IV/Akhenaten (1360–1340 B.C.E.). This occasion clarified this distinction for the entire structure of a religion. Akhenaten's revolution was the first example of the founding of a religion in the history of humankind. It displayed features of a radical enlightenment as well as of an exclusive monotheism. In the texts of this period, which profoundly altered Egyptian religion, though it was a brief episode of no more than twenty years in the entire history of Egypt, there is only one realm: that of the here and now, of the reality lit up by the sun god. There is no talk of the mythical, primeval time when the cosmos came into being, when the present-day world was produced after many changes related in the myths, or of a next world, where the dead go. This silence is so striking that some have understood it as a systematic exclusion. Akhenaten's monotheism was a radical doctrine of a single realm. Amarna religion abolished the afterlife. The dead continued to live, but they dwelled in their tomb, not in the netherworld; by day, they visited the temples of Amarna in an invisible or altered form, and by night, they returned to their tomb.[29] When Amarna religion failed and the traditional religion was restored, those aspects of it which Akhenaten had particularly persecuted and excluded were now placed center stage and elaborated on. Thus, it was at this time that the genre of "books of the netherworld," in which knowledge about the afterlife was systematically codified and handed down, experienced an enormous upswing. To the classic work known as the Amduat, which had been employed in the decoration of the funerary chambers of the royal tombs of Dynasty 18, there was now added a series of similar compositions depicting the next world in pictures and written descriptions: the Book of Gates, the Enigmatic Book, the Book of Caverns, the Book of the Earth, the Book of Nut, the Book of the Heavenly Cow, the Book of the Day, and the Book of the Night.[30] All these books are surrounded by an aura of strictest mystery, and thus secrecy: in the New Kingdom, they occur almost exclusively in royal tombs, which were located in hidden places in the Valley of the Kings, where no human foot was supposed to tread.

From these dramatic events, which wrought far-reaching changes in the Egyptian world in the course of less than fifty years, we see that there are connections between the "demystification of the world" and Akhenaten's doctrine of a single realm, connections familiar to us from the intellectual history of our own culture, and we see that death plays a decisive role in the genesis and formation of concepts regarding an "other world." With equal clarity, the Egyptian findings also show us that this "other world," which is connected with death, is bathed in the aura of mystery. Death generates mystery; it is the threshold to another world and also a veil that hides it. This aspect of death will be treated in chapter 9. With its radical denial of a next world, the Amarna Period robbed death of its mystery, and by way of a reaction, the notion of mystery moved into the center of Egyptian beliefs about death. Knowledge of this mystery was now the royal path to immortality, and the royal tombs became repositories of this knowledge that brought deliverance.

d) Images and Counterimages, Death and Counterworld

Were the Egyptians obsessed with death, did they have an aversion to life? Or did they, on the contrary, merely suppress death under a mass of cultural forms and symbols? In this regard, we can perhaps distinguish between two ideal cultural types: cultures that accept death and cultures that rebel against it.[31] Cultures that accept death tend to accord no special status to man among living beings, but rather to place him on the same level as everything alive and to view him as a part of nature, born of dust and returning to dust, sinking into nature's great cycle of life and death. Cultures that deny death, however, view man as a spiritual being and place him in sharp contrast to the rest of nature. Uniqueness, intellectuality, and immortality are related concepts that characterize such cultures' view of humankind. Like the two basic attitudes, the two types of culture—those that accept death and those that deny it—are ideal types that have not found pure expression in historical reality. In reality, all is mixed, for in any given culture, people differ according to era, social level, geography, and even the times they assign to religious and to profane concerns. With regard to this ideal distinction, I wish to propose three theses that can characterize the world of Egypt by way, as it were, of contrastive diagnosis.

My first thesis is that Egypt was one of the cultures of denial, one of the societies that do not accept death and thus, in their concept of man, draw a sharp boundary between the spirit, immortality, uniqueness, and the remainder of nature. But did they in fact do so? An objection immediately arises: What about the animal cults? As we know, the Egyptians mummified many kinds of animals in large quantities, and they evidently ascribed immortality to animals as well. Thus, they cannot have drawn so very sharp a distinction between animal and man. In response, it must be noted that it matters not so much whether they drew a distinction between man and animal, but rather that they drew it between the mortal and the immortal, between the perishable and the imperishable. For the Egyptians, the distinction was different from ours; for them, under certain circumstances, animals were part of the circle of the immortal, the spiritual, the imperishable. What is decisive is the fact that they made the distinction.

Another objection concerns the unique presence of death in Egyptian culture. Death must have continually preoccupied the Egyptians—with the construction of pyramids for kings and huge burial monuments for high officials, with the decoration and outfitting of these tombs, cenotaphs, and commemorative chapels, with the preparation of statues, stelae, offering tables, sarcophagi, wooden coffins, and Books of the Dead, with the procurement of mortuary offerings and the conducting of mortuary rituals—and we wonder how a society that so constantly and in so many ways made death the object of all possible actions supposedly did not accept death. Moreover, as a rule, a high-ranking Egyptian would spend many years of his life constructing and outfitting a monumental tomb. How can someone who did not accept death invest so much of his lifetime, not to mention his material resources, on death?

Here, we must be specific. The Egyptians certainly did not accept death, but they also did not repress it. It was on their minds in many ways, unlike us, who also do not accept it. In Egyptian culture, as in no other, we may observe what it means not to accept death and yet to place it at the center of every thought and deed, every plan and act, to make it, in every possible way, the theme of the culture they created. The Egyptians hated death and loved life. "As you hate death and love life . . .": with this formula, visitors to a tomb were enjoined to recite an offering formula on behalf of its owner. "Given that death humbles us, given that death exalts us," we read in the Instruction of Djedefhor, the oldest example of wisdom literature preserved to us, which goes on to say, as is typical, "the

17

house of death (i.e., the tomb) is for life."[32] The Egyptians hated death, and in a sense, they built their tombs as a countermeasure to it. In ancient Egypt, more so than in any other culture, we encounter death in many forms, in mummies, statues, reliefs, buildings, and texts; but these were not images of death, they were counterimages, articulations of its negation, not of its affirmation. This is my second thesis. If we wish to learn something about the experience of death in Egypt, we must turn these images inside out. They depict the deceased as he appeared in life: well dressed, bejeweled, in the bloom of youth, always accompanied by his wife and often also by his children, carrying out the duties of his office, worshiping the gods, and engaging in the leisurely pursuits of the well-born, such as fishing, fowling, and hunting, and receiving rich offerings. And the texts speak of his successful outcome in the Judgment of the Dead, his acceptance into the realm of the gods, his ability to transform himself and to return to earth in all sorts of forms, to visit his house, to stroll in his garden, to participate in religious festivals, and above all, to be close to the gods in the sky, the netherworld, and the temples on earth. These pictures and texts might tempt us to think that for the Egyptians, death was nothing other than a gentle transition into an even finer, more fulfilling, richer life. Perhaps it was, but not in and of itself. Rather, it was the distant goal of countless efforts, without which death would be an absolute opposition: isolation, termination, end, disappearance, darkness, filth, defectiveness, distance from the divine, decomposition, dismemberment, dissolution, in short, all that constitutes the opposite of those radiant images of a transfigured existence. The Egyptian experience of death was not, overall, much different from that elsewhere in the world, except for the astonishing, and in this respect probably unique, attitude that the Egyptians assumed toward this experience, an attitude based on trust in the power of counterimages, or rather in the power of speech, of representation, and of ritual acts, to be able to make these counterimages real and to create a counterworld through the medium of symbols.

The world of Egyptian mortuary religion was indeed a counterworld. But what was special, and perhaps unique, about this Egyptian counterworld is that it was not a construct of fantasy and belief, but one that required planning and architecture, along with all sorts of other arts, including anatomy, pharmacology, linen weaving, and everything else that the mummification process entailed, all of it set into motion, visible, tangible, massive, even colossal, with all its resultant costs and side effects. There has probably never been so this-worldly a next world, this-worldly not in the sense that the Egyptians envisioned Paradise, as Muslims do, after the fashion of an earthly pleasure house, but in the sense that in this world, Egyptians were obliged to keep their hands full building it, conceptually colonizing it, and ritually keeping it in motion.

As our first thesis stresses, Egyptian culture was one of those societies that do not accept death but rather rebel against death as an empirical fact with all the power at their disposal. This rebellion assumed the form of religion, that is, the creation of a counterworld. That was our second thesis. I do not mean, however, that these counterimages sketched by religion cover up the empirical world and make it disappear; on the contrary, rather, they generate an excitement for the always remembered, and in this excitement all the more brightly illuminated, factual world. This was especially true of Egyptian mortuary religion. The original experience of death was in no way covered up or suppressed by the counterimages of religion. These counterimages made that which they negated, the darker aspects of the theme of death, all the more intensely borne in mind. Along with the transfiguring texts of the mortuary religion, which sketch magnificent, linguistically articulated images, there are other texts that speak of loneliness and darkness, lack, deprivation, and paralysis. The dark side of death was not covered over but remained present. The counterimages generated an excitement that sounded a call to action. This impetus was what was special about Egyptian religion. Where others sat back and let matters take their course, the Egyptians took things into their own hands. For them, death was a call to action, the beginning and the end of a major realm of cultural praxis. My third thesis thus states that the Egyptians did not locate the counterimages they placed in opposition to their experience of death in a distant "next world" but rather realized them in this world with the means at their disposal, and that they believed that even if they could not defeat death, they could thus at least "handle" it, handle in the sense of healing, of a bridge to a culturally healthful form.

In its central and normative, sophisticated aspects and motifs, culture is nothing other than the symbolic realization of a comprehensive horizon without which man cannot live. This point is also true of societies that have on all points believed the opposite of what was true for the Egyptians, and it is the culture-theoretical hypothesis that underlies this book. To substantiate it, there must be comparative studies, and these in turn must be built on "thick descriptions" of culture-specific phenomena. Here, a step in this direction will be undertaken. This contribution can be built on earlier works but not on earlier models. For a long time now, there has been no comprehensive book on Egyptian mortuary religion. The fundamental and oft-cited book by Hermann Kees, *Totenglauben und Jenseitsvorstellungen der alten Ägypter,* which has achieved the status of a classic, is a rich and especially philological collection of material, but it is without contour or perspective, and it is essentially confined to the Old and Middle Kingdoms. The first edition of 1926 must now be viewed as outdated, for many important sources were not yet published at the time of its appearance. As best he could, Kees worked the Coffin Texts, which began to be published in 1938, into the second edition of 1956, though in the process, his account lost much of its readability. Jan Zandee's book *Death as an Enemy* is a lexical study confined to just one out of many different images of death. The useful dissertation by Gretel Wirz, *Tod und Vergänglichkeit im alten Ägypten,* deals only with literary sources, omitting the rituals and recitations of the mortuary cult, which stand at the center of this volume. A. J. Spencer's *Death in Ancient Egypt* treats the theme exclusively from the perspective of archaeology.[33] In its pages, customs are dealt with in terms of their archaeological and architectonic traces, omitting the world of texts. Quite comprehensive, but also concentrated on the material culture of the Egyptian religion of death, is the recent book by John H. Taylor, *Death and the Afterlife in Ancient Egypt,* which unfolds all the riches of the world of objects in which Egyptian mortuary belief is manifested with the help of examples from the British Museum. The present book, however, seeks to venture into the realm of the cultural semantics on which this rich array of customs once fed. In this regard, Erik Hornung has paved the way more than any other scholar in the introductions and commentaries of his various text editions and anthologies.[34] The essays by Alan Gardiner,[35] Constantin Sander-Hansen,[36] Philippe Derchain,[37] and many others[38] are confined to individual aspects. There is no lack of literature on the theme,[39] but there is no comprehensive treatment of this phenomenon, which is not only important in and of itself, but which also opens the way to insights, insights with wide-ranging consequences, into the relationship between death and culture.

PART ONE ◆

IMAGES OF DEATH

CHAPTER ONE

Death as Dismemberment

1. The Opening Scene of the Osiris Myth

In ancient Egyptian tradition, at least as it is preserved to us, the Osiris
myth was never recounted as a coherent whole; rather, it served as a
source of allusions for a large number of religious texts. We may,
indeed we must, conclude from these allusions and circumstances, that it
was not a coherent story but rather a sequence of scenes that was unmistakably rooted in the mortuary cult. The only texts that furnish us with a
continuous narrative are written in Greek, by Diodorus[1] and especially by
Plutarch.[2] But in the coherence of their narratives, in their care about a
single, meaningful, stimulating story, these authors seem to have strayed
far from the Egyptian form of the myth.

The myth had both a prehistory and a starting point. The prehistory is
never narrated in the Egyptian texts, yet it is the necessary precondition
for all that follows. Osiris was king of Egypt, the successor of his father,
the god Geb. Unlike his divine predecessors in the royal office—the sun
god Re, the air god Shu, and the earth god Geb—Osiris did not come to
the throne as an only child but rather with a brother and rival, Seth. That
was his undoing. But his salvation lay in the fact that he also had two
sisters, Isis and Nephthys. And there was also Horus, who brought the
number of the children of Nut to five, though strictly speaking, he was

the child of Osiris and Isis. For the time being, we shall leave aside this contradiction. That the "children of Nut" were five in number was ritually conditioned. It corresponded to the constellation of ritual roles into which the complex phenomenon of death unfolded: the murder, the sacrifice, the two mourning women, and the son.

Osiris' rule plays a great role in Egyptian texts. They almost always speak of him as ruler of the realm of the dead, an office he assumed only as a dead god, and almost never about his earthly kingship, which he exercised over gods and men in the world above as successor of Geb.[3] Osiris' reign came to a violent end, for he was slain by his brother, Seth. Thus did death come into the world, confronting the gods with a great problem. This is the prehistory, of which there is no coherent narrative in the Egyptian texts.

As stated above, we encounter the actual myth, which begins at this point, not as a continuous narrative in the texts but as a cycle of scenes. The first scene depicts the slain Osiris, his life destroyed and annihilated in the grossest of ways. For Seth did not just slay Osiris, he hacked him to pieces and threw the individual limbs into the water, with the result that the Nile carried them to various places throughout the land. This is the first image to which we shall turn: death as dismemberment. It depicts death in its physical, bodily, biological form of manifestation. This scene is the common theme of a large corpus of texts, which do not actually describe it but rather presuppose it as the trigger for various actions whose aim is to cope with this catastrophe. Just as it was Osiris' undoing that he was the first of the divine rulers to have a brother and thus a rival for the throne, so his sisters became his salvation. Isis, his sister-wife, was the first to take action. She traversed the land to collect his scattered body parts. A hymn to Osiris from Dynasty 18 (stela Louvre C 286) narrates her actions in the form of two scenes:

1. Isis' search and her care for the body:

Isis the powerful, protectress of her brother,
who sought him tirelessly,
who traversed this land in mourning
and did not rest until she found him;

who gave him shade with her feathers
and air with her wings;
who cried out, the mourning woman of her brother
who summoned dancers for the Weary of Heart;

2. The conception, birth, and childhood of Horus:

who took in his seed and created the heir,
who suckled the child in solitude, no one knew where,

who brought him, when his arm was strong,
into the hall of Geb—
the Ennead rejoiced:
"Welcome, Osiris' son,
Horus, stout of heart, justified,
son of Isis, heir of Osiris."

Isis' activities with regard to the corpse of Osiris culminate in the posthumous conception of Horus. In the accounts of Diodorus and Plutarch, Isis recovered all the body parts of the slain god except for his virile member, which had been swallowed by a fish. She was thus obliged to replace this member with an artificial one that she was able to make into the instrument of a posthumous insemination. The Egyptian texts, which seldom mention this scene, know nothing of this detail. The *locus classicus* is a passage in Pyramid Texts spell 366:

Isis comes to you,
rejoicing for love of you,
that her seed might issue into her,
it being sharp as Sothis.

Horus, the sharp one, who comes forth from you
in his name "Horus, who is in Sothis,"
may it be well with you through him
in your name "Spirit in the *ḏnḏrw*-barque."

Horus has protected you
in his name "Horus protector of his father."

The pyramid text describes the transition from the first stage of salvation from death, which is concentrated on the image of death as dismemberment and on the corpse of the deceased, to the second stage, which has to do with the image of death as social isolation and is concerned with the restoration of the social person of the dead individual. Isis and Nephthys are the protagonists of the first phase; it ends with the conception and birth of Horus, who assumes direction of the second phase as "Horus protector of his father." We shall discuss these matters in the next two chapters.

The texts do not speak of Osiris' condition but rather of the actions aimed at remedying it. They speak of searching and finding, of gathering and putting together, of joining the head to the bones, of reinserting the heart, of replacing discharged fluids, of mourning Osiris, transfiguring him, and breathing life into him, in short, of a host of activities, all of them related to the body of the dismembered god, and in which we can easily recognize the mythic counterpart to the embalming ritual. Behind

25

them lies not an actual dismemberment and rejoining of the corpse, as some scholars once assumed, but rather a specific image of the body, one that was quite characteristic of Egyptian culture and of the ancient Egyptian style of thinking.

2. The Egyptian Image of the Body

The image of death as dismemberment is derived (a) from the Egyptian image of the body as a multiplicity of members joined through the connective medium of blood into a living unity and (b) from the counterimage of redemption from death through collecting, joining, uniting, and knotting together. Here, we touch on an area of extremely basic cultural attitudes, which Emma Brunner-Traut, in particular, has dealt with in studies that have major theoretical implications.

In her influential book *Frühformen des Erkennens* (early forms of conceptualization), Brunner-Traut postulates a psychological, cognitive basis for certain especially striking peculiarities of Egyptian art, which she sets in parallelism with other phenomena in Egyptian culture, as well as with the art of other primitive peoples and with forms of children's art.[4] She groups these peculiarities together under the rubric of the "aspective." This erudite concept, which is the opposite of "perspective," designates a purely additive stringing together or aggregating of elements without organizing, structuring principles that would make them appear to be parts of a superordinate whole. These peculiarities are particularly clear in Egyptian art; Brunner-Traut, though, would like to see in them a trait that reaches far beyond art and into Egyptian thought, perception, and conceptualization in general. According to her theory, Egyptians cast a dissecting glance at the world, one that perceived only individual details and was incapable of seeing larger unities. In other words, they did not see the forest for the trees. Thus, in the case of the body, they saw a "marionette," an aggregated multiplicity of individual limbs, not an organic whole controlled from the center outward.[5] "The body is 'put together,' 'knotted together' out of a number of parts; it is, so to say, what we call a 'marionette.'"[6] In language, this dissecting style of thought is expressed in the lack of generic terms. Thus, for example, there is no word for world, cosmos, *mundus*. Instead, Egyptians said "sky and earth." Egypt was "Upper and Lower Egypt." Egyptian grammar has few conjunctions; the typical form of joining clauses is parataxis. Brunner-Traut qualifies Egyptian society as an "aggregated" society that had no structure but was rather an aggregated mass of individuals, an agglomeration of individual persons.[7] This mass was hierarchically assembled, to be sure, but no one could "survey this whole and understand it as a unity and in its all-around functional interdependence." The hierarchic construct was not fitted together into a "structure" but merely into an aggregate, an "aggregation (Latin *grex*, "herd") of individuals but not into an organic body in which all the parts are reciprocally related to one another and thus woven into a whole by means of warp and weft."[8] These are astute observations. Without doubt, behind Brunner-Traut's concept of the "aspective" stand deep, far-reaching insights into certain central phenomena of ancient Egyptian culture and their inner relationship. The psychological, cognitive interpretation, however, is too one-sided. It is true that the Egyptians cast a dissecting gaze on the world; but at the same time, there was always a question of connective principles, and these were what mattered most to them.

With the French sociologist Emile Durkheim, we can distinguish two different forms of thinking about the relationship between unity and multiplicity: the "organic" and the "mechanical," or perhaps better, the "connective."[9] What Emma Brunner-Traut rightly notes is the absence of the organic model, in which the relation between the one and the many is conceived after the model of an organism, whose parts are functionally interdependent. In this model, all the parts of the whole work on one another, every movement and change is to a greater or lesser extent taken up and reflected by all of them. This model seems in fact to have played no special role in Egypt. We do not encounter collective identities such as clan, tribe, kinship group, or people, which are regarded as organically predetermined. Such units must of course have existed in prehistoric Egypt, as in all tribal societies, but under the Egyptian state, they retreated into the background, at least in the official semantics. This semantics was so universally dominant that it allowed for no "organic" forms of social grouping outside the bureaucratic-administrative and priestly, and later also the military, professional hierarchies. Brunner-Traut quite rightly maintains, "Extended families, as we still often find them in the Middle and Far East, did not exist, not even kinship groups with a collective identity through a series of generations."[10] But that did not mean that the individual was to be understood as an isolated element in an "amorphous" or "aggregated mass." Here, the connective model comes into play, the concept of a medium that binds elements thought to be unbound into a comprehensive unity. We have a definite impression that the connective model was in the service of the state and the form it assumed, that of a pharaonic monocracy. The Egyptians developed a sort of connective ethic aimed at binding the individual into the structure of the state. To the principle of the aspective, which does not perceive a unity as such but rather breaks it down into its components, there corresponds a "connective thought" that inquires as to the binding elements. With regard to the theme of death, the presence of connective thinking is especially clear on two levels: on that of the Egyptian image of the body, which has to do with dismemberment and piecing together, and on that of the Egyptian image of social structure, which has to do with isolation and integration. As in many other societies, in ancient Egypt there was a correspondence between the image of the body and that of social structure.[11]

In this chapter, we shall first consider the image of the body. If the body presents itself to the aspective, dissecting gaze as a marionette, what are the binding elements, the connective media that integrate this puppet into a living body? The French physician and Egyptologist Thierry Bardinet has been able to supply a conclusive answer to this question. The connective thinking is especially clear from the Egyptian theory, as deduced by him, of the circulation of blood. The Egyptians recognized the function of the blood and blood vessels in integrating the limbs into a body. So long as the heart pumps blood through the vessels and its beating is perceptible ("speaks," as the Egyptians put it) in all the veins, the parts of the body remain integrated and thus alive.[12]

The heart was thus the epitome and the guarantor or generator of connectivity in the bodily sphere.[13] We must therefore deal with it in some detail. As a dead god, Osiris' epithet was wrḏ-jb, the "weary of heart." Weariness of the heart belongs to the image of death as decay and dismemberment. To unite the limbs and animate the body, the heart must be (a) "alive" or "awake," and (b) "in its place." The heart must thus be (a) stimulated, awakened, animated and (b) securely set in place. The corresponding opposite conditions are (a) the "weary heart" or weariness of heart, the designation of the condition of death noted just above, and (b) the removed or absent heart. In both conditions, that of weariness and that of absence, the heart fails to perform its centralizing function, and the person dissolves into a disparate multiplicity. The description of old age in the Instruction of Ptahhotep furnishes a well known example of such dissolution:

> Frailty has come, old age has arrived,
> weakness has come, childish helplessness returns,
> strength diminishes, for my heart is weary.
> The mouth is silenced and speaks no more,
> the eyes are dim, the ears are deaf,
> sleep comes with difficulty, day after day;
> the heart is forgetful, it no longer remembers yesterday,
> the bone aches due to the length (of years),
> the nose is stopped up, it cannot breathe,
> for standing and sitting are difficult.
> Good becomes bad,
> all sense of taste is gone.
> What old age does to man: bad in every way.[14]

Here, old age is described as the disintegration of the liveliness made possible by the heart, and it is ascribed to weariness of the heart. Death is a wearying of the heart. Thus Osiris, the dead god of the realm of the dead, bears the epithet "weary of heart."

The Egyptians had rituals and recitations whose goal was to restore, in a new form, the corporeal unity that had disintegrated in death. The most important prerequisite was to restore the heart to its former place and to awaken it, so that it could again assume its centralizing and organizing functions. Without this personal center and source of direction, the new, divine constellations into which the self was now to be inserted for a new unfolding would not have been serviceable. From spells that deal with the restitution of the heart, we learn a great deal about the connective function of that organ:

> My heart, it creates my limbs,
> my flesh obeys me and raises me up.[15]

In these texts, the heart stands not only for life-giving integration through the blood that it pumps through the "vessels" (*mt.wt*), but also and above all for will, consciousness, and memory as mental media of connectivity:

> Your heart is placed in your body for you,
> that you might recall what you have forgotten.[16]

The Egyptian language had two words for "heart," which have long been regarded as synonyms. The one is *jb* and is related to the Hebrew word for "heart," *leb, lebab*. The other is *ḥꜣ.tj*, Coptic *het*, and it displaced the apparently older Semitic word *jb* in the course of the history of the Egyptian language. The one is thus taken to be the older, and the other the newer expression for the same thing. Thierry Bardinet has found a plausible explanation for this terminological doubling or distinction.[17] Bardinet understands *jb* as the "insides" and as a collective term for the internal organs, such as the lungs, the heart, the liver, the spleen, and the stomach. *Jb* thus metaphorically, or better, metonymically (*pars pro toto*) designates the emotional and cognitive inner life of a person, his "inner being." The Egyptians assumed that this complex of internal organs was inherited by the child from its mother at birth, through a physical, biological process of transfer. The expression *jb n mw.t=j* "heart of my mother" rests on this physiological assumption. The word *ḥꜣ.tj*, by way of contrast, refers to the heart in the narrower, more literal sense. *Ḥꜣ.tj* thus designates metonymically mental phenomena, such as consciousness and recollection, which are not biologically inherited, but instead are developed during the course of one's existence. The $ḥ3.tj$-heart is connected with concepts of individuality, consciousness, and personal identity that can be held liable, the "moral self." Thus, in the Judgment of the Dead, it is weighed on a scale. The jb-insides were removed during the embalming process and placed in canopic jars, while the $ḥ3.tj$-heart was restored to the deceased.[18] Thus, in spell 30 of the Book of the Dead, the $ḥ3.tj$-heart is specified as $ḥ3.tj=j$ n $ḫpr.w=j$, "my heart of my $ḫpr.w$," with the variant in spell 30A, $ḥ3.tj=j$ n $wn=j$ $tp-t3$, "my heart of my existence on earth."[19] Scholars have usually taken the term $ḫpr.w$ as referring to phases of development during a lifetime, but recent research has made it plausible that this explanation rests on shaky ground. Evidently, we are to render it here as "form."[20] It must thus be maintained that where we find the jb-heart specified as "of the mother," the $ḥ3.tj$-heart must be taken as referring, in contradistinction, to the $ḏ.t$-body, the $ḫpr.w$-form, and existence on earth. The jb-heart ensures the biological continuity that binds a person to his parents and children and enables the person to live on in his descendants, while the $ḥ3.tj$-heart ensures the mental and personal identity that enables the deceased to recall his earthly life and to retain his personality in the afterlife.

Here as well, it is clear that for the Egyptians, this principle of "connectivity," the attachment of an individual to a whole, was what characterized life in general. Life was connection, death was disintegration and isolation. But to be able to consider this connection, we must determine the entities between which the life-giving connectivity is to be in effect. It was for just that reason that the Egyptians cast a dissecting gaze on the world, so as all the more keenly to grasp its connectedness, that is, the connective structures and principles. They conceived of the body as a marionette only in order to catch sight of the life-giving and life-maintaining function of the circulatory system. The Egyptians thus did not really view the world with a dissecting gaze but with an integrating, one might almost say, an "embalming" gaze. For the embalming ritual was specifically intended to remedy the condition of dismemberment and decomposition that set in with the stopping of the heart and the ceasing of the circulation of the blood, and to benefit the marionette of the body by substituting a new, symbolic connectivity by means of ritual and chemistry. Because we ourselves do not have this embalming glance, what we see in Egyptian art and in other phenomena of Egyptian culture is primarily the additive, the isolating, and the paratactic. We are blind to the animating, the connective. Just as the Egyptian reader had to supply the vowels, for the writing system noted only the consonants, so also he had to supply the conjunctions, for the connection between clauses was mostly paratactic, and in both cases he had no difficulty. In both cases, the reader breathed a connective life into the elements.

From this distinction and this interplay of dissolution and integration, we see that in Egypt, the boundaries between life and death ran in directions different from those to which we are accustomed. Death was the principle of dismembering, dissolving, isolating disintegration, while life was the principle of integrating animation, which conferred unity and wholeness. Thus, something lethal and fatal was inherent in all that served to isolate, while something life-conferring was inherent in all that integrated. And this principle in no way stopped at the body. The individual, too, was conceived of as a member of a whole, one who was alive only in so far as he was integrated in with others. This principle of integration was the Egyptian idea of justice, which we shall discuss in the next chapter. This preoccupation with the principle of integration is what I wish to call the embalming glance. For in Egyptian thought, that which integrated was also that which preserved, that which conferred continued existence.

3. Salvation from Death by Piecing Together

We now understand why the embalming ritual had to portray the corpse not just as a lifeless body but as a dismembered one. The purpose was none other than to indicate the lack of connectivity, which had been supplied during life by the heart and the blood. The stopping of the heart brought an end to the integration of the limbs, which now fell apart into a disparate multiplicity. The myth dramatized this condition, telling how Seth slew his brother Osiris, tore his body into pieces, and scattered his limbs throughout all of Egypt. In the embalming ritual, this myth was played out for each deceased person, even if he had in no way been killed and dismembered but rather had died a peaceful, natural death. In mythic thought, there was no such thing as a natural death. Each death was a violent assault, and to the Egyptians, who thought in terms of dismemberment and connectivity, it represented a tearing of limb from limb. Scholars once thought that the dead were in fact carved into pieces, presumably to render them harmless and to protect posterity from revenants.[21] Myths of dismemberment are attested throughout the world, especially in the context of shamanistic rituals, and they have been interpreted as reflections of this sort of burial customs.[22] In the meantime, it has been recognized that in Egyptian texts, this talk of the collecting and piecing together of that which had been torn up and scattered is to be understood symbolically. The mythic image of the dismembered body represented a starting point for action. Mythic images have the function of overcoming paralysis and making it possible for action to be taken.

The Egyptian embalming ritual ideally took seventy days. It was the Egyptian equivalent of all the rituals, throughout the world, by means of which the dead assume the "eternal" form in which they can at last enter into the company of their ancestors.[23] This transformation occurs in a great many ways (reduction to a skeleton, dismemberment, maceration, mummification, cremation, exposure, etc.), but the basic concept seems always to be the same. Many societies entrust this process of transformation entirely to nature; this leads to classic forms of double burial, in which, after a certain time, the corpse, now ripened into its final, eternal form, is exhumed and given its final burial. Other cultures, the most extreme of which is that of Egypt, take this process into their own hands and prepare the corpse for eternity by artificial (surgical, chemical, magical) means. This process was conceived of as, and represented by, the image of *membra disiecta* reunited into a new entity.

The dead body as *membra disiecta* was thus a metaphor, a metaphorical image of death that served as a foil for the image of life, into which the dead body was to be transported by carrying out the embalming ritual. The initial, surgical-anatomical phase of this seventy-day process was not free of violent intrusion. The body was of course not cut into pieces, but for the purpose of preserving it, it was treated anything but "conservatively," in the medical sense of the term. The brain was fished out through the nose, and the internal organs were removed through an incision in the side. Only the heart was wrapped up and set back in place; the other organs were placed in canopic jars, vases with lids in the form of an animal or human head. The remaining soft tissue and fluids were dissolved by a solution of natron and resin and pumped out of the body through the anus. This first phase was carried out in the name of purification. Everything "foul," that is, everything perishable that could represent a danger to the goal of achieving an eternal form, was removed from the body. For this reason, in the few representations of the embalming ritual, this phase is represented as a purifying bath. The corpse lay "on" (that is, in) a basin, and water was poured over it. The Egyptian word for such a basin is *šj*, "lake," and such a "lake" is mentioned repeatedly in the accompanying spells, some of which we shall cite in chapter 5. Old Kingdom inscriptions describe the deceased's crossing into the afterlife with turns of expression such as the following:

Going down into his house of eternity in very great peace,
that he might be provisioned by Anubis and Khentamentiu
after a mortuary offering is brought for him at the opening of the shaft,
after crossing the lake after he is transfigured by the lector priests.[24]

Setting out to the western mountain,
after crossing the lake while he was transfigured by the lector priest
and the rites were carried out for him by the embalmer in the presence of
Anubis.[25]

May the crossing of the lake be carried out for him,
may he be transfigured through the carrying out of the rites by the lector priest.[26]

"Crossing the lake" and "transfigured," that is, being changed into a transfigured ancestral spirit by the lector priest, who recited the funerary liturgies from a roll of papyrus, often go closely together. Both turns of expression refer to the embalming, the one to its physical and the other to its spiritual-magical aspect. The phrase "crossing the lake" refers to passing safe and sound through the purification phase.

Then began the phase of desiccation (drying and salting), which extended over about forty days. Next, the corpse, which was by then reduced to skin and bones, was built back up during the mummification ritual, by anointing it with balsamic oils that made the skin supple again, by stuffing it with resins, gum arabic, cloths, wood-wool, chaff, and other substances, by adorning it with artificial eyes, make-up, and a wig, and lastly, by wrapping it in mummy bandages of fine linen that were partly inscribed with magical formulas and had amulets interspersed among them. The end result of this elaborate treatment was a mummy.[27] The mummy was more than a corpse, it was an image of the god Osiris and a sort of hieroglyph of the entire person, one that, as the Egyptians put it, was "filled with magic." Just as the magic of writing made it possible to make meaning visible and to preserve it, so in the mummy as a symbolic form or hieroglyph, the person of the deceased was made visible and preserved.

But far more important than the surgical intervention and chemical treatment was the verbal treatment of the deceased. The inscriptions cited above summarize this aspect of the embalming with the phrase "transfiguration by the lector priest." The lector priest—literally translated, the Egyptian title means "he who carries the book-roll"—accompanied the activities of the embalmers with the recitation of mortuary liturgies that he read from a roll of papyrus. This merging of action and speech, and specifically, speech set down in writing, is entirely characteristic of the Egyptian mortuary cult. We shall deal with this topic several times in the second part of this book. In the Egyptian language, this "talking therapy" for the dead is designated by an essentially untranslatable word that is rendered in English and French as "transfiguration" and in German as "Verklärung." In this treatment, the deceased is constantly talked to. This stream of speech apparently had the function of a connective medium that was deployed, in connection with rituals and amulets, as a means of endowing with life. The deceased thus became a being endowed with consciousness and physical strength, capable of returning to life in a number of forms. One of these many different forms was the mummy, the reintegrated body, the *corpus* into which the gathered *membra disiecta* of the deceased were united. By means of these "transfiguring" recitations, the limbs of the body, which were conceived of as scattered, were gathered, as it were, into a single text, which described them as a new entity.

The verbal accompaniment to the embalming process centered on the theme of reuniting what had been torn apart. One by one, limbs and organs were given back to the deceased. He got back his eyes so as to see, his mouth so as to speak, his arms so as to receive what was given to him, his heart so as to recollect who he was and what his name was, his legs so as to walk, and so forth. In these spells, it is recounted how the missing connectivity could be restored:

> Your eyes are given you so as to see,
> your ears, so as to hear was is said,
> your mouth, so as to speak,
> and your legs, so as to walk.
> Your hands and arms are to serve you.
> May your flesh be firm, and your vessels be well.
> May you have enjoyment of all your limbs!
> May you have control of your limbs, they being all present and intact,
> and there being no evil in you.
> May your *jb*-heart be with you, truly,
> and your *ḥꜣ.tj*-heart in its former condition,
> as you return in your condition of strength.[28]

The Egyptian concept of the world rested on an unusually firm belief in the binding power of symbols. Osiris was wakened to new life, though his heart had once and for all stopped beating. His constant epithet was, as stated, the "weary of heart," which meant precisely this: the god whose heart does not beat but who nevertheless lives. The Osiris myth transports life-giving connectivity out of the sphere of the natural, physiological, and organic and into the sphere of culture, institutions, and symbols. It was rituals, images, and texts that awakened Osiris to new life and kept him alive. With the help of symbolic forms, what was torn apart was gathered back together, and the boundaries between life and death, this world and the next one, were overcome. Yet the mystery of this connectivity that overcame death lay not in the symbolic forms but in the love they set in motion. The connection between love and speech was the most potent connective energy the Egyptians knew, and at the same time, the most potent elixir of life.

Thus, saving the dead Osiris from his dismembered condition was first and foremost a matter for Isis, the loving sister and wife, who searched for her missing husband and busied herself with his corpse, collecting it, protecting it, and endowing it with life. In this initial scene of redemption from death, Isis embodies the life-giving powers that stem from romantic attachment, and her care works like an animating sphere that can wake the dead with light and air. Thus the preference for depicting Isis on the walls of coffins: her presence was supposed to transform the coffin into a sphere of life in which the deceased could see, breathe, and experience pleasure. In Egyptian mortuary belief, Osiris was the prototype of every deceased individual. Everyone would become Osiris in death and be endowed with life by Isis. In the Coffin Texts, the mortuary texts of the Middle Kingdom, there are brief hymns to Isis as embodiment of the end of the coffin where the head rested:

> . . . who knots the *ba* and fashions the shadow
> that gives breath to the Weary of Heart
> in this your name of "She who is under the head of her lord"!
> May you place my head on my neck,
> may you gather life for my throat.
> May you transfigure me, may you join my limbs,
> may you tie on my face,
> may you form my *ba* . . .[29]

Isis was the goddess of physical restoration. All her life-giving actions were aimed at the body and its vitality. The most important weapon that Isis could deploy against death was speech, the recitation of magical spells that could create a reality. One function of Isis' "transfiguring" recitations was to gather the limbs of the body, which were conceived of as scattered, into, as it were, a single text that described them as a new entity. As a rule, such descriptions enumerate the individual parts of the body, beginning with the head, from top to bottom, and they compare them with deities:

> Your head is Re,
> your face is Wepwawet,
> your nose is the jackal (= Anubis),
> your lips are the two children (Shu and Tefnut).
> Your two ears are Isis and Nephthys.
> Your two eyes are the two children of Re-Atum (Shu and Tefnut),
> your tongue is Thoth,
> your throat is Nut,
> your neck is Geb,
> your shoulders are Horus,
> your breast is He-who-gladdens-the-*ka*-of-Re-the-great-god-who-is-in-you.
> Your rib cage is Hu and Kheperi,
> your navel is the jackal and the two Ruty,
> your back is Anubis,
> and your belly is Ruty.
> Your two arms are the two sons of Horus,
> Hapy and Imset,

your fingers and your fingernails are the children of Horus.
Your back is Spreader-of-sunlight,
your leg is Anubis,
your breasts are Isis and Nephthys.
Your legs are Duamutef and Qebehsenuf.
There is no limb of yours that is free of a god.
Raise yourself, O this Osiris N.![30]

The deceased can thus say of himself:

My limbs are gods,
I am entirely a god,
no limb of mine is without a god.
I walk as a god,
I come out as a god.
The gods have transformed themselves into my body,
I am one whose form changes, lord of transfiguration.

My limbs lead me,
my flesh clears the way for me.
Those which arose from me protect me,
they are pleased with what they formed.
I am indeed the one who formed them,
I am indeed the one who engendered them,
I am indeed the one who caused them to arise.[31]

In Egyptian, the same expression meant both "to transform into" and "to arise from." The text plays on this double meaning: limb by limb, the gods turned into the body of the deceased, but they also arose from this body, and the deceased could say of himself that he formed, engendered, and brought forth the gods. In this way, the scattered limbs became a single body again, and he himself was in full control of the divine community he had formed. This process was not just a matter of reuniting the individual *membra disiecta* into the "text" of a body but of bringing this text into the form of a community of gods: that is the symbolic connectivity by means of which the sundered limbs were to be reunited into a single, living body.[32]

In the mouth of Isis and Nephthys, the liturgical recitation of the deification of the limbs was combined with the lyrical language of yearning, thus approaching the form and mood of a love lyric:

Your head is anointed, my lord, when you travel north,
like the tresses of an Asiatic woman,
and *your face* is brighter than the house of the moon.
Your torso is of lapis lazuli,

your locks are blacker than the doors of that star on the day of eclipse . . .
Re shines on your face so that it is clothed in gold . . .
Your brows are the two sisters who have united,
and Horus has covered them with lapis lazuli.
Your nose is provided with breath,
and air is at your nose like the winds in the sky.
Your two eyes behold the eastern mountain,
your lashes remain always,
their eyelids are of genuine lapis lazuli.
Your two cheeks are offering bearers,
their lids are full of eye paint.
Your two lips give you *maat* (i.e., truth, justice),
they report *maat* to Re,
they pacify the heart of the gods.
Your teeth are those in the mouth of the *ouroboros*, with which the two lords
   have played.
Your tongue speaks sensibly,
and what you say is more penetrating than the cry of the bird in the marsh.
Your jaws are the starry realm, your breasts are firm in their place,
when they traverse the western wastes.
O see, you are mourned, you are mourned![33]

The text continues with an enumeration from head to foot. It is not by chance that these songs remind us of the descriptive genre in Egyptian love poetry and in Near Eastern love poetry more generally. In such poems, the body of the beloved is praised, limb by limb, and from head to toe in poetic, often highly ingenious comparisons.[34] The most famous example is the Song of Songs,[35] but there were also such poems in Egypt:

> Shining bright, fair of skin,
> Lovely the look of her eyes,
> Sweet the speech of her lips,
> She has not a word too much.
> Upright neck, shining breast,
> Hair true lapis lazuli;
> Arms surpassing gold,
> Fingers like lotus buds.
> Heavy thighs, narrow waist,
> her legs parade her beauty;
> With graceful step she treads the ground,
> Captures my heart by her movements.[36]

In the embalming texts that deify the limbs, what is involved is a style of description that individualizes each discrete part of the body. In the love poetry, the body of the beloved is also dissected so as to be gathered anew through the medium of the texts, though on an entirely different level of poetic images. But in the love poems, as in the case of mummification, it is not a matter of dismemberment but of bringing to life. Just as the "transfiguration spells" breathe life into the corpse of the deceased, so the love poems breathe life into the body of the beloved.

From this example, we see in how many ways certain images of the dead worked their way into the lives of the Egyptians, influencing their culture. The image of death as disintegration left its mark on the experience of the body in the realm of the living, and it led to concepts of mortality that ascribed death to the weakening or breakdown of connective elements. And conversely, the corresponding image of life as unity, harmony, and coordination resulting from functional means of connectivity left its mark on concepts of death as something that could be remedied by restoring the lost connectivity by other means. Philosophy and practice were mutually dependent.

But restoration of corporal unity was only one side of the complex events that occurred during the Egyptian funerary ritual. The other was the restoration of the social person of the deceased, his respect, his dignity, his status, his recognition. Horus, the son, was responsible for this aspect of redemption from death. In its gender differentiation, this division of labor seems especially meaningful to me. In the mythic distribution of roles, activities aimed at restoration of the person to the corporal sphere was associated with the feminine, while those aimed at restoring him to the social sphere were associated with the masculine. The conjugal and sibling love between Isis, Nephthys, and Osiris overcame death by endowing the body with life, while the filial love of Horus for Osiris overcame death by challenging the enemy, by indicting and passing judgment on him, thus vindicating and rehabilitating the slain one.

CHAPTER TWO

Death as Social Isolation

1. The Physical and Social Sphere of Man

Just as the image of death as dismemberment arises from the image of the body as a marionette brought to life as a unity by the heart and blood as a connective medium, so the image of death as isolation is inferred from the image of life as social connectivity. This image of life can best be reconstructed from two maxims already mentioned at the outset of this book. One of them reads, "One lives, if another guides him" and refers above all to life *before* death. The other is, "One lives, if his name is mentioned,"[1] and it refers above all to life *after* death. But both refer to a single concept of life, one that is based on the principle of social "connectivity." A solitary person is not capable of life, that is, alive in the full sense of the word. There must be someone else to take him by the hand and guide him. By the same token, he is also not dead, so long as there are others to mention his name, so long as the bond of connectivity is not broken. Thus, as the Egyptians understood it, a person lived in two spheres, which we can distinguish as the "physical sphere" and the "social sphere." In both spheres, the principle of connectivity worked to confer and maintain life, and correspondingly, the principle of disconnectivity threatened and wrought death. Thus, for instance, the punishments with which tomb violators are threatened in tomb inscriptions above all concern the name and the posterity of the perpetrator, his banishment from the community both of the transfigured in the afterlife and of posterity in this life, his isolation from all connective ties to humans, gods, and spirits. In many such curse inscriptions, the punishments touch solely on the social sphere of the perpetrator:

> As for any rebel who might rebel and plan in his heart to desecrate this tomb and what it contains, who might destroy the inscriptions and damage the statues in the tombs of the ancestors and the temple of Ra-Qerert with no fear of the court, he shall not be transfigured in the necropolis, the place of the transfigured ones, his property shall not endure in the necropolis, his children shall be expelled from their tombs, he shall be an enemy to the transfigured ones, one whom the lord of the necropolis does not know, *his name shall not be mentioned among the transfigured ones, his memory shall not endure among the living on earth,* water shall not be poured for him, offerings shall not be brought for him on the *wag*-festival or on any other goodly festival of the necropolis. He shall be handed over to the law court, he shall be an abomination to his city god, he shall be an abomination to his relations, his courtyard shall be committed to the flames, his house to the consuming fire. All that comes out of his mouth shall be repudiated by the gods of the necropolis.[2]

During life, persons feared damage to their social sphere at least as much as harm to their physical existence. Thus, in prayers of the New Kingdom, we often find requests for "deliverance from the mouth of men."[3] Evidently, a bad reputation was one of the worst things that could happen to a person. Even the wisdom literature warned of being talked about.[4] As the Egyptians saw it, someone's personality could be as badly harmed by negative words as by a physical attack.[5] Death threatened not only physical but also social integrity. The following passage from spell 214 of the Pyramid Texts mentions risk to the name that the king left behind on earth when he ascended to the sky:

> Anyone who shall speak badly of the name of Wenis when you ascend,
> Geb has condemned him to contempt in his city,
> so that he must retreat from it and come to naught.[6]

Another spell leaves us to understand that even the king's dead condition as he lay in the liminal state of the embalming process, during which he had not yet become an ancestral spirit, was in no way to be made known:

> It is Horus, who has come to claim his father Osiris.
> It is dangerous for him that the king is passing over the places of Anubis;[7]
> no one who hears of this shall live.

O Thoth, spare no one who hates the king.
O Thoth, hasten and see whether the father is passing, for it is dangerous
  to him.[8]

To the image of death as dismemberment in the physical sphere,
there corresponds, in the social sphere, the image of death as isolation,
in which death represents the principle of expulsion, dishonoring, and
degradation:

It (i.e., death) is taking a man from his house to cast him into the desert.[9]

By transforming the deceased into a transfigured ancestral spirit, the
ritual of transfiguration affects both his physical and his social sphere.
The names of Isis, Nephthys, and Anubis stand for the former, and the
names of Horus and Thoth for the latter.

2. *"One Lives, if His Name is Mentioned"*

The principle of social connectivity endows the individual with life by
integrating him into the community, just as the principle of physical connectivity, realized in life through the blood and during the mummification process through the magic of texts and amulets, integrates the
multiplicity of limbs and thus endows the individual with life. Internally,
man is a *multiplicity of members* that must be joined into a unity, while exter-
nally, he is a *member of a multiplicity*, who is brought fully to life by the
process of socialization, by integrating him into the constellations of social
life as a member of the community. To this image of life as integration,
there corresponds the image of death as isolation. Just as Isis is able to
restore the physical unity of Osiris by searching for and joining his limbs
and by mourning and transfiguring his body, so Horus is responsible for
restoring the personal identity of Osiris by resocializing him into the community of the gods. The restoration of the body is the stuff of the constellation of man and wife, brother and sister, and thus of conjugal love,
while the restoration of the social personality is the stuff of the constellation of father and son, filial love, and piety, which the Egyptians
regarded as no less strong an emotion, and which, just like conjugal love,
had the power to overcome the boundaries of death and to commence
and sustain a connection between the living and an individual in the
realm of the dead. The two themes, the horizontal theme of conjugal love
and the vertical theme of parental and filial love, constituted the basic
texture of Egyptian society, and in each case, it was the boundary of death
that was crossed and overcome in both directions.

There are ritual texts that express the responsibility of the son for restoring the social person of his father. Pyramid Texts spell 371 is an example of what I wish to call these "Horus-texts":

> O Osiris Khentamentiu,
> Horus has set you at the forefront of the gods,
> he has bidden that you seize the white crown, the Mistress (or, "all that is
>   yours").
> Horus has found you, and it fares well (*akh*) with him through you.
>
> Go out against your enemy, you are greater than he,
> in your name "Great House."
> Horus has bidden that he carry you
> in your name "Great Mat."
> He has saved you from your enemy,
> he has protected you as one who is protected in his time.
>
> Geb has beheld your form
> and has placed you on his throne.
> Horus has stretched out your enemy under you,
> you are older than he, you came forth before he (did).
>
> You are the father of Horus, his engenderer,
> in your name "Engenderer."
> The heart of Horus is happy (lit., "prominent") with you
> in your name "Khentamentiu."

All of Horus' activities on behalf of Osiris are aimed at restoring his honor, status, and dignity. Horus sets Osiris at the forefront of the gods, he restores him to the rulership by means of the *wrr.t*-crown, he raises up the one who has been laid low so that he may go out against his enemy, and he has humiliated the enemy by obliging him to carry Osiris—the humiliation of the enemy has to do with the restoration of honor—and protects Osiris from any further assault by the enemy, so that the latter is unable to attack him again. He also sees to it that Geb beholds and acknowledges Osiris in the status to which he has been restored. Geb is the authority who has the final word in the succession to the rulership, for after the death of Osiris, the royal office reverts to him as predecessor of Osiris and father of the brothers who are in contention. The first and last strophes lay stress on an important constellation, the togetherness of father and son. It is *akh* (in this context an untranslatable word, and one to which we shall often return) with the son in the presence of Osiris, and his heart turns to his dead father.

Another important, typical Horus-text is Pyramid Texts spell 364, in which we again find a number of the motifs dealt with just above:

O Osiris Khentamentiu, arise!
Horus has come to you to claim you from the gods.
Horus has loved you,
he has perfected you as a god.
Horus has attached his eye to you.
. . .
Horus will not be far from you: you are his *ka*.
May your countenance be gracious to him, so long as you exist.

Hasten, accept the word of Horus,
that you may be pleased with it.
Listen to Horus: he will not harm you.
He has bidden the gods to follow you.

. . . Horus has found you, and it goes well with him through you.
Horus has caused the gods to ascend to you.
He has given them to you, that they may brighten your face.

Horus has set you at the forefront of the gods,
he has bidden that you seize the white crown, the Mistress (or, "all that is
   yours").
. . . Horus has assembled the gods for you,
and they will not abandon you in the place to which you have gone.
Horus has mustered the gods for you,
and they will not abandon you in the place where you have drifted in the
   water.
. . .
O Osiris Khentamentiu,
lift up your *jb*-heart for him, may your *ḥȝ.tj*-heart be great.
Open your mouth! Horus has stood up for you,
he has not failed to stand up for you.

O Osiris Khentamentiu,
you are a mighty god, and there is no god like you.
Horus has given you his children, that they may convey you,
He has given you all the gods,
that they may follow you, that you may have power over them.
. . . You are transfigured in your name "Horizon from which Re arises."
   You are honored and prepared,
   ba-like and *sekhem*-mighty,
   forever and ever.

Horus' goal is the restoration of the social relationships of the deceased,
the social connectivity that restores him as a person. Horus demands him
back from the gods, evidently inimical gods, perhaps confederates of Seth,
who have stolen his corpse, and with his deceased father, he enters into
a constellation that is described by invoking the concept of *ka*. We shall
deal with this concept in detail in chapter 4. Here, it is of special interest

as the symbol of a connectivity that crosses both the boundary between the generations and the threshold of death. The deceased father is the *ka* of Horus. Pyramid Texts spell 356, another typical Horus-text, closes with an address that once again employs the concept of *ka* in summarizing the roles of the deceased father and the son left behind:

> O Osiris N., Horus has intervened for you,
> he has acted on behalf of his *ka*, which is you,
> that you may be satisfied in your name "Satisfied *Ka*."

Ka is a sort of spirit, genius, or vital energy, a legitimizing, dynastic principle that is passed along from father to son; for it, the son is dependent on the father. The hieroglyph for *ka* depicts a pair of arms stretched upward (Figure 1), probably indicating a gesture in which the arms are extended outward to embrace another person. With this gesture, *ka* is

Figure 1.
Hieroglyph for *ka*.

transferred from the father to the son. Thus, for example, the creator god Atum embraces Shu and Tefnut, the twins who have emerged from him:

> You have placed your arms around them as the arms of *ka*,
> that your *ka* may be in them.[10]

We are also told of this embrace in a document known as the "Memphite Theology." There, the story ends with the discovery of Osiris and his resurrection by means of a mutual embrace that causes Horus to "appear as king":

> And so Osiris entered the earth in the royal mountain
> at the north of this land, where he had arrived.
> His son Horus appeared as king of Upper and Lower Egypt
> in the arms of his father Osiris,
> in the midst of the gods who were before and behind him.[11]

The next section begins with a motif that is central to the Osiris-Horus constellation: the speech that Horus addresses to Osiris, the "great word." It is often mentioned in the texts, including the following solemn example from a Coffin Text of the Middle Kingdom:

> Be silent, be silent, you men,
> hear, hear, you men,
> hear this great speech
> that Horus made for his father Osiris,

that he may live by means of it, that he may be a *ba* by means of it, that he
may be honored by means of it![12]

This speech, or command, is to be recognized as the actual proclamation
of the restored honor of the deceased. It culminates in the deeds of Horus
for Osiris. He creates respect for his father by means of the royal authority that he acquires after ascending the throne. The verses that follow
center on the motif of the integration of Osiris into the realm of the gods,
who are to follow him, serve him, and remain loyal to him.

From a somewhat later period stems a mortuary text in which the scene
of the social rehabilitation of Osiris by his son unfolds in dramatic form,
and which also indicates what possible cause for conflict lay decided in
this constellation of father and son that overcame the threshold of death:
Coffin Texts spell 312 = Book of the Dead chapter 78.[13] This is a lengthy
text, and here, we can consider only those passages that refer directly to
the theme of the restoration of the person. The spell begins with an
address to Horus by the deceased Osiris in the netherworld:

> O Horus, come to Busiris,
> . . . that you may behold me and raise me up!
> Spread reverence of me, create respect for me,
> so that the gods of the netherworld fear me,
> so that they defend their gates for me,
> so that the one who harmed me not draw near to me,
> when he sees me in the House of Darkness
> and discovers my weakness, which is (now) hidden from him.

Osiris no longer lies slain and dismembered in Nedit. He is now in the
House of Darkness, that is, in the tomb, in the netherworld, physically
restored and provided for, but also threatened by Seth, who has the power
to slay him a second time and thus annihilate Osiris forever. Osiris is helpless against this potential second attack so long as reverence and respect
for him are not restored, so that those in the netherworld will support his
paramount position and stake all on not allowing Seth to lay his hands
on him. Isis and Nephthys had the power to reconstitute, mourn, and
bury him. But only his son, for whom Osiris therefore longs, can create
respect and recognition for him and reconstruct him as a social person.
All the interests of the father thus lie in bringing his son to him in the
netherworld. But the latter protests:

> Take back (the word) that came from your mouth!
> Care for yourself and make use of your power!
> Let me set out and have power over my legs,
> that I may be like the All-lord there (i.e., in the world above)!

> Then will the gods of the netherworld fear me,
> then will they defend their gates for me.
> Let me move about there with those who move about,
> that I may remain on my perch like the Lord of Life
> and join with the divine Isis
> when I have healed what the one who injured you did
> when he came and saw your weakness.
> I shall set out and come to the confines of the sky,
> that I may consult with Geb
> and request authority from the All-lord,
> that the gods of the netherworld might fear me,
> that they might defend their gates for me,
> that they might see what you have brought in to me!

What Horus wishes to make clear to his father is that in the world above, he can speak up for him and restore his honor far more effectively than by coming to him in the netherworld. He thus dispatches a sunbeam as a messenger to look after Osiris in the netherworld. After many stops along the way, where he must prove that he is an authorized messenger of Horus, he comes to Osiris:

> O lord of *ba*, great of honor,
> see, it is I!
> . . . Your heart is glad, your desire is enduring,
> and happy is the heart of your entourage:
> for you are lasting as Bull of the West,
> while your son Horus has ascended your throne
> and all life belongs to him.
> Millions serve him, millions fear him;
> the Ennead serves him, the Ennead fears him.

The dignity of Osiris, the father, rests in the position of his son Horus. The respect the latter acquires for himself on earth and in the sky also benefits Osiris in the netherworld. This is a fact that Osiris must learn. He must understand that it is in his own interest to allow his son to remain in this world, to maintain his position there and "speak up for him." There was even a ritual whose exclusive goal was to dissuade the deceased father from his understandable wish to summon his son to himself in the netherworld.[14] In the course of the ritual, the son turns to the deceased with the following words:

> O my father, who are in the West!
> . . . Have you said that I am to be carried off to this illustrious land
> in which you are,
> so that your house (on earth) will be destroyed and your gateway torn
> down,

so that your heir is lacking and your enemy exults over you?
I am here in this land to assume your throne,
to hold together your despondent ones, to raise your orphans,
to secure your gate, to keep your name alive
on earth in the mouth of the living.
Have patience, have patience,
O you who are divine in that illustrious land where you are!
I am here in this land of the living,
to construct your altars, to establish your mortuary offerings
in your house of eternity on the Isle of Flame!
. . . You are content in that land
as my supporter in the tribunal of the god!
I, however, am here as an advocate in the tribunal of men,
setting up your boundary stone, holding together your despondent ones,
and serving as your image on earth,
while your gateway is secured by means of that which I do.[15]

Father and son are dependent on one another. They stand by one another, the one in the afterlife, and the other in this life. Such was the Egyptian form of the contract between the generations. Its meaning lay in the fact that the boundary between the two worlds could be overcome. In order to do that, however, the father had to remain in the netherworld and not roam about haunting uncontrollably in the world above, while the son had to remain in the world above and not be summoned to the netherworld by the father. Additionally, in the mortuary beliefs of the royal Pyramid Texts of the Old Kingdom, father and son divided the rulership between them, kingship over the dead going to the god Osiris, while Horus inherited kingship over the living from his deceased father:

May you arise, O N., protected and complete as a god,
outfitted with the regalia of Osiris on the throne of the Foremost of the
    Westerners,
as you do what he (once) did among the transfigured ones, the
    imperishable stars.
May your son Horus arise in your place, outfitted with your regalia,
that he may do what you once did at the head of the living
at the behest of Re, the great god.[16]

This mutual dependence that crosses the threshold of death leads to the citation of an aphorism in a spell that accompanies an offering:

"*Akh*" is a father for his son,
"*akh*" is a son for his father.[17]

The son is *akh* for his father when he stands up in support of him in this world and maintains contact with him. Chapter 173 of the Book of the

Dead[18] depicts "Horus' greeting of his father when he entered (the place of embalming) to gaze upon his father," when "the one embraced the other, that he might become *akh* in the realm of the dead." Horus ends by enumerating the actions that he performed for his father in the context of the transfiguration ritual:

> O Osiris, I am your son Horus!
> I have come   that I might transfigure you,
> I have come   that I might give you your *bas*,
> I have come   that I might make you strong,
> I have come   that I might create respect for you
> I have come   that I might spread fear of you!

An especially impressive and eloquent example of this filial piety that makes it possible to maintain contact with the deceased father and integrate him into the community of the living is a text of Sethos I, which he ordered carved on the stela of a chapel he erected for his father Ramesses I in Abydos. Abydos was the principal cult center of Osiris, the mythic archetype of all deceased fathers. Sethos I erected a great temple to that god in Abydos, and to this day, it remains one of the best preserved and most impressive temples in Egypt. But he also remembered his actual father, Ramesses I, with a small memorial chapel.[19] In it, he wrote about his father and the actions the latter performed on his behalf:

> It was he who created my beauty (i.e., appointed me to the royal office),
> after he made my family great in the hearts (of men).
> He gave me his advice (i.e., instructed me in wisdom)
> to protect me,
> his teaching is a rampart in my heart.
> I am his son, *akh* for the one who brought me forth,
> keeping his name alive.
> . . . After he joined himself to the sky, I took his place,
> for it is I who keep his name alive.
> . . . I am king on the seat that he made broad,
> on the throne on which he sat.
> This land is in my hand, as it was in my father's.
> But now, he has begun to be a god.

As the one in charge of his father's burial, Sethos built him a chapel "in the places of Abydos," dedicated a cult statue to him, provided it with food offerings, and commanded that it be a part the procession that took place during the festival of Osiris:

> When the majesty of this august god Wennefer goes out[20] to tarry there,
> he will honor my father as (he does) the ancestors.

48

... I will praise the god who is in the netherworld,
that he may accept my father into the following of his *ka*.
May he go out with him and settle down in his house in the Sacred Land.

In all that he did, Sethos obeyed a principle:

It is good to be active for one who is in the netherworld (*d³.t*).
It attests to a son who stands up for his father.

What enabled the son to take action on behalf of his deceased father was
his heart, a theme that would later be constantly evoked:

See, *my heart* wearies not of thinking
of the one who begot me.
His name is with me like my light-eye.
... (In the burial procession) I went with my father,
while the mourning women sang transfiguration hymns for him
and beat their faces with their hands for him.
The children of his children will recall his virtue,[21]
and they will mourn him from generation to generation.
The sayings of the forefathers relate true things,
the one who heeds them arises in his place,[22]
awake and gazing at the sun.
They (i.e., the sayings) gladden his heart in the netherworld,
for this is an excellent state of affairs.[23]

My heart led me to work in his house,
it being splendidly erected in the places of eternity,
proper and beautiful,
while I thought of him and the members of his family.
The perfection of his character has gladdened *my heart*.
I spoke with my mouth,
and *my heart* was at work on his house of eternity,
that I might worship his body, which is in the chapel.

In what follows, Sethos goes into detail regarding the chapel and its
decoration, supplying one of the few verbal descriptions of artistic
representations preserved to us from Egypt:

I shall erect a resting place for his *ka*,
decorated with pictures engraved with a gouge,
with depictions of the one who created me
made in his image.
His mother is with him, not leaving his side.
Those who passed away before him
are gathered in front of him.

> The brother of the king, whom he loved,
> stands face to face with him.
> I, his son, keep his name alive.
> The god's mother, her arms are around him
> like (the arms of) Isis
> when she accompanies her father.
> All his brothers are (represented) according to their rank.
> He rejoices that his people are around him.

The decoration of the chapel, as it is described in this text, constitutes the exact antithesis of the image of death as isolation. Not only does the son take on the task of making contact with his father who has passed away, acting for him out of the love and devotion of his heart, his actions are first and foremost aimed at restoring the social constellations of the deceased by reuniting him with his loved ones. As the one who is now head of the household, it is the son who is responsible for seeing to it that the deceased and his family remain in contact with one another.

The following stanzas, which begin with the words "I am a son" and "he is a god," are related to one another and describe the two partners of the father-son constellation in their respective roles. The role of the heart is again stressed:

> My *jb*-heart turns the one who is weary,
> my *ḥ3.tj*-heart cares for my true father,
> I being like Horus at the side of his father,
> and I commemorate the name of my engenderer.

> ... While my heart hangs[24] so heavy at the condition of his place,
> my *jb*-heart knows no surfeit with regard to him.
> My *ḥ3.tj*-heart strives for his perfection,
> while I (hover) over my father like a falcon,
> my wings (spread) over him in flight,
> I protect his figure like He (i.e., Horus) of Edfu
> in his image at the place of Edfu,
> when he appears on earth
> and joins his father.
> His form is stretched out on the ground;
> my eye beholds the figure of the god
> searching for the body of the Great God.

The memorial chapel was included in the festival processions of Abydos, so that it would be visited by the gods. The deceased father was thus not only united with his family but also integrated into the realm of the gods:

> I cause the majesty of Wennefer to appear,
> that he may visit his house eternally.

I have made it the foremost of the memorial chapels of the kings
that have been erected since the time of Re.
I have made the heart of the lord of This gracious,
so that they may tarry in his illustrious house,
the assemblage of those who have long since passed away.
They honor my father because of his excellence.
I cause my mother to join my father,
like Isis at the side of the one who wakes hale.

To keep a deceased person alive, it was above all important for the son to turn his heart to him. This is also said of Ramesses II, who for his part continued and completed the temple of his father Sethos I:

His countenance was friendly towards his begetter,
his heart was turned to the one who raised him.

In his dedicatory inscription, he goes into the special attachment of his heart to his father, which prompted him to complete the latter's work:

Pleasing, good, and compassionate
is a son who turns his heart to his father.
My heart leads me to perform good deeds for my father, Sethos I.
I will cause that one forever says,
"It was his son who kept his name alive!"[25]

This inscription even includes a dialogue between father and son. Ramesses says:

See, I keep your name alive, I have acted on your behalf!
... May you now say to Re:
"Grant a lifetime filled with jubilee festivals to King Ramesses."
It is good for you when I am king.
A good son is he who commemorates his father.

Sethos responds to his son "as a father speaks on earth with his son." He has in fact intervened on his behalf with the sun god and is able to bring him glad tidings:

Rejoice, my son, whom I love, King Ramesses!
... I shall say to Re with a loving heart:
"Grant him eternity on earth like Khepri!"
I repeat to Osiris, as often as I appear before him:
"Grant him double the lifetime of your son Horus!"

With his concluding words, Sethos again stresses what is especially important about the intervention of the son: to restore the honor and status of his father, to restore him as a social person:

I am exalted through all that you have done for me,
I stand at the forefront of the realm of the dead,
I have become divine and have increased perfection
since your heart turned to me,
while I am in the netherworld,
in the company of the gods in the following of the sun god.[26]

In these texts, it is clear how father and son are interdependent and lend support to one another. The father needs the son to "stand up (i.e., intervene) for him."[27] What is meant is the entire spectrum of activities aimed at restoring the dignity, honor, and social status of the deceased, from revenge on his assassin down to care for his tomb and the preservation of his reputation. The son, for his part, needs the father to speak up for him to the gods and obtain their needed blessing on his activities on earth. All this is what is meant when it is said that father and son are *akh* for one another.

The untranslatable word *akh* refers to a salutary effectiveness that crosses the threshold of death, from this world into the next and vice versa. The precondition of this redemptive force lies in the heart of the son and its bond with the father. The Egyptian expression for this phenomenon is *tkn-jb*, which literally means, "approach of the heart." The heart of the loving and beloved son has the power to create this "approach" that crosses the boundary of death. We are informed about this approach of the heart in a text that warns against enriching oneself through unjust means:

The riches of the dishonest one cannot last.
His children find no store.
He who proceeds unjustly, at the end of his life,
there will be no child of his with "bonding of the heart" (*tkn-jb*).
Only he who can control himself has next of kin,
while the unrestrained one (lit., "he whose heart is torn out") has no
   heirs.[28]

The punishment of the greedy one and the deceiver is a social isolation that begins with his own children. They lack the needed "bonding of the heart" whose redemptive effectiveness reaches into the world beyond. Belief in the possibility of such an effectiveness is the central tenet of Egyptian religion. The basic statement that "one lives if his name is mentioned" defines the state of being alive as a social category. This state is not a matter of an inner, autonomous life force but of constellative integration and acknowledgment. In other words, the state of being alive depends on the extent to which a person is recognized by others as being alive: it is a status.

3. *"One Lives, if Another Guides Him"*

No aspect of the Egyptians' experience of life was as intensely stamped by death as their ethics. This fact is especially clear in two phenomena, one of which was specifically Egyptian, while the other was characteristic of the entire ancient Near East. The specifically Egyptian phenomenon was the close, indeed indissoluble relationship between tomb and right-eousness. With its autobiographical inscriptions, the tomb was the place where moral discourse first occurred in Egypt; it was the tomb that first mentioned social virtue, which later became the theme of the instructional texts that constituted the most important genre of ancient Egyptian literature. In Egypt, the tomb was the "pre-school" of both ethics and literature. The more general phenomenon in which ethics and the image of death were embedded was the framework or setting of these instructions. In this literature, it was always a father who was the teacher, instructing his son in the rules of living with others. This instruction had an unmistakably testamentary character: it was a bequest of the father to the son, who was supposed to take his place among the living and see to the continued existence of his father.

In the previous chapter, we cited the description of old age from the Instruction of Ptahhotep as an example of the physical experience of mortality. Here, we wish to consider it in its context, where it serves as the motive for the instruction of the son. Ptahhotep's reference to his old age leads to his request for the king's permission to instruct his son:

> May this servant be commanded to make himself a "staff of old age"![29]
> Then shall I tell him the words of the "hearers,"
> the thoughts of the predecessors
> who once heeded the gods (var.: who once served the ancestor-kings).

Then the majesty of this god spoke:

> If you instruct him in the words of the past,[30]
> he will be a model for the sons of high officials.
> What is heard will enter him, along with all the reliability of the one who
> speaks to him.
> For no one is born wise.[31]

On the threshold of death, an old man passes a summary of his knowledge along to his son.[32] This was the typical situation in which Egyptian wisdom was handed down. It had both an initiatory and a testamentary character, for the mortuary cult and wisdom had the same root: the father-son constellation.

The point of the father-son constellation was mutual endowing with life. The son endowed his deceased father with life by pronouncing his name, intervening on his behalf, restoring and maintaining his place and status in society. The father endowed his son with life first by introducing him into society, by raising him into a life in society and thereby socializing him. This is the meaning of the maxim "one lives, if an other guides him."[33] Here, we are dealing with connectivity during life: just as a deceased person lives again if his name is mentioned, so a living person is alive in the full sense of the word only if another is there to give him guidance. True life requires at least two persons. Obviously, the condition the Egyptians called "life" in its full sense did not begin with birth, but only when someone else was there to provide guidance.[34] A man was alive by virtue of his entering into a constellative community that included his family, friends, superiors, and subordinates. Egyptian ethics was connective because it arose from the image of death as disconnectedness, and thus of death as isolation and the collapse of connection. Its goal was to make a person alive through integration. A pupil who was unable to hear was thus incapable of being guided by others, he was like one of the "living dead":

> But the foolish one who does not heed,
> . . . he views knowledge as ignorance,
> usefulness as harmfulness.
> . . . He lives on what one dies of,
> his condition is . . . (that of the) living dead, day by day.[35]

One incapable of understanding cannot distinguish between good and evil. He views what is harmful as useful, and what is useful as harmful. His social incompetence isolates him from the structure of life-giving connectivity. Someone unable to heed another is condemned to isolation and thus to death. The ideal was the "hearing heart."[36] Speech was the most important connective medium and life-giving element of a human being, and that is why it played so central a role in communicating with the dead, and why someone incapable of good speech and of heeding was one of the "living dead."

The other case of a failed integration of the individual into the constellations of society was the greedy one. Here, too, the Egyptians saw a deadly form of disconnective behavior. Another section of the Instruction of Ptahhotep deals with this theme:

> Greed is a serious, incurable sickness
> that cannot be treated.
> It alienates fathers, mothers, and full brothers;
> it drives out the wife.
> . . .
> But that man endures who lives up to *maat*

and who departs (i.e., dies) at his own pace.
It is he who can thus make a testament,
while the greedy one has no tomb.[37]

Just as obstinacy is called death, here, greed is diagnosed as an incurable illness. It sunders even the closest ties of blood relationship and marriage, leading to isolation and loneliness in the social dimension. In this passage, Ptahhotep brings the threshold of death into play. The foolish one who will not allow himself to be guided is dead while still alive. The greedy one who destroys his social ties gambles away any chance of enduring in the memory of society: "the greedy one has no tomb." In the eyes of the Egyptians, as we have seen, this was the mystery of connectivity: it survived death, it meant immortality. Obstinacy and greed, not death, had the power to rend this net asunder. This hope was the fundamental principle of Egyptian society. The Egyptian ideal of *maat* (truth, justice, order) was not only the principle of social but also of temporal connectivity, of permanence, endurance, and remembrance, of the continuity of past and future. The egoist not only had no friends, he had no future. He had no prospect of his name being mentioned, and thus no prospect of a tomb. For without such incorporation into the memory of society, the physical tomb had no meaning, it was a meaningless signifier, a rubber check, something abandoned and left to die. The true monument of a person was not a tomb of stone but his righteousness and the love of his fellow man. There is a maxim that reads,

> The monument of a man is his virtue,
> the one with bad character is forgotten.[38]

In the Instruction for Merikare, it is said that a tomb is built through virtue and righteousness. These were the investments in remembrance: the tomb was only an external sign of the remembrance that was attached to a life lived in virtue and righteousness. Remembrance presupposed these qualities. An important text of the early second millennium, the Story of the Eloquent Peasant, has this to say:

> Righteousness is eternal.
> It descends into the realm of the dead in the hand of the one who
>   practiced it.
> He will be buried, and he will join the earth;
> but his name will not be erased on earth,
> he will be remembered because of his virtue.

Righteousness was a social principle. So also was the remembrance that it conferred and in which the individual hoped to live on, that is to say, a social remembrance, the remembrance of the group. The inscriptions and representations in the tomb were directed toward this remembrance, to the extent that they were not connected with rituals, which constituted another medium of survival. Tombs were intended to be visited by posterity. They impressed the visitor not only by displaying the high rank of the tomb owner, that is, the royal favor he obtained during life as reward for the honesty, the virtue, and the professional efficiency with which he conducted himself; they also show clearly that this reward fell to a truly righteous person who looked after the poor and the dependent, who fed the hungry, gave drink to the thirsty, clothed the naked, ferried the boatless, protected the widow, and raised the orphan, in short, who did everything in his power to take action against injustice on earth, to vindicate the poor man against the rich one, to oppose the oppression of the weak by the strong, to assure the just distribution of the means of sustenance, and to spread harmony, solidarity, and friendship in society. An elaborate rhetoric of virtue, righteousness, and social responsibility was developed in connection with these tomb biographies, or rather, these apologia of the tomb owner before the tribunal of posterity, and this rhetoric led to the development of a discourse on wisdom that constituted the core of Egyptian literature. As the Egyptians saw it, wisdom was the art of living righteously, and the epitome of a righteous life was living with others. To the Egyptians, life meant connectivity, integration into the group, so that the individual thought and acted for others, so that they might think and act for him for all time. Death was to be forgotten, to fall loose from the social net of mutual thought and action. It was needful to struggle against such a death so as not to be forgotten, not through heroic deeds that exceeded all norms, but through a righteous and virtuous life that fulfilled the norms.

These wisdom texts imply that life is an art to be learned, and specifically, an art of living together with others. "We can only live together"; this formula, to which Theo Sundermeier has reduced the quintessence of the black African experience of life, also serves to characterize ancient Egyptian ethics.[39] Life is a question of being able to live, and this ability is dependent on the ability to live with others, on the connective virtues that make one competent to live in society.

4. Subjection to Death through Social Isolation

It is clear that competence to live in society was a question of good upbringing and specific social virtues. But the Egyptian texts go one step further still, a step we can understand only with difficulty. Peter Seibert has distinguished a concept of subjection to death in texts that deal not with inner virtue but with external circumstances, the "satires on the trades." In them, various occupations are derided with regard to the "subjection to death" they entail, and in particular, the fact that they interfere with the competence of those who exercise them to live in society by dirtying them, tiring them out, making them sick, isolating them from their loved ones, and so forth, thus exerting as disconnective an effect as foolishness and greed. The unkind, derisive glance that the satires on the trades cast on these occupations isolates the exercise of them from the structure of meaning inherent in social activity and represents them as lonesome ones, absurd à la Sisyphus or Beckett in the circular nature of their activity: the fisherman fishes, the washer washes, the barber barbers, with nothing whatsoever resulting from all this labor except that in the end, they are worn out, wet, and dirty, and no one wants to have anything at all to do with them. We may console ourselves with the thought that those so mocked repaid the mockery with mockery of their own, for there was no trade that could escape it. These satires are evidently not entirely serious, though the comic effect of their characterization is not altogether clear to us.[40] These texts are intended to recruit individuals into the scribal profession. The scribe was the only man who did not dirty himself with his work, the only one whose work did not isolate him; quite the contrary, it intensively integrated him into society, for it was he who communicated orders and exercised control. The intent of the mockery is thus to attract children born into the various trades to the scribal profession. The difference between the scribal elite and the working masses is stressed not to promote the solidarity of the masses but to encourage individuals to strive for upward social mobility.

We thus maintain that just as the principle of connectivity breathed life into the body, binding the individual limbs into a body, so it breathed life into an individual as a person by integrating him into the constellations of society. It is easy to see that this concept of the person corresponded perfectly with the structure of a polytheistic religion. Deities, too, existed as persons in reciprocal relationships in which they acted on and spoke with one another. They were what they were as persons only with respect to one another. Constellative theology and anthropology mirror and model themselves on one another, stressing the ties, roles, and functions that bind the constituent members of the group. What they view as the worst evil are the concepts of isolation, loneliness, self-sufficiency, and independence. From their point of view, these are symptoms of death, dissolution, and destruction. Even for godhood, loneliness is an unbearable condition.

5. "I Am One of You": Salvation from Death through Inclusion

To the image of death as isolation, there corresponds the counterimage of acceptance of the deceased into the world beyond and his complete, heartfelt inclusion in the social constellations of the afterlife. Thus, in the Egyptian texts, the world beyond is not a spatially conceived landscape but rather a social sphere that needs to integrate the deceased into itself as a newcomer.

In the Pyramid Texts of the Old Kingdom, this integration has two quite different, even contrary aspects. The narrower circle of the highest gods and goddesses, who constitute the deceased's family—Re, Geb, Nut, and the goddess of the West (Isis)—receive him with gestures of joyous recognition, embrace him, and lead him to the place where he will exercise his rule. The other gods, however, react with astonishment, fear, and even terror at the appearance of a powerful being whose like they have never seen:

> Tumult reigns in the sky.
> "We see something new!" say the primeval gods.
> O Ennead, Horus is in the sunlight!
> The lords of forms greet him,
> and the Ennead serves him.[41]

> The sky is clouded, the stars are veiled,
> the arches (of the sky) quake, the bones of the earth god tremble,
> the movements (of the stars) are stilled,
> for they have seen the king, how he appears, *ba*-mighty,
> as a god who lives on his fathers
> and consumes his mothers.[42]

In this well-known spell, which is known as the Cannibal Hymn, the king is described as a being who physically incorporates the realm of the gods into himself:

> He it is who eats men and lives on the gods,
> ... The one he finds on his way he eats piecemeal.

This violent form of integration through incorporation occurs only in the Pyramid Texts. But it is important that through the process of "sacramental explanation," which we shall discuss in chapter 15, the taking of nourishment came to be generally associated with the incorporation of the deceased into the realm of the gods. Eating and drinking were social acts that incorporated the recipient of what was given into a community that took meals together, a sort of "round table." We know that the offerings of the deceased came from the temples and altars of the gods, for example, from the altar of Re at Heliopolis, with the result that the deceased thereby entered into a relationship with the gods. This relationship was more important than the nourishment itself. This provisioning was first and foremost a symbolic expression of his social integration and inclusion in the realm of the gods.

In the Coffin Texts, the violent characteristics of the Old Kingdom retreat into the background, though the Cannibal Hymn does occur on two coffins as spell 573.[43] But the deceased appears as ruler of the netherworldly realm in these texts as well:

> "This is Osiris, this is your king!
> Give him praise,
> rejoice at the sight of him,
> he who has come from the land of life
> to his place of justification!"
> —so says Osiris, the Bull of the West.[44]

The appearance of the deceased as king and ruler of those in the netherworld is the exact reversal not only of isolation but also of his loss of honor and status as a result of death. It is for this reason that praise of the deceased plays so important a role. A mortuary liturgy first attested at a relatively late date, which was intended for the cult of Osiris and thus written in the name of the god Osiris-Khentamentiu and not in that of a private "Osiris N.," supplies the earliest spell that serves to "instill fear of Osiris-Khentamentiu":

> O Osiris-Khentamentiu,
> fear of you seizes the dead spirits,
> reverence for you prevails among the divine spirits;
> the fear of you among the gods of the realm of the dead is as great
> as (the fear of) Anubis, the foremost of the westerners,
> and Osiris, the foremost of the westerners.
> . . . May you appear as King of Upper and Lower Egypt
> and assume power over the Ennead
> and their food and provisions.
>
> O Osiris-Khentamentiu,
> sky and earth are yours,
> life and death are yours,
> supremacy over the realm of the dead is yours!

In the mortuary texts of the New Kingdom, however, the deceased turns to the inhabitants of the realm of the dead as peers and expresses the wish that he be accepted into their circle as one of them:

> I have come to you, my arms full of *maat*,
> and no contrariness in my body.
> I have not knowingly told a lie,
> I have not coveted the belongings of another.
> I have done *maat* for the lord of *maat*
> and have calmed the Light-eye for its lord.
> I have given divine offerings to the Ennead
> and mortuary offerings to the ancestral spirits.
> Open up for me, that I may enter into your midst,
> I am one of you![45]

In this period, the idea of a Judgment of the Dead (see chapter 3), which lent a strongly ethical character to the mortuary beliefs, became the decisive center of Egyptian mortuary religion. The deceased no longer made his appearance before the inhabitants of the netherworld in the intimidating splendor of his royal insignia but rather in possession of the virtue and righteousness that proved him worthy to join their circle.

The Theban ruling house of Dynasty 21 invented a special form of integration into the society of those in the netherworld. This was the era of the divine state, ruled by Amun through oracular decisions in the form of a direct theocracy. The members of the royal family went to their tombs with a document from this god, a decree that concerned their next-worldly destiny and assured them the status to which they aspired. After a grandiose royal titulary that represents the culmination of Egyptian hymnic writing,[46] Amun determines, for example:

§ 1. Amonrasonther has issued his great, august oracle in order to deify Neskhons in the West.

§ 2. I shall deify Neskhons in the West; I shall deify her in the realm of the dead. I shall command that she receive water in the West; I shall decree that she receives alimentation offerings in the necropolis. I shall deify her *ba* and her body in the necropolis and shall not allow that her *ba* be destroyed in the realm of the dead. . . .

I shall command that every god and every goddess and all that is divine in the realm of the dead receive her.

I shall command that all that is good be done for her, that a person approach when she is in the condition in which she is, transported to the necropolis and deified, and every good thing is done for her, and she is able to receive water and alimentary offerings, and she receives her *p3w.t*-bread when it is *p3w.t*-bread that the deified ones have received, and a temple offering when it is a temple offering that the deified have received.

§ 3. I shall command that Neskhons eat and drink in the same way as every god and every goddess in the realm of the dead.

I shall command that Neskhons be in every good state that accrues to a god
or a goddess in the realm of the dead, and I shall protect my servant
Pinudjem from any complaint regarding this matter. . . .
I shall cause that her *ba* go out and in as it wishes, without hindrance.[47]

Another seven paragraphs follow, in which, among other things, Pinudjem is exculpated from any complaints and gripes on the part of the
deceased Neskhons. The genre of divine decrees continued to develop in
the Late Period, when they were copied onto a wooden stela and
deposited in the tomb to assure the deceased acceptance, recognition,
freedom of movement, and provisions.[48]

In the especially richly decorated tombs of the Late Period (eighth to
sixth centuries B.C.E.), it was customary to inscribe the doorposts and
thicknesses of the many interior doorways with spells whose most important theme was the integration of the tomb owner into the social sphere
of the next world:[49]

> The Great Ennead praises you,
> the Lesser Ennead carries you,
> the southern chapels praise you,
> the northern chapels carry you . . .[50]

In all the regions of the cosmos, a place is erected for the deceased, for
each of the forms in which he will spend eternity:

> You who remain in the entourage of the night barque (of the sun god)
> and in the entourage of Re in the day barque,
> a seat will be set up for you in the temple of Sokar,
> you will join the Ennead.[51]

Not only is acceptance into the society of those in the next world especially important but also participation in the divine festivals of this world,
especially the festival of Osiris at Abydos:

> You will be summoned into the following of the *neshmet*-barque
> when it journeys to U-Poqer.
> You will be given the garland of vindication,
> as something that the lord of Abydos has taken off.[52]

In another spell, the deceased turns to the deities who surround the sun
god when he rises:

> Open up for me, that I may join you:
> I am one of you![53]

One of the most popular mortuary spells of the Late Period depicts the integration of the deceased and his acceptance into the world beyond in the form of an initiation into a temple. Here, the autocratic appearance of the deceased king, as it is depicted in the Pyramid Texts, is turned on its head:

> May you appear in the place where the god is,
> in the sacred place where the god is.
> May the followers (of the god) bring you,
> and may the ushers usher you,
> may the gods rejoice in your presence.
> May you eat bread from the altar of Re,
> may your *ka* take nourishment from the offering table of Nun.
> May the "Shorn One" announce you
> and the "Greatest of Seers" introduce you,
> may your (every) step be furthered in the "Great House."
> May you leave and enter among the gods,
> accepted into the divine family.
>
> You find the gods dancing before your gaze,
> the Ennead calling your welcome.
> Your hand will be taken by Re himself,
> the crew of his barque escorts you.
> The gods rejoice when they see you,
> they exult at your coming.
>
> They say to you, Osiris-Khentamentiu,
> when they join you in peace,
> "Welcome in peace to the sacred place":
> thus do those in their chapels cry out to you in joy,
> when they see you, making your appearance as a god,
> and how tall you stand in the form of a god.
>
> "Come with us to the chapel,
> that you may take (your) place at the side of Re,
> that you may see the god, and the god see you,
> and the one god rejoices over the other.
> Welcome in peace to the All-lord,"
> say the gods who follow Re.
>
> The god of Light-land extends his hands to you,
> you receive offerings on the altar of Re.
> Your hands are grasped by the primeval ones.
> The god conducts you to the barque.
> You take your place in it, wherever you desire.
> You sit down, your legs unhindered.
>
> You fly up as a Horus falcon,
> you roam (i.e., glide down) as a goose,

a star that cannot set.
Yours is *nḥḥ*-eternity, your sustenance is *ḏ.t*-eternity.
A place has been granted you at the side of the Sole Lord,
you are his companion in the fields of Light-land.[54]

The common concept underlying these wishes (to which innumerable others could easily be added) is relief from the isolation into which death has plunged the individual. All these texts conjure up images of social connectivity, with the aim of reintegrating the deceased into a community that will take in the one who has been torn from the land of the living.

CHAPTER THREE

Death as Enemy

1. The Lawsuit in Heliopolis

The image of death as enemy[1] finds Osiris confronted by Seth, his murderer. It is also closely connected with the second image of death, that of social isolation and the activities of the son. But the contending of Osiris with his murderer constitutes a constellation of its own, one that came to acquire an especially central status during the course of the history of Egyptian mortuary religion. In the narrative unfolding of the mythic events, these three images of death are arranged into successive stages in the action. The first stage is the finding of and care for the body and the restoration of its physical connectivity by Isis and Nephthys, and the second is the restoration of the person and his social connectivity by Horus. The third stage, or better, the culmination of the second, is the legal contending with Seth, the murderer. The hymn to Osiris on stela Louvre 286 contains the most detailed continuous description of these three stages. We have cited the first two, (1) Isis' search and her care for the body, and (2) the conception, birth, and upbringing of Horus at the end of the first section of chapter 1. The hymn continues:

> 3. The Lawsuit between Horus and Seth
>
> The judicial council of *maat* was gathered for him,
> the Ennead and the All-lord himself,

the lords of *maat,* who despise wrong, were gathered in it,
sitting in council in the hall of Geb,
to give the office to the one to whom it belonged,
the kingship to the one who was entitled to it.
Horus was found in the right,
to him was the office of his father given.

In the stanzas that follow, the hymn depicts the triumph of Horus:

He emerged garlanded at the command of Geb;
he seized the rulership over the Two Banks,
the White Crown firm on his head;
he laid claim to the entire land,
sky and earth were under his supervision.
Men were commended to him: subjects, officials, sky-people,
Egypt and northerners,
what the sun encircles was subject to his plans.

Next, we are told of the beneficent rule of Horus:

The north wind, the (Nile) river, the flood,
all plants, all vegetables;
the god of grain, he granted all his herbage,
the nourishment of the earth;
he raised repleteness and granted it in all the lands.

The whole world rejoiced, their hearts were glad,
their breast was full of rapture,
all faces exulted, while everyone prayed to his beauty:
"How sweet for us is love of him!
His charm penetrates hearts!"
Great was the love of him in every breast.

The hymn then portrays the humiliation and punishment of the enemy, and with the same stroke, the restoration of the honor of Osiris:

They have delivered his enemy to the son of Isis,
fallen through his (own) violence.
Evil has befallen the troublemaker
who committed violence, his judgment has overtaken him.
The son of Isis, he has avenged his father,
he (i.e., Horus) who has sanctified his name and made it splendid.

The dignitaries have taken their place,
reverence is firmly established according to his laws;
the street is free, the roads are open,
how happy are the Two Banks!

> The illness has perished, the slanderer has flown;
> the land is in peace under its lord,
> *maat* is firm for its lord,
> the back is turned to evil.

With his son's acquittal and the punishment of Seth, Osiris is once again fully alive. Now it is death, which had torn him limb from limb, isolated him, and robbed him of his dignity, that is conquered.

> Rejoice, Wennefer!
> The son of Isis, he has received the crown,
> the office of his father has been granted him
> in the hall of Geb.
> Re, he has declared it,
> Thoth, he has written it,
> the council is satisfied.
> Your father Geb has decreed in your favor,
> and it has been done as he said.

Osiris is resurrected to a new form of life. He remains the "weary of heart," and he remains in the netherworld. But he is not dead: his limbs are reunited into a single body, his person is restored through his integration into the social constellation of the divine realm, and the wrong done to him by death is atoned for by the trial, conviction, and punishment of Seth, the embodiment of the cause of death.

This splitting up of death into the five roles of Osiris, Isis, Nephthys, Horus, and Seth represents a specific feature of mythic thought, one that conceptually overcomes a complex crisis experience and renders it manageable through ritual.

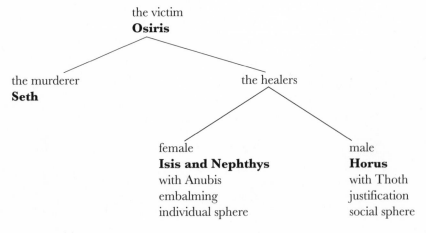

the victim
Osiris

the murderer
Seth

the healers

female
Isis and Nephthys
with Anubis
embalming
individual sphere

male
Horus
with Thoth
justification
social sphere

Death—in the person of Seth—is overcome and eliminated. The deceased regains his disintegrated integrity, and he is ritually integrated into the triangular constellation Osiris-Isis-Horus. Isis (with Nephthys) is the feminine principle that gathers and breathes life into the disparate multiplicity of body parts, while Horus is the masculine principle that maintains his rank in the realm of the living and looks after his rights. Osiris embodies the deceased himself, and Seth is the death—the murder, the violence, the wrong—that is to be channeled away from Osiris. In mythic thought, as already noted, there is no such thing as a natural death. Every death is a violent assault that always meets with blame, an extremely widespread concept that Thomas Macho views as "the most ancient explanation" of death; as he puts it, summarizing this point of view, "every death is perhaps actually a murder."[2] Every death is to be traced back to the influence of something evil. This evil is personified by Seth, who is held accountable. The Egyptian myth, however, goes one step further. It not only portrays the violent character of death but also its injustice. It constructs its image of death on the basis of the distinction between right and wrong, thus providing an opening for ritual action. Every death is an offense against what is right, the truth/justice/order that the Egyptians called *maat*. It was thus possible for them to call it to account, to denounce it, to bring it to justice. They could do something about it and restore the order that had been destroyed. Because death was not natural, because it did not lie in the nature of things, they could not accept it, they could and had to do something to counter it. And so, they initiated a legal proceeding against death, with Seth as the accused and Osiris the complainant. Pyramid Texts spell 477 has to do with this proceeding:[3]

> Think of it, Seth,
> place in your heart
> these words that Geb has pronounced against you,
> and these accusations that the gods have raised against you
> in the House of the Prince in Heliopolis,
> for you cast Osiris to the ground,
>
> and you said, Seth, "I have not done it,"
> so that you might gain power thereby and wriggle out of it
> and be more powerful than Horus,
> as you said, Seth,
> "it was he who provoked me,"
> and there came into being his (i.e., Osiris') name "*iku-ta*,"
> as you said, Seth,
> "it is he who approached me,"
> and there came into being his name "Orion,"
> long of leg and broad of stride at the head of Upper Egypt.

Raise yourself, Osiris,
for Seth has raised himself.
He has heard the accusations of the gods,
which were spoken on behalf of my father, the god.
Your arm belongs to Isis, your hand belongs to Nephthys,
and you go between them.
To you is the sky given,
to you is the earth given,
to you is the Field of Reeds given,
the Horian places and the Sethian places,
the towns are given to you, and the nomes are gathered for you.
So said Atum. The one who pleaded for it was Geb.

Thus is death prosecuted. Death, in the person of Seth, is defeated, while the deceased, Osiris, gets his due and is installed as ruler of the nether-world, and his son Horus inherits his throne on earth. In the Coffin Texts of the Middle Kingdom, we encounter this spell from the Pyramid Texts at the end of an extremely comprehensive mortuary liturgy, that is, a series of spells that were recited on behalf of the dead in a particular cultic framework.[4] We are thus able to get a picture of the accompanying rites. From the Coffin Texts version, it emerges clearly that the legal conflict with Seth and the latter's condemnation were accompanied by a ritual slaughter. Seth's execution was symbolically carried out in the form of the slaughter of an ox. Nearly two thousand years later, we again encounter these same spells at the end of a different mortuary liturgy on papyri of the Graeco-Roman era.[5] We can thus conclude that this ritual slaughter was the typical conclusion of a mortuary liturgy. With the execution of the enemy, the healing of the deceased was completed.[6] This fact is made clear in the concluding text, in which the ritualist presents himself and explains his cultic acts:

See, I have come, my father Osiris,
I am your son, I am Horus.
I have come, that I may bring you these enemies
whom the Ennead has subjected to you.
. . .
Atum has slain him (i.e., your enemy Seth) for you
in that name of his, "Bull."
Atum has destroyed him for you
in that name of his, "Long-horned Bull . . . ."
Atum has delivered him to you as a bad one.
He will be bound in the care of the sun-people,
in this name of his, "Sacrificial Bull."
I have brought him to you as a bull
with a rope around his neck.

Eat it, devour his head,
for all your things belong to you.
His leg of beef belongs to me, for I am your heir on your throne,
since you have fortified your house, which is on earth.

This is clearly the description of a ritual slaughter that closes the recitation of the spell, and thus the entire mortuary liturgy, and which is explained as the punishment of the enemy.

The decisive difference between the second image of death, in which Osiris and Horus form a constellation, while Seth is only the object of Horus' actions, and the third image of death, in which Osiris is directly confronted by Seth, lies in the fact that here, Osiris is active for the first time. Supported by Isis and Nephthys, and led by Horus and Thoth, he has regained his mobility and can make his appearance before the gods. Without an active encounter with his enemy, Osiris cannot come back to life; this encounter is the decisive threshold he must cross in order to conquer death. With his public vindication against his enemy—that is, death as assassin—Osiris regains both rulership and life, for in this image of death, these two things are closely related. The crown that Osiris regains symbolizes eternal life and ultimate salvation from death.

Of all the gods, Osiris is the paradigmatic king. Hymns to this god indulge in enumerations of royal titles. All his other aspects—as moon, as the constellation Orion, as the Nile, as the seed that is buried and reborn—take second place to his role as king. This thoroughly political aspect of Osiris as a royal god polarizes the divine realm into friend and foe. Rebellion is the inevitable dark side of rulership. When claim to rulership is made, counterclaim is also made. This dialectic is played out in solar myth as well as in the myth of Osiris. Rulership must always be asserted against opposition. The power of a ruler is proportionate to, and manifests itself in, his capacity to assert himself against his enemy. Rulership is a violent power that provokes opposition, and in Egyptian mythology, this opponent is called Apopis in the case of the sun, and Seth in that of Osiris.

As the Egyptians conceived it, the sun traversed the sky in the daytime and the netherworld by night. This movement had not only a cosmic character as the source of light, warmth, and time but also an eminently political meaning, as the establishment of right and order (*maat*).[7] With his unceasing realization of *maat*, the sun god was the prototype of the king, who imitated the sun god's activity on earth. In the mythic construction of reality, this political aspect of the sun's course was stressed by the fact that Re had an enemy who ever and again threatened his claim to rulership. This enemy was Apopis, a huge serpent that threatened to gulp down the celestial waters and leave the sun barque stranded on the sandbanks of the heavens. In this confrontation with Apopis, the course of the sun assumed the character of a victory, or as the Egyptians saw it, a "vindication (or "justification") against." Re had to justify himself against Apopis, and Osiris against Seth, to maintain the rulership. The task of the sun god was to keep the cosmic cycle going, while that of Osiris consisted in overcoming death. The cosmic cycle was politicized, interpreted as the establishment of rule and thus as justification against an enemy. In the Osiris myth, the overcoming of death was politicized by depicting it as a justification against Seth.

Seth played contrasting roles in the solar and the Osirian myths. In the solar myth, he fought at the side of the sun god. He stood at the prow of the sun barque and pierced the dragon Apopis with his mighty spear, with the result that all the water the latter had swallowed gushed forth from his body. Seth's double role demonstrates that the Egyptians considered death as an enemy and an embodiment of evil, but not as the absolute evil. Death was also a part of the cosmic order; it did not threaten the cosmos from without but only life from within.

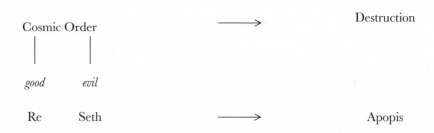

In his constant struggle against the destructive powers opposing his effort to keep the cosmic order in motion, Re makes use of death, mustering it against Apopis, the personification of absolute destruction. Seth cannot be eliminated from the cosmos without bringing it to a standstill. Death is inevitable, but—and of this, the Egyptians were convinced—something could be done about it, especially in that it embodied evil only in a this-worldly, relative sense.

Osiris triumphed over Seth before the divine tribunal and thereby regained the rulership. On the existential level, this mythic episode became the archetype for triumph over death. Just as Osiris triumphed over Seth, so every deceased person would triumph over death. Encountering the enemy and achieving vindication against him constituted the last, decisive step in the overcoming of death.

The mythic model of legal wrangling over the succession to the throne had its natural place in the royal mortuary cult, and it could easily be applied to the nonroyal level. At the royal level, the point was first and foremost continuity of the kingship after the death of the king, according to the principle of "the king is dead, long live the king." This point found expression in the triangular relationship between Osiris, death (Seth), and Horus. On the more general, human level, the point was not continuity of office but the continuity of life itself, the overcoming of death and the vindication of the deceased against the powers responsible for his death, as personified by the figure of the enemy. In the Coffin Texts, there is a spell, spell 149, that describes this contending of the deceased with his enemy at some length.[8] The spell bears the title "Becoming a Falcon-Man, Transfiguring a Man in the Realm of the Dead, Giving Him Power over His Enemies," and it begins with the remark, "A man shall speak while shod with sandals and clothed in red linen and his breastplate." The expression "human falcon" or "falcon-man" presumably designates a being that can shape-shift back and forth between a human and a falcon form, just as a werewolf shifts back and forth between the form of a man and that of a wolf.

> I have a human body
> that comes raging from the Isle of Fire (i.e., the world above).
> May (admittance) be opened for me in(to) the tribunal
> on account of what has been done to me,
> the wrong (done) by my enemy.
> I desire for myself (the ability to) transform into a falcon-man
> that goes about among men,
> that I may go out in it (i.e., in this form)
> with no god hindering me.
> I am a human falcon
> who moves among men and whom no one can take to court.
> I am on the pathway of Horus,
> that I may shoot at my enemy among men,
> as I go out against him from the tribunal of Khentamentiu.
>
> I have spent the night being judged with him
> and his people in the realm of the dead.
> His advocate in the tribunal arose,
> his hands pressed tight against his face,
> when he saw that I was vindicated
> and that that enemy of mine was delivered into my power,
> that I might seize him, at the side of the men
> who came with me to do battle
> with magical spells on their lips.
>
> I have appeared as a great falcon
> and seized him with my talons.
> My lips are against him like a flashing knife,

my talons are against him like the arrows of Sakhmet,
my horns are against him like (those of) a great wild bull,
my wings are against him like (those of) a kite,
my tail is against him like (that of) a living *ba*.

I fly up and alight on his spine,
I strangle him in the presence of his family,
I seize his heart without their noticing it.

I am truly a human falcon,
to whom transforming into a falcon has been granted
in the house of Khentamentiu upon the true testimony,
after I gave it concerning what was done to me,
the wrong (done) by that enemy of mine.

But now I speak from my heart:
How transfigured am I, how strong is my son (var., my *ba*)!
I shall turn to his family,
that I may cut them off from their grief (?).

But now I speak from my heart
to those in the tribunal in the house of Khentamentiu:
"See, I have come
and have driven out my enemy and his family,
I have torn down his house and driven out his survivors."

Then the transfigured ones rejoice,
and the heart of Osiris is joyful,
when he sees me and how I mount up as a falcon,
after I walked on my legs
when I was among men.

I am truly a human falcon
who speaks in the caverns of Osiris (i.e., the netherworld).
I speak at the side of Osiris,
as I spoke on the Isle of Fire (i.e., the world above).

"How very transfigured is he, this god!" said Khentamentiu with regard
    to me.
The command exists in the tribunal,
the confirmation is at the side of the two goddesses of Truth,
that my enemy is delivered into my power:
"Condemned are those who are and who are not (yet)
who will battle against you and demand him (i.e., the enemy) back
    from you."

There is reason to think that this scene has to do with the vindication of
the deceased against a symbolic enemy, and that like Seth in the myth of
Osiris, this enemy symbolizes death. Here, though, there is a break with
the mythic model of the lawsuit about the succession to the throne, and

the same basic concept, the confrontation of the deceased with his enemy as his death, is expressed in quite different terms.

2. *The Moralizing of Death: The Idea of the Judgment of the Dead*

Within a few centuries, the idea of a "Judgment of the Dead" evolved from this model of vindication.[9] The wrong that was responsible for the death of the deceased, and which in the mythic model was separated off from him and called to account, was now sought within himself, and specifically as a guilt for which he had to answer and from which he had to purify himself. Confrontation of the deceased with his enemy thus became confrontation with his own guilt. Originally, the deceased distanced himself from death and vindicated himself against it, but at the end of this centuries-long process of evolution, he had to separate himself from his guilt and vindicate himself before a divine judge. "Vindication against" became "vindication before." The emergence of a Judgment of the Dead from the archaic image of death as an enemy was one of the most significant developments in the history of Egyptian religion, and the idea of such a judgment was one of the central religious ideas of Egypt, one whose influence would spread far beyond that land. The concept of the Judgment of the Dead came to acquire a towering importance among the images of death that influenced the reality of life for the ancient Egyptians.

This concept evolved at the beginning of the second millennium B.C.E., and it found its clearest expression in the Instruction for Merikare, a wisdom text of this period:

> The judges who judge the wretch,
> you know they are not lenient
> on that day of judging the miserable one,
> in the hour of fulfilling what is prescribed.
> Awful is the accuser who has knowledge.

> Trust not in the length of the years!
> They view a lifetime as but an hour.
> When a man remains over after "landing" (i.e., his death),
> his deeds are set beside him as a sum.

> Being there lasts forever.
> A fool is he who does what they reproach.
> He who reaches them without sin
> will be there as a god,
> striding freely like the lords of eternity.[10]

Here, it is clear that we are dealing with a court of law before which each person had to appear after death. He was accountable, before a "knowing" judge, for a lifetime that played before their eyes in a single hour, as though it were a biographical film. Death as an enemy who had wronged the deceased became personal guilt for which he had to answer before a knowing god. Here, we already see the Judgment of the Dead in its classic form: as a scene in which the deceased is confronted no longer by his enemy but by his own life, his own guilt, and by his judge.

The question is thus only one of how widespread and normative this concept already was at that time, and how greatly it influenced the conduct of life in the various strata of society in the Middle Kingdom. The text is addressed to a king. Perhaps the Judgment of the Dead was still a highly exclusive concept.

On this point, recent research into the Coffin Texts has enabled the reconstruction of a cultic context within whose framework the Judgment of the Dead was ritually enacted.[11] From these texts, it emerges that the ceremony of the Judgment of the Dead occurred at the end of the embalming ritual. On the night before the burial, the embalming ritual was concluded with a "wake" that was celebrated with offerings, libations, censings, purifications, and above all, with recitations. These recitations confront us with a concept of the Judgment of the Dead that was still largely based on the old royal model of the mythic lawsuit between Horus and Seth. As Osiris, the deceased was fully vindicated against Seth, that is, death, in this lawsuit. In the myth, Osiris became king of the netherworld and ruler of the dead. The ordinary deceased was a follower of Osiris, was called Osiris and compared to him, and became a member of his following. He came into possession not only of life but also of personal status and recognition. He bore the name of the god, along with his own titles and his personal name, as well as the epithet "justified/vindicated." He smote Seth, which meant that he had conquered death. Not only had Seth once killed him, he also continued to threaten his offerings with an irrevocably annihilating attack. At the heart of this concept of death as an enemy lay the distinction between the first and the second death. The first death was the work of Seth, which we have described in the first two chapters as dismemberment and isolation. Osiris could be cured of this death through the combined efforts of Isis and Nephthys, Horus, Thoth, and Anubis. But Seth did not give up, he continued to threaten Osiris with annihilation. This was the second death, which had by all means to be warded off. Seth therefore had to be repelled, humiliated, condemned, and punished. Just like the vindication of the deceased in the Judgment of the Dead, the contending with Seth was tantamount to the warding off of the second death. Victory over the enemy had the same meaning as acquittal from the accusation of sin, and therein lay the distinctive common ground of the older and the newer concepts. Through his victory over Seth in the lawsuit over the succession to the throne, and also through his acquittal in the Judgment of the Dead, the deceased, who had suffered the first death, was saved from the second, ultimate death. For him, the first death was a transition into an immortality that immunized him against that further, ultimate death. The Judgment of the Dead determined the transition into that other realm in which he regained his integrity, his identity, and his personality.

The Coffin Texts give us an unexpected insight into the ritual enactment of the Judgment of the Dead in the form of liturgical recitations. They closely connect the concept of vindication with the process of embalming and mummification. Guilt, accusation, enmity, and so forth are treated as forms of impurity and decay—as, so to say, immaterial but harmful substances—that must be eliminated so as to transpose the deceased into a condition of purity that can withstand decay and dissolution. Vindication was moral mummification. When the embalmer's work on the corpse was done, the priests took over and extended the work of purification and preservation to the entirety of the person. The Egyptian word for "mummy," *sᶜḥ*, also meant "worthy" and "aristocrat." In this last stage of the mummification process, the deceased experienced the Judgment of the Dead and received the aristocratic status of a follower of Osiris in the netherworld. He was vindicated against all accusations and absolved of any and all guilt, of any sin that could hinder his transition into the next life, even the foolishness of early childhood.

In many respects, the concept of the Judgment of the Dead, as codified in chapter 125 of the Book of the Dead, was the opposite of the original mythic model. In chapter 125, the deceased was not the plaintiff but rather the defendant, and he had to vindicate himself before the divine judges, reciting a long list of potential transgressions and testifying that he had not committed them. In the process, his heart was placed on a scale and weighed against a feather, the symbol of *maat* (truth/justice/order). With every lie, the pan in which his heart lay would have sunk, and his lying heart would have been swallowed by a monster. In this monster, we are to see the personification of the second death. This monster, though, did not stand for evil, but rather, defense against evil. It acted on the side of Osiris, not Seth. If the deceased was swallowed, it was because he had been exposed as an element of evil, a follower of Seth. With this increasing moralization, the afterlife became ever more ambivalent and threatening. It was divided not into a physical heaven and hell but into two aspects, one of which spelled annihilation for evildoers, and the other, salvation for the righteous.

In a late inscription from the fourth century B.C.E., the Judgment of the Dead is described in the following words:

75

> There is no distinction there between poor and rich,
> what matters is being found without fault.
> Scale and weight stand before the lord of Eternity,
> no one is free of the need to settle accounts.[12]

These words clearly emphasize the inescapable, obligatory character of the Judgment of the Dead.

The Judgment of the Dead represented an extreme spiritualizing and ethicizing of the mythical concept of vindicating the deceased against death. Here, too, a division was drawn and a distinction made. Here, the figure of Seth was split into the guilt of the deceased, on the one hand, and on the other, the heart-swallowing monster. The guilt of the deceased was that which stood in the way of his transformation into the eternal form of a "transfigured ancestral spirit." It was the Egyptian form of the Pauline concept, "the wages of sin is death" (Romans 6:23). Guilt was a sweeping charge against which the deceased had to vindicate himself. Quite the opposite of contemporary legal practice, the burden of proof was on him: he had to prove his innocence. What mattered was whether he had lived righteously, already judging himself during life against the norms of the next world. Here, however, the gods were favorable to him. Anubis saw to it that the scale remained in plumb, Thoth registered a favorable result, and Horus himself pled for the deceased. But the gods were powerless against evil. If condemned, the deceased could not become a transfigured spirit; rather, he had to vanish from the created cosmos, and *that* was the second death.

We often encounter the concept of a second death in the context of funerary customs that entail a secondary burial. The second burial in fact had the sense of a rebirth, a return to existence, not of the living but of the transfigured spirits, the ancestors. If this transformation of the deceased into his eternal form of an ancestral spirit did not succeed, the second, ultimate death transpired. In Egypt, embalmment, coffin, and funeral played a transfiguring role, while the secondary, that is to say, the ultimate burial, signified birth into eternity.

The mythic model made it possible to break down the complex experience of death and make it "manageable" through differentiation. The deceased was explained as the victim of a murder; death—or the cause of death—was personified in the figure of Seth. The condition of lifelessness was explained as a liminal phase of the crisis of "betwixt and between,"[13] here and not-here, of earthly life and the life to come. The life to come was made dependent on moral purity. It was life in another realm, but the tomb was a contact zone, an interface between here and not-here. The connection between the two realms was symbolized and personified in the mythical figure of Horus, the son and avenger of Osiris.

The liminal status of the deceased was transformed into a blessed, final state by two events: the deceased himself became a "transfigured spirit" in the other world, and his son was installed in the position of his father on the model of Horus, to whom the royal throne of Egypt had been granted. Both events were the result of the Judgment of the Dead and vindication. Vindication meant restoration of personal identity and integrity. As the Egyptians saw it, however, a person was part of a multiplicity, a constellation. The myth of Osiris, Isis, Horus, and Seth supplied the model for this constellation. Death, in the person of Seth, was overcome and eliminated. His disintegrated integrity was restored to the deceased by inserting him into the triangular constellation of Osiris-Isis-Horus.

3. Death as Enemy and the Life-giving Significance of the Judgment of the Dead

If, as we did with the images of death treated earlier, we pose the question of how this image of death as enemy had an effect on life, determining the conduct of the individual, a problem with the mythical model immediately leaps to the eye: it fails to make explicit the moral expectations of the one who judged the dead. One could never be sure of remaining blameless; no one had exact knowledge of which moral investments counted in the project of death. There was no code of written or unwritten laws to serve as the basis for the verdict in the Judgment of the Dead, laws that persons could follow during life with the hope of satisfying the judge.

This problem was solved by the classical, or canonical, form that the Judgment of the Dead assumed in the New Kingdom. In that period, it was entirely clear that the Judgment of the Dead was regarded as general and inescapable. Everyone had to pass over this threshold. Now, however, the regulations for admission into the other realm were codified. The mythic model vanished entirely. The entire procedure now seemed more like an examination than a lawsuit.

The deceased now stood before Osiris, who presided over the Judgment of the Dead, and his forty-two fellow judges. He no longer needed to make himself secure against any possible accusation that any complainant whatsoever might happen to make against him. He knew the charges in advance, and he had only to declare his innocence. All possible crimes and misdemeanors that could represent a hindrance to his admission into the next world were enumerated and set down in two lists, one containing forty sins and the other forty-two, with a number of overlaps between the lists. The deceased had to recite these lists and explicitly declare his

77

innocence of each and every sin. The one list must have been recited before Osiris and the other before the forty-two judges. During this recitation, his heart lay on the scale.[14]

With the recitation of this list of negations—"I did not do x, I did not do y"—the deceased cleansed himself of all burdens that represented "moral pollution" and had the power to bring about his ultimate annihilation. Thus, he entered the next world in a condition of imperishable purity. Book of the Dead chapter 125 spell is entitled,

> Purifying N. from all the evils he committed.
> Gazing upon the face of the gods.

This was no matter of innocence and purity. No one is innocent. What was important was whether or not someone was in a position to cleanse himself of his sins.

In the title of chapter 125, the motive for the purification is brought into close connection with gazing directly upon the gods. The Egyptians believed that no one (with the possible exception of the king) was capable, during life, of looking at the gods, of having a vision, or of entering the realm of the gods. Prior to the Graeco-Roman Period, there are no traces of shamanism, prophecy, or mysticism in Egypt. All forms of immediate contact with the divine realm refer to life after death. Thus, in a harper's song from Theban Tomb 50, we read:

> Every god you have served on earth
> you now meet face to face.[15]

But never did death entail automatic access to the divine presence. Quite the contrary: the realm into which, according to Egyptian belief, an individual passed after death was a reversed world in which divine order was suspended. The deceased was obliged to pass through this state in order to be able to enter the sphere of divine presence that he longed for. The decisive precondition for doing this was moral conduct during life, which meant not violating any of the eighty-two negative commandments. Any sin or fault from which the deceased could not cleanse himself in the Judgment of the Dead would have excluded him from beholding the gods. He would have been banished from the divine presence into a region where the rays of the night sun did not penetrate.[16]

Because we are inquiring here about Egyptian concepts of death, not morality, we need not go into the details of each of the eighty-two forbidden acts of which the deceased protested his innocence.[17] We may content ourselves with noting that they fall into three categories:

(a) very general rules, such as "I have not killed," "I have committed no false-hood against anyone," and so forth;

(b) more specific taboos, such as "I have not dammed up running water, I have not put out a burning fire"; and

(c) rules of correct professional behavior, especially in connection with weights and measures: "I have added nothing to the weights of the hand-held scale, I have removed nothing from the weights of the standing scale."

This classical form of the concept of the Judgment of the Dead, as we find it in chapter 125 of the Book of the Dead, presumably had a great influence on how individuals conducted their lives. The Book of the Dead, in which these concepts were codified, belonged to the mortuary literature and thus to the magical objects with which the dead were provided. But nothing speaks against the idea that this form of postmortem judgment, with its precise list of transgressions to be avoided, were of importance to the living. An individual could prepare himself for this form of judgment by making the approximately eighty forbidden acts listed in the negative confession the basis for his conduct during life. The Book of the Dead could thus have served as a manual for the moral invest-ment with which the Egyptians were obliged to complement the material expenses of preparing a tomb and arranging for a mortuary cult, which were to provide a serviceable basis for life after death. I hold this view to be essentially more plausible than the idea that chapter 125 of the Book of the Dead had the sole purpose of "magically outflanking" the Judg-ment of the Dead.[18] To be sure, there can be no doubt that this chapter was magical, like all the mortuary literature. These texts were magical in the sense that they brought to bear the "healing power" of religious action and speech, and not for the good of society but on behalf of an individ-ual and with the goal of personal vindication. I in no way contest the magical character of these texts. I contest only the notion that the Egyp-tians relied exclusively on magic in these matters. Nothing compels us to think this. It is, in fact, extremely improbable, for it can easily be shown that in comparable circumstances, the Egyptians in no way relied exclu-sively on magic. During the mummification process, they did not just use amulets and magical spells; rather, they brought into play the entirety of their anatomical and chemical knowledge. In cases of accident or illness, physicians, who were also magicians, first used all the practical means of their professional art before they resorted to magical means in certain cases. Medicine was never replaced by magic but only complemented by it. Thus, in my view, everything speaks against the notion that in the case of the Judgment of the Dead, the Egyptians "outflanked" morality through magic, rather than employing it in a complementary fashion in this instance as well.

We may thus with some certainty start out from the assumption that the Judgment of the Dead and the laws of the "Hall of the Two Truths" where the judgment was passed did not just decide the future fate of the soul but also to a certain extent determined the earthly conduct of the individual. The concept of the Judgment of the Dead cast a long shadow over the life of the individual, just as did the task of preparing and outfitting a monumental tomb. The moral investment in the project of death was presumably no smaller than the material investment. There is even an Egyptian text, a stela with an autobiographical tomb inscription from the fourteenth century B.C.E., that explicitly states that its author made the "laws" of the Judgment of the Dead the basis of his conduct during life:

> I am a truly righteous man, free of transgressions,
> who has placed the god in his heart
> and is aware of his power.
> I have come to the "city in eternity,"
> after doing good on earth.
> I have not sinned, I am blameless,
> my name has not been questioned because of misconduct
> any more than because of injustice (*jzf.t*).

> I rejoice at speaking *maat*,
> for I know that it is valuable
> for the one who does it on earth,
> from birth until the "landing."
> It is an excellent protective wall for the one who speaks it,
> on that day when he arrives at the court
> that judges the wretch and uncovers his character,
> and punishes the sinner (*jzf.tj*) and cuts off his *ba*.

> I existed without blame,
> so that there is no complaint against me and no sin of mine before them,
> and so that I might emerge vindicated
> and praised among those provided with a tomb,
> who have gone to their *ka*.

> . . .[19]

> I am a worthy who is fortunate because of *maat*,
> one who emulated the laws of the Hall of the Two Truths,
> for I intended to reach the realm of the dead
> without my name being attached to any meanness,
> without having done anything evil to any man,
> or anything that their gods censure.[20]

What Baki, the owner of the stela, calls the "laws of the Hall of the Two Truths" are nothing other than the eighty-two transgressions from which persons were obliged to distance themselves in the Judgment of the Dead.

In this inscription, an Egyptian thus for once states expressly that from the beginning on, he had made the norms of the Judgment of the Dead the basis of his conduct during his lifetime on earth.

An entirely different connection between the concept of the Judgment of the Dead and the realm of the living has been uncovered by the Cologne papyrologist Reinhold Merkelbach. In a Greek papyrus from Egypt, he discovered the text of an oath that priests had to swear when they were accepted into the priesthood of a temple:

I shall eat nothing that is forbidden to priests,
I shall cut nothing with a knife . . . nor ask anyone else
to do what is forbidden.
I have cut off the head of no living being,
I have killed no man,
I have had nothing to do with unclean men,
I have slept with no youth,
I have not slept with the wife of another, . . .
I shall not eat or drink what is forbidden or is listed (as forbidden) in the
    books.
Nothing will stick to my fingers.
I shall weigh out no grain on the threshing floor.
I shall take no scale in my hand.
I shall measure no land.
I shall visit no unclean place.
I shall touch no sheep's wool.
I shall seize no knife, to the day I die.[21]

These formulas are amazingly similar to the negative formulations of chapter 125 of the Book of the Dead. While all the formulas in the latter text are in the perfect tense, here, many are in the future tense, and others in the perfect. Merkelbach explains the difference thusly: "All the transgressions indicated by means of the perfect are major sins; a candidate for priestly office must never have committed them. . . . All the other affirmations have to do with acts that one was no longer to commit in the future."[22] Both categories of sins are run in together in list A of Book of the Dead chapter 125, the major sins that no one may commit and that a priori exclude a candidate from priestly office, and the more special transgressions that priests had to give up upon entering office. Reinhard Grieshammer has adopted Merkelbach's discovery and interpreted it as the real-life origin of chapter 125 of the Book of the Dead and thus of the concept of the Judgment of the Dead in its classical form and formulation. In my book *Ma'at: Gerechtigkeit und Unsterblichkeit in Alten Ägypten* (*maat*: righteousness and immortality in ancient Egypt), I also adopted this explanation. All three of us had to endure a great deal of criticism for having leaped over the chronology and adduced a text preserved only in the Greek language to interpret a chapter of the Book of the Dead that is attested one and a half millennia earlier. Meanwhile, Joachim F. Quack has discovered the Egyptian original of the Greek priestly oath in the published fragments of a comprehensive temple handbook, the Book of the Temple, thus pulling the rug out from under this criticism. The Book of the Temple is written in hieratic and in pure Middle Egyptian. Quack dates the text to the Middle Kingdom. I would not myself go that far, but the institution of the priestly oath, whose formulation is so astonishingly similar to that of Book of the Dead chapter 125, is in any case demonstrated for the classical periods of Egyptian history.[23]

It is unimportant whether the Judgment of the Dead was conceived on the model of induction into a priesthood, or whether the latter was organized on the model of the concept of the Judgment of the Dead. Here, what is important is the connection as such, the influence of an image of death on the world of the living and the association between acceptance into the realm of the dead and acceptance into the priesthood of a temple. The common denominator of both forms of acceptance is the closeness to the gods that they entail. In the temple cult, as well as in the netherworld, the goal was to "gaze upon the face of the gods."

One characteristic of the Judgment of the Dead, at least in the canonical form lent it by chapter 125 of the Book of the Dead, could have no counterpart in the priestly oath: the stress on publicity. The deceased was obliged to make his declaration of innocence before "all the world," that is, the entire land of Egypt. This nationwide publicity was symbolically represented by the forty-two members of the judicial tribunal. They stood for the forty-two "nomes," the districts into which Egypt was divided; we have already encountered their sacral importance for the idea of Egypt as a sacred land in connection with the "embalming glance" with which the Egyptians beheld the world. Egypt's internal administrative divisions were changed from time to time between the Old Kingdom and the Byzantine Period; but the number forty-two, along with the names of the nomes and the nome capitals, became at some point in time canonical and attained the rank of a sacred ordering. This "sacred geography" played an important role in the temples of the later periods of Egyptian history; we shall deal with this point in chapter 15. It had its basis already in the forty-two judges of the Judgment of the Dead. These figures clearly represented the entire land, the widest imaginable public for a confession. This point was especially important to the Egyptians in the formation of their concept of a Judgment of the Dead: when the deceased declared his guilt or innocence before all the world, the public nature of this declaration endowed his pronouncement with the sanction of law.

With the formulation of the concept of a postmortem judgment and its canonization in chapter 125 of the Book of the Dead in the second millennium B.C.E., the Egyptians took two momentous steps. They transferred the horizon of the fulfillment of human action and effort to the next world, and they placed the ultimate judgment of earthly conduct not in the hands of the state or posterity but in the hands of the gods. Thus, they took an important step in the direction of a sacralization of ethics, which could no longer remain a matter of human philosophy of life but was now one of divine judgment and thus also divine will. This step made its complete breakthrough only in biblical religion, where God appears not only as judge but also as lawgiver. But the Egyptian idea of the Judgment of the Dead removed final judgment regarding the success of a human life decisively away from worldly powers and interests and placed the norms of social existence on a transcendental basis. With this step, there began an evolution in the area of images of death and in that of mortuary rituals, one that quickly affected the entire culture and ultimately radiated out into the world beyond Egypt.

Having dealt with the emergence of the concept of a Judgment of the Dead, I wish to close with a glance at the history of its effect. In the West, there was an enduring tradition that Egypt was the home of this concept. The sources for this Western knowledge about the Egyptian Judgment of the Dead were above all the writings of Diodorus and Porphyry.

Porphyry discussed the Judgment of the Dead in his treatise *De abstinentia*. In an aristocratic burial, he wrote, the entrails were separately removed and placed in a chest (*kibotos*). After all the other rites were carried out on behalf of the deceased, the embalmers took hold of this chest and called the sun as witness. One of the embalmers began to speak:

> He says something like this, as Euphantos translated it from the language of his homeland: "O Lord Sun and all the gods who give life to humans, receive me and present me to the eternal gods to reside with them. The gods of whom my parents told me I have reverenced for all the time I lived under their rule, and I have always honoured those who begot my body. I have neither killed any other human being, nor stolen from any what he had entrusted to me, nor done any other unpardonable act. And if during my life I have been at fault by eating or drinking something forbidden, I did not do it myself, but through these," showing the box which contains the belly. Having said this he throws it into the river, and embalms the rest of the body as being pure. In this way they thought that a speech for the defence was owed to the divinity about what they had eaten and drunk, and on account of this violence should be done.[24]

This account gives an impression that is not unqualifiedly authentic. The entrails as scapegoat: this is an entirely un-Egyptian concept. They were in fact removed, not to dispose of them as unclean, but rather to bury them with the deceased in special vessels, the so-called canopic jars. We are also baffled by what Porphyry meant by the "apology" of the deceased. It seems to correspond roughly to the "negative confession" in Book of the Dead chapter 125. But eating and drinking, and thus what is called *kashrut* in the Jewish faith, played no special role, not even in the priestly oath so closely related to this chapter of the Book of the Dead. Still, this situation could have changed in the later historical periods, when each nome had its own dietary taboos. Especially interesting is the close connection between vindication and embalming in Porphyry's account, which gives the impression that vindication was a constitutive element of the embalming procedure, and that the body was to be cleansed of sin in the sense of immaterial pollutants. Porphyry seems to make the Judgment of the Dead into a specifically physical purificatory procedure, one whose goal was improved preservation. With the entrails, sins were removed from the body. That this connection between the embalming process and the Judgment of the Dead in fact closely corresponds with the original ritual context of the concept of the Judgment is something I have already indicated, and I shall discuss this matter at greater length in chapter 12.

Porphyry's information served as the basis for John Marsham's portrayal of the Egyptian *ethica et civilis disciplina* (ethical and civil teaching). Marsham's book *Canon chronicus Aegyptiacus, Ebraicus, Graecus* appeared in 1672 and was often reprinted. Through the seventeenth and eighteenth centuries, it remained one of the most influential works on ancient history. Marsham referred to the negative confession as the *Apologia funebris* (funerary apology) and compared its importance as the foundation of an ethics to that of the Decalogue. Thus, long before the decipherment of the hieroglyphs and the publication of Egyptian Books of the Dead, scholars were already debating the level of Egyptian ethics and were able to make comparisons between the negative confession and biblical Law.[25] Porphyry's information about the *apologia funebris* of the ancient Egyptians led Marsham to the following commandments, which we here compare to the Decalogue in the Jewish enumeration:

Apologia funebris Aegyptiorum	*Decalogus Hebraeorum*
1. Honor the gods	1. No other gods
	2. No graven images
	3. Take not the name in vain
	4. Keep the Sabbath holy
2. Honor one's father and mother	5. Honor your father and your mother
3. Do not kill	6. You shall not kill
	7. You shall not commit adultery
4. Do not steal	8. You shall not steal

5. Do not commit any other transgression	9. You shall not bear false witness
	10. You shall not covet

For Marsham, this "Pentalogue" was not only the common denominator of the Egyptian "funerary apology" and the biblical Decalogue but also the origin of the latter. It is the ethics that the Hebrews learned during their sojourn in Egypt and took with them when they left. The comparison also shows how correct Jewish tradition was in counting the Fifth Commandment ("honor your father and your mother") among those which concerned the relationship between man and God and were engraved on the first tablet, and not among the commandments regarding social behavior, to which the second tablet was devoted.

Diodorus supplies an entirely different description of the Judgment of the Dead ritual in the first book of his *Bibliotheca historica* (library of history).[26] According to him, the Judgment of the Dead occurred between the embalming and the burial. The body was conveyed by boat over a pond, probably to an island where forty-two judges were waiting on the shore. At this point, everyone who had something to bring against the deceased made their complaint. If guilt was proved, the corpse could not be buried. But if no complainants made their appearance, or if their complaint was unjustified, the deceased was extolled by all present and then buried with honors. From the New Kingdom in particular, we have numerous representations of a funerary celebration in a garden with a pool, and in these cases, the mummy of the tomb owner was in fact conveyed to an island.[27] I know of no representation of the forty-two judges on this island, however. Perhaps Diodorus did not derive his version of the Egyptian ritual from his own observation of such a procedure but rather from representations in tombs, thereby somewhat confusing the two. But Reinhold Merkelbach has compared Diodorus' account with the texts in the two Rhind funerary papyri, which he understands as a record of the burial ceremonies for Menthesuphis and his wife, who both died in the year 9 B.C.E.[28] In these papyri, there clearly emerges a sequence of ceremonies in the form of a dramatic presentation in which priests played the role of gods. If we combine this information with Diodorus' description of the burial ceremonies, we get the picture of a "Baroque spectacle." The Baroque period was itself influenced by Diodorus' account. Jacque-Bénigne Bossuet made detailed use of it in his *Discours sur l'histoire universelle* (discourse on universal history, 1681),[29] and Abbé Jean Terrasson lent it a fictitious touch in his novel *Séthos* (1731).[30]

Bossuet and Terrasson made clear the connection between the concept of a Judgment of the Dead and the state. The Egyptians were the first to recognize (so it was assumed in the seventeenth and eighteenth centuries, not altogether incorrectly) that a state can only be founded on the basis of an unshakeable belief in the immortality of the soul. Such an idea not only represented the interests of the state, it has also stood at the center of the Christian picture of the world. In Christianity, too, the worthiness of the individual to enter the realm of God is measured by the social norms of interpersonal relations, and in it, too, the next-worldly sanction of eternal damnation is ascribed to norms that cannot be sanctioned on earth.[31] Both concepts base their postulation of man as *zoon politikon* (social animal) on a belief in divine judgment and life after death.

The concepts of a life to come and a reward or punishment in the next world are foreign to the Old Testament. This fact, too, was first noted toward the end of the seventeenth century, in the same decade in which Bossuet and others stressed that Egypt was their homeland. Spinoza was the first to draw attention to this circumstance in his *Tractatus politico-theologicus*, and the Anglican Bishop William Warburton confirmed it from the Christian side in his nine-volume work *The Divine Legation of Moses.*[32] But if these ideas were already as central for ancient Egypt as for the Christian world, were the ancient Egyptians better Christians than the Israelites? Was *heilsgeschichte* to be sought in Egypt rather than in Israel? Was it necessary to abandon the distinction between *heilsgeschichte* and profane history? These were among the questions that shook the foundations of the Christian picture of the world in the seventeenth and eighteenth centuries, and which arose from insights into ancient Egyptian concepts of death and immortality that modern Egyptology can only confirm. The Egyptian concept of salvation from death through vindication has never ceased to fascinate the human mind. If Egypt has succeeded in remaining present in the cultural memory of Europe, it is above all because of its concepts of death and of the ability to overcome death through moral investment.

CHAPTER FOUR

Death as Dissociation

The Person of the Deceased and Its Constituent Elements

The concept of the person played an important role in the three preceding chapters. Concerns about managing death and restoring life were not just concentrated on the body and the soul but also on the person of the deceased, which included other, in particular social, aspects such as rank, status, and honor. As I use it here, the concept of the person is a modern one, and there is nothing in the ancient Egyptian language that corresponds to it. I mean by it a collection of individual aspects of a human being for which ancient Egyptian expressions do in fact exist. These Egyptian concepts occur often in mortuary texts. The spells of the mortuary liturgies and texts prove to be the locus of an "anthropological discourse" about the aspects or constituent elements of the person. In death, it seems, the person of the deceased emerged in its various aspects or constituent elements, which now took on a life of their own. I call this process of emergence *dissociation*. Unlike the images of death as dismemberment and isolation, the process of dissociation was not catastrophic and destructive but rather, in a certain sense, desired and necessary. What was crucial was that when they emerged and went off in different directions, these aspects of the person entered into a new relationship with, and remained connected to, one another.

These elements of the person, which are ubiquitous in the mortuary texts, include especially the concepts of *ba* and the *ka*, which have to do with what is covered by our own concept of "soul," as well as words for body, corpse, and mummy ($\underline{d}.t$, $\underline{h}^3.t$, s^ch). They also include the concept *akh*, which I here render "transfigured ancestral spirit," as well as the concepts "heart," "shadow," and "name." The principal goal was to maintain the unity of the person, even under conditions of dissociation, with the connection of the *ba* and the corpse playing an especially important role in this regard.

On anthropoid stone sarcophagi of the Late Period, there is a spell that appears with almost canonical regularity on the upper surface, the breast of the mummy, where the *ba* was supposed to land when it came to unite with the corpse. All the important elements of the person make their appearance in this spell:

> O you who drag away *bas* and cut off shadows,
> O you gods, lords of the living heads (or, heads of the living),
> may you bring the *ba* of Osiris-Khentamentiu to him,
> may you join his *$\underline{d}.t$*-body to him, that his heart may be glad!
>
> May his *ba* come to his *$\underline{d}.t$*-body and to his heart,
> may his *ba* swoop down on his *$\underline{d}.t$*-body and his heart.
>
> Bring it to him, O gods,
> in the *benben*-house of Heliopolis,
> at the side of Shu, Geb, and Atum.
> May his *jb*-heart belong to him like Re,
> may his *$\underline{h}^3.tj$*-heart belong to him like Khepri.
>
> Purity for your *ka*, for your *$\underline{d}.t$*-body,
> for your *ba*, for your corpse,
> for your shadow, and for your illustrious mummy,
> O Osiris-Khentamentiu![1]

Here, the concern is with the uniting of the *ba* and the corpse, and further, with the reintegration of the person, which is composed of no fewer than eight different elements, components, or aspects. First (verses 3–4), we see the constellation of the *ba* and the *$\underline{d}.t$*-body, which appears here instead of the more usual juxtaposition or combination of *ba* and *$\underline{h}^3.t$*-corpse. Then, in verses 5–6, the heart appears, turning the duo into a trio. In verses 10–11, the concept "heart" is divided into the *jb*-heart and the *$\underline{h}^3.tj$*-heart. Turning away from the heart, the concluding verses 12–15 enumerate, after the fashion of a litany, six aspects/components of the person: *ka*, *$\underline{d}.t$*-body, *ba*, *$\underline{h}^3.t$*-corpse, shadow, and mummy.

In the tomb of the grain assessor Amenemhet from Dynasty 18 (Theban Tomb 82), no fewer than fourteen constituents of the person are adduced (two of which are lost in a lacuna).[2] On the south wall of the chapel, "stela" and "tomb" appear, along with five personifications of destiny (*š³jj* "destiny," *ʿḥʿw* "lifetime," *Msḫn.t* "birthplace," *Rnn.t* "development," and *Ḫnmw*, the personal creator god),[3] while on the north wall, we find *ʿbꜣ* "offering stone" (in parallelism with *ʿḥʿ* "stela") and, after a lacuna that might well have contained "*ba*" and "heart," *ꜣḫ* "dead spirit," *ḥꜣ.t* "corpse," *šw.t* "shadow," and *ḫpr.w = f nb.w* "all his forms of manifestation."[4] This scene, however, is a unique instance, unparalleled in any other tomb. More widespread and representative is a scene that appears in three Theban tombs of the Ramesside Period,[5] in the early Hellenistic tomb of Petosiris,[6] and on coffins of the Late and Ptolemaic Periods.[7] Here, the four Sons of Horus bring the deceased his heart,[8] his *ba*,[9] his *ka*,[10] and his body or mummy. In the ritual texts of the Osiris chapels at Dendara, the king says to Osiris:

> I bring you the capitals of the nomes: they are your body,
> they are your *ka*, which is with you.
> I bring you your name, your *ba*, your shadow,
> your form (*qj*), and your image: the capitals of the nomes.[11]

These texts and scenes afford us only an introductory glimpse at the concerns of this theme, which plays so great a role in the mortuary literature.

In our own understanding of the human being, the decisive distinction is between body and soul, or between mind and body. The Egyptians drew a wider and apparently even more decisive distinction. They distinguished between the physical sphere and the social sphere of the person. To the physical sphere belonged, naturally, the concepts of body, limbs, and corpse, as well as *ba* and "shadow." To the social sphere belonged the concepts of *ka*, name, and even "mummy," for the word for "mummy," which also meant "aristocrat," "dignitary," "worthy," was first and foremost a designation of status. The mummy was the body as bearer of an identifying sign, in particular, a sign of rulership, which had an effect on the social sphere and created respect for the dead in the netherworld. The heart was the "interface" between the personal sphere and the social sphere, and its work consisted in the integration of these two spheres into the entirety of a person.

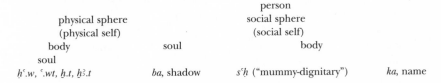

		person	
physical sphere		social sphere	
(physical self)		(social self)	
body	soul	body	
soul			
ḥʿ.w, ʿ.wt, ḥ.t, ḥꜣ.t	*ba*, shadow	*sʿḥ* ("mummy-dignitary")	*ka*, name

It might seem surprising that the *ba* is ascribed to the physical sphere. Was *ba* not a soul-like concept? To be sure: the conventional translation of the Egyptian term *ba* as "soul" (German "Seele," French "âme") was not created out of thin air. It is based on the figure of a bird (a heron with a feathered breast) used to indicate the word in the writing system, and which serves in art (in the form of a falcon with a human head) to represent this aspect of the person. It is also based on the concept of freedom of movement connected with the *ba*. In the form of a *ba*, the deceased passed through the realm of death, and from there, into the hall of the Judgment of the Dead, into the house of Osiris, into the Field of Reeds and the Field of Offerings, and into the sun barque. As a *ba*, he also enjoyed the ability to assume various forms (including that of a "living *ba*") in which he could return to the world of the living. From an ethnological perspective, the *ba* belongs to the category of a "free soul" that could separate itself from the body.

It would seem, then, that in Egyptian thought, *ba* and body were opposites. Yet, when we look at the texts, we see that they form a pair and are most often cited together. In the Dialogue of a Man with His Soul (Papyrus Berlin 3024), there is even a reference to the "corpse" of the *ba*. The verses in question lay stress on the corporeality of the *ba*, and on its close connection with the shadow:

> I shall make a cooling over your corpse,
> so that you may make another *ba*, one that is weary, envious.
> I shall make a cooling, though not too cold,
> so that you may make another *ba*, one that is hot, envious.
> I shall drink water at the well and set up a protection for the shadow,
> so that you may make another *ba*, one that is hungry, envious.[12]

Ba and body constituted a unity that was broken up in death and had to be restored by mortuary rituals under conditions of separation.

1. The Ba

a) The *Ba* in the Sky, the Corpse in the Netherworld

The goal of the funerary rites was to bring about the separation of *ba* and corpse, so that they could once again be placed into a relationship with one another. The last act of the burial procession, before the actual interment, was the making of an offering to the mummy under the open sky. Thus, in an oft-used offering spell, we find the *ka*, the mummy, the *ba*, and the corpse all mentioned:

> One shall cut off a foreleg for your *ka*,
> and a heart for your mummy.
> May your *ba* ascend,
> may your *corpse* descend.[13]

Before the coffin containing the mummy was deposited in the sarcophagus chamber, and thus in the netherworld, the *ba* was supposed to
ascend to the sky during this rite carried out in the sunlight. Dozens of
text passages can be cited in support of this point:

> Your *ba* to the sky,
> your corpse to the netherworld![14]

Such formulas are ubiquitous in the mortuary texts of the New Kingdom
and later periods,[15] where they lay stress on the positive aspect of the
dissociation. The separation of *ba* and corpse was one of the goals of
the transfiguration rituals, and it was part of the transformation of the
deceased into a transfigured ancestral spirit. Other wishes on behalf of
the deceased added the statue, in whose form the deceased was present
on earth. For the most part, the reference was not to the tomb statue, but
to one or more statues that meritorious officials were allowed to set up in
a temple by special favor of the king, so as to be able to enjoy, on earth,
the blessings of divine presence:

> Your *ba* endures in the sky,
> your corpse in the netherworld,
> your statues in the temples.[16]

Temple statues first appeared in the Middle Kingdom (ca. 2000–1700
B.C.E.). At first, they were a rare privilege, granted by the king to his
highest dignitaries. In the New Kingdom, the custom of setting up temple
statues became more widespread, to the point where, in the first millennium, they surpassed the monumental tomb as a medium of continuance,
for a time even taking its place. In the form of their statue, those accorded
this privilege remained close to their god, breathing incense, listening to
the chanting of hymns, and taking part in the festivals. Such images most
commonly took the form of a "block statue," a cuboidal representation
of a man, wrapped in his mantle, squatting on the ground with upraised
knees. In the New Kingdom (beginning ca. 1500 B.C.E.), there appeared
variations on this theme, depicting the deceased in connection with a
divine emblem (naos, divine statue or symbol, etc.), thus iconographically
laying stress on his relationship to the deity in question. When this custom
was in its heyday, we can see to what an extent Egyptian temples served
the quest to overcome human mortality. In any case, this was true for the
king; when he erected a temple, it was for a deity, to be sure, but it was
also his "personal monument," as the dedication inscriptions stress, and
much the same became true for the growing number of those who were
allowed to take up residence, in the form of a temple statue, in this ter-

restrial enclave of divine immortality. In the later stages of Egyptian history, the image of the block statue served as a hieroglyph in the writing of the word "praised one."

During the embalming ritual, "those in the land" went to the sky and the netherworld, where they busied themselves with the preparation of the body:

> Your *ba* is in the sky,
> your corpse is in the netherworld.
> Those in the land make your body magnificent,
> you receive ointment in the Place of Unction.[17]

Through the medium of his representations as statue, on stelae, and so forth, the offering cult turned the double form of the deceased as *ba* and corpse into a triple one, in which he was present in the sky, on earth, and in the netherworld. This is how we are to understand the text passage that served as our departure point. The sacrificial offering of the heart and foreleg of a bull was a part of the tomb cult, where it was performed before the mummy, as it stood propped up in the forecourt of the tomb during the Opening of the Mouth ritual. The offering was thus intended for the *ka* and the mummy, the forms in which the deceased was present in the tomb and received cult attention. As tomb owner, he remained a member of the community that included his posterity, and the cult in the tomb had to do with his social sphere on earth. The tomb was the special place of the *ka*, a topic to which we shall return.

The *ba* and the *ḥꜣ.t* (corpse), however, belonged to the otherworldly spheres of the sky and the netherworld, where they shared in the cosmic existence of the sun god. As early as the Coffin Texts, there are text passages that compare the relationship between the deceased and his *ba* and corpse to the course of the sun:

> May you control your *ba*,
> and your flesh and your corpse in Heliopolis.[18]

On the model of a deceased human being, the sun was conceived of as a *ba* that traversed the sky by day and at night visited his corpse, which was resting in the netherworld of Heliopolis. It is thus that we are to understand this wish that the deceased, like the sun god, might cross the sky and come to rest in Heliopolis as a corpse.[19]

The New Kingdom solar hymns and Books of the Netherworld constantly affirm that the *ba* of the sun god is in the sky and his corpse in the netherworld, precisely as stated of human beings in the mortuary spells. Thus, in a solar hymn from the tomb of Apuia, which was constructed at Saqqara in the immediate wake of the Amarna Period, we read,

> *Ba* to the sky,
> corpse to the netherworld.[20]

Such wishes are typical in the Books of the Netherworld, for example:

> The sky for your *ba*, that it may rest there,
> the earth for your corpse, O Lord of Provisioning![21]

Clearly, then, the point of the dissociation of the *ba* and the *ḥȝ.t*, and of their assignment to the sky and the netherworld, was to enable the deceased to have a share in the sun god's form of existence. In the daytime, this god traversed the sky, visible to all in the form of his *ba*, the sun disk, and in the evening, he sank into the netherworld, where, invisibly, mysteriously, and beyond any human perception, he united with his corpse. From this union, the *ba* absorbed the power to renew itself, after which it once again ascended to the sky to begin another day. The *ba* and the *ḥȝ.t* were partners in this cycle of regeneration; they worked together in a process that would otherwise have been inconceivable. The body needed its *ba*, and the *ba* needed its body. Together, the two were an indissoluble pair.

During the embalming process, the *ba* hovered over the corpse, ascending to the sky only at its end, at the time of the Opening of the Mouth and the offering in front of the entrance to the tomb. This is what we see, for instance, in a scene in the tomb of the vizier Paser. In a liturgy from the Coffin Texts that refers to the embalming ritual, the *ba* and the corpse are both said to be still on earth, and it is made clear how both these aspects are a part of the physical sphere of the deceased:

> May Geb open your sightless eyes,
> may he straighten your bended knees.
> May your *jb*-heart be given you by your mother,
> and your *ḥȝ.tj*-heart, which belongs to your *ḏ.t*-body,
> your *ba*, which is on earth,
> your corpse, which is on the ground.
> Bread for your body,
> water for your throat,
> sweet breath of life for your nostrils.[22]

These verses refer to the process of embalmment, when the corpse was not yet buried and the *ba* had not yet ascended to the sky, as depicted in the tomb of Paser.

In the Coffin Texts, there are portions of a liturgy whose aim was to enable the *ba* to separate itself from the corpse and to exit the netherworld unhindered. Spells 94–96 and 488–500 are part of this liturgy. Spell 94 is entitled "Causing the *Ba* to Depart from the Corpse,"[23] a sentiment that runs counter to the fear, frequently expressed in later texts, that the *ba* might distance itself from the corpse. In this spell, the *ba* is still in close contact with the body. Osiris has created it out of the discharges of his flesh and the semen of his phallus; it is the "*ba* in its blood." From his bodily fluids, Osiris creates a *ba* that is to emerge into the light of day and take sexual pleasure in the world above. This was a role the deceased wished to play. In spell 96, the deceased calls himself "that great *ba* of Osiris, on whose behalf the gods have ordained that he copulate by means of (etc.)." The corresponding divine commandment reads, "Come out and copulate by means of your *ba*."[24] This concept shows clearly that the *ba* belonged to the physical sphere. The sequence of spells 488–500 belong to a liturgy dealing with the *ba*'s freedom of movement. The *ba* was to descend, unhindered, all the way to Osiris in the depths of the netherworld, and to ascend all the way to Re in the celestial heights. It was to approach both these gods, which was the most pressing need of every deceased person: the sun god as dispenser of truth/justice/order, for whose functioning on earth man himself was responsible, and Osiris as healer of his affliction.

The *ba* left the corpse through the head. On many coffins, the end that sheltered the head is inscribed with a hymn to the goddess Isis (Coffin Texts spell 229), who stood by the head of the deceased in the embalming ritual. In this hymn, we read, for example, "May you form my *ba*!" In the latter part of the text, the deceased affirms aspects of his well-being that are connected with his head and entail the unbroken connection between the *ba* and the corpse:

> My neck will not be severed, my name will not be ignored
> among the transfigured ancestral spirits,
> I shall not be caught in the fish net,
> the word of power will not be snatched from my mouth,
> my *jb*-heart and my *ḥꜣ.tj*-heart will not be cut out.
> My face is not sad, my heart is not forgetful,
> my *ba* will spend the night watching over my corpse;
> my face will not be sad, my heart will not be forgetful,
> I shall not be ignorant of the path to the realm of the dead.
> I am one with a spirit-powerful mouth and unscathed magic,
> one who has outfitted himself with the needs of his heart.[25]

This passage makes it clear that the *ba* was closely related to the body and to concerns regarding corporal integrity and vitality.

b) The Uniting of *Ba* and Corpse

After the *ba* was separated from the body, it acquired its own freedom of movement and could roam about in the celestial and netherworldly spaces of the afterlife. It was then necessary for it to remember its connection with the corpse, so that the personal unity of the deceased would remain preserved, even under conditions of separation. In a funerary liturgy from the Coffin Texts, it is said to the deceased,

> The heart of your *ba*, may it remember your corpse,
> that it may gladden the egg that brought you forth.[26]

The vague allusion to the "egg" plays on the mystery of regeneration in the coffin, which will be treated in chapter 7. The placing of the body in the coffin was explained as a return to the uterus.[27] The comparison of the mummy with the egg "that brought you forth," and thus with the symbol and epitome of origin, points in this direction. The *ba* "gladdens" the mummy when it returns to it.

Especially important here is the *ba*'s "remembering" the corpse, whereby the continuity of the person is maintained. There is a similar statement in another funerary liturgy:

> Your heart comes to you, it is not far from you,
> your *ba* remembers you and unites with you.[28]

Here, we again encounter the theme of life-giving connectivity (see chapter 2), which worked against death as isolation and was above all a matter of the heart:

> Truly, so long as your *ba* exists, your heart will exist with you!
> May Anubis think of you in Busiris,
> may your *ba* rejoice in Abydos,
> may your corpse, which is in the necropolis (of Abydos), be glad.[29]

Every bit as important as the separation of the *ba* from the corpse, without which the desired freedom of movement could not be gained, was the unhindered return of the *ba* to the body.[30] It is often stated that this communication between the *ba* and the corpse is not to be hindered, with the result that the *ba* would be locked in or out:

> May my *ba* not be guarded (= locked in) on my corpse,
> may I not be hindered from drinking water from the flood.[31]

The concept of the *ba* spending the night upon the corpse now became one of the central leitmotifs of mortuary belief. Chapter 89 of the Book of the Dead is devoted to this theme, and its accompanying vignettes depict the *ba* hovering over the corpse. The text states:

> May it (i.e., my *ba*) gaze upon my corpse,
> may it alight upon my mummy,
> may it never be destroyed or perish.

In the cult of Osiris at Dendara, the union of the *ba* and the corpse was celebrated during the festival of Khoiak, when a "grain mummy" was prepared and set out in the sunlight in the court of the rooftop temple. There is a reference to this practice in a text that makes use of an oft-attested mortuary offering spell:[32]

> Rejoice, you gods and goddesses:
> the *ba* of Osiris has come,
> and it rests on his corpse.[33]

2. *The Deceased and His* Ka

A great deal, much of it contradictory, has been written about the *ka*.[34] Scarcely any other Egyptian concept has received so many or such different explanations. The reason is that this concept played a central role not only in the conception of man but also in that of the king and of the gods, and that over time, it underwent changes in all three cases. Given these circumstances, it is not to be expected that we can arrive at an accurate definition of the *ka* concept that would satisfy all its occurrences in the texts. For every attempt at a definition, contrary examples can easily be adduced. We shall therefore confine ourselves here to the meaning of the *ka* concept in the framework of conceptions of death, singling out some central points that can shed light, above all, on the different meanings of the *ba* and the *ka*. In this connection, I hold the following differences to be essential:

1. "Freedom of movement," an essential element of the *ba* concept, played no role with regard to the *ka*.
2. The *ka* had nothing to do with the corpse; it was not part of the "physical sphere" of the individual.

Ka and *ba* are often mentioned together but seldom in a way that highlights the different roles of these two aspects of the person. One example is the formula with which the sage Djedi greets Prince Hardjedef in the "tales of wonder" from Papyrus Westcar:

> May your *ka* prevail over your enemy,
> and may your *ba* know the path, in the world beyond,
> to the portal of the place that conceals the weary![35]

It was the *ba* that could move freely between this realm and the next and, thanks to its knowledge, led the deceased out of the realm of death to Osiris and Elysium. The *ka*, however, was the vehicle of the vindication that restored the individual's status as a social person, which had been destroyed by death. In other words, the *ba* belonged to the physical sphere of the deceased, restoring his movement and his ability to take on form, while the *ka* belonged to his social sphere and restored his status, honor, and dignity.

From the point of view of comparative religion, the *ba* obviously fell into the category of a "free soul," for freedom of movement was its prime characteristic. Nevertheless, it was closer to the body than was the *ka*. Mobility is a physical ability. The *ka*, for its part, did not form a pair with the body but with the "self" of a person. It was soul, protective spirit, and doppelgänger, all rolled into one. It was said that the deceased "went to his *ka*." This was also a matter of uniting, just as when the *ba* alighted on the corpse. But when the deceased united with his *ba*, it was not body and soul that were united, it was the deceased himself and his alter ego.

Here, I should like to cite some texts that describe this union. The oldest one, a classic that continued to be cited down into the latest periods of Egyptian history, is spell 25 of the Pyramid Texts, a censing spell. In it, the rising scent of the incense is "sacramentally explained" (on this concept, see chapter 15) as a departure or ascent of the deceased king to his *ka*:

> A departer departs with his *ka*,
> Horus departs with his *ka*.
> Seth departs with his *ka*.
> Thoth departs with his *ka*.
> Dewen-anwy departs with his *ka*.
> Osiris departs with his *ka*.
> Khenty-en-irty departs with his *ka*.
> You yourself depart with your *ka*.
>
> O N., the arms of your *ka* are in front of you,
> O N., the arms of your *ka* are behind you,
> O N., one foot of your *ka* is in front of you,
> O N., one foot of your *ka* is behind you.

Osiris N., I have given you the Eye of Horus,
that your face may be complete by means of it.
To be spoken four times: May the aroma of the Eye of Horus waft its way
    to you.

In Pyramid Texts spell 447, we find the same concept of the deceased
"going with his *ka*" in the context of a text that describes the uniting of
the deceased with the sky and mother goddess Nut, as embodied in the
coffin. This is thus a "sacramental explanation" of the laying of the body
in the coffin. The deceased enters the coffin as sky and must therefore
"depart" from the earth. As in spell 25, this departure occurs in the
company of his *ka*:

A departer departs with his *ka*,
Osiris departs with his *ka*,
Seth departs with his *ka*,
Khenty-en-irty departs with his *ka*,
You yourself have departed with your *ka*.

O Osiris N., a comer comes, that you may not suffer need,
your mother comes, that you may not suffer need,
Nut (comes), that you may not suffer need,
the Great Protectress (comes), that you may not suffer need.
The protectress of the fearful (comes), that you may not suffer need,
to protect you, to prevent that you suffer need,
to give you your head,
to gather your bones for you,
to unite your limbs for you,
to give you your heart in your body,
that you may be at the head of those who are before you
and give commands to those who are behind you,
that you may secure your house behind you
and keep your children from mourning.
Your purity is the purity of the gods who have gone to their *ka*s,
your purity is the purity of the gods who have gone so as not to suffer (?).[36]

From this text, we learn two things: first, that "departing in the company
of the *ka*" is a specifically divine action that has something to do with
purity, and second, that this motif was not necessarily connected with the
rite of censing but could also occur in spells mentioning Nut that presumably refer to the ritual placing of the body in the coffin. To be in the
company of the *ka* was the end, the high point, and the epitome of personal reintegration as expressed on the physical level by the motif of
uniting the limbs.

In the Coffin Texts, this spell has only a single, rather badly preserved
variant, in which it is stated that the deceased goes, not "with" but "to"

his *ka*.[37] This is a reference to a blessed existence in death, corresponding to the biblical expression "gathered to his people." In the Hebrew Bible, this expression refers to a real situation: interment in a family tomb. These family tombs were extensive caverns in the hillside. With each new interment, the last to have been buried was shoved aside and the disarticulated body, of which only the bones remained, was tossed onto a huge heap of bones at the back of the cave.[38] In ancient Egypt, the formula "going to one's *ka*" also referred to the individual's joining his forebears. This meaning is made clear in tomb inscriptions of the Old Kingdom:

> Ferrying the forebears in very beautiful peace,
> setting out for the hills of the necropolis;
> grasping the hand by the fathers, namely his *kas*,
> each (of them) a provisioned one;
> bringing an offering to him above the shaft
> in his house of eternity.[39]

In these inscriptions, going to one's *ka* is also closely connected with burial. "Going to the *ka*" meant being buried in one's tomb as a "provisioned one." There are numerous examples of this formulation, especially from the Old Kingdom.[40] The following text, however, which also mentions the *ba*, is from the Dynasty 18 tomb of Khaemhet (Theban Tomb 57):[41]

> May the sacred place be opened to you,
> may you die as one who goes to his *ka*.
> May you receive your offering in the Great House,
> may your *ba* rest in the House of the Phoenix.
> May you carry out a purification in the Lake of *Maat*.
> May Anubis himself wrap you with bandages.

Here, the *ba* is connected with Heliopolis. There stood the House of the Phoenix, and also the Great House, in which the deceased, surely in the form of his *ba*, is to receive offerings. In this text, the *ka* makes its appearance as a sort of doppelgänger of the deceased, and to go to it is the epitome of the kind of death one hoped for. An inscription from the temple of Sethos I at Kanais is especially informative regarding the sense of this usage. It contains a blessing on any official who will respect the king's edict and keep it in force under future kings: "His end will be peaceful, (the end) of one who goes to his *ka*."[42] By way of contrast, on the statue of the high steward Amenophis from Memphis, there is a curse on the potential wrongdoer: "His *ka* shall be far from him."[43] Just as the separation of *ka* and self was the epitome of a dreadful, cursed death, so the togetherness of *ka* and self was the epitome of a goodly, blessed death.

Because the *ka* and the self were created simultaneously, they had a symbiotic relationship in this life, one that fell apart at death and had to be restored, albeit in a different form, by ritual.

The text of Khaemhet refers to the relationship between the deceased and the sun god, in the sun barque as well as in the temples of Heliopolis. In another, unfortunately badly destroyed inscription in his tomb, Khaemhet speaks again of union with his *ka*: "You will unite with your *ka* of your earthly existence."[44] The additional phrase "of your earthly existence" usually refers to the heart.[45] What is meant is a consciousness, or recollection, of existence on earth that the deceased is to maintain, thus assuring his personal continuity.[46]

Book of the Dead spell 105, entitled "Spell for Satisfying the *Ka* of a Man in the Realm of the Dead," connects the *ka* with existence on earth and also with the Judgment of the Dead and its moral assessment of the guilt or innocence of the deceased. The vignette depicts a man offering an incense vessel and a libation vase before his *ka*, which is represented as the hieroglyph for *ka* resting on a standard:

> Greetings to you, my *ka*, my lifetime!
> Lo, I have come to you,
> having appeared and being strong,
> *ba*-mighty, and powerful.
> I have brought you natron and incense,
> that I may purify you therewith and purify your sweat therewith.
> Every evil statement I have made,
> every evil deed I have done,
> (they) will not be reckoned against me;
> for I am that amulet
> that is around the throat of Re
> and is given to the horizon dwellers.
> When they thrive, I also thrive,
> and my *ka* thrives like theirs,
> and my *ka* is fed like theirs.

The *ka* of the deceased is equated with lifetime, just like "the heart of my existence on earth," thus assuring an equation of the heart with the *ka*. This aspect of the *ka* seems to underlie the meaning of the verb *k3j* "to think, intend, plan."[47] The meaning "spirit, consciousness, will" can be connected with the concept that the *ka* was created together with the individual and accompanied it as a protective spirit or doppelgänger (Latin *genius*). It is this aspect of the *ka* that is evidently invoked with the mention of the "*ka* of your existence on earth."

In Book of the Dead chapter 105, the *ka* is soothed from the worry that it might reject the "I" who is addressing it and dissociate itself from him on the grounds of potential moral burdens, just like the heart, which the deceased implores not to abandon him and testify against him (see below, section 3). In this chapter, concern about the possibility that the *ka* might distance itself from the "I," not as a witness for the prosecution, like the heart when it is placed on the scale, but as a lifetime companion who might end his association with one who has been found guilty. He assures the *ka* that it will not come to a verdict of guilty. Like the heart, the *ka* thus belongs to the moral, and thus the social, aspect of the person. Notwithstanding the association of the root *k₃* with the word "bull," the *ka* does not designate physical strength but rather the moral personality, the "normative" doppelgänger, a sort of superego connected with social categories of honor, dignity, and status, just as the heart is connected with the categories of virtue and righteousness.

The meaning "bull" seems to be connected with the original, central concept that the *ka* was handed down from father to son, specifically in the form of the embrace that the hieroglyph seems to depict, for it is not a matter of upraised but rather of horizontally outstretched arms.[48] We have mentioned this embrace in Chapter 2. This aspect of the *ka* can be called a paternal, dynastic principle, one that reproduced itself through the genealogical line; this principle includes the concept that the god Horus manifested himself in the *ka* of the king.[49]

The wish for union involves both the *ba* and the *ka*. In both cases, death means dissociation. The *ba* separates itself from the body and ascends to the sky, while the *ka* returns to the social sphere from which it came, to the ancestors who have already died. What had been a unity during life could no longer sustain itself as such, that is, as constituents of the person joined together symbiotically in a single body. Thus, as the Egyptians conceived it, the parts of the body, which had come apart at death, had to be brought into a new connection with one another.[50] As we can see, this, too, is a matter of integration and connectivity. Life is integration, community, and interaction, while death is decay, dissolution, and isolation. Just as decline and isolation could befall an individual even during life, the Egyptians held it as possible that there could be integration and association after death. In order to overcome the state of death and attain the blessed status of a transfigured ancestral spirit, it was necessary to facilitate the continued interaction of the various aspects or components of the person, though now under the altered circumstances wrought by physical death. These aspects or constituent elements were no longer united in the body, but separated. This fact created the possibility of new forms of cosmic existence that were not at the disposal of the individual during his lifetime. But to make this happen, these various aspects had to be placed into a relationship with one another so that they could remain connected to the "I" as an organizing personal center. It was necessary not only to maintain these elements as such and thus preserve the corpse from decay and the *ba* from destruction but also to construct a network of relationships that created specific connections between the "I" and the *ka*, the "I" and the heart, the *ba* and the corpse, and the *ba* and the shadow.[51] The *ba*, the *ka*, the corpse, the heart, and the shadow, all separated by death, had now to be reunited.

3. The Heart

Surprisingly, this need for reunion was also true for the heart. Deities were implored to help the deceased recover his heart. The goddess who regularly appears in this connection is the mother and sky goddess Nut:

> I give you back the heart of your mother,
> I set it in its place in your body,
> you being fresh and rejuvenated.[52]

This motif is closely connected with the mummification process. Anubis, the god of embalming, played a special role in the concept of the reinsertion of the heart into the body. A number of vignettes to chapter 26 of the Book of the Dead depict him giving the deceased his heart; in Theban Tomb 359, he even places it in his mouth, which reminds us of the episode in the Tale of Two Brothers in which the older brother, whose name is Anubis, causes his younger brother Bata to drink his heart. On the Anubis shrine of Tutankhamun, the god says,

> I bring you your heart
> and give it to you in its place in your body.[53]

In the mummification ritual, the heart was the only internal organ that was not removed.

But even when the deceased recovered his heart, there was still the danger of a further—and this time, a final—disassociation. This was the situation at the Judgment of the Dead, when the deceased was obliged to answer for his conduct during life before a divine tribunal. What the mouth averred, the heart had to confirm, or it would be exposed as lip service, that is, as a lie. All depended on the heart's not deviating from the mouth, and thus from the speaking "I." The deceased thus implored his own heart:

> O my *jb*-heart of my mother,
> O my *jb*-heart of my mother,
> O my *ḥ3.tj*-heart of my earthly existence:

> Arise not against me as witness
> before the "lords of demand"!
> Say not against me,
> "He actually did it" according to what I have done—
> let no complaint against me arise
> before the Great God, the Lord of the West.[54]

> O my *jb*-heart of my mother,
> O my *jb*-heart of my mother,
> O my *ḥꜣ.tj*-heart of my changing forms:
> Arise not against me as witness,
> oppose me not in the court,
> turn not against me before the master of the balance!

> You are my *ka*, which is in my body,
> my Khnum (= creator), who makes my limbs hale.
> May you go forth to the good
> that is prepared for us there![55]

> Do not make my name stink for the officials
> who reduce men to "sums."[56]

Thus, with regard to the heart, death is also pictured as dissociation, and salvation from the latter is represented as reintegration. The deceased speaks to his heart, as he does to his *ba*, promoting the notion of solidarity. He "comes" to his heart and unites with it, as with his *ka*. And, what is more, he has his heart restored to him by deities such as Nut and Anubis, as is never said of the *ba* or the *ka*, though it is said of organs and body parts.

The Egyptians considered a dissociation between self and heart while still alive to be a life-threatening symptom. This was especially true of physical circumstances. One love song, for instance, describes lovesickness as an absence of the heart.[57] In another text, a man complains of longing for his home town.[58] In the healing spells on the Metternich Stela, Isis wails over her child Horus, who has been bitten by a scorpion.[59] The motif of the absent heart also makes its appearance in the Story of Sinuhe, which describes the state of extreme fear that overcame Sinuhe in the presence of Pharaoh:

> I was like a man in the grip of darkness.
> My *ba* was gone, my limbs trembled,
> my heart was no longer in my body
> that I might be able to distinguish death from life.[60]

For the Egyptians, lovesickness, homesickness, worry, and fear were physical conditions that seemed like the grip of death, for to them, death was the ultimate dissociation of the heart and the self. To them, to be a person meant to be able to exercise self-control. But this control was lost when the heart, the *ba*, or some other aspect of the person was dissociated from the self. Such a dissociation resulted in powerlessness, unconsciousness, or sleep, all of which were compared to the state of death. The deceased was promised the ability to regain self-control. In this connection, the concept of *d.t*, which we have rendered above as "cult body," was invoked:

> A great one is awakened, a great one wakes,
> Osiris has raised himself onto his side;
> he who hates sleep and loves not weariness,
> the god gains power, the god gains control of his *d.t*-body.[61]
> Horus has set him upright,
> the one in Nedit, he has lifted himself.

Just as it is said to the deceased that he is to gather his limbs in the framework of the image of death as dismemberment, so here he is bidden to become conscious, and above all, to wake up:

> The sleeper awakes,
> Osiris-Khentamentiu awakes here with his *ka*,
> he who sleeps on his left side, the sleeper![62]

Such sentiments, along with spells for the provisioning of the deceased and the presentation of offerings, go back to an early date, to the third millennium B.C.E., when the deceased was pictured as sleeping in his tomb.[63] Later, the deceased was pictured as being in the next world, and he was summoned to receive his offerings (see chapter 14). In the New Kingdom, we encounter the image of death as sleep especially in the Books of the Netherworld, where the sun, during his nightly journey, awakens his mummy, which is slumbering in the netherworld, from the sleep of death. It awakens in the sunlight, which for a short while restores its consciousness, life, speech, and personality. When the sunlight passes, it sinks back into sleep.

The image of death as sleep is a familiar one in Western tradition. *Hypnos* and *Thanatos*, Sleep and Death, were twin brothers in Greek mythology. But while this image represents a blessed ultimate condition in the Western mythology of death, in Egypt, it was an image—like those of dismemberment, isolation, and dissociation—of a helplessness that had to be reversed through ritual. The deceased slept, but he was not to remain asleep; he was to awaken, just as he was to be gathered together, out of his dismemberment, into a single body, and to be integrated, out of his isolation, into a community. Sleep was not a goal, but a starting point.

4. *Image and Body*

a) Image and Death, Statue and Mummy

The primary experience of death included the idea that in death, the body became not only a corpse but also an "image" of the deceased.[64] The original image of the deceased was his own corpse.

> Death itself always already appears as an image, for even the corpse has already become an image that merely resembles the body of the living person. . . . It is no longer a body, but only an image of a body. . . .
>
> The true meaning of an image lies in the fact that it represents something that is absent and thus can only exist in the image. It makes something appear that is not in the image, but can only appear in the image. Under these circumstances, the image of a deceased person is not an anomaly, but the original meaning of what an image is. Dead, a person is always already absent, death is an unbearable absence that is quickly filled with an image so as to make it bearable.
>
> This is now an artificial image, summoned to counter the other image, the corpse. Making an image, one becomes active so as no longer to remain passively delivered to the experience of death and its terror.[65]

There was thus a concern to preserve the appearance of the corpse as image of the deceased, for instance, by covering it with a coat of plaster so as permanently to preserve the features. Such techniques were employed at a very early date at Jericho and in other neolithic cemeteries of the Fertile Crescent, and they are also attested from Old Kingdom Egypt as a preliminary step in the direction of mummification and tomb statues. The beginnings of mummification, with its "masking" of the face and sometimes the entire body with a thin layer of plaster, show how the masking of the body stemmed from the need to preserve the external forms, to change into the unchangeable. The early stages of mummification did not yet aim at the chemical preservation of the corpse but rather, and above all, at the preservation of the external form by means of padding and wrapping, makeup, and paint. The corpse thus became an image of the deceased, one that was as lifelike as possible, and it was dressed in the clothing of the living. From this common origin sprang mummy wrappings and anthropoid coffins, on the one hand, and on the other, tomb statues.[66] The characteristic form of the mummy, in which the deceased was made to resemble the god Osiris, became the goal of mummification only in the First Intermediate Period, and it was at that time that tomb statues and mummification went their separate ways. Tomb statues, which depicted the deceased in the form and the clothing of the living, left the hidden spaces of the tomb and were increasingly set up in the accessible cult rooms, until, with the end of the Old Kingdom, the *serdab* disappeared altogether. The corpse, however, which remained in the hidden spaces, assumed the form of the god Osiris.

In the matter of "treating" the dead, art played as great a role as language. One principle reigned supreme: a depiction was not a depiction of a body, it was itself a body. This was true not only for statues of the dead in their tombs but also for those of gods in their temples. In the course of the daily cult, they were anointed and clothed, and they benefited from all the actions that were normally carried out on behalf of a genuine body. The Egyptian language had a term that erased the distinction between representation and body: the word $\underline{d}.t$, which we usually translate as "body," actually referred to both.

Words for "corpse" (mummy, body) and "representation" (statue, picture, form, etc.) were determined by one and the same hieroglyph in the Egyptian writing system. Standing upright, this sign indicated a "depiction," and recumbent, it meant "corpse" (Figure 2). This hieroglyph is a clear indication of the relationship, even the equivalence, of the two concepts in Egyptian thought. Lift a body up on its own two legs, and it is a representation, lay a statue down on its back, and it is a corpse. Central, in this connection, is the symbolism of horizontality and verticality in Egyptian mortuary texts and rituals. To be upright was synonymous with life and renewal.

Figure 2. Hieroglyph used as determinative in words for (a) depiction and (b) corpse.

Throughout the history of Egyptian tomb statues, the analogy between statue and corpse is clear. In Old Kingdom tombs, the statue was not set up in the accessible cult chambers but rather in a special, walled off room that Egyptologists call a "*serdab*," an Arabic word meaning "cellar."[67] In the wall between the *serdab* and the cult chamber, there was often a peephole that enabled the statue to participate in the rituals and inhale the aroma of the incense without itself being seen. In this period, the statue was thus part of the "hidden functioning" of the tomb (see chapter 8), just like the corpse in its coffin. It was only at the very end of the Old Kingdom that the statue began to leave the "personal sphere" of the *serdab* and to be set up in the cult chamber, where it was visible.[68]

b) Reserve Head and Mummy Mask

In tombs of Dynasty 4, life-size heads of limestone were deposited in the sarcophagus chamber; the sculptors endeavored to make them true portraits of the deceased. These "reserve heads" were not deposited with the statue in the *serdab,* yet they fulfilled its function in a different manner. Like mummification, they sprang from the impulse to preserve the corporeal form. Scholars have assumed they were created from plaster masks that were made either before or after death.

The mummy mask reminds us of the "reserve head" of Dynasty 4. The Egyptian term for this important element in the mummification process is *tp n sšt3* or *tp št3,* "head of mystery (= corpse)" or "mysterious head." The following stanzas from the mortuary liturgy refer to this mummy mask:

> He sees, the one who sees with the head of a god.
> He sees: N. (Osiris-Khentamentiu) with the head of a god.
> He gives instructions to the gods.
> He gives them to them as the foremost among them,
> as the greatest one of the council.
> The *mks*-scepter is in his hand.
> His *nḥb.t*-mace is in his hand.
> He gives instructions to the gods,
> and they do what he says, trusting in them,
> and satisfied with what you say to them.[69]

The mummy mask was thus no "mask" in the sense of dissimulation, of hiding a true identity; rather, it was the "head of a god," a head that enabled the deceased to see and act as a god. What the expression "you see with the head of a god" is supposed to mean is revealed in chapter 151 of the Book of the Dead, which deals with the mummification of the deceased. It is a spell for the mummy mask, entitled "spell for the mysterious head" or "the head of mystery":[70]

> Anubis speaks, the embalmer, lord of the divine hall,
> when he has placed his hands on the coffin of N.
> and equipped him with what (he) needs:
> Hail, O beautiful of face, lord of vision,
> whom Ptah-Sokar has gathered together and whom Anubis has upraised,
> to whom Shu gave support (that is, impetus),
> O beautiful of face among the gods!
>
> Your right eye is the night barque,
> your left eye is the day barque,
> your eyebrows are the Ennead.
> The crown of your head is Anubis,
> the back of your head is Horus,
> your lock of hair Ptah-Sokar.

You (the mask)[71] are in front of N., he sees by means of you.
(You) lead him to the goodly ways,
you repel Seth's band for him
and cast his enemies under his feet for him
in front of the Ennead in the great House of the Noble in Heliopolis.
You take the goodly way to the presence of Horus, the lord of the nobles.

From the Middle Kingdom on, this spell was written on the inner surface of mummy masks; it is even on the famous golden mask of Tutankhamun.[72] Its focus is in fact on sight. The mask is called "lord of vision," and it is stated, "he sees by means of you." The apotropaic aspect of the mask is also stressed: it repels enemies for him. The expression "with the head of a god" becomes understandable when we note that all the details of the mask—eyes, eyebrows, crown and back of the head, "finger" (understand: nose), and hair—are divinized. "With the head of a god" is thus tantamount to saying, "with a thoroughly godly head." The designation of the mask as "head," and not "face," is entirely justified. It refers to a helmet-style mask that did not just cover the face but enclosed the entire head and was worn on the shoulders.

There are many mummy masks, and also faces on anthropoid sarcophagi, that are in no way second-rate sculpture in their quality, and sometimes even in their portrait-like nature. The mummy was treated like a statue, and the statue was treated like a mummy; both served the deceased as bodies, that is, as instruments of his continued life, which was conceivable only in the medium of corporeality. The statue and the mummy are both to be understood as representations of the deceased, representations that served to keep the deceased present while at the same time also presupposing his absence.[73]

For this reason, the Opening of the Mouth ritual was carried out on both the statue and the mummy of the deceased. Though it doubtless originated in the preparation of statues, for mummification and its accompanying rituals developed at a later date, by the time that our written and pictorial evidence for it were created, the ritual had long since been applied to mummies as well. In any case, unlike Mesopotamia, where there was a like-named ritual, the Opening of the Mouth ritual originated in the mortuary cult. It was a matter of a representation of the deceased father, which was to be prepared and endowed with life under the supervision of the son. The preparation of a statue was unequivocally connected to the management of death, and the statue cult had its origin in the mortuary cult.

Like corpses, statues could be buried. In the mortuary temple of Mentuhotpe II, the king who reunited Egypt at the end of the First Intermediate Period, there is a grave known as *Bab el-Hosan,* "(Tomb-)Entrance of the Horseman," which Howard Carter sank into while riding his horse one morning, thus discovering it. It is a passageway nearly 500 feet deep. In what would normally be the sarcophagus chamber, the archaeologists found a seated statue of the king, wrapped in linen bandages and lying on its side.[74] In the cults of Osiris and Sokar, artificial "corpses" were annually prepared and buried. At Karnak, in recent years, archaeologists excavated a cemetery in which artificial corpses of the god Osiris were buried by the hundreds. The figurines were made out of a certain cohesive mixture of sand that was then covered with plaster and decorated. The Osiris mysteries, along with the Khoiak mysteries that were inseparably connected with them from the New Kingdom on, were nothing other than the embalming·and burial rituals of the mortuary cult, transposed onto the divine level. These mysteries centered on a statue, not a corpse, but this distinction played no role and was ritually rescinded. In this connection, priests in certain temples prepared "grain mummies" that also had the intermediate status of both representation and corpse. To a great extent, and all the more so in the later stages of Egyptian history, the divine cult was a mortuary cult, not because the Egyptians believed their gods were dead (and that their dead were gods), but because there was no distinction between corpse and statue. Rites carried out to transfigure the corpse and endow it with life could thus epitomize all the ritual activity aimed at life-endowing renewal that was deemed appropriate for gods and their images. The burial ritual was thus the epitome of the ritual activity that, in these later periods, centered on the "synthetic" corpses of Osiris and Sokar, and on the bodies of the sacred animals of certain other gods.

Because of the equivalence of image and body, sacred animals also counted as images or bodies of gods. The gods were powers whose identity or life force could occupy a host of physical receptacles, both statues and, in certain cases, animals. This power to be incarnated in representations and in theriomorphic "transformations" was also ascribed to the dead in their status of transfigured ancestral spirits. For the dead, the statue was the medium of physical self-multiplication. There were thus often multiple statues, especially in the *serdabs* of the Old Kingdom.[75] In this period, there were even double and triple group statues that depicted the deceased in the company of himself.[76] During life, the individual's presence in his body stood in the way of such self-multiplication; in death, his absence dissolved this barrier, and the single body, which itself had become a statue through the mummification process, could now be multiplied into a host of statues that served as bodies.

c) *Shabty* and Golem

In this connection, we must also consider the well-known figurines called "*shabty*" or "*ushabty*."[77] Made of clay, faïence, wood, or hard stone, they were deposited in tombs in large quantities. Along with beautiful, carefully modeled and inscribed figurines, there are also grotesque examples that are scarcely more than lumps of clay rolled out between the palms of the hands. They were placed in a small wooden chest. Intact finds show that the ideal number of these figurines was 401: 365, one for each day of the year, and 36 "overseers," one for each ten-day period. The year in question was a period of possible obligatory labor in the afterlife. For each day of this year, it was supposed to be possible for the tomb owner to send a substitute in the form of a *shabty*-figure. *Shabty*s are thus not to be understood as a means of avoiding obligatory labor, but rather, as a means of enabling the deceased to participate in this labor. In Egyptian beliefs about the magic of representations, the distinction between "(mere) representation" and "(true) self" was entirely dissolved. If it had been desired to avoid such duty, there would have been appropriate spells: "O you overseers of the afterlife, who call those obliged to serve to their work, you shall have no power over me, for I am a worthy in the household of Osiris, free of any obligation to serve!" I know of no such spells.[78] The deceased created substitutes for the sake of taking his place, and thus to participate, not for the sake of avoidance.

A spell was written on the bodies of these figures to activate them. The spell became chapter 6 of the Book of the Dead,[79] and it also appears in the mortuary liturgy of Pa-aa,[80] which means it was recited in the mortuary cult:

> O this *shabty*, if the scribe Pa-aa is conscripted
> for any work that is carried out in the realm of the dead,
> as a man who is obliged to do his work,
> to till (the fields) and to water the banks,
> to carry sand from the east to the west,
> you will say, "I shall do it, here I am!"[81]

On a Late Period wooden chest used for storing *shabty* figures, there is the following text:[82]

> Spoken by Thoth, lord of hieroglyphs,
> scribe of Truth of the lord of eternity.
> He says: O *ushabty*-figure (*rpjj*),
> and you great officials of the realm of the dead,
> when one calls, when one commands N.
> to transport sand from west to east,

to transport sand from east to west,
you will say, "Yes, I shall do it,"
in sunlight and moonlight,
at the beginning and the end of the year,
in summer, in winter, on the 365 days of the year,
to secure (him) in his activity (*r rwḏ m jrr=f*),
like the great gods who lie in (their) coffins in the crypt
in the sacred district of the divine region.

That such *shabty*-figures could serve other forms of sharing and participation emerges from an archaeological find, a burial "in effigy" that the
overseer of domains Qenamun, who had shared a wet nurse with King
Amenophis II and also been his companion at arms, had arranged for
himself by special favor of the king in the most sacred part of Abydos, so
as to be buried in the immediate vicinity of the tomb of Osiris and the
entrance to the netherworld.[83] The *shabty* thus represented the deceased
not only for the purpose of compulsory labor but also could serve as a
bearer of his extended identity in other connections, such as here, in the
proximity of Osiris.[84]

From here, it is but a small step to the medieval Jewish concept of the
golem, the artificial clay man who could be brought to life by means of
letters written on his forehead and the recitation of secret spells, and
whom its creator could send in his place on various missions.[85] An Egyptian story from the New Kingdom, fragmentarily preserved on a papyrus
of the Late Period, tells of just such a case. It is prophesied to a king that
he has only a short time left to live. But there is the possibility that another
can go to the netherworld in his stead. Only one person, General Merire,
an extremely wise, virtuous, and learned man, is capable of doing this.
He receives a promise from the king to care for his widow and his son,
and he goes in his place to the realm of the dead. There, he immediately
learns that the king has most thoughtlessly broken all his promises. The
king has made his wife the Great Royal Wife, given his house to a rival,
and had his son killed. As a deceased person, Merire is not in a position
to return to the world above to look after his family. But he forms a man
of dirt, whom he is able to send in his place, with appropriate instructions, to the world above.[86]

The "organic" unity in which the various constituent elements were
integrated with one another during life could not be restored by the mortuary rituals, nor was this attempted. In the condition of death, they
entered into entirely new forms of connection that opened up, for the
deceased as a transfigured ancestral spirit, new forms of continued life in
the sky, the earth, and the netherworld. This new connectivity, which held
his person as such together, thus took on cosmic dimensions. His body,

which earlier had all the elements united inside it, now became only one element out of several. Along with the *ba*, the *ka*, and the heart, with which we have concerned ourselves in this chapter, these included the shadow and the name. The shadow belonged with the *ba*, but it did not follow it to the sky. The name lived on in the world above, in the memory of posterity; it had a certain affinity to the *ka*. What the Egyptian aimed for was a life in and with all these aspects of his person, which he now no longer "embodied" but rather combined. With the construction of a tomb with its statues and symbols, with the carrying out of rituals, and with the depositing of "mortuary literature" (see chapter 10), he endeavored to construct a network of connections that was supposed to facilitate a postmortem relationship between the individual elements of his personality.

Moreover, the tomb served as a medium of social integration. Each tomb was part of a network of significant relationships with other tombs, with a temple, and with the city of the living. Its location was determined, for the most part, by social, not topographical or astronomical, factors. In every necropolis, there were principal tombs, dominating structures for correspondingly dominating personalities, around which smaller tombs were grouped. In cemeteries of rock-cut tombs, the highest-ranking tombs were often above, near the top of the hillside, while clients and dependants located their tombs below it. At el-Bersha, one tomb inscription stresses that the owner had constructed his tomb "at the feet of his lord." There were also many group tombs that sheltered the wife, the father, or other close relatives in their upper stratum, and in the middle stratum, larger groups of relatives and dependants. At Deir el-Gabrawi, the Dynasty 6 nomarch Djau stressed in his tomb inscription that he had prepared his tomb together with his father, not because he lacked the means to make a tomb of his own, but because it suited him to be together with his father in the next life: "I have made my burial in a single tomb together with this (senior) Djau, so as to be together with him in a common place. This happened, not because means were lacking to make two tombs; I did this because I wanted to see this Djau daily and to be together with him in a single place."[87] In this respect, the tomb was the "house of the *ka*": first and foremost, it was at the service of the social self of the deceased, preventing his isolation by integrating him into both the sphere of those who owned tombs and the sphere of those yet to be born.[88]

CHAPTER FIVE

Death as Separation and Reversal

1. Separation from Life: Death as Parting and Inversion

a) The Widow's Lament

Death as separation is the most natural and the most widespread form in which death is experienced, out of sight of those left behind. We thus encounter this image of death most often in the dirges that accompany scenes of mourning in private tombs. Such representations and captions are attested as early as the Old Kingdom.

In the earlier tomb inscriptions, the words attributed to the pallbearers and mourning women refer mostly to the procession to the tomb, which they depict as a crossing over to the "beautiful West" and accompany with exclamations such as "Welcome to the presence of Osiris!"[1] and "May the Desert extend her arms to you"[2] or "O goddess of the West, extend your hand to him!"[3] The following is an oft-attested song:

> Giving a goodly burial to N.,
> causing the god to ascend to his Light-land,
> accompanying him to the staircase of the realm of the dead.
> Welcome in peace to the presence of the Great God!
> Pass in peace to the sky, to Light-land,

to the Field of Reeds, to the netherworld, to the *sšm.t*-hall,
to the place where this god dwells![4]

Clearly, these words explain the burial procession as a passage through
the realm of death and into the place of eternal life. Firm belief in immortality made it impossible to include songs expressive of pain and sadness,
songs that would have immortalized the negative side of death and the
realm of death. In the immediate wake of the Amarna Period, however,
this taboo was lifted, and the texts sound an entirely new note expressive
of pain and sadness. In them, we encounter the image of death as reversal. Thus, from the reign of Aya (ca. 1320 B.C.E.), we have the tomb of a
man named Neferhotep (Theban Tomb 49). In it, his widow mourns:

> Go away—how can you do that?
> I walk alone, see, I am behind you!
> O you who loved to chat with me,
> you are silent, you do not speak![5]

> The good shepherd is gone to the land of eternity . . .[6]
> You, who were rich in people, are in the land that loves loneliness.
> He who loved to stretch his legs and walk
> is bound, wrapped up, hemmed in!
> He who loved to clothe himself in fabrics
> is sleeping in yesterday's cast-off clothing![7]

In the tomb of Nefersekheru at Zawyet es-Sultan, from the reign of
Ramesses II, the following caption accompanies the mourning women:

> The glib one, silence has befallen him.
> The wakeful one is asleep.
> The one who took no sleep at night
> is weary every day.

> The house of those in the West
> is deep and dark.
> There is no door, no window in it,
> no light to brighten,
> no north wind to refresh the heart.
> The sun does not rise there.
> They lie forever in sleep
> because of the darkness, even in the daytime (?).
> Oh, woe! May the dear one be safe and sound, breathing air!

> The one with the booming voice is silent, he does not speak.
> The self-aware one (*p³ jp d̠.t = f*) is unknowing. . . .

> Those in the West are in difficulty, their condition is bad.
> How motionless is the one who has gone to them.

He cannot describe his condition.
He rests in his lonely place,
and eternity is with him in darkness.[8]

The mythic prototype of the widow's lament was the mourning of Isis over the corpse of Osiris. Her songs speak the same language as the widows' laments in the tomb inscriptions. These laments belong to the female, to the Isis-Nephthys, aspect of bestowing life on the deceased, and thus to the physical side of the efforts to restore life and personhood. Horus does not mourn: his words describe the restoration of honor, the punishment of the enemy, the elevation and enthronement of Osiris, but never longing, love, or grief. Mourning occurs in the intimate space of the physical constellation of spouses, not in the social space of honor, sovereignty, and vindication, for which the son is responsible. Lyric, the language of emotions, is a sensuous, feminine language, and its earliest expression—at least, in the texts preserved to us—is to be found in the laments of Isis and Nephthys. In the organization of the life-endowing and renewing activities by means of which ritual endeavored to treat and to heal death, there was a strict differentiation of the sexes. Even a deceased woman played the role of Osiris, and in the rituals, Isis, Nephthys, and Horus acted on her behalf, as well. Grief, and specifically *female* grief, was an unconditional form of handling death by bestowing life. Only the two women, the two "mourning birds," as they were called, had the power to wake the dead in this way. In this respect, the myth of Isis and Osiris is the exact reversal of the myth of Orpheus and Eurydice. The manly grief of Orpheus could master Orcus, the god of death, but it could not reach Eurydice herself and call her back to life, or help her in the netherworld. But Isis' womanly grief was directed squarely at Osiris. Crossing the boundary of death, Orpheus' masculine grief constituted the enormous exception that overturned the established order of things. Isis' feminine grief did not infringe upon the order of things, but rather, restored it. Her love did not fetch Osiris back from the netherworld, but it made it possible for him to come back to life there. What was important was for Osiris to go to the netherworld and remain there. Only thus, in the realm of death, could he become the center of a sphere of eternal life that held out the promise of salvation from the realm of death and the promise of eternal life for every deceased person who followed him. "Salvation" and "eternal life" are Christian concepts, and we might think that the Egyptian myth can all too easily be viewed through the lens of Christian tradition. Quite the contrary, in my opinion, Christian myth is itself thoroughly stamped by Egyptian tradition, by the myth of Isis and Osiris, which from the very beginning had to do with salvation and eternal life. It thus seems legitimate to me to reconstruct the Egyptian symbolism with the help of Christian concepts. As with Orpheus and Eurydice, the constellation of Isis and Osiris can also be compared with Mary and Jesus. The scene of the Pietà, in which Mary holds the corpse of the crucified Jesus on her lap and mourns, is a comparable depiction of the body-centered intensity of female grief, in which Mary is assisted by Mary Magdalene, just as Isis is assisted by Nephthys. Jesus also descended into the realm of death, though he did not remain there, and Mary had nothing to do with his resurrection. Osiris remained in the netherworld, but he was resurrected and alive. With this, Isis had a great deal to do. What she accomplished was to maintain the relationship that kept her husband and brother inserted into a solid constellation, even beyond the boundary of death. His son could do the same in his own way, by the specific means of his filial love. Even in the netherworld, Osiris remained bound up in the life-endowing connectivity of the basic constellation of his family. With their constellative thought, the Egyptians invoked all the human ties and relationships that had the power to extend their effects beyond the boundary of death. First and foremost among these was womanly grief.

Here, I shall cite some examples from these ritual lamentations of Isis and Nephthys before returning to the laments in private inscriptions. They stem from papyri of the Late Period, but they surely go back further in time, at least to the New Kingdom:

> Come to your house, O Heliopolitan!
> Come to your house! You have no enemy.
> O beautiful boy, come to your house, that you may see me.
> I am your wife, who loves you.
> Part not from me, beautiful youth,
> come straight to your house! I cannot see you.
> My heart beseeches you. My eyes desire you.
> I seek you, to see you.
>
> Come to the one who loves you, Wennefer,
> come to your wife!
> Come to your wife, O powerless one,
> come to the mistress of your house!
>
> I am your bodily sister,
> go not far from me.
> Gods and men have turned their face to you,
> and together, they bewail you, for they see me.
>
> I call to you wailing to the heights of the sky.
> Do you not hear my voice?
> I am your wife on earth, the one you love,
> you love none besides me, O my husband![9]

In another liturgical lamentation, we read:

> Come quickly to me!
> For I wish to see you, after not seeing you.
> Before me is darkness, though Re is in the sky.
> Sky and earth are one,
> today, shadow lies over the land.
> My heart burns, for you depart into evil,
> my heart burns, for you turn away from me,
> though there is nothing that you have found against me.
>
> Destroyed are the homes, turned back are the pathways.
> I seek, for I wish to see you.
> I am in a city that has no walls.
>
> I mourn your love for me.
> O, be not far, be not far!
> See, your son drives the enemy to the place of execution.[10]

Seeing, a longing for the sight of the beloved, is a leitmotif in these lamentations. For the widow robbed of this sight, darkness reigns, though the sun is in the sky. In another lamentation, in her despair, Isis goes so far as to demand the opening of the sarcophagus chamber, the mysterious crypt, so that she may gaze upon the corpse:

> It is too long for me to spend the night here,
> one month after another.
> Woe, woe, loneliness is upon me,
> (I) who spent the night alone!
>
> May the crypt be opened for me, that I may see Osiris:
> I am his sister, I am his wife,
> I am his companion, I am his beloved.[11]

For Isis, the world is darkened, it is destroyed, collapsed, impassable terrain, it is like a city that has no walls, delivered defenseless to the powers of darkness. When light disappears from the world, sky and earth are joined together. This motif occurs often in the lamentations:

> O come to me,
> the sky is joined to the earth;
> there are shadows on the earth today,
> the sky is brought down upon the earth![12]

Not only are personal need and grief, darkness, and deprivation themes of these laments but also empathetic depictions of the situation that has befallen the deceased. For him as well, everything is turned upside down:

You, who love life,
should not go to darkness.
You, who love company,
should not go to loneliness.

Where are you going, child of the Golden One,
who love the noise of company?
We call, but the Land of Silence,
its gateways lead into a house of darkness.[13]

Speak to me, Osiris! I am Isis.
I woke your house with the harp.
I gladdened you with the lute.[14]

She cries: The lonely one is husband,
brother, and companion.
Where are you going, child of the Golden One,
who, born yesterday, are going off today
to those whose land lies in darkness,
whose fields are sand,
whose tombs serve silence,
whose call is not heard?

Those who lie there without standing,
whose coffin is girded by bonds,
whose limbs are hindered;
those whose water is so distant,
whose air slips away—when does it come back to them?
To those whose chapel locks are secured with bronze,
whose steps are weighed down under silence?[15]

Reflected in these lamentations of Isis is the human experience of death, which sunders the togetherness of a couple in life. Here, too, the image of death as inversion is central.

The laments in the mortuary ritual and in the inscriptions of private persons on tomb walls, coffins, and stelae draw on the same conceptual fund and belong to the same text genre. In both groups of texts, we find the same laments over the inversion of life. From the Late Period, we have the coffin of Ankhpakhrod (Berlin 20132). Here, the talk is about death as isolation and the turning of social intercourse into its opposite, loneliness. Yet there is also a companionship beyond this separation. The widow remains close to her husband—"your hand is in my hand"—she can contact him with her drink offering, and she can implore the dead spirits in the world beyond not to deny the deceased the conviviality he so loves:

Your hand is in my hand.
One (who) took joy in a crowd—

in the meanwhile, you betake yourself to barren places.
Your heart is with me (*jb=k m-ʿ=j*),
while you spend the day in the realm of the dead (*jgr.t*, literally, "land of
 silence"),
when the (or, "without that the" ?) time comes for you to drink what will
 be given at the (right) time,[16]
when it (the water) joins with the soil.
O you dead spirits who rejoice,
do not repel all men from him.
His heart is pleased by the sight of many.[17]

This lament touches on three themes: first, the theme of separation; second, that of a dreary conception of the netherworld; and third, the theme of the reversal of the deceased's situation into the opposite of what it had been during life. Death meant a total change from what was habitual, a radical discontinuity of life. These motifs are surely far older than the Amarna Period, when they are first mentioned in tomb inscriptions. It was not their formulation, but the fact that they were recorded in the monumental form of tomb inscriptions, that was new in the post-Amarna era.

b) Death—"Come!" is His Name

It is surely no accident that at the same point in time, another innovation in the canon of tomb decoration made its appearance, one that also represented the afterlife as a realm of death and not a paradise. These were songs sung at banquets by harpers and lute players. In this case, there is even a text that goes into the matter explicitly. In Theban Tomb 50, the tomb of the "god's father" (a priestly title) Neferhotep, from the reign of Haremhab, there are three such songs. In one of them, we read:

I have heard these songs that are in the tombs of the forebears
and what they say, extolling this life and belittling the afterlife.
Why is such a thing done to the land of eternity?
. . . our people have rested in it since the beginning of time,
and they shall be there for endless years,
all go there. There is no tarrying in Egypt.
There is none who does not arrive there.
The time one spends on earth is but a dream.
But "Welcome, safe and sound!" is said to the one who has reached the
 West.[18]

This song about the afterlife has little to say that is comforting. That all must go there, and that time there is so endlessly long that a lifetime spent on earth seems, by comparison, to shrivel up into a dream image, still does not make the afterlife into a desirable place. Important, though, is the explicit reference to other songs in the tombs of the forebears, songs that "extol this life and belittle the afterlife." We can get a clear picture of these; the reference is doubtless to the Antef Song, the classic harper's song, the model of all the others,[19] which read like variations on it.[20] This song appears in the tomb of a Paatenemheb from the Amarna Period,[21] as well as on a papyrus containing love songs,[22] another genre of songs sung at banquets, and it in fact expresses itself bluntly regarding the transitoriness of earthly life and the inevitability of death:

> Song which is in the tomb of King Antef, the justified, in front of the
>   singer with the harp.
> He is happy, this good prince!
> Death is a kindly fate.
> A generation passes,
> Another stays,[23]
> Since the time of the ancestors.
> The gods who were before rest in their tombs,
> Blessed nobles too are buried in their tombs.
> (Yet) those who built tombs,
> Their places are gone,
> What has become of them?
> I have heard the words of Imhotep and Hardedef,
> Whose sayings are recited whole.
> What of their places?
> Their walls have crumbled,
> Their places are gone,
> As though they had never been!
> None comes from there,
> To tell of their state,
> To tell of their needs,
> To calm our hearts,
> Until we go where they have gone!
> Hence rejoice in your heart!
> Forgetfulness profits you,
> Follow your heart as long as you live!
> Put myrrh on your head,
> Dress in fine linen,
> Anoint yourself with oils fit for a god.
> Heap up your joys,
> Let your heart not sink!
> Follow your heart and your happiness,
> Do your things on earth as your heart commands!
> When there comes to you that day of mourning,

The Weary-hearted hears not their mourning,
Wailing saves no man from the pit!

Refrain: Make holiday,
Do not weary of it!
Lo, none is allowed to take his goods with him,
Lo, none who departs comes back again![24]

The theme of this song is none other than the sage advice of Siduri, the divine barmaid who attempted to dissuade Gilgamesh from his futile quest for eternal life:

> Thou, O Gilgamesh, let thy belly be full;
> Day and night be thou merry;
> Make every day (a day of) rejoicing.
> Day and night do thou dance and play.
>
> ... This is the lot of [mankind . . .].[25]

The image of death as separation, as the complete termination of any continuity of life, is a theme common to both feasting and laments. Someone convinced that he will be able to celebrate again in the afterlife, or that he will only then be able genuinely to celebrate, does not have the correct attitude toward the irretrievability of the present moment, which lends the feast its unquotidian, intoxicating luster. Such apparently heretical views thus found expression even on festive occasions. And in this case as well, as in that of laments, these views were immortalized for the first time only in the tombs of the Amarna Period.

In this case, we can demonstrate that these views were much older. From the Middle Kingdom, we have Papyrus Berlin 3024; the text it contains, the well-known Dialogue of a Man with His Ba, is perhaps older still, possibly stemming from the First Intermediate Period. This text, which we shall discuss in the last section of chapter 16, is a dispute about attitudes toward death. In it, the *ba* represents the position of the harpers' songs. The image of death as separation, termination, and reversal could not have been expressed more bluntly, for Egyptian ears, than in the words of the *ba* in this text.

There is yet another text that portrays the netherworld as a realm of death (Hebrew Sheol), not as an Elysium. It is a dialogue between Atum and Osiris that occurs in chapter 175 of the Book of the Dead. This text also presumably stems from the Middle Kingdom (we find citations from it already in the Coffin Texts), but in the Book of the Dead tradition, it first appears at the end of Dynasty 18, in a Book of the Dead belonging to a man named Kha. I cite only the portion that interests us here:

(Osiris speaks)
O Atum, how is it
that I must travel to the wasteland of the realm of the dead?
It has no water, it has no air,
it is utterly deep, dark, and endless!

Atum supplies a profound response to this question, and the dialogue
continues in an extremely interesting manner, to which we shall return
later. Here, our interest is only in Osiris' question, which again treats the
Sheol aspect of the netherworld as an absolute, thus contradicting all that
the mortuary texts have to say about air, light, and water in the netherworld. The Egyptians did not repress this question; rather, they allowed
it to be expressed, with all its radical skepticism. They conceived a terror
of the realm of the dead that was every bit as unqualified as that of the
other peoples of the Mediterranean world—Sumerians, Babylonians,
Israelites, Greeks, and Romans. The Egyptian realm of the dead was essentially none other than a land of no return, a Sheol or a Hades. The counterimage of a paradise in no way covered over the dreadful image of a
Sheol.

Siduri's wise advice to enjoy life, in consideration of its finality and its
irretrievability, is discernible in some inscriptions on statues that were set
up in temples during Dynasty 22. In this period, such statues were considered a more potent assurance of continuance in the memory of posterity than the construction of a monumental tomb. In the inscriptions
on a statue of this period, the wife of the man represented says:

To see a moment of sunlight is worth more than eternity as ruler of the realm
of the dead.[26]

Adriaan de Buck has referred to this aphorism as the "Egyptian version
of Achilles' lament."[27] In book 11 of the *Odyssey*, which relates Odysseus'
journey to the netherworld, Achilles says to him:

I would rather be the most common slave in the fields for some landless
peasant than rule these lifeless dead as their king.

The Egyptian aphorism in fact amounts to a similar pronouncement. To
be sure, the opposition is not that between "slaves" and "ruler," but rather
between "moment" and "eternity": better a moment here than an eternity there. Such an opposition seems to be a crass contradiction of the
official Egyptian view: in the widow's lament, sentiments are expressed
that could be classified as "heretical." But in Egypt, there was no ortho-
doxy. The aphorism had its reality in the mouth of the wife, who wished

to live here on earth in the company of her husband, and this intimacy, however brief it might have been, took priority over all the promises of the mortuary religion.

From the same period, we have the inscription of a Nebnetjeru, also on a statue that was set up in a temple. This text also expresses a rather pessimistic view of life after death:

> I made my days festive with wine and myrrh,
> I eradicated weariness from my heart.
> For I knew that darkness reigns in the valley (of the dead).
> The one who follows his heart is thus not foolish.
>
> . . .
>
> Be not stingy with what you have,
> or miserly with your fortune!
> Sit not in a tent of sorrow,[28]
> predicting the morrow before it has come.
> Deny not your eye its tear,
> so that it does not come three times.
> Sleep not when the sun rises in the east,
> suffer no thirst in the presence of beer!
> The West commands: Give reward to the one who follows his heart.
> The heart is a god,
> the belly is his chapel,
> he rejoices when the limbs are in festival.[29]

Nebnetjeru also advises living life in this world fully and deliberately and not denying any wish ("follow the heart"), so long as it is day.

The boldest and most moving text of this sort is again placed in the mouth of a woman. Here, however, it is not a bereaved widow who speaks to her deceased husband, but rather, a deceased woman to her bereaved husband. The text occurs on a mortuary stela and stems from the first century B.C.E.:

> O my brother, my husband,
> my friend, high priest!
> Your heart will not weary of drinking and eating,
> of intoxication and lovemaking!
>
> Spend a good day, follow your heart
> day and night!
> Let no care into your heart!
> What are years not (spent) on earth?
>
> The West, it is the land of slumber, a burdensome darkness,
> the dwelling place of those who are there (i.e., the dead).
> Sleep is their occupation,

they wake not to see their brothers.
They cannot gaze upon their fathers and mothers.
Their hearts miss their wives and their children.

The water of life, in which (= which) is the nourishment of every mouth,
it is thirst for me.
It comes only to the one who is on earth.
I thirst, though there is water beside me.[30]

I do not know the place where I am
since I came to this valley.
Give me flowing water!
Say to me: "May your form not be far from water!"
Turn my face to the north wind on the bank of the water!
Surely my heart will be cooled in its grief.

Death, "Come!" is his name, whoever he calls to himself,
they come immediately,
though their hearts shudder in fear of him.
No one sees him among gods and men.

Great and small alike are in his hand.
No one staves off his curse from the one he chooses.
He steals the son from his mother,
rather than the old man who is drawing nigh to him.

All the fearful plead before him,
but he turns not his face to them;
he does not come to the one who prays to him,
he does not heed the one who praises him.
He is not seen, so no gift can be given to him.[31]

This moving text begins with Siduri's carpe diem motif, justifying it by alluding to the end of all celebration, and indeed, of all life in the netherworld, which is here mercilessly depicted as a realm of death. In any event, it is indicated that even here, the libation and the prayer of the bereaved can have some good effect. Its conclusion consists of impressive verses concerning death, which mercilessly and indiscriminately summons all.

That "Come!" is death's name is known to other texts, for example, a harper's song in the tomb of the vizier Paser:[32]

> Think not of that day of "Come!"
> until you go to the West as a praised one.

In other texts, this "Come!" refers to the summons to the Judgment of the Dead, before which every deceased person had to present himself immediately, as, for example, in two prayers from the reign of Ramesses II:

Would that I have Thoth
as supporter tomorrow!
"Come!" it is said,
when I have entered into the presence of the lords of righteousness,
"that you may emerge vindicated!"[33]

Would that I have Amun
as supporter tomorrow,
when "Come!" is said.[34]

Already in Coffin Texts spell 335 (which became chapter 17 of the Book of the Dead), there is mention of the Judgment of the Dead as the day of "Come, then!"[35] This is the most widely attested mortuary text from ancient Egypt, so it is presumably the origin of this turn of expression. These texts, however, conceive of "that day 'Come!'" differently from the stela of Taimhotep. Taimhotep was not thinking of the Judgment of the Dead but of death as the inescapable end of all life. To be sure, death spares no one. But the concept of the Judgment of the Dead harbors the promise of redemption. It is now clear that this is a matter of salvation from a fate of death that awaited everyone, and which even the Egyptians took note of with perfect clarity. Thanks to the idea of the Judgment of the Dead, however, this fate did not remain the final word that religion in Egypt had to say about death.

With regard to this capacity to think both of death as inescapable and of the Judgment of the Dead as a path to salvation, toward which Egyptian thought was developing in the course of the New Kingdom, we may cite one of the most splendid hymns to the god Osiris that is preserved to us. It is from the Ramesside Period (thirteenth century B.C.E.), and it has come down to us in several versions.[36] Here, for once, the god is not praised in the splendor of his mythological epithets but as the god of death:

Those who exist are with you,
gods and men.
You prepare their places in the realm of the dead,
and they beseech your *ka*.

They come in millions and millions,
in the end, there is the landing in your presence.
Those in their mothers' womb already have their face turned towards you,
there is no tarrying in Egypt.[37]

They are in your hands, they all come to you,
great and small.
Yours is what lives on earth.
All the world comes to you alike,

you are their lord, there is none other than you.
All this, it belongs to you.

Whether one sails upstream or downstream in the course of a lifetime—
morning by morning, your majesty is there as Re,
and all that is and is not yet follows you.

I have come to you, knowing your will
and aware of your role in the netherworld.
You sit (in judgment), *maat* before you,
and judge the hearts on the scale.
Here am I, before you, my *jb*-heart full of *maat*,
no lie in my *ḥ₃.ty*-heart.
I pray to your might, for you are so strong,
I soothe the Ennead who surround you.
I give you praise and rejoice before you,
I kiss the ground tirelessly.

Chapter 154 of the Book of the Dead concerns the theme of distancing from death in connection with the deceased's arrival in the presence of Osiris and with his similarity to this god. Death, from which the deceased distances himself, is depicted in an uncommonly drastic manner, and this motif of distancing takes on the allure of salvation:

Hail to you, my father Osiris!
I have come to you to treat you—
may you also treat this flesh of mine.
. . .
I have done nothing that you abhor—
may your *ka* therefore love me and not reject me.
May you accept me into your following, that I not decay,
as you have ordained for every god and every goddess,
for all cattle and all worms that must perish.
His *ba* ascends, after he is dead,
and it descends, after he passes away:
this means he will be swollen, all his bones will rot,
the limbs are destroyed and fallen away (?),
the bones are softened and the flesh is a stinking mass;
he reeks, he decays and turns into a mass of worms, nothing but worms.
. . .
All that has lived is dead there,
has dwindled away when all the worms have done their work.
. . .
Greetings to you, my father Osiris!
Your body continues, you do not decay,
you do not rot, you do not disintegrate,
you do not stink and decompose,
you will not turn into worms.

I am Khepri, and my limbs continue forever.
I do not decay, I do not swell up,
I do not decompose and turn into worms.
. . . I have awakened in peace,
I am not swollen up and perished in my entrails,
I am not injured, my eye is not swollen,
my skull is not crushed, my ears have not grown deaf,
my head has not been severed from my neck,
my tongue has not been torn out, my hair has not been cut,
my eyebrows have not fallen off, no harm has befallen me.
My body continues, it does not perish,
it is not destroyed in this land, forever.

This depiction of salvation from death alludes to the process of embalming, of preserving the corpse from decomposition and decay, which turns it into the imperishable body of Khepri, the morning sun. But true salvation from death is not achieved through this transformation but rather by command of Osiris, into whom the deceased is transformed through the embalming ritual. The deceased owes his redemption from death to the grace of the god, who recognizes him as a peer and receives him into his kingdom.

Laments, harpers' songs, and many other texts as well depict death as a transition from the realm of the living to that of death and draw a blatantly merciless contrast between the two. Yet in the ritual texts intended to transform the deceased into a transfigured ancestral spirit, we read of a passage from the realm of death into a paradise, from death into a transfigured state. The deceased managed this transition—this was the great hope and promise—by means of his moral righteousness ("I have done nothing that you abhor") and his knowledge. This is what the deceased says in chapter 17 of the Book of the Dead, which we have already cited several times in this connection:

> I am in my kingdom, having come from my city.
> My evil is eliminated, my sin is driven out.
> I transform on the path, which I know,
> to the isle of the blessed.
> I arrive at the island of the Light-land dwellers,
> I emerge from the shielded gateway.[38]

For the deceased, it was important only to leave death as such behind him and to press on toward life everlasting. The realm of death was "another land, which men do not know."[39] The deceased, however, forged ahead to the "place that he knows."

2. *Out of the Realm of Death and into the Place of Eternal Nourishment*

a) The Food of Life

The texts that depict the condition and the realm of death most vividly and drastically as the reversal of the life and order of the realm of the living are those concerned with providing for the deceased in the after-life. From these texts, it clearly emerges that the deceased first arrives in a realm of death that is anything but a paradise but also not a hell, a place of punishment where sinners are annihilated, but simply a place where the dead are dead. This state of death was an inversion of life. The dead walked upside down, they ate excrement and drank urine. Understandably, the deceased wanted to have nothing to do with this. To avoid this fate, the deceased was provided with spells such as Book of the Dead chapter 51, whose title is "Not Walking Upside Down in the Realm of the Dead," and chapter 52, "Not to Eat Excrement in the Realm of the Dead":

> My abomination, my abomination,
> I will not eat my abomination—
> my abomination is excrement, I do not eat it!
> And filth, it shall not enter my body!
> I will not touch it with my hands,
> I will not walk on it with my feet.[40]

The gods of the realm of the dead subject the newcomer to an interrogation. In spell 173 of the Coffin Texts, they first ask him about the reasons why he refuses the nourishment—feces and urine—that has been offered him:

> "Eat, then!" they say to me.
> "I shall not eat for you!"
> "Why?" they say to me.
> "For I am shod with the sandals of Sokar."
> "Eat, then!" they say to me.
> "I shall not eat for you!"
> "Why?" they say to me.
> "For the staff that divides sky and earth is in my hand."
> "Eat, then!" they say to me.
> "I shall not eat for you!"
> "Why?" they say to me.
> "For I have approached the stick[41] that is on the acacia."[42]
> "Eat the excrement that comes from Osiris' behind!"
>
> "On what do you live?" these gods say to me,
> "What have you come to eat
> in this land to which you have come?"

"I eat bread of pale spelt,
I drink beer of yellow spelt."
"Bread of pale spelt perishes,
beer of yellow spelt perishes.
On what do you live?"
"There are seven meals on earth,
Four meals come to me above, with Re,
and three meals below, with Geb."[43]

The gods inform the deceased that the bread and beer on which he desires to live are perishable. He thereupon explains to them that it is not a matter of a single ration but of daily deliveries. Seven times a day, he receives something to eat, that is, four times during the day and three times during the night. "Above" and "below" are probably to be understood in this way.

The next question has to do with the place where nourishment is taken. In Book of the Dead chapter 52, the gods ask:

"Where are you allowed to eat?"
say they, the gods, to me.
"I eat under that sycamore of Hathor, my mistress,
and I give the rest of it to her dancing girls.
My fields have been assigned to me in Busiris,
and my green plants in Heliopolis.
I live on bread of pale wheat,
my beer is of yellow barley.
The servants of my father and my mother are given over to me."

The deceased makes himself out to be a member of a landholding aristocracy in the afterlife, someone who has property of his own, so as to cultivate grain, as well as his own farmhands to prepare bread and beer out of it. Once again, there is a tree that marks the place where nourishment is taken: in Book of the Dead chapter 52 it is a sycamore, in Coffin Texts spell 173, an *ima*-palm. Both are manifestations of the tree goddess, who has already been mentioned. The tree goddess is a personification of the nourishment on which the transfigured ancestral spirits live in the afterlife.

In Book of the Dead chapter 68 (=Coffin Texts spell 225), the deceased rejects the demand that he eat the "bread of Geb," presumably dirt. Here, too, the tree goddess is mentioned:

I dwell under the branches of the palm tree of Hathor,
who has command over the broad sun disk—
she has betaken herself to Heliopolis,
carrying the writings of the divine word, the books of Thoth.[44]

In another spell, the question about the place is answered thus:

> "Where is it,
> where do you eat?"
> say the primeval gods to him.
>
> "I eat under the sycamore that I know,
> the beautiful one, verdant and many-leaved!
> My mouth truly belongs to me, that I may speak with it,
> my nose, which was in Busiris,
> that I may breathe air and take in the north wind.
> I live on the divine dew.[45]

In this spell, we then learn the decision of the gods, which constitutes the end of the interrogation:[46]

> "So hasten to the chapel, like these!"
> say the gods to you, O Osiris-Khentamentiu,
> "you live on what we live on,
> and you drink of what we drink of.
> You sit where we sit!"

The netherworld is a space of death, as these texts make clear. But beyond this space in which the dead are dead and forced to walk upside down, to live on their excrement and wander around in dirt and filth, there is a place of eternal life. That is the place of the tree goddess. There, the transfigured deceased, who has become an ancestral spirit, is secure in the face of death. In certain spells, this place is described as a city, the very sight of which spells salvation from death:

> He beholds, the one who beholds in the vicinity of the city—
> you behold in the vicinity of that city
> of which it is true that no one who beholds it lands (=dies),
> but everyone who has come to it has become a god.
> You see yourself there, O Osiris-Khentamentiu,
> and you become a god in their midst.
> You walk on your legs,
> not going upside down, not eating what you abominate.
> The food that is given you is the food of Re,
> and water is given you from the lord of the Inundation.[47]

In the Coffin Texts, this place that makes someone a god, this place of eternal life, is also described as a shore on the far side of a body of water that the deceased desires to cross in the form of a bird:

130

> I have flown up as a swallow,
> I have cried out as a goose,
> I have alighted on that great shore;
> what it means for the one who alights there: he does not "land" (=die),
> and the one whom its arms shelter is regarded as a god.[48]

This theme[49] appears similarly, but in more detail, in spells that deal with transformation into a goose, such as the following spells, all of which are formulated according to the same scheme: (1) transformation into a goose and a swallow, (2) swooping down onto the shore, and (3) making one's appearance there as an immortal god. Despite their many repetitions, it is sensible to draw these spells together here, so as to give an impression of these motifs, which stem from an almost canonical composition:

Theme	Spell 278	Spell 287	Spell 581[50]
Transformation	I flew up as a swallow, I cackled as a goose	I flew up as a swallow, I cackled as a goose	I flew up as a swallow, I cackled as a goose
Landing	I was granted an alighting on the shore of the great island	I came down on that great shore, the northern, the powerful (one) of the sky	I received a place to stand on the great shore north of the great island
Deification	I stood up on it and did (not) "land," I alighted on it, and I appear as a god.	He who sees it does not "land," he who alights on it appears as a god.	He who sees you does not "land," he who alights on you appears as a god. I have seen you, I have alighted on you.

This body of water that the deceased must cross in order to attain eternal life separates the two aspects of the netherworld as a place of death and a place of life. The idea of distancing from death is here turned into a matter of spaces, while the idea of the Judgment of the Dead turns it into a matter of ethics and law. In the conceptual horizon of the Judgment of the Dead, the deceased was obliged to distance himself from his guilt so as not to fall victim to the Devouress. Here, mortal danger threatened him from the guardians and "policemen" in the netherworld, whom Osiris had bidden to ward off evil. In the horizon of overcoming space, he was threatened by bird catchers who had spread a giant net over this body of water. He escapes this danger, for he is able to name all the individual elements of this net in a mysterious spirit language, which proves him to be an initiated member of the divine realm, a transfigured ancestral spirit:

I know the name of the peg in it (i.e., the net):
it is the middle finger of Sokar.
I know the tension-peg in it:
It is the leg of Shesemu.
I know the strut in it:
it is the hand of Isis.
I know the name of the blade in it:
it is the butcher's knife of Isis, with which she cut the intestines of Horus.
I know the names of the float and the plumb-bob in it:
They are the kneecaps of Ruty.
I know the names of the cords that make it snap shut:
They are the sinews of Atum
(etc.).[51]

Another means of crossing the water and arriving at the place of eternal life was a ferryboat. Book of the Dead chapter 98 is a spell for fetching the ferry. Here, too, that far shore the deceased longs for is a place of divine immortality:

> Hail to you, O that strand
> that is in the northern sky, on the great isle![52]
> He who sees you does not "land" (=die),
> he who stands on you appears as a god.
> I have seen you, I do not "land,"
> I stand on you, I appear as a god.
> I have cackled as a goose,
> I fly there as that falcon.[53]

In order to use this ferry, the deceased must wake the ferryman, who proves to be quite unwilling and again subjects the deceased to a lengthy interrogation. Here, too, the deceased succeeds in compelling the ferryman to take him across, for he is able to name all the parts of his boat in the spirit language.

First, the deceased is asked who he is, where he wishes to go, and what he intends to do there, and then, who is to bring him the ferry, which lies disassembled in the dockyard and must now be put together by the force of language:

"Take her starboard side (says the deceased to the ferryman) and attach it
    to her prow,
take her port side and fix it to her stern."
"But she has no rushes, no ropes, no *hsfw*, no straps!"
"Her ropes are the locks on the tail of Seth,
her rushes are the bandages on the mouth of Babai,
her *hsfw* is the skin on the ribs of Babai,

her rudder blades (?) are the two hands of the images of the goddesses. It is Horus who has made it.[54]

And so it continues, endlessly; one by one, the parts of the ferry are enumerated and identified with elements of the divine world. There are also spells in which the objects themselves speak up and ask the deceased to name them. Thus, in spell 404 of the Coffin Texts, the parts of the boat make their appearance in the Field of Reeds:

> "Say my name," says the fore-rope.
> "O that Lock of Isis, which Anubis tied with the craft of the embalmer."
> "Say my name," says the mooring-post.
> "Mistress of the Two Lands in the Shrine" is your name.
> "Say my name," says the mallet.
> "It is Haunch of the Steer."
> "Say our name," say the poling shafts.
> "It is Tent-poles of the Divine Realm."
> "Say my name," says the *hpt*-apparatus.
> "Aker is your name."
> "Say my name," says the mast.
> "It is He Who Retrieved the Great One, after She Distanced Herself."
> (etc.).

This dialogue also continues at great length.[55] The principle is overall the same: a list of this-worldly things on one side, and a list of other-worldly things, persons, and events on the other side. Between the two, there is a relationship of reference and meaning. It is knowledge, knowledge of the language into which reference and meaning are sublimated, that connects the two worlds. The *tertium comparationis* in these texts has less to do with wordplay than with formal or functional equivalencies, and with similarities in appearance or function. The specifics are not important; the main thing is that the two worlds can somehow be placed into a relationship. We shall return to these interrogations later, in another context. Here, they interest us in connection with the themes of "transition" and "distancing." The deceased must cross a boundary, the boundary between the realm of death and the place of eternal life. He must demonstrate that he is someone who belongs not in the realm of death but in that of the gods, and he succeeds in this by means of his knowledge.

Chapter 99B of the Book of the Dead, another spell "for fetching the ferry in the Realm of the Dead," makes it entirely clear that the deceased, who is coming out of this world, first lands in the realm of death, from which he wants to be redeemed as quickly as possible:

133

> O you guardian of the mysterious ferryboat . . . ,
> bring me the ferryboat,
> tie on the prow-rope for me,
> so as to escape it, this horrible land
> in which the stars fall, overturned, on their faces
> and do not know how to rise again![56]

Finally, the ferryman responds:

> Come, O transfigured one, my brother,
> and go to the place that you know![57]

The deceased's journey in the next world has a goal, and the journey is a success for the one who knows this goal. Knowledge is redemption from death, and it points the way to eternal life. It was for this reason that Egyptian mortuary religion had the character of a "branch of knowledge," a science, as the Egyptians understood such matters. In chapter 10, whose topic is the origin and function of Egyptian mortuary literature, and especially in chapter 17, which sheds light on the concept of redemptive knowledge from the point of view of the royal Books of the Netherworld, we shall return to the "scientific" character of this mortuary literature.

b) The Dialogue between Atum and Osiris

In Chapter 175 of the Book of the Dead, we find a highly unusual solution to this problem of redemption from the realm of the dead. We have already cited the anxious question of Osiris, as he trembled before the netherworld as a realm of death, and now, we shall consider the continuation of his dialogue with Atum, the creator god. Here is Atum's answer to Osiris' question as to what it means that he is to descend into the immeasurably deep, dark netherworld:

> Atum:
> You live there in contentment of heart.
> Osiris:
> But there is no making love there.
> Atum:
> I have granted transfiguration in place of water, air, and making love, and
>   contentment of heart in place of bread and beer.

Atum gives an entirely different answer from what we would have expected, given all that we have heard to this point about the realm of death. He does not say that he will immediately redeem Osiris from the realm of the dead and transplant him to an Elysian place where he will rule and find eternal satisfaction of his wishes. Instead, he says that he will transform these very wishes, so that Osiris will no longer yearn for water, air, bread, beer, and sexual pleasure, but rather live in a condition of transfiguration and peace of heart.[58] Osiris thus does not reach the place of eternal nourishment; rather, his physical desires are sublimated in such a way that he no longer has need of such things. Atum has conceived of death not as an outer but as an inner inversion. He has replaced desires with peace of heart, and human nature with transfiguration.

Osiris asks further:

> Osiris:
> And gaze upon your face?
> Atum:
> I will not tolerate that you suffer need.

Osiris' concern has to do with beholding the sun god. Atum promises that he will have no lack of that. He is thus playing on the nocturnal journey of the sun, and he is understood by Osiris in such a way that the latter asks in response:

> Osiris:
> But every (other) god has taken a place in the Barque of Millions.

Osiris means that every other god follows the sun god on his cyclic journey through the sky and the netherworld. Only he, Osiris, remains bound to the netherworld. Here, Atum's answer is unusual. He must have assigned Osiris, too, a place in the Barque of Millions, for at the end, he boasts of this beneficent deed. That is, Osiris is also awarded an existence as a star; from early on, he was thought to be the constellation Orion in the southern sky. Osiris' next question is also unusual, and Atum gives it the following answer:

> Your throne belongs to your son Horus, so said Atum.

Osiris is concerned about the future destiny of the kingship he left behind, which has been usurped by Seth.

> Osiris:
> But will he also be able to dispatch the Elders?

That is to say, will he also possess the authority to issue orders to gods who are greater than he?

Atum:

He rules on your throne and will inherit the throne on the Isle of Fire.

Osiris:

Command, then, that one god sees the other! My countenance shall
    behold the countenance of the All-lord.

The text passes over Atum's response and continues with a further question of Osiris:

Osiris:

How does it stand with the lifetime that is spent there?—so asked Osiris.

Atum:

You will (spend) millions of millions (of years),
a long time of millions (of years).
But I shall destroy everything I have created.
This world will return to primeval waters,
to the primeval flood, as at its beginning.
(Only) I shall be left, together with Osiris,
after I have transformed into another serpent,
which men do not know and gods do not see.[59]

This announcement of an end to the world is rather unique in the
Egyptian tradition. But the end is deferred to a far distant time. At any
rate, the world is not endless. It once came into being, and it will come
to an end, just as it began, that is, it will return to its origin, and Atum,
the god of preexistence, will return to his primeval form. But the lifetime
of Osiris will be coextensive with this endlessly long span of cosmic
existence.

How good is what I have done for Osiris!
More than for all the other gods.
I have granted that he rule the desert,
and his son Horus is indeed his heir on his throne on the Isle of Fire.
And I have assigned him a place in the Barque of Millions,
while Horus remains on his royal throne
to erect his monuments.

The form of existence that Atum has created for Osiris, and which he
wants to impress him as worth aspiring to, is precisely the form in which
every human deceased person endeavored to follow Osiris: as illustrious
a place as possible in the netherworld, a place in the Barque of Millions,
so as to follow the sun god in the sky as a *ba*, while in the world above,
his son was his successor in his profession and his house.

    But Osiris' concerns are not yet allayed:

Osiris:
But will the *ba* of Seth not be sent to the West,
unlike all (the other) gods?
Atum:
I have seen to it that his *ba* remains confined to the barque,
so that he does not terrify the god's body.

Osiris and Seth must remain forever separated. Osiris' netherworld is a place where the deadly power of Seth may not encroach. Thus, the *ba* of Seth remains confined to the barque. There, he is useful indeed: the sun god employs his Typhonic power in the struggle to defend himself against Apopis. Seth, or his *ba*, must therefore travel in the sun barque. But he is confined to it, so that he does not come too close to Osiris; again, we have the familiar theme of the distancing of the deceased from his enemy, from death as assassin:

O my lord Atum, said Osiris,
may Seth be in fear before me,
when he sees that my form is the same as your form.
May men come to me,
all the noble ones and all the commoners, all those who dwell in the sky,
gods, transfigured ones, and the dead
together, when they see me,
for you have spread the fear of me and created respect for me.
And Re did all that he (i.e., Osiris) said.

Shouts of praise ring out in Herakleopolis,
joy reigns in Naref.
Osiris has risen as Re,
he has inherited his throne and reigns over the Two Banks.
The Ennead is pleased with that,
while Seth (is in great sorrow).

At the end, the deceased himself speaks up and prays to Osiris:

O my father, may you do for me
what your father Re has done for you,
that I may remain on earth and prepare my coronation,
that my heir may remain healthy and my tomb endure,
(for) my retainers are on earth.
May my enemies be made into "fruits,"
and may Selkis keep watch over their bonds.
I am your son, O my father Re,
may you grant me life, prosperity, and health
so long as Horus remains on his throne.
Grant that my lifetime equal yours,
and be brought to venerability.[60]

3. Inversion as a State of Death

The image of death as inversion, as the reversal of the familiar order of life, intensely affected the Egyptians' perception of reality during their lifetimes. As already noted, we owe our recognition of this point to Peter Seibert, who has demonstrated that certain works of Egyptian literature make use of the "once–now" formulation that is otherwise characteristic of funerary laments.[61] These works are laments over the collapse of social order, and they typically claim that "he who was once below is now above":

> He who was (once) weak
> is (now) mighty.[62]

> He who (once) never built a boat for himself
> is now the owner of ships.[63]

> He who (once) could not afford a coffin
> (now) has a tomb.[64]

> A woman who (once) had to gaze on her face in the water
> now has a mirror.[65]

> He who (once) did not sing for himself
> now praises the goddess of song.[66]

The rise of the lowly corresponds to the fall of the mighty:

> The ones who (once) owned clothes
> are now in rags.[67]

> He who was (once) rich
> is (now) one who has nothing.[68]

These sentences are from the Admonitions of Ipuwer. We shall not wonder at length over the uniqueness of a lament that seems to intimate a utopian condition or a Golden Age. Why is it lamentable that the weak are mighty and that servants are elevated, that beggars heap up riches and poor people eat bread? Bertolt Brecht put together his "Song of Chaos" from portions of this text; the judge Azdak sings:

> Big men are full of complaint
> And small men full of joy.
> The city says:
> "Let us drive the strong ones from our midst!"
> Offices are raided. Lists of serfs are destroyed.
> They have set Master's nose to the grindstone.
> They who lived in the dark have seen the light.
> The ebony poorbox is broken.

Sesnem wood is sawed up for beds.
Who had no bread have barns full.
Who begged for alms of corn now mete it out.
. . .
The nobleman's son can no longer be recognized;
The lady's child becomes the son of her slave.
The councilors meet in a shed.
Once, this man was barely allowed to sleep on the wall;
Now, he stretches his limbs in a bed.
Once, this man rowed a boat; now, he owns ships.
Their owner looks for them, but they're his no longer.[69]

In Brecht's play, the lament has become a revolutionary song of triumph, one that contains some slight changes that Brecht made to Erman's German translation.[70] The Egyptian text is a depiction of a topsy-turvy world that is not intended to be as utopian or carnivalesque as it seems to us. Originally, it had to do with laments, and the use of the "once–now style," which was familiar to every Egyptian reader or listener from funeral laments, was supposed, as Seibert has shown, to present the changes it depicts as comparable to the state of death. This point is clearly stated in the best-known text of this genre, the Prophecy of Neferti:

I show you the land in deep sickness:
the weak is now strong,
one greets the one who once greeted.
I show you the undermost uppermost,
what lay on its back now has its belly below.
One will live in the realm of the dead.[71]
The beggar will heap up riches.
. . . The poor will eat bread,
servants will be elevated.[72]

"Sickness" seems to be the Egyptian word for this sort of death-stricken condition that can overcome an entire society. When the social order is overturned, men live in a topsy-turvy world, a realm of death.

The most gripping testimony to such an experience is preserved to us in the Dialogue of a Man with His *Ba*. The man bewails the collapse of that kind of society. He feels himself pressed into a deadly isolation, one in which physical death appears to be a redemption. The well-known song whose stanzas begin with the words "death stands before me today" (see chapter 16, section 3) compares death to recovery from a serious illness, the scent of myrrh, and return home from a military expedition or from imprisonment. This text, too, treats the *topos* of a topsy-turvy world. The word for death used in the text has, in the Egyptian language, a hateful and fearsome tone and is usually avoided and replaced by euphemisms such as "to land." Tomb inscriptions employ this word to move visitors to recite a prayer on behalf of the deceased. "You who hate death and love life," they say. To the protagonist of this text, this hateful death seems like recovery from an illness, return from a military expedition. With that, all the traditional values of Egyptian culture are turned upside down. Death seems like recovery from a state of death that has afflicted this earthly realm.

To the "I" who speaks here, this world of the living has become a realm of death from which the life-giving connectivity of fraternal love and justice has disappeared. Thus, to him, death seems like redemption from a dead world: the afterlife, to which death alone gives access, does not seem to him to be a realm of death, but rather, a realm of closeness to the divine and of intensified life. Immediately after the poem cited above, there follows the last one: "The one who is there will be a living god . . . ," in which the existence of a transfigured ancestral spirit is described with the help of three images: the punishment of evil, the allocation of offerings, and conversing with the sun god. The word "there" refers to the afterlife of the realm of death, in which the speaker believes himself to be even here, in this world, in which there are no friends, no intimacy, no dialogue, and from which what we have designated as "connectivity," and represented as the Egyptian epitome of the condition of life, has disappeared. If life is so dead, then must death be all the more alive. Death thus seems like redemption to the speaker, a release from a this-worldly realm of death into a next-worldly life, in which life-giving *maat* rules as "connective justice," as the verdict that checks evil, as provisioning, and as wisdom whose advice finds a hearing in the presence of the sun god.

CHAPTER SIX

Death as Transition

1. Transition as Ascent to the Sky

Death as transition, as passage: this image of death had its influence even on tomb architecture. The Theban tombs of the Middle Kingdom are laid out in the form of a long passageway leading westward into the mountain to the cult chamber. This corridor symbolizes the transition from the realm of the living to the realm of the dead. In the New Kingdom, a transverse chamber was placed in front of the corridor; scenes from the life of the tomb owner, and especially scenes of a banquet that he enjoyed in the company of his family, were placed on the wall of this "reception room." Rituals of transition were depicted on the walls of the corridor: on the left side, the burial, and on the right side, the Opening of the Mouth ritual. These rituals will be dealt with in chapter 13. One of the earliest tombs of this type, the Theban tomb of the vizier Antefoqer and his wife Senet from the twentieth century B.C.E., already displays the burial procession on the left wall of the corridor leading to the chapel. A caption accompanying the depiction of the persons who drag the sarcophagus records their song:

> Welcome, in peace, to the West!
> O endowed one . . . !
> You have not departed dead,
> you have departed alive.
> Seat yourself on the throne of Osiris,
> your *aba*-scepter in your hand,
> that you may command the living![1]

Thus begins the oldest and most widespread, indeed, the classic mortuary liturgy that we find already in the sequence of Pyramid Text spells that begins with spell 213,[2] and which introduces us to the theme of transition. The text begins with termination and departure:

> O N., you have not departed dead,
> you have departed alive!
> Seat yourself on the throne of Osiris,
> your *aba*-scepter in your (one) hand,
> that you may command the living;
> your *mekes*- and your "bud"-scepter are in your (other) hand,
> that you may command those whose seats are hidden.

The deceased has departed, there is no doubting this fact. But we learn of two comforting aspects of this departure. One is that he has not departed dead, but rather, alive. The other is that he has not ventured into the unknown, but rather, has a goal: the throne of Osiris, and with it, rulership over the living and the dead ("those whose seats are hidden").[3]

He sits on this throne in the form of a man ("Atum") with a jackal's head and receives the homage of the "places" of Horus and Seth, that is, the two parts of the land, which together comprise the realm of Egypt:

> Your arms are Atum,
> your shoulders are Atum,
> your belly is Atum, your back is Atum,
> your rear end is Atum,
> Your legs are Atum,
> your face is a jackal.
>
> The places of Horus serve you,
> the places of Seth wait on you.[4]

His passage into the next world is at the same time a transformation into an eternal form (the Egyptian word $\underline{d}.t$ means both "body" and "eternity").

The next spell (Pyramid Texts spell 214) begins with a warning that is to be repeated four times:

O N., beware of the lake (four times)!

It is thus made clear that this departure entails danger. What matters is not to end up on the side of death. The afterlife that the deceased aspires to attain is a place of life, not of death, a place where a person escapes death.

The following extract from Pyramid Texts spell 665D lends detailed expression to this point:[5]

> O N., beware of the great lake that leads to the transfigured ones,
> that watercourse that leads to the dead!
> Beware of those people of the house of that *ba*,
> who are terrible and inimical in that name of theirs, "Female Antagonists."
> Let them not seize your hand in the house of that *ba*!
> It is dangerous, it is painful.

This warning is presented at greater length in Coffin Texts spell 839, which is not preserved in the Pyramid Texts, but presumably stems from the same period, the late Old Kingdom:

> O Osiris N.,
> beware of the great lake.[6]
> Beware of abomination in the presence of the dead.
> Beware of the bloodbath in the presence of the ancestral spirits.
> Beware of that man
> in that council of that eastern *ba*
> —they are evil and unpleasant—
> may you escape them.

The journey thus begins with a decided distancing from places of danger and evil. Here, we encounter another image of confrontation with death as an enemy, as we have learned in chapter 3. Here, it is not a matter of a legal wrangling but of avoidance and escape. That this dangerous place and the evil beings that inhabit it and try to draw the deceased onto their side have to do with death is clearly expressed in one of the Coffin Texts:

> O this N., beware of the great lake!
> As for death, you are to escape it.
> May you avoid the route to it.
> They shall not drag you off to the house of that *ba*,
> they shall not oppose you
> in their name of "Opposers."[7]

The deceased has departed, and the continuation of his journey to the afterlife thus entails, first and foremost, a distancing from death. The "great lake" that the traveler must cross harbors the danger of foundering along the way, and it is important to escape this peril. The embalming ritual, which is called "Crossing the Lake" in contemporary inscriptions (see chapter 1), mentions this body of water. Above all, the deceased had to survive the purification phase that was imaged as a "lake" in which his body was "gutted" and thus cleansed of all harmful, perishable substances.

We do not know who "that *ba*" and his accomplices were.[8] But it is clear that the "house of that *ba*" was precisely that aspect of the realm of the dead that was negated by Egyptian mortuary beliefs: the place where the dead were dead, where they spent their dead existence. It corresponded to the Hebrew Sheol, the Mesopotamian Land of No Return, the Greek Hades, and the Roman Orcus. It was a place far from the divine, where the rays of the nocturnal sun did not penetrate. The deceased did not want to be abducted to that place. The difference between the afterlife that was desired and that which was abhorrent is made entirely clear. The boundary is drawn, and the deceased is conveyed securely to the correct side: what this means is that the deceased leaves alive, not dead.[9]

The deceased is certain he will be saved from death, for he began his journey not of his own volition but at the bidding of a god.[10] He can produce a message that was sent to him by his father, the sun god:

> A message of your *ka* comes to you,
> a message of your father comes to you,
> a message of Re comes to you (as follows):
>
> "Set out quickly, after the days on which you are purified,
> for your bones are those of the divine female falcon in the sky.
> May you abide at the side of the god
> and leave your house to your son, your offspring!
> Whoever speaks badly of the name of N. when you go out/go up,
> Geb has determined that he will be in misery in his city,
> so that he shrinks back and sinks down exhausted."

This message makes a great difference. The deceased will not be driven out of the land of the living and cast into the realm of death, but rather, conveyed to the side of the gods. His journey has, as it were, the character of an official trip on a matter of the utmost importance, and thus with maximum protection. New, still greater tasks and ties await him so that he can break his old, earthly ties and leave his house to his heir. He must not fear that after his departure, ill will be spoken of him, that is, that his enemies will profit from his absence. Geb has already issued the command that any defamation of his character will be punished by total loss of status.

The continuation of the spell deals with the purification of the king "in the cool sky of the stars," with his boarding the "*henu*-barque," and with his ascent

> to the place where your father is,
> to the place where Geb is,
> that he may give you what is on the brow of Horus (i.e., the royal diadem)
> and that you may thus become a "*ba*" and gain "*sekhem*"-power,
> and become the Foremost of the Westerners.[11]

Just as the king is setting out on a commission of his father, one that calls him up to the sky, so he himself dispatches his own messengers, who are to announce him there. Spell 215 begins with this motif:

> O N.,
> your messengers hasten, your heralds run
> to your father, to Atum.
> O Atum, let him ascend to you,
> take him in your embrace!
> For there is no star god who has no supporter.
> I shall be your supporter.

This measure also serves to assure the correct route and to avoid unpleasant alternatives:

> O Osiris N., you shall not go to those eastern lands!
> May you rather go to those western lands
> on the road of the followers of Re!
> May your messengers run and your sprinters race,
> and your vanguard make haste
> to announce you to Re, who swings his left arm.[12]

What is in any case important is that the deceased end up in the arms of his father, Atum. In this early spell, he is not yet Osiris, but rather, Horus and Seth. He embodies both gods, and apparently, according to this early concept, his fate depends upon the fact that the two brothers became estranged and wounded one another. Seth tore out the eye of Horus, and Horus ripped off Seth's testicles. Atum will heal these wounds.

> Look at me! You have also seen the form of the children of their fathers,
> who know their spell, the imperishable (stars).
> May you now also see the palace dwellers,
> namely, Horus and Seth.
> May you see the face of Horus spit for him
> and the wounds on him go away.

May you catch the testicles of Seth for him
and drive away his pain.
That one is born for you, this one is captured for you.

Spell 215 continues with the motif of distancing, which is once again clearly discernible:

Re-Atum will not give you to Osiris,
he will not examine this *jb*-heart of yours,
he will not have your *ḥꜣ.tj*-heart at his disposal.
Re-Atum will not hand you over to Horus,
he will not examine this *jb*-heart of yours,
he will not have your *ḥꜣ.tj*-heart at his disposal.
Osiris, you have no power over him,
your son has no power over him.
Horus, you have no power over him,
your father has no power over him.

Here, oddly enough, Osiris and Horus are the gods of the realm of the dead from which the king distances himself. This double role of Osiris is unfamiliar and scarcely comprehensible to us. On the one hand, Osiris was the god on whose throne the deceased king was to sit, the ruler of the afterlife, and into whom the king himself transformed. On the other hand, Osiris was also god of the dead, among whom the king in no way wished to be counted. This early text stems from the formative phase of Egyptian images of death and concepts of the afterlife, and it is geared entirely to the king. Here, the difference between the life and the death sides of the transition into the next world is bound up with the difference between the royal fate in the afterlife and that of ordinary mortals. This point is clearly stated in another Pyramid Texts spell from this early period: "Men hide, gods fly up."[13] Osiris was god of the dead for ordinary men, but he was to have no power over the deceased king. This fact does not contradict the concept that the king laid claim to Osiris' power for himself. The king wanted to become Osiris but not to be subject to this god. He wanted to rule over the dead, like Osiris, but not to be one of the dead over whom Osiris ruled. In other spells of the Pyramid Texts, the god of the dead from whom the deceased wished to escape is called Kherti:

I have saved you from the hand of Kherti,
who lives on the hearts of men;
I will not deliver you to *Nwt.k-nw*.[14]

Later, with the collapse of the Old Kingdom, the royal mortuary texts became available to other social strata, and this motif of distancing from Osiris disappeared.

146

The liturgy continues at length. In spell 216, the deceased presents himself before the night barque of the sun god and requests that it remember those who belong to it, that is, that it recognize and accept him as a rightful passenger during the nocturnal journey. Like Orion and Sirius-Sothis, he wanted to set, to be embraced by the netherworld, and to rise again in Light-land in the arms of his father, the night sun Atum. The two spells that follow were recited by the officiant, who presented the deceased to the gods. Spell 217 addresses Re-Atum and introduces the deceased king as his son:

> O Re-Atum, this N. comes to you,
> an imperishable spirit, . . .
> your son comes to you, this N. comes to you!
> May (the two of) you traverse the sky,
> united in the darkness!
> May you rise in Light-land
> in the place where it is well (*akh*) with you!

The gods of the south (Seth and Nephthys), the north (Osiris and Isis), the west (Thoth), and the east (Dewen-anwy) are dispatched to all the cardinal directions to announce the arrival and enthronement of the king. The spell closes with the paternal embrace with which Re-Atum is to receive his son:

> O Re-Atum, your son comes to you, N. comes to you!
> Let him ascend to you, take him into your embrace,
> he is the son of your body, forever.

Spell 218 announces to Osiris, in the form of a litany, the king's arrival and assumption of power, while spell 219 is addressed to all the deities of the "great" and "lesser" Enneads and portrays the king as Osiris in the appropriate relationships: as son of Atum, Shu, Tefnut, Geb, and Nut; as brother of Isis, Seth, Nephthys, and Thoth; and as father of Horus. The spell closes with a description of the king receiving an offering meal.

2. Transition as Journey to Osiris

After the end of the Old Kingdom, with the spread of the mortuary texts into the nonroyal mortuary cult, the theme of distancing, as we have seen, experienced an astonishing transformation. Now, it could no longer be a matter of distinguishing the destiny of the deceased king from that of ordinary mortals. Instead of the distinction between high and low, divine and human, royal and nonroyal, there was the distinction between good and evil, as well as that between the knowing and the unknowing. With that, the entire picture of the cosmos was altered. Now, sky and earth no longer represented the distinction between afterlife and this life. The cosmos became three-tiered. Contrasted with the earth as this world was a next world that included both sky and netherworld. As before, the deceased soared aloft to the sky, but now, the netherworld was equally important to him. A formula that made its appearance in the Middle Kingdom and is attested to us hundreds of times, down to the end of the history of Egyptian religion, describes the status to which he aspired as

> Transfigured (*akh*) in the sky with Re,
> powerful on earth with Geb,
> vindicated in the realm of the dead with Osiris.

Thus arose the concept of the next world as a place to which only the just and the knowing were admitted. This "moralizing" of the afterlife was a necessary consequence of the extension of the royal idea of the afterlife to lower social classes. The image of the enemy was also split, and "death as enemy" acquired a double aspect. On the one hand, the image continued to bear the features of Seth, personifying death as a murderous attack, against which the deceased turned to the judgment in the afterlife for protection and acquired what was due him. On the other hand, the image now entailed guardians who were supposed to stand at the side of Osiris, warding off Seth and his band, along with all evil more generally, and it also entailed Seth's thugs and henchmen, who hauled evildoers off to the law court and cut off their heads. The netherworld thus came to be peopled by beings scarcely less terrifying than Seth and his band, and scarcely less dangerous to the deceased. In the netherworld, the deceased was threatened from two directions: from that of the "gangsters" who had killed him and now were attempting his second death, and from that of the "policemen" whom Osiris, Isis, and Horus had mustered to combat these gangsters, and who roamed around the netherworld brandishing their knives. They acted on the side of good, not evil, and they belonged to Osiris, not Seth.

In Book of the Dead chapter 127, these guardians are addressed as follows:

> O doormen, O doormen, who guard the gates,
> who gulp down *ba*s and devour the bodies of the dead
> who pass by them, when they are condemned to the place of annihilation!
> Give good guidance to the *ba* of the excellent transfigured one,
> he being well protected in the places of the realm of the deceased,
> filled with *ba*-power like Re,
> praised like Osiris!

In chapter 71, there is an address to "those seven counselors,"

> who carry the balance
> on that night on which the *udjat*-eye is examined,
> who knock off heads and tear out throats,
> who seize hearts and rip them from the chest,
> who make a bloodbath on the Lake of Fire—
> I know you, I know your names![15]

In the New Kingdom, this new aspect of death as enemy was condensed into the "Devouress," the monster that sat beside the scale at the Judgment of the Dead, ready to swallow the heart of any deceased person if it was laden with guilt when examined and thus found to be too heavy.

We may wonder why we always encounter this fearsome monster in representations of the Judgment of the Dead, why the mortuary texts so dramatically portray the terrors of the realm of the dead, and why it was important to the Egyptians not only to populate the netherworld with horrible monsters but to have these monsters around them in the afterlife, in texts and in representations. The answer is that here, as before, it was a matter of distancing and dissociation, but now in a moral sense. These powers could do no harm to the righteous. The entire Judgment of the Dead was none other than an articulation and an acting out of this distancing of the deceased from death. All of it—the scale, the Devouress, the thugs, and the henchmen—belonged to the threshold the deceased needed to cross so as to remain forever protected from death. For this reason, the threshold could never be high enough, the boundary could never be secure enough, and the character of the guardians could never be terrifying enough. For if the deceased could get there safe and sound, threat turned into protection for him, and the more fearsome the threat, the more effective was his protection, the more unassailable his security, the more insuperable the distance he put between himself and death.

In the Pyramid Texts, the deceased king strove to unite with the sun god. His path led him unequivocally upward, to the sky, to the "imperishable" stars in the northern sky, the stars that never set. But in the Coffin Texts, it was a matter of a passage through the netherworld and admittance into the presence of Osiris. The difference between the older, royal and the newer, common concept of death as transition can best be illustrated by comparing two liturgies, one of them from the Pyramid Texts, and the other one representing the later version of the concept.

Pyramid Texts spell 254 begins, after some opening verses, with a presentation of the deceased king, who arrives in the sky and makes dire threats to compel the gods to make a place for him:

> O lord of Light-land, prepare a place here for N.,
> for if you do not prepare him a place,
> N. will lay a curse on his father Geb:
> the earth will no longer speak,
> Geb will no longer be able to protect himself;
> whomever N. finds on his path,
> he will devour him, skin and hair.

The threats intensify to the point of predicting a cosmic catastrophe. The highlands will be joined together, the riverbanks will be united, the roads will be impassable to travelers, and slopes will be inaccessible to those who wish to climb. The gods react to this epiphany with startled outcries. "Have fear," it is said to them, "tremble, you slaughterers, before the storm-cloud of the sky! He has split open the earth with what he knew on the day he wanted to come!"

The spell then turns to the deceased himself:

> See, she comes to meet you,
> the beautiful West (a goddess), to meet you,
> with her beautiful locks, and she says:
> "Here comes the one I have borne,
> whose horn gleams, the eye-painted pillar,
> the Bull of the sky!
> Your form is noble, pass in peace,
> herewith, I have taken you in!"
> So says she, the beautiful West, to N.
> "So hurry and row to the field of offerings,
> navigate to the one who is on his *Qat*-plant!"
> So says (the doorman) Khentimenitef.

The text continues at some length, but here end the correspondences to the later liturgy, which we now wish to consider. In the version on Coffin T1L, it bears the title:

> To be recited: Being at the side of the great god.
> Causing that the goddess of the West extend her arms to so-and-so.[16]

The title clearly alludes to the burial procession. In the tomb of Renni at el-Kab (beginning of Dynasty 18), the pallbearers recite:

> May the goddess of the West open her arms to you,
> may she extend her arms to you!
> The goddess of the West rejoices at you.
> To the West, to the West![17]

The Coffin Texts liturgy begins with spell 30:

> A cry goes out from the mouth of the great ones, the lords of the *rḥy.t*,
> a plaintive cry sounds in the mouth of the veiled ones
> at the thunderclap of the gods in Light-land,
> when they see the terror on their faces,
> the like of which they have never seen before,
> when they see Osiris N.,
> how he fares in peace on the roads of the West
> in his form of a divine ancestral spirit,
> after he has equipped himself with all the power of spirits,
> when the great ones at the head of Light-land said to him:
>
> "Welcome in peace, rejuvenated god,
> born of the beautiful goddess of the West,
> (you who have) come here today from the land of the living,
> after you have shaken off your dust,
> filled your body with magic,
> and quenched your thirst with it.
> Your attendants tremble before you like birds."

So say they to this N., the gods of Light-land.

The appearance of the deceased in the realm of the dead arouses surprise, astonishment, and even terror. To those who are there, it is clear that a great one is coming, the like of whom they have never seen. This arrival does not have the character of a return home to one's family. And yet the chiefs of Light-land, that is, of the liminal area between sky, earth, and netherworld, where the sun rises and sets, greet the newcomer as son of the "beautiful West" (which we render "goddess of the West,"[18] for in the Egyptian language, the word for "west," as well as for its corresponding personification, are grammatically feminine), and thus as the son of the deity into whose realm he enters when he is buried. The West is the realm of the dead.

In what follows, the gods invite the new arrival to penetrate into the realm beyond and to visit the mysterious places:

> They say to him: "So hurry,
> row to the field of offerings within the isles of the sky;
> may you navigate there to the one who is on his *qꜣd.t*-plant."
> So say the gods to this Osiris.

This speech corresponds to the words with which the doorman Khentimenitef greets the newcomer in the Pyramid Texts.

(spell 31):
They say to him: "Oh, may you see the falcons in their nests—
you are entitled to that, Osiris N.!
Oh, may you gaze upon the birth of the Apis bull in the herd of the
    spotted cows—
you are entitled to that, Osiris N.!
Oh, may you gaze upon Osiris in Busiris
in his rank of Bull of the West—
you are entitled to that, O rejuvenated god!"

The scene now shifts to Osiris in Busiris, which we must imagine as the center of the netherworld, for the following verses are to be understood as an address of the priest to Osiris:

(spell 32):
Greetings to you, he will relieve your suffering,
O Osiris in Busiris!
This N. has come to the place where Your Majesty dwells
to drive away your suffering, to set fear into your enemies,
to offer you your insignia as a nobleman of the summer's heat.

May you let the goddess of the West know
that he is your son, whom she has borne to you,
whom she has taken to herself and loved,
your son, the fruit of your loins,
whom you yourself have created.

Out of all the journey in the afterlife, of the transition from this world into the next, and in the next world to the place of ultimate security, this text seizes on a single scene: the scene of arrival in the presence of Osiris. What matters is the reception of the deceased, his recognition as son, and his acceptance as one of those in the afterlife. After these words of the priest, Osiris turns to the goddess of the West:

"Listen to this with your ears!"
says Osiris to the beautiful goddess of the West.

The goddess of the West now greets the deceased:

"Welcome in peace, have a good journey,
that I may take you to myself!"—
says she, the beautiful goddess of the West, to this Osiris.

This brief greeting has three crucial terms. One is "welcome." The second is the word that indicates the transition, which we have translated here as "journey," and which occurs only in reference to the transition of the deceased into the afterlife. The third is *ḥnm* "to take someone to oneself," a word that concisely indicates the relationship into which the deceased wishes to enter with the realm that now accepts him. The text continues with a description of the goddess of the West:

> She has come to meet him
> with her adornment of *sndw*,
> with her necklace of carnelian.
> Her offerings are spread on her hands,
> her meals are behind her, with her entourage.

The goddess of the West appears in the role of provisioner of the deceased. In all its variations, this is the principal motif of the idea of transition: the deceased's journey into the afterlife always leads to a place where he is forever provided with food and drink. Along with the goddess of the West, Nut and Hathor also play the role of the goddess of provisions; the three goddesses are indistinguishable in this role. There is also the tree goddess, who is usually a manifestation of Nut but who can also be Hathor. This is a goddess in the form of a tree that dispenses eternal nourishment to the deceased. We shall encounter her again several times in this book.

The goddess of the West greets the deceased exactly as he wishes—as the son of Osiris:

> She says to him: "Come, welcome!
> Be a god in the following of the Bull of the West,
> may your rank be as you wish.
> You are the son of the lord of the house!"

The priest now speaks, announcing to even the most distant gods that the goddess of the West has recognized the deceased as the son of Osiris:

> (spell 33):
> O gods in endless airspace,
> O Ennead in the mysteries:
> Behold him, O gods,
> this divine ancestral spirit
> whom Osiris has made his son,
> whom Isis has made her child.
>
> Give him praise,
> come and behold him,
> how he has come out in peace, vindicated.
> Rejoice at him!

> She comes, the majesty of the goddess of the West herself,
> to meet this Osiris N.,
> and says to him: "Welcome,
> my son, O *ba* with gleaming horn,
> proceed in peace, that I may take you to myself!
> For thus has Osiris commanded."

This extract is derived almost verbatim from the pyramid text. The goddess of the West recognizes the newcomer as her own son, and the arrival of the deceased thus assumes the character of a homecoming. We shall occupy ourselves with this motif again in chapter 7: it is itself an image of death, and there are many texts devoted solely to this image. Here, however, it is embedded in the larger context of transition, designating the third phase of the transition, the arrival. Even in the royal conceptual universe of the Old Kingdom, the deceased king ascends to the sky as a son, and he joins his father, who is called both the sun god Re and the earth god Geb.

The priest now turns to the goddess of the West and introduces the deceased to her as her son:

> Greetings, beautiful goddess of the West:
> see, this N. has come to you
> to greet you daily
> as your son, your child,
> whom you have borne to Osiris.
>
> He has come from the Isle of Flame (in the world above) to greet you,
>
> he has shaken the dust off himself,
> filled his body with magic,
> and quenched his thirst.
> His attendants tremble before him like birds.

It is again clearly stated that the deceased is the son not only of Osiris but also of the goddess of the West, so that the latter is none other than Isis herself, the wife of Osiris. In the pyramid text, Osiris plays no role; the goddess of the West simply greets the newcomer as her son. Here, the theme of transition is retrospective, and the focus is on the arrival of the newly deceased, who has just arrived from the world above, which is called the "Isle of Flame," both here and in similar texts. Three turns of expression that will recur in what follows—shaking off dust, filling with magic, and quenching thirst—allude to the ritual of embalming and transfiguration, through which the deceased is transformed into a "transfigured one," a "divine ancestral spirit." The text continues:

He has equipped the land with what it had not known,[19]
like the one to whom he has descended,
saying to her:
"Greetings, O beautiful goddess of the West, in the following of Osiris!
Greetings, O following of Osiris, in the beautiful goddess of the West!
I have come here,
for I wished to dispel the suffering of Osiris
and to set fear into his enemies."

The deceased presents himself as a healer and avenger, and thus in the role of Horus, which we have encountered before in chapter 3, in spell 312 of the Coffin Texts. He wishes to heal the wounds that Seth has inflicted on Osiris and to restore his dignity.

There follows a lengthy speech of the goddess of the West, in which she promises to initiate the deceased into the various mysteries of the netherworld:

"Come in peace, that I may take you to myself!"
says the beautiful goddess of the West to this N.

(spell 34):
I shall show you:
Osiris in Busiris,
and how you travel with him to Abydos.
That is what you are entitled to, you rejuvenated god!

I shall show you:
the god of the winepress, Shesemu, with his knives,
in his form of slaughterer.
That is what you are entitled to, you rejuvenated god!

I shall show you:
the fields full of birds.
That is what you are entitled to, you rejuvenated god!

I shall show you:
the god of magic, decked out in his insignia,
and how he brings offerings to the provisioned ones.
That is what you are entitled to, you rejuvenated god!

I shall show you:
Nut, and how she equips the offering table for you,
acting as the one in charge of the offerings.
That is what you are entitled to, you rejuvenated god!

Welcome in peace, O you whom Osiris has sent!
Behold these gods!
Because of the words that the beautiful goddess of the West spoke to this
    Osiris,

to that father of mine, that supporter of mine,
that protector of mine, to whom I have descended among the provisioned
   ones.[20]

With these words, the officiant strides forcefully into the foreground, commenting on the speech made by the goddess of the West. He presents himself as the son of the deceased, describing this role with formal turns of expression that would regularly recur in texts from that time on (omitted in the translation). The father was to act as the supporter and protector of the bereaved son, and to do so in the afterlife, among the "provisioned ones," that is, the other dead, who, as ancestral spirits, were the recipients of provisions and capable of exerting influence. The son promises to arrange for six things. The first three have to do with purification, and the last three with initiation. In Egyptian cult, purification and initiation went hand in hand. These promises are followed by a refrain having to do with the deceased and describing the relationship of the son to his father.

(spell 35):
I shall cause that he be purified in the Jackal Lake among the provisioned
   ones.
Your four (?)[21] are on me in life and lastingness.
I am your progeny on earth,
I am your living *ba* on earth,
who brings you mortuary offerings on earth
in your house on the Isle of Flame.

I shall cause that he be loosened (i.e., purified) on the isle of the
   netherworldly ones,
among the provisioned ones (etc.).
I shall cause that the two Great of Magic (the goddesses of the crowns)
   cense him
among the provisioned ones (etc.).

Thus far the three purifications; now, there follow the three initiations:

I shall cause that he enter the Great Chapel
among the provisioned ones (etc.).
I shall cause that he enter into the mysteries
among the provisioned ones (etc.).
I shall cause that he enter the place of the crossing
among the provisioned ones (etc.).

What matters to the son is the connection, but at the same time also the distance, that is to prevail between him and his deceased father. In the refrain, he stresses four times that his place is "on earth" or "on the Isle of Flame," and he promises to see to it that his father will pass deeper into the netherworld, and that he will be initiated into the mysteries and be accepted among the transfigured deceased, the "provisioned ones."

The two spells that follow contain nothing new; once again, they depict the scene of the deceased's reception and recognition as son by Osiris and the goddess of the West. At the end, Osiris declares his decision:

> "He shall enter, after you (the goddess of the West) have dispelled the grief
> from among his family on earth.[22]
> He shall not cry out, but shall think of my abomination:
> My abomination is outcry.
> It may not enter my house."

Osiris is thus declared to be the lord of silence. Outcry and mourning are taboo in his home. If the deceased is to enter into his realm of silence, mourning must stop. Perhaps the allusion is to the mourning of the deceased himself, who still pines for the family he has left behind on earth. The next spell is also concerned with the mourning of the deceased. The goddess of the West utters a solemn formula that was pronounced on the occasion of processions:

> "A god comes; beware, O earth!
> Come in peace, that I may take you to myself!"
> says the beautiful goddess of the West to this N.

In the following spell (spell 37), the deceased is bidden to comfort himself and to rid himself of his grief:

> Voice your grief, that it may be banished,
> and things will be done according to what you say.
> . . .
> Cry not, for outcry is the abomination of Osiris,
> and it may not enter his house.

Finally, the officiant again speaks, commending his father to the god Osiris:

> Greetings, Osiris in Busiris,
> in your rank of Bull of the West.
> See, this N. is here with you!
> May you promote his position and fix his rank,
> and hear his words and banish his grief,

> may you vindicate him against his enemies,
> and may his arm be strong in your tribunal
> when he speaks up for his family (which I am) on earth.

With that, the final state is reached and sealed. The deceased father is brought in to Osiris and accepted into the tribunal of the god, where he can now effectively represent his bereaved son.

This ritual teaches us a great deal about the concept of death as a transition into another space and another condition. The deceased now has behind him the rites that have transformed him into a deified ancestral spirit. So equipped, he begins the journey into the beyond. His appearance at the boundary between this realm and the next causes a sensation. Those in the netherworld have never seen so powerful a being. Suddenly, he reaches Osiris and Isis, who is here called the "beautiful goddess of the West," and requests admission into their realm. The officiant concludes by representing himself as the bereaved son; having accompanied him as far as this threshold, he introduces him to Osiris and the goddess of the West, not as his father but as their son. It is now a matter of affiliating the deceased with the world of the gods. The deceased can cross the threshold only when he ceases grieving. He must express his grief in order to find consolation. Only when this is done will it be possible, on the basis of this separation and of the bilateral social connection, on the one hand with the society of the netherworld and on the other with that of the world above, for the tie between father and son to be built anew to their mutual benefit.

3. Assistance from Beyond: The Image of Death as Transition and the Realm of the Living

This situation is then immediately put to use. At the conclusion of the lengthy ritual, there is again talk of a clash with an enemy. But this is not the enemy of the deceased. The latter has already been vindicated against him, he has all that behind him. It is the enemy of the bereaved son, whom the son denounces before the tribunal of Osiris, using his father, who has now become a part of it, as his legal representative or "joint plaintiff." The officiant thus turns first to the father:

> Behold, that enemy etc.[23] among men and (among) the gods of the
>   netherworld
> and (among) all creatures has come
> to destroy your house and smash down your door
> and to cause that your enemies gloat over you on the Isle of Flame.

He then also denounces this enemy to Osiris. To do this, he must interpret his evil machinations within the conceptual framework of the myth of Osiris, representing him as an ally of Seth. In him, Osiris is to recognize his own enemy and take action against him:

> O Osiris, behold that enemy of mine among men,
> in the netherworld, and among all creatures,
> he has allied himself with Seth,
> he has spread tidings of your weakness,
> he has blabbed about your hidden wounds
> and said that the illness is grave,
> your suffering that is on you (var., your shoulder).
>
> As sure as your *ba* will be praised, you must behold your enemies,
> the rebels, how they display honor for you and redouble your honor!
> May you ruin him and bring him to collapse, that enemy etc.,
> may you place him under you (var., your soles).
> Osiris, act for yourself, for your *ka*, that it may be satisfied.

Postscript: To be recited over a waxen representation of an enemy, inscribed with the name of that enemy on its breast, with the bone of a *wḥˁ*-fish (synodontis); put it in the earth at the place of Osiris.

The deceased passes into an afterlife from which he is able to care for those he has left behind, a place where he has status and position. A connection can be established with him; he has not disappeared from the world, he is merely "beyond," on the other side of a boundary that, within the framework of a culturally regulated border traffic, can be crossed in either direction. One can "descend" to him and call upon him, and he himself, though he perhaps cannot return in person, can be effective for his family from the world beyond. In Egypt, people made much use of this possibility.

From ancient Egypt, we have letters to the dead, which those who remained behind deposited in the tomb of the deceased to lay claim to his assistance in such cases.[24] By way of an example, a late Old Kingdom letter to the dead from Naga ed-Deir is addressed by an eldest son to his deceased father and requests his assistance against someone else, from whom harmful acts are feared. The letter was found in situ in the father's tomb:

> A servant speaks before his lord,
> (namely) his son Heni,
> saying: Take heed a million times,
> for taking heed is useful for the one who provides you with offerings,
> because of that which your servant Seni is doing,

(namely, because) it was caused that your servant there[25] see himself in a
    dream in a city together with you.
See, it was his character that demolished him!
See, that which happened to him did not happen through the action of
    this servant there!
There are no limits to what occurs;
but see: It was not I who first did harm to him.
Others acted before your servant there.
May his lord take heed that he not rebelliously do harm,
he being guarded, so that he no longer sees the servant there.[26]

Heni had reason to worry. In a dream, he had seen himself together with
his father, and he must have feared that he would be carted off to the
latter in the netherworld. He attributed this situation to the machinations
of a servant, Seni, who evidently had come to his death with Heni not
entirely without a share of the blame[27] Meri is to see to it that this Seni
will be closely watched.

Another letter, also from the late Old Kingdom, was written by a widow
and her son to her deceased husband on a piece of linen. Here, the
deceased's assistance is called upon against living persons whose greed
has robbed the writer of her share of the inheritance:

A sister speaks to her brother,
a son speaks to his father!
Your condition is like that of a (genuinely) living one, a million times . . . .
This is a communication that the messenger of Behedjti came to the
    bed-chair
when I was sitting at its head
and Iri's son Ay was called to be recognized by the messenger of Behedjti,
and you said, "Protect him, out of respect, from Ay the elder!
The wood of this bed of mine would rot
if any man would carry it, who would keep the son of a man from his
    bedstead (?)!"

But look, Wabuet has now come with Isesi.
They have ravaged your house, and they have removed everything that
    was in it,
in order to enrich Isesi,
for they wished to ruin your son through Isesi's enrichment.
Yea, she has taken away Yaazi, Yeti, and Anankhi;
she has taken away all the servants of your majesty.
Will your heart remain cool about this?
I would rather that you take to you she who is here with you,
than see your son subject to the son of Isesi.
Rouse your father Ay against Behedjti,
raise yourself, come quickly against him—

you know who has come to you here
in a legal process with Behedjti's and Aai's son Anankhi.
Raise yourself up against them, along with your fathers, your brothers,
    and your friends,
and bring down Behedjti and Aai's son Anankhi.
Remember what you said to Irti's son Ay:
"The houses of the fathers should be kept standing,"
when you said, "House of the son and further house of the son."
May your son manage your house, as you managed the house of your
    father.
O Seakhenptah, my father, may it please you to command
that Ini be called to you so as to take away the house of Anankhi, son of
    Wabuet.[28]

The deceased is reminded of his last words on his deathbed, when he expressly confirmed his wish to see his son Ay as heir of his house. He should also intervene now, for an inimical party has appropriated the entire household and plunged his son Ay into misery.

A third example stems from the end of Dynasty 11. As was common from the end of the Old Kingdom to the end of Dynasty 18, this letter was not written on papyrus but on a dish that was probably used to pour water as an offering to the deceased; the importance of water as a medium of contact with the realm of the dead will be discussed in chapter 14:

That which Dedi gives to the priest Antef, born of Iu-nakht:
as for this (female) servant Imu, who is sick:
Neither by day nor by night do you (the *akh*) stand up for her,
for you do not combat the one who does evil to her.
Why do you wish the destruction of your house?
Fight for her again today,
that her household may be safe and that water be poured for you.
If you do not do it, your house will be destroyed.
Can it be that you do not know that it is this (female) servant who cares
    for your house among men?
Fight for her, watch over her.
Protect her from all, male and female, who act against you!
Then will your house and your children again be well established.
May you heed well![29]

The illness from which the servant is suffering is not attributed to the influence of the ancestral spirit who is addressed in this letter. He is merely reproached for having failed to help. He is to bring charges in a court of law in the realm beyond the grave and prosecute the guilty. The role of an ancestral spirit is that of a legal adviser and joint plaintiff in that otherworldly realm. He is supposed to look after the affairs of his house. In exchange, the bereaved, in this case his widow, will look after the affairs of the deceased, tending to both his house among the living and his tomb in the necropolis, and "pouring water" for him, that is, making mortuary offerings.

From these examples, we see what an important and concrete reality the afterlife represented in the beliefs of the Egyptians. The deceased were powerful ancestral spirits, and we see what possibilities were ascribed to them to lend support to those they had left behind in the realm of the living. This world and the next were two realms that were intimately interconnected. Tombs were places where people contacted the dead and could "descend to them," as the Coffin Text puts it.

The afterlife was an ordered world, with clear hierarchical and legal structures. As one who was "provisioned in the afterlife" and an "ancestral spirit," the deceased could attain power, influence, and status there, at the court and in the tribunal of Osiris. It is necessary to make this point clear if we are to understand the Egyptian idea of transition. This transition had a clear goal that it was necessary to reach. The deceased did not sink indiscriminately into a dusty realm of shadows, nor did they free themselves gradually from the living and vanish into a cosmic distance; rather, they made their way, consciously and well equipped, to the court of Osiris in hope of recognition, provisioning, and promotion. Once arrived and accepted into the tribunal, they were in a position to enter into a relationship with the world of the living and effectively support their interests.

Instead of citing further letters to the dead, I should like to close with a rather unique text. An ostracon from Deir el-Medina preserves a text that is addressed to a deceased person.[30] The verses are separated by red "verse points." It is a liturgy for placating an ancestral spirit:

> When you enter into the presence of the sun god,
> you shall refer so-and-so (the name of the person on whose behalf this
>   spell is recited is to be inserted here) to him.
> You shall not punish him for any offense,
> rather, you shall recollect his good deeds.
> May you assent that his cow has freedom to roam,
> without wandering from the pathway.
> May you permit the srmt-beer there to be sweet in the jug,
> and food and feathered game to be in the storeroom.
> May you spread satisfaction within his house,
> without complaint[31] being brought forward.
> May you eliminate disaster and display clemency,
> what you say is done.
> May you remove the harmful and dispense the useful,
> without your plan being dilatory.

May you let plowed land become fields of grain,
that they may bring forth uncountable yields.

To understand this text, it suffices to cite a passage from the Instruction
of Any:

> Satisfy the ancestral spirit, do what he wishes.
> Keep yourself clear of what he abominates,
> that you may remain unscathed by his many hurts.
> Beware of every sort of damage.
> The cow in the field was stolen?
> It is he who does the like.
> As for any loss from the threshing floor in the field—
> "That is the ancestral spirit!" one says.
> The moment he causes strife in his house,
> hearts are set against one another.[32]

CHAPTER SEVEN

Death as Return

The images of death considered to this point—dismemberment, isolation, enemy, dissociation, transition, and reversal—have revealed
the ambivalence of Egyptian concepts regarding death and the
afterlife. They portray death as a destructive attack on the continuity of
life, while at the same time, they depict counterimages of salvation and
restoration. They depict the realm of death as a place of loneliness and
darkness, in which all life is extinguished, while at the same time, they
point the way to an Elysian realm in which the individual is forever
redeemed from death and becomes a living god. These images derive
their meaning from the actions they are supposed to incite and
enable. The negative images of death—dismemberment, isolation, and
inversion—are counterimages of the ultimate, salutary aims of the rituals,
in which the body of the deceased is restored from dismemberment to
unity, his person restored from isolation to integration, and his legal status
restored by means of vindication, first "against" the enemy, and then
"before" the divine judges. These images of death are points of departure
for ritual acts aimed at completely reversing them and overcoming death.

Entirely different, however, is the image of death to which we turn in
this chapter. Here it is a matter not of a stimulus but of a result. Unlike
the images considered to this point, the goal is not the reversal of a con-

dition caused by death. Here, death is not a forceful distancing, an abduction from which the deceased is rescued by ritual; this is in no way the case, though the texts indeed invoke the images of dismemberment, isolation, reversal, and inimical attacks. The image of return does not constitute a counterimage in which we are to recognize the true image of death; rather, it is itself a comprehensive image of death. But as we shall see, this image, too, is firmly rooted in a ritual context. The texts that elaborate this image in greatest detail are inscriptions on coffins, in which the coffin itself speaks to the deceased.

1. *Nut Texts: Laying to Rest in the Coffin as Return to the Womb*

a) The Inscription on the Coffin of King Merneptah

In Egypt, as elsewhere, there is truth to the expression *saxa loquuntur*, "the stones speak." They speak, for they are inscribed: the walls of tombs, the bases of statues, altars, offering tables, stelae (which were intended purely to be inscribed), and "false doors"—all of which indicated places where offerings were made—as well as coffins and sarcophagi. On coffins, a deity speaks to the deceased, both as coffin and as mother. She greets him as her son, whom she accepts forever into her body. Thus, we read in the oldest coffin inscriptions, those on the coffins of kings of the Old Kingdom: "King Teti is my eldest son, who has opened my womb, my beloved, in whom I take pleasure." We have such speeches of the mother to her son in the thousands; they are the canonical kernel of the inscriptions on coffins. In the course of time, they became more detailed. By far the most comprehensive speech of the coffin- and mother-goddess to the deceased is that on the lid of the outermost of the three granite sarcophagi of King Merneptah, from the end of the thirteenth century B.C.E.[1] Here, and here only, to the best of my knowledge, it is the goddess Neith, not Nut, who appears in this role. Notwithstanding this unusual circumstance, this text can count as representative of the concepts associated with the coffin. Neith speaks as mother and sky:

> I am your mother, who nurses your beauty,
> I am pregnant with you in the morning,
> and I deliver you as Re in the evening.[2]
>
> I carry you, you being on my back,
> I elevate your mummy, my arms under you,
> I continually take your beauty into myself.

In the second stanza, the goddess explicitly identifies herself with the coffin:

> When you enter me, I embrace your image,
> I am the coffin that shelters your mysterious form.

The coffin becomes the body of the goddess of the sky, and this body encloses an entire divine realm, as we have already seen in an entirely different context, in the texts that deal with the deification of the limbs, which have to do with the body of the deceased:

> My entrails[3] are your protective gods,
> my kidneys are yours as the Two Sisters,
> in order to prepare your protection with their magic.
> I shall supply you with air from my nose
> and exhale the north wind for you from my throat.
> My birthing brick and my fulfillment are with you,
> my Khnum forms your body
> and repeats birth for you as the great lotus bud.
> If you desire to breathe the south wind, I open the way for it;
> I bring you the west wind in its place.
> I raise the sun for you on my skin,
> so that its image drifts by on your breast.

To the body of the goddess belong the genies "birthing brick" (Meskhenet), "fulfillment" (Renenutet), and creator (Khnum). These are creative powers that determine personality in its external appearance, its development, and its destiny, which every person bears in himself, and apparently every god, as well. Neith wishes to place these powers at the disposal of the deceased.

The stanza that follows deals with the embalming and mummification of the deceased:

> I unite your limbs, I hold your discharges together,
> I surround your flesh, I drive away the fluids of your decay,
> I sweep away your $b\jmath w$, I wipe away your tears,
> I heal all your limbs, each being united with the other;
> I surround you with the work of the weaving goddess,
> I complete you and form you as Re;
> I lift you up on my arms,
> I shine on your head,
> I repeat for you my form as uraeus,
> I make your form of appearance like that of the lord of sunshine.

Here ends the first part of the text, which depicts the constellation of coffin and corpse as the union of mother and child. The second part includes other deities. In the preceding verses, it was a matter of healing physical dismemberment and restoring the body, while the verses that follow deal with the healing of social isolation and with the reintegration of the deceased into constellations of protective deities. Behind all this is a ritual that followed immediately upon the embalming and mummification, the ritual of the nocturnal wake. This was the night during which the deceased was vindicated, the night of the wake that was to protect him for the long run from any further pursuit by evil, that is, by death. We shall deal with this matter in chapter 12. Here, our principal interest is in the role of coffin as mother, as it is described in unique detail in this text. The first deity whom Neith presents to the king is the sun god Re:

> Re comes to you to embrace you;
> he lowers himself onto your illustrious image.
> He shines on you, he gives you light,
> his radiance illuminates the cavern dwellers.

There follows a group in whom we are probably to recognize the four torches or the four magical bricks that were deposited in the burial chamber:

> I cause the four noble women to come to you,
> that they may make light for you on all your ways,
> that they may repel your enemies for you every day
> and drive away the rebel, the evil one, for you.[4]
> I place you on his back,
> he will not escape you,
> you will not be disgusted by him, ever.

The humiliation of the enemy, who was compelled to carry Osiris, was part and parcel of the latter's social rehabilitation, which we have already encountered in chapters 2 and 4. Isis' and Nephthys' mourning over the deceased is described in detail in what follows:

> I bring you the two kites
> with their sistra and necklaces;
> they will bind the headcloth around your head
> and beat for you on the two copper gongs.[5]
> I cause you to hear the mourning of Isis,
> the cries of the great king maker,
> as she cries for you, her arms on her knee,
> before your body on the bier.
> I cause that Nephthys mourn for you,
> wailing at the top of her voice.
> I place (for you) the two sisters at (your) head and (your) feet.

In fact, Isis and Nephthys often appear at the head and foot ends on royal sarcophagi of the New Kingdom. We begin to understand that the goddess is describing the decoration of the coffin. Because she is herself the coffin, she can justifiably say of herself that she causes the deities represented on the coffin to appear for the king. Retrospectively, we must also thus understand the mention of the sun god; he, too, is represented on the coffin. The following verses name the deities of the side walls of the coffin:

> I bring you Shu with his august *ba* (= the wind),
> that he may endure on your right side,
> going up and down in your body
> and in and out of your nostrils.
> I bring you Geb to look after you;
> I cause him to say to you "my eldest son!" and to say regarding you, "my office belongs to him!"
> "May the bad one suffer, may the deficient one suffer lack,
> seized by annihilation, may he have no livelihood!"

The mention of Geb calls to mind the mythic lawsuit over the succession to the throne, the classic form in which the struggle with death as enemy was depicted:

> Geb says to Osiris
> in the presence of the Ennead and the two chapels of the land:
> "I know the condition of my child,
> for a man should know about what has sprung from him.
> Vindication belong to
> King Merneptah.
> He praises you as king of the gods.
> Netherworld and West are in his hand,
> while the Two Lands belong to his son Horus,
> vindicated as your fully empowered representative.
> Thoth makes note of it,
> according to what Re-Atum says."

On the left wall of the coffin, corresponding to the gods Shu and Geb, who are depicted on the right wall, are the goddesses Tefnut and Nut. Just as Geb evokes the topic of the lawsuit over the succession to the throne, so Nut evokes the topic of the Nut texts: the coffin as mother, the mother as coffin. The fact that Neith has here usurped the traditional role of Nut does not prevent Nut from herself appearing in this role. Perhaps Neith was conceived as embodying the outer, box-shaped sarcophagus, while Nut embodied the inner, mummiform sarcophagus.

> I call your mother Nut to you,
> and Tefnut on your left side,
> that they may throw their arms around you
> and recognize their son in you.
> I cause your mother to spread herself over you,
> and I cause her to take you into herself as "She Who Takes the Great One
> into Herself."

Shu and Geb are thus on the right side of the deceased, and Nut and Tefnut on his left. From the Middle Kingdom, we indeed have coffins on which these deities are so arranged on the side walls. Neith's speech is a description of the decorative program of a coffin, but of one that belongs to a period six hundred years in the past.

Next, Neith causes Horus to make his appearance, and in accordance with his traditional role as son, he addresses his speech to his deceased father, restoring his dignity and status by humiliating and annihilating his enemies:

> I bring you Horus, that he may worship you,
> I set you upright and let him speak to you.
> He brings you your enemies as prisoners
> and annihilates them beneath you, forever.

Lastly, she turns to her son, the god Osiris, to pray on behalf of the Osiris King Merneptah:

> To me, to me, my son with hidden name,
> Osiris, king of the gods!

> May you grant that the Osiris King (beloved of Amun, *ba* of Re),
> the son of Re (Merneptah, satisfied with *maat*) remain
> in the following of the Great God,
> while the gods of the netherworld are the protection of his body
> and lay low his enemies.

This lengthy text is a unique document. It testifies to a special relationship of King Merneptah to Neith, the goddess of Sais, whom he has chosen as the protective deity of his corpse. But the role played by Neith in this text is entirely typical: that of a mother goddess who embodies the coffin and welcomes the deceased, as he enters her, as her son. This inscription is to be understood as a text that the coffin itself, that is, the deity who embodies it, addresses to the deceased.

b) Goddess of the Coffin, Goddess of the West, Goddess of the Tree:
Figurations of the Great Mother

Normally, as already noted, it is Nut, and not Neith, who appears in the
role of the mother goddess who is embodied in the coffin. In a text from
about a thousand years later, it is said of her:

> My beloved son, Osiris N.,
> come and rest in me!
> I am your mother who protects you daily.
> I protect your body from all evil,
> I guard your body from all evil.
> I make your flesh perfectly hale.[6]

Often, the goddess promises the deceased, whom she receives into her
womb, that he will be reborn as a star, as in the following text from the
Late Period:

> I place you within me, I bear you a second time,
> that you may go out and in among the Imperishable Stars
> and be elevated, alive, and rejuvenated like the sun god, daily.
> . . . I surround you in my name "Coffin,"
> I give you the sweet breath of the north wind,
> . . . your existence lasts forever, O Osiris N.![7]

But once, in another text, the mother goddess also says to the deceased:

> Your (earthly) mother carried you for ten months,
> she nourished you for three years.
> I carry you for an undetermined length of time,
> I shall never bear you.[8]

These words seem to contradict the promise of rebirth as the sun or
a star, as stated in other speeches of this sort. Yet they only serve to
underscore the idea of eternal security. The mother who speaks here
is not only the coffin but also the goddess of the sky. Rebirth, rejuvenation, and renewal occur in the coffin and in the sky, this womb is the
world. In coffins of the Late Period, a representation of this mother
goddess often appears on the inside of the lid, sometimes even naked,
spreading herself over the deceased so as to embrace him in her arms
and incorporate him into herself.[9] In a late mortuary papyrus, this
representation is captioned:

The inscription of the representation of Nut inside the coffin:
Welcome in peace to your coffin,
the place of your heart (i.e., dearest wish), forever!
My arms are spread to surround your divine body,
I desire to protect your body and guard your mummy
and breathe life into your soul forever.[10]

Hymns praise her:

> O mother! O great one!
> O cheerful one from whom I emerged!
> O goodly nurse who does not weary,
> O goodly nourisher into whom one must enter,
> O you into whom everyone goes daily.
> O great mother, whose children are not delivered,
> O great goddess within the netherworld,
> mysterious, mysterious, whom no one knows,
> O great goddess whose mummy wrappings are not loosened,[11]
> O looser of the bonds, O concealer,
> the way to whom cannot be pointed out.[12]

In the coffin, the vindicated deceased experiences a revelation of the great mother, the sky goddess, who incorporates him into herself for eternal regeneration. But the deceased encounters her in many forms, not just that of the coffin. She is the tomb, the necropolis, the West, and the realm of the dead; all the spaces that receive him, from the smallest to the largest, are manifestations of the womb into which the transfigured deceased enters. In all these welcoming and embracing forms, she promises the deceased security, eternal renewal, air, water, and nourishment. As nurse and nourisher, she manifests herself as a sycamore, the tree of life, who dispenses eternal nourishment to the deceased.

In New Kingdom tombs, we often encounter a scene in which the goddess of the West embraces the deceased and welcomes him as her son.[13] Thus, for example, Hathor greets a Djehutiemheb in a tomb from the reign of Ramesses II (ca. 1250 B.C.E.):

> Welcome, Djehutiemheb!
> . . . I have broadened the space for your mummy
> and sanctified the place for your body.
> I shall announce you to the Great God,
> that he may welcome you.[14]

The goddess then lists a lengthy series of deities to whom she will "commend" the deceased, so that they will care for him in every way possible. What is at stake here is the incorporation of the deceased into the realm of the gods, and thus the reversal of isolation; the goddess, who here welcomes the deceased as one who is returning home, plays the role of intercessor. In the neighboring tomb of Nakhtdjehuti (Theban Tomb 189), we encounter a similar scene. The goddess of the West invites the deceased into his tomb with a gesture of welcome that the Egyptians called *nini*, which means, "to me, to me":[15]

> Welcome, Nakhtdjehuti . . .!
> My arms make the *nini*-gesture to receive you,
> my heart is filled with your being.
> I shall announce you to the Great God,
> that he may welcome you.
> I broaden the place for your mummy,
> I sanctify the place for your body.
> I shall place you among the righteous, next to the praised ones,
> for I know that you are a truly righteous one,
> the son of one who does *maat!*[16]

In the tomb of the vizier Paser, in the same scene, the tomb owner is embraced by his own mother.[17] Her identity is made clear in the caption, yet Paser addresses his mother as a manifestation of the goddess of the West:

> Rejoice, O great city,
> you region of the dead, from which I have gone forth!
> See, I have come to be at rest with you.

The mother responds to her son with the words:

> How good it is! My heart is full of joy,
> My longing has been fulfilled.

The interpretation of the coffin, the tomb, and the necropolis by reference to the mother goddess Nut is also transparent in the reference to the physical mother. The deceased's own mother is also a manifestation of this ever maternal entity that is to receive the deceased in the form of the coffin, the tomb, and the West. Nut, the goddess of the sky, the dead, the coffin, and the tree, was the Egyptian manifestation of the Great Mother, who has perhaps never made her appearance in so many forms, or otherwise been so unequivocally a figuration of death.

Death as return to the womb was a central concept, one that extended into every area of Egyptian culture, every bit as much as that of the Judgment of the Dead, which belonged to the other image of death, that of death as enemy. But while the concept of the Judgment of the Dead experienced considerable development over time, that of death as return to the womb exhibited an astonishing consistency. It found verbal expression already in the inscriptions on royal coffins of the twenty-fourth and twenty-third centuries B.C.E., but it was presumably older still, for in all likelihood, the crouched position of prehistoric burials, in Egypt and probably also elsewhere, was intended to imitate the position of the embryo in the womb. The concept of archetype comes to mind in this connection, and in fact, this Egyptian image of death did not escape the attention of Carl Gustav Jung. As early as 1912, he attempted to demonstrate that behind the Oedipal desire for an incestuous union with the mother, as postulated by Freud, there actually lay the desire for immortality.[18] It is this drive for immortality that I wish to understand as a sort of generator of culture and meaning, as the necessary complement to the unbearable knowledge of mortality that is unique to humankind.

c) Renewal and Vindication: Re and Osiris

The two images of death—as enemy and as return to the womb—are, to our way of thinking, as opposed as two images could possibly be. The one has to do with confirmation and preservation of identity, individuality, and personality, while the other has to do with the dissolution of these categories. In the one case, the deceased gains immortality as a social and moral individual, with all the titles and offices he acquired in life, according to the virtues he had practiced during life, while in the other case, the deceased disappears as an individual into the sheltering and homogenizing womb of the Great Mother, and the personality he had developed during life retreats back into the original, unindividualized, symbiotic form of his embryonic preexistence.

Nevertheless, these two images of death as enemy and as return do not stand in opposition to one another as alternative solutions; rather, they belong together, and the entirety of their culture-forming significance unfolds only in their complementary connection. They are not spread out over different periods of the history of Egyptian religion, or different levels of Egyptian society, or even over different ritual contexts. They belong to one and the same context, they presuppose and complete one another, and they illuminate one another. The one image is presided over by the god Osiris, and the vindication of the deceased against his enemy, death, represents an emulation of Osiris, an *Imitatio Osiridis*. The other image is presided over by the sun god. The union of the deceased with the mother is an *Imitatio Solis*, and specifically, of the setting of the sun and its nocturnal journey through the netherworld. Hymns to the sun describe its setting with precisely the same images and turns of expression as those used by the mortuary texts to describe the placing of the deceased in his coffin.[19]

The mystery of solar immortality is the circular path that leads the sun god from birth to death in the course of each and every cycle of day and night. The mother goddess Nut gives birth to him in the morning and receives him again in the evening.[20] For the Egyptians, this interpretation of the apparent course of the sun around the earth served as natural evidence for their hope of immortality. The sun set an example that everyone wished to follow: a cyclical course of life, return to the origin, overcoming death, consummation as conception, and restoration through (re)birth.

Here, longing for immortality is fulfilled in the cyclical time of endless renewal, as an *imitatio solis*. By way of contrast, there is the other image of death as vindication, which has to do with the historical time of earthly existence, with the preservation of one's achievements during life, of one's status, and of one's individual identity. Imitating the sun, the deceased will become his own father, always engendering himself in the womb of the mother goddess. Imitating Osiris, however, he will assume the form of the "deceased father" whose son occupies his place in this world and preserves his memory. He desires to overcome death by bringing it to account and obtaining its condemnation in the next-worldly court, or later, by freeing himself of accountability at the Judgment of the Dead, by being acquitted of guilt and passing vindicated into the world beyond. Osiris represents the paternal principle, the norms of culture, the linear time of human action and suffering. The destiny of the sun, however, represents the maternal principle, the cycle of the regeneration of nature, the cyclical, reversible time of the life of the cosmos. The wonder of these figurations of death is their dual unity, their complementary relationship, their *complexio oppositorum*.

But unlike the apparent course of the sun around the earth, a lifetime does not, by its nature, complete a cyclical course, and it bears little resemblance to the solar course. The individual must exert all his powers to achieve a similarity to the cyclical. The maternal concept of a return to the origin has a normative, ideal component, and this is the point where the two images of death coincide. For it is the righteous individual who has lived according to the norms of *maat* who vindicates himself at the Judgment of the Dead and thus turns his life into a cyclical course. Return to the origin and union with the maternal womb of the tomb—this is death as fulfillment, as *summum bonum*, as the most lofty goal of all longing and effort. In hymns to the Great Mother, the two concepts of union and vindication come together:

To the goddess of the West:
Greetings! To you belong the righteous,
those who do wrong do not reach you.
I know that you are the place of eternity,
one reaches you and endures.
You stand open daily,
the god of the dead sails "to you."
Your gates stand open, they are not closed,
in order to open for the righteous.
Who is here who will not be in you,
who is here who does not belong to you?
. . .
Behold, I am yours in praise,
I am a righteous one who did no wrong
while I was here on earth.
Praised is everyone who is in you!
I am the first among them.[21]

"Who is here who will not be in you?"—all the living are consigned to death. No one can escape this destiny. But mimesis of the solar course is granted only to the righteous, it is only they who may be rejuvenated in her womb and be included forever in the cycle of the sun. Here again we encounter the common concept of general subjection to death and the individual hope of salvation through the Judgment of the Dead, as in the first section of the previous chapter.

Even the gods enter the womb of the Great Mother, in particular, the sun god Re. Entry into the mother does not signify continuation, but rather, immortality. The dead now share the life of the gods, which consists of an endless circular passage over the thresholds of birth and death.

Another hymn to the Great Mother expressly stresses the parallels between the course of the sun and the fate of the deceased:

Greetings, Great One,
mistress of the sky, ruler of all the gods!

She who takes Re-Harakhty-Atum into herself at his beautiful setting,
mistress of the tip of the western mountain;
she who conceives her father Re in peace,
mother of the gods who go to rest in her.

Mistress of those who exist, she to whom they who do not yet exist belong;
she loves the coming in and abhors the going out.[22]
The land longs to be there.
May you embrace me in the company of the praised ones,
may you shelter me within you forever.

I come to you bearing *maat*,
I did no wrong on earth.
I have done what pleases the king and that with which the gods are
content.[23]

The Egyptians felt equally bound and obligated to both principles, the
normative, moral, paternal principle and the cosmic, regenerative, maternal principle.

2. *"The Place Where My Heart Returns": The Tomb in the Homeland*

a) Return to the Tomb

Egypt was a culture of "life permeated by death," not of "death pieced
on." Its images of death penetrated intensely into life, and we have found
this principle affirmed in the case of every image we have considered to
this point. This point is especially impressive in the case of death as return.
For the Egyptians, the greatest horror was to be buried not in their homeland but in foreign territory. They called this "the terror of the foreign"
in inscriptions intended to move visitors to the tomb to say a mortuary
prayer for the tomb owner:

> As you love life and forget death,
> your city gods will praise you,
> you will not taste the terror of another land,
> you will be buried in your (own) tombs,
> and your offices will be assigned to your children . . .[24]

These texts always refer to the ultimate death, not the threshold represented by physical death. For the latter leads to life for one who is buried
in his tomb in the homeland, while his children hold his position in this
life.[25] This point is already made in the Instruction of Hardjedef, the
oldest preserved work of wisdom literature:

> Accept: death is worthless (lit., "low") to us,
> accept: life is exalted for us—
> but the house of death (i.e., the tomb) serves life.[26]

Burial in one's hometown was an ambitious goal that was granted only
to the righteous. The one who achieved it was praised after death:

> One lands as a praised one in Thebes,
> the nome of truth, the land of silence.
> Those who do evil do not enter there,

the Place of Truth;
the ferry that conveys the doers of right,
its ferryman does not convey sinners.
Happy is he who lands there!
He becomes a divine *ba* like the Ennead.[27]

The highest aspiration of an ancient Egyptian was to grow old and be
buried in his hometown:

It is good to tread the way of the god.
... He who places his (i.e., the god's) way in his heart flourishes on it, ...
he grows old in his city as a worthy of his nome.
... He arrives at the necropolis with blissful heart,
in a beautiful embalming, the work of Anubis.
The children of his children praise him ... :
"This is a follower of Osiris,
no divine reproach is upon him!"[28]

This connection between return and burial is a theme of the two best-
known literary narratives of the Middle Kingdom, the Tale of the Shipwrecked Sailor and the Story of Sinuhe. The Tale of the Shipwrecked
Sailor tells of an expedition leader who was shipwrecked and cast onto a
distant island. There, he encountered a god, in the form of a serpent,
who prophesied his return:

A ship will come from the Residence
with sailors whom you know.
You will go with them to the Residence
and die in your city.[29]

At the end, the god again predicts his successful return, connecting it
closely with death and burial:

See, you will reach the Residence in two days,
you will embrace your children,
you will be rejuvenated in your coffin![30]

He who was buried in his homeland, in a tomb long since prepared, was
received in his coffin by the Mother Goddess, into whose womb he
returned for eternal rejuvenation.

The Story of Sinuhe, which is widely viewed as the most important work
of literature from ancient Egypt, stems from early Dynasty 12, and thus
from the twentieth century B.C.E. It has the form of an autobiographical
tomb inscription; the first-person narrator is to be pictured as a deceased

person who, as the owner of a tomb, is looking back on the entirety of his life. The story begins with the description of a death, that of King Amenemhet I (1962 B.C.E.), which is described as a return to the origin:

> King Amenemhet I flew up to the sky
> and united with the sun.
> The god's body united with the one who created him.[31]

The biography of Sinuhe that follows relates an entirely different return and death. As a court official, he was a member of the retinue of the crown prince Senwosret, and by chance, he was witness to the report of Amenemhet I's death. This news filled Sinuhe with panic. He deserted the army and quietly fled, always fearing discovery, beyond the eastern border and into Palestine. There, he earned the trust of an educated Bedouin sheikh who understood Egyptian; the latter took in the refugee and even married him to his daughter. Sinuhe acquired power, respect, and riches. The middle of the story, its turning point, depicts a duel with a rival tribal chieftain. Sinuhe interpreted his victory as a divine judgment, as a sign of reconciliation with the unknown god who, he believed, had driven him to flight and cast him out of Egypt. He turned to this god, giving thanks on the battlefield and begging for his return to Egypt. The battle had raised the specter of death before his eyes, and with it, the "terror of the foreign." Now, he had only one wish: to return to Egypt so as to die and be buried there:

> O god, whoever you are, who decreed this flight!
> May you be merciful and take me to the Residence!
> Surely you will let me see once again the place where my heart still dwells.
> What is more important than that my body be buried
> in the land where I was born?
> . . .
> Ah, may my body be young again,
> for old age has come.
> Weakness has overtaken me,
> my eyes are bad and my arms feeble,
> My legs have stopped following my weary heart,
> I am nearing the point of passing away.
> May I be taken to the city of eternity,
> that I may follow the Mistress of All (= the sky and mother goddess).
> Then will she say to me what is good for her children (= Nut texts)
> and spend eternity over me (i.e., as coffin).[32]

His prayer is heard, and he receives a letter from the king, inviting him to return:

Come back to Egypt, that you may again see the Residence,
in which you grew up. . . .
Now, you have begun to grow old and to lose your manly strength.
Recall the day of burial,
on which a person is brought to a venerable state!
A night will be prepared for you with ointment
and wrappings from the hands of the weaving goddess.
A funeral procession will be carried out for you on the day of burial.
The inner coffin will be of gold, its head of lapis lazuli.
. . .[33] It must not be that you die in a foreign land.
Asiatics shall not bury you,
you shall not be wrapped in a ram's skin, no heap of stones shall be made
    for you.
Put an end to your wandering!
Think of your corpse and come back![34]

Upon receipt of this letter, Sinuhe rejoices: "Good is the kindheartedness that preserves me from death!" In his reply, he even gives the king the title "who saves from the West," as though he could redeem a man from death. And this is indeed what is meant, for dying abroad would be death, while dying in the homeland, in the favor of the king, and being buried in a tomb presented by the king, is life.

In a work of literature written two thousand years later, there is again talk of bringing home a wanderer, and again, the thought of burial in her hometown is the strongest argument. This time, the action takes place on the divine level. Tefnut, the daughter of the sun god, leaves Egypt in a rage (the reason for which is unspecified) and journeys south into Nubia. But then, all joy and festivity vanishes from Egypt. Shu, Tefnut's brother, along with Thoth the scribe, who knows how to muster the entire arsenal of cultural memory, are dispatched to soothe the raging goddess and bring her home. To do this, Thoth has recourse to the moral of Sinuhe, that nothing is more important than to be buried in the homeland. "For of what is on earth, one loves nothing more than his native town, that is, the place where I was born," says Thoth to the distant goddess, and he continues:

> It happens that he (i.e., the creator god) has guided the heart(s) of gods and men to their resting place (i.e., the tomb), the place where they were born and where they also go to rest. This happens not only to men, he causes it to happen to everything on earth, if they remain in their place, that is, in the place where they were born.[35]

The creator has guided the hearts of his creatures to the tomb. The concept of life permeated by death cannot be more clearly expressed. In an important spell from the Coffin Texts, again two thousand years earlier, the creator states:

> I have ordained that their hearts not forget the West,
> that offerings may be brought to the gods of the nomes (i.e., the local, native deities).[36]

To think of the tomb means to think of one's hometown and its local god—and vice versa. In the Demotic myth, Thoth sings a song that explains the concept of burial in one's birthplace in poetic form:

> You fall on your threshing floor,
> you find your sycamore—
> so says destiny to its darling.
> You die in your village, in which you were born.
> You find your burial, you are buried and go to rest
> in your coffin, which is your sycamore, of which he has spoken.
> For if a crocodile has grown old in any place,
> so he will die in the canal, which is his city.
> If a serpent wishes to take rest,
> it seeks its hole, so as to creep in.[37]

It was not unusual for death, and thus also birthplace, to be thought of even in the realm of the gods, especially in the Late Period, when each temple had tombs of its divine forefathers (= the cemeteries of the sacred animals). In a libation spell from the "wake" of the Ptolemaic cult of Osiris, we read:

> It happened that the god hurried to his Two Lands,
> to the primeval place (*bw p3wtj*) where he was born,
> where he came into being out of Re (*ḫpr.n.f jm m R^cw*).
> This means that every god, when they become old . . . ,
> they go to the lands in which they were born,
> the primeval land (*t3 zp-tpj*) in which they came into being out of Re,
> where they lived, were small, and became youths.[38]

For an Egyptian, his hometown was the place not only of his own tomb but also of the tombs for which he, as descendant, was responsible. The meaning of this concept of burial in one's place of origin was that in this way, the deceased did not fall out of the "connective," life-giving structure of affiliation but rather remained included in his community. This inclusion took many forms. The most important, but also the briefest and least certain form was the organized mortuary cult; it seldom lasted more than one or two generations. Another form was the festivals of the necropolis, when the tombs of ancestors were visited; these were festivals that the inhabitants of a city celebrated along with their gods and with the dead. A third form was spontaneous, unorganized visits to tombs; we have evidence of these from numerous graffiti left behind by literate Egyptians, not in all tombs but in certain, evidently famous ones. Such visitors were the object of tomb inscriptions that related the biography of the tomb owner and asked visitors for an offering prayer. By means of a monumental, inscribed tomb, the deceased remained present in the memory of society and continued to exist as a member of the structures of affiliation of the community, which was first and foremost a community of family and town. In a strange place, where no one had known the deceased during his lifetime, this affiliation beyond death through the medium of a tomb was more difficult; in foreign lands, where an inscribed tomb could not be prepared for lack of literate craftsmen, and where no one could have read such inscriptions, such social connectivity was entirely excluded.

For an Egyptian, a proper burial was thus a burial in his hometown. For him, such a burial was the *summum bonum*, the most worthwhile goal. But to reach this goal was in no way just a matter of personal endeavor. A tomb in this sense, that is, an inscribed monumental tomb, could be had only through the king, and by way of royal service. The king was "lord of burial." For the one who turned his back on the king, as we read in the Story of Sinuhe, there was no "end," that is, no tomb.[39] In a Middle Kingdom wisdom text, we read:

> He who follows the king becomes owner of a tomb.
> He who opposes the king, for him there is no tomb.
> His corpse is cast into the water.[40]
> . . .
> (Therefore) enter the earth through what the king gives,
> and rest in the place of enduring,
> and join the caverns of eternity,
> while the dwellings of your progeny preserve love of you,
> and your heirs remain in your places.[41]

This passage is to be understood literally. In Egypt, the crafts were a royal monopoly, and one could employ artists and craftsmen only with royal authorization. In this way, royalty disposed of the means that, in the eyes of the Egyptians, opened the way to immortality and thus represented a means of salvation of the highest order. Royalty thus had at hand a strong incentive not only for loyalty but also for its subjects' sense of obligation to the Residence, that is to say, a means of binding the individual to his city. This situation must be seen against the background of the recurrent problem of anachoresis, that is, flight from the workplace and internal migration.[42] This constant tendency to wander off because of high taxation, obligatory labor, and other burdens imposed by the state worked against the ideology of a connection with one's place of birth. Just as Thoth wishes to bring the wandering goddess back to Egypt in the Demotic tale of the Solar Eye, so the Story of Sinuhe solicits the return of officials who fled in connection with the assassination of Amenemhet I, and so instructional texts solicit loyalty to the king and to the land, and in all these cases, the strongest argument is the tomb in the homeland. We must not lose sight of the blatant political interests behind this structure of affiliation that centered on the tomb. Much like modern totalitarian regimes, the Egyptian state had to keep its people under control.

Still, the meaning of a conviction so central and so deep as that of the redemptive power of a burial in one's place of birth did not stop with its usefulness as a political instrument. The image of death as return was an image of life, a counterimage of death, and specifically, of death as isolation and expulsion from the community of the living.

b) Death as Return and the Mystery of Regeneration

Aristotle preserves the following, enigmatic sentence written by the Greek physician and philosopher, Alcmaeon of Croton, a pupil of Pythagoras:

> Alcmaeon says, that men perish because they do not have the strength to connect the end to the beginning.[43]

Did the image of death as return not strive for precisely this: to connect the end to the beginning? It seems to me that Alcmaeon's sentence yields a comprehensible sense only in light of the Egyptian concept of death. Nature, and especially the sun, draw the power of renewal from their cyclicality. The Egyptians strove according to this model, while the Greeks already recognized that man had fallen irredeemably out of the cyclical time of nature. Forming the course of a life into a circle, returning to the origin, returning to the all-encompassing One from which we emerged at birth, these are images of longing, counterimages of the linearity of perishability, in which life is experienced as a prelude to death. Yet it does not seem meaningful to me to classify the image of death as return as a counterimage in the same sense as the images of physical joining together (as counterimage to dismemberment) and social reunion (as counterimage to isolation). The image of death as return is no counterimage in this sense, for it does not turn an irredeemable original condition into its redemptive opposite. Alcmaeon's sentence refers to longing for renewal, for regeneration in cyclical time. This was in fact the Egyptians' most important hope for the afterlife, and the image of death as return had to do with precisely this concept.

Erik Hornung has shown that the Books of the Netherworld deal above all with the concept of renewal and the reversibility of time.[44] Without death and without descent into the deepest depths of the netherworld, regeneration cannot be achieved. The great model of regeneration is the sun god, who descends nightly into these depths to unite with his corpse, which is resting there, and to renew himself through this union. Just as the royal mortuary texts of the Old Kingdom are dominated by the image of *ascensio*, of ascent to the sky, so the royal mortuary texts of the New Kingdom are dominated by the image of *descensus*, of descent into the netherworld. In each case, the goal is the same: union with the sun god and entry into the course of the sun, that is, the cyclical time of renewal. The books of the Netherworld are descriptions of the sun's course, specifically its nocturnal phase, in which the sun god sinks into the cosmic depths. The Amduat, the earliest and the classical Book of the Netherworld, employs an especially vivid symbol to express the idea of cyclical time. It depicts the sun god and his entourage (in which the deceased king wishes to be included) passing through a gigantic serpent, and doing so the wrong way around: he enters through the tail and exits via the mouth. Time is thus reversed, and the mystery of renewal is effected.

Hornung connects the idea of the reversibility of time with the motif of the netherworld as a topsy-turvy realm in which the orderly processes of life are reversed. We have dealt with this image of death in the preceding chapter, and in my opinion, it belongs to an entirely different context. Inversion is an image of death, while renewal is the epitome of life, and I do not believe that the concept of the reversibility of time belongs to the motif of a topsy-turvy world. For the deceased, it was of greatest importance to have nothing to do with inversion: it was the embodiment of that from which he wished to distance himself, to free himself, in order to win eternal life. The concept of temporal reversibility, of cyclical renewal, did not belong to the properties of a reversed world but to the order of the cosmos, which could not endure without cyclical time. The mystery of the connection of the end to the beginning does not stand the order of this world on its head. The seed corn knew this mystery, as did the Nile, the moon, and the sun, it was an overwhelmingly obvious phenomenon of nature. In the image of death as return, man, too, laid claim to this mystery. The concept of cyclical time combined circularity and reversibility. Thus, motifs of inversion make their appearance in this connection but without any fundamental reversal of the cosmic order. Evening and morning, west and east, and night barque and day

barque sometimes exchange roles in sun hymns, intimating the coincid-
ing of end and beginning, death and birth.[45] Regeneration did not mean
traveling a reversed path from death to birth, but rather, being born anew
through death. The sun god himself did not reverse direction when he
united with Osiris in the depths of the cosmos; rather, he gained the
strength to make yet another cycle.

It seems to me that there is another central motif here, one that
Hornung has also connected with the idea of regeneration: the motif of
the primeval waters. In the netherworld, the deceased, just like the sun
god, comes into contact with elements of the pre-cosmos or preexistence,
that "primal matter" (so Hornung) out of which the cosmos emerged at
the beginning and which remained ever present as the source of regeneration. Every morning, the sun god emerged from the primeval waters,
and the annual Nile inundation that renewed the fertility of the land also
fed on these netherworldly primeval waters. There was even a concept
that while they were asleep, people were already immersed in the primeval
ocean from which the cosmos emerged at its beginning. "How beautiful
you are," sang one poet, "when you rise in Light-land,"

> we live again anew,
> after we enter the primeval water,
> and it has rejuvenated us into one who is young for the first time.
> The old man is shed, a new one is made.[46]

The Egyptians thus believed that even during their lifetimes, they had a
share in the rejuvenating circularity of cosmic time.

The image of death as return arises from the paradoxical desire to turn,
by dint of culture, the natural, biological temporality of man, which
marches relentlessly and linearly toward death, into a cyclical path that
follows the model of nature. Man, who dies by nature, wishes to share in
the regeneration of this nature, and to that end, he makes use of symbolic forms of culture: rituals, images, and language. What this image
of death does not imply—and this needs to be stressed by way of a
conclusion—is the concept suggested by the expression "passing on":
existence on earth as an exile from which the soul returns to its real home,
the divine and heavenly sphere. The Egyptians did not normally view existence on earth as a foreign exile from which death was a release—with
the sole possible exception of one text that is extraordinary in every
respect, the Dialogue of a Man with His *Ba*, in which, among other things,
it is stated:

> Death is before me today
> like the passing of rain (or: like a beaten path),
> as when a man returns from an expedition.

. . .
Death is before me today
as when a man longs to see his house again
after he has spent many years in captivity.[47]

Here, we have to do with an intentional inversion, with a sort of reversed world. Death was not normally viewed in this way. These verses refer to a borderline situation in human experience, one in which this life has become something foreign.

CHAPTER EIGHT

Death as Mystery

1. The Mystery of the Sun: Renewal and Rebirth

The image of death as return has led us to the mystery of the circuit of the sun god and his nightly renewal in the depths of the world. He is able to join the end to the beginning, so that each morning, he emerges from the realm of the dead rejuvenated and glorious, as on the "first occasion." That this renewal is a mystery, and perhaps even the deepest mystery in Egyptian religion, is assured by the texts and representations that depict it. Unlike the images of death treated to this point, which occur in all the mortuary texts of all periods, the mystery of the nocturnal regeneration of the sun occurs in a single text genre, one that is thoroughly exclusive and cloaked in the aura of mystery: the texts in the royal tombs of the New Kingdom. For their part, these royal tombs were architectonic realizations of the mysterious, crypts where no human foot was to tread after the burial. Thus, the external fact of the place where it was represented already reveals that the renewal of the sun god in the depths of the world has to do with a mystery. In hymns, mortuary texts, and other genres of Egyptian literature, only brief turns of expression allude to this mystery, which receives detailed verbal and visual representation in only one genre: the Books of the Netherworld. We thus have to do with three closely connected phenomena: the theme of solar renewal, that of the mysterious seclusion of the places where it is depicted, and that of the royal tomb and the relationship of this mystery to death.

The Egyptian tomb—not just the royal tomb but the tomb in general—served two functions that were diametrically opposite and mutually exclusive: "mystery" and "memory." On the one hand, the tomb served as a visible sign intended to keep the recollection of the deceased alive in the memory of posterity. This function of the tomb required visibility and openness. On the other hand, the tomb was supposed to shelter the mummy and, to the extent possible, to keep it safe from any profaning touch. It was supposed to be a hidden, inaccessible place where the deceased was protected forever. Thus, a typical monumental Egyptian tomb contained accessible rooms but also shafts that led more or less deeply down into the rock bed, to a sarcophagus chamber that was walled up after the burial. In most cases, the shaft was filled up as well so as to shut off the sarcophagus chamber all the more effectively. In this architectonic attempt to create a mysterious, inaccessible, protective space for the mummy, we can perceive the tangible expression of the image of death as mystery. Embalmed and mummified, the deceased vanished from the profane world of the living and entered the mystery of the netherworld. Architectonically realized by the sarcophagus chamber of a monumental tomb, this mystery had two aspects: the solar aspect of renewal and the Osirian aspect of protection, of absolute hiddenness.

Let us first consider the solar aspect of renewal. As noted, it determined the decoration of the royal tombs of the New Kingdom, in which the antagonistic double function of the tomb—mystery and memory—emerges far more clearly than in the tombs of officials. In the case of royal burials, the two functions are strictly separated, and each is realized in a special structure. The cult and memorial function was realized in the form of a mortuary temple, or "mansion of millions of years,"[1] which was constructed visibly and on as monumental a scale as possible at the edge of the cultivation. The mystery function was assured by a rock-cut tomb in the Valley of the Kings, a tomb that was hermetically sealed, rigorously guarded, and located in as hidden a place as possible.[2] If we wish to understand the Egyptian concept of mystery, we need only consider the royal tombs and their decoration. This decoration is devoted almost exclusively to a single theme: the nocturnal journey of the sun through the netherworld.[3] During this journey, the sun god descends into the netherworld, waking the dead from their sleep, giving them light and air, and addressing them with his regal words; he grants them nourishment, judges the evil, overcomes the dragon Apopis, who opposes him even here, decides the fate of the dead, and unites himself with Osiris, who is his corpse. From this union, he gains the power of renewal. In Osiris and Re, the beginning is joined to the end, as are yesterday and tomorrow, as stated in chapter 17 of the Book of the Dead.[4] In a sun hymn from the Book of the Dead, this union is described thus:

> Re sets in the western mountain
> and lights the netherworld with his rays.
> This means: Re rests in Osiris,
> Osiris rests in Re, this means.[5]

This description can be connected with the representation of a ram-headed mummy, as depicted in the tomb of Nefertari and in Theban Tombs 335 and 336, standing upright between Isis and Nephthys, who protectively flank him.[6] The caption uses this same formula to explain this representation: to the left of the mummy are the words "Osiris, who rests in Re," and to the right, "It is Re, who rests in Osiris." We must thus recognize this mummy as the form of the dead sun god, who does not become Osiris, like the other dead, but who "rests in Osiris," that is, who unites with Osiris only temporarily and then once again separates himself from him. This form, which comprises the two gods, is called the "United Ba":

> United Ba Re-Osiris,
> Great God who is at the head of the West in Abydos.[7]

Another name of this ram-headed mummy is "He with the ram's head." This being was the center of a ritual that served to maintain life in Egypt; it was performed in the House of Life, the school and scriptorium of the temple, and we read of it:

> He who divulges it dies a sudden death,
> for it is a great mystery:
> it is Re and it is Osiris.[8]

Here, we are witness to a tremendous mystery. As we have seen, the renewal of the sun god in death, in the depths of the netherworld at midnight, was indeed the most mysterious thing known to Egyptian religion. The concept of regeneration was enormously widespread in Egypt, as widespread as the scarabs and the many other amulets and symbols that lent it expression. But all the texts and representations that deal with it in detail are associated with mystery and secrecy: as noted, in the New Kingdom, they occur almost exclusively in royal tombs. For this reason alone, we must consider them to be a sort of secret literature and lore, removed from common use by the very place where they were recorded.

A strict boundary was drawn that on the one hand separated royal and nonroyal mortuary literature, and on the other hand, among the royal texts themselves, also distinguished what a king could cause to be represented in his mortuary temple from what was represented in his tomb.

In these and related texts, the Egyptian word for "mystery" also has the extended meaning "corpse."[9] The sun god, for instance, is called "the one whose mystery is hidden," referring to his corpse, which rests in the depths as Osiris.[10] The netherworld is called "that which conceals the mystery." At midnight, the Book of Gates has the sun god reach the "guardians of the mystery," of whom it is said:

> They guard the mystery of the Great God,
> which those in the netherworld do not see.
> Re says to them:
> You have embraced my image,
> you have grasped my mystery.
> You rest in the house of the *benben*,
> in the place that shelters my corpse, which I am.[11]

During the night, however, the sun god does not just unite with his mystery, that is, with Osiris as his corpse; as we have seen, he also enters the body of the great mother- and sky-goddess, who gives birth to him anew each morning. In this aspect, he unites himself in a different sense with Osiris, for like him, he becomes the son of Nut, who returns in death to the womb of the sky goddess.

As the texts cited to this point indicate, the mystery of the sun god is on the one hand his corpse, which rests in the depths of the world, and on the other hand, the process of renewal that he himself undergoes when he unites with this corpse and experiences rebirth in the womb of the mother- and sky-goddess. These images exist together, they lend expression to the idea of renewal, and they are also prototypes for man, who desires, like the sun god, to return to the womb of the mother goddess and unite himself nightly as a *ba* with his corpse, which is lying in his tomb.

2. *The Mystery of Osiris*

Every reader of Herodotus' *Histories* has been struck by the extreme care with which this author avoids mentioning the name of Osiris. He imposes no comparable taboo on any other divine name or any other religion, only on Osiris and only on Egyptian religion. Neither the other classical writers nor the Egyptian texts themselves know of such a taboo regarding a divine name. It is evidently a matter of a misunderstanding. Nevertheless, Herodotus was entirely correct in surrounding this particular god with the aura of special mystery. While the cult of Osiris knew no taboo regarding the god's name, it was filled with other taboos. One, the most important, we have already encountered in a Coffin Text: outcry. Osiris was lord of silence, and no one was to raise his voice in his vicinity. All the taboos and mysteries surrounding the god Osiris had something to do with death. There were many of these in the institution of the "Abaton," a sacred grove containing a tomb of Osiris, which was so inaccessible that even birds could not alight on its trees.[12] In the later periods of Egyptian history, all the larger temples seem to have had such an Abaton. It was the locus of the reliquary cult of the parts of Osiris' body, which had been torn asunder by Seth and then buried by Isis in each of the nomes.[13] In this connection, Diodorus relates a story that anticipates Lessing's parable of the ring. Isis desired that Osiris' tomb be secret and yet revered by all the inhabitants of Egypt. She therefore created a corpse in the form of Osiris around each individual limb and prepared the priesthood of each nome by disclosing that she had entrusted to them alone the burial of her husband under conditions of strictest secrecy. Each nome thus believed it possessed the true corpse and guarded this knowledge as a great mystery. It is not the name but the death of Osiris that Diodorus designates as *aporrhetos*, a mystery not to be spoken of. This word is aptly chosen. The rituals that had to do with the death and "resurrection" of Osiris were shrouded with mystery, for the corpse had to be protected from attacks by Seth (Greek *Typhon*). The "mystery of Osiris" was the fact of his death.

In this connection, death and mystery obviously went hand in hand. The condition of Osiris demanded the strictest secrecy. Hence the long and dangerous road to reach Osiris in "Busiris," which we must picture as located in the heart of the netherworld. The netherworldly Busiris was the place of embalming that was prepared for Osiris in the afterlife. Every tomb of Osiris was a gateway to the netherworld. This was especially true of the most sacred of all the sacred locales: Busiris, Heliopolis, and Abydos. At Abydos, the tomb of Osiris was located in the necropolis "She Who Harbors Her Lord" in the mountains called "Mysterious Mountain." A decree of Nectanebo II forbade, on pain of mutilation, the quarrying of stone in this area, which was a place of the greatest sanctity.[14]

At this point, we must return to the theme of transition. Transition led the deceased into the mystery of Osiris.

In the Tales of Wonder from Papyrus Westcar, the sage Djedi wishes Prince Djedefhor:

> May your *ba* know the roads of the afterlife,
> to the portal of the place that conceals the Weary One![15]

The gate or portal symbolizes transition. It leads the *ba*, which travels the roadway, to the "place that conceals the Weary One." The Weary One is Osiris, and it is his weakness that must be concealed. The concealment of the Weary One is another image for the protective embrace of the mother goddess. Here, this idea is connected with the symbol of the gate, through which the deceased wishes to enter into the concealed mystery of Osiris. In chapter 145 of the Book of the Dead, the symbol of the gate is extended into a series of twenty-one gates through which the deceased must pass. Chapter 146 reduces the number to fourteen or fifteen. In chapters 144 and 147, there are seven "gateways."[16] The number is not important. Other chapters of the Book of the Dead describe this transition zone as twelve caves or fourteen places. This image of death found expression in the land of the living in the form of a board game that was itself called "passage" (*zn.t*). This was a game for two persons to play. Against his opponent, the player had to make his passage through thirty fields and into the presence of a god who granted provisions (bread and water) and vindication.[17] In the tomb of Sennedjem, the tomb owner is ostentatiously represented on a door leaf playing this board game called "passage." Next to the table on which the game is being played, there is a table laden with offerings, one that symbolizes the goal of the "passage": access to and enjoyment of eternal nourishment.[18]

The gates were guarded by monsters that, despite their hideous appearance, did not embody evil but rather served good, the next-worldly "police force" that was supposed to protect Osiris from the attacks of Seth. The deceased averted the terror of the guardians by naming their names and also by knowing the names of the gates, and he obtained free passage through the gates by demonstrating his purity. He knew the mythical meaning of the water in which he had bathed, and he wore the correct clothing. The gates and their guardians constituted a 21-, 15-, 14-, or 7-fold protective wall around the "Weary One," whom they "concealed." In the Demotic Story of Setne, Osiris sat enthroned in the seventh of seven halls through which the deceased had to pass in order to arrive at the place of vindication. A series of seven gates was also a central concept in the temple architecture of the later periods of Egyptian history.[19] This is death as mystery, and the deceased identified himself with it. In the innermost ring of this most secluded and hence most sacred cosmic sphere, he will dwell with and as Osiris. He will share in his mystery, and the terrifying figures at the gates will be his guardians as well, protecting him from all evil.

3. The Tomb as Sacred Place

While the decoration of the royal tombs refers mainly to the solar aspect of the mystery of regeneration, the sarcophagus chambers of the tombs of officials are connected with the Osirian aspect of absolute hiddenness. In other words, with their architecture and their decoration, the royal tombs realize a symbolic description of the netherworld and the nocturnal journey of the sun, while the private tombs realize a cavern or crypt in the depths of the earth. The sarcophagus chambers of the private tombs were seldom decorated, but in the Book of the Dead, there are two vignettes that are to be understood as representations of an ideal sarcophagus chamber. One belongs to chapter 182.[20] Here, we see a mummified Osiris lying on a lion bed. The caption identifies him as *sˁḥ špss*, "august mummy." Above and below, six guardian monsters are represented, apotropaic protective spirits holding lizards, serpents, or knives in their defensively upraised hands. The deceased, in the role of Thoth, recites the accompanying spell, saying, among other things,

> I cause Re to enter Osiris,
> I cause Osiris to enter Re.
> I cause him to enter the mysterious vault,
> so as to breathe life into the heart of the Weary of Heart,
> the sheltered *ba* who is in the West.[21]

This "mysterious vault" in which Osiris lies as a "sheltered *ba*" is depicted in the vignette. It is also the mythic prototype of the sarcophagus chamber of a monumental tomb. Chapter 151 of the Book of the Dead also refers to this sarcophagus chamber/crypt (Figure 3). It consists of a ground plan with opened-up walls. In the middle, the mummified deceased is lying on a bier, cared for by Anubis, who lays his hands on him. Under the bier is the *ba*-bird of the deceased, while Isis and Nephthys kneel to the left and the right, reciting protective spells for the deceased. On the walls are the four "magical bricks," symbols bearing inscriptions that are supposed to ward off the enemy. In the corners, the four Sons of Horus are represented, each with a spell that assures the protection of the deceased. The entire spell bears a title that scholars translate "spell for the mummy mask."[22] The word for mummy mask, which is attested only here, can be rendered "head of the mystery," or even "mysterious head." The word "mystery" is especially closely connected with Anubis, the embalmer,[23] whose characteristic epithet is "He who is over the mystery." This epithet also occurs as a title of officials, in which case we usually translate it as "confidential adviser." In reference to Anubis, however, it has a different meaning. The mystery over which Anubis watches is the mummified

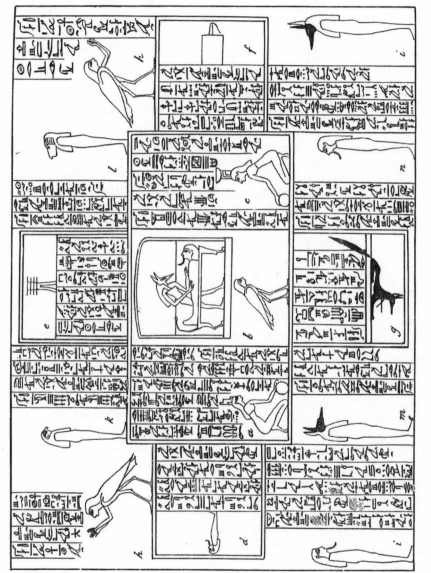

Figure 3. Vignette to Book of the Dead chapter 151. From E. Naville, *Das ägyptische Totenbuch der XVIII. bis XX. Dynastie,* vol. 1, *Text und Vignetten* (Berlin, 1886), pl. 173.

corpse. The mystery of Anubis imparts divine presence as protection against disintegration and decay. The gods who watch over the corpse heap sacredness and divinity on it, just as embalming and mummification impregnate it with imperishable substances. This protective divine presence as a maternal sphere of extreme hiddenness had its place in the hermetically sealed, inaccessible sarcophagus chamber.

The decorative program of an Egyptian tomb traditionally consisted of four thematic areas:

1. The biographical representation of the tomb owner (name, titles, biographical inscription, scenes of the exercise of office, scenes from daily life)
2. The provisioning of the tomb owner in the tomb (preparation, delivery, and presentation of the offerings)
3. Rites of passage into the tomb (burial, Opening of the Mouth)
4. Life in the next world (Judgment of the Dead and the gates of the netherworld; the deceased worshiping the gods; Field of Reeds and solar barque, etc.). This fourth area was connected with concepts of the sacred and the mysterious.

In the Old and Middle Kingdoms, the decoration was confined to thematic areas (1) and (2), and less often, (3). In the Old Kingdom, thematic area (4) occurred only in the royal sphere, and specifically, in the form of texts carved on the walls of the subterranean chambers of the pyramids beginning with Wenis, the last king of Dynasty 5. Their theme is the next-worldly life of the dead king and the way there from the tomb. In the Middle Kingdom, nonroyal deceased also acquired a share in this mortuary literature, which was inscribed on the interior walls of their coffins. From that time on, we can see that thematic area (4), which was connected with the concept of mystery, was regularly connected with the sarcophagus chamber of the tomb, the place where the corpse lay and which, as we have seen, was the epitome of protection and mystery.

In Dynasty 18, thematic area (3) became canonical, along with (1) and (2). The corresponding scenes from (3) were located in the passage (the long corridor) of the tomb, where as a rule, the funeral was represented on the left (on the south wall, for the tomb was oriented toward the west) and the Opening of the Mouth on the right. Scenes of cultic provisioning (2) were connected with the statue chapel at the far end of the east–west axis but also with the false door and the stela in the transverse chamber at the front of the tomb, with the false door mostly on the south wall and the stela mostly on the north wall of the chamber. Here, the predominant theme was the memory of the tomb owner, which was preserved in the texts and scenes of his biographical representation (1). Two scenes that already belonged to (4) were taken up anew: adoration of the sun god, mostly on the architrave of the entrance, and adoration of Osiris, mostly at the end of the funeral procession. Otherwise, thematic area (4) remained strictly confined to the mortuary texts, which were now deposited with the deceased in the sarcophagus chamber, in the form of a papyrus roll (Book of the Dead).

It can thus be maintained that as a rule, until the end of Dynasty 18, thematic area (4) was confined to the hermetically sealed sarcophagus chamber. The next-worldly life of the deceased in the company of the gods was a mystery confined to the inaccessible, interior realm of the tomb and recorded only in the form of texts, with few exceptions, such as the famous burial chamber of Sennefer (Theban Tomb 96).[24] The great innovation in the decorative program of the tombs of the Ramesside Period was that thematic area (4) now also became canonical and came to dominate the decorative program of the tombs, even in their outer areas, while in most tombs of this period, scenes of biographical representation (1) disappeared almost entirely. This means that now, the cult chambers of the tomb shared in the sacredness and the mysteriousness of the sarcophagus chamber, and this innovation put an end to the uncrossable boundary between the sarcophagus chamber and the cult chambers, which until then had determined the layout of the tomb. Instead of the inaccessible shaft, an easily accessible, winding passageway with stairs now led from the upper cult chambers to the entrance to the sarcophagus chamber, which remained walled up. This profound and dramatic change in the Egyptian concept of the tomb can be explained in various ways. One of these had to do with the image of death as mystery, which acquired an entirely new meaning in this period.

The character of the tomb as a temple was emphasized by a number of new scenes in which the tomb owner is depicted not as the object of the mortuary cult (2), but as the subject of divine cult (4). To integrate these new scenes into the decorative program, it was necessary to introduce a new principle of arranging scenes on the walls, one that was based on the opposition of and the relationship between above to below. Thematic areas (2) and (3) had to be retained, of course. The problem was resolved in such a way that, for the most part, scenes of worshiping deities were represented above, while scenes of the mortuary cult (2) and of transition (3) were represented below.

The vertical axis above/below was foreign to the older tomb decoration, in which there prevailed the horizontal relationships between outer and inner, east and west, and north and south. The fundamental unity of the tomb decoration lay in the representations on the walls, which filled a wall from top to bottom. A representation was often divided into several "registers" that had no spatial meaning but merely served as lines for the figures represented to stand on; these rows of figures divided up the picture and made it "readable," without disrupting its semantic unity. The registers were located within a scene; they did not serve to separate different scenes. For the most part, they were oriented toward a huge figure of the tomb owner that was several registers tall, lending unity to the representations on the wall. This principle was now gradually abandoned in favor of a new principle of rows of representations that occupied only a part of a wall and, along with one or two further rows, filled the available space between the ceiling and the colored stripe that served as a "baseboard." These rows of representations, in which various scenes were arranged side by side, were now often no longer confined to a single wall but continued onto other walls of the room. It was thus possible to arrange various scenes in different rows of representations, one above the other. This new principle was used in particular to subordinate the traditional scenes of transition and mortuary cult to the new scenes depicting the worship of deities.

By way of an example, in the transverse chamber of the tomb of Djehutimes, a chief intendant of domains from the reign of Ramesses II (Theban Tomb 32), the front (east) and rear (west) walls are each divided into three rows of representations, whose scenes continue on both sides of the passageway.[25] In the upper row, the tomb owner is represented worshiping the gates of the netherworld and their guardians. This pictorial concept belongs to thematic area (4) and corresponds to chapter 145 of the Book of the Dead. It represents the transition, not from the realm of the living into the tomb (3) but from the tomb into the realm of Osiris, and the action thus takes place in the afterlife. The middle row contains scenes of the Opening of the Mouth ritual, which belong to thematic area (3), for they refer to rites that consummate the transition into the tomb. In the bottom row, we find scenes of the mortuary cult, which are here complemented by a scene in which a female lute player performs two songs.[26] The meaning of this arrangement is clear: the most sacred scenes, the ones pertaining to the sacral aspect of the tomb as temple, are at the top. They stem from the repertoire of themes and scenes in the mortuary literature. The scenes below them refer to a ritual that seldom occurs in tombs in this full form, with its representations and recitations; they also count as sacral but in a more restricted sense, for here, the tomb owner is the object, not the subject of the cult. There is now an obvious semantic relationship between the scenes above and those below. Both refer to a transition: above, from the tomb into the afterlife, and below, from this world into the tomb. We are not, however, to conclude from this relationship that the upper scenes continue the scenes below: that would be a horizontal form of relationship. The upper scenes are rather to be understood as an interpretation of those below. The scenes below are played out in the visible realm of the cult, and those above in the invisible realm of the afterlife.

This principle of above and below stems from another type of monument, in which it appeared already in Dynasty 18: the stela. A whole series of Dynasty 18 stelae display two fields of decoration, one above the other, and on not a few of these, the upper field contains a scene of worship, in which the deceased addresses Osiris enthroned in a shrine, and the one below a scene of provisioning, in which the deceased sits at an offering table and receives a libation or some other form of offering from a priest or family member.[27] On many stelae, the upper field of decoration consists of an antithetical scene of worship, in which Osiris and Anubis, or Osiris and Re-Harakhty, sit back to back in the middle, while the deceased approaches them, praying, from both edges of the stela.[28]

In a tomb from the transitional period from Dynasty 18 to Dynasty 19, whose architecture already lays considerable stress on the new, sacral character but from which the principle of rows of representations is still missing, the vertical axis of the wall decoration found a solution from which the origin of the principle of rows of representation clearly emerged. This tomb, which belonged to a predecessor of Djehutimes, the chief intendant of the domains of Amun, Amenemope (Theban Tomb 41), contains no fewer than five large stelae with scenes of divine worship and of the mortuary cult. Here, the older form was exploited to represent the semantic subordination of the mortuary cult. In later tombs, the principle of the stela decoration was extended to the walls. The tomb of Amenemope is highly interesting in yet another respect. It already occurred to the tomb owner, or to the artists in his employ, to connect the scenes of transition from this world into the tomb with scenes of transition from the tomb into the next life. As the principle of above and below and the form of rows of representation had not yet been conceived, a highly original solution was found. The funeral scenes were represented in five registers on the south wall of the transverse chamber, and the register lines were continued around the corner and onto the west wall: this arrangement would have been entirely impossible according to the decorative principles of the traditional style of wall decoration. On the west wall, these registers are filled with scenes of the transition from the tomb into the afterlife and of life in the next world: the embrace by the goddess of the West, provisioning by the tree goddess, passing through the gates, greeting the gods who presided over the Judgment of the Dead, the weighing of the heart, the Field of Reeds, the adoration of the barque of Sokar, and so forth. Here, on the south and east walls, there stand what would later be arranged in two rows of representations, one above the other. But below these scenes, in the southwestern corner of the transverse chamber, there begins the stairway down into the crypt of the tomb, which is in this way integrated into the semantics of the wall decoration.[29]

A tomb of this new type included not only cult chambers and accessible crypts but also a sometimes sunken forecourt closed off by a pylon, and in most cases a superstructure in the form of a pyramid.[30] The cult chambers and crypt were connected with Osiris (or the Memphite funerary god Sokar, who in this period was entirely merged with Osiris), while the court and the pyramid were connected with the sun god. Here, the vertical axis was repeated on a large, three-dimensional scale, integrating the tomb into the layered cosmic structure of sky, earth, and netherworld, into the mysteries of the course of the sun and of Osiris, as well as into the world above illuminated by the light of the sun, which, as we shall see in the following chapter, stood at the center of concepts of the afterlife in the New Kingdom.

In the Ramesside Period, the mystery aspect of the tomb as a place of divine presence came to the fore, determining its decoration and architecture. This change took place at the expense of the memorial aspect of the tomb. The wish for representation and continuation in the memory of society gave way before the wish for divine presence. In a harper's song from Theban Tomb 50, we read:

> The gods you served on earth,
> you now step face to face with them.[31]

We encounter this "face to face" in scenes that depict the tomb owner worshiping deities and which now, after the Amarna Period, constituted the main theme of the tomb decoration. The accessible portions of the tomb were interpreted as a sort of fictive temple, in which the deceased served the gods in the role of a priest. This notion was taken to such an extreme that in certain tombs, the statues of the tomb owner and his family in the chapel at the rear were replaced by representations of Osiris, Isis, and Horus.[32]

In the tomb of Djehutiemheb (Theban Tomb 194) from the reign of Ramesses II, there is a highly unusual inscription that clearly expresses the concept of the special sanctity of the tomb as a place of divine presence, even in its outer chambers. It has to do with a hymn to Hathor as goddess of the Theban necropolis, in which it is related that the goddess appeared to the tomb owner in a dream to reveal the place where he was to locate his tomb. Now he asks the goddess to remain present for him in his tomb, so that he may pray to her there forever:

Djehutiemheb, the vindicated, says:
I have come to you, O mistress of the Two Lands, Hathor, O beloved one!
Behold, I am in praise before your beautiful visage
and kiss the earth before your *ka.*
I am truly a servant of yours
and am upon the water of your command.
I do not reject the speech of your mouth, I do not disregard your teaching.
I am on the way that you yourself have ordained,
on the path that you yourself have prepared.
Blessed be he who knows you!
He who beholds you is blessed.
How happy is he who rests at your side,
who enters into your shadow.
It is you who prophesied my tomb at the beginning,
when it was first planned.
What you said has been realized through you,
a place for my mummy has been founded.
. . . It is you who spoke to me with your own mouth:
"I am the beautiful Heli, my form is . . . my mother.
I have come to instruct you.
Behold your place, seize it for yourself,
without traveling north- or southwards,"
while I slept and the earth lay in silence
in the depths of the night.
In the morning, my heart jubilated, I rejoiced,
and I went to the western side
to do what you said.
You are a goddess whose word must be carried out,
a lady who must be obeyed.
I have not dismissed your words and I have not ignored your plan.
As you have said, so I do.
Give me your countenance, let me praise it,
grant your beauty, that I may gaze upon your form in my tomb,
so as to proclaim your power, so as to let posterity know of your might.[33]

This text once again makes clear the paramount importance of the tomb, which could haunt the mind of an Egyptian even in his dreams. What is especially important in our context here is the prayer for divine presence. The description of a face-to-face of the goddess and the tomb owner gives expression to the hope that the goddess will inhabit her image and allow the tomb owner to see her in the flesh and adore her. Here, a single concept becomes the basis of nearly all the tomb decoration, one that has its place of origin in the decoration of the coffin: the deceased in the womb of the mother- and sky-goddess Nut, who as coffin has taken him into herself, surrounded by the group of protective deities who are represented on the coffin walls.

4. Initiation and Death

In accordance with the image of death as mystery, the deceased not only crossed over, or returned, to the netherworld, he was initiated into it. In their rubrics, many spells of the Book of the Dead identify themselves as initiations into the mysteries of the netherworld. The following rubric, for instance, accompanies a whole series of spells:

> The mysteries of the netherworld,
> initiation into the mysteries of the realm of the dead.[34]

Chapter 137 A of the Book of the Dead continues:

> Let it be done for no one
> except yourself,
> by your father or by your son.
> For it is a great mystery of the West,
> an initiation into the mysteries of the netherworld,
> for the gods, the transfigured spirits, and the dead view it as service for
>   Khentamentiu.
> . . .
> What is carried out in the hiddenness of the netherworld,
> the mysteries of the netherworld,
> an initiation into the mysteries of the realm of the dead.[35]

The rubric to chapter 137 B of the Book of the Dead reads:

> A great mystery of the West,
> an initiation into the mysteries of The-One-in-the-Netherworld.[36]

In particular, the Books of the Netherworld in the royal tombs purport to be initiations into the mysteries of the realm of the dead. They were part of the decorative program of the royal tombs, and in them, the king is greeted by the gods as one

> who knows our forms and our past,
> who knows the initiation into the mysteries of the netherworld,
> for you are one who has penetrated into the sacredness of the mysteries.[37]

The concepts employed here—"mysteries," "initiation"—also occur constantly in temple texts. It is thus reasonable to suppose that the initiation of priests into certain cults was the prototype for the initiation of the deceased into the world beyond. If we look more closely into the spells of the Book of the Dead, this analogy is confirmed. The deceased is initiated into the afterlife as into a temple, and the divine presence in which he shares has the character of cultic service. He enters into an other-worldly cultic community. The most detailed version of this title occurs in the introduction to a hymn to the nocturnal sun:

> The mysteries of the netherworld,
> an initiation into the mysteries of the realm of the dead,
> a breaking up of the mountains, an opening up of the valleys,
> mysteries that absolutely no one knows
> for the treatment of the transfigured dead,
> to lengthen his stride, to restore his gait,
> to drive deafness out of him, to open his face along with the god.
>
> You do this, without letting any man see,
> aside from the one who is truly your intimate and a lector priest.
> Let no one else see and no servant from outside come in.
> You make it in a tent of linen cloth
> that is entirely studded with stars.[38]

The deceased is thus inducted into a "Secret Service," into the nightly service rendered by those in the netherworld to the sun god, who has descended to them.[39]

If we close by again posing the question, in what form the image of death as mystery participated in the world of the living in Egypt, the analogy of the temple cult presents itself. Is it conceivable that initiation into the mysteries of the netherworld, as it was granted to the deceased by the Book of the Dead and the mortuary rituals, was modeled on the prototype of initiation into temple mysteries, as it was granted to the living? Here, we touch upon one of the most controversial problems of Egyptology. Though esoteric circles cling to the notion of "Egyptian mysteries," academic Egyptology almost unanimously rejects this idea. In his book *The Secret Lore of Egypt*, Erik Hornung[40] makes it clear that this "secret lore" is a projection of the Greeks, who conceived their image of Egyptian culture on the model of their own mystery cults. The problem raises itself differently in the light of the question of how the image of death as mystery might have influenced the living reality of the Egyptians. It is difficult to believe that the mystery into which the deceased was initiated and the mystery into which the living priest was initiated could have been entirely unrelated to one another, considering that the concept of "initiation" played so great a role in both spheres. Might it not be that already during his lifetime, a priest experienced his introduction into the mysterious cultic presence of the divine as a sort of foretaste of his postmortem introduction to Osiris?

It seems to me that an especially conclusive response to this question is afforded by the harper's song from the tomb of the God's Father

Neferhotep (Theban Tomb 50) from the reign of Haremhab, two verses
of which we have already cited above:[41]

Beginning of the song to remind the heart
of that day of landing,[42]
that it (the day of death) may be placed in the heart of the buried one (?),
for there is no one that escapes it,
strong and weak alike,
whether one fares upstream or downstream in life,[43]
one lands (i.e., dies) inevitably after this.

O God's Father, how great is your bliss!
You go in to the lords of eternity. . . .
All the gods you served on earth,
you now step face to face with them.
They are ready to receive your *ba*, to protect your mummy,
they repay you double the work of your hands,
they will gather your beauty,
they will establish offerings for (your) mummy,
each god brings his food.
They say to you, "Welcome in peace,
you servant who are *akh*-effective for our *ka*!"
O God's Father, I have heard your praise in the presence of the lords of
    eternity!
It is said about you, "He has dragged Sokar,
he[44] has placed the *henu*-barque on its stand
and circled the walls in its following.
The sparkling pendant on his breast,
he has raised the *djed*-pillar in Busiris,
a *sem*-priest in his function,
who grasps the hoe at the end of the Hacking of the Earth;
he has recited the festival scroll in Busiris!"
Perfect was your encounter with the gods;
your (family) will also be well regarded because of your perfection,
for you are one who may enter Heliopolis and know the mysteries
that are therein!

O God's Father, . . .
may Anubis lay his arm upon you,
may the Two Sisters join with you;
may you be anointed again,
being made complete in the work of permanence:
precious stone of the god in its genuine form,
salve in the hands of the god of the press,
clothing of the work of the weaver goddess;
the Sons of Horus as your protection,
the two mourning kites sit outside[45] for you

and raise cries in your name,
for you are one who was *akh*-effective, when you were on earth,
for your lord Amun.

O God's Father, may your (family) be well regarded in Heliopolis,
may you be protected in Thebes,
may you not be missed in eternity,
may your name not be erased,
for you are a righteous one in Memphis,
one who may enter face to face in the holy of holies,
who is perfect in the knowledge of its great images!

Already during one's lifetime, participation in the festival rites, or initiation into the "mysteries" of the sacred places—Abydos, Busiris, Saqqara, Heliopolis, Memphis, and Thebes—affords opportunities to be serviceable to the gods in a way that is decisive for the next-worldly fate of the one who does it, for these gods will in turn care for him after death. One who has served the gods during life will behold them "face to face" in the afterlife.

Certain motifs associated with this concept are old, going back to the Coffin Texts. The "spells for knowing the souls of the sacred places"[46] show that in the afterlife, it was of the greatest importance to be initiated into the mysteries of the sacred places, an initiation that we are probably to imagine took place during life. Particularly relevant for our text is Coffin Texts spell 314 = Book of the Dead chapter 1, certain of whose formulations have even been adopted verbatim in the harper's song. In this spell, just as in the harper's song, it is a matter of carrying out festival rituals that require a certain liturgical competence:

> I am a *wab*-priest in Busiris,
> one who elevates (?) He-on-the-Hill.[47]
> I am a priest of Abydos
> on the day the earth becomes high.
> It is I who see the mysteries in Rasetau,
> it is I who recite the festival scroll for the *Ba* of Mendes,
> I am the *sem*-priest in his office,
> I am the high priest of Memphis
> on the day the barque of Sokar is placed on its sledge.
> It is I who grasp the hoe
> on the day of Hacking the Earth in Herakleopolis.

Earlier in the spell, the deceased, who appears in the role of Thoth, and thus as the divine lector priest, declares to the god Osiris, who is being addressed, that he has participated along with Horus in the sacred rituals in Rasetau, Letopolis, and Heliopolis. In Rasetau, these mysteries consist of the embalming of Osiris:

> I was together with Horus
> on the day of covering the dismembered one,[48]
> when the caverns were opened and the Weary of Heart was washed,[49]
> when the entrance to the "Mysterious Place" was opened in Rasetau.[50]

At Letopolis, the ritual had to do with the left shoulder of Osiris:

> I was together with Horus
> as protector of that left[51] shoulder of Osiris in Letopolis,
> I went in and came out among those who are there[52]
> on the day on which the rebels were driven out in Letopolis.

At Heliopolis, the cult of the embalmed and buried Osiris was carried out in the form of the festival of the lunar month:

> I was together with Horus
> on the day of the festival of Osiris, when offerings were given[53]
> on the festival of the sixth and seventh lunar day at Heliopolis.

Whatever the original meaning of this text might have been in the Middle Kingdom, the harper's song in any case shows how relevant these statements were both before and after the Amarna Period, and it shows the extraordinary, even canonical, popularity that chapter 1 of the Book of the Dead had acquired at that time.[54] To judge from the title and the vignettes that accompany this chapter, it was recited on the day of burial.

The critical point was the concept that actual, earthly priesthood opened a way to immortality, for already during life, it conveyed divine presence through service of a god, a presence that extended beyond death and came to full fruition only after death, for the deceased only then actually came "face to face" with the gods, whereas during his lifetime, he had only been able to relate to their images. Initiation into the temples and cults of Egypt anticipated and prefigured the ultimate initiation into the mysteries of the realm of the dead. This initiation did not benefit only the priests. The major festivals also enabled the laity to serve the gods by assuming certain roles, and thus to enter into a relationship with them during life, a relationship they could then call on in the afterlife. This fact explains the important role that festivals and participation in them played in the mortuary beliefs of the New Kingdom. We shall return to this point in the next chapter.

The Egyptian texts, however, tell us nothing about the initiation of a priest into the mysteries of the sacred places. It is not until the reign of

Hadrian, that is, in the first half of the second century C.E., that we encounter such a text, and we find ourselves no longer in an Egyptian, but an Egyptianizing, context. But the text is so rich in genuinely Egyptian allusions, and it touches so closely on our theme that it is well worth considering here.

The text in question deals with the initiation of Lucius into the mysteries of Isis, as related by Apuleius in his novel *The Golden Ass.*[55] The scene is not Egypt but Cenchreae, the harbor of Corinth, where there was an Isis sanctuary. In the Hellenistic Isis religion, the goddess embodied her adherents' hope for eternal life, and she brought a great deal from her Egyptian past to this role. It was she who had awakened Osiris to new life through the power of her magical spells. And since, according to Egyptian belief, every individual became an Osiris by means of the mortuary rituals, his hope for immortality depended on Isis as well. There is good reason to think that ancient Egyptian burial customs lived on in the Hellenistic Isis mysteries, though in the latter case, they were enacted and interpreted not as a burial of the deceased but as an initiation of the living.

When Lucius, who has been transformed back from an ass into a man, wishes to be initiated into the mysteries of Isis, the priest advises caution:

> For the doorbolt of the netherworld and its saving protection lie in the hand of the goddess, and the ordination itself is celebrated as the reflection of a voluntary death and a salvation granted upon request. For when a lifetime is over and men stand on the threshold where light ends, then the goddess calls back from the netherworld those to whom the great mystery of religion was confidently entrusted, and she sets those who have in a certain sense been reborn through their providence once again on the course of a new life.

Initiation thus clearly had the sense of a prefiguration of death, one that conveyed to the mystic a divine presence that otherwise, according to the Egyptian view of things, was imparted only to the ritually "transfigured" dead. By voluntarily experiencing this symbolic death, the mystic qualified himself to be brought back to life by Isis on the day of his actual death.

When the day of the initiation finally comes, Lucius is first bathed (baptized), and the priest "expresses the forgiveness of the gods." The bath thus has the sacramental sense of a remission of sins. On the evening of the same day, there is the initiation, of which Apuleius gives only intimations:

> I entered the region of death
> and set my foot on the threshold of Proserpina,

and after I passed through all the elements, I turned back again.
In the middle of the night I saw
the sun shining in white light,
and I encountered the gods above and below
face to face and addressed them at close quarters.

Lucius is initiated into the mysteries of the netherworld. He carries out the *descensus* of the sun god, descending into the netherworld and beholding the sun at midnight. With these sentences, we cannot help but think of the Books of the Netherworld that are to be found on the walls of the Ramesside royal tombs and in the Osireion at Abydos.[56] We may imagine that the mystic was led into similarly decorated rooms—perhaps the crypts—of a temple. In any case, the process seems to be a symbolic journey through the netherworld, in which the netherworld is depicted, in an entirely Egyptian sense, as the subterranean realm of the midnight sun.

Such crypts existed in temples of the pharaonic era. At the Sacred Lake of Karnak, there is an edifice constructed by King Taharqa, a Kushite king of Dynasty 25 (end of the eighth century B.C.E.). Of this edifice, there remains only the subterranean portion, which is richly decorated with representations of solar and other rituals. The Osireion of the Osiris temple of Sethos I at Abydos is also such a crypt, though it is located next to, not under, the temple. It is entirely decorated with Books of the Netherworld. It seems quite likely to me that there were also such crypts decorated with Books of the Netherworld at Heliopolis. To me, it seems that in Egypt, the mystery of death and the mystery of cult and the holy coexisted so closely that they probably even interpenetrated one another.

The Books of the Netherworld were not, however, just patterns for the decoration of the royal tombs. They were also a sort of scholarly literature whose purpose was to codify and transmit knowledge of the netherworld. This knowledge was placed in the tomb along with the deceased king. But there is much in favor of, and nothing against, the idea that they also served in the instruction or initiation of the living. Certain scholars even see this as their actual purpose and consider their use as tomb decoration to be a secondary application. Such scholarly literature regarding the world beyond is also to be found in the nonroyal mortuary literature. The oldest work of this sort is the Book of Two Ways, a map with integrated texts; in the Middle Kingdom, and exclusively at el-Bersha, it was depicted on the floors of inner coffins. In the Book of the Dead of the New Kingdom, this literature consisted of all the spells that furnished the deceased with topographical knowledge of the world beyond, including the twelve caves (chapter 168), the seven gateway structures (144, 147), the twenty-one portals (145–146), the entrance to Rasetau

(117–119), the fourteen mounds (149), and the "Field of Reeds" (110). Would it be entirely erroneous to imagine that this image of death, too, had an influence on life, to the extent that some of this knowledge of the afterlilfe was acquired during life, in the sense of a preparation for death and its overcoming?

We encounter such a relationship between initiation during life and grave goods in Greece, in the framework of the Orphic and Dionysian mysteries. Small golden plaques were placed in the tombs of initiates, plaques incised with texts sketching a detailed scenery of the next world and affording the deceased orienting indications, precisely in the sense of a guidebook to the world beyond. They mention the house of Hades, to the right of which are two springs. Next to one of them is a brightly shining cypress tree (a manifestation of a topsy-turvy world, for cypresses are dark), while guards stand over the other. This other spring is fed by the Lake of Memory, from which the thirsty souls drink. To do this, they must enter into a dialogue with the guards, like those we know from dialogues in the Egyptian sources. They then arrive at a sacred road that they travel with other initiates. Other texts contain a dialogue of the deceased with the queen of the netherworld and describe a road that leads him or them to the sacred grove and meadow of Persephone.[57] These sources reveal a connection between death, initiation, and next-worldly topography that we should take into account, *mutatis mutandis*, at least as a possibility, with regard to Egyptian mortuary religion and its relationship to life.

From the Roman Period, though still from Egypt, we have shrouds that depict the deceased in the bloom of youth, in the clothing of the living, his unusually lively, portrait-like face represented frontally, looking straight at the viewer, between Anubis on the right and Osiris on the left. Osiris is mummiform and also represented frontally, while the jackal-headed Anubis is depicted in profile, holding the deceased by the hand.[58] These representations have found two contradictory interpretations. Siegfried Morenz interpreted them as "becoming Osiris." The deceased is supposedly represented twice: once in his individual form as a living person, and once as an Osirian mummy with the mask as the "head of a god." Anubis would then symbolize embalming as the process of transition that transformed the deceased into Osiris, the desired form of a transfigured ancestral spirit.[59] Klaus Parlasca, however, has interpreted these representations as the deceased being led by Anubis into the presence of Osiris. In this case, the figure on the left does not represent the deceased transformed into Osiris, but rather, the god to whom Anubis as psychopomp conducts the deceased.[60] In light of the image of death as mystery, especially in its late Hellenistic form, the two interpretations seem to be the two sides of a single coin. Initiation into the mysteries of a deity entailed the deification of the mystic. "Conducting into the presence of" and "becoming" Osiris comprise precisely these two aspects of initiation into the mysteries of Osiris. Egyptians of the Roman Period might easily have assented to both interpretations. This type of representation is the most beautiful and the most impressive expression of that dissociation and doubling that lies in the experience of death, and which we discussed in chapter 4 under the rubric "image and death."

In the Egyptian idea of the netherworld and its organization in the Books of the Netherworld, Erik Hornung would like to see a baring of the unconscious and of the depths of the human soul.[61] He sees the image of death as corresponding, in this life, to the unconscious, to the depths of the soul, to which, in his opinion, the descriptions of the Books of the Netherworld actually refer. This "baring" remained unknown to the Egyptians themselves, however, for they held what they depicted and described to be a next-worldly space in the depths of the netherworld. Dare we say that in doing so, in reality (and without knowing or desiring it), they were depicting the "depths" of the human soul? Or that they projected images from the depths of the soul into a cosmic next-worldly realm? I think it is essentially less risky to view the Books of the Netherworld and the guides to the world beyond as initiation literature, a secret knowledge guarded by special priests, probably priests of Heliopolis, and then placed with the king in his tomb. In any event, the Egyptian texts say one thing clearly enough: that all rituals, and especially those centered on Osiris and the sun god, were cloaked in mystery. And it is also clear that there is a relationship between initiation into these (ritual) mysteries and life in the next world. He who knew these things overcame the dangers of the realm of death and managed the passage into Elysium and the "going forth by day."

CHAPTER NINE

Going Forth by Day

1. This Life as the Afterlife: The "Reversed Polarity" of Mortuary Belief in the New Kingdom

All eight images of death considered to this point have centered on the transition from the condition of death to a new, higher form of life, transition from the realm of death to Elysium, and transition from the destruction wrought by physical death to a healthful restoration of body and person. This transition was accompanied by rituals whose purpose was to transform the deceased into a "transfigured ancestral spirit." But the mortuary rituals did not all end with the funeral; quite the contrary, there now began the offering cult at or in the tomb, a cult that was potentially supposed to last for all eternity. One idea underlay these rituals, and more than any other, it characterizes Egyptian mortuary belief: the concept of "going forth by day" (*pr.t m hrw*).

In the beginning, this concept did not have the absolutely paramount status it assumed from the New Kingdom on. Today, when we turn from the images of death to the images of the life of the tomb owner in the next world, we not only change theme but also feel that we are dealing with a far-reaching historical change. In the Old Kingdom, the idea of going forth by day does not yet seem to have played a role—in any event, it found no textual expression. When "going forth" is mentioned in the Pyramid Texts, it mostly refers to ascent to the sky; the Egyptian word *prj* means both "to go out" and "to go up." In the Old Kingdom, the verb *prj* was associated with the idea of a "departure into the world beyond," either (in the case of the king) an ascent to the sky or (in the case of normal deceased persons) in the form of a transition from the realm of the living to the "Beautiful West," and not, as later, the reversed idea of a "return to this world." The concept of going forth by day presupposed the netherworld, which first asserted itself in the Middle Kingdom as the place of the dead. The deceased desired to go forth from the netherworld to behold the light of day and communicate with the living. In the Pyramid Texts, the king, who had ascended to the sky, had no such wishes.

In the Middle Kingdom, the motif of going forth by day appeared sporadically, but at that time, along with a number of other motifs having to do with the deceased's freedom of movement in the afterlife. It was only in the New Kingdom that the idea of going forth by day came to prevail over all other concepts of life after death. Not only does the Book of the Dead bear this formula as its title ("The Spells of Going Forth by Day"), but one-seventh of its spells are also so titled. This change mirrors the development from the mortuary belief of kings, as codified in the Pyramid Texts, to the mortuary belief of the people, which asserted itself ever more strongly with the spread of the mortuary literature. Just as ascent to the sky and distancing from earth and the world of man was the central idea of royal mortuary belief, going forth by day and return to the world above was the central idea of popular mortuary belief.

We can tell the folk character of this idea by the oldest, most widespread, and longest lived symbol of Egyptian mortuary religion: the false door. This is the door through which the deceased, or his *ka* or *ba*, emerged to receive his offerings. The symbol of the door thus stood in complementary opposition to the symbol of the tomb mound, the stony mastabas and pyramids, or, in other cultures, to the symbol of the memorial slab, which shut the tomb off from the outside and the world above. By way of contrast, the door created an opening, a passageway, or, to express it in the language of computer technology, an "interface" between the netherworld and the world above.

During the New Kingdom, as the concept of going forth by day moved center stage in Egyptian mortuary belief, the false door also changed its form.[1] It now acquired a twofold frame and thereby a threefold division that expressed the concept of transition from inside to outside. In the inscriptions of the "outer" and "inner frames," there was a regular distinction in the choice of the gods mentioned and the acts of grace requested of them. Both frames were inscribed with "offering formulas." On the outer frame, they were directed to the sun god in two different forms, at Osiris in two forms, or, quite often, at the sun god and Osiris. The lines of the inner frame never mention the sun god; here, Anubis dominates, along with Osiris, Sokar, and Ptah-Sokar. Alone or in connection with Osiris, the sun god stands for the world above and this life, into which the deceased hopes to return in altered form in the daytime: this is unequivocally a "going forth by day." The requests that the tomb owner directs to these gods refer to offerings, and thus concern things brought from outside into the tomb, and which the deceased hoped to receive by emerging from the world beyond. Anubis, however, alone or in connection with Osiris, Sokar, or Ptah-Sokar, stands for the sarcophagus chamber, the netherworld, and the next life, into which the deceased hoped to enter for eternal rest, hiddenness, and divine presence. The wishes in the lines of the inner frame had to do with leaving and entering, and with the welfare of the deceased in the afterlife. The inscriptions in the lines of the outer frame are closely analogous to the decoration of the entrance to the tomb, where the tomb owner was often depicted reciting hymns to the sun god in two forms or to the sun god and Osiris, with the left lines of the frame and the left (southern) wall decoration corresponding to the right frame lines and the right (northern) wall decorations. The innermost inscribed vertical strips, the "door posts," contain *jmȝḫjj ḫr* formulas intended to place the deceased in the care of the Sons of Horus. The Sons of Horus, deities of embalming like Anubis, stand for the innermost zone. By means of this differentiation between inside and outside, the false door acquired a spatial significance that reflected the tomb itself. The false door of Dynasty 18 can be described as a "mise en abîme" (a small-scale reproduction) of the tomb. The false door can thus be clearly and unequivocally interpreted as a two-dimensional projection of the three zones of the tomb. The outer frame corresponds to the entrance of the tomb, with its courtyard and (in some cases) superstructure, the inner frame corresponds to the accessible spaces of the tomb chapel (as interface between this world and the world beyond), and the door posts correspond to the sarcophagus chamber, in which the Sons of Horus keep watch over the mummy of the deceased. In its arrangement and its inscriptions, the false door realizes the same triple semantics of outside and inside that underlies the overall concept of the Dynasty 18 tomb.

After the Amarna Period, the false door disappeared from Theban tomb architecture, making way for a new form: the false door stela. Here, a stela featuring projections and recesses similar to what had previously framed the false door was placed in the cult chamber. Characteristic of these stelae was the fact that their decoration was not organized according to the scheme of outside and inside but to that of above and below. For the most part, the stela now had two representational fields. In the upper field, the tomb owner addresses the gods, while in the lower field, he is the beneficiary of the mortuary cult. As in the decoration of false doors, the theme is the receiving of offerings: the false door stela marks the cult place where offerings were deposited. But in this case, the concept of passage and emergence is less important than that of divine presence and of the analogy between the mortuary cult, in which the tomb owner participated as object (recipient) and the divine cult, in which he was the subject (officiant).

A sure indication of this development is supplied by the requests attached to the mortuary prayer known as the "ḥtp-dj-njswt formula." This prayer begins with the words "an offering that the king gives to this or that god . . . that he may give," followed by a series of requests. Over the course of the centuries, these requests changed. Sporadic requests to go forth by day first appear in the Middle Kingdom. On one stela, the deceased expresses the wish to "go forth by day on every festival."[2] The wish to return to the realm of the living is thus attached to the notion of festival. Offering formulas appear mainly on false doors, and lists of festivals are a favorite theme in these offering formulas. We may thus conclude that it was on the occasion of religious festivals that the deceased expected to receive offerings from those he had left behind. The wish to return was originally, and especially, a wish to receive mortuary offerings, and thus for cultic contact with the world above. Various expressions of this request appear already in Dynasties 13 and 14: one person wishes to "go forth by day on every beautiful festival of Osiris,"[3] another to "go forth by day from the realm of the dead,"[4] and a third to "go forth by day on the Great Festival of Vindication at Abydos, together with the venerated ones."[5] In this third case, it is no longer a matter of receiving offerings, but of participating in the "Osiris mysteries" at Abydos. In the Middle Kingdom, there began the practice of erecting offering chapels at Abydos for the purpose of postmortem participation in the processional festival of Osiris. Connected with this practice was the concept of religious festival as a sacred interval of time in which the gates of the netherworld were open, and the deceased were able to return to the world above to celebrate along with the living. Later, we shall return to this concept in greater detail. In the New Kingdom, this wish was related to other festivals: "to go forth by day to see Amun on his Beautiful Festival of the Valley,"[6] or "to go forth by day in the following of His Majesty on this day of circumambulating the walls on the festival of Sokar."[7] Above all, the concept of going forth by day was connected with that of transformation, which was the central concept of Egyptian mortuary belief in the New Kingdom. Thus, we encounter wishes such as "to go forth by day in any form he wishes,"[8] or "to go forth by day as a living ba to behold the sun disk when it rises"[9] and "to go forth from the earth as a living ba."[10] "Changing into a living ba" was one of the transformations to which the deceased aspired, and the term *ba* denoted the capacity to change into any form whatsoever.

From the Egyptian point of view, the capacity to transform was one of the most important means of freeing oneself from the realm of death. In the Pyramid Texts, the king assumes various forms in order to ascend from the earth to the sky and to free himself from the realm of the dead, and in the Middle Kingdom, the deceased attempted a host of transformations in order to be saved from the realm of death and enter Elysium. The ability to transform saved the deceased from the topsy-turvy world, prevented him from having to eat excrement, and freed him from the motionless state of rigor mortis, from being locked up in the coffin and the sarcophagus chamber, from the bonds of the mummy bandages. It endowed him with the freedom to move about in all the realms of the cosmos, including occasionally, but in no way centrally, the world above:

(may he grant) that N. enter his house and look at his nestlings,
that he "do what is pleasant"[11] in his grove in the company of those in the
    world above, for ever and ever,
that he assume all the forms he wishes to assume.
Truly, the illustrious god, the one in his egg, has ordained
that N. is to breathe on the day of the great ceremony (*jrw* ꜥ).[12]

Similar words conclude Coffin Texts spell 405, which deals with the Field of Offerings, an Elysian realm in the afterlife. The deceased who wishes to reach it must undergo various interrogations. At the end, the tribunal of this field announces its findings:[13]

> He shall drink water in the place of drinking!
> Grant that he "does what is pleasant":
> that he sing and dance and put on jewelry;
> that he play the board game with those in the world above,
> his voice being heard without his being seen;
> that he go to his house and look at his nestlings,
> forever and ever.

Typically, it is the Field of Offerings or the Field of Reeds, the Elysian goal of the deceased's journey in the world beyond, to which he is granted the ability to return, as though it were a matter of an especially this-worldly place in the world beyond. The person who arrives there finds it easy to "go out and go in," as it is put in Egyptian, that is, to leave the realm of death each morning, and visit the realm of the living, and to return each night to the netherworld. Elysium is thus pervious to the realm of the living. Here, the inversions of the realm of death are erased, and the world is restored to order, eminently habitable and beneficial to life. In the texts that deal with the Field of Reeds and the Field of Offerings, we encounter a curious interpenetrability between this world and the world beyond, a fact that is also true of the concept of life after death.

The transfigured ancestral spirit accomplishes this shuttling back and forth between the two realms through his capacity to assume various forms. In the New Kingdom, and in the conceptual world of the Book of the Dead, this aspect became predominant. The formula "going forth by day" no longer referred to a single occasion of salvation from the realm of death, but to the deceased's daily preoccupation with his freedom of movement between the world above and the world below.

Chapter 86 of the Book of the Dead enables the deceased to change into a swallow. The postscript elucidates the purpose of this transformation:

> The one who knows this spell enters (again), after going forth by day,
> in any form in which he wishes to emerge from the Field of Reeds.[14]

The spell itself deals with the deceased's return to the netherworld in the evening. To the doorkeepers of the realm of the dead, he says:

> Give me your hand,
> I have spent the day on the "Isle of Fire" (i.e., the world above).
> I left with instructions,
> and I have returned on a mission.
> Open up to me, that I may relate what I have seen!

In what follows, the deceased reports to those in the netherworld what things are like in the realm above:

> Horus is the helmsman of the boat,
> the throne of his father Osiris has been transferred to him,
> and that Seth, the son of Nut,
> is in the chains he had intended for him.
> I have checked what is in Letopolis:
> it is the left shoulder of Osiris.
> I have gone forth to check,
> and I have returned to report.
> Let me by, that I may deliver my message!

The deceased also refers to his status as a transfigured spirit, which was bestowed on him at the Judgment of the Dead:

> I am one who goes in examined
> and goes forth confirmed from the gate of the All-lord.

I have been purified in that great district,
I have eliminated my evil and know no wrong,
I have power over the course of the light.

I know the inaccessible ways
and the gates of the Field of Reeds.
Behold, I am there—
I have brought down my earthly enemies,
and my corpse is buried.

The deceased has behind him all that is connected with transformation into an ancestral spirit and with transition into eternal life. Now, his desire is to lead this life. He wishes to leave the netherworld each morning to visit the world above and to return again each evening. Spell 340 of the Coffin Texts already expresses the wish to "enter after going forth." Its postscript reads, "The one who recites this spell finds entry into the West after his exit; but the one who does not know this spell as one who understands how to go out by day finds no entry thereafter."[15]

A typical Dynasty 18 wish on behalf of the deceased expresses this desire to go forth and go in as follows:

> May you go forth and go in according to your desire,
> in all the forms you wish to assume.[16]

The deceased leaves the netherworld as neither a mummy nor a ghost. Nor is he reborn to a new life on earth. Transformation is the medium of his freedom of movement between the two realms. The Egyptian word *ba*, which we translate as "soul," is a concept having to do with power, and it refers first and foremost to the capacity to assume or breathe life into various forms:

> May your *b3* be *3ḫ*-effective[17] for you in the realm of the dead
> and assume forms daily.[18]

These forms include the statues in the tomb chapel. Mortuary belief assumed that the *ba*s of the deceased inhabited the statues, and that they could also assume, that is, breathe life into, all other possible forms in the world above. Twelve such forms are canonized in chapters 76–88 of the Book of the Dead. Spell 76 has the title "Spell for assuming any form one wishes," and it functions as an introduction to the cycle of spells that follows. Spell 77 serves to "assume the form of the golden falcon," 78 to transform into a "divine falcon," 79 enables transformation into the "greatest of the divine tribunal," 80 has the title "Transforming into a god and lighting the darkness," 81 is entitled "Assuming form as a lotus blossom," 82 is "Assuming form as Ptah," 83 is "Assuming form as a phoenix," 84 is "Assuming form as a heron," 85 is "Assuming form as a living *ba*, not going to the Place of Slaughter," 86 is "Assuming form as a swallow," 87 is "Assuming form as a *Sa-ta*-serpent," and 88 is "Assuming form as a crocodile." These 1 + 12 spells constitute a consistent sequence within the Book of the Dead and a book in its own right, which might have been called "Book of Transformations."[19]

In tomb inscriptions, the wish to transform into a "living *ba*" is expressed thus:

> Transforming into a living *ba*
> so as to alight on his grove
> and enjoy the shade of its sycamores
> and sit in the rear part of the pyramid,
> while his statues endure in his house
> and receive the offerings,
> and while his corpse remains, without being lost
> to the Lord of Life (= coffin),
> after he (i.e., the deceased) has taken his seat . . . for the future.[20]

> Transforming into a living *ba*
> that has disposal over water, bread, and air,
> changing into a phoenix and a swallow
> . . . to receive the offerings set (before the god)
> and what is proffered to the lord of the sacred district.[21]

> . . . transforming into a living *ba*.
> May he again see his house of the living,
> so as to be a protection to his children daily,
> forever and ever.[22]

The purpose of this return to the world above was first and foremost to receive offerings. Deceased persons wanted to return to earth and participate in the offering cult in their tomb. This return is the topic of a text from Theban Tomb 72, which can stand here for many similar statements:

> Going out as a living *ba*
> to eat what is given him on earth,
> going in and out of Imhet,
> striding freely out through the gates of the netherworld.[23]

Egyptians thus did not conceive of the dead as dwelling in their tomb, but rather in a distant realm beyond, from which they emerged and came to their tomb in the land of the living to receive their mortuary meals. In all periods, taking a meal was interpreted as an act that created a sense of community, freeing the deceased from his isolation and integrating him into a tightly knit social sphere. In the Old and Middle Kingdoms, this sphere was the society of the sun god and other celestial deities. In Dynasty 18, the tomb owner took his mortuary meal in the company of his relatives and friends. This idea dominated the scenes on the walls of tombs, where now, the traditional scene of offering nourishment to the deceased often became a depiction of a festive banquet. These scenes emphasized the this-worldly character of the mortuary meal and its meaning as a reunion of the deceased with his family and friends. Festivals, in particular the "Beautiful Festival of the Valley," played a predominant role as occasions for reunions.[24] Just as a tomb was a sacred place enabling contact to be made between this world and the next one, a festival was a sacred time that facilitated such contact. To the "this-worldliness" of the concept of the next life, there corresponded a "next-worldliness," or sacralization, of this life. The more explicitly the deceased were believed to make their way back into the world of the living, the more intensely this world became laden with sacral meaning.

The introduction of "this-worldliness" was the decisive change in Egyptian mortuary belief. It characterized the New Kingdom, the centuries from 1500 to 1100 B.C.E. The decisive indication of this change is to be found in the texts from Amarna.[25] Amarna religion is renowned above all for its exclusive monotheism. Amenophis IV/Akhenaten abolished all the temples and festivals of traditional religion in favor of his new cult of a single god, the sun (Aten).[26] This upheaval also had decisive consequences for mortuary religion. At Amarna, belief in the afterlife represented, as Hornung formulates it, "a total reversal in the polarity of mortuary belief, from west to east, from the next world to this one." The dead no longer rested in a realm that was believed to be subterranean, where the sun temporarily aroused them during its nightly journey, but in the tomb, which they left in the morning, just like the living, to move about in the world of the living in the form of their *ba*. As Hornung writes, "beliefs regarding the afterlife at Amarna can thus be summarized quite simply: the dead slept at night, and in the daytime they accompanied the Aten and the royal family to the Great Temple, where all were provisioned."[27] The dead no longer lived in the sky and the netherworld, but at Amarna. They shared in the offerings in the temple, accompanied the king on his excursions, and strolled in their gardens. A text from the tomb of Pentu is typical of this new mortuary belief:

> May you grant that I rest in my place of eternity,
> that I join my cavern of everlastingness,
> entering and leaving my house
> without my *ba* being blocked from what it desires,

that I may stroll as I wish
in the garden I have made on earth,
that I may drink water at the edge of my pond,
day after day, without cease.[28]

In another text, we read,

May you set me forever in the place of the praised ones,
in my house of vindication.
My *ba*, may it go forth to behold your rays,
and to eat of its offerings.
May one call on my name,
may one (= my *ba?*) come at the call,
may I receive the offerings that go forth from the Presence (= from the
    temple),
may I partake of the nourishment of bread and beer,
roasted and boiled meat,
cool water, wine, and milk,
that go out from the temple of the Aten at Akhetaten.[29]

Hornung is entirely correct in drawing attention to the revolutionary character of this mortuary belief. In fact, it entailed a reversal of the polarity of hopes for the afterlife, which were now directed entirely toward the realm of the living. This belief, however, was not an achievement of the Amarna Period; rather, it characterized all the mortuary belief of the New Kingdom, and it was in precisely this respect that it signified a revolutionizing of the traditional mortuary religion. What was revolutionary in the Amarna texts was the absolutizing of this aspect at the cost of all other conceptions of life after death. Before and after Amarna, these new ideas were embedded in a host of traditional concepts and were only a part of the total thematic spectrum of the mortuary texts, whereas at Amarna, they constituted the totality of the postmortem existence to which the deceased aspired. At Amarna, the world of the living replaced the traditional concepts of a next-worldly realm, whereas otherwise in the New Kingdom, it complemented the "classical" realms of sky and netherworld, playing the principal role in hopes for life after death.

2. *Festival and Garden as Elysian Aspects of the Realm of the Living*

a) Visits Home

The motif of going forth by day is connected with the wish to return to the world above, and in particular, to four places:

- the tomb, for the purpose of receiving offerings;
- one's home, for the purpose of visiting one's posterity;
- the garden, so as to alight as a bird on the sycamore and stroll in its shadow; and
- on the occasion of festivals, first and foremost that of Osiris at Abydos, but also the festival of Sokar at Memphis and the Festival of the Valley at Thebes, for the purpose of participating in processions along with the living.

Visits home are the topic of chapter 132 of the Book of the Dead, which is entitled, "Spell for Turning Back into a Man so as to See His House Again." The vignette depicts a man striding, staff in hand, toward a house. But the spell itself seems to be in no way related to this theme:

> I am the lion who set out with a bow,
> I have shot and I have shackled.
> I am the Eye of Horus,
> and I have spread open the Eye of Horus at this time.

No one would suspect that this is a description of a visit home. And yet, this motif is clearly stated in tomb inscriptions. Thus, in a mortuary spell that was especially popular in early Dynasty 18, we read:

> One says to you, "Welcome, welcome!"
> in this your house of the living.[30]

In the tomb of Tjanuni (Theban Tomb 76, reign of Tuthmosis IV, ca. 1420 B.C.E.), the tomb owner is depicted on the right thickness of the entrance, making just such a visit to his home. The accompanying text explains the scene:

> Going in and out of the realm of the dead,
> without being turned away at the gate of the *Duat.*
> Transforming, as desired,
> to visit his family of the living.[31]

In a text from a tomb dating to the reign of Tuthmosis III, the deceased is wished:

> May you open the mound of the realm of the dead,
> so as to see your house of the living again.
> May you hear the sound of song and music
> in your (dwelling?-)house[32] in this land.
> May you be a protection for your children,
> forever and ever.[33]

On a group statue from Dynasty 18, the deceased prays

> to go forth as a living *ba* in order to open the mound
> on the day of the fighting of the Two Lands,[34]
> to see his house of the living again,
> as was his custom on earth.[35]

To this wish to return home, there was connected the age-old concept of the ancestral spirit as protector of his family, a concept that lay at the heart of the Letters to the Dead. At first, it was believed that in the afterlife, the deceased would come to the aid of his bereaved relatives in the law court of the netherworldly gods. Now, there was added the idea of entering and leaving, and that of a return to the world above. Thus, in an inscription on a door post in the Memphite tomb of a man named Paser, we read:

> May you alight upon your place on the western mountain (i.e., the tomb).
> May you incriminate (your enemies) and heed the petitions
> of the children and the servants of your house.[36]

In a number of New Kingdom Theban tombs, there are representations of such a visit by the tomb owner to his house. These are elaborate versions of the vignette to chapter 32 of the Book of the Dead, and they are our most important source for house architecture in the New Kingdom.[37] But these are mostly scenes from the life of the tomb owner, as in Theban Tomb 23, from the reign of Merneptah (ca. 1220 B.C.E.), where the following inscription accompanies the representation of a visit by the tomb owner to his home:

> May you enter your house of the living,
> rejoicing and jubilating.
> May you receive the favor of the king,
> coming out vindicated.
> Amun-Re protects you daily,
> Mut drives away your enemies,
> Khons-in-Thebes is the protection of your body,
> the moon keeps you healthy daily.
> May they grant you the West of old age,
> for you are *akh*-effective for their *ka*.[38]

These are the words with which the wife of the tomb owner greets him as he returns home, but they clearly refer to the living, not the dead. Still, we may presume that the tomb owner commissioned this scene from his existence on earth because he wished to keep repeating it in his capacity as a transfigured deceased person.

b) Visiting the Garden

In the mortuary wishes of the New Kingdom, a visit to the garden played an even greater role than a visit to the house itself. The two motifs are combined in the following text, which is a prayer to Osiris:

> May I go forth and enter to see my people,
> may I stroll around my "canal pond,"
> may my *ba* sit on that sycamore,
> may I be refreshed in its shade and drink its water.[39]

Such a visit of the tomb owner to his garden is represented on a pillar in the tomb of Amenemheb (Theban Tomb 85 [Cd]). The accompanying text reads:

> Going forth to the city to see Amun,
> that I may enjoy the radiance of his sun disk.
> Cheering the heart in the western lea,
> going into and out of the garden with its pond
> to cool the heart under its trees.
> Performing (?) the work of the goddess of the fields [. . .] of her flower,
> drinking water from his bird pond,
> smelling lotus blossoms and plucking buds
> by N.[40]

The following text, which occurs with many variants in Dynasty 18, can be viewed as the classic expression of this wish:

> Going into and out of my tomb
> to refresh myself in its shadow,
> to drink water from my pond daily,
> that all my limbs may flourish.
> May Hapi supply me with nourishment and offerings,
> and vegetables in their season.
> May I stroll at the edge of my pond
> daily, without cease,[41]
> may my *ba* alight[42] on the branches of the trees I have planted,
> may I refresh myself under the branches of my sycamores
> and eat the bread that they give.[43]

This text describes the garden as a paradise, just like the Field of Reeds and the Field of Offerings, which the deceased visits in the Coffin Texts;

it is a place of refreshment and unending plenitude of nourishment. Here, however, it is unequivocally a garden in the realm of the living, one planted by the tomb owner himself, and not a place in the next world. Here are two further examples of this motif from inscriptions of Dynasty 18:

> May you go as you please
> to the beautiful shore of your lake.
> May your heart rejoice in your wooded garden,
> when you cool yourself under the sycamores.
> May your heart take satisfaction in the Nun[44]
> in the fountain you have created,
> for ever and ever.[45]

> Transforming into a living *ba*,
> oh, may he glide down onto his grove,
> may he enjoy the shadow of his sycamores,
> may he rest (*sndm*) at the corner of his pool,
> while his statues remain in his house,
> and receive what is given on earth,
> while his corpse rests in the tomb chamber.[46]

Such a tomb garden, one that corresponds exactly to the descriptions in the mortuary wishes, is in fact archaeologically known: in the forecourt of the mortuary temple of Amenhotep son of Hapu at Medinet Habu. It represents the ideal tomb garden, as described in the texts, but which in most cases was realized only cursorily.[47] In the middle of the forecourt, there was a rectangular basin, eighty-five feet long, surrounded by twenty trees, presumably sycamores. The remains of fish were found inside the basin. The following text from a tomb of the Ramesside Period refers unequivocally to a tomb garden of this sort, which in this case, as undoubtedly in most other cases, could be realized only symbolically:

> May your house that is on earth thrive
> in the district of Ahmose-Nofretari.[48]
> May your trees blossom and not wither.
> May you alight on their branches.
> May your pond be full, without fail . . .
> May you go about on your pond at your usual times,
> may you be conveyed on the body of water you have dug.
> May you snare its *r3*-geese and catch its fish in (your) net,
> May you sit at its fish pond.[49]
> May one fashion for you a *neshmet*-barque from (the wood) of your
>   sycamores.
> May one prepare offerings for you from its *pr.t*-fruits

and its *jšd*-fruits for every sacrifice.
Its dried fruits are intended for you as summer produce,
and its bread loaves are intended for you as winter produce.[50]

The expression "your house in the district of Ahmose-Nofretari" can only
refer to the tomb, for the district was part of the Theban necropolis. The
garden the text goes on to describe must therefore have belonged to this
tomb. Here, the pond served not only to refresh the deceased and provision him with fish and birds but also as a place for sacral processions by
water. The *neshmet*-barque that was to be constructed for the deceased out
of the wood of his sycamores was a ritual boat employed during the mysteries of Osiris at Abydos. Tomb representations show that boats were
indeed used in such garden ponds. Such scenes, known as "Totenfeier im
Garten" (celebrations of the deceased in the garden) occur in Theban
and Memphite tombs, in connection with the funeral and with various
festivals.[51] The type of boat depicted in these representations is regularly
the *neshmet*-barque. The garden thus had an unmistakably sacral character. It was a place in this world, not in the next one, like the Field of Reeds
and the Field of Offerings, but it was a sacred place where rituals were
carried out, and where deities important to the deceased were present.

The garden with its pool was first and foremost a place of plenitude, a
source of never-ending nourishment.[52] It shared this quality with the
Egyptian Elysium, the Field of Reeds and the Field of Offerings. From as
early as Dynasty 11, we have a representation of the tomb owner in a
garden with a pool, with the caption:

> Birds from what the goddess of the fields brings you,
> fresh vegetables from what Hapy brings you.[53]

A libation spell that was widespread in Dynasty 18 contains the following
wish on behalf of the deceased:

> May the goddess of the fields come to you with her fish,
> and the mistress of fishing with her geese.[54]

As personifications of fertility and provisioning, the goddess of the fields
and Hapy (the Nile inundation), along with the "mistress of fishing," represented the most important aspect of Elysium in the eyes of the Egyptians: plenitude of nourishment and eternal inexhaustibility of provisions
for the deceased. In earlier periods, the Egyptian sought these essentials
for his immortality especially in the next world; now, in the New Kingdom,
he sought it in this world, in the world of the living, which thus assumed
traits of paradise.

We can elucidate the shift of accent between this world and the next one with the help of a single detail: the figure of the tree goddess. In the Pyramid Texts, and then in the Coffin Texts, the tree goddess appears as an absolutely next-worldly figure in the form of a sycamore, whom the deceased approaches and under whose branches he will live on inexhaustible nourishment.[55] In mortuary wishes of Dynasty 18, however, the sycamore under which the deceased wishes to rest in the form of a *ba*[56] stands in a this-worldly (*tp-t3*) garden:

. . .[57]

> May my *ba* alight on the branches of the trees I have planted,
> may I refresh myself under the branches of my sycamores
> and eat of the bread that they give.[58]

Clearly, these texts speak not of the tree goddess but of an entirely this-worldly tree, whose real-worldly, profane character is emphasized by the possessive pronoun ("your sycamores"). Dynasty 18 was the high point of the this-worldly orientation of mortuary belief, which, as we have seen, reached its culmination in the religion of Amarna. Afterwards, the theme of the garden continued into the Ramesside Period. Ramesside texts also speak of the sycamore in this world, but they make note of the great tree goddess:

> May I go to my "canal pool,"
> may my *ba* sit on that sycamore,
> may I refresh myself in its shadow and drink its water.[59]

Here again, it is clearly a matter of a this-worldly garden with a pool.[60] But at the same time, the turn of expression "*that* sycamore" clearly alludes to the tree goddess. The garden and its pool now seem to be not just a source of provisioning and refreshment but also a place of festival occasions, and thus a sacral place. The texts of the Ramesside Period represent this aspect of the garden. They do not defer events into the next world; rather, they express the religious meaning of things that occur in this world. The actual sycamore of the tomb garden now became the manifestation, or, as the Egyptians put it, the "name" of the goddess Nut. The tree goddess was often depicted in the tombs of the post-Amarna and Ramesside Periods. For example, in the tomb of the vizier Paser (Theban Tomb 106), she is called:

> Nut, the great, with saving power,
> in that name of hers "sycamore."[61]

In Theban Tomb 41, Amenemope turns to her with the following prayer:

> Grant that my *ba* alight on your leaves,
> that it sit in your shadow and drink your water.[62]

With this development, the tomb garden, and this world in general, have become a sacred place where the deceased wishes to return. We must thus acknowledge an unmistakable "sacralization" of the tomb, which now became a this-worldly locus of divine presence.

c) Participation in Major Divine Festivals

If we can understand the garden as a this-worldly god of divine presence, given that in the Egyptian imagination, it assumed ever stronger traits of an Elysium, the same is even more unequivocally true in the case of festivals. The sacralization of the world of the living was clearest in the festival culture of the New Kingdom. As the Egyptians conceived it, for the duration of a festival, the opposition between this world and the next was eliminated, or at the very least, diminished.[63] The god appeared to men, the tombs of the dead were visited, and the tomb owners were involved in the festival events. This joining of the two realms took place in a temporally and spatially defined framework: in the sacred time of the festival and the sacred space of the city. Around this idea, which went back to the Middle Kingdom and the "mysteries" of Osiris at Abydos, there developed a new form of festival culture and mortuary belief, one that became predominant in the New Kingdom. The festival was an otherworldly enclave in the realm of the living. In this sense, the concept of "mystery," as it gained currency in the festival of Abydos, is entirely justified.

In the Middle Kingdom, the wish to participate in festivals after death was connected exclusively with the so-called Osiris mysteries at Abydos:[64]

> May he go out with the Great God
> in the divine procession to Poqer.[65]
> May he go out on the great festival of vindication
> at Abydos in the company of those provisioned in the afterlife (*jmȝḫw*).[66]

These wishes found their most important and most explicit expression in the so-called Abydos formula, which is attested from the Middle Kingdom in any number of variants.[67] The version that follows is from the stela of the sealbearer Meri (Louvre C3), from year 9 of Senwosret I:

I: Arrival and Welcome at Abydos:

May hands heaped with offerings be extended to him
on the festivals of the necropolis,
together with the followers of Osiris.
May the great ones of Busiris transfigure him,
and the household in Abydos.
May he open the ways he strives for
in peace, in peace.
May the inhabitants of Ta-wer elevate him,
and the *wab*-priests of the Great God.

II. Participation in the Journey of the *Neshmet*-barque

May arms be reached out to him in the *neshmet*-barque
on the ways of the West;
may he ply the rudder in the night barque,
and may he sail in the day-barque.
May "welcome!" be said to him
by the great ones of Abydos,
when he crosses with the Great God to Ra-poqer,
and the great *neshmet*-barque maintains its course
during the festivals of the necropolis.
May the Bull of the West transfigure him,
may he help him with his oars.

III. Participation in the Nocturnal Rites of the *Haker*-festival:

May he hear the acclamations from the mouth of Ta-wer
during the *"Haker"*-festival on the night of sleep,
during the wake of Horus *"Shen."*

IV. Transfiguration in the Place of Birth (*Meskhenet*):[68]

May he traverse the beautiful ways to the opening in the western horizon,
to the district where offerings are brought,
and to the gateway "Great of Praise."
May Khnum and Heqet transfigure him,[69]
the ancestors who originated formerly,
on the birthing place (*Meskhenet*) on which Abydos lies,
which came out of the mouth of Re himself
when Abydos was sanctified on it (by means of it?).

V. Provision of Offerings at Abydos

May they give him pure offerings,
together with the followers of Osiris.
May the inhabitants of Ta-wer acclaim him,
may Osiris advance his position
before the great ones in the Sacred Land.
May he have a superfluity of offerings and food

and Osiris' abundance of food
on the *Wag*-festival and the Thoth festival,
on the "torch" festival, on the New Year's festival,
on the great festivals of the First One and of the Great Procession,
and on all festivals that are celebrated for the Great God.

May the *mhwn*-priest extend his arm to him
with offerings of the Great God.
May he sit at the right of Osiris
at the head of the illustrious nobles.
May he arrive at the tribunal of the god,
and may he follow him (the god) on all the pure roads in the Sacred
    Land.
May he receive offerings on the great offering slab
as his daily requirement, every day.[70]

Without this lengthy text and its history, we would be unable to make
a correct evaluation of the theme of "festival participation" in the mortuary belief of the New Kingdom. Many (though by no means all) of the
stelae bearing this text come from Abydos, while a great many of them
come from Thebes and other places. It is thus clear that the prominence
of Abydos and its rituals in this spell was not conditioned by where the
stelae were set up, or by the function of the stelae; rather, they reflect the
general meaning of the theme "Abydos" in Egyptian mortuary belief in
that period. On stelae of the New Kingdom, this theme of festival participation continued to play a role, one that was extended to other religious
centers, though Abydos remained the most prominent in this connection.

We owe most of our information regarding the sequence of events in
this festival to Ikhernofret, a high official under Senwosret III, whom the
king sent to Abydos with the task of restoring the temple of Osiris and
organizing the festival there. According to Ikhernofret's stela, the festivi-
ties included the following four acts:[71]

I. The Procession of Wepwawet ("Opener-of-the-Ways"):

I arranged the procession of Wepwawet, when he went to the aid of his father.
I beat back those who rebelled against the *neshmet*-barque and subdued the
enemies of Osiris.[72]

Wepwawet was represented as a jackal standing on a standard that was
carried in front of the king in processions during the Archaic Period for
the purpose of "opening the way" for him during his processions. In the
festival at Abydos, Wepwawet was a manifestation of the "victorious Horus"
who came to the aid of his father by subduing his enemies. This subduing of the enemy was a ritual that consisted of recitations accompanied

by actions, such as mutilation and burning of wax figures, or "breaking the red pots," or a ritual slaughter.[73]

II. The "Great Procession" in the *Neshmet*-barque:

I arranged the Great Procession and accompanied the god on his way. I caused the divine barque to sail, and Thoth granted that the journey went well. I outfitted the barque "Appearing in Maat" of the lord of Abydos with a cabin and put on his crown. How beautiful was his procession to the district of U-poqer! I sanctified the ways of the god to his grave at the peak of U-poqer.[74]

What is described here is the funeral procession of Osiris. For the deceased, participating in this procession, traveling in the *neshmet*-barque crowned with the "wreath of vindication," was the highest goal. Spells of the Middle Kingdom contain such wishes on behalf of the deceased:

> May he travel with the Great God
> on the divine crossing to Ra-poqer.
> (May he follow) the *neshmet*-barque on its journey
> during the festivals of the necropolis.[75]

III. The Night of the "Battling Horus": The Haker Festival

I took action for Wennefer on that day of the great battle. I subdued all his enemies on the sand bank of Nedyt.[76]

Here, we think first of the battle that was enacted to accompany the funeral procession of the god to U-poqer; other inscriptions inform us of ritual battles at Abydos:

> I am one at the head of the fighters.
> I rejoiced . . .
> when Horus killed the crooked of heart.[77]

> I directed the work in the barque
> and repelled the one who rose up against His Majesty.[78]

> May you seize the tow rope at the prow of the divine barque
> when it crosses in Ta-wer to U-poqer.
> May you rejoice there with the Following of Horus
> when the enemies are smitten for him.[79]

The meaning of this act, however, is something else entirely. "That day of battle" alludes to the contending of Horus and Seth, that part of the festival drama which is called "the night of the battling Horus" or "the night of the Haker festival" in other texts.[80] In the mortuary cult, this night corresponds to the "night of vindication,"[81] when the Judgment of the Dead occurred at the conclusion of the embalming process. On this night, a wake was held:

> May he hear the cries of joy in the mouth of Ta-wer
> on the occasion of the Haker festival during the night of sleep
> and the night wake of the battling Horus.[82]

IV. The Procession to the Temple of Osiris

I caused him to go out in procession to the interior of the "Great One" (i.e., the *neshmet*-barque); it bore his beauty. I broadened the heart of the eastern desert, I created jubilation in the western desert, when they saw the beauty of the *neshmet*-barque, after it put in at Abydos in order to bring Osiris Khentamentiu to his palace (in the temple). I conducted the god to his house. His purification was carried out, his places were made broad. . . .[83]

The last act of the festival was the return of the god to the temple. Just as the procession to U-poqer was celebrated as a funeral procession and the night spent there as the "night of vindication," so the return was interpreted as a triumphal entry of the vindicated and resurrected Osiris into his palace.[84]

The sanctity of Abydos dates back to the First Intermediate Period, the period after the collapse of the Old Kingdom and a time of deep-reaching cultural reorientation, as Egyptians reached back in time to before the Old Kingdom, to the earliest Egyptian royal necropolis, interpreting it as the ideal necropolis and the center of mortuary belief, where the netherworld and the world above communicated in a mysterious manner. The sanctity of Abydos was thus a matter of reaching back over a thousand years in time. In the Old Kingdom, this center had been Memphis, with its Residence cemeteries stretching out along the edge of the western desert. Here, Sokar was the god of the dead, and his name survives in the place name Saqqara. With the end of the Old Kingdom, the institution of Residence cemeteries disappeared, and the pyramid rituals came to an end. They were succeeded by Abydos and its Osiris mysteries, which were none other than the annually repeated royal funerary ritual of the Pyramid age, now transposed to the divine level. The idea and function of a "Residence cemetery," which, by means of its royal tomb and mortuary cult, imparted divine presence upon all the officials buried there, were now transferred to the age-old cemetery of Abydos, with its tombs of the kings of the Archaic Period, while Osiris was made the royal lord and "Great God" of this cemetery.[85] The same was also true of the festival of Sokar, the great festival of the Memphite necropolis, which also went back to the funeral ritual of the pyramid era and thus displayed the same basic structure as the Osiris mysteries of Abydos: "embalming," which was carried out in the form of an eight-day preparation of a "grain mummy,"[86] wake (at Abydos, the night of the "Haker" festival, at Memphis, the night of the *Ntry.t* festival), and funeral procession (at Abydos, the journey by water in the *neshmet*-barque, at Memphis, the "procession around the walls" in the Henu-barque).

In the New Kingdom, when Memphis regained its importance, the festival of Sokar was elevated into a mortuary festival of importance throughout Egypt.[87] Thebes also laid claim to this rank with its mortuary festival, the "Beautiful Festival of the Valley." In the New Kingdom, the wish to participate in festivals thus spread to other festivals, in Theban texts especially to the Valley Festival,[88] and from the reign of Amenophis III on, to the festival of Sokar[89] as well. In the tombs at Amarna, wishes of this sort were unthinkable, for the festivals and the gods they celebrated had been done away with.[90] At Amarna, the presence of the king took the place of divine presence on festival occasions:

> May you grant me a beautiful burial, by command of your *ka*, in my house, which you have given me, so as to rest in it in the mountains of Akhetaten, the place of the praised ones. May I hear your sweet voice in the house of the *benben*, when you do what your father Aten praises.[91]

In the texts of the post-Amarna and the Ramesside Periods, the wish to participate in festivals was extended to an even greater number of festivals and religious centers. It seems that at this time, there took shape a canon of major festivals in which the deceased wished to participate after their death. In its opening verses, the following text establishes a connection between the motif of transformation and the wish to participate in festivals:

> May I travel north to Busiris as a living *ba*,
> and south to Abydos as a falcon.
> May I be given a seat in the *neshmet*-barque
> on the day of the Wag festival,
> and may I eat a bunch of *hsjjt*-plants
> on the morning of the Neheb-kau festival.
> May I follow Sokar with onions around my neck
> on the day of the *Ntrj.t*-festival.
> May a torch be prepared for me in the place
> next to the lords of Imhet,
> and may I receive offerings at the beginning of the inundation
> on the morning of the New Year festival.
> May I be brought ships full of offerings
> on the day of the Tjahet-festival (?).
> May I receive offerings on the night of the dinner.[92]

The most explicit text is the already oft-cited prayer to Osiris in the tombs of Paser (Theban Tomb 106), Tjay (Theban Tomb 23), and Heqmaatrenakht (Theban Tomb 222).[93] It demonstrates the inner connection between the themes of receiving offerings, returning to the living, strolling in the garden, and participating in festivals:

> May a seat be prepared for me in the *neshmet*-barque
> on the day of the Wag festival.
> May I play the helmsman in the god's boat like the Following of Horus.
> May my *ba* come out and alight on the earth
> when its name is called.
> May I go forth and in to see my people,
> may I stroll by my "canal pond,"
> may my *ba* sit on that sycamore,
> may I refresh myself in its shade and drink its water.[94]

This wish to participate in major festivals was typically expressed by representations and texts that imaged the deceased at the center of the festival events. In her research on "extrasepulchral shawabti deposits," that is, on mortuary figurines that have been found in places other than tombs, Frauke Pumpenmeier has established that such places were mostly connected with the mysteries of Osiris and Sokar and with other important festival processions.[95] Stephan Seidlmayer has been able to demonstrate that many graffiti at Elephantine and its environs are connected with the events of the Satet procession.[96] The representations of the journey to Abydos in Theban tombs were supposed to enable the deceased to participate in the mysteries of Osiris. They refer to rituals involving model boats and mortuary figurines that carried out this journey symbolically (on this journey, see chapter 13, section 2b of this volume.).

A typical motif in this topic of participation in festivals is the calling out of the name and its "being found" (in a list). We may imagine that at this time, it was the custom, during the major festivals of the necropolis, to bring a list of prominent tomb owners and to call out their names, evidently in connection with visits to their tombs. In this way, the deceased were involved in festival events that the living celebrated together with the dead.[97] Presumably, those who went on pilgrimage to these festivals during their lifetimes and played a particular role in them could have had themselves included in such a list, which was supposed to guarantee their participation in the festival forever. We may think of this inclusion in a list as a rudimentary initiation into the permanent society of those who celebrated the festival of the deity. In this way, the festival was the medium of an advantage in the next life that was already acquired on earth, as was also the case later with the Orphic and Eleusinian mysteries. Here, for the first time, we are able to grasp a central point in the connection between

Egyptian festivals and Greek mysteries that Greek writers constantly stressed. During life, the festival already opened up a next-worldly space where the deceased could hope to return after death.

These texts tell us of the special roles that individuals wished to play in these festivals, such as that of the helmsman in the *neshmet*-barque; of specific insignia they wished to wear, such as the faïence pendant and the clothing of red material during the festival of Sakhmet or the wreath of onions during the *henu* procession; and the taking of nourishment particular to a festival, such as a cake of *khesait* plants on the Neheb-kau festival. If we wish to learn something about the customs observed during Egyptian festivals, we must turn to these wishes on the part of the deceased. What all this finally amounted to becomes clear when we follow the historical development down into the later periods of Egyptian history. It ends with the Book of Traversing Eternity, a veritable festival calendar containing wishes for the deceased to participate in thirty-nine Theban festivals, thirty-nine Abydene festivals, seventy-eight Memphite festivals, and other festivals as well. This text is not a guidebook to the world beyond, as scholars have always assumed, but rather a guidebook to this world. But it conducts us through a specific aspect of this world: through its sacred times and spaces, or, so to speak, through the next-worldly areas of the world of the living. These wishes have to do with divine presence: not a presence that awaited the deceased in the afterlife but one imparted to the individual during festivals celebrated on earth. It was thus not just a matter of bringing beliefs about the afterlife into the world of the living, but, at the same time, of sacralizing the world of the living.

As we noted at the outset, going forth by day was connected with the symbol of the false door. From its very beginning, the false door served to connect the realm of the dead to that of the living, the next world to this one, whatever the concept of the afterlife in the various eras of the history of Egyptian religion. The deceased was a wanderer between two worlds, and the world of the living was, above all, a place where a tomb was built, a structure that gave access to the world beyond. This image of interpenetrability became ever more vivid over the course of time. Here again, we come upon the concept of the "most sacred land," which we encountered in connection with the image of death as mystery. When we said that in the New Kingdom, the concept of Elysium began to shift between this world and the next, the statement was also true of the concept of this world, which took on Elysian aspects. This was the point that impressed the Greeks so strongly.

In book 1, chapters 96–97 of his *Bibliotheca historica*, Diodorus Siculus conjectures that the Greeks obtained their concept of the Islands of the Blessed from their encounter with Egypt. From the experience of the beauty of this land in the midst of endless wastes, and from the sight of the dead crossing to their burial places in ships, their fantasy created the myth of the Elysian Fields. Orpheus had already brought this idea of Elysium from Egypt to Greece, along with the Egyptian mysteries. Homer described them thus;[98] his "Meadow of Asphodel," where "souls dwelled," was supposedly the place on the "Acherusian lake" in the vicinity of Memphis, where there were wonderfully beautiful meadows, marshes, lotus blossoms, and reeds; and it was true that the dead lived there, for the most beautiful burial places in Egypt were there, and the deceased were conveyed there over the river and the Acherusian lake.[99] We have here the familiar image of the garden with its pool and its mortuary festivals, which we have encountered in the iconography and texts of the New Kingdom.

In fact, it emerges from a newly discovered and as yet unpublished Egyptian text that in the vicinity of Memphis, there was an area with watercourses and gardens that had the Egyptian name *sḥ.t jȝr.w*, "Field of Reeds," the Egyptian designation of Elysium as a place where the blessed dead enjoyed eternal bliss, peace, and eternal plenitude. This discovery is a surprise, for normally, this Field of Reeds was not localized on earth but in the world beyond. The sun god visited it in the ninth hour of the day, so it lay in the southwest sky, but it was also connected with the netherworld. It was not easy to get there, and in no case did the living catch a glimpse of it. The Field of Reeds was a place of plenitude. The grain grew unbelievably high there, and the deceased received a field that he cultivated himself so as to lead a carefree life, consuming its yield forever. From the point of view of our own concepts, it was quite a fertile and active paradise; there could be no question of meadows filled with flowers or of idleness. But for the Egyptians, it was a place they longed for, and its paradisiacal, superworldly, and counterworldly aspect lay not only in the plenitude and the imperishability of the nourishment it yielded but also in the immortality that the very sight of it conferred. Anyone who saw it became a god, so state the texts we treated in chapter 5. Thus, as its inhabitants conceived it, Egypt became a land where not only men lived, but where the blessed dead also returned to stroll by the pool in their garden. They returned in the form of their *ba*, a bird-shaped soul of which it was said that it "alit" on the trees and sat on their branches.

In the latest periods of ancient Egyptian history, when Greeks and Romans ruled in Egypt, these concepts were also applied to the gods. They, too, had a *ba*, a bird-shaped soul that swooped down from the celestial heights to alight, not on trees, but on their cult images, so as to breathe life into them. This late theurgy was dominated by the idea of origin. The cult was an event, and the gods were invited daily to fly down to their earthly temples and attend it, just as was believed regarding the souls of the dead. From this practice, there emerged the idea that all Egypt was the *templum mundi*, the temple of the world, a sacred place of divine presence, *hierotate chora*, the land that was a holy of holies, as Porphyry called it, in relation to which the surrounding world was a place of relative profanity. In late Egyptian thought, all Egypt was an "other-worldly realm in the world of the living." The origin of this concept lay in the reversed polarity of mortuary belief in the New Kingdom. The concept of "going forth by day" thus ended by transforming the reality of life in Egypt.

PART TWO ◆

RITUALS AND RECITATIONS

CHAPTER TEN

Mortuary Liturgies and Mortuary Literature

1. Provisioning and Transfiguration: The Recording of Recitation Texts in Old Kingdom Pyramids

The images of death treated in Part One of this book underlay a number of actions whose purpose was to treat death in the way an illness is treated. The function of such images was to lead to action, opening up a horizon of meaningful possibilities for such action, a horizon in which a person could deal with and overcome the problems of existence by means of subjectively and intersubjectively meaningful action. By far the most important, and the central, medium of this treatment of death was language. In Part Two of this book, we shall use selected examples to demonstrate how the images of death expounded in Part One were ritually and verbally deployed, and in doing so, we shall above all study the instrument of language and the forms in which it was employed and recorded.

In dealing with death, language was deployed in two forms: in the form of cultic recitation and in the form of written recording. With regard to this distinction, we should begin by noting that the concept of written words as a form of verbal activity that exercises salutary effects is quite foreign to us. From analytic philosophy, we have learned "how to do things with words"[1] and how to classify such "speech acts."[2] "Acts of

237

writing," however, are scarcely mentioned in this connection, though this category is of fundamental importance to the understanding of Egyptian texts. Most of these texts have come down to us recorded in highly concrete and meaningful contexts. They belong where they are, and the context in which they were recorded is a part of their meaning. They are not in books but on mummy bandages, shrouds, coffins, tomb walls, papyri that were to be kept in prescribed places, stelae, statues, offering tables, and so forth, and the place and the context in which they were recorded bears a correlation with what these texts were supposed to say and do. In ancient Egypt, it was possible to "do things with words" by writing specific texts in specific places, and productive use was made of this means of dealing with death.

Along with the distinction between writing and the spoken word, there is another that will play an important role in this chapter: the distinction between mortuary literature and mortuary liturgy. I understand *mortuary liturgies* to be texts intended to be recited in the mortuary cult and *mortuary literature* to be texts placed in the tomb in order to be of use to the deceased in the afterlife. Mortuary liturgies are thus literature recited in the cult. The *place where they were performed* belonged to the realm of the living, in the place of embalming and in the accessible cult chambers of the tomb, though the *place where they were recorded* was in many cases the inaccessible sarcophagus chamber. Mortuary literature, however, belonged where it was recorded: on the walls of the sarcophagus chamber (Pyramid Texts),[3] on the coffin (Coffin Texts),[4] or on Book of the Dead papyri.[5] Mortuary literature drew on many sources, including even mortuary liturgies. Nevertheless, we must observe the distinction between mortuary liturgies and mortuary literature. Mortuary liturgies belonged in the accessible outer part of tombs, and mortuary literature in the inaccessible inner part. Mortuary liturgies were intended to be carried out on behalf of the deceased, while mortuary literature was intended to equip him magically.

Egyptian mortuary literature is a unique phenomenon among the mortuary customs of the world. In other places, of course, there has been the custom of accompanying death by words, and in some cases subsequent processes as well, addressing a person even after his death and thereby keeping him present in the community of the living as the addressee of human speech. Even the practice of placing certain texts in the tomb for the benefit of the deceased is attested outside Egypt. Thus, for example, the tombs of members of Bacchic mystery cults contained gold tablets with instructions for their postmortem journey, the so-called mortuary passports, and a charred papyrus has even been found.[6] But nowhere else has the use of speech and writing in connection with the cult of the dead assumed such forms as it did in Egypt.

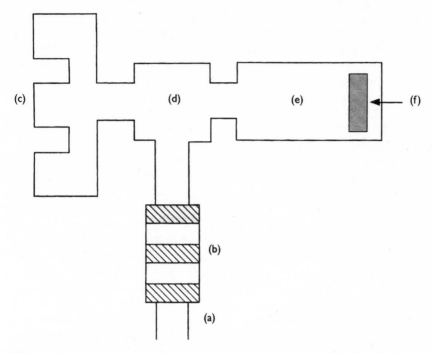

Figure 4. The subterranean portion of the pyramid of Wenis: (a) entrance corridor, (b) three portcullises, (c) three statue niches, (d) antechamber, (e) sarcophagus chamber, (f) sarcophagus. Adapted from Kurt Sethe, *Die altägyptischen Pyramidentexte*, vol. 3 (Leipzig, 1922), p. 116. Drawing by David Lorton.

The Egyptian custom of mortuary literature goes back to Wenis, the last king of Dynasty 5, who ruled in the middle of the twenty-fourth century B.C.E. It was during his reign that someone came up with the idea of inscribing the subterranean chambers of his pyramid with texts that were characterized as "spells" by the constantly repeated phrase "to be recited." The pyramid of Wenis contains 227 spells, a number that was increased to 759 in the later pyramids.[7] The wall inscriptions in the subterranean chambers (Figure 4) were thus conceived as a permanent recitation that was to surround the deceased on all sides. With this step of making the walls of the subterranean chambers—the sarcophagus chamber, the antechamber, and the entrance corridor—speak by means of inscriptions, thereby swathing the deceased in a permanent (though silent) recitation, there began a tradition that remained alive in various forms—wall inscriptions, coffin inscriptions, and inscribed rolls of papyrus—until the end of pharaonic history. New texts were created in the course of time, but the old content also continued to be handed down, and these texts constitute the overwhelming majority of all the texts preserved to us from ancient Egypt. We designate these texts collectively as *mortuary literature*.[8] If we wish to trace the function of the mortuary literature, we need to return to the original situation in the pyramid of Wenis and examine their form, their themes, and where they were distributed in the chambers.[9]

The sarcophagus chamber of the pyramid of Wenis is entered from the east. On the other side of the chamber, the sarcophagus is in front of the west wall. This wall is uninscribed; only in the tympanum are there protective spells against serpents. The inscriptions thus address the king beginning from the east. To the right, on the north wall, is the ritual for the funerary meals, with its seemingly endless list of offerings presented to the king, offerings that are accompanied by brief spells (spells 23–212). To the left, on the south wall, are spells addressed to the king, describing his transformation into a jackal-headed star god and his entry into the course of the sun (spells 213–219).[10] This is a fixed sequence of spells that always occurs in the same order, down to the Late Period. It appears in all the pyramids of the Old Kingdom, on many coffins of the Middle Kingdom, and then again in tombs of the Saite Period; it is thus the oldest, and also the most widespread and classical example of a mortuary liturgy. The Egyptian term for this text genre was *s3ḥw*, "making an *akh*," and it referred to a recitation whose goal was to transform the deceased into a transfigured ancestral spirit. In English, the Egyptian concept *s3ḥw* is rendered as "transfiguration." Scholars have connected the root *3ḥ* with the verb *j3ḥ* "to shine," which adds the idea of light to that of transfiguration. The decoration of the sarcophagus chamber of Wenis is thus concerned entirely with provisioning (north wall) and transfiguration (south wall). The transfiguration spells continue onto the eastern (entrance) wall (spells 219–224) and the southern wall of the entrance, while the offering spells continue onto the northern wall of the entrance and into the antechamber (225–246).

The antechamber is inscribed with spells (247–312) whose theme is ascent to the sky and crossing it. Here, the deceased is no longer addressed: he himself speaks, or he is proclaimed in the third person; in a number of texts, an original first person has been secondarily transposed into the third person. These texts deal with the appearance of the king in the realm of the gods, and they are not intended for liturgical use. They occur in later pyramids, on coffins, on mortuary papyri, and so forth, but no longer in the same sequence. We have the impression that these texts present the deceased to the realm of the gods as a powerful being, while the spells in the sarcophagus chamber address the deceased, making him into a powerful being through provisioning and transfiguration, and confirming him permanently in this status. The entrance corridor is inscribed with spells (313–321) whose concern is the opening of the gates of the sky and the appearance of the deceased in powerful forms of manifestation: baboon, crocodile, serpent, bull, star, and so forth. Perhaps we are to see these many "transformations" as a presentiment of the later idea of "going forth by day."[11]

The voice that is permanently frozen in the inscriptions of Wenis thus addresses the deceased in the sarcophagus chamber, while in the antechamber and in the entrance corridor, it addresses the realm of the gods. In the sarcophagus chamber, we hear/read the voice of the priest; in the spells of the antechamber and the entrance corridor, it is, at least originally, mostly the voice of the deceased himself. The distribution of the spells in the pyramid of Wenis thus not only takes account of their themes but also of their "interpersonal form," the shifting reference between speaker and addressee that they respectively realize. For the most part, we can make out four such interpersonal forms:

1. An unidentified speaker (0) speaks to a specified addressee (2) about the latter himself (0:2:2)
2. An unidentified speaker (0) speaks to an unspecified addressee (0) about a third party (0:0:3)
3. A specified speaker (1) speaks to an unspecified addressee (0) about himself (1:0:1)
4. A specified speaker (1) speaks to a specified addressee (2) about himself (1) or about a third party (3) (1:2:1 or 1:2:3)

Theoretically, a number of other interpersonal forms could be created using these three variables, but it is the four just enumerated that play an important role in the texts we are considering. The typical form of the mortuary liturgy, or transfiguration, is the form 0:2:2; an unnamed speaker turns to the deceased, speaking about the latter himself.

To the complete invisibility of the speaker, there thus corresponds an equally absolute dominance of the addressee. The texts have the unmistakable character of an appeal, and the "you" of the addressee is present in nearly every line. Thus, for example, we read:

> Raise yourself, Teti,
> take your head, bind your bones,
> collect your members,
> wipe the earth off your flesh,
> take your bread, which cannot go moldy,
> and your beer, which cannot go sour.
> May you approach the door leaves that keep out the *rḥjj.t*![12]

These statements are thus not to be understood as descriptive or narrative in nature but rather as appellative. Where an imperative is lacking, the statement is formulated as a wish:

May the sky open to you,
may the earth open to you,
may the ways in the realm of the dead open to you.
(the ways) on which you go forth and enter with Re,
striding freely like the lords of eternity.
Receive offerings as a gift of Ptah,
pure bread from the altar of Hathor.
May your *ba* live, your vessels thrive,
may your face be open on the ways of the darkness.[13]

The interpersonal form of the transfiguration is thus to be described as a wish that expresses an intense appeal, one that strives to maintain explicit contact with the addressee in every single verse. This form of address by an invisible speaker is here designated "0:2:2."

The typical interpersonal form of mortuary *liturgies* is 0:2:2, with occasional third parties (0:0:3). These are clearly distinguished from two other forms that do not appear, or appear only exceptionally, in this text genre: 1:0:1 and 1:2:1/2. In form 1:0:1 the deceased speaks about himself without turning to a specified addressee (as, for example, in prayers or appeals addressed to the living). The latter form is extremely widespread in the mortuary *literature*, and it is the usual form assumed by nonliturgical mortuary spells. The form 1:2:1/2 (the deceased speaks to a next-worldly being about himself and/or him) is also quite common in the mortuary literature. More interesting in our context here is the form 1:2:2, in which an explicitly identified speaker addresses the deceased. In the context of mortuary liturgies, this form performs two different functions: as a "concluding text," in which the speaker finally sets aside his incognito and reveals his identity and his relationship to the addressee, and as "lamentations" put in the mouth of Isis and Nephthys, a typical element in the liturgy of the wake. We shall deal with the latter in the next chapter.

The connection between an anonymously recited spell that addresses a hearer and deals only with the latter, and a concluding text in which the speaker identifies himself and clarifies his relationship to the hearer is also characteristic of hymns to the gods.[14] But there are also important differences between hymns and mortuary liturgies. Hymns lack, for instance, the appellative element, or, in any event, it does not play the same dominant role in them. The form of address is also different. Mortuary liturgies employ the expression *hꜣ wsjr N. pn*, "O this Osiris N." The interjection *hꜣ* "O" seems to be confined almost exclusively to mortuary liturgies, and it is used neither for the living[15] nor (at least in earlier texts) for deities.[16] The word might be derived from the verb *hꜣj* "to go down"; perhaps it was originally the imperative "descend!" It is often determined by the pair of walking legs, like the verb "to go down." It is in any case not a greeting like *jj.tj* or *jj-wj-tw* "welcome!" or *jnd-ḥr=k* "greetings!" but rather an interjection employed in addresses. The demonstrative pronoun after the personal name has the character of a vocative and refers to the presumed proximity of the addressee: "N. here . . ." Deities are never addressed in this fashion. So much for the interpersonal form of the transfiguration spells.

In what follows, I wish to deal with the pragmatic aspect of transfiguring speech. What sort of action was carried out when spells were recited, and, in this regard, what was the relationship between oral recitation and the use of writing? With these questions, we touch on the above-mentioned theory of the speech act, which treats speech as a form of social activity. Egyptology is especially inviting for such considerations, for Egyptian texts are in so many ways embedded in ritual, magical, and other relationships of social life. It is thus certainly no accident that Sir Alan Gardiner, the great Egyptologist, was also one of the founding fathers of linguistic pragmatism and the theory of the speech act. His book *The Theory of Speech and Language* appeared as early as 1932. Gardiner recognized the linguist Philipp Wegener as his predecessor, dedicating his book to him and citing the latter's work *Untersuchungen über die Grundfragen des Sprachlebens* more often than any other.[17] The thesis is that the meaning of the statement we utter is determined by the situation in which we find ourselves along with the listener, and that it is thus not only dependent on grammar and vocabulary but on the frameworks and the settings of social life. Thus, claims Gardiner, the discipline most closely related to linguistics is neither logic nor psychology but rather sociology.[18]

An important indication of how mortuary liturgies were used (their "situational embedding") is supplied by representations. We have depictions of offering rituals with the recitation of mortuary liturgies from all periods, though we most often encounter them in tombs of the Old Kingdom. Mostly depicted are three "lector priests" (*ḥrj.w-ḥꜣb*), whom we recognize by their long hair and their sash, and who kneel on the ground, alternately beating their breast with each of their two fists. This is a form of "corporal music"; the muffled, rhythmic sound created by this drumming was supposed to accompany the recitations. In Egyptian, this gesture was called *hnw*,[19] this term is mostly rendered "jubilation," though the rendering does not suit the context here. *Hnw* was not an expression of joy but rather of emotion at the presence of a superhuman power, such as the pharaoh, a deceased person, or a god.[20] The caption to this gesture is usually *šd.t sꜣḥ.w ꜥšꜣ.w jn ḥrj-ḥꜣb* "reciting many transfigurations by the lector priest(s)." From the especially detailed representation in the tomb of Kagemni, it emerges that a standing lector priest recited the transfigurations from a papyrus roll, while the three kneeling priests accompanied him, beating their breasts in the *hnw*-gesture.

"Transfigurations," or mortuary liturgies, were thus lengthy texts that were read out loud from rolls of papyrus. The Egyptian word s³ḫ.w is the causative form of the root ³ḫ, which means something along the lines of "to have spirit power." The causative formation of the designation of this text genre itself indicates that these are effective texts whose recitation resulted in a transformation, and specifically, transformation into a transfigured ancestral spirit. The fact that they were handed down in writing and recited from written copies demonstrates the special status of their language. It was sacrosanct, and writing served as the means of preserving the texts. When it came to these spells, no failure of memory could be allowed to slip in. The priest and his roll of papyrus guaranteed the exactitude of the recitation, just like the conductor and his score in a modern concert. In the functional context of "recitation literature," writing served only as an aid to memory. The actual communication act was the oral performance. The writing was not "read" but "sung." In this way as well, this sort of ritual writing corresponds perfectly to a musical score, which also is not read but performed. Of course, instead of being written down, the text could be learned by heart. Theoretically, it made no difference; in this connection, human recollection serves as a memory cache and "notation system," just like writing or other systems of notation, such as knots on a string, pictures, notches, and so forth. The Brahmans of India are known to have been distrustful of writing and to have preferred recollection as a memory cache. From the very beginning, the Egyptians made the opposite choice. They distrusted recollection, and they made use of writing as the memory cache for their cultic texts.

In the Berlin Museum, there is an early Ptolemaic papyrus containing a collection of "transfigurations"; its opening remark identifies it as a copy of a manuscript from the reign of Amenophis III (ca. 1400–1360 B.C.E.).[21] Naturally, scholars have considered this claim to be exaggerated, but a glance at the text reveals that this collection is much older than its alleged original, and that its contents are already to be found on coffins of the early second millennium. The individual texts already occur in the pyramids of Dynasty 6 (twenty-fourth century B.C.E.). The textual tradition is astonishingly good. Here, in fact, a mortuary liturgy was accurately cached in the framework of ritual writings for two thousand years and more and could be performed verbatim in the cult over and over again. What had been "normal" Egyptian around 2300 b.c.e. had become essentially a foreign language by around 300 b.c.e., one used only in the cult. It is difficult to date this gulf between normally spoken and written Egyptian and the stage of the language preserved in the papyrus rolls of the lector priests. Undoubtedly, it was a matter of an ongoing process of drifting apart. For a long time, the difference between the language employed in the cult and everyday language was experienced only as dialectical variants. But by the post-Amarna Period (ca. 1350 B.C.E.) at the latest, it was clear to the Egyptians that there were two distinct languages. Now, the old written language was something that was learned at school.[22] Late in Egyptian history, knowledge of this language was the exclusive prerogative of the priests, and the language itself became the exclusive language of the cult, along with the hieroglyphic writing system and its cursive variant, hieratic, which were used to record it. At this time, the old expression *md.t nṯr*, "divine language," which had designated the hieroglyphs, must have been extended to refer to Old and Middle Egyptian, which had become foreign languages: the language of the cult was the language of the gods, and thus a foreign language.[23]

All actions performed in the cult were also performed in the realm of the gods. As in heaven, so on earth was the principle.[24] Had Isis not awakened her husband, Osiris, with her laments and turned him into a powerful, immortal spirit with her transfigurations, all earthly, cultic actions and recitations in this regard would have been pointless. If the sun god did not daily defeat Apopis, the dragon of chaos, who threatened him with darkness and with coming to a standstill, the protective rituals carried out daily in the temples to ward off the domestic and foreign enemies of Pharaoh and to maintain the order and well-being of the state would have had no effect. The name of the text genre that comprised these protective rituals was indicative: they were called *bꜣ.w Rꜥ.w* "demonstrations of the power of Re," for it was believed that by reciting them, the power of the sun god himself was brought into play, the power with which he overcame cosmic opposition during his daily course around the earth.

The verbal treatment of death was only one (albeit central) special case of ritual recitation of the "demonstrations of the power of Re." In general, this was nothing less than the attempt to keep the world in motion through language. The cosmos, and the divine realm that embodied it, was conceived of as a drama, and cultic actions and recitations as the carrying out of divine interaction. Cult was thus not carried out in the sense of a communication between man and god but as the enacting of a drama in the divine world, between god and gods. If we do not shy away from an anachronistic usage first coined in late classical antiquity, we can call this principle of enacting events in the divine realm through the medium of cultic action and recitation "theurgic." What the most important advocate of theurgy, the Neoplatonic philosopher Iamblichus, wrote about these matters in his *On the Egyptian Mysteries* rests on deep insights into the meaning and function of cultic language, insights that are, *mutatis mutandis*, entirely appropriate to ancient Egypt.[25] Iamblichus never tires of making up new formulations to shed light on the principle of theurgic communication for the purpose of refuting the objection that the theurgist wished to threaten the gods, so as to compel them or, at least, to influence them according to his will. His argumentation rests on the concept that the theurgist did not approach the gods as a man but from an ecstatic position that had a share in divinity. He did not drag the gods down to his level but rather raised himself to theirs: "For an invocation of this kind does not draw down the impassive and pure Gods, to that which is passive and impure; but, on the contrary, it renders us, who have become passive through generation, pure and immutable."[26] He thus insists, "that divine work is not effected when two contrary and different parties (man and God) confront one another; rather, this kind of divine work is accomplished in agreement, unity, and accord (between god and God)."[27] "The theurgist, through the power of arcane signatures, commands mundane natures, no longer as a man, nor as employing a human soul; but as existing superior to them in the order of the Gods, he makes use of greater mandates than pertain to himself, so far as he is human."[28] The basic principle of ancient Egyptian ritual practice could not be expressed more clearly. This theurgic principle was valid for ritual action, and it was especially valid for ritual language, which was inseparable from this action. The transforming, transfiguring power of the performance lay in the recitations that accompanied the actions. This is why the lector priest was always there with his papyrus roll. He directed the oral side of the proceedings, the recitation that, in the mouth of the priest and in the moment of cultic action, became divine speech. When the priest spoke, one god spoke to another, and the words manifested their transforming, performative, theurgic power, that is, their power to create divine presence. That was the performance. What the lector priest held in his hand was the score.

In its meaning and its essence, sacred recitation was thus divine speech, cached in the medium of writing and realized in the context of cultic role playing. The priest did not utter it as something of his own, and he did not approach a divine image as a man. Rather, he slipped into a role in the context of a "constellation" in the divine realm. The cosmos—reality—was made up of such "constellations." They were the structural elements comprising the entirety of the "world," which was continuously coming into being. Language made it possible to describe them and to integrate them through narrative: this was the origin of myths. But language also made it possible to articulate and dramatically represent the words spoken, as it were intra-constellatively, in this acting in combination: this was the origin of liturgies or cult recitations.

The life-giving, animating effect of the divine word finds its clearest expression in the Books of the Netherworld. In them, we encounter yet another image of death, one to which we have not devoted a chapter but which we wish to mention here, at least briefly. The image is connected with the nocturnal journey of the sun god through the netherworld. In the Books of the Netherworld, death is a condition of sleep and unconsciousness, out of which the dead are awakened every night by the sun god as he passes by them, endowing them with life by means of his light, but above all, by means of his words. They live, as it is repeatedly stated, "on the breath of his words." He dispenses justice upon them and grants them their provisions, and they thank him with "transfiguring" addresses that considerably resemble mortuary spells. This nightly exchange between the sun god and the deceased in the netherworld, as recorded in the Books of the Netherworld, makes the life-giving role of speech in Egyptian mortuary belief especially clear. After the sun god has passed by them, the deceased break out into lamentations and then fall back into their sleep. This image of death as "Sleeping Beauty slumber" (E. Hornung) stands in strange opposition to the concept of the lasting abode in Elysium of the transfigured spirits saved from death, and also to that of going forth by day; perhaps it concerns only the mummified bodies of the transfigured spirits, while the image of eternal life after being saved from death is connected with the *ba*. Along with their representations and descriptions of the netherworld, the Books of the Netherworld also codify the life-giving speeches that the sun god addresses to those dwelling in the netherworld and with which they answer him. Recorded on the walls of the royal tombs, they constitute the artificial recollection of the king, who had to know these speeches in order to join in the course of the sun and play a collaborative role there.

These texts had a salvatory, transfiguring power, they awakened those lying in the sleep of death, they raised those who were stretched out, they opened the netherworld and effected divine presence:

> The spells of the ancestors relate true things.
> He who hears them stands erect in his place,
> awake and gazing upon the sun.
> They (i.e., the spells) gladden his heart in the netherworld,
> for this is a splendid condition.[29]

The *recording* of such texts thus belongs in the area we connected in chapter 8 with the mystery function of the tomb—the coffin and the sarcophagus chamber—notwithstanding the fact that we are to imagine their *performance* as having occurred in the areas accessible to ritual activity.

2. Writing as Voice and Recollection: The Recording of Mortuary Texts in Middle Kingdom Coffins and in the Book of the Dead

In the Middle Kingdom, the Old Kingdom situation was reversed: the pyramids of the kings remained anepigraphic, while the insides of the coffins of private persons were regularly inscribed with mortuary texts.[30]

The Coffin Texts were edited by Adriaan de Buck in seven volumes, which appeared from 1935 to 1961. This edition is a masterpiece of philological care. Its only disadvantage is that it is confined to the "new" spells that are not attested in the pyramids, leaving out all the texts that have parallels in the pyramids, and thus creating an entirely false impression of the textual content. One gets the impression of a sharp discontinuity, as though the Middle Kingdom in no way continued the tradition of the pyramids of the Old Kingdom and instead created entirely new texts. But this is an optical illusion created by the selection of texts in de Buck's edition. In reality, the Coffin Texts combine old and new texts. The tradition was seamlessly continued, and it was enriched by a host of new texts.

One innovation in the Coffin Texts leaps immediately to the eye. They belong to a different writing culture from that of the Pyramid Texts of the Old Kingdom. The Pyramid Texts are *inscriptions*, while the Coffin Texts are *manuscripts*, displaying all the refinement in the art of manuscript writing that had developed in the offices of the administrative bureaucracy. This refinement includes the use of lists and tables, and especially of red and black ink to make it possible to distinguish "texts" and "paratexts" from one another. The "texts" are the actual spells; these are written in black and correspond to what the decorators of the pyramids had (or would have) written on the walls. The "paratexts," written in red, have no counterpart in the pyramids. These are titles and postscripts that inform us of the purpose and the effects of the respective spells, as well as instructions for reciting them, in cases where the spell was to be recited under specific conditions or with the use of specific objects. Typical goals, for instance, are "not to die a second time," "not to eat excrement in the realm of the dead," "not to go upside down," "to transform into . . . ," "to have disposal of air and water," "to vindicate a man," and so forth and so on.

This innovation shows that the principal purpose of the coffin decoration was no longer, as in the pyramids, the recording of a voice that permanently addressed the deceased or with which the deceased himself wished permanently to speak. The voice was unable to express this distinction between text and paratext, red and black ink. These bureaucratic forms of recording texts are directed at the eye of the reader. Here, it is not a recitation that is made permanent but a store of knowledge that is put on stand-by. In other words: here, writing functions not as a prosthesis of the voice but as artificial recollection.

It is thus imperative to make the distinction between mortuary *liturgy* and mortuary *literature* if we are to find our way through the labyrinth of the Egyptian mortuary texts. In the case of the mortuary *literature*, it is a matter of written codification of a store of knowledge that is placed in the tomb along with the deceased for the purpose of equipping him for the afterlife; in the case of the mortuary *liturgies*, however, it is a matter of recording cultic recitations whose salutary effect is to surround the deceased permanently. In the one case, writing serves as an artificial prosthesis of recollection that is to replace the recollection that has disintegrated in death, while in the other case, it serves as a prosthesis of the voice, specifically the voice of the reciting priest, which it will cause to ring out forever in the depths of the sarcophagus chamber.

As artificial recollection, writing was intended to equip the deceased with a repertoire of texts that he needed in the afterlife so that, with their help, he could free himself from the realm of death and enter Elysium. Knowledge of these spells made him a "transfigured ancestral spirit," "one who knows his spell"; this was magical knowledge that writing held ready for him as a replacement for his natural recollection. Writing served here as a cache of magical knowledge. To foster easy command of this knowledge, and for the purpose of quick orientation, the means of bureaucratic written culture, such as rubrics and tables, were brought into play.

As artificial voice, writing was intended to extend cultic recitation beyond the time span of its ritual performance and to keep the deceased forever within the range of the priestly voice. In this function, it served to realize a permanent recitation. This function, too, was continued in the Coffin Texts. We constantly come upon the two liturgies we already know from the pyramids, the liturgy Pyramid Texts spells 213–219 + 220–222/223/224 (in what follows: "liturgy A") and the liturgy Pyramid Texts spells 539 + 356–357 + 363 + 677 + 365 + 373, and so forth (in what follows: "liturgy B"), as well as new liturgies. In the Coffin Texts, they now acquired titles such as "Book of Transfigurations" and the like.

It can be seen that liturgy B and the new mortuary liturgies belong to a ritual context that differs from the provisioning liturgies. The next two chapters will shed light on this context, which has to do with the embalming ritual. We shall establish that there is a thematic connection between embalming as a *context of performance* and inscription on the coffin as *place of recording*. And this is true not only for the coffins of the Middle Kingdom but also for the coffin inscriptions of later epochs, down to the Ptolemaic Period. In these cases as well, it can be shown that the spells were created out of mortuary liturgies whose emphasis, at least, lay on the embalming ritual. Clearly, it does not much matter whether mortuary texts were recorded on tomb walls, on coffins, or on mortuary papyri. When coffins came to be inscribed, a special thematic reference came into play, one that had to do with the ritual of embalming.

Coffins were, of course, a place of recording that stood in the closest of relationships with the place where embalming was carried out. The body was placed in the coffin in the chamber where the embalming took place, and in a sense, the coffin carried the salutary effects of this ritual out of the embalming chamber and into the sarcophagus chamber. We can define this ritual context even more closely. It was not a matter of the entire embalming, a process that took seventy days, but of the nocturnal "wake" that seems to have concluded the embalming ritual, and in the midst of which was the corpse of the deceased, already in its coffin. The ritual of the wake, with its comprehensive mortuary liturgies, was thus presumably carried out over the coffin. All this will be demonstrated and explained in detail in the following chapters.

We are thus dealing with two entirely different ritual contexts for mortuary liturgies or "transfigurations": with the mortuary offering cult and with the wake at the end of the embalming process. By the very bias of the place where they were recorded, the mortuary liturgies in the Coffin Texts refer, with the exception of liturgy A taken over from the pyramids, exclusively to the nocturnal rites in the embalming chamber.

From the beginning of the New Kingdom (ca. 1540 B.C.E.) on, mortuary texts were no longer written in coffins but rather on rolls of papyrus. We call these rolls "Books of the Dead."[31] The designation "Book of the Dead" is misleading for two reasons. First, this is not the Egyptian title, which is "Spells of Going Forth by Day," and second, it is not a matter of a "book" in the sense of a constant text reproduced in many copies but rather of a repertoire of mortuary texts from which scribes selected only some spells to put together their own individual compositions. It was not until Dynasty 26 that a specific selection, sequence, and text version was canonized, it is only at this time that we are dealing with a "book."[32] Nevertheless, for the sake of simplicity, we shall maintain the conventional designation "Book of the Dead" here.

The Book of the Dead contains hardly any Pyramid Texts. It is now that we see the break in tradition that de Buck's edition of the Coffin Texts incorrectly leads the reader to think occurred in the Middle Kingdom. The number of spells in the Coffin Texts is reduced to a sixth; instead of more than a thousand, there are now barely two hundred. The liturgical element, in which writing functions as the recording of the voice, is also highly reduced compared to the Coffin Texts. The few remnants of mortuary liturgies to be found, such as spells 151, 169, and 172, are clearly related to embalming. Each spell now regularly has a title stating its purpose, and the entire collection bears the title "Spells of Going Forth by Day."

The major innovation of the Book of the Dead consists in the vignettes. Many spells are now accompanied by representations, either in a strip of their own above the text fields, as in spells 1 and 17, or in a small field within the text field, or, finally, they occupy the entire height of the papyrus. Often, these are veritable masterworks of book illumination. Curiously enough, the return to the traditional religion after the end of the Amarna Period entailed a breakthrough in the use of illustrations. In many other ways, as well, the post-Amarna era was something quite other than a retrogressive period of pure restoration. This breakthrough of representations was a reaction to the deiconization of Egyptian religion during the Amarna Period. This is as true of verbal images as it is of art itself. Of the nine images of death we treated in Part One, in the Amarna Period, only the ninth, "going forth by day," remained. During the Ramesside Period, Egyptian mortuary religion became ever richer in images, until in Dynasty 21, the images managed to displace the texts entirely, and there appeared a new type of mortuary papyrus that consisted solely of pictures. Here, images appear as a third element added to the functions of writing as "voice" and "recollection." What the representations introduce is the intensity of situative visualization: context, space, action, the embedding of the words to be spoken and the spells to be recollected in a concrete scene. The words are always only a part of the whole; with the image, their reality is intensified.

There was something magical, in my opinion, about this intensity. The Book of the Dead is a book of magic. It contains rituals for domestic use.[33] Magical spells were typically to be recited to or over an image in order to be effective. The magic of images and the magic of words complemented one another in their effectiveness, so as to visualize the sacred. Thus, in the New Kingdom, the subterranean ramps and chambers of the royal tombs were decorated with compositions consisting of images and texts. At Deir el-Medina, the village of the workmen who created the royal tombs, the inhabitants adopted this principle for their own tombs and decorated their subterranean chambers with vignettes from the Book of the Dead. The sarcophagus chamber was thus laden with sacredness and made into a sacred space of divine presence, where the things and beings talked about in the texts were actually present in their images. In the tomb chambers of Deir el-Medina, the deceased was no longer surrounded by writing that spoke to him from all sides and held him forever within the scope of effective liturgical recitations. Now, he was surrounded by representations that inserted him directly into the realm of Elysium. The Book of the Dead, too, gained three-dimensionality and the power of magical imagination through its images.

The mortuary liturgies are mostly excluded from this context. In the New Kingdom, they found another place, in the decoration of the accessible areas of the tomb. But the liturgies of the wake, which had been written on the interiors of coffins in the Middle Kingdom, of course did not belong there. In the cult spaces of the tombs, there were spells that were recited during the offering cult; they dealt with the provisioning of the dead. Chapters 14 and 15 of this volume will treat their themes and their significance.

The mortuary liturgies are essentially more accessible to our comprehension than the mortuary literature. They have the considerable advantage of a ritual context and a textual coherence that seem to be absent from the texts dealing with magical knowledge. Their ritual context is often unclear to us, but we can guess at what is going on in them and bring the allusions in the texts into an at least general connection with the goals of activities such as embalming, vindication, protection, purification, and placement in the coffin. In the case of the mortuary liturgies, it is never a question of individual spells but always of a series. It is clear that the understanding of an individual spell gains decisively if one looks at the series and observes the spell's position within a sequence. For the mortuary liturgies, we thus have two keys or "determinatives" that approximately establish the meaning of the spell and help orient our interpretation: the ritual context and the context of the composition.

3. Greetings, Requests, and Wishes

That mortuary liturgies are generally easier to understand than mortuary literature, that they are more "exoteric" compared to the "esoteric" character of the Book of the Dead, that they seem to be written in plain language, as opposed to the mysterious language of the magical mortuary spells, appears to have something to do with the fact that they are, above all, a form of wish. Unlike magical conjurations, wishes are a speech act that occurs in everyday life. Ancient Egyptian manners seem to have been rich in elaborate wishes. The Egyptian art of the wish began already with greetings. A nice example occurs in the tomb of the royal epistolary scribe *Tȝjj* (Tjay, Theban Tomb 23), which is also rich in mortuary spells. In scenes of "foreign service" that represent real-life relationships, the tomb owner is greeted with the words:

> May Thoth praise you, may he grant you (many) years,
> may he grant you a lifetime,
> with your name enduring in the royal palace
> and you free of dread of the king.[34]

Tjay's interlocutor then continues with wishes for himself, uttering a prayer to Amun-Re and then saying to Thoth:

> Thoth, you judge of *maat*,
> may you grant me the West for my old age,
> after 110 years in the favor of men,
> I being free of dread of the king.

252

Such wishes are only meaningful in the mouth of one who is alive, and the corresponding wishes addressed to him are also only meaningful if the tomb owner is alive. We are also to view the wishes with which Tjay is greeted when he visits his home[35] as addressed to him in life, not death, notwithstanding the fact that they are recorded in his tomb. Such wishes were the stuff of ancient Egyptian courtesy. There is a famous scene in which Prince Djedefhor greets Djedi, the sage and magician, in the Tales of Wonder from Papyrus Westcar. The prince approaches the sage, an old man of 110 years, with the words:

> Your condition is like that of one who lives
> before aging and being old,
> before dying, being enwrapped, and being buried,
> one who sleeps until dawn,
> free of illness,
> without the coughing of old age.[36]

"Thus does one greet someone provisioned for the afterlife (*jm₃ḫjj*)," adds the narrator by way of explanation. The sage Djedi responds:

> Welcome, Djedefhor,
> king's son, whom his father loves!
> May your father praise you,
> Cheops, the vindicated!
> May he advance your position among the elders.
> May your *ka* file suit against your enemies,
> and may your *ba* know the ways, in the next world,
> to the portal of the place that conceals the weary![37]

The narrator again adds a comment: "Thus does one greet a king's son." Similar wishes were employed at the beginning of letters.[38]

In literary letters, such wishes are expanded into lengthy lists that can scarcely be distinguished from mortuary liturgies. The best known example is the much-copied "epistolary contest" from Papyrus Anastasi I:

May you live, prosper, and be healthy, my goodly brother,
may you be provisioned, and may you endure without wishes,
may your need of life and provisioning be satisfied,
may joy and rejoicing be placed in your path,
may your "holes" overflow with daily abundance,
your fortune and your fulfillment remaining and enduring,
may the sickness demons not attack you in your hour of destiny.
May you see the rays of the sun and be strengthened by them [. . .],
may they brighten your eyes by the sight of their light.
[. . .]

May you be provisioned after old age,
may you be anointed with top-quality oil, like the righteous,
you being treated in the house of embalming until the end of your period
   (i.e., of 70 days),
may you enter your tomb in the Sacred Land,
may you mingle with the excellent *ba*s and mix with them.
May you be vindicated in Busiris in the presence of Osiris,
enduring in Abydos before Shu and Onuris (?),
may you cross over to U-poqer in the divine retinue,
may you traverse the divine mound in the retinue of Sokar,
may you join the crew of the *neshmet*-barque without being turned away,
may you see the sun in the sky when it opens the year,
may Anubis join your head to your bones,
may you come out of the hidden chamber without being annihilated,
may you see the radiance of the sun in the netherworld when it passes
   over you,
may Nun overflow in your house and flood your path,
may it stand seven cubits high beside your tomb,
may you sit on the bank of the river at the hour of rest,
may you wash your face and hands when you receive offerings,
may your nose inhale air and your throat breathe,
may the clothing of the weaver goddess [. . .],
may the grain god give you bread, and Hathor beer,
may you nurse at the breast of the milk goddess,
may you open (the house) of the hearts,
may you enter it, take what is yours, and put it in its place,
may your *shawabti* figurines receive you,
may they carry sand (for you) from east to west,
may you [. . .] grasp your sycamore goddess,
may she moisten your throat, may you repel [. . .],
[may you be strong] on the earth, may you be transfigured [in the
   netherworld],
[. . .] air,
may you be vindicated in the sky, the stars [. . .],
may you transform yourself as you wish, like the phoenix,
each of your forms being a god according to your desire.[39]

This passage draws on the repertoire of formulas found in the mortuary liturgies, and the latter two-thirds of it could have been inscribed in a private tomb of the Ramesside Period.[40]

The "compliments addressed to a high official" in the schoolboys' anthologies ("miscellanies") also belong here:

May your condition be that of one who lives a million times.
May the Primeval One of the Two Lands, Amun-Re, creator of the gods,
   act on your behalf,

may he provide you with the grace that goes out from the king,
your mouth being hale and no mistake being found on your lips,[41]
and you being in the grace of the king of your time,
of the Horus who loves *maat.*
May you live 110 years on earth,
may you go to rest on the mountain top
whose lord[42] is in the west of Thebes,
may your *ba* be divine among[43] the living.[44]
May you mingle with the excellent *bas*[45]
and follow[46] Osiris in Rasetau on the day of the Sokar festival.
May a libation be poured for you on the two banks
in the presence of Wennefer,
may you go up[47] into the *neshmet*-barque without being turned back,
may you cross over to U-poqer and be justified in the Presence (of the
   god).
May your *ba* be divine until drunkenness (?),[48]
as is done for a first-rate student
who is happy to do *maat.*[49]

Though these texts are the spitting image of mortuary spells, they are
addressed to the living, not the dead, and they are thus not examples of
mortuary spells or liturgies.

That the spells in mortuary liturgies and other tomb inscriptions so
closely resemble these elaborate greeting formulas lies in the fact that in
both cases, they are expressions of the same art: the art of the wish.
Certain mortuary spells, just like the greeting formulas of letters and
verbal intercourse, belong to the culture of Egyptian politeness: spells that
the tomb owner puts into the mouth of visitors to his tomb. The interpersonal form of transfiguration, form 0:2:2, was especially well suited
to spells of this sort. Any speaker could step into the role of the anony-
mous reciter.

In the case of spells that the tomb owner puts into the mouth of visitors
to his tomb, writing functions rather obviously and explicitly as "frozen
speech" that the visitor was to bring to life with "the breath of his mouth"
as he read them out loud. It is indeed just "a breath of the mouth" that
the tomb owner asks of the visitor to his tomb. It will make them no poorer,
nor will their hands be burdened. It costs them nothing. But the words
are salutary (*akh*) to the transfigured one. The tomb owner especially
hoped that visitors would read the texts on the tomb stela. They, and not
a priestly officiant, are implicitly, and often enough also explicitly,
addressed as readers, that is, as persons who read out loud and thus as
reciters of the recorded texts. They are requested to say an offering prayer
for the deceased. Often, a transfiguration spell is also placed in their
mouth, as for instance in the tomb of Nefersekheru at Zawyet el-Sultan:

All you people who will come,
you young people in the distant future,
may you care for my statue in my august tomb,
my lifelike image—
its form is truly my appearance.
May you say to it, after seeing it
while passing by my tomb:
"Breath for your nose,
blessed Nefersekheru!
A libation for your *ka*!
May your *ba* live, may your corpse endure.
May your name remain on earth,
and your goodly memory of a happy day,
may all bad things be far from you!"
Thus will the same be done by those (who come) after you.[50]

Mortuary spells, in the sense of addresses to the deceased with wishes for well-being in the afterlife, were thus not necessarily liturgical and intended for cultic recitation; they could also be recited by anyone who visited the tomb.[51] As noted, this was especially true of the texts on stelae. A typical example of such a tomb stela is afforded by the tomb of Paheri in el-Kab from early Dynasty 18 (ca. 1500 B.C.E.). The text begins with the offering formula to be recited by the visitor: "An offering that the king gives to god N., that he may grant this and that to the tomb owner"; this list of impersonally formulated gifts requested of the gods is immediately followed by wishes of form 0:2:2, which are addressed to the deceased himself:

May pure clothing of *paqet*-material be placed on you,
and bandages (?) of what has been removed from the god's body.
May pure oil be poured out for you,
may you drink water from the edge of the altar,
may you receive offerings among them,
you being equipped with the rank of a "foremost of the praised ones." . . .
May you come in and may you go forth with broad heart
in the favor of the lord of the gods!
A goodly burial after old age,
provisioning for the afterlife, when old age has come.

May you take your place in the "lord of life" (i.e., the coffin)
and be buried in your rock-cut tomb in the west.
Becoming a living *ba*,
that it may have disposal over bread, water, and air.
Transforming into a phoenix and a swallow,
and, according to your wish, into a falcon and a heron.[52]

May you cross over in the barque without being hindered.
May you sail the tide of the (open) sea and the inland waters.
May it happen that you live anew.
Your *ba* will not turn away from your corpse,
may your *ba* be divine, together with the transfigured ones.
The excellent *ba*s[53] will speak with you.
May your statues be among them
and receive what is dispensed on earth.
May you have disposal of water, and may you inhale the winds.
May you have an abundance of the needs of your heart.

May your eyes be given to you so as to see,
and your ears so as to hear what is spoken,
your mouth, it speaking,
and your legs, they walking.
Your hands and arms will serve you.
May your flesh be firm, and may your vessels be hale.
May you enjoy yourself in all your limbs!
May you test your limbs, they being complete and uninjured.
May nothing bad be given to you.
May your *ib*-heart be with you rightly,
may your *ḥȝ.tj*-heart be yours in its former condition.

May you ascend to the sky and may you open the netherworld
in all the transformations you have desired.
May one call out (the offering list) for you daily
at the offering table of Wennefer,
may you receive the offering loaves that have lain before (the god)
and the offerings of the Lord of the Sacred Land,
. . .
May you eat *šns*-cakes by the side of the god
at the great staircase of the lord of the Ennead.

May you break away from it at the place where he tarries in the first *ḏȝḏȝ.t*.
May you walk with them, and may you befriend the Following of Horus!
You will ascend and descend without being restrained,
without being turned away at the gate of the netherworld.
The two door leaves of the horizon will be opened for you,
and the doorbolts will open for you on their own.

You will enter the hall of the Two Truths,
while the god who is in it greets you.
May you alight within Imhet,
may you step out freely in the city of Hapy.
May your heart be broad in your tilling the field
on your plot in the Field of Reeds.
May your livelihood arise from what you have created,
may crops come to you in abundance.

A tow rope will be furnished for you at the ferry,
that you may cross as your heart desires.

May you go forth every morning,
and may you turn back every evening.
A torch will be burned for you in the night,
until sunlight rises on your breast.
"Welcome, welcome!" is said to you
in this your house of the living.
May you see Re in the horizon of the sky,
and may you behold Amun as he rises.

May you waken beautiful every day!
Every burden will be cast from you to the ground.
You will live for *nḥḥ*-eternity in joy
and in the favor of the god who is in you.
Your heart is with you, without abandoning you.
Your food will last in its place.

The typical stela text, however, is not a transfiguration or mortuary spell addressed to the deceased but rather a biographical inscription, and to the extent that mortuary spells appear on stelae, they are mostly embedded in a larger textual context that also contains biographical texts. Even in the case of the text just cited, the biography of the tomb owner immediately follows the quoted passage. The framework of what can be mentioned on a stela thus extends well beyond the offering situation. Every bit as general and comprehensive is the determining power of the stela as a place of recording: it removes boundaries rather than establishing them. It is thus not surprising that typical stela texts include a general sketch of life in the world beyond. We may go so far as to assume there is a connection between the biographical inscription typical of stelae and the mortuary spells that appear on them. The mortuary spells complement the representation of the life of the deceased in this world by means of their reference to the next-worldly existence of the transfigured one, suggesting a connection between this-worldly action and his well-being in the next world.[54] This connection is expressed explicitly in a form of mortuary wish attested only on stelae. The wish is always of the form "As surely as one is transfigured because he did this and that during life, may this and that be granted to me in the afterlife," for example:

> As surely as one is transfigured (*akh*) for having been *akh*-effective,
> my *ba* will follow Wennefer
> and transform into a divine falcon,
> come up out of the earth and open the netherworld
> so as to gaze upon Re at his rising
> on the morning of the New Year festival.

As surely as one is transfigured for having been *akh*-effective,
my *ba* will follow Hathor
and turn into a swallow of God's Land
so as to gather (seeds) under the myrrh trees,
and transform into a living *ba*
so as to gaze upon Re in his morning.[55]

The mortuary wishes in the tomb inscriptions no longer belong just to the semantics and pragmatics of a single, specific scene in the framework of the embalming or mortuary cult; rather, they concern the general semantics of the tomb and of existence after death. Here, too, we thus have to do with comparatively "situationally abstracted," disembedded, universally valid texts suited to a form of recording whose determining function removes rather than establishes boundaries. The special interest of the mortuary spells of the New Kingdom lies in this situative removal of boundaries. In this text genre, the New Kingdom created a medium in which the concept of life after death could be represented in a general, comprehensive manner, beyond all the specific cult situations—the embalming, Opening of the Mouth, funeral, and offering rituals—that entailed special sacramental explanations of specific acts, objects, and procedures. This general, basic, and comprehensive view of the questions of existence in the afterlife was characteristic of the mortuary spells of the New Kingdom, and it constituted the great innovation of this period, in contrast to the mortuary liturgies of the Middle Kingdom.

There was thus a great diversity in the ways that death was handled by language. We must distinguish between two different functions of written recording: whether they were to replace the recollection of the deceased, holding a store of knowledge for him, or whether they were to preserve the effectiveness of recitation, replacing the voice of the priest. We must note who is speaking to whom, and how this interpersonal relationship is verbally expressed. We must distinguish between the places and the contexts of the recording: whether they belong to the "secret area" of the sarcophagus chamber or to the accessible area of the cult chambers, which were themselves divided into an inner and outer area. We constantly have occasion to refer to the general validity of the dictum *saxa loquuntur,* "the stones speak," in Egypt. They speak, for they are inscribed, but before they can speak to us, we must reconstruct what they had to say within the world of ancient Egypt, and what the meaning and function of their inscribing was for the Egyptians themselves.

CHAPTER ELEVEN

In the Sign of the Enemy

The Protective Wake in the Place of Embalming

1. The Night before the Funeral

O f all the contexts in which mortuary liturgies were performed, the most important was the embalming ritual. Important information about this ritual is supplied by several inscriptions of the Middle Kingdom:

> Further, I have contractually obligated (*ḥtm*) the chief lector priest *Jnj-jtj=f*, son of *Nj-sw-Mnṯw*, son of *Jnj-jtj=f*, son of *Ṯtw*, to perform the liturgy in the place of embalming (*r jr.t jr.t m wˁb.t*) and to read (*šd.t*) the festival roll (*ḥȝb.t*) for my majesty at the month festival and the mid-month festival, that my name might be beautiful and that recollection of me might endure to the present day.[1]

> That she be embalmed in her place of embalming, that the work of the embalmer and the art of the chief lector priest be performed for her.[2]

Especially important among the rituals in the place of embalming was a night that was celebrated with hourly rituals and invocations. In all likelihood, this was the night that preceded the solemn burial procession from the place of embalming to the tomb. The importance of these nocturnal rites is made clear in the Story of Sinuhe. The story cites a letter from the king, inviting the émigré to return to Egypt and recounting the advantages of an Egyptian burial. One of these was the carrying out of a wake:

A wake will be divided up for you with unguent and four-threaded fabric of Tayt.[3]

The mention of unguent and fabric shows that we are in the context of the embalming ritual, while the key word *wḏ^c* "to divide" refers to the division of the night into hours. There is a rather clear reference to this division in a spell from the Coffin Texts that, as we shall see, belongs precisely to the context of this wake. It is spell 49, which contains an invocation of the protective deities of the wake:

Trembling befalls the eastern Light-land
at the mourning cry from the hall of embalming.
Isis is in great mourning,
Nephthys bewails
this eldest god, the lord of the gods.
An attack is planned against his invigilation in the hall of embalming
by the one who did something to him,
after he transformed into a flea against him,
so as to creep under his flanks.

Be watchful, O you in the hall of purification,
pay attention, oh you in the hall of embalming,
see, the god, his body is in fear
of the enemies, who have transformed themselves!
Light the torches, O you guardians of the chamber,
you gods in the darkness!
Lend your protection to your lord,
divide the hours for the lord of the white crown,
until Horus comes from Heliopolis,
to whom the great Atef-crowns were given![4]
The power of the *Jm.j-w.t* appears,
the guardians of the chamber rejoice,
the eldest ones have received their panther skins,
and the staffs are set up in front of the place of embalming
for[5] Anubis, who has come in peace,
appearing as vizier.

He says, "You shall provide protection, O you with attentive faces,
you who watch over the hall of purification and come in the following of
    Nebedj (the demon of darkness)
who enter into the most select ones, who create your[6] breath,

who prepare the daily offering of this great god, the lord of the gods,
who guard the doors[7] for their lord!
Hurry and lend a hand in the palace!
Great weariness reigns in the embalming chamber (*sṯ.t*),
because of this god who is here before me,
filled with fear in his (own) palace!"
So says Anubis.

It is not good in the opinion of those who are present,
that which is said in their midst:
"He (i.e., Osiris) will be harmed in his palace
by the one who (already) did something to him!"
(Rather:) seized is the demon who is in the darkness,
harm was done to his band.

This spell, along with the statement cited from the Story of Sinuhe, refer to the night before the funeral, which was celebrated in the form of a wake. The night was divided into hours, and each hour had a protective deity of its own. Priests played the roles of these deities. Such a ritual is preserved to us in its entirety, with all its rites and recitations, only from the Osiris cult of the Ptolemaic temples.[8] There, the wake went on around the clock, and thus, also during the twelve hours of the daytime. The rituals carried out during each hour consisted of the recitation of a "transfiguration" by the chief lector priest, the carrying out of a censing, or (during the day) an anointing, or (during the night) a libation by an officiant, and the recitation of a dirge by Isis or Nephthys. But the passages just cited, along with a host of other references, especially in the Coffin Texts, show that in the mortuary cult, the wake goes back to the beginning of the second millennium B.C.E.

Typical of these spells are invocations to the presiding deities to encourage them to the utmost watchfulness and attentiveness. It was of the utmost importance that Seth, the murderer of Osiris, not penetrate into the embalming chamber. The situation was all the more dangerous in that the enemy was able to transform himself and could appear in a tiny, scarcely visible form, such as that of a flea. The wake during the night before the funeral thus took place against a background of protection from attack by the enemy, and thus against the image of death that I have called "death as enemy." The night before the funeral was spent enacting a ritual of intense watchfulness.

In a wake liturgy preserved to us on a late papyrus in the British Museum,[9] the guardians are called "those with piercing eyes," a reference to the sharpness of their eyesight, and they are given names:

Ho, you gods there,
with piercing eyes in the following of Osiris,

"Nedjehnedjeh," "Qed-ka,"
"He to whom the flame prophesies on the tip of his fire (?),"
"Redeye, who is in the house of the red fabric,"
"Flaming one, who comes out backwards,"
"He who gazes before him on what is brought to him by day,"
whom Re appointed to protect Osiris
for he did not want Seth to see him.

Arise, you gods in your hours,
give protection, you gods in the darkness!
You shall smite Seth for him,
you shall turn back his following for him.
Do not allow the attack to succeed a second time.

We also encounter this group of protective deities in the decoration of coffins from the later stages of Egyptian history,[10] where there are usually eight of them. On the coffin of Ankhhapy in Cairo, the eight are divided into two groups of four, led on the right by Horus and Isis and on the left by Thoth and Nephthys, all striding toward, a scarab in the center.[11] The deities who lead them say to the guardians:

O you gods with piercing eyes in the following of Osiris!
(To be recited.) Keep watch, O you who are in your hours,
be attentive, O you who are in your darkness,
you shall give protection for Osiris N.,
you shall smite those who rise up against him,
you shall turn back for him those who band together against him.
Do not allow the disaster to happen a second time.
Do not allow them to rise up against you (= him)
and penetrate into that sacred chamber in which he is.

Their role is similarly described in a text in the Sokar chamber of the Temple of Edfu:

The gods with piercing eyes in the following of Osiris,
the household of the Weary-of-heart,
the lords of the knife who live on bloodbaths,
who lead the enemies to the slaughter,
whom Re has appointed to protect His Majesty,
for he does not wish that Seth see him,
who protect the bier, who drive away the rebel,
who sanctify the gate of the place,
who watch over him at the beginning of the darkness,
who divide the night into hours for him,
who arrange his protection in the morning,
until Re goes into his mother.[12]

Their task is to prevent the "second time." Seth has struck once, killing Osiris and dismembering his corpse. Combining their powers, Isis and Nephthys, Horus, Thoth and Anubis, and the other gods of the embalming ritual have been able to rectify this attack. Now, all depends on avoiding a second attack. The point of the wake is to build, by ritual means, a wall around Osiris-Khentamentiu/N. to protect him against further attacks by Death, a wall that will last forever. Above all, Seth must be prevented from seeing Osiris in his helpless condition. We have already come upon this motif in spell 312 of the Coffin Texts (= Book of the Dead chapter 78), which has to do with transforming into a "divine falcon" and crossing over into the realm of Osiris:

> (Osiris speaks)
>
> Spread fear of me, create respect for me,
> so that the gods of the netherworld fear me
> and defend the gates for me,
> so that the one who wounded me does not approach me
> and see me in the house of darkness
> and discover my weakness, which is hidden from him.[13]

After invoking the guardians, the wake liturgy of the London papyrus turns to the enemy himself, who must be kept away from the embalming chamber:

> Back, you wicked rebel,
> step not into this sacred chamber where Osiris is!
> Six excellent *akh*-spirits[14] are there
> to protect this illustrious god.
> Greetings, you gods in your mysteriousness!
> They punish you with what is in their hands,
> they fell you with what is in their mouth.
>
> Back, wretched rebel,
> come not to that tomb where Osiris is!
> Anubis has arisen against you,
> to lodge that punishment against you,
> for you have planned
> to gaze upon the hiddenness of the Great God on that night.
> His son Horus,
> he [. . .] you in that awful place of execution
> in the custody of [. . .],
> according to that which Geb has ordained to be done to you.
>
> Back, O Nebedj, son of Nut!
> Come not to that palace of Osiris.
> Thoth [. . .] against him,

264

in that his true form of Isdes.
The Two Sisters go out against you.
A flame goes out against you to the sky,
and wrath against you out of the earth,
they drive your *ba* in the sky in the presence of Re,
they punish your *ka* in the earth in the presence of Geb,
they mourn you in the presence of the *ka*s at the head of the living,
according to that which Re commanded to do to you.

Back, rebel
of wretched character, Redeye!
Enter not into that embalming chamber where Osiris is!
Shesemu has arisen to drive you away,
with the sister who is great of regard;
she it is who mourns for her brother Osiris.
She has driven away your *ba* and annihilated your *ka*;
you cannot escape from that awful place of execution
in the custody of Geb, forever,
according to that which the great tribunal in the realm of the dead has
   commanded to be done to you.

Many indications in the texts point to the fact that this wake was celebrated during the night before the funeral. Thus, it is not only stated that
the wake will last until morning and the sunrise but also that the deceased
will leave the place of embalming in the morning: "Come, let us mourn
this Osiris N until he leaves us early in the morning!"[15] Or:

> Bastet, the daughter of Atum,
> the first-born daughter of the All-lord,
> she is your protection until the earth brightens
> and you enter the realm of the dead.[16]

In mortuary liturgy CT.2, Coffin Texts spell 50 describes the morning
departure from the embalming chamber, after the concluding rites of the
wake and the procession to the tomb:

> The god appears in his shrine
> when he hears how the two gongs have been rung for him.
> His protection is effected among the gods and the children of Horus-
>   Avenger-of-His-Father.
>
> Geb is there for your protection,
> your own father, to whom you were born.
> The arms of Nut, who bore you, are behind you, elevating your beauty.
> Your *ba*, which is in Mendes, lives.

Those who are ill-disposed are held in check for you,
Seth is in fear when he sees you.
He casts his uproar to the ground,
for the fear that radiates from him befalls his own limbs.

Ptah, Beautiful-of-face among the gods,
and Sokar are at the prow of your barque,
their arms are on the divine seal.

Bastet, the daughter of Atum,
the first-born daughter of the All-lord,
she is your protection until the earth brightens
and you enter the realm of the dead.

The Eye of Horus beams for you,
and it goes with you into the realm of the dead.
May you live on their hearts,
(the hearts of those) who are in the following of your brother Seth.

That which is said to He-in-his-Shrine,
(namely, to) Re himself as All-lord,
when he bids the coming of the gods in his following.

The barque travels, towed is the rope.[17]
With happy heart, the god enters the realm of the dead.

Horus is king,
after he has played the role of *sa-meref*-priest for him:
the opponent is silent when he sees you.
The *sem*-priest, the chief lector priest,
and the embalmer: each one of them casts down the enemy.[18]

The nurse of the souls of Heliopolis has come,
laden with the revenue of the All-lord.
Anubis, foremost of the divine booth,
offers the necessities on behalf of the chief lector priest
until morning, when the day dawns,
when the god comes out of the hall of embalming.

The last two verses furnish a clear indication of exactly when this ritual was performed. There is much evidence that the wake took place at the end of the embalming rituals, during the night before the funeral. The great processions of the two major festivals that went back to the royal burial rituals of the Old Kingdom—the Abydos mysteries and the Memphite Sokar festival—were also preceded by a night filled with rituals. In the case of the festival of Sokar, it was the night called *Ntry.t*, "the Divine," when the participants wore garlands of onions, while in the case of the Abydos festival, the nocturnal festival that preceded the procession in the morning bore the enigmatic name "Haker."[19] *Sdr.t* or *sdrj.t* "spending the night" designates what is to be understood as "wake":

> May he hear the *hnw*-cries in the mouth of Ta-Wer
> at the Haker festival during the night of spending the night,
> the wake of the battling Horus.[20]

Chapter 18 of the Book of the Dead, which draws together all these nocturnal rituals so as to draw a parallel between them and the wake of the deceased, also mentions the Haker festival:

> O Thoth, who vindicates Osiris against his enemies,
> vindicate N. as well against his enemies
> in the great tribunal that is in Abydos
> on that night of the Haker festival,
> when the damned are singled out and the blessed are counted,
> when there is dancing in This.[21]

Just as the Haker festival took place during the night before the procession at Abydos and the *ntrj.t* "divine" festival occurred the night before the *henu* procession, the wake was held on the night before the funeral procession.

We are well informed regarding the rituals of the *ntrj.t* festival during the night that preceded the procession of the *henu*-barque during the Sokar festival. A recently published Ptolemaic Period papyrus in New York[22] begins with a ritual that was expressly to be celebrated during this night:

> The great decree that is issued in reference to the nome of the
>   netherworld (*jgr.t*),
> fixed in the night of the diadem
> to cause that Osiris be installed as ruler in the nome of the netherworld,
> . . . while his *ba* appears in the Hale Eye (variant, in the temple of Sokar)
> and is transformed atop his corpse.
> What is carried out during the *ntrj.t*-night, in the dreadful night,
> that night of going away and becoming distant,
> that night of the going forth of the voice,
> that night of lonely sleep,
> that night of great defensive magic,
> that night of hacking the earth in tears,
> that night of loneliness,
> that night of mourning,
> that night of hacking the earth, when the whole land gazes upon Sokar,
> Upper and Lower Egypt are in silence,
> and the entrance to the closed place remains at rest.[23]

In the ritual cycle of the Sokar festival, this night corresponded to the night before the burial procession in the mortuary cult. The ritual of the

New York papyrus begins with a "Great Appeal" to be sung in the third hour of the night, called "the secluded wake, when all the gods and goddesses are overcome by hunger and thirst."[24] We are dealing here with an address to those in the netherworld, to whom Osiris is presented as their new ruler. The high priest directs the ceremony, presenting libations and censings to those in the netherworld.

Next, a double chorus composed of those from the "northern" and the "southern sanctuary" begins to sing an antiphonal processional that is to accompany Osiris' arrival in the netherworld:

> The southern sanctuary: Let us go to the King of Upper Egypt, for he has departed from you! To be recited ten times.
> The northern sanctuary: Where is he, the King of the Two Lands, that we may receive him? To be recited ten times.
> The southern sanctuary: He is landing at the great crypt in the nome of the realm of the dead! To be recited five times.
> The northern sanctuary: O, his temple creates the forms! To be recited five times.
> The southern sanctuary: Receive the tears of Isis, the plaintive cries of Nephthys! To be recited five times.
> The northern sanctuary: O, he who keeps himself far from you, he will always be distant from you![25]

At this point, Isis makes her appearance, and, accompanied by Nephthys, she begins to sing highly lyrical and emotional dirges;[26] we have cited extracts from these in chapter 5. From time to time, the chorus, called "men and women," breaks into their songs of mourning. Even Pharaoh, probably played by a priest, appears and joins the two sisters in mourning Osiris.[27] This great mourning scene extends over several columns of text. The dirges are intended to induce Osiris to come forth. His death is represented as a departure and distancing, and this night is thus celebrated as the "Night of Loneliness." The deities are gathered together, to be sure, but they have been left alone by the departure of Osiris. Their moaning and wailing is intended to bring him back. Finally, Anubis offers an explanation: "This god is arriving at the great entrance to the nome of the realm of the dead."[28] Now begins the second part of the ritual, which is devoted to escorting Osiris through the twenty-one gates of the realm of the dead. At each portal, the priest recites a ceremonious greeting to the gateway and the deities who guard it, either Isis or Nephthys sings a dirge, Anubis bids the gods who are present to show reverence to the arriving Osiris, and Horus greets the gate and the deity who guards it, gives proof of his purity, and is granted admittance. The procession then moves on to the next gateway. At the seventeenth gate, Isis can no longer control herself:

Isis remains alone with the shrine.
She opens it and beholds the god.
She prostrates herself before him and says:
"I have opened the Golden Shrine,
but my eye is sealed by darkness,
though it sees to the four corners.
I have opened the Golden Shrine,
but my heart is in despair and anguish,
it has strewn wounds in my body.
I have opened the shrine and want to compel him,
I call to him, and when he answers,
I shall live on his voice.
I have opened the shrine,
ah, would that there were opening without closing,
would that there were answering without silence!"[29]

But the procession and the mourning go on, all the way to the twentieth gate. When they arrive there, an actor designated "The-one-in-the-chest" speaks. We are probably to view him as the spokesman of the dead Osiris himself; the word "chest" can also mean "coffin."[30]

Why should loneliness be bad for me?
Is the earth anxious about me?
Is it the people to whom I turn?
Is what lies before me inaccessible?
Is it not rather what lies behind me?
Are Busiris and Abydos without me?
Oh, would that I be able to see Memphis
and be able to go to Heliopolis!
Are the cities and nomes anxious about me?
I shall go and see all the faces in another form,
without their realizing it, on another occasion.
See, the earth, whose sight I have sampled,
I shall spread a cloud (*ḏj=j gb.t*) when it (i.e., the earth) turns to me.[31]

In this ritual, the entry of Osiris (and thus also of the deceased) into the netherworld is celebrated as a striding through portals in the sense of a transition from this realm, via the realm of death, into the place of eternal, salutary security, as we have seen in chapter 6 with the help of other examples. Here, this transition is enacted in anticipation of the procession (the "circuit around the walls" or the funeral procession) that will follow on the next morning. During the night, there is a rehearsal of what will be publicly enacted in the morning, and whose result is to last forever.

The reference of this anticipatory enactment also connects the ritual of the wake with the resting of the coffin in the sarcophagus chamber, which from the next night on, is to stretch into all eternity. There seems to be a close connection between the nocturnal rites and recitations of the wake and the decoration of Egyptian coffins. It seems that the coffin was to keep the attentiveness and watchfulness of the gods stored effectively around the deceased forever. We have already encountered the principle of breathing life into objects by inscribing them—*saxa loquuntur*—in reference to the decoration of coffins, in connection with the image of death as return. In that image, the coffin addressed the deceased with the words of Nut, the sky- and mother-goddess, greeting him as her son. The most detailed text of this sort is on the lid of the huge granite outer sarcophagus of King Merneptah. This text, too, makes reference to the wake. Neith, who addresses the deceased as mother and coffin, assures him that the deities of the nocturnal rites will gather to protect him, and in precisely the same order in which they appear on coffins of the Middle Kingdom.

The coffins of the Middle Kingdom have the peculiarity that they were not only decorated on the outside but also again and again inscribed on the inside. Among the texts chosen for these inscriptions, a central position is occupied by spells that clearly were recited in connection with the nocturnal wake.

2. *Coffin Texts Spell 62*

Coffin Texts spell 62 mentions three such sequences of spells, or mortuary liturgies, that were to be recited in the context of the wake. In this spell, which is found only on the coffin of the nomarch Amenemhet but occurs there five times, Horus himself makes his appearance as the god of the coffin and addresses the deceased, just as the goddess Neith does in the inscription on the sarcophagus lid of King Merneptah. Spell 62 is evidently not a traditional text but was written specifically for the nomarch Amenemhet, as is also the case with the Merneptah inscription, which is another individual composition with no parallels whatsoever on other sarcophagi or other types of monument.

In what follows, I wish to take a close look at this splendid text. In its unusually clear structure and the poetic power of its imagery, it stands out from the mass of ordinary mortuary texts. Moreover, from this spell, it becomes particularly clear what the mortuary liturgies recited during the night before the burial were concerned with.

> Greetings to you, my father Osiris!
> See, I have come, I am Horus.
> I shall open your mouth together with Ptah,
> I shall transfigure you together with Thoth.

I shall give you your heart in your body,
that you may recollect what you have forgotten.
I shall cause that you eat bread as often as you want,
more than you did on earth.

I shall give you your legs,
that you may be able to walk and let your soles "roar."
I shall cause that you travel with the south wind
and that you hurry with the north wind.
Your steps are (faster) than a glance of the face,
you hurry there (faster) than the wink of an eye.

I shall cause that you transform yourself in the company of the *dwj.t*-bird,
and cause that you fare over the *ptr.wj*-waters and over the lake.
You shall cross the sea on foot,
as you have done on land.
You shall rule the streams in the company of the phoenix,
with no one opposing you on the bank.
I shall cause that you act as one who plumbs the depths[32] with a pole of
    forty cubits
that grew on a cedar of Byblos
as you stand in the barque of Re
after crossing the "Lake of the Subjects (*rḫjj.t*)."

You will be vindicated on the Day of Judgment
in the tribunal of the lord of rigor mortis.
(The liturgy) "The Earth is Hacked Up" will be recited for you,
the rebel will be repulsed,
the one who comes in the night,
and the robber in the early morning.
The nocturnal ceremony will be performed in the form of (the liturgy)
    "The Great *Ṯhb* comes"
and (the liturgy) "*ḥnm.w*" of the house of Isis.

You will cross the steppes with Re,
he will show you the places of enjoyment.
You will find the wadis full of water
and wash yourself to your refreshment.
You will pluck papyrus and reeds,
and lotus blooms with buds.
Water fowl will come to you in the thousands,
lying on your way.
When you have cast your throwstick at them,
a thousand are felled by the sound of its flight,
gray geese and green-breasted geese,
trp-geese and *st*-geese
The young of the gazelle will be brought to you,
and herds of white male antelopes (?).
The "cow" of the ibex will be brought to you, fattened with grain,

and the male of the woolly sheep.
A ladder to the sky will be knotted together for you,
and Nut will stretch her arms out to you.
You will fare on the Winding Lake
and set sail in the "eight-boat."[33]
Those two crews will navigate you,
the imperishable ones and the unwearying ones.
They will punt you and tow you
to the bank with their ropes of bronze.

I know of only one other text that addresses the deceased with the solemn formula "greetings to you": the inscription on the sarcophagus lid of Merneptah.[34]

> Greetings, my son Osiris,
> King and Lord of the Two Lands

The Merneptah text is in fact entitled *dw3.w* "hymn." If we compare Coffin Texts spell 62 with the inscription on the sarcophagus lid of Merneptah, we note major similarities. These texts obviously belong to the same genre. Both texts are lengthy speeches that a deity addresses to the deceased. Both depict the beneficent deeds they wish to have done for the deceased in the form of cause and effect. In both cases a deity speaks, promising to care for the well-being of the deceased in the afterlife in a comprehensive sense that also includes the other gods. In the case of Merneptah, Neith appears in this superordinate role, representing the entire realm of the gods, while in the case of Amenemhet, it is Horus. In the case of Merneptah, Neith addresses the deceased, who is equated with Osiris, as her son, while in the case of Amenemhet, Horus addresses his father. In this regard, it is quite surprising that in two of the five versions, Horus speaks to the god Osiris; in these versions, the name of the deceased does not even occur.

Horus makes his appearance and describes all that he will do for the deceased. His first acts (verses 3–4) are "Opening of the Mouth," together with Ptah, and "transfiguration," along with Thoth. The "Opening of the Mouth" was a matter of artisans, for it was carried out in the "house of gold" at the conclusion of the preparation of a statue, and it thus fell in the domain of artists, artisans, and Ptah, their patron god. Transfiguration, however, was a matter of writing and magical recitation, for which Thoth, the scribe, ritualist, and magician, was responsible.

The next act is the replacing of the heart (verses 5–6) in the body so as to restore the ability to recollect. This is usually a matter for Nut, the mother- and sky-goddess;[35] here, Horus assumes her role. The special point of this passage lies in the motif of recollection. Placing the heart in the body restores the deceased's ability to recollect, and with that, his personal identity.[36] In the Egyptian Elysium, the Field of Reeds, there is also talk of "recollection":[37]

> I have disposal of this very great magic of mine,
> which is in my body and my place.
> I recollect what I have forgotten.[38]

> My spells are secure,
> for I recollect what I have forgotten.[39]

The deceased recollects the spells with which he outfitted himself for his journey in the afterlife. And in the texts of the Bacchic mysteries, the mystic is to recollect what he learned about the afterlife in the mysteries.

After the replacement of the heart and the restoration of recollection, knowledge, and personality, verses 7–8 mention eating, the first and most important basis of life. Here, for the first time, we encounter the motif of an intensification of the possibilities of earthly life. The deceased will not just live as he did during his lifetime on earth but far better and more luxuriously. Verses 9–14 continue this point with regard to the motif of movement, employing images that make it clear we are dealing with a composition of unusually poetic, expressive power. Transfiguration spells constantly mention the restoration of the deceased's ability to move about, especially in connection with the embalming process. But so far as I can see, never is anything meant other than the normal ability of the living to move about. I know of no other passage in which the locomotive power bestowed on the deceased intensifies into the supernatural. Therein lies the unusual interest of this passage, as well as in the unusually poetic metaphors with which this superhuman locomotive power is described.

The next ten verses (15–24) describe movement toward water. Typical is the connection of the theme of transformation with that of freedom to move and to cross. The deceased assumes the form of a bird so as to cross the body of water that separates him and the realm of death from Elysium. The miracle of movement finds expression above all in the motif of "walking on water,"[40] as well as in the gigantic proportions of the steering pole that the deceased is to ply at the prow of the sun barque.[41] In verses 19–20, the deceased appears "in the company" of the phoenix and not "as" a phoenix, as later in the Book of the Dead, where spell 83 serves to "transform (him) into a phoenix."[42]

The next verses (21–24) transplant the deceased into the sun barque. Because of its changing water levels, the Nile was difficult to navigate; it changed its course, and new sand banks and shoals were constantly forming. In the case of boats of some draft, the depth of the water had to be measured constantly. To this end, a man stood at the prow of the boat, poking a pole into the water. This practice can still be observed today, though in the absence of the inundation, thanks to the High Dam at Aswan, the river is largely under control. Our text transposes this scene into the boat with which the sun god crosses the sky, for even there, the formation of sand banks had to be reckoned with. In the celestial ocean, there lurked a giant sea serpent that drank up the waters. If it was not exorcised and speared by Seth at the right time, so that it disgorged the water it had swallowed, the sun barque ran the risk of being stranded.[43] It thus becomes clear that his transformation did not return the deceased to the world above but rather led him into regions of the world beyond. Crossing the Lake of the Subjects, the deceased distanced himself from the realm of the living, as well as from the realm of death of ordinary mortals, and entered into the divine presence of Elysium. These verses conclude the magnificent depiction of locomotive capacity that Horus promises to bestow on the deceased, and the sentences containing the turn of expression "I shall cause" also come to an end. The things that follow are not the gifts of Horus alone; they require the assistance of other gods.

First, there follows a stanza of eight verses (25–32) that constitutes the exact middle of the entire spell. This stanza gives us decisive indications of the function of the mortuary liturgies that were recited during the night before the funeral. The theme of this stanza is vindication in the Judgment of the Dead. All the preceding—the corporal and mental restoration of the person of the deceased, the bestowing of freedom of movement, and the crossing of bodies of water in the next world—are prerequisites that enable the deceased to face the Judgment. As can be seen, this is not the actual Judgment of the Dead but rather its ritual enactment. This is perhaps the most interesting stanza in the entire text, for it deals with the mortuary liturgies and their performance on behalf of the deceased:

> (The liturgy) "The Earth is Hacked up" will be recited for you,
> the rebel will be repulsed,
> the one who comes in the night,
> and the robber in the early morning.
> The nocturnal ceremony will be performed in the form of (the liturgy)
>   "The Great *Thb* comes"
> and (the liturgy) "*hnm.w*" of the house of Isis.

The liturgies mentioned in verses 25–27 can only be those consisting of Coffin Texts spells 1–26. Every single word in these verses is a key word from these liturgies: the concepts "vindication" and "judgment" occur passim, the "tribunal of the lord of sighs" is a citation from Coffin Texts spell 13,[44] and the key words "the earth is hacked up" (*ḥbs-tꜣ*) and "recite" or "dig" (*šdj*) begin the great judgment scene in Coffin Texts spell 7,[45] which we shall deal with in the following chapter:

> *The earth is hacked up* after the two companions have battled,
> after their two feet have *dug up* the divine pond in Heliopolis.[46]

If this interpretation is correct, this passage sheds a unique light on the purpose of these liturgies and on the context in which they were performed. The purpose was the vindication of the deceased "on the Day of Judgment," and thus a liturgical enactment of the Judgment of the Dead, with a successful outcome, as later in Book of the Dead chapter 125. This agrees fully with the titles of the liturgies that have come down to us. The context in which they were performed was the nocturnal wake, for only on that occasion was the repelling of the enemy a central concern, with the belief that he might make his way into the embalming chamber and do harm to the corpse.

This interpretation also supplies the key to the three verses that follow, which would otherwise remain thoroughly unclear: "The wake will be carried out in the form of (the liturgy) 'The Great *Ṯhb* comes' and (the liturgy) '*ḥnm.w*.'" The first phrase consists of the enigmatic opening words of the liturgy CT no. 3 (Coffin Texts spells 63–74). The second concept occurs repeatedly as a refrain in the liturgy CT no. 2 (Coffin Texts spells 51–59).[47]

The brief stanza referring to the nocturnal wake, which is understood here as an enactment of the Judgment of the Dead, is followed in verses 32–48 by a sprawling, colorful depiction of the joys of paradise that await those who are vindicated. This text has long since[48] been interpreted as a depiction of certain scenes from life in the next world, which also occur in tomb decoration: journeying by boat and plucking papyrus in the thickets of the marshes, fishing and fowling, and hunting in the desert. In the captions to these tomb scenes, they are classified generically as *sḥmḥ-jb*, with the verb probably to be understood as a causative of *ḥm* "to forget" and the phrase as meaning "to cause the heart to forget (its cares)." This expression sums up the Egyptian concept of leisure. As in other cultures, leisure in Egypt was a characteristic of the upper, or "leisure" class. This aristocratic aspect of the culture of leisure was visualized by a cycle of representations that included, in particular, hunting in the desert and fishing and fowling in the marshes. In all periods, the hunt was the most genteel form of the culture of aristocratic leisure.[49] Our text does not employ the expression *sḥmḥ-jb* from the tomb captions but rather the essentially synonymous but even more comprehensive *šms-jb* "to follow the heart." The Instruction of Ptahhotep devotes an entire maxim to the concept of *šms-jb*:

> Follow your heart so long as you live,
> and do not multiply concerns.[50]
> Do not cut back the time of leisure (*šms-jb*):
> it is an abomination for the *ka*, if its time is reduced.
> Do not waste time on daily needs,[51]
> above and beyond taking care of your household.
> If possessions exist, then follow your heart,
> for possessions are of no use if it is unwilling.[52]

Here, "following the heart" (*šms-jb*) is placed in opposition to concerns and to taking care of one's household, and it seems perfectly clear to me that it refers to the concept of leisure. The Coffin Text images the concept of "following the heart" by means of hunting scenes from the tomb decoration, which it expounds verbally. Of course, the text does not "describe" any actual tomb scenes; rather, it sketches an imaginary scenario that the tomb scenes depict using their own means. In this regard, it is again characteristic that the text does not simply describe "pleasures of fishing and fowling" in this life but rather sublimates them into the supernatural. Amenemhet's throwstick does not just hit something; the very sound of its flight fells "thousands" of water fowl. The hunt succeeds on its own by means of supernatural, magical power (thereby, of course, losing much of its sporting character).[53] In the later stages of Egyptian history, the expression "roaming the marshes filled with birds," that is, a pleasure trip to the thickets of the marshes, served as an expression of leisure and enjoyment: "I spent even more time sitting at leisure (*ḥmsj m whʿ*) and roaming the marshes filled with birds (*sꜣb sšw*) in the course of what I did."[54]

We would love to know whether these "places of pleasing the heart" are to be pictured as being in this world or the next. Here, it does not seem to be a matter of the Field of Reeds. Is it already a matter of "coming out by day," a return to the world of the living? The pictorial representations of fishing and fowling in the tombs of the Old, Middle, and New Kingdoms probably refer to this world. The tomb owner had himself represented engaging in activities he had enjoyed during life, and which he wished to continue enjoying after death. Yet by adding traits of the wondrous, our text displaces these activities into a realm beyond. In an offering text in the tomb of Rekhmire (Theban Tomb 100),[55] the following words are addressed to the deceased:

> You will cross the river and traverse the Great Green,
> a shank of beef in your mouth.
> The goddess of the fields (comes to you) with her fish,
> and the mistress of fishing with her geese.
> May you ascend to the sky

garlanded with faïence pendants
and clad in turquoise.

Here, we encounter the motif of fishing and fowling in a comparable context. Here, too, the reference is next-worldly. The crossing of the water occurs in a context of festive abundance, as festive as the ascent to the sky in what follows, an ascent in which the deceased wears the festive jewelry of Sakhmet.[56]

After the lengthy stanza dedicated to *šms-jb*, our Coffin Text also closes with an ascent to the sky in verses 49–56. Reception by Nut and entry into the course of the sun constitute the conclusion of the text. The ladder to the sky is attested countless times in the Pyramid Texts,[57] and reception by the sky goddess is mentioned equally often. The "Winding Lake" surely refers to the body of water called *mr n-ḫ}* in the Pyramid Texts, on which the sun god crosses the heavens.[58] The "imperishable ones" and the "unwearying ones" are the sun god's typical crew members. The "towing" of the solar barque is mentioned in sun hymns. In the ritual of the wake, the eleventh hour of the day is the time for "fixing the tow rope."[59]

The text is clearly organized, far more so than is otherwise usual in mortuary liturgies. It is clearly a poetic text. Throughout, the verses are connected into pairs, and the verse pairs into stanzas of 4, 6, or 8 verses, and in two cases, the stanzas are joined together into larger stanzas of 16 verses:

		self presentation	2	greeting
	8		2	opening of the mouth, transfiguration
			2	placing the heart in the body
24			2	feeding
	16	movement	6	on land
				in the air
			6	on water
			4	in the sun barque
8	8	wake with mortuary liturgies	2	vindication
			4	*ḥbs-t}* liturgy
			2	*jj ṯhb-wr* and *ḥnmw* liturgy
24	16	*šms-ib* in the company of the sun god	6	roving through the desert
			6	fowling with the throwstick
			4	hunting in the desert
	8	ascent to the sky	2	ascent to the sky
			4	crossing in the sun barque
			2	nocturnal journey

The whole is centrally structured:

24	actions of Horus on behalf of the deceased
8	recitation of mortuary liturgies
24	actions of the deceased in the company of the sun god

The significance of the central stanza of eight verses as a hinge between the two sections of 24 verses each is now clear. The recitation of the liturgies proves to be the act that is decisive for the destiny of the deceased in the afterlife.

The first person of the speaker appears only in the first part. The central stanza is formulated in the passive: "is recited," "is performed." In the last part, the deceased himself acts. The agential "I" of the speaking Horus is now completely withdrawn. The central stanza marks the turning point. By means of the "vindication," full personal sovereignty is restored to the deceased, and he can move about as he wishes in the company of the gods, "striding freely like the lords of eternity," as we read in the Instruction for Merikare. For its part, the vindication before the judges of the dead was, if not exactly magically forced, at least accompanied in a supportive manner by the nocturnal recitation of the three mortuary liturgies. The text is therefore of fundamental importance to our understanding of the function of these liturgies.

3. Wakes and Coffin Decoration

Coffin Texts spell 62 is a key text for the function of mortuary liturgies. It furnishes us with a first and decisive answer to the question of what a mortuary liturgy was and to that of how we are to pick out such texts in the mass of the mortuary literature, naming three of these liturgies and describing their ritual function. These three liturgies are preserved in extenso, and they can give us a detailed impression of what such mortuary liturgies recited during the night before the burial were like.

1. The liturgy "The Earth is Hacked Up" (*khebes-ta*) consists of spells 1–26 (or 28) in de Buck's edition
2. The liturgy "The Great *Tjeheb* Comes" corresponds to spells 63–74
3. The liturgy *Khenemu* comprises de Buck's spells 44–61

What spell 62 tells us about this genre is its ritual setting in the embalming chamber and in the night, the liturgies in all likelihood occurring after the wake during the night before the funeral. But spell 62 itself, which furnishes us with so much information about the mortuary liturgies, does not belong to this genre. It is an independent text and a divine speech that was probably not composed as a record of an actual recitation, but rather as a virtual recitation that existed only in writing. The genre "divine speech" is widespread on coffins. It is in fact the earliest form of coffin inscription, in the form of texts in which the sky goddess Nut addresses the deceased as embodiment of coffin and mother. This genre thus constitutes the canonical form of coffin inscription. In the Old

Kingdom, it was above all Nut and Geb who addressed and welcomed the deceased as their son. At a later date, the most splendid example is afforded by the lengthy divine speech of Neith, which fills the entire lid of the outer sarcophagus of King Merneptah. In the later periods of Egyptian history, divine speeches developed into a new form of coffin texts. Here, it is the gods who stood watch over the hours of the wake who address the deceased with lengthy speeches. For the most part, these speeches are taken from chapter 169 of the Book of the Dead, and for its own part, this chapter goes back to a Coffin Texts liturgy that we shall study in detail in the following chapter. The coffin was thus the classic location for the recording of divine speeches.

Divine speeches on coffins can be interpreted in two ways:

(a) as recording a speech that was recited by a priest playing the role of a deity in the context of the wake, as is certainly the case with the divine speeches drawn from Book of the Dead chapter 169; and

(b) as the speech of an actual deity (and not a priestly recitation), and thus a "virtual speech" that was actualized by writing. This is the case with Coffin Texts spell 62, in which the god Horus addressees the nomarch Amenemhet as his father, just as the goddess Neith addresses the king as her son in the Merneptah inscription.

It is thus clear why the nomarch Amenemhet had this spell copied five times on his coffin. In this spell, Horus speaks as chief of the entire operation, as orchestrater of the wake and guarantor of the salvation of the deceased in the afterlife. This is the principal text of the entire coffin, and in it, the coffin in a certain sense itself speaks to the deceased, dedicating to him all that is otherwise recorded on it. This is the decisive point in which Horus here usurps the role of Nut, as Neith does in the Merneptah inscription. The nomarch Amenemhet has replaced the mother-child relationship, which otherwise served deceased persons as the relationship that welcomed them into the enveloping coffin, with the father-son relationship. For Amenemhet, the role of the deceased father was the more important, and the son's address was thus the most important guarantee of his continued existence.

Horus was god of the mortuary cult. Nut personified the Elysian realm the deceased hoped to enter, while Horus embodied life on earth, the community of the living, the society to which the deceased wished still to belong through the mediation of his son. Horus was also the god of vindication, "he who intervenes on behalf of his father" (*nḏ.tj jtj=f*), who went into battle against the enemy on behalf of his dead father, for the purpose of restoring his life, his honor, his respect, his prestige, and his dignity— in short, his social and moral personhood. For the nomarch Amenemhet, this was apparently the highest value and goal as he prepared for his existence in the afterlife.

CHAPTER TWELVE

The Night of Vindication

1. Liturgy A, Part 1: The Judgment Scene

The Osirian liturgy of the "Divine Night," which we cited in the previous chapter, recounts the carrying out of a wake for Osiris:

> When this misfortune struck the first time,
> an embalming place was set up for you in Busiris,
> to mummify you and make your scent pleasant.
> For you, Anubis was enacted
> carrying out his rituals in the pure place.
> I and my sister Nephthys lit the torch
> at the entrance to the embalming chamber,
> so as to drive Seth into the darkness.
> Anubis emerged from the area of the house of embalming
> to smite all your enemies.
> The mourning women sang their dirges for you,
> your son Horus felled the rebels and placed Seth in fetters.
> The gods stood up and mourned
> because of the great suffering that was inflicted on you.
> They let their cries of mourning mount up to the sky,

so that those in the horizon heard
how the goddess mourned and wailed.
They saw what that one did to you;
Thoth stood at the entrance of the pure place and recited his rituals
so as to breathe life into your *ba* daily.
The great Hacking of the Earth was carried out for you,
and on day 25 of the fourth month of the inundation season, you were
    conveyed
when you went out in the night, borne by the sons of Horus,
and Horus before you, the rope in his hand.
Your ways were prepared.
The god's servants have been purified at the opening of your mouth with
    the Opening of the Mouth ritual,
the chief lector priest and the *wab*-priests hold their transfiguration books
    in their hands
and recite from them before you.
The *sem*-priest opens your mouth (with the words)
"Sokar in the *henu*-barque is vindicated!
Your enemies are smitten!"[1]

This text describes the rituals carried out during the night before the funeral. The rituals are dated to day 25 of Khoiak, the eve of the procession of the *henu*-barque and the funeral of the god Sokar-Osiris in the context of the Sokar festival. Among these rituals, the "Great Hacking of the Earth" is mentioned. Coffin Texts spell 62 makes use of this concept to designate one of the three mortuary liturgies that were recited during the night before the funeral:

> You will be vindicated on the Day of Judgment
> in the tribunal of the lord of sighs.
> (The liturgy) "The Earth is Hacked up" will be recited for you,
> the rebel will be repulsed,
> the one who comes in the night,
> and the robber in the early morning.

This liturgy is thus unequivocally connected to the vindication of the deceased in the Judgment of the Dead and to the repelling of the enemy. In the context of the nocturnal wake, the Judgment is reenacted by reciting the liturgy *khebes-ta*, "The Earth is Hacked up." In what form did the Judgment of the Dead play a role in this liturgy? Was it a vindication "against," or a vindication "before"? Was it the conflict with the enemy, with death as murderer, that stood in the foreground, or was it the accounting for his earthly life that the deceased had to make before the divine judge? As we have seen, the Egyptian idea of the Judgment of the Dead experienced a process of evolution from the former to the latter, and we wish to determine the position of the *khebes-ta* liturgy in this development.

In de Buck's edition of the Coffin Texts, spell 7 begins with the words *khebes-ta*. As the history of the transmission of this spell reveals, it is the actual beginning of the liturgy. This history also reveals that the sequence of spells, as assembled by de Buck, combines two originally independent liturgies. Liturgy A originally began with the words *khebes-ta*, and it is the one cited in spell 62 as a liturgy for vindicating the deceased and repelling the enemy. Liturgy B begins with spell 1 and then continues in spells 20–25. The contents of liturgies A and B are organized quite differently. The theme of vindication plays no role in liturgy B, which has to do exclusively with embalming, freedom of movement, and provisioning, and thus with a physically oriented treatment of the deceased, as opposed to the treatment of the deceased as a person in the Judgment of the Dead. Ultimately, at el-Bersha, there was a version that combined the two liturgies into a single liturgy AB.

This textual history leads us emphatically to an inner connection between two themes that at first glance seem quite unrelated: vindication (liturgy A) and embalming (liturgy B). Both themes pertain to what happened during the night before the funeral. The latter has to do with the restoration of the body, and the former with the restoration of the social person, the honor and the rank of the deceased. The one theme looks back to the embalming and the mummification, which have been completed, while the other complements this treatment of the body with a treatment of the mental-spiritual-moral aspects of the person. The figure of the god Anubis, who plays a major role in both themes, clarifies their inner connection. On the one hand, he was the god of the embalming process, working together with Isis and Nephthys in the endeavor to restore the corpse and breathe life into the deceased. On the other hand, he was the master of the scale, and he appears in every single representation of the Judgment of the Dead and the weighing of the heart. It was he who operated the scale, and in this role, he received the title "counter of hearts" or "controller of hearts."[2] The heart required more than mere embalming. In Egyptian anthropology, the heart was the seat of both emotions and consciousness, and it was the nucleus of the identity, the social and moral personality that the deceased wished to carry with him, under any and all circumstances, into his postmortem existence. This goal required an entirely different sort of treatment: purification from guilt and public recognition, in the realm of the gods, of his purity and merit. The themes of embalming and vindication were thus related to one another, and liturgy AB, which is attested only on coffins from el-Bersha, illustrates this relationship.

Let us now consider the liturgy *khebes-ta* in detail. The first scene begins with the following stanza (Coffin Texts spell 7):

> The earth is hacked up after the two companions have battled,
> after their feet have dug up the divine pond in Heliopolis.
> Thoth comes, equipped with his rank,
> after Atum has distinguished him with (the requirements of) power
> and the two Great Ones (i.e., the Enneads) are satisfied with him.
> The battle is over, strife is finished,
> the flame that emerged is put out.
> Censed (= calmed?) is the reddening (= wrath) before the tribunal of the
>   god,
> so that it is seated to speak justice before Geb.

There is talk of battle and law court, as we expect in a liturgy having to do with vindication. Obviously, we are dealing with a vindication "against." But what is the meaning of the words "the earth is hacked up," which gave the entire liturgy its name? In the context of the scene, they describe the condition of the area at the end of a battle that must have been quite violent. But these words have an entirely different meaning.

Book of the Dead chapter 18, which draws together nocturnal rituals dealing with the vindication of Osiris against his enemy, connects the hacking up of the earth with the nocturnal rituals in Busiris:

> O Thoth, who vindicate Osiris against his enemies,
> vindicate N. against his enemies
> in the great tribunal that is in the Great Hacking Up of the Earth in Busiris
> on that night when the earth and its blood was drunk up
> and Osiris was vindicated against his enemies.

The text offers the following commentary on the passage:

> "The great tribunal that is in the Great Hacking Up of the Earth in
>   Busiris,"
> this means: The band of Seth came, after they transformed themselves
>   into goats.
> They were slaughtered in the presence of these gods,
> and their blood flowed down from them.
> Then they were given over to those who are in Busiris.

This is obviously a slaughtering ritual. This is also true of the many places in the Pyramid Texts that mention the hacking of the earth in connection with offering rites:

> May the earth be hacked up for you and an offering brought before you.[3]

The ritual of hacking the earth is often attested in the cycle of the Sokar festival. In classical antiquity, an agrarian meaning was imputed to it. The earth was hacked up for sowing, and the seed grain was mourned as it was placed in the ground like a corpse, for it was bewailed as a manifestation of the slain and buried Osiris. Firmicus Maternus describes the ritual thus:

> In the holy of holies of their temples, they buried an idol. They mourned it annually; they shaved their head, beat their breast, scratched their limbs, and so forth, so as to bewail the pitiful death of their king. . . . The defenders of this mourning and burial offer a physical explanation. The seed grain, they say, is Osiris, the earth Isis, and the heat Typhon. And because the fruit ripens through the effect of heat, it is gathered for the support of man and separated from its companionship with the earth. And when winter comes, it is sowed in the earth in what they call the death and burial of Osiris. The earth becomes pregnant and bears new fruit.[4]

The "idol" of Osiris was the "grain Osiris," a wooden mold filled with earth and sowed with seeds of barley; after eight days, when the seeds sprouted, it was buried. This explanation suits the date of the festival, at the end of the season of inundation, when the land reappeared and was sown. In any event, this passage makes it clear that the initial words of our liturgy, "the earth is hacked up," form a catch phrase laden with meaning.

The earth was hacked up as a result of the battle, and Thoth made his appearance to settle the conflict. The verses describe the condition of peace caused by Thoth's arrival, which made it possible to institute a judicial proceeding. Law took the place of brute force, and Thoth's intervention caused this transformation. The text continues:

> Greetings, you magistrates of the gods!
> May Osiris N. be vindicated by you on this day,
> as Horus was vindicated against his enemies
> on his beautiful day of ascending the throne.
> May his heart be gladdened by you,
> as the heart of Isis was gladdened
> on her beautiful day of playing the sistrum,
> when her son Horus took possession of his Two Lands in triumph.

This scene sets the vindication of the deceased N. in parallelism with the mythical lawsuit between Horus and Seth over the succession to Osiris, which was mentioned in the first stanza. It is thus clear that the first stanza does not refer to the actual scene "on this day," but to the mythical scene "on that day," which is invoked as a mythic precedent.

The invocation of the court is continued in the next stanza:

Greetings, tribunal of the god,
which will judge Osiris N.
because of what he said when he was inexperienced and young,
when it went well with him, before he became wretched.
Rally around him, place yourselves behind him,
may this Osiris N. be vindicated before Geb,
the hereditary noble of the gods,
in the presence of that god who judges him according to what he knows,
after he has appeared before the court, his feather on his head,
his *maat* on his brow.
His enemies are in grief,
for he has taken possession of all his property in triumph.

This passage clearly has to do with vindication before the knowing god, not vindication against the enemy. This enactment of the Judgment of the Dead thus combines both concepts, relating them to one another through mythic parallelism. Just as Osiris was vindicated against Seth, and just as Horus triumphed over him in the tribunal of Heliopolis, so shall the deceased N. now be vindicated before the divine judge who will call him to account for what he knows, and even for transgressions committed unknowingly in childhood. These are specifically religious transgressions, impure acts and violations of taboos, a "guilt" for which Egyptians feared they would have to answer before an offended god.

This is the only place in the liturgy where mention is made of the guilt of the deceased. Compared with the "enemies," its very possibility is ignored. Enmity, hate, and calumny drive the liturgy, not the wish to make amends for wrongs that have been incurred. The liturgy is imbued with the figure of the god Seth, who in any event has wrong on his side. But the knowing god knows the offenses of the deceased, which the latter does not dispute, though he acknowledges only that he committed them in a condition of ignorance. The deceased knows that the god will not call him to account for this guilt. The reference is to the ten years of childhood, which were understood as a period when a sense of morality was lacking. As Papyrus Insinger puts it, a man spends ten years as a child before he can distinguish between life and death.[5] In this context, the phrase "life and death" is tantamount to "good and evil." This capacity for making a distinction does not make man godlike, as in the Bible, but simply makes him a man, a responsible, accountable member of civilized society.

The concept of guilt that underlies our liturgy is ritualistic and magical. Guilt arises and is accumulated by the one affected, whether he wishes it or not. The concepts of guilt and regret were not yet known. The individual can do nothing of his own accord to remove his guilt, whether overcoming it, confessing it, or atoning for it. In this situation, the concept of a knowing god appears as a relief, offering the possibility of ridding oneself of the guilt by nonaccountability and forgiveness. Man can confidently leave to the judgment of this knowing god all the guilt he might have accumulated when he was underage and not responsible for his actions.

The next stanza is addressed to Thoth, the prosecutor who will bring N. to justice "according to what he knows." It has a caption of its own:

> Greeting Thoth and his tribunal.

> Greetings, Thoth, with whom the gods are satisfied,
> along with that tribunal that is with you!
> May you command that they come out to meet him, this Osiris N.,
> that they may listen well to all that he says on this day.

> For you are that feather that goes up in God's Land,
> that Osiris brought to Horus
> that he might tie it to his head as a sign of vindication
> against his male and female enemies.
> It is he who squeezed out the testicles of Seth,
> he has not perished, he has not died.
> You are that star that the Goddess of the West bore,
> which does not perish, which is not destroyed;
> so has this N. not perished and not been destroyed,
> no sort of evil recrimination has been brought forth
> against this Osiris N., so said Atum.
> As for all evil that they plan (lit., "say") to do
> against this Osiris N. before Geb:
> It is (itself directed) against them, it remains (itself turned) against them.

This spell returns to the level of the mythic scene. Thoth is equated with a "feather," that is, he is addressed as the lord of the feather, which is the sign of victory. The victory again refers to the battle between Horus and Seth. For the deceased N., this victory means that no charge has been brought against him and that he thus will not perish. Just as Horus triumphed over Seth, N. triumphs over death. Because this confirmation is placed in the mouth of Atum, we must recognize it as the decisive verdict of acquittal in the court. The deceased is acquitted, for no accusation has been raised. The final verse is an excommunication formula, as also occurs in the sarcophagus inscription of Merneptah:

> May it go badly with the evil one, may the deficient one suffer lack.
> Seized by annihilation, may he have no sustenance![6]

Here ends the actual judgment scene that is enacted in spells 7–9. In the later version, this core scene is preceded by an introduction that we wish to examine, at least in the form of excerpts. The point of the text is to rouse the deceased from his unconscious state. He is to betake himself to the place where the Judgment of the Dead occurs, so as to be vindicated against his enemies. In what follows, this formula is constantly repeated as a refrain.

> Osiris N., raise yourself from your left side,
> place yourself on your right side!
> Geb has commanded, Ruti has proclaimed (*wḥm*),
> that your *ba*, which is in the earth, be given to you,
> as well as your shadow, which is in hiding.
> O Osiris N., raise yourself,
> that you may be vindicated against your enemies!

> O Osiris N., take your staff,
> your kilt, and your sandals
> to go down to the tribunal,
> that you may be vindicated against your male and female enemies,
> who act against you (manly and womanly),
> who will take legal action against you
> on this beautiful day in the tribunal.
> . . .
> May you go to the Great Staircase,
> may you come to the Great City!
> May you pour your warmth to the ground,
> may you become (an) Osiris!

The deceased's journey to the Great Staircase and the Great City belong to the image of death as transition. The Great Staircase is Abydos as the place where the Judgment of the Dead takes place, and Great City is the usual designation of the Elysium where the vindicated deceased went. "Warmth" is used metaphorically for passion; the deceased is to free himself from it. Before the law court of Osiris, he will himself make his appearance as Osiris, playing the role of the god.

The next verses lend the deceased encouragement for the journey. In the role of Osiris, he will appear before the court as a mighty god:

> May your great ones stand up before you,
> may the scribes on their mats tremble before you,
> for you have attached to yourself the heads of the multicolored serpents
>   in Heliopolis.
> Seize the sky,
> take possession of the earth as heir.
> Who will take this sky away from you
> as a god who has rejuvenated himself and is thereby beautiful?

2. Liturgy A, Part 2: The Transfiguration of the Vindicated One

The judgment scene is followed by transfiguring invocations of the deceased. Their goal is to affirm the successful outcome of the Judgment of the Dead and the triumph of the deceased:

> O Osiris N., may the gate be opened to you by Seshat,
> and may the goodly ways be opened to you by Wepwawet!
> There is no god who renounces what he has said.
> This is what he said: Osiris N. is vindicated
> against his male and female enemies,
> against those who wished to take
> legal action against him on this day.

The world stands open to the one who has been vindicated. He will "stride freely," as stated in the Instruction for Merikare:

> He who arrives without doing evil,
> he will be like a god there,
> striding freely like the lords of eternity.[7]

Yet again, the irrevocable decision of the gods is repeated.

In the verses that follow, the deceased is entreated to return. We recall that he had set off for Abydos to stand before the "tribunal of the god" and achieve vindication against his enemies. Now, he must return to his tomb:

> May you come, may you come, may you return (lit., "bring yourself"),
> O may you come, may you come,
> may you return, O great one!

This is the language of the dirges of Isis and Nephthys, whose goal is none other than to induce the deceased to return. The dirges rest on the image of death as separation and distancing. They repeatedly beseech the deceased: "Come! Come back! Come to your house, that of your sister, of your wife, of your beloved! Do not remain distant! Do not separate yourself from us!" The thematic developed in the recitations on the night before the funeral is complex and ambivalent. On the one hand, it is a matter of furthering the deceased along the way through the realm of death to the saving shore of bliss to which the Judgment of the Dead opens decisive access. On the other hand, Isis and Nephthys constantly call the deceased back into this realm in their laments. The deceased must set out and manage the transition, free himself from all the confining and impeding aspects of embalming and mummification, placement in the coffin, and burial, and become an ancestral spirit whose true place is in the realm of the gods. But at the same time, he must maintain a relationship with those he has left behind, he must not depart entirely from his tomb and his mummy, he must remain accessible to the cult and to the love of the bereaved. The Osirian liturgy of the "Divine Night" expresses this ambivalence with wonderful clarity. While Horus and Anubis accompany the deceased Osiris through the twenty-one gates of the netherworld, Isis and Nephthys summon him back to this world with their dirges and their constantly repeated "Come!" This liturgy culminates in the solemn speech in which the newly arrived Osiris is presented to the gods of the netherworld as their new ruler:

> Rally round this N., do all he bids.
> Give praise to him, O gods,
> come, O gods,
> behold him, how he has gone forth in peace,
> vindicated against his enemies!
> He has taken hold of the Great Ones, he has traversed the places of Geb,
> having prevented any other from doing them harm.

With his vindication, the deceased regains the honor and the status of which death had robbed him. He leaves the court as a crowned ruler ("Great Ones" is a designation of the royal crowns), and he traverses his realm, seizing it back from the usurper.

The following stanzas all begin with the cry "Come out!" referring to the triumphal emergence of the victor from the tribunal:

> Osiris N., come out, you being great and mighty,
> like the emergence of Re, he being great and mighty,
> on the eastern side of the sky.
> The gods who spoke in favor of Horus,
> that they might fell Seth for him,
> it is they who have spoken in favor of this Osiris N.,
> that they may fell his male and female enemies for him.
>
> O Osiris N., come out from your house, from your place,
> from the place where you are,
> like Horus, who was vindicated,
> after he took possession of the inheritance and grasped the leg of an ox.
> Come out, justified before that tribunal
> of the gods of Buto and Heliopolis,
> as Horus came out, justified against Seth,
> before that tribunal of the lord of rigor mortis.[8]

The final stanza is a sort of excommunication formula. The deceased, vindicated and acquitted in the Judgment of the Dead, is sacrosanct; he is accepted into the realm of the gods, and he himself becomes a judge in the Heliopolitan tribunal and thus inviolate. Potential enemies have no chance against him:

> There emerges from the law suit
> the one who emerges from the law suit.
> It is Horus who emerges from the law suit.
> You are far from this N., you who should be far from this N.
> Do not approach this N., you who wish to approach him!
> This Osiris N. is in the habit of judging "whomever he pleases" in
>   Heliopolis.

The apotropaic character of this excommunication formula results from the ritual context of the liturgy, the nocturnal wake. Its central purpose is to repel the enemy, whose attempts to approach were feared; the rituals of the wake were intended to exclude the possibility of his ever attacking the body of the deceased. The stanza that follows is also to be understood as an excommunication formula. It is in any event written in a dark, mysterious language that we cannot make out. This ends the sequence of spells that bid the deceased to emerge from the hall of judgment and return to his tomb.

3. Liturgy A, Part 3: The Vindicated One as Companion of the Gods

The final section of liturgy A describes the royal status of the vindicated deceased. Though he is constantly designated Osiris N., he appears here, as in the liturgy as a whole, in the role of Horus.

> Osiris N. sits before Geb, the hereditary noble of the gods.
> You are Horus, his white crown on his head!
> Isis bore him,
> Khabyt brought him up,
> the Horus-nurse nursed him,
> while the powers of Seth, over and above his own powers, served him.
> His father Osiris gave him these two staffs of his.
> Osiris N. has come, jubilating with them in triumph.

> These his two great and powerful Enneads have granted
> that he threaten the gods with his *sekhem*-scepter.
> It is he who leads life[9] to the gods,
> and recitation offerings for Re in the form of *maat*.
> It is Horus, foremost of the living, who protects his father Osiris;
> he has hindered the steps of the one who killed his father Osiris.
> As for those who will commit any evil theft against this Osiris N.,

this N. will topple the uppermost among their great ones
in Heliopolis, at the side of Osiris when he has appeared.
This N., he has taken his Two Lands in triumph.
You are Horus, lord of *maat.*

This description of the vindicated Horus sketches a brief biography of his
birth and upbringing, to the point when he was outfitted with two *jꜣ.t-*
staffs by Osiris. The "sitting before Geb" has been pictured as the exercise of the office of judge, to which the deceased was appointed when he
was vindicated before the tribunal. With the deceased characterized as
having the status of an earthly ruler, toward the end, a threat of punishment is again inserted. This threat underscores the apotropaic character
of the ritual as a component of the wake. On the mythic level, the "theft"
refers to Seth, who threatened to plunder the corpse of Osiris; on the
level of the real world, the threat formula could have been directed at
those who might desecrate the tomb. Finally, the deceased is addressed
as "lord of *maat.*"

The final stanza contrasts this earthly rulership in the company of Geb
with the deceased's arrival in the sky and his participation in the course
of the sun:

O Osiris N. here,
may you fare in the sky and cross the firmament,
may the inhabitants of the Winding Canal worship you
when they see you, how you rise in the eastern Light-land.
Those in the netherworld sing "beautiful is your rising"
when you emerge from the *mesektet*-barque
and enter the *mandjet*-barque,
as Horus, lord of the *pat*, himself commanded to you.
O Osiris N. here, where you have ascended
is over the great starboard side of the sky,
where you have descended is over the great port side of the earth,
among those gods in the following of Osiris.
Welcome, welcome to the presence of Re, he who dwells in the sky.

"Faring in the sky and crossing the firmament" is a formally established
turn of expression for the sun god's crossing of the sky, and it is at the
same time a "basic principle" of Egyptian mortuary belief.[10] The funeral
procession is thus "sacramentally explained" as a crossing of the sky:

May he fare in the firmament and cross the sky,
may he join with the earth in the western Light-land,
may he ascend to the Great God.[11]

It is thus not by chance that our stanza begins with this formula. A crossing of the sky, celebrated in the form of the burial procession, stands at the beginning of the deceased's entry into the course of the sun.

The deceased is greeted, like the sun god, by those near the Winding Canal when he rises and by those in the netherworld when he sets. These and the following verses describe the circular journey of the deceased in the course of the sun by means of polar concepts that stand for the two phases of the sun's course.

The conclusion of the text stresses once again that inclusion among the "followers of Osiris" is synonymous with entry into the company of the sun god:

> O Osiris N. here,
> you are a god, you endure as a god,
> you have no enemy, you have no rival
> in the presence of Re, who is in the sky,
> or in the presence of Osiris, the Great God, who is in Abydos.

By vindicating the deceased against his enemy or enemies and thus ridding him of them, the court grants him the status of a god. The goal of passing through the Judgment of the Dead is entry into the course of the sun and membership in the tribunal of Osiris.

4. Liturgy B: Embalming and Provisioning

Like liturgy A in the newer version, liturgy B begins with spell 1; then, it continues with spell 20.

> O Osiris N. here,
> may Geb open your blind eyes,
> may he stretch out your bent knees.
> May your *jb*-heart from your mother be given to you,
> and your *ḥ3.tj*-heart, which belongs to your *ḏ.t*-body,
> and your *ba*, which is on the earth,
> and your corpse, which is on the ground.
> Bread for your body,
> water for your throat,
> and sweet breath for your nostrils.

Here, we are clearly in the horizon of the image of death as corporal vulnerability. This much is shown by the list of body parts enumerated in the spell: eyes, knees, *jb*-heart, *ḥ3.tj*-heart, *ba*, corpse, body, throat, and nose. The unity of the person has collapsed, and it must be restored to the deceased. Even the *ba* belongs to this group of physical aspects and elements; it is one of the personal items that must be returned to the deceased. His new neighbors, owners of tombs and coffins, also belong to this personal sphere:

> May those in their tomb chambers be gracious to you,
> may those who possess coffins open up to you.
> May they bring you your limbs, which have distanced themselves from you,
> may you be ever secure in your possessions.

The next spell builds on this restoration of life through the rejoining of elements. It treats the theme of unhindered movement and of provisioning, which otherwise also belong closely together: not to have to go upside down or suffer hunger and thirst:

> O Osiris N. here, come,
> that you may ascend to the sky:
> a ladder will be knotted together for you
> beside Re, among the gods.
> The epidemic of the rivers will be driven away for you,
> that you may be able to drink water from them.
> May you walk on your feet,
> may you not walk upside down.
> Where you go out is from the midst of the earth,
> but you do not go out of the gate,
> so that your walls collapse,
> (the walls) that surround your tomb, which your city gods have built for
>   you.

These verses make it clear that the reference is to the deceased as owner of a tomb. I presume that here, it is a matter of the form in which the deceased will receive his offerings in the tomb. In the following chapters, we shall see that this theme is connected with the motif of ascent to the sky. The spell closes with a stress on purity, which is the common denominator of the offering cult and the embalming process:

> You are pure, you are pure,
> as truly as Re lives, you are pure!
> Your brow is in purity,
> your hind-part is in purity,
> your place is purified for you
> with natron and incense,
> with Apis-milk and *tnm*-beer.

The spells that follow also deal with the provisioning of the deceased and with his freedom of movement. They refer to the offering cult in the tomb

293

and to its "sacramental explanation" as sharing in the food of the gods. First, there is a spell with a note, "A wax representation of a goddess, which drives away evil." The spell was evidently to be recited over such a representation. The goddess was presumably Tefnut, who is mentioned at the beginning:

> May Tefnut, the daughter of Re, present you
> with what her father Re has given her.
> May the goddess of the valley give you bread
> from the grave goods of her father Osiris.
> When Re bites into something sweet,
> he will give it to you.
> Your three (rations) are in the sky with Re,
> of Lower Egyptian snh-barley.
> Your four (rations) are on earth with Geb,
> of Lower Egyptian jbw-barley.
> The two miller-women grind it for you.
> The Field of Offerings, it makes offerings before you.

The provisioning of the deceased is entrusted to two goddesses. Tefnut, the daughter of Re, will care for him in the sky, and the "goddess of the valley," the personification of the necropolis and the daughter of Osiris, will care for him on and in the earth. Like an official in the bureaucracy, the deceased draws a stipend in the form of grain rations, three in the sky from the sun god and four on earth from the god of the earth; the grain will be ground for him and served as a meal by the Field of Offerings, personification of the table. His provisioning is thus assured for all time.

The next spell again takes up the theme of unhindered freedom of movement, which is as immediately connected with the concept of physical restoration as the theme of nourishment:

> O Osiris N. here, may you go forth/ascend in the daytime,
> having power over your feet in the morning,
> having power over your feet by torchlight,
> having power over your feet at all times
> and at any hour you wish to go forth,
> (O Osiris N.), you having power over your feet
> in every tribunal and in every doorway,
> (Osiris N. here), you having power over your feet in every place
> to which your heart desires to go at any time.

The theme is then considered again, this time negatively:

> O Osiris N. here, you will not be examined, you will not be
> locked up, you will not be taken prisoner,

you will not be bound, you will not be guarded,
you will not be set in the place of execution, to which rebels are consigned,
sand will not be placed on your face,
so as to prevent it from weighing on you.
No barrier will be set before your face,
so as to prevent you from being able to go out.
Take your staff,
your *dꜣjw*-garment, your sandals,
and your weapon for the street!
May you cut off the head and separate the neck
of your male and female enemies,
who hasten your death and divert your coming,
who say to the god, "bring him here" on the day of execution.

The topic here is not the deceased's transition through the realm of death and into Elysium but rather his going forth by day and his daily visit to his tomb and his offerings. The tomb is not to restrict him, the earth is not to weigh on him, and Osiris' thugs, who keep evil away from the realm of the dead and protect Osiris, are not to seize him and take him off to be executed. This is not a matter of the Judgment of the Dead but of the dangers in the world beyond, dangers to which the deceased remains exposed, notwithstanding the fact that he has been vindicated in the Judgment and has acquired the status of a transfigured ancestral spirit.

At the conclusion of the liturgy, two stanzas of nine verses each juxtapose the nocturnal rites of the wake and the opening up of the ends of the earth for the going forth by day:

> O Osiris N. here, the falcon mourned over you,
> the goose gabbled over you.
> An arm was stretched out to you by Thoth,
> it was the arm of your enemy, cut off for you.
> The two kites mourned over you,
> they were Isis and Nephthys,
> the two gongs were struck for you.
> The two arms of Anubis are upon you, protecting you,
> Wepwawet, he opens the beautiful ways for you.

Mourning, punishment of the enemy, beating the gongs, and embalming by Anubis are typical themes of the nocturnal rituals. But with equal clarity, the stanza that follows refers to the deceased's freedom of movement when he receives his mortuary offerings:

> O Osiris N. here, may the door leaves of the sky be opened for you by Re,
> may the door leaves be opened before you by Geb.
> The door leaves are opened for you in Abydos,

> the door leaves of the "cool place" are opened for you
> by your mother Nut;
> this is because of the greatness of your *akh*-power.
> Opened for you are the doors
> in the earth by Geb;
> this is because of the excellence of the knowledge of your name.

As we shall see in the next chapter, the theme of opening, not for entering, but, as here, for exiting, belongs to the semantics of offering. The final verses make this reference clear:

> O Osiris N. here,
> a plot of land was given to you in the desert valley,
> that you might eat the bread of the Westerners.

In the real world, the "plot of land in the desert valley" can refer only to the tomb in the necropolis. But we must also think of the plot of land in the Field of Reeds or the Field of Offerings, which was assigned to the vindicated one for his eternal provisioning as a result of his triumph in the Judgment of the Dead.[12]

I understand the final verses as a sort of postscript that was not recited, but rather was intended to comment on the effectiveness (in Egyptian, *akh*) of the text to be recited:

> *Akh* is it, this speech, it is a starting in the West,
> pleasing to the heart of Re,
> gratifying to the heart of his tribunal, which watches over humankind.

> "Give to him," says Re, "lead him (in?)."
> May he be gracious to you at the staircase, in the tribunal,
> at the door, at the crossroads (?),
> at that place where your god is gracious[13] to you.

The last verses evidently comment on Re's satisfaction with the deceased, which is evoked by reciting the liturgy and citing the verdict that Re utters on behalf of the deceased. "Staircase" refers to the place of the judgment, to which the words "tribunal" and "door" also refer. The words of the sun god again make the initiatory character of the ceremony clear. "Give to him": the provisioning in the afterlife that is due to him; "lead him": that is, into the next-worldly society as "one vindicated in the presence of Osiris in the netherworld, a powerful one in the presence of Geb in the earth and a transfigured spirit in the presence of Re in the sky," as a well-attested formula puts it. In the weighing of the heart scene in the Book of the Dead papyrus of Ani, the judgment of the gods is similarly formulated:[14]

Let food be given to him
that comes from the table of Osiris,
and a plot of land permanently in the Field of Offerings, as for the
Followers of Horus.

By being acquitted in the Judgment of the Dead, the deceased is accepted into the next-worldly aristocracy of the Followers of Horus. As such, he has a claim to land and to food from the table of Osiris. This form of provisioning in the next life is clearly based on the earthly model of royal service. Osiris takes the place of the king, while the altar and provisioning by the temple replace the royal table and kitchen. In our text, it is the sun god Re who speaks the decisive words: "Give to him, lead him in."

Thus ends liturgy B, which centers on the themes of physical restoration and provisioning with offerings. This liturgy B had a long and (for us) instructive history. While both versions of liturgy A are confined to the Coffin Texts and do not appear in the later mortuary literature, liturgy B became chapter 169 of the Book of the Dead. The title of the chapter clearly states its goal: "Spell for Setting Up the Bier." Its liturgical use in the framework of the embalming process is thus made clear. The bier is the lion bed used in the embalming process. Despite its many references to provisioning and offerings, the liturgy thus does not belong in the framework of either the daily or the festival offering cult in the accessible area of the tomb but rather to the isolated realm of the embalming chamber and the sarcophagus chamber. It is thus again clear that the original two liturgies, A and B, have a common ritual framework. The relationship of liturgy B/Book of the Dead chapter 169 to the embalming process becomes clearer still in the Late Period, when the protective deities of the wake were often depicted on the outer walls of coffins, along with their speeches, which assured the deceased of their assistance. A good half of these speeches are drawn from the text of this liturgy,[15] making it clear that this liturgy belongs in the context of the wake and thus in the same framework in which liturgy A is also anchored. The two liturgies serve a complementary function, with liturgy A referring to the social aspect of the salvation of the deceased, to vindication as restitution of his social person, and liturgy B referring to the physical aspects in the form of embalming and provisioning.

Liturgy A already understands the Judgment of the Dead as a liminal ritual aimed at entry into life in the next world in the presence of Osiris and Re. The deceased, however, did not have to vindicate himself "before" Osiris but "against" potential opponents ("male and female enemies") who might make accusations against him.[16] Moreover, the deceased appears in the role of Horus not as the accused but rather as the accuser. This is the image of death as enemy. With his death, harm has been done

to the deceased, and this harm is mythically ascribed to Seth. As personification of death, Seth struck the first blow. Now, it is a matter of taking
him to court and receiving vindication against him, as well as preventing
him from striking the second blow and getting hold of the corpse. This
is the meaning of the wake. The Judgment of the Dead, or rather, its
enactment, thus belongs in the context of the rituals of the wake, whose
most important goal, along with breathing life into the deceased, is to
repel either the mythic enemy (Seth) or all possible actual enemies and
their hostility. The ritual is intended to compensate for the helplessness
of the deceased, who is exposed, defenseless, to his enemies, and at the
same time in a certain way to overcome death, which is traced back to
inimical effects and personified in the form of the mythic enemy. Vindication thus means two things: triumph over possible opponents who
might accuse the deceased before the tribunal and triumph over the
mythic enemy who himself brings the deceased before the tribunal and
accuses him of being responsible for his own death. The condemnation
of Seth is thus to be understood as compensation for death. The ritual
applies this meaning, as derived from the myth of Osiris, to N., who is
equated with Osiris. To the extent that the vindication of the deceased is
understood as an integral part of his ritual revivification, as it is effected
by the rituals of embalming, mummification, Opening of the Mouth,
placement in the coffin, and burial, the ritual enactment of the Judgment
of the Dead also belongs in this context. It was only in the New Kingdom
that the Judgment of the Dead complex became an independent cycle of
texts and representations.

CHAPTER THIRTEEN

Rituals of Transition from Home to Tomb

1. Artistic and Textual Depictions of the Funeral

A lmost no Egyptian ritual was depicted as often or as richly as that of the funeral. Representations of rites clearly connected with the funeral are to be found in tombs from the Old Kingdom down to the latest periods of Egyptian history, as well as on Book of the Dead papyri and coffins.[1] We thus have the impression of being well informed regarding these matters, but it quickly emerges that the multitude of representations yield scarcely any insight into what actually happened. The depictions present us with a picture, sanctified by tradition, of something that might actually have occurred at an early point in time, but which is only marginally related to what was done later. It was only in the course of the New Kingdom, in the fourteenth century B.C.E., that an attempt was made to bring the representations of the funeral into accord with the actual conduct of the rites. A great number of the representations had thus long since lost their connection with reality.

From the transitional period around 1300 B.C.E., we have the tomb of a high official, the chief domain administrator of Amun, Amenemope (Theban Tomb 41), in which both representational conventions are combined, both the old scenes, which had disappeared from the repertoire some decades earlier, and the new, "realistic" type of funeral ritual.[2] The old scenes refer to rituals performed with and on various objects and to pieces of scenery pertaining to a cultic drama with a number of individual episodes. The new scenes, however, depict the actual funeral procession, which included three major segments:

1. crossing the Nile from the city of the living on the east bank to the necropolis on the west bank;
2. the procession from the embalming hall to the tomb; and
3. the rites in front of the tomb.

In the tomb of Amenemope, the sequences of scenes continues from the entrance into an area we are probably to recognize as the next-worldly realm. We see the tomb owner embraced by the goddess of the West and provided with food by the tree goddess. We also see him praying to various deities and tending to his occupations in the Field of Reeds. And, finally, we see him addressing the deities of the nomes, that is, the judges at the Judgment of the Dead (Book of the Dead chapter 18), undergoing the Judgment in the form of the weighing of the heart, and, at the end, acquitted and saved from death, seated before Osiris.[3]

In the decorative program of this tomb, we can distinguish three levels of representation in terms of their relationship to reality: (1) the level of "old scenes," which refer to an age-old cult drama from early in the historical period, one that was stored in the cultural memory; (2) the level of "new scenes" that represent the three major segments of the funeral ritual as it was actually performed; and (3) the level of scenes of the afterlife, which do not refer to ritual acts but to events that occur in the next world, after the funeral, or rather, are intended to represent the meaning or "sacramental explanation" of these events in the realm of the gods. In the visible world, the deceased was conveyed to the tomb and buried in the sarcophagus chamber, while in the next world, he penetrated into the spaces of the realm of the dead, finally arriving at the paradise of the Field of Reeds and Osiris in the hall where the Judgment of the Dead occurred.

The depiction of the funeral in the tomb of Amenemope, which is unique in its complexity, can serve as a key to understanding both the older and the newer representations. In older tombs, we find only scenes from representational levels 1 and 2, while in later tombs, only levels 2 and 3 are combined with one another. If we turn from the tomb of Amenemope to the older tombs, we encounter, along with scenes of the archaic cult drama, representational level 1, scenes that correspond to the "new scenes" of level 2. We see the journey across the Nile (the journey to the West) represented, along with the procession to the tomb, which is often divided into three processions: the sled bearing the sarcophagus, which is drawn by cattle, is accompanied by two smaller processions, one bearing a shrine containing the canopic jars, and the other bearing an unshapely object identified in the captions as *tekenu*, which probably contained remnants of the embalming process sewn into an animal skin.[4] In all periods, the dragging of the coffin, with the cattle, the mourners, and the accompanying priests remained the canonical core of the funeral procession.

Texts also lay stress on this procession as the core of a splendid burial, as in the description of a state funeral at the Residence in the Story of Sinuhe, by means of which the king endeavors to persuade the protagonist, who had fled to Palestine, to return:

> Think of the day of burial, of passing into a revered state!
> A nocturnal wake is divided for you with ointment and the four-threaded
>   cloth of Tayt.
> A burial procession is made for you on the day of the funeral.
> The mummy case is of gold, the mask of lapis-lazuli,
> the sky (i.e., the baldachin) is above you as you lie on the sledge.
> Cattle draw you and singers precede you.
> The dance of the *muu* is performed for you at the entrance to your tomb.
> The offering list is recited for you,
> and a sacrifice is made on your offering-stone.

Here, too, the funeral is divided into three major sections: the embalming, the procession to the tomb, and welcome to the tomb by means of the dance of the *muu*[5] and a large offering. Dances played an important role in Egyptian festival rituals, expressing the emotion aroused by the appearance of a sacred being. Ritual dancing at the entrance to the tomb is also mentioned in funerary spells of the New Kingdom: "The dance of the dwarfs is performed for you at the entrance to your tomb"[6] and "May the dance of the dwarfs be performed for me at the entrance to my tomb."[7]

The funeral rites are described in far greater detail in a stela text from early Dynasty 18 (ca. 1500 B.C.E.):

> The beautiful burial, may it come in peace
> after your seventy days are completed in your embalming hall.
> May you be laid out on a bier in the house of rest
> and be drawn by white oxen.
> May the ways be opened with milk[8]
> until your arrival at the entrance to your tomb.
> May the children of your children all be assembled
> and wail with loving heart.
>
> May your mouth be opened by the chief lector priest,
> may you be purified by the *sem*-priest,

may Horus weigh your mouth for you,
after he has opened your eyes and ears.
May your limbs and your bones all be present on you.
May the transfiguration spells be read for you
and the mortuary offering (*ḥtp-dj-nswt*) be performed for you.

May your *jb*-heart be with you in the right way,
and your *ḥȝ.tj*-heart of your existence on earth,
you being restored to your previous form,
as on the day when you were born.

May the *sȝ-mr*-priest be brought to you,
may the friends sing the litany "Beware, O earth!,"
the entry into the earth that the king grants,[9]
in the coffin of the western side.

May you be given an escort like the ancestors,
may the *muu* come to you in jubilation.

The god's favor for the one he loves is
to be imperishable forever and ever.[10]

Here, we find the same segments of the ritual: (1) the seventy day embalming process, (2) the procession with cattle, here specified as "white oxen," which are preceded by a priest who libates with milk to "open the way," and (3) the reception at the tomb, which is described with special detail: the mourning of the family, the Opening of the Mouth, purification by the *sem*-priest and the chief lector priest, the Opening of the Mouth by Horus (which again refers to rites carried out by the *sem*-priest), the recitation of transfiguration spells (which again refers to the chief lector priest), the carrying out of the offering ritual, and placement in the tomb with the help of the *sa-mer*-priest (literally translated, "loving son"), the "friends," and the *muu*, whose dance was already mentioned in the Story of Sinuhe.

Here, we must add a few words regarding the various priests who concerned themselves with the deceased. As we can see, the Opening of the Mouth and funeral rituals were complex affairs in which a number of persons participated in various roles. A mortuary spell from the tomb of the royal epistolary scribe Tjay (Theban Tomb 23, ca. 1220 B.C.E.) contains a list of the "dramatis personae" of these rituals:

Chief lector priest, *sem*-priest,
imy-is-priest, *imy-khent*-priest,
nine friends, *sa-meref*-priest,
follower of Horus,

sculptor, carver,
craftsman (?), carpenter,
the two mourning birds, mourning women, the bereaved,
who are present in the hall . . .[11]

Of all these, we see only the *sem*-priest and the chief lector priest engaging in other activities, in particular, the mortuary offerings. Both wore special clothing: the *sem*-priest a panther skin, and the chief lector priest a special wig and a sash that crossed the breast. Only these two were mortuary priests in the strict sense of the term; the others bore their titles as roles in the cult drama but not in their professional life. In the offering ritual, there was a third participant, the "embalmer"; he is often represented in Old Kingdom tombs, and he is perhaps to be recognized in the figure of "Anubis," who supports the upright mummy at the entrance to the tomb in New Kingdom representations, and who is the only one of the three who wears a mask as his characteristic garb. The other two priests also played divine roles. The *sem*-priest was Horus, the mythic son, the successor to the priest of the Archaic Period who bore the title "seeker/embracer of the ancestral spirit." The chief lector priest was Thoth, the mythic savant, ritualist, and magus, the master of the sacred texts.

With their many participants, these rituals differed from the normal mortuary cult in the tomb. The latter was always carried out by a single participant whom we often see represented wearing the panther skin of the *sem*-priest. He was the actual mortuary priest who was responsible, after the funeral, for carrying out the mortuary cult. In life, he bore the title "*ka*-servant" (*ḥm-kꜣ*), in analogy with the title "servant of the god" in the temple cult, and in the representations in the tombs, he played the role of *sem*-priest. His duties consisted of making libations and censings over such food offerings as vegetables, meat, grapes, figs, bread, beer, and similar foods, but which might never or only seldom have actually been brought, as opposed to simply representing them on offering tables, ready to be activated on behalf of the deceased by the pouring of water.

The figure of the *sem*-priest was systematically hacked out of tombs dating to before the Amarna Period. Amarna art did away with all historical costumes: only reality was to be represented. Representational level 1 of the "virtual ritual," which recalled the Old Kingdom and was more a medium of cultural memory than a representation of reality, was banned from the canon of Amarna art. The *sem*-priest with his linen panther skin was an especially striking manifestation of this principle of shunning historical costumes.

2. *From Home to Tomb*

a) Crossing Over to the West

We have information regarding the first stage of the funeral, the crossing of the Nile from the place of death to the embalming hall, exclusively from representations in tombs at Thebes. In the captions that comment on the action (e.g., in tomb 133), the boat carrying the coffin is sometimes equated with the "great ferry" that the deceased will use in the afterlife to make the transition from the realm of death to Elysium. The crossing to the necropolis was thus interpreted as a passage that brought salvation from death and led to immortality. But, as the text indicates, this salvation was only for the righteous:

> Fare across, great ferry of the West.
> Fare in peace across to the West!
> I gave bread to the hungry,
> water to the thirsty,
> clothing to the naked . . .[12]

In Theban Tomb 347, there is a caption that designates the boat carrying the coffin as *neshmet*. This was the name of the sacred barque of Osiris that was used in the mysteries at Abydos. In fact, the depictions on the walls of tombs always represent the boat carrying the coffin in the form of a *neshmet* barque, a papyrus boat with a high prow and stern, whose ends take the form of large papyrus blossoms. In the barque, the coffin lies on a lion bed under a baldachin, with statues of Isis and Nephthys at its head and foot. In most cases, the mummy is accompanied by mourners. This purely ceremonial vessel was towed by a normal, river-worthy boat equipped with sail and oars.

> What the pilot at the prow of the *neshmet*-barque of the West says:
> Ply to the West, the harbor of the righteous,
> Khefethernebes, the city of Amun;
> he (Amun) has given it over to N.,
> the landing place of your silent one.
> How the place (i.e., the tomb) rejoices at it!
> Hathor, mistress of the West,
> protectress (?) of the western side,
> she who prepares a place for every righteous one,
> may she take N. in her embrace![13]

In this text as well, the crossing to the west bank is interpreted as a transition into a sphere of security and divine presence that is granted only to the righteous. This "sacramental explanation," along with the use of a ceremonial boat, shows that the crossing to the West was not a mere physical transfer of the corpse from one place to another but rather a ritual riverine procession.

b) Embalming, Cult Drama in the Sacred Temenos, and Rituals in the Garden

Except for a single scene in the above-mentioned tomb of Amenemope, which was later copied by the owner of the neighboring Theban Tomb 23, the embalming process itself was never represented in the tombs. For that reason, the depictions of what occurred before and after the embalming play an even more important role in the decoration of the older tombs. Before the embalming, there was the "procession to the divine tent of Anubis," that is, to the embalming hall, and after the embalming, but before the actual procession to the tomb, a cultic drama was performed in the "sacred temenos." The latter was above all a symbolic journey by boat to various places in Lower Egypt:

> Giving a goodly burial to N., vindicated, after the landing.
> Going to the necropolis, accompanying N. to the beautiful West,
> to the divine tent of Anubis (i.e., the place of embalming) in the western desert.
> Accompanying N. to the cult barque.
> Going upstream to the uniting hall of Rekhmire.
> Turning around and sailing downstream, accompanying N. to Sais,
> traveling downstream to the gates of Buto.
> Arriving at the House of the Noble (in Heliopolis).
> Conducting N. upstream and stopping in the middle of the water.
> Going on land by N. in the presence of the inhabitants of Buto.[14]

Perhaps, in remote prehistory, there really were such journeys to the sacred places of the land during the funerals of Lower Egyptian chieftains or kings. In the older tombs of Dynasty 18, they were represented as an archaic cult drama in the sacred temenos (in the sense of representational level 1), while in the later tombs (in the sense of representational level 2), they became the "mortuary celebration in the garden with its pool."[15] The rites in the garden might have included the "journey to Abydos," a scene that was depicted in many tombs from the Middle Kingdom down to the later stages of Egyptian history, always in connection with the funeral. In any event, it was represented as an actual journey by boat and not as a merely symbolic journey in a ceremonial barque, as it undoubtedly was in fact carried out. In the "journey to the West," we see a larger, river-worthy boat towing a barque. Depending on the geographical location of the necropolis, either the trip there was by sail (with the north wind, but against the current) and the return trip by oar (with the current, but against the wind), or vice versa. In the barque sat the statues of the tomb owner and his wife. In so far as the brief captions yield information, the journey to Abydos was connected with the desire to participate in the cultic dramas of Osiris that were celebrated there. In inscriptions of the New Kingdom, we often encounter the wish to travel to Abydos and Busiris in a transformed state in order to participate in the major festivals of Osiris:

> Traveling downstream to Busiris as a living *ba*,
> traveling upstream to Abydos as a phoenix,
> following Wennefer in U-poqer
> at his festival of the beginning of the year.
> A seat is prepared for me in the *neshmet*-barque
> on the day of the ferrying of the god.
> May my name be called out when he is found
> before the one who decides *maat*.[16]

Behind the journey to Abydos stood the concept of the special sacredness of this place, a sacredness in which the deceased wished to share unconditionally at his transition into the netherworld. The necropolis of Abydos was the oldest Egyptian royal necropolis; here lay the kings of Dynasties 1 and 2, and modern excavations have discovered a "Dynasty 0" that makes it possible to extend the series of royal tombs back well into late prehistory. Even after other places in the north and the south came to be used as royal cemeteries, Abydos retained its paramount sanctity, which it had perhaps first won as a semi-mythical place of origins. Though there were cemeteries everywhere in the land, there was thus a place that was closer to the netherworld than any other, just as Heliopolis was closer to the sky than any other city in Egypt. That place was Abydos. The concept of transition from home to tomb thus included a journey to the one place on earth with an especially close connection to Osiris and the netherworld. More generally speaking, the concept of a sacred place in Egypt included the fact that it opened into the netherworld. In Heliopolis lay the body of the sun god, at Busiris there was a netherworldly counterpart in which Osiris lay, at Thebes there was the mortuary cult of the primeval gods at Medinet Habu, while in the later periods of history, fourteen or sixteen—the numbers varied—religious centers in Egypt had a tomb of Osiris. This idea of a sacred city as entrance to the netherworld had its origin and model in Abydos. Abydos was sometimes also the location of the Judgment of the Dead. Certain texts give the "day of examining the dead" as the date of the journey to Abydos.[17]

In the tomb of the god's father Neferhotep from the reign of Haremhab (end of the fourteenth century), there is a festival calendar that contains not only dates but also additional information and even recitations for various important mortuary festivals,[18] including the journey to Abydos. The journey there is described:

> First month of the inundation season, day 18:
> Staying up by the chief lector priest half the night.
> Steering the prow of this barque downstream,
> reefing its sail.
> Censing and libating for Osiris N. in front of it.
> Spell for the journey to Abydos.
>
> To be spoken by Osiris N.:
> Quickly, I bring you your sins and your rotting discharges.
> Your father Atum allows you to ascend to him.
> He takes you in his arms.
> Bringing the meat of the god to the [. . .] daily.

This spell seems, in fact, to refer to the Judgment of the Dead. As we saw in chapter 4, the idea of the Judgment was rooted in the embalming ritual, whose purpose was to remove the traces of moral and physical pollution, both sins and rotting discharges. Only then could the vindicated one ascend to the sky and enter the embrace of his father Atum. The return from Abydos is described:[19]

> First month of the inundation season, day [1]9:
> Staying up by the chief lector priest half the night.
> Turning this barque southwards.
> Setting its sail,
> pouring the libation and the incense that they love (?).
>
> Spell for faring upstream to (read: from) Abydos.
> Come down, Osiris N.,
> in the company of the northern gods in a goodly wind.
> May the southern gods receive you,
> may the eastern gods feed you,
> may the western gods embrace you!
> To the West, to the West,
> to the place you desire to be.
> Welcome in peace to the West!
> Come to your tomb,
> return to your tomb,
> to the place where your father, where Geb is,
> that he may give you the bandage on the brow of Horus.
> O Osiris N.,

> may you have power there, as a beloved one there, as Foremost of the
>   Westerners,
> may you be there, Osiris N.

The cult drama of the journey to Abydos seems to have been performed in connection with the funeral, given that the two are regularly depicted together in the representations in tombs of Dynasty 18. But it was undoubtedly also repeated later, as emerges, for example, from this text, according to which the journey to Abydos was enacted every year on the eighteenth and nineteenth day of the first month of the inundation season. This was the date of the *wag*-festival. At Abydos, this was the day of the great river procession of the *neshmet*-barque to U-poqer, the holy place of the tomb of Osiris, where the festival participants received the "wreath of justification":

> A wreath is placed round your neck
> on the day of the *wag*-festival.[20]

This is the "bandage" that is also mentioned in the text considered here. Adorned with it, the deceased was supposed to return to his tomb.

c) The Procession to the Tomb

The deceased was conveyed from the embalming hall to the tomb in a solemn procession. The sledge bearing the sarcophagus, again drawn by cattle, was accompanied by the shrine containing the canopic jars and the mysterious *tekenu*.[21] As already noted, the *tekenu* might have been a sack containing materials left over from the embalming process. Another plausible explanation of the *tekenu* that has been proposed by Hermann Kees, who sees it as "a sort of scapegoat" that "was supposed to attract the evil powers that won control over a person in death, so that the transfigured body would remain free of them," that is, it was the embodiment of the noxious substances (Egyptian *dw.t nb.t* "everything evil") removed during the embalming process.[22]

The threefold procession was accompanied by an age-old song that was also sung during processions of deities: "Beware, O earth: a god is coming!"[23] The song is another sign that the funeral procession was celebrated as a hierophany, an appearance of a sacred being. The captions identify the active participants who helped to drag the sledge as "people of Pe and Dep (= Buto), of Hermopolis, Iseum, Sais, and *Ḥw.t-wr-jḥw*," and they are also globally referred to as *rḥy.t nb.t*, "all the subjects." The funeral was thus a public one for all the land to see, as least as far as Lower Egypt was concerned. "Your arms on your ropes!" the chief lector priest called out to them. "South, north, west, east: accompany N. to his place!"[24] The burial procession of a high-ranking, though in no way royal, Egyptian thus took the form of a festival drama whose theme was the funeral of a Lower Egyptian king or chieftain in late prehistory. Are we in fact to think that the Thebans who accompanied the vizier Rekhmire and other New Kingdom notables to the tomb played the role of inhabitants of the delta? Surely not; the event assumed the character of a festival drama only in the representations, which intentionally transposed what actually happened into an archaic scenery.

This discrepancy between what was represented and what was actually done was given up in the course of the New Kingdom. What disappeared were the scenes of representational level 1, which depicted persons performing actions in clothing dating back a millennium and a half before the New Kingdom, and what came to dominate were scenes of representational level 2, which depicted actual, contemporary clothing and actions. In the Ramesside Period representations, the deceased was no longer borne to the tomb by inhabitants of delta cities but by his relatives, friends, and professional colleagues. In the tomb of Amenemope, we see the two viziers, the highest officials of the state, while in others, we also see the generalissimo and ministers of the highest rank.[25] As before, it was a matter of status and openness to the public. A typical motif of the "realistic" funeral scenes of the Ramesside Period consists of arbors containing food and drink, which were set up on both sides of the processional way. These arbors served two purposes: on the one hand, they constituted a gigantic offering structure, out of which gifts accompanied by libations, censings, and acclamations were presented to the sarcophagus as it passed by, while on the other hand, they served as hospitality for the participants, who were able to help themselves to the food and drink after the sledge passed by. We also see arbors of this sort in representations of the processions that occurred on major religious festivals. In Egypt, all the great divine festivals were celebrated in the form of a procession in which the local inhabitants were involved as participants or spectators and in which, as we saw in chapter 9, even the deceased wished to continue to participate. On this model, aristocratic burials were conducted in the form of a private processional festival that quite possibly involved the entire city in its proceedings.

Also characteristic of this type of representation are the many ways in which grief was expressed. In the older representations, there was only one artistic formula for grief: upraised arms. Now, we see a broad spectrum of gestures of grief, from streams of tears, arms gashed in the heat of passion, and hands beating the brow or placed on the head, to the gesture of composed mourning, with the hand supporting the chin and the cheeks, which was now characteristic of high officials.[26] There was a

309

distinction in the way in which men and women were depicted displaying grief. The women display intense pain, while the men grieve calmly. In the Amarna and post-Amarna Periods, however, artists did not hesitate to depict even high-ranking men making gestures of passionate mourning. In the royal tomb at Amarna, we see Akhenaten by the bier of his deceased daughter Meketaten, holding his head in the same gesture of despair as Nefertiti, while in a newly acquired relief in Munich, one of the two viziers is depicted turning away crying and holding a hand to his face.[27]

This change in the representations from depictions of an image sanctified by tradition to depictions of actions that really took place occurred at the same time as the open expression of pain and mourning, and the negative images of death in the songs of mourning sung at funerals, a few of which were cited in chapter 5. These far-reaching changes in the iconography of the funeral ritual do not point to a change in the ritual itself, which had undoubtedly been carried out in the same way for some centuries, but rather to a change in the pictorial and textual representations' relationship to reality. Earlier, the desire had been to stress the funeral's ritual and cultic aspect as a canonical festival drama that rested on an age-old ancestral tradition. Now, the desire was to emphasize its ritual and above all its emotional character. The individual importance of the deceased was shown by the intensity and variety of the emotions expressed: theatricality and authenticity were always closely connected in these representations. But whereas previously the authenticity was seen in the reference (preserved only in pictures) to rituals from prehistoric times, now it was seen in the liveliness and articulateness of expressions of emotion in language, mime, and gesture.

3. The Rites of Opening the Mouth at the Entrance of the Tomb

a) The Opening of the Mouth Ritual

The different files of the burial procession, which towed the sledge bearing the coffin, the shrine containing the canopic jars, and the *tekenu* (which disappeared from the representations at the beginning of the Ramesside Period), ended in front of the tomb, which was usually represented as a pyramid with a vestibule and a stela. Here, the mummy was taken one last time out of its coffin or sarcophagus and set upright in front of the stela, facing south, in the forecourt of the tomb. In the representations, it is often supported from behind by Anubis (Figure 5).[28] It is generally thought that this was a priest wearing a dog-headed mask: depicting the god himself in these scenes would not have suited the relationship to reality otherwise found in these representations. The

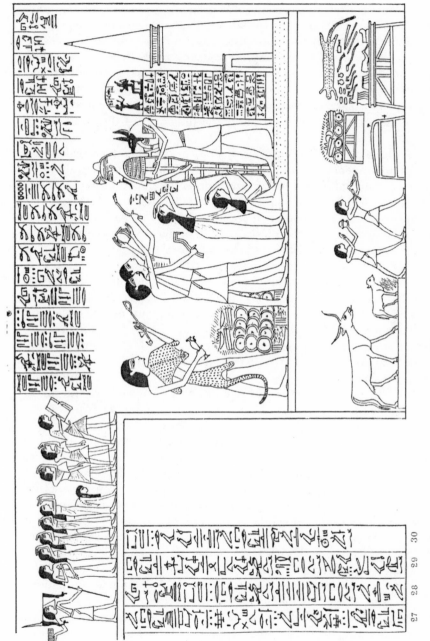

Figure 5. Vignette to Book of the Dead chapter 1. From E. Naville, *Das ägyptische Totenbunch der XVII. bis XX. Dynastie*, vol. 1, *Text und Vignetten* (Berlin, 1886), pl. 2

depictions in the tombs mostly show two mummies set up in front of the tomb, and scholars have taken these to be the mummies of the tomb owner and his wife. The wife thus plays a double role in these depictions. She appears in the role of widow bewailing her husband, which was the role of Isis, and she is also represented as already deceased, standing mummiform next to the mummy of her husband, just as she also sits and stands next to him in the other representations on the walls of the tomb, receiving mortuary offerings, adoring the gods, striding through the gates of the netherworld, and undergoing the Judgment of the Dead before Osiris.

The Opening of the Mouth (Egyptian *wp.t-r³*) ritual was carried out on the mummies set up in front of the tomb.[29] This was originally a ritual for bringing the tomb statue to life, and it then developed into a consecration ritual carried out on all possible sacred objects, from offering stands to an entire temple, in order to dedicate them to their sacred purpose. The ritual transformed the statue from an object crafted by artisans into a cultic body that was capable of being animated by a god or an ancestral spirit in the framework of sacred actions.

None of our sources is older than the New Kingdom, but the ritual itself must have been much older than that. A number of its spells are already attested in the Pyramid Texts of the Old Kingdom, and many scenes display a vocabulary and a form that point to an even older period, perhaps that of the first two dynasties, in which the preparation of divine statues was such an important activity that it was used in the names of years. Eberhard Otto, to whom we owe the definitive publication and study of the ritual, was thus motivated by an understandable interest in establishing the oldest layers of the text and making out the various stages in its development. This proved to be an impossible task, and the ritual of the Archaic Period cannot be reconstructed. It thus appears more meaningful to understand the ritual as an element of the mortuary cult in the New Kingdom, regardless of the differing ages of its various components. The modern edition of the ritual with its seventy-five scenes is an abstraction put together from various versions. We prefer here to proceed from a single one of these concrete versions, that in the tomb of the royal domain administrator Nebsumenu from the reign of Ramesses II (ca. 1250 B.C.E.). In this tomb, the scenes of the Opening of the Mouth ritual are spread out over four walls, so that there is already a division into four sequences that prove upon close examination to be entirely meaningful. The first sequence (scenes 1–8) stands, looking at it from the entrance, on the left rear wall (west wall, southern portion), the second (scenes 9–25, omitting 20–22 and 24) on the left entrance wall (east wall, southern portion), the third (scenes 28–32, remainder destroyed but presumably, with omissions, to 42) on the right rear wall (west wall, northern portion), and the fourth (scenes 43–59, with omissions) on the right entrance wall (east wall, northern portion).

First sequence: scenes 1–6 all consist of purifications. The accompanying spells begin with the formula "Pure, pure!", which is to be repeated four times. So far as the representations are preserved (scenes 4–6), they depict censings. In scenes 5 and 6, the statue is circled four times and censed with different kinds of aromatic substances. This sequence includes above all a purification with four *nemset*-jars, which must be assumed here in the destroyed portion. In this purification as well, the statue was circled four times and water was poured out. This sequence clearly has the character of an initial purification ritual. In the daily temple cult as well, the offering sequence was preceded by purifications with incense and water.

The seventh scene bears the title "Entering, gazing upon him." "Entering, gazing upon the god" is also a scene in the daily temple ritual. The eighth scene is entitled "Going to the tomb" (*šm.t r jz*). The priests who participate in it are the *jmj-ḫnt* (chamberlain) and the lector priest. As depicted, the tomb looks like a tall base with sloping walls resting on a pedestal, the hieroglyph for the typical tomb of the Old Kingdom, which we designate with the Arabic word "mastaba." The tomb is captioned "tomb of the Osiris, the domain administrator Nebsumenu."

The second sequence on the opposite east wall begins on the right with a series of scenes that belong to the core material of the ritual. They are unique in the history of Egyptian religion; they are an instance of trance or meditation, for which there are no parallels whatsoever in Egypt. In our tomb, these scenes are unfortunately badly damaged, so that we are obliged to consult better-preserved variants. A *sem*-priest is depicted wrapped in a mantle and squatting on a bed or chair. In the tomb of Nebsumenu, he is depicted kneeling. According to the caption, he is "sleeping" or "spending the night" (*sḏr*). "The *sem*-priest, sitting before him (i.e., the statue)" says, "He has *sḏ* (shattered?) me," and the *jmj-jz*, who is standing behind him, says, "He has *dḏw* (Otto suggests 'shoved') me." The *jmj-jz* then says four times "My father! My father! My father! My father!" Finally, we read, "Waking the sleeping one, the *sem*-priest. Finding the *jmjw-ḫnt* priests." In the following scene 10, the *sem*-priest, still squatting on his chair, conducts a dialogue with the *jmjw-ḫnt*: "To be spoken by the *sem*-priest: 'I have seen my father in all his outlines!'" The word *qd* "outline" is a play on *qd* "sleep." "The *jmjw-ḫnt* say to the *sem*: 'Your father shall not depart from you!' The *sem* says to the *jmjw-ḫnt*: 'The face hunters have captured him.' The *jmjw-ḫnt* say to the *sem*: 'I have seen my father in all his outlines. Beware lest he perish. Let there be no damage to him!'"

The *sem*-priest plays the role of the son of the deceased, or vice versa. Only the son was capable of doing what is happening here: seeing the form of his father in a trance or in meditative concentration and capturing it in its outlines so that artisans can render it in stone or wood. Scene 11 is entitled, "Standing up by the *sem*. He takes his staff. He wears the *qnj*-breastplate." The *sem* thus dresses himself, putting on a garment whose name means "embracer." Scene 12 depicts him facing three "wood-carvers" (*qs.tjw*). He says to them: "Brand my father! Make my father for me! Make it like my father! Who is it who makes it similar for me?" In scene 13, the *sem* addresses three other artisans, the bone-carver, the woodchopper, and the craftsman who wielded the polishing stone, with the words: "Who are they who wish to approach my father? Do not smite my father! Do not touch his head!" The artisans' activities on the statue entail violence that must be neutralized. Scene 14 depicts the *sem* making a symbolic gesture designated "adding the mouth"; he extends his arm to the statue and touches its mouth with his little finger. The Egyptian term rendered "adding" here is a carpenter's term that means putting two pieces together in such a way that they interlock. He then recites (in the Rekhmire version):

> I have come to seek/embrace you, I am Horus.
> I have added your mouth.
> I am your son, who loves you!

Scene 15 also has the purpose of averting the disagreeable consequences of unavoidable violence. The *sem* says to the artisans, "Come, smite my father for me!" and the artisans say, "Let those who smite your father be protected!" In scene 16, the *sem* says to a woodchopper, "I am Horus and Seth; I do not allow you to make the head of my father white!" In scene 17, the *jmyw-ḥnt* say to a priest called "the one behind Horus," "Isis, go to Horus, that he may seek his father!" In scene 18, the chief lector priest stands before the *sem* and says, "Hurry and see your father!" The statue is now ready, and it is to be recognized by the son as a portrait of his father.

The sequence of scenes involving artisans comes to an end here, and with scenes 19–21, something new begins. The *sem* must change his clothes; he removes the *qnj*-breastplate and dons the panther skin that is his characteristic item of clothing. His recitation is devoted solely to this action: "I have saved his eye from his mouth! I have ripped off his leg." The chief lector priest says to the statue, "O N., I have branded your eye for you, so that you may be brought to life by it!" The words "brand" and "be brought to life" are puns on the word for panther skin.

Like most of the other versions, the one in tomb 183 proceeds immediately to scene 23. This is the beginning of the chief portion of the entire ritual, the actual opening of the mouth. Scene 23 prescribes a slaughter. Later, we shall go into this in detail, so we shall merely summarize it here.

One leg and the heart are removed from a bull, and the heads of a goat and a goose are cut off. In scene 24, the chief lector priest and the *semer*-priest quickly bring the leg and the heart to the statue and place them, along with the goat and the goose, on the ground in front of it. This scene has been misunderstood by Otto and others as an offering scene. It is clearly titled "opening of the mouth and eyes." The *sem* does not offer the leg to the statue but rather uses it as an implement to open its mouth. In this regard, we must note that in the writing system, the hieroglyph depicting a bull's leg resembles an adz, the actual implement for opening the mouth, which is employed in the following scenes 26 and 27 (which are lost in tomb 183). The slaughter is thus a part of the opening of the mouth, which begins with scene 23 and ends with scene 27. We can now grasp the scenes on the left entrance wall as a unity: they include the sleep sequence in which the *sem* beholds the father (9–12), the artisan sequence 13–18, and the opening of the mouth sequence 23–27. Scene 19, in which the *sem*-priest changes his garb, serves as an intermission.

Third sequence: the ritual continues on the right rear wall. In scene 28, the *jmj-ḥnt* and a priest called *jrj-pꜥ.t* "hereditary noble" (again a son's role) stand facing one another. The recitation here yields no sense and is (as will later become clear) displaced to here from the opening of the mouth scenes: "I smite him for his mother, so that she bewails him. I smite him for his consort." Scene 29 is a repetition of scene 17. The *jmj-ḥnt* again says to "the one behind Horus," "Isis, go to Horus, that he may embrace his father!" Scene 30 repeats scene 16. Scene 31 is a double scene. The first part has to do with "finding the 'son who loves,' who is standing outside," and the second part with "bringing the 'son who loves' inside the tomb." We see the *sem* take the "son who loves," who precedes him, by the hand and guides him into the tomb. Behind them stands the lector priest, and behind the tomb the statue, which is present in all the scenes. The recitation reads: "O N., I bring you your loving son, that he may open your mouth for you!" In scene 32, the "loving son" goes into action to open the mouth and the eyes: "Carrying out the opening of the mouth and eyes, first with the *ḏdft*-implement, and then with the finger of electrum." The lector priest recites, "O N., I have attached your mouth for you! This cleaning out of the mouth of your father N. in your name 'Sokar' (etc.)." In scene 33, there follows the "opening of the mouth with the little finger," in which, as in scene 14 , the *sem* touches the mouth of the statue with his little finger. In scenes 34–39 and 41 (40 is a doublet) various objects are extended to the statue, objects that are to have a life-endowing, "mouth opening" effect: a *nemes* (scene 34), at whose offering the chief lector priest says, "I clean out your mouth, I open your eyes for you," four *ꜥb.t*-grains (35 and 36), at whose offering it is again said, "cleaning out the mouth and the eyes, opening the mouth and the eyes with each of them, twice," the *psš-k3=f*-implement, a kind of flint knife (37) with the words "I have opened your mouth for you with the *psš-k3=f*, with which the mouth of every god and every goddess is opened," grapes (38), with the words "O N., take the Eye of Horus, seize it; if you seize it, it will not pass by," an ostrich feather (39), with the words "take the Eye of Horus, may your face not be devoid of it," and a bowl of water (41), with the words "take the Eye of Horus, take the water that is in it!" These are symbolic gifts that do not nourish the deceased but rather are to open the mouth and eyes of his statue.

The final sequence of scenes is on the right entrance wall (east wall, northern portion). It begins with the rare scene 40, a repetition of scene 20 with the recitation "I have saved the Eye of Horus from his mouth. I have torn off his leg! I have desired this Eye of Horus for you, so that you may be *ba* by means of it," the last an allusion to the *sem*-priest's panther skin. In the following scenes, there are also repetitions of actions from the second sequence, which is on the southern portion of the east wall. The correspondences are as follows:

no. 20	intermission	no. 40
no. 23	slaughtering scene	no. 43
no. 24	presentation of the heart and leg	no. 44
no. 25	presentation of the leg	no. 45
no. 26/27	opening of the mouth with the adz	no. 46

The core of the ritual, the opening of the mouth with the leg of the freshly slaughtered bull, is thus carried out twice, which undoubtedly corresponds to an intent of the tomb owner that these two most important scenes stand opposite one another on the eastern wall, to the left and right of the entrance. On the southern side, these principal scenes are preceded by the sequences involving the sleeping *sem*-priest and his dialogue with the artisans. On the northern side, the scenes are preceded by scenes that conclude the ritual in this version. These begin with scene 55, in which the *sem* anoints the statue, touching its mouth with the index finger of his right hand. The following spell is then recited (in the version in a mortuary liturgy on a papyrus of the Late Period;[30] in tomb 183, only the first three verses are preserved):

O Osiris N., your mother has given birth to you today!
You have been made into one who knows what was not known.
Geb at the head of the corporation of the Great Ennead has healed you,
joining your head to your bones.
Then he speaks to you, and the Great Ennead
among the living hears it on this day.

316

May Geb be gracious to you
and give you your head
and join your limbs together.
May Horus be gracious to you
and give you your head
and join your limbs together, that you may endure.

May you receive it, your *ka*, your god.
May your *ka* be gracious to you,
may your god be gracious to you,
your *ka* being in front of you
and your god being behind you.
May you receive your head.

The anointing has the effect of uniting the limbs; the entire effect of the embalming ritual is contained in this single gesture that the *sem*-priest carries out with his index finger. After the anointing, there follows a purification with incense (scene 47), and a classic spell that is often attested outside the ritual is recited. Then the statue is given a garment (scene 50), as well as a scepter and a mace (scene 57). In tomb 183, the conclusion is a censing in front of the uraeus-serpent (scene 59). The structure of the entire ritual can now be summarized as follows:

Sequence 1 west wall south	Sequence 2 east wall south	Sequence 3 west wall north	Sequence 4 east wall north
Opening: a) purification with libations and censings b) going to the tomb, entering it	a) endowing with life (sleep of the *sem*) b) transfer to the statue (artisan scenes) c) first opening of the mouth with slaughter	opening of the mouth with various objects	a) second opening of mouth with slaughter (= sequence 2 c) b) "investiture" of the statue by means of anointing, clothing, and insignia

In some tombs, this actual Opening of the Mouth is followed by the carrying out of a food offering, a ritual of its own with preliminary censings and libations, as well as a litany to the sun god that we shall discuss further below.

b) Setting up the Mummy "before Re"

The Opening of the Mouth ritual was carried out in the forecourt of the tomb on the mummies of the tomb owner and his wife, with a concentration on certain central rites. Captions make it clear that the mummies were to be set upright:

The day of burial, striding freely to his tomb.
Performing the Opening of the Mouth at the [. . .] in the House of Gold,
set upright on the desert soil,
its face turned to the south,
bathed in light on earth on the day of being clothed (i.e., the
"investiture").[31]

Censing and libating to Osiris N.
in order to open the mouth for the statue of N.,
it being oriented with its face to the south on the desert sand.
May you be bathed in light on the day of being clothed (i.e., the
"investiture").[32]

The turning of the face towards the south probably means that the mummy or statue was set up at midday, facing the sun, which was in the south at that hour. Since the procession began in the early morning, at the embalming hall, we must conclude that it arrived at the tomb around 12 noon. The meaning of this setting up of the statue or mummy is that it was bathed in light and "charged" by the rays of the sun.

It is thus often stressed in mortuary spells that the mummy is to be set up at the entrance of the tomb "before" or "for" Re.[33] These formulas appear at the same point in time as the representations: at the end of Dynasty 18, around 1300 B.C.E. The earliest mention is in a harper's song in the tomb of the god's father Neferhotep from the reign of Aya:

> Their mummies are set up before Re,
> while their people mourn ceaselessly.
> Death comes at its time,
> Shay (i.e., fate, lifetime) counts his days.[34]

In Theban Tomb 224, and similarly in the tomb of the vizier Paser (Theban Tomb 106) from the early Ramesside Period, the deceased expresses the wish:

> May my august mummy be set up in the sight of Re
> and a great offering placed at the entrance to my tomb.
> Then those in the Secluded Land will say,
> "See the praised one, N.!"[35]

There is constant stress on contact with the sunlight. The mummy is set up "for" or "before" Re, and the entrance, or more often, the court (wsḥ.t) of the tomb is specified as the place where this takes place:

> Your mummy is set up for Re
> in the forecourt of your tomb.[36]

A text attested in two tombs of the late thirteenth century connects this rite with a clear allusion to the Judgment of the Dead:

> Your mummy is set up for Re
> in the court of your tomb,
> you being given over to the scale of the necropolis.
> May you emerge vindicated.[37]

Here, setting up the mummy in the court of the tomb was taken as the signal for an enactment of the Judgment of the Dead, which perhaps consisted of a recitation of chapter 125 of the Book of the Dead. This was presumably a repetition of the vindication of the deceased that had been carried out in the framework of the embalming ritual.

As we have seen, the forecourt of the tomb is mentioned as the place where these proceedings took place. When we consider the development of the Egyptian monumental tomb in the course of the New Kingdom, we take note of an astonishing coincidence. Just when the textual formulas describing the setting up of the mummy and the artistic representations of the rites made their appearance, that is, at the end of Dynasty 18, there was a change in the appearance of the forecourt of the tomb.[38] It was now surrounded by a high wall that protected it from the outside world, and often enough, its character as a sacred place was emphasized by pillars, decorated façades, and stelae. The tomb of Amenemope, which was the starting point for our treatment of the funeral rituals, furnishes a good example of this new type of court. In this case, the court is sunken, and it is entered by a staircase leading down from the east. The south, east, and north sides are surrounded by pillars, and the pillars on the south side are decorated with mummiform, mezzo-rilievo statues of the tomb owner, while the pillars of the other two sides would undoubtedly also have had such statues had their preparation been completed. The motif of setting up the mummy in the forecourt "before Re" is thus architectonically realized in this instance. Tomb 183, which served as our model for the reconstruction of the Opening of the Mouth ritual, also has a richly decorated forecourt. It was entered from a second court through a pylon. On all sides, including the west side, it is surrounded by pillars, and on the sides facing the court, these pillars are decorated with figures of the tomb owner. Similar figures flank the façade of the entrance to the transverse chamber (where the Opening of the Mouth ritual is located), as well as the doorway from the transverse chamber to the passage.

This change in tomb architecture serves as an important indication that with the transition from Dynasty 18 to Dynasty 19, not only did the conventions of representing the funeral change but also the ritual itself.

Perhaps the mummy had been set up at the entrance to the tomb before being buried from time immemorial, or at least since the beginning of the New Kingdom; we have no way of knowing, for the earlier representations do not depict the rituals that were actually carried out but rather a sort of pictorial recollection of the time of origins. Now, however, what actually happened assumed so much importance that the architecture took note of it and furnished an appropriate cultic stage for it. The most important aspect of the rite was probably the contact with the sunlight. This emerges from the passages cited above, describing how the mummy or statue was set up "facing south," and the point is also stressed in mortuary spells that refer to this scene of the Opening of the Mouth at the tomb:

> May you stand erect on the sand of Rasetau,
> may you be greeted when the sun shines on you
> so as to carry out your purification.[39]

> Your mouth will be opened, your limbs will be purified
> before Re when he rises!
> May he transfigure you, may he grant that you be rejuvenated,
> living among the gods![40]

The cult of the sun flourished in New Kingdom Egypt, culminating in late Dynasty 18 and early Dynasty 19, and solar religion also grew ever more important in funerary beliefs. Tomb owners often had themselves represented on the southern thickness of the entrance to their tomb, striding out to greet the rising sun with a hymn. On the opposite thickness, they returned into their tomb with a hymn to the evening sun or to Osiris.[41] In this way, the tomb decoration expressed the idea of "going forth by day" and connected it with the sun god. During this period, stelae with solar hymns and representations of the Opening of the Mouth ritual were often placed on the façades of tombs.[42] The tomb of Amenemope is again a good example of this practice. Not only did it have three stelae in front of its façade, two on the south side with solar hymns and one on the north side with a hymn to Osiris, but the south side was itself decorated with a representation of the sun god and a lengthy hymn to him.[43] The motif of the deceased's association with the sun god, which played so great a role in the transfiguration texts of this period, found its iconographic and architectonic expression in this tomb. Its ritual expression, however, was in the rite of setting up the mummy "before Re."

Also connected with this motif was the practice of setting up stelae decorated with sun hymns and representations of the Opening of the Mouth ritual in the forecourts of tombs, in front of the façade, as first attested in the reign of Amenophis III. Association with the sun god, which played so great a role in the transfiguration spells, had its cultic equivalent in this rite: setting up the mummy in front of the entrance to the tomb was thus well suited to the period in which it was first mentioned and represented.

The rite can also be connected with a tradition dating back to the Pyramid Texts, from the period when the Opening of the Mouth ritual is also first mentioned. Pyramid Texts spell 222 is especially well suited to the framework of a comparable rite. Here, too, the deceased, in the form of a statue, coffin, or mummy, stands face to face with the sun. This spell stems from the liturgy whose initial spells (213–216) were cited in chapter 6. I cite it here in a version from a tomb of Dynasty 18, from which it is clear that it was also used in the cult at this time:

> May you stand up on it, on this land
> from which Atum emerged,
> on the sputum that came out of Kheprer.
> May you come into being on it, may you come on high on it,
> so that your father sees you,
> so that Re sees you.

The stanza that follows is addressed to the sun god, describing the deceased, who has been set up in front of him:

> He has come to you, his father,
>   He has come to you, O Re.
> He has come to you, his father,
>   he has come to you, O *Ndj*.[44]
> He has come to you, his father,
>   he has come to you, O *Dndn*.[45]
> He has come to you, his father,
>   he has come to you, O Great Wild Bull.
> He has come to you, his father,
>   he has come to you, O Great Reed Float.
> He has come you, his father,
>   he has come to you, O Equipped One.
> He has come to you, his father,
>   he has come to you, O Sharp-toothed One.
> May you grant that this N. seize his sky![46]
> May you grant that this N. rule the Nine Bows and make the Ennead
>   complete,
> may you place the shepherd's staff in N.'s hand (as) a divine gift,
> may you grant (him) Upper and Lower Egypt.

The next stanzas once again address the deceased, describing his participation in the course of the sun. The first depicts his association with the sun god when the latter rises and the daily journey across the sky, and the second his participation in the nocturnal journey of the sun through the netherworld:

> May you shed your impurity for Atum in Heliopolis,
> may you go down with him and loose the bonds of Naunet,
> may you sit on the throne of Nui.
> May you come into being with Atum,
> may you come on high with Atum,
> may you rise with Atum.
> May the bonds be loosed for you,
> may your head belong to the lady of Heliopolis.[47]
> May you ascend and clear the way for yourself in the bones of Shu,
> and may the arms of Nut embrace you.
> May you purify yourself in Light-land,
> may you shed your impurity in the lakes of Shu.
>
> May you rise and set,
> may you rise with Re,
> may you join[48] with Nedi.
> May you rise and set,
> may you rise with Re,
> may you rise with the Great Reed Float.
> May you rise and set,
> may you rise with Nephthys,
> may you join[49] the night barque.
> May you rise and set,
> may you rise with Isis,
> may you rise with the morning barque.
>
> May you have power over your body, may there be no hindering of you.
> May you be born like Re
> and carried in pregnancy like Thoth.[50]
> Purify yourself for yourself in the western nome,
> receive your purification in the Heliopolitan nome with Atum.
> Come into being for yourself, come on high for yourself,
> may it be well with you, may it be pure for you
> in the embrace of your father Re-Atum.
>
> O Atum, take him
> in your embrace, together with your *ka*!
> He is the son of your body, forever.[51]

There is good reason to view this ritual of setting up the mummy before Re and carrying out the Opening of the Mouth in the sunlight as the origin of a ritual that played a major role in the temple cult of the late stages of Egyptian history. This ritual, called "Uniting with the Sun" (*ḫnm-jtn*), consisted of a procession in which the statues were taken to the temple roof on specified occasions and set out in the sunlight.[52] Here, the illumination by the sunlight seems to have taken the place of the Opening of the Mouth ritual and its consecrating, life-endowing function. This history of transmission, which spanned three millennia, reveals a creative power that began with the royal and then the nonroyal funerary cults and finally extended to the temple cult of the gods.

The setting up of mummies before Re and his shining down on them was thus already an important, even central rite, one that was entirely independent of the further rites that were carried out on the mummy after it was set up. These consisted first of all of a purification scene that we often see represented in the tombs. In this rite, water was poured over the mummy from the so-called *nemset*-jars. In a mortuary spell that appears above a representation of the *sem*-priest and the mourners in Theban Tomb 23, the rite is described in detail:

> May you stand up on the sand of Rasetau,[53]
> may you be greeted when the sun shines on you,
> and may your purification be carried out for you as a daily performance.
> May Nun purify you,
> may cool water come forth for you from Elephantine,
> may you be greeted with the *nemset*-jar.
> Take incense for yourself,
> receive natron!
> May the divine words purify you,[54]
> may your mouth be opened by the chisel of Ptah.[55]
> May your two eyes be opened for you.
> May the requirements of an aristocrat be brought to you,[56]
> so that their work can be carried out for you.
> May the lector priest come to you with his book rolls[57]
> and the *sem*-priest with his transfiguration spells.
> May the pieces of carpentry be granted to you by Ptah,
> namely, the chest, provided with its implements.[58]
> May Anubis place his arms on you,
> may the *jwn-mw.t=f*[59] priest libate for you.
> May the Great Mourning Birds (i.e., mourning women playing the roles
>   of Isis and Nephthys) come to you and punish your enemies.
> The *s3-mr=f*-priest stands in front of the tomb behind you.
> May the four-threaded cloth that Tayt has woven come to you.
> May your *jb*-heart mount up to its place for you
> and may your *ḥ3.tj*-heart be as it was.
> May your body be transfigured, and may your *b3* be divine.
> May you keep company with the god in the sky.
> May the sky belong to your *b3*,
> may the netherworld belong to your corpse.[60]

May linen belong to your mummy
and breath be at your nose, that you not suffocate.[61]
May you renew yourself daily[62]
and assume any form you wish.
May you emerge as a living $b\!\!\!/^3$.

c) Offering of the Heart and Leg

The central rite of the Opening of the Mouth ritual was celebrated with an offering, which we shall consider in some detail here. This was an unusually ghastly offering scene, first attested in tombs and Book of the Dead papyri from after the Amarna Period. A foreleg of a living calf was amputated while its mother stood behind it, mourning her young with upraised head and her tongue stuck out. A priest went running with the leg, carrying it to the mummy: evidently, it was important that it be presented while it was still warm with life. Sometimes, a second slaughter was depicted, and another priest went running to the mummy with a heart.

In two tombs, this scene has a caption from which it emerges that not only did the warm flesh of the calf play a role in this rite but also the mournful bellowing of its mother:

> The spell of that which the cow says:
> Weeping over you, O dearly beloved!
> The cow is sorrowful (at) your tomb,
> her heart grieves over her lord.[63]

Both of these, the fresh meat and the bellowing of the bereaved cow, which was interpreted as mourning over the deceased, were supposed to have a life-endowing, "mouth-opening" effect on the mummy.

Among the scenes of the Opening of the Mouth Ritual, as we have seen, it is the scenes of slaughtering and of presenting the heart and leg that occur twice.[64] In each case, the presentation of the heart and leg is followed immediately by the central scenes of the entire ritual, the "opening of the mouth" with the carpenter's tool specific to that purpose. Though the texts that accompany the archaic ritual are unclear, they furnish indications as to the meaning of the slaughtering scene, which does not serve to feed the statue but rather to endow it with life. As usual, the slaughter of the animal is explained as punishment of the enemy. The woman playing the role of Isis whispers into the ear of the offering animal, who evidently represents Seth, that he has brought the judgment on himself. This statement alludes to the scene in the House of the Nobles at Heliopolis, where Seth, attempting to defend himself before the gods, tries to shift the blame to his offering and in the process signs his own death warrant (Pyramid spell 477, see chapter 3).[65]

scene 23 = 43:
Sem-priest: laying a hand on the male Upper Egyptian steer.
Slaughterer: descending on it, removing its leg, taking out its heart.
Reciting in its ear by the "Great Kite" (i.e., Isis as mourning woman):
"It is your lips that have done this to you through the cleverness of your
   mouth!"
Bringing a goat; cutting off its head. Bringing a goose; cutting off its head.

It is said to the enemy incorporated in the animal to be slaughtered that
he has pronounced his own judgment![66]
   In the scenes that follow, the leg and heart are given to two priests, who
hurry to the statue with them. It is thus clear that this is still a matter of
the cow-calf scenes, in which the speed of the delivery plays so great a role:

Scene 24 = 44:
Slaughterer: giving the leg to the chief lector priest, the heart to the *semer*.
The heart is thus in the hand of the *semer*, the leg in the hand of the chief
   lector priest.
They run quickly with them.[67] Laying the leg and the heart down before N.

Recitation: Take the leg, the Eye of Horus!
I have brought you the heart that was in him (i.e., Seth).
Do not approach that god!
I have brought you the goat, its head cut off.
I have brought you the goose, its head cut off.

Just what this offering rite is about is made clear in the scene that follows.
The severed, hastily delivered leg is held to the face of the statue so that
the still warm vital energy streaming out of it will open its mouth and eyes,
that is, endow it with life. There is an allusion to Seth, in the third person
and without mention of his name, an allusion that acquires meaning only
from the scene with the cow and the calf:[68]

scene 25 = 45
Sem-*Priest* and *Chief lector priest*:
Taking the leg, opening the mouth and eyes.

Reciting: O N., I have come in search of you (to embrace you)!
I am Horus, and I have supplied your mouth.
I am your beloved son, and I have opened your mouth for you.
How he (i.e., Seth, the animal being offered) is slain for his mother, who
   bewails him,
how slain he is for his companion.
How *hng* (the meaning of this word is unknown) is your mouth!
I have fit your mouth on your bones.
O N.! I have opened your mouth for you with the leg/Eye of Horus!

The offering of a heart and leg is also mentioned in mortuary spells of the New Kingdom. It is clear that this was not just a rite connected with a ritual that endowed a statue with life, but that in a more general sense, it had to do with bringing the deceased himself to life:

> A leg is cut off for you;
> a leg is cut off for your *ka*,
> and a *ḥꜣ.tj*-heart for your mummy.[69]

In an oft-attested text that accompanied food offerings, the rite that interests us here is mentioned in the fourth stanza:

> An offering litany with incense will be brought to you
> at the entrance to your tomb.
> A foreleg will be cut off for your *ka*,
> and a heart for your mummy.
> May your *ba* go above
> and your corpse below.[70]

The rite is expressly connected with the Opening of the Mouth in the following mortuary spell:

> Opening of the Mouth and rejoicing
> for your *ka* in every beautiful place,
> while the *sem*-priest carries out the (ritual) of Opening the Mouth
> and the Great Leader of the Craftsmen exalts your *ka*.
> May a leg be cut off for your *ba*,
> that it may be divine in the realm of the dead.[71]

The essential point is that this presentation of the heart and leg, which is carried out twice during the Opening of the Mouth ritual, has nothing to do with an ordinary food offering. This offering occurs later: after a series of censings and libations (scenes 58–64), the offering meal (scenes 65–70) serves as the crowning point of this last segment of the funeral. In most representations, we thus see not only the Opening of the Mouth implements in front of the deceased but also a huge pile of offerings. This offering is both an end and a beginning: it completes the procession to the tomb, and it inaugurates the offering cult that from now on will be regularly carried out in the tomb.

Scene 71 is a censing for Re-Harakhty, an act that again integrates the ritual performance into the course of the sun. The priest addresses a litany invoking *maat*:

> O Re, lord of *maat!* O Re, who lives on *maat!*
> O Re, who rejoices over *maat!* O Re, who loves *maat!*

After a lengthy series of additional epithets compounded with *maat*, there is a concluding text in which the priest presents himself and explains his ritual actions:

> I have come to you, I am Thoth, who is your equal!
> I have come forth for you, appointed for this occasion.
> I have purified myself in Hermopolis.
> What is healthful to me is what is also healthful to you.
> What is known to me is what is also known to you.
> I have drawn on your strength,
> on that power that is in your mouth.
> I have come to you to bring *maat* to you,
> that you may live on it and rejoice over it,
> that you may feed on it and become powerful by means of it,
> and endure by means of it, be hale by means of it, be adorned by means
> of it,
> and rise with it, shine with it, and set with it. . . .

Finally, the priest speaks of the rites that he has carried out on the deceased:

> I have given breath to those who are in hiding,
> I have enabled those who are in the netherworld to breathe.
> I have shaped the gods, each according to his form.
> I have caused them to rest in their chapels and their offerings to endure.
> I have equipped the ancestral spirits with their images,
> mortuary offerings will be brought to them in hecatombs,
> set out at every bidding as praiseworthy action.
> The one in Light-land rejoices over N.:
> I have formed him as well.
> I have created his divine form.
> The breath of life, it comes and creates his image,
> his mouth is opened, I have made him the equal of the righteous.
> His name endures forever,
> because he is an excellent ancestral spirit in the netherworld.
> He hears the call of those among his relatives.
> He protects the body of the one who pours water for him.
> He has power over bread!
> He has power over beer!
> He emerges as a living *ba*, he assumes its form
> according to the wish of his heart, wherever his *ka* wishes to tarry![72]

This declaration is followed by the rite of carrying—in the statue ritual, the statue into its shrine, and in the burial ritual, the coffin into the sarcophagus chamber (scene 73):

Carrying by nine *smrw*.

O *smrw*, carry him on your arms!
Recitation: O sons of Horus, hurry with your father, carry him.
He is not to be far from you, carry him!
O N., Horus has placed your children under you,
that they may carry you and that you may have power over them.
O you sons of Horus, Imset, Hapi,
Duamutef, Qebehsenuf!
Hurry with your father!
He is not to be far from you.
O N., they carry you like Sokar in the *henu*-barque.
It (the barque) elevates you as a god in your name Sokar.
O N., you are embraced; you have power over Upper and Lower Egypt
as this Horus, with whom you are united.[73]

This scene occurs in a number of Middle and New Kingdom tombs.[74]

Playing the role of the nine friends, the sons of Horus also carry the corpse of Osiris in the ritual of the Osiris chapels at Dendara:

The god is then carried in on their shoulders, on those of the sons of
 Horus,
whose name refers to nine gods.[75]

This act concluded the funeral ritual. After being set up before Re in the forecourt of the tomb, the mummy was again placed in its coffin, which was transferred from the sledge to carrying poles. A group of participants lifted it onto their shoulders and carried it from the forecourt to the sarcophagus chamber. In a representation in the Middle Kingdom tomb of Inyotefoqer (Theban Tomb 60), this scene occurs in front of the entrance to the tomb, where the *muu*-dancers greeted the coffin. At the beginning of this chapter, we cited texts that mention their dance. In the tomb of Amenemhet (Theban Tomb 82) from the reign of Tuthmosis III, the scene occurs in front of the false door, in the interior of the tomb.[76] At the end, the coffin was brought to its proper place in the sarcophagus chamber. The "friends" and "royal dependents" then took the coffin and placed it on a sledge. Two priests took turns dragging the sledge, one to the south and the other to the north, until it reached its final position. In the tomb of Rekhmire, we read the following:

To be spoken by the *ka*-servant: It is I who drag it to the south!
To be spoken by the embalmer: It is I who drag it to the north![77]

In the tomb of Mentuherkhopshef (Theban Tomb 20), this scene occurs in a space that might well represent the sarcophagus chamber. Seven priests crouch around the coffin, among them a *sem*-priest, a chief lector priest, an embalmer, an *imy-khent,* and a "royal dependent." A caption specifies that recitations are to be spoken, "first to the west, second to the east, third to the south, and fourth to the north." Apparently, a wake was again carried out here so as to place the coffin under the care of protective deities and their spells, which drove off the enemy, on all four sides.[78] After this was done, the priests left the room and the sarcophagus chamber was bricked up and sealed, so that—this was surely always the pious wish—no one would ever again set foot in it.

CHAPTER FOURTEEN

Provisioning the Dead

here were two important frameworks for the recitation of mortuary liturgies: the rites in the embalming chamber during the night
before the funeral and the offering service in the cult place in the
tomb. The Egyptian expression for "mortuary offering," translated literally into English, is "coming out at the voice."[1] The idea was that at the
sound of the mortuary priest's voice, the *ba* of the deceased would "come
out" from the netherworld, the sky, or wherever it was conceived of as
being, and receive the offering. The term for making an offering is *wȝḥ*
jḫ.t, literally, "to set things down."[2] The offerings are sometimes accompanied by "transfigurations" (*sȝḫw.w*).[3]

Offerings were made to the *ba* of the deceased, the aspect of his person
that made it possible for him to "emerge" from the next-worldly realm to
receive the offering. In the texts of the New Kingdom, the characteristic
formula is *ḥr ḥrw njs n wȝḥ jḫ.t*, "(emerging) at the sound of the call of
the making of offerings" or "at the sound of the call of the one making
the offerings,"[4] as in the following example:

> May my *ba* emerge, at the sound of its mortuary priest,
> to receive the offering that has been brought to it.[5]

We can thus see that in Egypt, a mortuary offering was first and foremost a matter of speech and sound. The offering rite entailed a recitation, and it was this verbal act that made the difference.

In this chapter, I wish to present some well-attested spells that were recited at the making of offerings. They all have a similar structure:

1. invitations to the deceased to ready himself to receive offerings;
2. formulas for presenting the offerings ("take to yourself . . .");
3. mention of further actions of the deceased that result from receiving the offering and represent the "sacramental explanation" of the offering.

Sometimes, there is also

4. a "concluding text" in which the officiant speaks of himself and his activities on behalf of the deceased.

There are hundreds of spells structured according to this scheme. The following three spells, which I would like to present in some detail, have been selected because of the frequency of their occurrences. From their popularity, it can be concluded that they are typical and representative of this form of mortuary liturgy.

1. Pyramid Texts Spell 373

The first spell is from the Pyramid Texts. It is first attested in the pyramid of Teti and is then repeatedly attested down into the later periods of Egyptian history. This spell also occurs in the context of a mortuary liturgy that we shall not treat in its entirety here.[6]

> Raise yourself, Osiris N.!
> take your head,
> gather your bones,
> collect your limbs,
> shake the soil from your flesh!
> Take your bread, which does not grow moldy,
> and your beer, which does not grow sour.
>
> You will step up before the door-leaves that keep out the subjects,
> and Khenti-menutef will go out to you
> to take you by the hand
> and lead you to the sky,
> to your father Geb.

He will rejoice at your presence
and extend his arms to you.
He will kiss you and feed you
and place you at the head of the transfigured spirits, the imperishable ones.

Those with hidden places will worship you,
the great ones will gather around you,
and the guardians will stand up before you.
I have threshed barley and reaped emmer for you,
that I may arrange your monthly festival with them
and arrange your full moon festival with them,
as your father Geb has commanded to be done for you.

Raise yourself, Osiris N., you have not died!

The text is divided into three stanzas of 7, 5, and 7 verses, to which there is added a concluding text of 5 verses. The first stanza consists of motifs 1 and 2, that is, the invitation to the deceased to come and receive the offering and the formula for presenting the items offered. The second and third stanzas are devoted to the third motif, the sacramental explanation of the offering, which thus takes up by far the most space in this spell. The last verse of the concluding text refers back to the first verse of the spell, repeating the invitation to the deceased to raise himself up.

The call to "Raise yourself!" appears a hundred times and more in mortuary texts. It refers to the common goal of all the ritual activities aimed at the deceased, from the embalming process to the mortuary offerings. It is a "wake-up call" intended to rouse the deceased from his unconscious state. Lying down and standing up are the clearest manifestations of death and life. To this wake-up call are added invitations to gather the limbs, as though the deceased, after the carrying out of the rituals of embalming, mummification, and burial did not have this stage long behind him. These rituals had been aimed at restoring his personal, that is, his physical and spiritual unity, and now, he had to rouse himself from his condition of physical decline, as described in chapter 1, which dealt with the image of "Death as Dismemberment." In the Pyramid Texts, the motif of waking and uniting the limbs is often connected with that of invitations to receive offerings, for example:

Wake, O N., raise yourself,
take your head,
gather your bones,
shake off your dust,
seat yourself on that brazen throne of yours!
You are to partake of an ox's leg,

put a piece of meat in your mouth;
partake of your rib-joints
in the sky in the company of the gods.[7]

Another text adds the motif of the bread that is not to grow moldy and
the beer that is not to grow sour:[8]

Raise yourself, O N. here,
take your water,
gather your bones,
get up on your feet,
transfigured at the head of the transfigured ones!
Raise yourself to this bread of yours that does not grow moldy
and to your beer that does not grow sour.[9]

The following verses begin a spell for presenting the deceased with four
jugs of water, evidently to purify him:

Stand up, raise yourself, O my father N.,
gather your bones,
take your limbs,
shake the soil from your flesh,
take these four *nemset*-jars, filled to the brim.[10]

Another spell begins with a presentation of water and incense:

Raise yourself, O N. there,
gather your bones,
bestir your members,
your water comes from Elephantine,
your incense from the palace of the god.[11]

The same formulas occur when more substantial offerings are presented,
for example, meat:

Raise yourself, O N. there,
gather your bones,
take your head,
the Ennead has commanded that you be seated at your *t-wr* bread
and that you cut off an ox's leg on the great slaughtering block,
for the rib-joints have been placed for you on the slaughtering block of
   Osiris.[12]

This combination of motifs, so typical of the Pyramid Texts, does not
occur later in texts having to do with food offerings. We might see in this

an indication that these spells stem from a period when the embalming ritual had not yet been fully developed.

In Pyramid Texts spell 373, these two verses constitute the actual presentation of the offering. What follows belongs to theme 3, the sacramental explanation, and it is thus the most important concern of the spell. By "sacramental explanation," I mean an interpretation of the offering in a sacred sense, one that has to do with the realm of the gods. A non-sacramental explanation would be one that connects the taking of bread and beer with the quenching of hunger and thirst or with some other form of physical refreshment. A sacramental explanation, by way of contrast, is one that brings the receiver of the offering into a relationship with the sphere of the gods, one that goes beyond the merely physical and concerns the social sphere, the "social sphere" of a deceased person transfigured into an ancestral spirit being, of course, the realm of the gods.

In our spell, the deceased's ascent to the sky serves as the sacramental explanation. Taking nourishment makes it possible, as though the nourishment were a supernatural drug, and the journey takes the deceased into a next-worldly, celestial realm, with stops along the way. First, the deceased arrives at a gate that separates this realm from the next one, a gate called "that which keeps out the *rḥy.t*." *Rḥy.t* is a designation of ordinary people, as opposed to *pꜥ.t*, "dignitary," and *ḥnmm.t*, an enigmatic term we usually translate "sun-folk," a group that also makes its appearance in the afterlife. The gate "that keeps out the *rḥy.t*" leads into a next-worldly sphere that is inaccessible to ordinary people. These door-leaves are also mentioned in Pyramid Texts §§ 876b, 1726b, 1914, and 1934; they refer to the theme of "distancing" and thus to the image of death as transition. The celestial destiny of the king in the next world has nothing to do with the continued earthly existence of the ordinary dead, who are not allowed to pass through this gate.[13]

The king is to stand before this gateway, and the guardians will come out to him. This scene occurs often in offering spells. One example can suffice here for many:

> O N.!
> Step before the two door-leaves that keep out the people.
> May the guardian of the two houses, Kenti-menutef, come out to you,
> you unique star without peer![14]

The door-leaves of the gate that separates this world from the next one, that separates sky and earth, open up to the one who receives the offerings. This close relationship between offering meal and gateway is probably not to be separated from the symbolism of the false door where offerings were placed in an Egyptian tomb. If this is the case, then the false door was not only an interface between the inaccessible and the accessible portions of the tomb, and between this realm and the next one, but also a symbol of the celestial gateway. Receiving the offerings set down in front of the false door enabled the deceased to pass through the gateway that led to the sky.

Passing through the gate with the assistance of its guardian, Khenti-menutef,[15] the deceased king ascended to the sky. This ascent thus took place within the structure to which the door-leaves gave access. We must therefore picture this gate as located in that liminal area between sky and earth that the Egyptians called *ʒḥ.t*, a term we conventionally render as "horizon." This translation is not entirely correct, for a horizon depends on the standpoint of the beholder, and it shifts as he moves along, so that it can never be reached. As the Egyptians conceived it, however, the *ʒḥ.t* could indeed be reached. It was the zone at the edge of the world, where the sun rose and set. Temples and pyramid complexes were often called *akhet*, with the result that this zone also had a symbolic value. The false door was therefore also such a symbol, that is, "sacramentally explainable."

The guardian of the gateway takes the king by the hand and "leads" him to the sky. The verb used here is *šdj* "to lead," which also means "to save." The king did not have to mount to the sky on his own; he was "led," which our text describes, in a single verse, as a rapid transition and not as a long and tedious journey. In a stanza consisting of seven verses, the spell proceeds to describe the scene in the sky that follows this transition.

The first four verses describe the heartfelt welcome accorded to the deceased by the god Geb. Geb "rejoices at his approach,"[16] he embraces[17] the newcomer, kissing him and thus acknowledging him as his son. The god makes him ruler over the "imperishable stars," granting him lordship over the northern reaches of the sky, where Elysium is located in the conceptual realm of the Pyramid Texts. The newly enthroned ruler is received and acclaimed by his subjects, the deceased ("those with hidden places") and the dignitaries (the "great ones" and the "guardians"[18]), as is often stated in similar contexts, for example:

> The great ones gather around you,
> the guardians stand before you,
> as before Horus, the protector of his father.[19]

The spell is divided symmetrically into three stanzas of 7, 5, and 7 verses each. The first stanza alludes to the earth. The deceased, who is lying in the tomb, is to stand up, gather his limbs together, and receive his nourishment of imperishable bread and beer. The second stanza leads him to a gate, and through it, up to the sky. The third stanza describes his enthronement by Geb, his celestial father, and his acclamation by the next-worldly beings over whom he has been appointed ruler. The sun god often appears in the role of celestial father; but when ascent to the sky and assumption of rulership is represented in the framework of the mythic model of the lawsuit over the succession to the throne, it is Geb, to whom this rulership has reverted after the murder of his son, who takes it away from the assassin who acted contrary to law, and who grants it to the rightful heir. With its clearly articulated structure, the text thus describes a coherent thematic line that leads from a catastrophic starting point, the deceased lying unconscious and with his limbs strewn about, to the triumphal ending point of his celestial rulership. Spatially, this line leads him out of the sarcophagus chamber, through the cult chamber, and up to the sky; socially, it leads him from the isolation and disintegration of a dead person to integration into the realm of the gods as its ruler. The structure of the spell can be represented thus (the numerals refer to the number of verses):

				1 raise yourself
		7 in the tomb	5 wake-up call	4 gathering the limbs
			2 meal	2 bread and beer
	19	5 the gate		1 approaching the gate
				4 ascent to the sky
24			4 reception	2 reception
		7 in the sky	by Geb	2 enthronement
			3 acclamation	
	5	5 conclusion		4 work in the fields, festivals
				1 raise yourself

This thematic line thus describes a total transformation. As a sacramental explanation, this transformation underlies many offering spells, but it seldom stands out as clearly as it does in this early, classic example. Not only does the offering nourish the deceased, it conveys him to the sky and to the status of ruler of the dead. This is the sacramental explanation that can only be expressed by the words that accompany the offering. We may even say that it was the words that were decisive. It is even possible that the offering itself was not real. Perhaps we are to understand this talk about bread that does not grow moldy and beer that does not grow sour quite literally, as an allusion to symbolic and thus imperishable representations of these offering items, in the reliefs, for example, or more likely, on the offering tray placed in front of the false door. These representations would have been activated by the recitation.

To judge from the structure of the spell, the decisive element that marks the change from earthly to celestial surroundings is the striding through the gate described in the middle stanza. Furthermore, the gate is probably symbolized by the false door, the place where offerings were made and spells recited. The relationship between the offering meal and ascent to the sky, the latter being the sacramental explanation of the former, is one of the fundamentals of the Egyptian mortuary cult. The offering was the ritual framework for the image of death as transition. Spells that mention the deceased's passage from the realm of death, where the conditions of life are reversed, into the Elysian realm, where the order of eternal life prevails, have especially to do with eating and drinking. In the realm of death, the deceased are obliged to live on feces and urine. The nourishment to which he had a claim demonstrated that the deceased no longer belonged to that realm but rather had been called to life eternal. He strove for a share of this nourishment in the Elysian realm, and he ate of this nourishment in order to belong to it. Means and end intertwined, with the result that the deceased's food became the medium of his salvation from the realm of death (the aspect of salvation is clearly expressed by the verb *šdj* "to take out, rescue"). The offerings therefore had to be pure, for only thus did they belong to the realm of the gods, into which the deceased was integrated by receiving them.

This initiatory, transformative aspect of taking nourishment is familiar to Christians through the ritual of Communion, though the latter rests on different traditions of offerings and sacred meals. The Egyptian rite of provisioning the dead was intended to integrate the deceased into the communal feasting of the gods and the transfigured ancestral spirits.

The final stanza is a concluding text that stands outside the actual transfiguration. Here, the officiant speaks of himself and explains his cultic actions. The last verse of the text repeats the introductory wake-up call of the first verse, establishing the coherence of the spell by means of this cyclic device.

2. Summoning the Dead

The second spell[20] bears the title "spell for summoning the transfigured one and causing that he be satisfied with his offering."[21]

> Are you in the sky?
> Are you in the earth?
> Come, step forth,
> you being *bꜣ* and transfigured,
> you being mighty and prepared.
>
> May your legs bring you,
> that you may see this house of yours, which Seshat has built for you
> and on whose walls Khnum has stood for you.

May the door-leaves of the myrrh chest open for you,
the door-leaves of the "cool place" are to stand open to you,
as (they do for) Horus, who protects his father.
3ḥ is a son for his father,
3ḥ is a father for his son; this means that they go forth.

May you be counted before Thoth
when he counts them for *Jḥss=f*,
mighty of counsel, Foremost of the Westerners.

May your bread be in the hall
and your food on the god's slaughtering block.

May you sit on your throne.
The places travel upstream to you,
the *mrw* are on the move for you and await you.

Feet stamp for you,
arms are outstretched for you,
the [. . .]²² dance for you,

large doves are slaughtered for you,
the sun people prepare²³ them for you.

The two kites, the mourning birds, are before you,
they are Isis and Nephthys.
O Osiris N., raise yourself!

This spell is not addressed to the deceased lying in the tomb, whom it is a matter of waking, but to an absent one who must be summoned from an unknown distance. This is an entirely different conception of the relationship that ritual establishes between the deceased and the offering that is brought to him. The deceased is to come from the distant reaches of his next-worldly existence and receive his offering, and he is to do this in his status of transfigured ancestral spirit, which is paraphrased by invoking four concepts having to do with power: *b3*, *3ḥ*, *sḥm*, and *spd*. Of these four, the first two refer to something spiritual and internal, while the last two refer to something visible that has an effect on what is outside the person. It is probably meant that the deceased is to appear in his tomb, breathing life into his statue. In temple inscriptions of the Graeco-Roman Period, the concepts *ba* and *sekhem* constantly form a pair. As *bas*, the gods are to swoop down from the sky and inhabit their cult statues (*sekhem*). This concept seems to have been taken over from the mortuary cult.

The next verses describe the tomb as the place where the deceased is to go:

May your legs bring you,
that you may see this house of yours, which Seshat has built for you
and on whose walls Khnum has stood for you.

The tomb has been built by gods and is thus a sacred place that the transfigured deceased is not to shy away from. In it, he remains close to the
gods. Seshat was the goddess of writing; she sketched the ground plan
and stretched the cord with which the lines indicating the walls of the
building were transferred from the plan to the ground itself. Khnum, the
god of the potter's wheel, was also lord of construction workers.

The next stanza contains the motif of the door-leaves, with which we
are already familiar from the first spell. While we do not know what is
meant by the "myrrh chest," the phrase "door-leaves of the cool place"
clearly refers to the gateway to the sky. As in the first spell, it might here
stand for the false door of the tomb, but it might also refer to the door-
leaves of a statue shrine. In any event, as in the first spell, there is an
opening and a passage that brings the addressee into immediate contact
with the offerings. Here, however, there are no guardians to greet the
deceased. Instead, the opening of the gate leads to an encounter of father
and son:

> ꜣḫ is a son for his father,
> ꜣḫ is a father for his son; this means that they go forth.

The expression "to be *akh* for someone" refers to helpful actions that
extend from one sphere into another, from this world into the next one
and vice versa. Typically, though not always, the partners in such a relationship are the deceased father and the son he has left behind, and, evidently on this model, the gods and the king. In the cult, the king played
the role of the son of all the deities of the Egyptian pantheon, acting on
their behalf on earth. The son was *akh* for his father by bringing him his
mortuary offerings and thus confirming his status as transfigured ancestral spirit, and also by assuming his father's position on earth and thereby
maintaining his honor, rank, and social status in the community of the
living. The father was *akh* for his son by legitimizing him in his earthly
position and by protecting his interests in the next-worldly law courts. The
Egyptian mortuary cult was based on this mutual *akh*-effectiveness of
father and son, which crossed the boundary of life and death, of this world
and the world beyond.[24] The son is mentioned first, for it is he who recites
the spell in his role of son, citing his ꜣḫ-effectiveness to induce his absent
father to come to him. This part of the sentence is already cited in a
mastaba of the Old Kingdom in the framework of a dedication inscrip-

tion of a son for his father.[25] I do not know precisely what is meant by the words "this means that they go forth"; in any event, it must refer to their encounter. The son greets his father at the celestial gateway, just as Khenti-menutef does in the first spell.

What follows in this spell is not the ascent to the sky but rather an allusion to a checking performed by Thoth, evidently in connection with the Judgment of the Dead. Anyone wishing to shuttle back and forth between this world and the next was obliged to be able to identify himself. Thus, in spell 86 of the Book of the Dead, when the deceased wishes to exit the netherworld by day in the form of a swallow and to return there in the evening, he says:

> I am one who enters after having been checked
> and who emerges, confirmed, from the gateway of the All-lord.

The text here must refer to just such a checking, which Thoth carries out on behalf of the Foremost of the Westerners, that is, for Osiris as lord of the Judgment of the Dead and ruler of the netherworld. The provisioning of the deceased is bound up, first and foremost, with the status he acquires as a result of his vindication in the Judgment. He is now entitled to "bread in the hall" and "meat on the god's slaughtering block." This is the only allusion to the provisioning of the dead in this version of the spell. Other versions are more explicit, as we shall see later.

As was the case in the first spell, the last portion of this one is devoted to the themes of enthronement and homage. But the scene is not necessarily in the sky; in particular, there is no celestial father who welcomes the deceased and seats him on his throne. Rather, the latter seats himself out of his own absolute power and receives the homage of his subjects. The homage includes dancing, slaughtering, and mourning, all of which suit the framework of the mortuary cult but not the concept of a ceremony in the celestial royal court. The spell closes with exactly the same request as the first spell: "O Osiris N., raise yourself!" In another version of the spell, this one attested, inter alia, in the somewhat earlier tomb of Senenmut,[26] the invitation to the tomb is followed by mention of the offerings:

> May your legs bring you,
> may you see this house of yours, which Seshat has built for you
> and on whose walls Thoth has stood for you,
> to this bread of yours and this beer of yours, which I have prepared for
> you!
>
> Are you in the south or the north,
> in the west or the east?

Come, lord of transfiguration (?),
hie yourself here, that you may see this house of yours,
which Seshat has built for you
and on whose walls Thoth has stood for you,
to this warm bread of yours and this warm beer of yours, which I have
    prepared for you!

Instead of the stanza dealing with the opening of the celestial gate and
the mutually beneficial actions of the father and son, in this version, the
son himself addresses his father:

O Osiris N. here, come,
I do for you
what Horus did for his father Osiris.
O Osiris N. here,
I have come to seek/embrace you.

The verb *zḥn* has several meanings, "to seek,"[27] "to meet, visit,"[28] and "to
embrace."[29] It thus designates a movement ("with outstretched arms," as
the determinative indicates) toward someone, which is a "seeking" if the
person is absent and a "meeting" and "embrace" if he is present. Here,
where the deceased is still conceived of as absent, we are probably to translate it as "seek." It is thus an effort to establish contact that underlies this
spell for beginning the mortuary offering ritual.

In the Senenmut version, what follows makes no mention of enthronement and homage. Rather, the spell returns to the questions with which
it began:

Are you in the sky?
Then your mother Nut shall open the door-leaves of the "cool place"
    for you.
Are you in the earth?
Then your father Geb shall open his doors to you.
Are you in the southern or northern places,
or the western or eastern places?
Then may you come in peace,
may you have power over your *ḏ.t*-body.
The door-leaves of Light-land will open to you,
and the door-leaves of the tomb will open for this N. here.
May you emerge from it, you being *ba*,
you being mighty and perfect.

The motif of the celestial gates thus comes at the conclusion here. The
deceased is not to enter them, but to exit. The offerings are to induce
him to return from the world beyond to the world above. This is an

entirely different concept from the sacramental explanation of the offering as the medium of transition into the world beyond. This change is connected to the importance that the concept of "going forth by day" had acquired by now. We must also not overlook the fact that this spell has an introductory character; the actual presentation of the offerings occurs in later spells.

From beginning to end, this version of the spell persistently bids the deceased to come, and the spell culminates in the wish, "may you have power over your $ḏ.t$-body."[30] The meaning is that the deceased is to get hold of a body and come to receive his offerings. This turn of expression has two meanings. On the one hand, it refers to the condition of consciousness, in which a person is aware of his body (and thus of himself; the Egyptian word has both meanings). On the other hand, it refers to having use of a body, as opposed to disembodied haunting. Thus, the second part of Pyramid Texts spell 690 begins with the statements,

> The god is let loose,
> the god gains *shm*-power over his body!

These statements apparently refer to release from the state of unconsciousness and the rigidity of the mummy bandages. This Pyramid Texts spell ends with the statement,

> O Osiris N.,
> may you be clad in your body when you come to me!

The connection between the expressions "to have disposal of the body" and "to be clad in the body" emerges from another Pyramid Texts spell that states:

> May you gain power over your body, you being clad in your body.[31]

Another spell ends with a request that is to be repeated four times:

> To be recited four times:
> clothe yourself in your body when you come to me.[32]

We are probably to suppose that this wish has to do with a "cultic body" that the deceased puts on, that he gets hold of, that he is to have disposal of, when he complies with the request of the priest and presents himself for the mortuary offering. What is meant is the symbol that makes him visible at the place where the offerings are made, either the statue or the false door.[33]

3. Presentation of Offerings

The third spell bears the title "spell for presenting offerings." From the New Kingdom down to the latest periods of Egyptian history, this was the most widespread mortuary spell of all. We have more than fifty variants or citations from it. I cite the spell here in the oldest version, which stems from the end of Dynasty 17 or the beginning of Dynasty 18, and which is written in hieratic on two bowls discovered in a tomb at Haraga.

> Spell for presenting offerings to the transfigured one,
> opening of the mouth at the beginning of reading many transfiguration
>   spells.
>
> May the sky open up to you,
> may the earth open up to you,
> may the ways open up to you in the netherworld.
> May you go forth and enter together with Re,
> may you stride freely out like the lords of eternity.
> Receive the offering cakes as a gift of Ptah,
> and the pure bread from the altars of Horus.
>
> May your *ba* live and your vessels be fresh,
> may your face be opened on the ways [of the darkness].
> Hapy: may he give water to you.
> Nepri: may he give bread to you.
> Hathor: may she give beer to you.
> Hesat: may she give milk to you.
>
> May you wash your feet on a bar of silver,
> in a turquoise basin.
> May you don pure clothing as a gift of Ptah to you.
> May he supply opening to your mummy wrappings.
> May you drink water from the altar of Re.
> May Osiris give you "things to do" (i.e., rites to be carried out).
> May you behold the light, without being kept at a distance
> in your house of darkness.
> May the Nile flood your fields to (a height of) seven cubits
> and in your house of thirst.
> May you drink a jugful of milk as a present from Seshat-Hor.
> May you put on pure clothing, removing the other (clothing),
> may the hands of Tayt clothe you.
> May you see the sun disk and may you worship Re,
> may you soothe the one who rises in Nun.
> You will be given bread in Memphis,
> and libation water on your offering table.[34]

This spell begins with a theme that stood closer to the middle of the first two: the opening of the celestial gates. Opening the spell, it has the same function as the call to awaken and gather the limbs in the first spell, and the imperative "come" and the request to acquire a cultic body in the second spell. The motif of opening has an especially close connection with the version of the second spell in the tomb of Senenmut. Senenmut's spell made mention of the opening of the cardinal directions, so that the deceased could leave them and go to the place where his offerings were. Here, too, sky, earth, and netherworld are to be open to the deceased, not so that he can enter them but so that he can leave them, wherever he might be. There is added a pair of verses that connects his unhindered freedom of movement with the course of the sun and includes a significant literary citation. In the company of the sun god, the deceased is to leave the netherworld in the morning and return to it in the evening, "striding freely like the lords of eternity." This is a citation from the Instruction for Merikare, where we read:

> Being there lasts forever.
> A fool is one who does what they reproach.
> He who reaches them without sin,
> he becomes like a god there,
> striding freely like the lords of eternity.[35]

The words of the offering, which follow the theme of awakening in the first spell and that of summoning in the second spell, here follow the theme of opening. The sacramental explanation of the offering items as divine gifts is taken up here: they are declared to be gifts of Ptah and Horus.

The presentation is not followed by a journey to the sky, as in the first spell, but by a descent into the netherworld. The words "ways of the darkness" can have no other meaning. These verses occur almost verbatim in a solar hymn that describes the nocturnal journey of the sun god:

> When you turn your face to the west,
> may your bones be counted, may your body be put together,
> and your flesh live, and *your vessels be sturdy*.
> *May your* ba *flourish* and your august image be praised.
> May your two feathers lead you *on the ways of the darkness*.
> May you hear the call of (those in) your following.[36]

There is an astonishing similarity between what is wished for the sun god and what is wished for the deceased. This correspondence is the basis for the hope of being able to enter and exit, or to rise and set, together with the sun.

After this brief allusion to a journey in the next world, our text returns rather abruptly to the theme of the offering meal. Though they mention

344

water and bread, and beer and milk, upon closer inspection, it emerges that these verses refer to the afterlife. More so than the preceding verses, they draw a connection between divinity and the offering items. Ptah and Horus pass along to the deceased what has been given to them. But the deities in these verses give the deceased what they themselves produce, independent of any human gifts. Hapy is the personification of the Nile inundation, and his natural gift is water. Nepri is the god and personification of grain, and his gift is bread.[37] Hathor is the goddess of drunkenness and hence the mistress of beer.[38] Hesat personifies the milk that she gives to the deceased. This unique quartet of deities present the deceased with imperishable nourishment, which was otherwise the function of the tree goddess.[39]

The scene is undoubtedly played out in Elysium, as is also the case with the scene that follows, which deals with the morning toilette of the deceased, with his purification and clothing. The journey into the afterlife thus leads the deceased, not to a celestial throne on which he receives the homage of his subjects, but rather, to the life style of an aristocratic Egyptian whose income is assured and who can put on clean clothes each morning after washing his feet in an expensive footbath.[40] Washing and clothing belong together, and these four verses thus constitute a unit of meaning.[41]

More than any others, Tayt, the goddess of weaving, and the weaving-women of Neith at Sais were responsible for the mummy bandages of the deceased. Ptah[42] will loosen these bandages and replace them with a pure garment. The Egyptians were quite conscious of the ambivalence of mummification. On the one hand, it protected the corpse from disarticulation and decay, transforming it into a durable object "filled with magical power" and richly decorated with salutary representations and texts. On the other hand, though, it signified binding and rigidity. The embalmed and mummified corpse was not the body that the transfigured deceased would use to "stride out freely like the lords of eternity," it was not the "$\underline{d}.t$-body" of which the deceased would "have disposal" in order to move between the world below and the world above and to come to his offering meals, as described in the previous spell. Erik Hornung has clearly demonstrated that the body of the deceased in the next world was not the mummy. He writes, "The Egyptian hoped that in the netherworld, which was where his body dwelled, he would be released from the rigid preservation of his mummiform condition. He wished to be freed from the bandages that wrapped, and even 'bound,' his body, he wished to be able once again to use his limbs and his organs of sex and intellection. The mummy mask, which protected but also concealed his face, was to be removed, his limbs were to awaken from their rigor mortis. He wished to stride freely in a form like the one he had on earth, a form that

345

had the needs and functions of a body on earth. Thus his wish to be provided with clothing in the afterlife, which would make no sense for a bandaged mummy."[43] By way of an example intended to stand for innumerable others, Hornung cites a text from the Book of Gates, in which the sun god, who has descended as the nocturnal sun to the deceased in the netherworld, addresses twelve mummies lying on a serpent-shaped bier:

> O you . . . followers of the one who rules the West,
> who lie outstretched . . . on your bier—
> your flesh is to be exalted,
> your bones are to be gathered together for you,
> your limbs are to be embraced for you,
> your flesh is to be united for you!
> May the pleasant breath of life be at your nose,
> loosening of your mummy bandages,
> and removal of your face masks!
> May there be light for your divine eyes,
> that you may see the glow by means of them!
> You are to rise from your weariness,
> that you may receive your fields![44]

This wondrous transformation of the rigid mummy into a breathing, seeing, freely moving body is, according to the Books of the Netherworld and many other texts of the New Kingdom, the work of the nocturnal sun, who awakens the dead from their "Sleeping Beauty" condition by means of his life-endowing light and above all by what he says to them.[45]

In the next two verses, Re and Osiris appear, along with Ptah. The transfigured one is to drink water from the "altar of Re," and thus at Heliopolis, and Osiris is to give him "things to do," that is, "rites to carry out."[46] The verses that follow speak of the tomb:

> May you behold light, without being kept at a distance
> in your house of the darkness.
> May the Nile flood your fields to (a height of) seven cubits
> and in your house of thirst.

The mortuary offering and the recitation are to transform this place of destitution into a place of abundance. The sacramental explanation of the offering refers here not to a next-worldly realm but to the transformation of this-worldly circumstances. The tomb is not to prevent the deceased from being able to go out and behold the light. The Nile is not to flow far from the desert valley but to reach the tomb, thanks to the

Figure 6. Offering table with a drain for water runoff and with a depiction of offerings. Heidelberg. Third century B.C.E. From J. Assmann, *Tod und Jenseits im Alten Ägypten* (Munich, 2003), p. 452.

power of the spell and the offering.[47] Such wishes are extremely frequent in mortuary spells of the New Kingdom and later periods. Sometimes Nun, the primeval ocean out of which the Egyptians believed the Nile inundation flowed, was itself to flood the tomb:

> Transfiguration for your *ba*!
> May you be called on the *wag*-festival,
> may Nun make a flood for you in your rock-cut tomb.[48]

But there are passages in which it is clear that the "Nile inundation" refers to nothing other than a stream of liquid poured from a libation vase:[49]

347

> Libation on the offering table! Receive the divine offering!
> May Hapy grant you all goodly foods.[50]

The concluding stanza brings no new themes; rather, it complements what has preceded. To Hapy, Nepri, Hathor, and Hesat, the four deities of food and drink, there are now added Seshat-Hor, the goddess of milk, while Tayt, the goddess of weaving, is now associated with Ptah as granter of a pure garment. The text strives to involve as many deities as possible in the provisioning of the deceased. The sacramental explanation of the offering items seeks to connect them with divine solicitude. The spell ends with a third mention of the sun god, making him the most important of these deities who are gathered around the deceased:

> May you see the sun disk and may you worship Re,
> may you soothe the one who rises in Nun.
> You will be given bread in Memphis,
> and libation water on your offering table.

The final verses return to the theme of offerings: bread in Memphis and water here, on the offering table in the tomb. The mention of Memphis once again alludes to the god Ptah. Re, Ptah, and Osiris (who is mentioned only once) are the major gods who care for the deceased, while Hapy, Nepri, Hathor, Hesat, Seshat-Hor, and Tayt are deities of provisioning who supply him with food, drink, and clothing. All that is implied by "bread in Memphis" belongs to the sacramental explanation of the offering items, and there is good reason why it is mentioned only in the final verse. An Egyptian offering table was decorated in such a way that the most important elements of the mortuary meal—bread, beer, goose, foreleg of an ox, vegetables—were represented lying on it. All of these were surrounded by a groove for liquids, with a drain in the middle of the front of the table (Figure 6). When the priest presented offerings, he poured water on the table and recited a spell. These actions activated the offering items represented on the table, endowing them with their life-giving power. In this way, a simple libation of water, together with its sacramental explanation in the form of an accompanying recitation, endowed the deceased with life, fortifying him and involving him in the provisioning of the gods in the realm beyond.

CHAPTER FIFTEEN

Sacramental Explanation

1. On the Semantics of Transfigurative Speech

The practice of loading an offering item with so much meaning in its accompanying spell that it not only supplied the recipient with food and drink, and anointed and clothed him, and so forth, but also endowed him with freedom of movement, ascent to the sky, the affection of the gods, and more besides, dominated the mortuary cult and that of the gods as well. But it seems to have originated in the mortuary cult, for only there was the distinction between this realm and the next one, and of the transition from the one to the other, of such fundamental importance. The distinction between this realm and the next one, the visible and the invisible realm, permeated the semantics of the mortuary liturgies and spells, endowing them with a characteristic ambiguity. "Here" became "there," and vice versa. A gradual shift between these two conceptual spheres can be observed in a textual detail in the Pyramid Texts that Siegfried Schott has called "extension of reference." The early texts use the demonstrative pronoun "this," pointing to a referent that is nearby, while later texts use the pronoun "that," pointing to one that is distant.[1] This shift between "here" and "there," between the realm where the cult is carried out and the realm of the gods, entails an ambiguity, a semantics that operates on two levels. This ambiguity impedes our comprehension, except when explicit commentaries come to our aid, as in the case of the Ramesseum Dramatic Papyrus. I wish to deal with this text in some detail here, for it offers an unparalleled illustration of the two-tiered semantics underlying the transfiguration spells.[2]

The papyrus[3] contains a copy of a ritual that was carried out for Senwosret I, either on the occasion of his coronation or on that of a jubilee festival. The manuscript is divided horizontally into a short strip of representations on the bottom that consist of line drawings illustrating the individual episodes of the ritual and above it, a taller strip of texts inscribed in vertical columns. The 139 preserved columns (the beginning of the papyrus is lost) contain the texts of 47 scenes, which correspond to 31 drawings in the lower strip, for several of the drawings serve to illustrate two of the scenes in the ritual. The scenes are all organized according to the same textual scheme. The text of each scene consists of five elements, A–E, with C–E sometimes appearing more than once:

A. description of an action: infinitival clause introduced by *ḫpr.n* "it happened that"
B. explanatory clause with the particle *pw*, "it means," "it is"
C. indication of who speaks to whom
D. speech
E. remarks regarding roles, cult objects, and places
F. a representation in the form of a sketchy line drawing that indicates the ritual action, often with captions that make it clear that what is represented is cultic activity, not a mythic event in the realm of the gods.

Points C–E can occur more than once, that is to say, the introductory clauses A and B can be followed by more than one divine speech (in the following example: 4 and 7), each of them framed by indications of who is speaking (3, 6, and 9) and remarks (5 and 8). Let us turn to an illustrative example:[4]

A	1	*ḫpr.n jnw qnj jn ḥrj-ḥ3b*	It happened that the *qnj*-breastplate was brought by the lector priest
B	2	*Ḥrw pw qnj.f jtj.f wḏb.f ḥr Gb*	It is Horus, who embraces his father and turns to Geb.
C	3	*Ḥrw > Gb ḏd mdw*	Horus to Geb, speaking:
D	4	*qnj.n<.j> jtj.j pn nnjw r*	"I embraced this my father, who was weary, until . . ."
E	5	| *Wsjr* | *qnj* |	| Osiris | the *qnj*-breastplate |
C	6	*Ḥrw > Gb ḏd mdw*	Horus to Geb, speaking:
D	7	*snbt.f r.f*	". . . he became hale again."
E	8	| *Wsjr* | *snb* | *P* |	| Osiris | *snb*-strands | Buto |
F	9		representation

The representation consists of a priest facing right, over him the caption *ḥrj-ḥȝb*, "lector priest," and in front of him the caption *ḏd mdw: jnj qnj zp sn*, "to be said: 'bring 12 breastplates, *srmt*-beer, six-threaded cloth, four-threaded cloth, clothing of purple cloth, and *ssf*-fabric!' "[5]

The correlation between the cultic realm and that of the gods is established through assonance. The decorative shawl (the *qnj*-breastplate) that is presented in this scene is called "that which embraces," for it surrounds its wearer like protective arms. It seems that this object is to be connected with the embrace (*qnj*) with which Horus takes his deceased father in his arms. With this embrace, the life force of the son enters the deceased father, while the *ka*, the legitimizing dynastic principle, passes from the father to his son. In this example, we can recognize the principle of "explanation" that drives the commentary.

The principle consists in the systematic distinction and correlation of the two referential levels, the "cultic realm" and the "divine realm." In the cultic realm, there are the king, priestly officiants, and objects. In the divine realm, there are the gods and their actions and words. In the divine realm, it is the speeches of the gods that comprise the central element, while in the realm of the cult, it is the ritual actions. The commentary (clause 2) supplies the explicit correlation of the two levels of reference. With the particle *pw* "it is," it points to the referential level of the cult, while the statement otherwise draws on the divine referential level as its explanation. The commentary thus only makes explicit that which implicitly connects the two levels of reference. The divine level is the explanation of the cultic level. The cultic actions are not in and of themselves invested with meaning—it is not simply a matter of bringing a breastplate—rather, they derive their meaning from the fact that they point to things that happen in the divine realm. Thus arises the two-tiered semantics; in analogy to "plural textual meanings," we could speak of "plural meanings of action." Cultic act and divine explanation are related to one another after the fashion of the *sensus literalis* and the *sensus mysticus* of medieval and early modern hermeneutics. Thus, an act such as purification (*sensus literalis*) is explained as rebirth (*sensus mysticus*), or provisioning (*sensus literalis*) as ascent to the sky (*sensus mysticus*). The process of sacramental explanation seems related, in many ways, to allegorizing. The fact that objects, persons, and actions derive their meaning from the realm of the gods constitutes a higher, hidden, secret level of meaning, a special knowledge.

It is not only a matter of explanation, however, but of a genuine transformation. From nourishment, an ascent to the sky comes into being, and from the presentation of the *qnj*-breastplate, an embrace that restores life. Transformation is achieved through the establishment of a relationship between the cultic realm and the realm of the gods: something that happens in the cult is transformed into an event in the divine realm. This transformative function of spells is expressed by the word *s³ḫ*. The recitation of spells with their sacramental explanation has a transformative power that rests on the interlocking of the two spheres of meaning.[6] What belongs to this realm is transparent to the realm of the gods, and what is in the realm of the gods is visible to what is in this realm.

The principle of sacramental explanation reigned supreme in Egyptian cult. The conceptual relationship between the realm of the gods and that of the cult could remain implicit, or it could be explicitly stated, and it could be stated in various ways. The commenting statement, as it appears in the Ramesseum Dramatic Papyrus, is only one of various possibilities. Another, much more common one was the "name formula." Here, an element in the realm of the cult—an object or a place—becomes the "name" of a deity, whom it "indicates" or "explains." In this way, the various statements and remarks of the Ramesseum Dramatic Papyrus become a continuous text. Thus, from a text (not preserved as such) *"The gods say to Seth, 'Carry one who is greater than you'; remark: 'it is the *Tf³-wr*-sanctuary,' " we get the statement, " 'Carry one who is greater than you,' they say to him in your name of *Jtf³-wr*."[7] Here again, it is clear that it is *language* that supplies this interlocking of the two conceptual spheres, and with it, the unity and meaningfulness of reality.

We maintain: the principle of sacramental explanation presupposes a *modus significandi* in which reality is divided into more than one conceptual sphere, with each referring to the other. In Egypt, there were two such conceptual spheres, ritual and myth,[8] and it was language that created the connection between them.

A similar principle underlies a second group of sources, to which we shall now turn. These are dialogues in which someone is asked about the divine or mythic meaning of specific objects. Such dialogues are preserved to us in mortuary texts that have to do with transition into the afterlife. The motif of transition seems to be constitutive here: these dialogues occur in the context of rituals of transition, *rites de passage*. I have therefore proposed to call them "initiatory examinations."[9] In them, the two realms connected by the mythic explanation have especially to do with this notion of transition. They have to do, on the one hand, with the ferryboat that is to convey the deceased into the next world, and on the other hand, with a net he wishes to escape. The net is stretched out between sky and earth, and it threatens the deceased, who wishes to pass from the latter to the former in the form of a bird. In both cases, the deceased must undergo an examination in which he demonstrates that he is able to call the individual parts of the ferryboat and the net by the names they bear in the divine realm.

Here, too, we are dealing with a doubling of the conceptual sphere. Everything has two designations, one in the real world and one in the world of the gods. But here, there is also the element of the mysterious and the esoteric, for the name in the world of the gods is known only to the initiated. It has the character of a password that can be used only by the one who knows it.[10] This secrecy is the most effective means of group formation and social bonding. In illiterate societies, all initiations and associations rest on secrets and on maintaining secrecy. It would be difficult to find any group or tradition that does not have secrets of this sort. In everyday life, initiatory examinations celebrate and seal admission into professional associations. In Egyptian mortuary belief, the acceptance was into a community of next-worldly, immortal beings conceived of as an association (specifically, a community that took meals together) of this sort. The initiatory examinations were a part of the transition from this world into the next one. The deceased qualified himself for the next world by demonstrating that he had this knowledge, and with it, a command of the language that connected the two worlds.

There is a close connection between cultic commentaries, with their principle of sacramental explanation, and initiatory examinations, with their principle of secret passwords that relate to the divine realm, and they are surely nothing more than distinct superficial articulations of a common deep structure. Dino Bidoli describes this commonality thus: "In both cases, a commentary with symbolic, mythic referents overlies an older textual base: in the one case (that is, in the Ramesseum Dramatic Papyrus), evidently an old coronation ritual, and in the other, in all likelihood a list of objects of a certain sort."[11] The heart of the matter is the ambiguity of the world, its separation into a phenomenological sense and a mystical sense. In the initiatory examinations, there is a secret language, and the initiate demonstrates his mastery of it. He who knows the secret language belongs to the secret world to which it refers, and he may enter it. In the cultic commentaries, there is a sacramental explanation of the ritual, by means of which the cultic acts are transposed into the context of the divine realm.

Especially significant for speech in the mystical sense is the examination that the deceased must undergo before he is allowed to enter the hall where the Judgment of the Dead will take place:

> "Let him come," they say regarding me.
> "Who are you," they say to me.
> I am the lower root of the papyrus plant,
> "The-one-in-the-olive-tree" is my name.
> "Where have you been?" they say to me.
> I have been to the places north of the thicket (variant, of the olive tree).

"What did you see there?"

It was a leg and a thigh.

"What did you say to them?"

I have seen rejoicing in those lands of the Phoenicians.

"What did they give you?"

It was a firebrand and a faïence amulet.

"What did you do with them?"

I buried them on the shore of the *maati*-water at the time of the evening offering.

"And what did you find on it, the shore of the *maati*-water?"

It was a scepter of flint, "Breath-giver" is its name.

"What did you do on account of this firebrand and this faïence amulet after you buried them?"

I wept on their account, I took them (out) again, I put out the fire, I broke the amulet and threw it in the water.

"Come, then, and enter this gate of the Hall of the Two Truths, for you know us!"[12]

This passage is not simply about secret names but also about complex actions. If we set aside the questions and put the answers together, we get one of those typical mortuary texts at whose meaning we despair. The result would look approximately as follows:

> I am the lower root of the papyrus plant,
> "The-one-in-the-olive-tree" is my name.
> I went to the places north of the thicket.
> What I saw was a leg and a thigh.
> "I have seen rejoicing in those lands of the Phoenicians,"
> said I to them.
> They gave me a firebrand and a faïence amulet . . . (etc.).

Such spells are written entirely in the secret language used by an initiate who wanted to present himself as such. We can understand these spells only if we know the specific rituals and myths to which they allude, and these would have been the local traditions of certain temples and festivals that granted the privilege of membership by initiation into their mysteries. Connected with every cult, there was a knowledge that was carefully guarded. In the later periods of Egyptian history, these local traditions were collected in written form, and certain of these handbooks have been preserved to us.[13]

The principle of sacramental explanation rests on the same basic assumption of a doubled conceptual sphere. Here, the object is not to demonstrate initiation and membership through knowledge of secret meanings that have to do with the realm of the gods. Rather, it is to establish a relationship between objects and actions in the real world of the cultic sphere and actions and events in the divine, mythic sphere. These texts have no esoteric character, any more so than the words of Jesus at the beginning of Communion: "This is my body, this is my blood." In this case as well, objects in this world, bread and wine, are sacramentally explained. The body and blood of Christ belong to a different conceptual sphere. What is important is the visualization of the relationship between the two spheres, which language makes possible.

2. The Discharge of the Corpse of Osiris: On the Sacramental Explanation of Water

"The Egyptians call not only the Nile, but all water in general, 'the discharge of Osiris (*Osiridos aporrhoe*),'" writes Plutarch in chapter 36 of his tractate "On Isis and Osiris."[14] This is perhaps the boldest, and in any case the oldest and longest-lived sacramental explanation that any offering object received in the Egyptian cult. "The discharge of the corpse of Osiris"—thus did the Egyptians designate water, especially when they offered it to the deceased in the mortuary cult in the form of a libation. Libation was the central rite in the mortuary cult, a fact to which there is an impressive witness: the papyrus of Nesmin in the British Museum (British Museum 10209).[15] This text is a collection of ten spells for presenting offerings in the mortuary cult, which, as the title of the text maintains, are taken from a scroll used in the Festival of the Valley.[16]

As a fully developed ritual, the mortuary cult could include a large number of different actions and offerings, including a number of highly divergent water rites.[17] But it could all be abbreviated and reduced to an allusion to a libation, for everything was contained *in nuce* in the libation. The papyrus of Nesmin stems from the beginning of the Graeco-Roman Period, when the mortuary cult at Thebes was the responsibility of the cultic association of the choachytes (water pourers), who were located at Medinet Habu—*Tꜣmw.t*, Coptic Djeme—and whose divine model was Amun of Luxor. Every ten days, Amun of Luxor crossed over to the west bank to bring an offering of water (designated *wꜣḥ jḥ.t, sfsfꜣw,* and *stj mw*) to his ancestors in the Dynasty 18 temple at Medinet Habu; this was thus a mortuary cult at the divine level. The choachytes were obliged to offer such a libation every ten days in the tombs of the deceased.[18] In this way, all the deceased buried in the west of Thebes were included in these libations made by Amun of Luxor: "May you accept the libations by Amun of Luxor in Djeme on all the first (days of the) decades," we read in a Demotic papyrus from the late Ptolemaic Period.[19] In his commentary on the Book of Traversing Eternity, J. F. Herbin has been able to adduce a good dozen variants of this formula in texts of the Graeco-Roman

Period.[20] The papyrus of Nesmin is a collection of spells that were recited during the choachytes' libations so as to make them the medium of a comprehensive presentation of offerings. We may thus easily imagine that this papyrus is derived from a handbook in the possession of one of the choachytes.[21]

The last of the ten spells on the papyrus of Nesmin begins with a reference to that curious comparison of water to the discharge from the corpse of Osiris that Plutarch stresses:

> O Sokar Osiris, take this libation,
> your libation from Horus,
> in your name of "Cataract-area."
> Take the discharges that have come out of you,
> which Horus gives you in that place where you were pushed into the water.

Of the ten spells in Nesmin's collection, this spell has the longest history, one that goes back to the Pyramid Texts. Here, I wish to take these water spells from the Pyramid Texts as a point of departure.

Pyramid Texts spell 436 is a purification spell. The libation has the sense of a washing of the hands before eating:

> May your water belong to you,
> May your inundation belong to you,
> the discharge that comes out of the god,
> the foul exudation that comes out of Osiris.
> Washed are your hands, opened are your eyes,
> transfigured is this mighty one for his *ba*.
> Wash yourself, may your *ka* wash itself,
> may your *ka* sit down to eat bread with you,
> without cease, forever.[22]

There are many purification spells of this sort. Especially typical and frequent, however, are libation spells, whose intention includes far more than just purifying the deceased or providing him with drink. The tenth spell from the papyrus of Nesmin is one of these spells. Here, the concern is to provide the deceased with water as a sacred, healing, life-endowing substance. The classic libation spell, attested a hundred times in all periods of Egyptian history, is spell 32 of the Pyramid Texts, which reads:

> This your libation water, Osiris,
> this your libation water, O Wenis,
> has come out from your son,
> has come out from Horus.

> I have come to bring you the Eye of Horus,
> that your heart may be radiant by means of it.
> I have brought it beneath you, under your feet.
>
> Take the discharge that has issued from you,
> may your heart not be weary of it.

The point here is neither to purify the deceased nor to provide him with drink. The libation is intended to bring him the water as a life-endowing substance. The spell is divided into three parts. In the first part, it is stressed that the water is from Horus; the concern is thus the bond between father and son. The water serves here as a sort of cement that is to restore the bond between Osiris and Horus, father and son, that has been torn asunder by death. This is true, of course, of every gift, and not just libations. Every gift creates a bond between giver and recipient. Water is especially suited to this purpose, perhaps because it seeps into the ground and thus (at least at an early date, when the dead were still buried in simple pits) could actually penetrate to the corpse. In many tombs of the Old and Middle Kingdoms, we can observe devices intended to lead the libation water poured out in the cult room down into the sarcophagus chamber.

The second part calls the water the "Eye of Horus" and states the goal of the libation: the water is supposed to make the heart of the deceased "radiant," that is, to freshen and revivify it. "Eye of Horus" is the cultic expression for every offering item, not just water. Every offering item was thus represented as a substance that restored something that had been lost, that returned something that had been stolen, that renewed something that had been used up, that replenished something that had been reduced, that put together something that had fallen apart—in short, it was the symbol of a reversibility that could heal everything, even death. The third part then explains the water as the discharge that flows out of the deceased himself, a reference to the deceased in his mythic role as Osiris. If the deceased is Osiris, then the water poured out to him has flowed out of himself as Osiris. The water symbolizes life force as a life-fluid that has flowed out of the deceased and is restored to him by means of the libation.

In the Pyramid Texts ritual, this spell is followed immediately by another libation spell that again represents water as a medium for placing the deceased in a relationship with the gods. This text delves somewhat more clearly into the mythic episode from which the motif of the corpse's discharge derives its reference:

> Osiris Wenis, take your libation!
> May it be cool for you with Horus

in your name "He-who-came-from-the-cool-place."
Take the discharge that issued from you.

Horus has caused that the gods assemble for you
at the place to which you have gone.
Horus has caused the Sons of Horus to gather for you
at the place where you were drowned.

Osiris Wenis, take your incense, that you may become divine,
for Nut has caused that you be divine
for your enemy in your name of "God."
Horus the rejuvenated has recognized you
in your name "Rejuvenated-water."[23]

The water is presented to a departed, distant being with the intention of bringing him back and establishing contact. Gods are to track the deceased to the place where he has distanced himself and bring him into contact with the one making the offering. This text adds that the deceased was "drowned" in this place. As we have seen, the tenth spell of the Nesmin papyrus also makes mention of this detail:

Take the discharges that have come out of you,
which Horus gives you in that place where you were pushed into the water.

These verses go back to Pyramid Texts spell 423, §§ 766b–767a, where we read:

Horus has caused all the gods to assemble
in the place where you have gone.
Take the discharge that has come out of you!
Horus has caused that his sons inspect you
in the place where you were drowned.
Horus the rejuvenated (?) inspects you
in your name of "Rejuvenated-water."

The passage alludes to the episode of the Osiris myth in which Seth cast the slain Osiris into the water. According to the myth, the Nile inundation had its origin in the exudations of the corpse of Osiris. The inundation is called "rejuvenated water," and the passage ends by making this expression a name of the deceased himself, for he is indeed Osiris, from whose corpse the inundation flowed. The idea of a cycle is crucial to this association of ideas. With the water, life-fluid is returned to the deceased, life-fluid that has flowed out of him, out of Osiris. The water is a discharge that is returned in the offering. The concept of "rejuvenation" results from this idea of a cycle.

The concept of "rejuvenation" points to the mystery of cyclical time, which runs back into itself. In fact, there was a close connection between water and time in Egyptian thought, a connection that resulted from the annual Nile inundation. The Egyptian year began (at least theoretically) with the onset of the inundation during the summer. Thus, in Egyptian thought, the concepts of "year," "Nile," and "rejuvenation" were closely connected in the sense of reversibility, return, and regeneration. The Egyptian word for "year" means "the rejuvenated/rejuvenating one," while the expression "rejuvenated/rejuvenating water" is a designation of the inundation. It was believed that with its annual rise, the Nile was rejuvenating itself, even as it also rejuvenated the fields. The Nile inundation was the central symbol of cyclical time, which did not flow irreversibly toward a goal but rather ran back into itself in a cycle, thus enabling renewal, repetition, and regeneration. For this reason, water was the most important of the libation offerings. In water lay the power of return.

These powers at work in the offerings can be called "sacramental potencies." The accompanying spell had the task of activating these sacramental potencies, and this is the principle of "sacramental explanation." As an especially detailed and typical example of such an explanation of water, I cite here a late bronze libation vessel. It is decorated with a scene in which the sky goddess, in her capacity as tree goddess, offers a libation to the deceased and says the following:[24]

To be spoken by Nut:
O Osiris N.,
take the libation
from my own arms!
I am your effective mother,
and I bring you a vessel containing much water
to satisfy your heart with libation.
Inhale the breath that goes out of me, that your flesh may live thereby,
for it is I who give water to every mummy
and breath to the one whose throat is empty,
who cover the corpses of those who have no tomb.
I shall be with you and unite you with your *ba*,
I shall not depart from you, forever.

O Osiris N.,
take this libation
that comes from Elephantine,
this discharge that comes from Osiris,
which Sothis (the goddess of the new year) brings with her own arms
as she associates Khnum with you.
A great Nile inundation has come to you,
its arms filled with rejuvenated water,

to bring you gifts
of all fresh things at their time,
with no delay.

Amun the Great strengthens your bones,
his goodly north wind wafts at your nose.
May he give you offerings on his altar every day,
and his jugs of beer will not leave your side.
Your body will live by means of the libation,
it being rejuvenated in your mystery (i.e., coffin).

The Foremost of the Westerners will make your name endure
among the nobles of the realm of the dead.
May he grant that your corpse endure among those provided with
    offerings,
your *ba* not being distant from you.

May Isis, the God's Mother, offer you her breasts,
that you may be flooded with life thereby.
May she grant you offerings in the hall of Osiris,
may she cause you to enter among the nobles of Thebes.
May your *ka* be sacred at the side of Wennefer,
may you not cease (being) in his service.

May you receive libation from the arms of your son
punctually every tenth day,
when the libator crosses over to the west of Thebes
to offer a libation of water at Medinet Habu
under the supervision of the father of his fathers.
May he remember your *ka* and decorate your limbs with a bandage
for all of time and eternity.
The heir and lord of libation for his father,
may he establish offerings for your *ka*.
If he is pleasing to his father and attends to his mother,
may his name be pronounced in the presence of his father.

The effective sister with established instructions,
may she equip your *ba* with her transfigurations,
may she cause (?) you to go forth and enter in the halls (of the
    netherworld),
may she sanctify you with her spells,
while the beauty of your name remains on all her scrolls,
and you are not barred from the sight of Osiris on his great festival.

These gods whose names I have pronounced,
may they grant you mortuary offerings,
while your name endures in their temples
at the time when praises are called out.
May you follow your heart at the source of the river
and drink of it as your heart desires,
forever.

Here, we have all the themes of the sacramental explanation of water: the socializing effect of water, which connects the deceased with the gods; its rejuvenating effect, which makes time run backward; and its space-opening effect, which provides him with freedom, movement, and breath. It is also made quite clear that these sacramental potencies are in the water because it is inundation water and comes from Elephantine, from the caves that are the sources of the Nile flood.

With this key word, we touch upon the mystery of the Nile inundation, which considerably preoccupied the mythic thinking of the Egyptians. In Egyptian belief, Elephantine, the region of the First Cataract, was the place where the Nile flowed out from the netherworld. We thus read in a libation text for Osiris:

> I purify Your Majesty with the water "Repeater of Life," which emerges from your leg, from the source-cave from which the Nile inundation springs forth, coming to your flesh, so that Your Majesty is rejuvenated.[25]

According to the myth, the annual inundation poured from a wound inflicted on Osiris' leg by his murderer, Seth. This left leg was for its part connected with Elephantine. A myth that took tangible form only in the later periods of history identified the forty-two nomes of Egypt with forty-two body parts of Osiris. Like the Pauline concept of the church as the body of Christ, according to this myth, the forty-two nomes of Egypt symbolized the body of Osiris.[26] When the reuniting and revivification of Osiris were celebrated during the annual Osiris mysteries, Egyptians were reassured of the unity of the land. In this mythic concept, all Egypt constituted the body from which the Nile inundation gushed forth like a bodily humor that brought life. We thus see that a correspondence of microcosm and macrocosm underlay the designation of water as the "discharge of Osiris." The world—or Egypt, at least—was conceived of as a body, and the water of the Nile as an elixir of life that gushed forth from it. In this system of assigning body parts to parts of the land, the wounded leg belonged to Elephantine. This was the place where the life juices flowed out of Osiris and flooded Egypt, giving rise to all the means of life. When it was offered to him in the cult, the water of the inundation, which had flowed out of the body of the slain god, made it possible to restore life to him, as well as to all the dead, who were equated with him.

> Take your cool water, which is in this land,
> which brings forth all living things, all the things that this land gives.
> It is the begetter of all living things.
> All things emerge from it,
> that you may have enjoyment of them, that you may live on them,

Figure 7. Libation water depicted as a chain of *ankh* ("life") hieroglyphs. From J.-F. Champollion, *Monuments de l'Égypte et de la Nubie*, vol. 1 (Paris, 1835), pl. 45.

> that it may go well with you by means of them,
> that you may breathe of the air that is in them.
> It has begotten you and you emerge,
> living on all the things that you desire.[27]

The inundation water that flowed from the wound of the god produced new life; it was a veritable elixir of life that brought forth and nourished all living things in the land. Thus, in many representations of water flowing out of a libation vessel, the water is depicted as a chain consisting of hieroglyphs for "life" (Figure 7).

The Nile flowed out of Nun, which was not only the primeval water from which everything sprang forth but also the water that surrounded the earth on all sides, in the sky, in the depths of the earth, and as an ocean that surrounded it. Since the primeval element from which all emerged was also continually present in the world, it was able to yield cyclical time, reversible processes, and complete rejuvenation and repetition. Immersion in the primeval water caused each hour to run backward. The morning sun bathed in this creative primeval water, drawing strength for a new day and a new ascent to the sky, and this water was poured out for the deceased so as to rejuvenate him, to connect him with the gods, to cause him to ascend to the sky, and to create a space where he could return for his offerings. This water was the water of creation, which contained the cosmogonic impulses and energies. A spell for purifying the king could thus proclaim:

> Pharaoh is Horus in the primeval water.
> Death has no power over him.
> The gods are satisfied with Pharaoh's purity.[28]

Whoever immersed himself in the primeval water escaped death and gained strength for new life. Death was the consequence of a pollution that could be erased by means of the primeval water. This water regenerated all that was decayed, and it turned back the hours. A world in which this water was effective needed no creator, for it was itself creative, divine, and holy, carrying within itself the mysteries of redemption.

3. Mortuary Rituals for Egypt

The most astonishing and wide-reaching instance of sacramental explanation was the political interpretation of the rites of Khoiak in the temples of the Graeco-Roman Period. We do not know how early this tradition reached back; in the sources, we first encounter it in the Ptolemaic Period. The rites of Khoiak were the most important in all of Egypt in the later periods of its history; they were celebrated in all the temples of the land, constituting a truly "national" ritual. At the center of the rites was the preparation and solemn burial of a "grain Osiris." A golden mold was filled with garden soil and seeds, and these were left to sprout for a period of eight days. In Papyrus Jumilhac, a genuine "priestly writing" in the biblical sense, which codifies all cultic knowledge regarding the eighteenth nome of Upper Egypt in a truly magnificent handwriting, the festival is called *Khebes-Ta*, "Hacking up of the Earth," a concept already familiar to us as the designation of the mortuary liturgy studied in chapter 12.[29] There, the festival period lasted for twelve days. This ritual was celebrated as the embalming and mummification of the corpse of Osiris. It entailed the reciting of the same mortuary liturgies that we already know from the mortuary cult: the wake with the laments of Isis and Nephthys, and the transfiguration spells of the lector priest. Here, though, the embalming process was replaced by an alchemistic preparation of all possible substances, which are minutely described, the grain mummy being only one of them, and all of them subjected to the transformative, sublimating process of "transfiguration." The decisive theme was the transformation from disunity to restored unity, which was celebrated in the form of a "canopic procession."[30] In the Osiris chapels at Dendara, this procession is depicted in the middle room of the western chapel.[31] Here, we see personifications of the forty-two nomes of the land, led by great and superordinate deities, each bringing a vase with a decorated lid (*canopus*). Each vase contains a limb from the body of the slain Osiris, out of which the body will be ritually put back together. Among the directions for carrying out the festival of Khoiak, there are exact instructions for preparing the limbs of Osiris' body. They were made of a special dough that was baked in wooden molds. We may thus presume that along with Nile water, each of the vases contained one of these limbs. The accompanying texts repeatedly make mention of the "discharges" of Osiris.[32] In the late stages of Egyptian history, the Nile and its inundation were ever more closely connected with Osiris. In each case, the offering is subjected to a double sacramental explanation. One explanation refers the offering to the specific limb of Osiris' body that is brought in it as a contribution by the respective nome to the restoration of the god's body. On the second level, the limb is explained as the nome and its capital, with the result that the body of Osiris, restored and brought back to life, represents the entirety of the land of Egypt. This point is expressed clearly in the speeches of the king, who accompanies this procession:

> I bring you the cities and nomes as your limbs.
> The gods are assigned to your body as your mystery.
> The divine limbs are the nome gods in their true form.
> I bring you the company of the gods of Upper Egypt in their entirety:
> Your divine limbs are gathered in their place.[33]

> I bring you the capitals of the nomes: they are your limbs,
> they are your *ka*, which is with you.
> I bring you your name, your *ba*, your shadow, your form ($qj=k$),
> your image, and the cities of your nomes.
> I bring you the chief gods of Lower Egypt, united together.
> All the limbs of your body, they are united.[34]

> (speech of the *meret* of the north:)
> I bring you the 42 cities and nomes:
> they are your limbs.
> The entire land is founded for you as the place of your body,

you go there, you come there.
I bring you the limbs, that you may live.[35]

(speech of Wepwawet of the north:)
I bring you your nomes,
the forty-two are with you: they are your body.
Your bones are joined together for you,
your name is "Ruler-of-the-capitals,"
the entire land preserves your grave.
As Re lives, you rest daily
in your name "He-who-lives-and-rests."[36]

Here, the embalming ritual is applied to the entire land of Egypt in order to heal its disunity, to unite it, to endow it with life, and to renew it. The festival period begins with the finding and embalming of the forty-two scattered limbs of the slain Osiris, which are brought from the forty-two nomes of the land and ritually joined together and brought to life, and it ends with the funeral of Osiris and the coronation of Horus, his son and avenger. This festival had its origin in the mortuary cult, in the embalming ritual. It was probably only in the later periods of history that its political dimension began to take on importance. There were other rituals that first acquired a political meaning at this time, for instance, the ritual of "pulling the four chests of fabric."[37] This ritual, in which four chests containing pieces of green, red, white, and *jrtjw*-linen were "consecrated" and then "pulled," originated in the festival of Sokar, from which the mysteries of Khoiak were also derived, and it was therefore closely related to the mortuary cult. The four kinds of linen were used in the god's embalming and burial.[38] In the Ptolemaic Period, the word *mrt*, "chest" was often understood as *t3-mrj*, "Egypt." The "consecration" of the chests was now explained as "leading" (in Egyptian, *ḥrp*, which also meant "to consecrate") the inhabitants of Egypt. In the accompanying spell, for instance, we read:

> Take Egypt, it being united.
> You have bound the Two Lands into a whole.

The motif of "binding" explains the "cords" wrapped around the chests. The word "Egypt" (*t3-mrj*) is a pun on the word "chest" (*mr.t*).

> I bring you Egypt,
> it being led to Your Majesty.
> The land magnifies the fear of you.[39]

Instead of "pulling the *meret*-chests for Amun," the ritual can be called "bringing Egypt to its father Amun."[40] The four chests can sometimes symbolize the enemies of Egypt:

> I take the scepter, I hold it in my right hand,
> I pull the containers before you.
> These rebels from the four corners of the earth are suffering,
> their eyes are blind to the realm of the dead.[41]

In the context of the Osiris cult, this ritual could also be extended to the limbs of Osiris. The pulling of the four chests symbolized the collecting and uniting of the limbs of Osiris' body.[42]

> I travel through the cities,
> I stride through the nomes,
> I travel through the places of Egypt.
> I seek what is hidden in the temples,
> I search for the limbs in Egypt (qbḥ.wj),
> I tread the two chambers (i.e., Egypt) in all their breadth,
> I make my city the equal of their places.
> I offer you the white and the green,
> the jrtjw and the red linen,
> to elevate your ka above their kas.[43]

The underlying image is that of death as dismemberment. The ritual of the canopic procession offers an especially good example of the "embalming glance" that the Egyptians cast at things, dissecting them and then putting them back together. This ritual stresses multiplicity; the forty-two nomes and their capitals are carefully distinguished and listed with all their local characteristics. An extreme regionalism is at work here, one that conceives of each nome as a cosmos in and of itself. This "liturgical geography" played a major role in the Ptolemaic temples. It supplied a central scheme for ordering the knowledge of the sacred traditions. Egypt was conceived of as a canon of forty-two bodies of knowledge, each of which constituted, in and of itself, a whole core library of sacred books. There were extracts from this canon in every temple. Every temple in and of itself constituted a cosmos, the entirety of Egypt being visualized in the form of comprehensive images of processions drawn from this canon, and this entirety was celebrated ritually in the mysteries of Khoiak. Multiplicity was stressed only for the purpose of ritually uniting, even "embalming," it into a unity.

The Egyptians thus projected the disarticulated body of Osiris onto the multiplicity of the nomes so as to celebrate, in the ritual of uniting the limbs, the unity, the completeness, and the intactness of the land of Egypt. It seems to me to be an error to think that this is merely a variant on the widespread vegetation myth of the dying and rising seed grain. This motif was, of course, a part of the original content of the Osiris myth. But it was certainly not concern with seeds and the return of vegetation that brought this myth, with its semantics of dismemberment and reunification, center stage in late Egyptian culture. Behind the myth, there lay a concern with the continuation of this culture itself, and specifically because of a crisis that was interpreted and experienced as a dismemberment. In the Graeco-Roman Period, Egyptian culture seemed like a conceptual complex that was ever more threatened with being forgotten or with falling asunder. It is important to remember that Seth, the murderer of Osiris and the butcher of his corpse, death as enemy, was also an Asiatic, a foreigner. Prior to the later stages of history, these aspects of Seth had been independent of one another, but now, they were joined together, and Seth's murderous attack acquired a new, political meaning. Seth's attack represented a danger that was seen as permanently threatening Egypt, and which was always localized in the north. In the great triumphal festival of Horus at Edfu, the myth was dramatized in such a way that Seth invaded Egypt from the north and then was beaten back by Horus from the south. The theme of "invasion from the north" played a major role in other myths during the later stages of history.[44] The political-sacramental explanation of these festivals and rituals, and especially those of the rites of Khoiak, articulated a nationalistic reaction to the foreign rule of the Persians, Greeks, and Romans. The rites of Khoiak attempted to stave off the "death" of Egyptian culture, uniting the forty-two nomes into the body of Osiris and preserving the immense cultural knowledge that had been assembled in these nomes by maintaining their presence in lists and liturgies.

At the end of this culture, there stands a text that describes its decline, the final forgetting and rendering asunder of this *officium memoriae*, as an apocalypse. Just as people now speak of the end of history, so this text speaks of the end of the rites and the end of the cosmogonic memory that ensures the cohesion of cosmos, order, and history. The text is from the Corpus Hermeticum:

> There will come a time when it will seem as though the Egyptians had honored the divine in vain with pious hearts and ceaseless devotion, and all sacred attention to the gods will be in vain and its fruits will be robbed. For divinity will ascend back from the earth to the sky and abandon Egypt. This land, once the seat of religion, will now be robbed of divine presence. Foreigners will people this land, and the old cults will not only be neglected, they will even be forbidden. Of Egyptian religion, only fables will remain, and inscribed stones. . . . In those days, men will grow weary of life and cease to marvel at the cosmos (*mundus*) and worship it. . . . The gods will separate themselves from men—O painful separation! . . . In those times, the earth will no longer be stable, and the sea no longer navigable, the sky will no longer be crossed by stars, and the stars will forsake their courses; every divine voice will be forced into silence. The fruits of the earth will be spoiled

and the soil no longer fruitful, and even the air will hang heavy and close. This is the old age of the world: lack of religion (*inreligio*), order (*inordinatio*), and meaning (*inrationabilitas*).

The termination of the rites and the end of the worship of the cosmos plunges the world into an acute, deathlike state. The rites are for the world what the circulation of the blood is for the body: they bind, they combine, they integrate, and they endow with life. Their decline ruins the unity of the world and leaves it to decay.

CHAPTER SIXTEEN

Freedom from the Yoke of Transitoriness

Resultativity and Continuance

T he Egyptians' hopes for freedom from the yoke of transitoriness ran in two very different directions that we must take care to distinguish, though they themselves perceived a connection between them, one that is difficult for us to understand. I wish to call one of these directions "continuance," and the other immortality. Continuance is focused on this world, and immortality on the next. Continuance was something in human existence, a prospect, realizable within the framework of human possibilities, of surviving death and somehow continuing to exist. Immortality was a privilege of the gods, something withheld from "mortals": one had to be transformed into a god in order to become immortal.

1. Resultativity

"So long as something is, it is not what it will have been." This sentence, which begins Martin Walser's novel *Ein springender Brunnen* (a gushing fountain), leads us directly to the distinction in question, for it is a matter of whether we are caught up in an event or whether we are looking back on it from the outside.[1] Often, it is only in retrospect that things take on the contours of a meaningful story that can be understood, recounted, and remembered. The individual events can be read only from the vantage point of the end. The end, the question of "whether anything came out of it" is what determines the meaning and the coherence of what has happened. Not that we must bat about in the dark while we are still in the midst of events. Even here, there is a light, more or less bright, that emerges from our presuppositions, our goals, our expectations, our recollections, and our intuitive orientation. But this illumination is essentially something other, and it can make things appear different from how they seem in the light that emerges at the end.

There are languages in which this distinction between "so long as something is" and "what it has been" is the basis of the system of tenses. In these languages, this distinction is more important than that between past, present, and future. We call these categories "aspect," as opposed to the three "tenses" just mentioned. Instead of three tenses, there are two aspects. The temporality of an event can be viewed only from within or from without. The aspect of "so long as something is" is called the "imperfective," and that of "what it has been" is the "perfective," with the perfective aspect indicating an event not only in its "having-been-ness" but also in its "not-yet-being-ness," at any rate when viewed from the outside. In the languages with which we are familiar, which lack aspectual opposition, aspect is expressed by means of periphrastic forms. The most common form of the imperfect is the progressive: "he is writing, was writing, will be writing." Our perfect tense comes closest to the perfective aspect: "he has written." The latter is a complex form, though, for here, the event is viewed not only from the outside but also in its "having-been-ness," as something in the past. But we find this same connection in Egyptian, as well. There, too, perfective aspect combines with past tense in a grammatical form I prefer to call "resultative." For what is important is the fact that the result of the completed action, writing, for example, is present in the form of a written document. The form "he has written" implies that the process of writing is completed and that what was written is available, can be "had." We connect the idea of completed action with the concept of "having," with something in our possession; in the resultative, we combine perfectivity and possession. This is precisely what happens in the Egyptian language. But in Egyptian, the concept of possession is not expressed by a verb, as in English (and in German, French, etc.), but by a preposition expressing affiliation, which corresponds to the indirect object in English. Instead of "he has written," Egyptian has "it is written to him." In this way, Egyptian combines the completedness of the action with the presence of its result.

These grammatical considerations might seem overly subtle and abstruse. Yet from them, there is a path leading straight to our theme of the relationship between death and time. The distinction between imperfective and resultative, between "so long as something is" and "what it has been," can be extended to life altogether. So long as a life is lived, it is not what it will have been after death. Needless to say, we cannot really cast an eye on our life from the perspective of what it has been. Yet Egyptians did, in a sense, attempt such a thing, for as soon as their income and position allowed for it, they prepared a tomb and had a biographical text inscribed in it. The institution of the Egyptian monumental tomb, with everything that belonged to it, from mummification of the body to the biographical inscription, rested on the principle of resultativity. We can understand the overwhelming cultural importance of this curious phenomenon for the Egyptian world only by understanding clearly what role the category of resultativity played in Egyptian thought and how centrally it was anchored in the Egyptian language. Resultativity entails two presuppositions: a linear concept of time and a concept of the end that represents the goal of the linear course of time. Unlike the cyclical concept of time, here, the end does not become, nor is it abolished by, a fresh beginning; rather, it remains an end, in the form of a result, and in Egypt, all cultural efforts were exerted from the perspective of preserving the result.

In the form of his tomb, the prominent Egyptian held a mirror before his eyes, one that reflected his life in the light of its "having-been-ness." In this mirror, he saw not what he was but what he wished to have been, in a final form that laid normative claims on the conduct of his life. For the Egyptian, the tomb was the instrument of a normative doubling of the self. In texts and representations, he could, in anticipation of his death, depict his life in the final form in which, removed from transitoriness and oblivion, he would be capable of continuing, forever unchangeable, in that time or eternity called *djet*.

As is well known, the Egyptians distinguished two concepts of time, *neheh* and *djet*. This distinction rested on aspectual opposition: *neheh* was the time of "so long as something is," which could be viewed only from within its course, which renewed and repeated itself regardless of the passing of the hours, the days, and the years. *Djet*, however, was the time in which "something will have been," the unchangeable duration in which everything completed was stored away. The two concepts of time were inseparably connected with the two gods with whom the Egyptians connected their hopes for the afterlife.

Re, the sun god, was the exponent of *neheh*-time, the cyclical concept of time, the time of unending ever-again, of ceaseless renewal and eternal return. The dead, too, strove for ceaseless renewal in the ever-again of *neheh*-time. They wished to "go forth and enter, in the company of the sun god"[2] and to indulge themselves daily in all sorts of transformations in the light of the sun. This desire to transform belonged entirely to the *neheh*-time of renewal; the Egyptian word *kheper*, "to become, to transform," written with the hieroglyph depicting a scarab, the symbol of this ceaseless power of regeneration, designates existence in the framework of *neheh*, of the "ever-again." Forming a pendant to *kheper* is the verb *wenen*, "to be, to exist, to last, to continue." The two verbs stand at the center of the Egyptian concept of the afterlife. Just as *kheper* belongs to Re, *wenen* is connected with Osiris. In his aspect of renewing transformation as the morning sun, Re is called Khepri, "the becoming one," and in his aspect of unchangeable continuation as mummy, Osiris is called Wennefer (Greek Onnophris), "the lasting, completed one." Osiris was the exponent of *djet*-time and the linear, or more precisely put, resultative concept of time, the time in which a ripened, completed result continues, stored away unchangeable. *Neheh*, the time of Re, was the time of renewal, while *djet*, the time of Osiris, was the time of remembrance.

The Egyptians wanted to overcome death in both kinds of time, and to do this, they relied on both Re and Osiris. They could move about as a *ba*, like Re, and endure as a mummy, like Osiris, in unchangeable completion. To achieve this goal of Osirian continuation, they needed embalming, mummification, and, above all, the Judgment of the Dead. The concept of completion/perfection, Egyptian *nfrw*, not only had connotations of beauty, perfection, and imperishability but also, and above all, connotations of virtue and righteousness, of moral perfection and conformance with the norms of *maat*. From *djet*-time, there arose a moral perspective. Only good could continue unchangeably; evil, bad, uncleanliness, and imperfection were given over to perishability. The moral qualities of a result, that is, its conformance to *maat*, decided its imperishability.

A text in the tomb of the vizier Amenuser, from the reign of Tuthmosis III, superbly exemplifies the resultative thinking of the Egyptians, which underlay the entirety of their tomb culture:

> I erected an excellent tomb for myself
> in my city of plenitude of time.
> I richly outfitted the place of my rock-cut tomb
> in the desert of eternity.
> May my name endure on it
> in the mouths of the living,
> while recollection of me is good among men
> in the years to come.
>
> Only a little of life is this world,
> (but) eternity is in the realm of the dead.[3]

This text begins with a classical citation. In the Instruction of Hardjedef, we read:

> Make your house in the west excellent,
> and richly outfit your seat in the necropolis.
> Heed this, for death is worth little to us,
> heed this, for life stands tall for us.
> But the house of death serves life![4]

This instruction is attributed to a prince of Dynasty 4, a son of Cheops, the builder of the Great Pyramid. Such attributions are fictitious; they tell us nothing about when the text was written but rather about its purposes. Because it is situated in the golden age of Egyptian monumental architecture and tomb building, the maxim just cited formulates the principle that underlay this flourishing period. This maxim was one of the most oft-cited verses of Egyptian literature, all the way down into the later stages of history.[5] The remainder of the preserved part of this instruction is dedicated to the theme of the tomb. One is not only to prepare a tomb and outfit it splendidly but also to acquire land from whose yields offerings are to be presented. These statements correspond to what was actually done in the Old Kingdom. An overseer was to be appointed for the land and for the delivery of the offering items, and a mortuary priest for making the offering: "This will be more useful to you than a bodily son. Promote him more than your heirs. Think of what is said: 'There is no heir who remembers forever.'"[6]

This instruction presumably had its origin in a period when Egyptians still assumed that such investments could assure the eternal continuation of their memory. But even here, there are already mentions of ethical considerations:

> If the death of a man approaches him on a day when he sins
> and sums up what he did earlier,
> then he is buried despised in the cemetery.
> From sadness emerges evil,
> his mortuary offerings become the god's punishment for him,
> and what was supposed to bring him joy becomes disgrace for him.[7]

The Instruction for King Merikare stems from a time when the decline of the Old Kingdom, the collapse of tombs, and the interruption of the cults was already a thing of the past. Here, the famous, oft-cited verses 11–12 of the Instruction of Hardjedef are given an ethical reinterpretation:

> Make excellent your house in the west,
> and richly prepare your seat in the necropolis
> as one who does right (or, "through righteousness")
> and as one who does *maat* (or, "and by the doing of *maat*"),
> for that alone is what the heart of a man can rely on.[8]

Not the monumentality of a tomb layout, but rather the righteousness and the conformity to *maat* of one's conduct during life was decisive for the unchangeable continuance of the resultative final form of a life in *djet*-time or eternity. For this continuance stood or fell with the recollection attached to the life that had been and to the tomb as the visible symbol of its resultative final form. The most splendid burial had no meaning without the memory that attached to the righteousness and the virtue of the tomb owner. That is the meaning of the second stanza of our text from the tomb of Amenuser. But the concluding verses give this Egyptian concept of resultative continuance in the memory of posterity a turn that seems to set the argument of Hardjedef on its head. The latter had stated, "death is worth little to us, life stands tall for us." Amenuser, however, says, "Only a little of life is this world, (but) eternity is in the realm of the dead." Here, it is not life and death that are contrasted but lifetime and *djet*-eternity. Amenuser justifies the extraordinary expenses of preparing a tomb and securing the remembrance of posterity on the grounds that time spent "on earth" (*tp t³*) is only "a little" compared to the "eternity" (*ḏ.t*) spent in the "realm of the dead" (*ḥr.t nṯr*). A lifetime on earth is short compared to the unending continuance of one's name in the recollection of posterity. In the light of "having-been-ness," "so long as something is" fades into a mere prehistory. Human life, threatened and bounded by death, receives its meaning only in the all-encompassing horizon of lastingness and eternity. This horizon, which found its expression in stone architecture, was based on the idea of righteousness. He who acted righteously was assimilating himself, already in the transitoriness of his existence on earth, into the sacred lastingness of his postmortem existence.

This connection between tomb architecture and resultative thought, that semantic complex of righteousness, remembrance, and imperishability, was described by Hecataeus of Abdera with incomparable precision, and we can only wonder how it was possible for a Greek of the late fourth century B.C.E. to reproduce so accurately a conceptual realm that had developed a full two millennia in the past. The unbelievable longevity of these concepts shows that we are here in the midst, in the innermost kernel, of the cultural memory of the Egyptians. Here, the powers of preservation, reinforcement, and canonization were at their strongest, inviting an excursus that ends by returning again to the thesis of "life permeated by death" and investigating the connections that arise, on the basis of the resultative view of life, between tomb architecture, the sense of time, and the consciousness of history. The monumental tomb constructed during one's lifetime was without doubt the most impressive and intensive form in which death permeated the life of the individual in Egypt.

Hecataeus lived in Alexandria at the beginning of the Ptolemaic Period, from 320 to 305. He wrote a major work about Egypt, which has been preserved to us only in extracts cited by other authors. In it, he writes:

> For the Egyptians regard the time spent in this life as completely worthless; but to be remembered for virtue after one's demise they hold to be of the highest value. Indeed, they refer to the houses of the living as "inns" (*kata-lyseis*), since we dwell in them but a short time, while the tombs of the dead they call "everlasting homes" (*aidioi oikoi*), since in Hades we remain for an endless span. For this reason, they trouble themselves little about the furnishings of their houses, but betray an excess of ostentation concerning their places of burial.[9]

Hecataeus was struck by the fact that the Egyptians built their dwellings out of sun-dried mud bricks, the cheapest and simplest building material imaginable. Even royal palaces were built of this material. But their tombs were made of stone. In his opinion, this phenomenon was based on the Egyptian construction of time, and this in turn stemmed from the Egyptian concepts of death and immortality. Knowledge of human mortality caused the Egyptians to view life as a brief moment, for which it was not worth the effort to make lavish provisions. They therefore invested all their intellectual and material means on eternity, or better, the endlessly long time during which they would be remembered, after death, for their virtue. Precisely like Amenuser twelve centuries before him, Hecataeus identified immortality with being remembered for one's virtue. The actual investment had to do with remembrance; the tomb was only the sign, the external symbol, of the memory that attached to a life led in virtue and righteousness. Thus, according to Hecataeus, there were two kinds of activity that stemmed from the Egyptian concept of death and the concept of time that was anchored in it: that of lavish stone architecture, and that of virtue, that is, of morality and righteousness.

So long as the tombs were accessible to visitors, the inscriptions were there to be read over the millennia, for the hieroglyphic writing system remained essentially unaltered for three thousand years: with unique consistency, it retained the lavish and impractically realistic pictorialness of its signs. The writing system could have functioned perfectly well without this pictorial aspect, as shown by the abstract, cursive system of signs that was developed for use on papyri. But the Egyptians stuck to the pictorial, hieroglyphic writing system for their monuments. Here, all change was excluded, and this was also true of the language written with the hieroglyphs, which was also frozen in a specific stage. There were various reasons for this fact, but one of them surely had to do with memory. This writing system was readable for millennia, its language was learned in the schools, creating a diachronically cultural transparence that made it possible for an educated Egyptian in Hecataeus' day to recognize his forebears in the tomb inscriptions of the Old Kingdom, to identify with the principles according to which they led their lives, and to bring them, out of gratitude, a small mortuary offering, one that probably consisted of no more than a prayer and a few drops of water.

The close relationship between tomb and writing can be further illustrated and extended. It was precisely in this respect that an Egyptian monumental tomb went far beyond what we would normally connect with the concept of mortuary cult and the culture of death in the narrower sense. Its place in the Egyptian world can only be compared with our own concepts of art, authorship, and work. This comparison might seem farfetched, yet the Roman poet Horace already compared his book of odes with the pyramids. Horace himself stands in a literary tradition that goes back to Egypt, for in a wisdom text dating to the thirteenth century B.C.E., we read the following lines regarding the great classical writers of the past:

> As for those learned scribes from the time of Re,
> . . . they did not build themselves pyramids of bronze,
> nor stelae of iron;
> they did not know how to leave heirs in the form of children
> to keep their names alive.
> Rather, they made books for themselves as heirs,
> and instructions that they composed.
> They appointed book rolls for themselves as lector priests,
> and writing boards as "loving son."
> Instructions are their pyramids,
> and reeds their son,
> smoothed stone surfaces their wife.
> . . . Doors and chapels were made for them—they are collapsed.
> Their mortuary priests are departed,
> their altars are muddied,
> their tomb chapels forgotten.
> But their names are pronounced over the writings they produced,
> for they endure because of their perfection.
> Their creators are remembered forever.
> . . . More worthwhile is a book than a graven stela
> or a solid tomb wall.
> It creates these tombs and pyramids
> in the hearts of those who pronounce their names.
> . . . Man passes away, his body becomes dust,
> all his family perishes.
> But a book causes him to be remembered,
> for one mouth passes it to another.
> Better is a book than a house that has been built,

or tomb chapels in the West.
Better is it than a well-founded palace,
better than a stela in the temple.
. . . They have hidden their magic from humankind,
who read in their writings.
They are gone, and their names would be forgotten,
but it is the book that keeps their memory alive.[10]

Here, literature appears to continue, or rather outdo, the stoniness of monumental architecture with other, intellectual means. But the decisive common denominator between tomb and book is the category of authorship. There are no parallels in any other cultures. Where else does a tomb owner make his appearance as "author" of his own tomb and the biography displayed in it? Tombs are erected by those left behind, under circumstances of long-term preparation and instigation on the part of the deceased. But they are scarcely to be understood as organs of a comprehensive textual and pictorial self-thematizing. Herein lies the special, "literary" element of an Egyptian monumental tomb. Art, literature, and tomb have a common root in resultative thought: in the idea of creating a result that will continue in the memory of men and will thus become the medium not only of self-thematizing but also of transcending and eternalizing the self.

Such continuance was based on the perfection of the result as well as on its diachronic cultural transparence, as mentioned just above. The texts had to be readable, even after thousands of years. Cultural memory had to form and to stabilize a long-term perspective in which it was possible for the dead to live on and engage in dialogue with the living over the centuries, and perhaps even the millennia. We have to assume there was a connection between the desire for immortality and what we are calling here "cultural memory."[11] This brings me back to the connection between death and culture, with which I began this study in the sense of a guiding hypothesis. Of all living creatures, it is man who must live with the consciousness of his own mortality. This knowledge, of course, was a pressing problem only for those who were not obliged to push it into the background because of their daily need to stay alive. As the philosopher Blaise Pascal once noted, "only such people tend to meditate about death (and thereby about immortality) who do not have to fight for their lives, sweat to gain their daily bread, struggle to bring up their children."[12] Like the cultivation of cultural memory, concern about continuance and immortality are elite concerns, but the two hang closely together. It seems to me that cultural memory is the most important of those "life strategies" that Zygmunt Bauman has emphasized in his book on death and immortality.[13]

Konrad Ehlich has reduced his definition of the concept "text" to a "need for tradition."[14] Texts do not arise ready-made in communication, in conversation, but only in cited communication, in reverting back to something that has been said. Texts do not live in the natural situation of conversation but in the "extended situation" of tradition, in which the participants are separated by a spatial and/or temporal distance. Ehlich develops this concept using the paradigmatic instance of the institution of the messenger ("The messenger is like the one who sent him"). But the possibilities of the extended situation experience a revolutionary expansion with the invention of writing. In Egypt, from the very beginning, this invention was used to institutionalize an "extended situation" that stretched beyond the threshold of death, permitting the dead to remain in contact with posterity. Behind the wish to "extend" the situation of dialogue beyond the boundary of death stood the wish for an extension of life. The living wished to remain in contact with the dead, and vice versa, and writing was viewed as a means of facilitating such communication. I take this power of written interaction with posterity as the decisive motive for the development of a cultural memory, and in no culture has this relationship between desire for continuance or immortality and the development of millennia-embracing "spaces of recollecting" cultural memory made its appearance more clearly than in ancient Egypt.

In such a millennia-encompassing space of recollection lived the Egyptians, whom Hecataeus questioned about the meaning of their curious custom of living in mud huts and having themselves buried in stone palaces, and who seemed to be so outstandingly informed regarding the millennia-old semantics connected with this practice. They looked back to a past whose depths the Greeks must have assumed was fabulous, for it went far beyond the boundaries reached by their own lineages, which in the case of the aristocracy went back to the world of heroes and gods. The Egyptians of Hecataeus' time must have been filled with a special sense and consciousness of the past, one that had its basis in the tomb culture and thus was again derived from death. What was special about this consciousness of the past was that the past had not become alien in the course of all that time. There had been plenty of opportunity for termination and radical change. The Old Kingdom had declined at the end of the third millennium, and the following century and a half saw the rise of a new political order and a new kind of cultural semantics. Nothing would have been easier for the Egyptians than to have distanced themselves from this past and to have looked back on the colossal ruins of the Old Kingdom as the work of giants or demigods, just as the Greeks ascribed the walls of the Mycenaean culture to the Cyclopes. But Egypt took an entirely different direction. Notwithstanding considerable changes in its cultural semantics, it was able to hang on to the tradition of the Old Kingdom and not to allow the past to become opaque. The same collapse repeated itself after the early centuries of the second millennium, this time exacerbated by the loss of political sovereignty to the Hyksos, West Semitic immigrants from Palestine. And again, the New Kingdom succeeded in renewing Egypt and reestablishing its connection with the past. At the end of the New Kingdom, Egypt entered into the general crisis of the Late Bronze and Early Iron Age, when a number of kingdoms and cultures, such as the Hittites and the Mycenaeans, disappeared. Under the foreign rule of Libyans and Kushites, Egypt again experienced major changes in its political structure and its cultural semantics, yet at just this time, there developed an especially intensive turn to the past, the distinct archaism of Dynasties 25 and 26, the latter the so-called Saite Renaissance.

We may ask whether this attachment to the past and this striving for individual immortality had a common root in the "need for tradition," and whether this need for tradition sprang from a desire for release from transitoriness and for overcoming death. This would be not merely a matter of an ancient Egyptian peculiarity but of a trait inherent in the nature of man as a creature aware of his own mortality. But that would also mean that our own interest in the past, in our cultural memory, springs from our aspiration to self-transcendence. We thus hold in our hand not just a key for understanding the ancient Egyptians but also our own interest in them. Our effort to remain in dialogue with the dead leads us ever further back, to dead persons who lived more than five thousand years ago.

2. *"Trust Not in the Length of the Years": Salvation through Righteousness*

> Trust not in the length of years!
> They view lifetime as an hour.
> When a man remains over after the landing,
> his deeds are set beside him as a sum.

So we read in the Instruction for Merikare. In these verses, a connection is made between the category of resultativity—the "sum of the deeds"— and human time. The judges of the dead regard this time as "an hour," in the mode of "having-been-ness," as a closed whole, and the living one who is responsible must be able to make this view of life his own; he must not, captive to the view of his ongoing life from within it, harbor the illusion of its endless continuation. Anyone who trusts in the length of the years falls prey to transitoriness. To live responsibly means to orient oneself to the "laws of *maat*." On this topic, Ptahhotep teaches:

379

> If you are a man in a leading position,
> who gives commands to many,
> then strive incessantly for right action,
> until your conduct is without fault.
>
> Great is *maat*, lasting and effective,
> it has not been disturbed since the time of Osiris.[15]
> He who transgresses its laws is punished,
> but this seems like something distant to the greedy.
>
> Meanness amasses riches,
> but never has unrighteousness succeeded and lasted.
> When the end has come, *maat* (alone) lasts,
> so that a man can say, "that is the property of my father."[16]

The greedy one trusts in the length of the years; to him, death and punishment seem like something distant. In his foolish trust, he does injury to the "laws of *maat*." The responsible one knows that "the end is there," and he keeps a timely eye on it. When the end is there, all that the greedy one has set his heart on proves to be transitory, and *maat* is the only thing remaining. *Maat* is the principle of continued existence, the foundation that lends permanence and continuance in the stream of perishing and disappearance. The somewhat puzzling statement, "that is the property of my father," becomes clear from another maxim that deals with conducting life in conformity with *maat*:

> The man who corresponds to *maat* endures,
> and he goes away (i.e., dies) according to his manner of conduct.[17]
> He alone is competent to make a testament about it,
> but the greedy one has no tomb.[18]

He who orients his conduct of life according to the laws of *maat* endures and does not perish. He becomes a tomb owner and an ancestral spirit, he can leave his goods to his children and remain protectively bound to his house.

Maat embodied the norms of the culture, and it displayed them in an unexpected light to which we, in the shadow of Nietzsche and Freud, must again accustom ourselves. Nietzsche denounced religion and morality as a system of cruelty, as a painful compulsion imposed by society on the individual to turn him into a "predictable individual," and Freud spoke of the "civilization and its discontents," which imposed a difficult renunciation of instincts on the individual.[19] Neither wished in any way to reverse the process of civilization, but rather, made up a reckoning of the cost to show how high a price man had to pay for these self-imposed efforts at sublimation. They dismissed the releasing and even redemptive aspects of religion and morality as ideological sugar tablets with which society attempted to sweeten the bitter pill of the self-sacrifice that was demanded. But Egyptian texts speak of the redemptive aspect of right-eousness with an intensity that we cannot dismiss as ideological padding. What the norms of *maat* imposed on the individual in the way of self-control and self-abnegation was based on the redemptive powers of these norms, which were believed to save human existence from transitoriness. This was an ethics conceived on the basis of death. Act always—so we can summarize the "categorical (or better: cultural) imperative" of the Egyptians—so that your actions need not fear examination in the Judgment of the Dead. Place your conduct of life and the style of your actions on a basis that has proved to be truly lasting in this life and also serves as a standard for lastingness in the next life. The norms of *maat* not only have the power to integrate the individual into society, they also endow life itself with temporal continuation. He who has lived according to the norms of *maat*, so we read in the Instruction of Ptahhotep, is in a position to leave a testament. The superficial meaning of this statement is that his property passes uncontested into the hands of his children; on a deeper level, it means that with his tomb, and with the recollection of his righteousness in the memory of posterity, he has achieved a lasting place. This point clarifies the statement that follows: the greedy one has no tomb. To have a tomb means to be saved forever from transitoriness. The reference is not to a tomb made by man from stone but to one made by dint of righteousness, as stated in the Instruction for Merikare.

The individual thus appears before his divine judges and avers that he has lived according to *maat*:

> See, I have come to you—
> there is no wrong, no guilt in me,
> no evil in me, no witness against me,
> and there is no one I have wronged.
> (For) I live on truth, I nourish myself on truth.
> I have done that which men advise
> and with which the gods are pleased.
> I have pleased the god with what he loves.
> I gave bread to the hungry,
> water to the thirsty,
> clothing to the naked,
> a ferry to the boatless.
> I gave divine offerings to the gods,
> and mortuary offerings to the transfigured spirits.

To the judges of the dead, the deceased reckons up the same sum of his life that, in anticipation of this step, he had already caused to be displayed in his tomb as an account to be read by later visitors to the tomb:

> I have gone forth from my city,
> I have gone down from my nome,
> after doing *maat* for its lord
> and pleasing the god with what he loves.
> I have spoken good and repeated good,
> I have spoken *maat* and done *maat*.
> I gave bread to the hungry
> and clothing to the naked.
> I have honored my father
> and been loved by my mother.
> I have said nothing bad,
> evil, or malicious against anyone,
> for I wished that it go well with me
> and that I might be an *jm³ḫjj* in the presence of the god and of men
>   forever.[20]

Miriam Lichtheim has drawn attention to the correspondences between the autobiographical tomb inscriptions and the texts from the mortuary literature.[21] There is no better evidence for this than the stela of the overseer of the granary, Baki, from Dynasty 18, which is often cited in this connection.[22] This text makes it clear that the idea of the Judgment of the Dead and the rules of conduct affirmed in the eighty-two declarations of innocence constituted the guiding principles of a responsible conduct of life in this world. In the following, I cite only the most important extracts from the lengthy inscription. It begins with a profession of righteousness:

> I am a truly upright one, free of transgression,
> who has placed the god in his heart
> and is aware of his might.
> I have come to the "city in eternity,"
> after doing good (*bw nfr*) on earth.
> I have not sinned, I am blameless,
> my name has not been questioned because of misconduct
> or because of injustice (*jzf.t*).

The stanza that follows is a praise of *maat* as the guiding principle of life and as a "rampart" in the Judgment of the Dead. It becomes clear how the idea of the Judgment of the Dead is a determining factor during life, "from birth to death":

> I rejoice at speaking *maat*,
> for I know that it is useful (*akh*)
> for the one who does it on earth,
> from birth until "landing."
> It is an excellent rampart for the one who speaks it

on that day when he reaches the court of judgment
that judges the distressed[23] and uncovers character,
that punishes the sinner (*jzf.tj*) and cuts off his *ba*.

I was without blame,
so that no complaint against me and no sin of mine was before them,
so that I emerged vindicated,
praised among those provisioned in the tomb,
who had gone to their *ka*.

After a summary of his professional accomplishments, Baki again expressly stresses that he made the "laws of the Hall of the Two Truths," that is, the norms of the Judgment of the Dead, the basis of his conduct in life:

I am a nobleman happy with *maat*,
who emulated the laws of the "Hall of the Two Truths,"
for I intended to reach the realm of the dead
without my name being connected with any meanness,
without having done evil to men,
or anything that their gods censure.

Baki closes his inscription with an appeal to emulate him. Whoever conducts himself according to *maat* will have the enjoyment of doing so daily, but above all, it will be useful to him after his death. Baki reinforces his advice with a citation from the Instruction for Merikare, showing that this passage from the instruction was in fact, for the ancient Egyptians, the classic exposition of the idea of the Judgment of the Dead:

Hear what I have said,
all you men who will exist!
Be happy with *maat* every day,
as with a grain with which one cannot be satisfied.
If you do it, it will be useful (*ȝḫ*) for you;
the god, the lord of Abydos, lives on it daily.
You will spend your lives in happiness
until you rest in the Beautiful West.
Your *ba*s will have the power to enter and go forth,
"striding freely like the lords of eternity,"
abiding with the forefathers.[24]

This is an ethics dominated by consciousness of the inevitability of death, of the transitoriness of earthly life, and of the reckoning of a lifetime that will be made in the Judgment of the Dead according to the concept of resultativity.

He who is vindicated in the Judgment of the Dead will "stride freely like the lords of eternity," he will be accepted among the gods. He will thus not only enjoy continuance on earth but also immortality in the next world. The idea of the Judgment of the Dead was thus entirely dominated by the concept of resultativity. When the judges of the dead view a lifetime "as an hour," they consider it under the aspect of "having-been-ness," and they reckon up the sum. It is as though an entire lifetime was the prehistory of this moment when the result, the final form that was reached, was determined. This was the moment when the process of life turned into the unchangeable and indestructible permanence of Wennefer, the "completed lasting one."

3. "Make Holiday! Forget Care!"

In chapter 5, we treated the opposite of resultative thought, and here, we wish to return briefly to the astonishing fact that the wisdom of Siduri was not foreign to the ancient Egyptians. Siduri's advice was to reject human longing for continuance and immortality, relegating man to his lot of mortality, of the finiteness of his existence. Egyptian culture also articulated this sentiment, which seems to be a radical contradiction of its central convictions, especially that of "resultative thought." We came across it first in the Dialogue of a Man Weary of Life with His *Ba*, and specifically from the mouth of the *ba*.[25] This astonishing text seems to be a debate about "continuance" and "immortality," with the man, the "I" of the text, representing at first the standpoint of continuance and then, in conversation with his *ba*, gradually adopting the standpoint of immortality. I have offered a detailed interpretation of the text in another context, and here, I wish to confine myself to the theme of "continuance versus immortality." The man's clearest plea on behalf of continuance stands at the end of the first part of the dialogue, in which the "I" attempts to induce the *ba*, who wants to depart, to remain:

> Truly, you are running away without caring for yourself.
> Every lackey says, "I'll seize you."
> Even when you are dead, your name lives.
> A resting place is the world beyond,
> where the heart leads one.
> A harbor is the West,
> when the voyage is difficult. . . .
> If my *ba* listens to me without misdeed,
> and its heart agrees with me, then it will be happy.
> I shall cause it to reach the West as owner of a tomb (lit., "one who is in his pyramid"),

after those who have survived him have attended his burial.
I shall make a cooling over your body,
so that you will make another *ba*, who is weary, envious.
I shall make a cooling, (but) not too cool,
so that you will make another *ba*, who is hot, envious.
I shall drink water at the pond and set up a sunshade,
so that you will make another *ba*, who is hungry, envious.
If you drag me away from such a death,
you will find no place on which to rest.
Have patience, my *ba*, my brother,
until there is an heir who will make offerings,
who will stand at the tomb on the day of burial,
so that he may watch over (or, "stretch out") the bier.

The "I" recites the promises of continuance—the "name," the "West," the "pyramid," cooling, shadow, water, repletion, the heir who carries out the mortuary cult—all the things that, according to the traditional anthropology, were included in the concept of human existence and came into effect here, on and in the earth, with no ascent to the sky or deification. The goodly death to which the "I" aspires is an end to life after preparations are made for continuance in the "beautiful West": the preparation of a tomb and the appointment of an heir. The "I" thinks entirely within the category of resultativity. Life is concerned entirely with care for continuance, it is devalued into preparation for landing in the "harbor" of the West. This concept of continuance includes the continued association of the "I," the *ba*, and the corpse in the altered conditions of the necropolis.

The *ba* now bluntly objects to the illusory character of resultative continuance that the "I" believes can be realized by preparing a tomb of stone and by carrying out the mortuary rites:

> If you think of burial, it is pitiful,
> it is drawing out tears by making a man grieve,
> it is taking a man from his house so as to cast him into the desert.
> You cannot come back to see the sun.
> Those who built in granite,
> who made chapels in beautiful pyramids,
> in perfect work,
> when their builders became gods,
> their offering stones remained empty like the weary ones
> who died on the embankment for lack of a survivor.
> The water has taken its share, the heat of the sun the same,
> The fish by the bank speak with them.
> Listen to me! It is good for men to listen.
> Make holiday! Forget care![26]

With these words, the *ba* addresses the most sacred and basic convictions of continuance: tombs, mummification, and expenditures on tomb equipment and the mortuary cult, all of which continued without interruption down into the Graeco-Roman Period and, according to Hecataeus, retained their meaning unchallenged until the end of Egyptian culture. One can think of no more radical an antithesis to the views of the "I," which represent the *communis opinio* of ancient Egyptian society. That a text could express so extreme a contrary voice and construct such a semantic tension demonstrates the greatness and the depth of Egyptian literature, as well as its ability to reflect on the fundamentals of the culture itself. In the context of this oration against resultative thinking, which sees the meaning of life only in the amassing of a "life's sum" that it believes will continue unchangeably, the *ba* offers Siduri's advice: "Make holiday! Forget care!" We have seen that this voice of opposition was expressed elsewhere as well. In chapter 5, we dealt with laments and harpers' songs and their savage criticism of the finite nature of earthly life, the perishability of tombs, the meaninglessness of resultative provisions, and the distant fate of the dead. The two motifs—criticism of resultative thinking ("forget care!") and the advice to enjoy life, for it is unique, finite, and incapable of continuation ("make holiday!")—are closely connected.

The *ba* illustrates his view of things with two parables, and the "I" responds with three poems. The first poem bewails his own situation ("See, my name stinks . . ."), and the second that of society ("To whom can I speak today?"), while the third sketches an altered view of death, at which the "I" has evidently arrived during the course of the dialogue:

Death stands before me today
as when a sick man recovers,
like going out into the open air after being confined.

Death stands before me today
like the scent of myrrh,
like sitting under a sail on a windy day.

Death stands before me today
like the scent of lotus blossoms,
like sitting on the riverbank of drunkenness.

Death stands before me today
like the stopping of rain (or, "like a well-trodden way"),
as when a man returns home from an expedition.

Death stands before me today
as when the sky clears,
as when a man is enlightened (?) regarding what was unknown to him.

Death stands before me today
as when a man longs to see his home again
after he has spent many years in captivity.[27]

This text is every bit as paradoxical and contrary to basic Egyptian convictions as the speech of the *ba* regarding the meaninglessness of care about continuance. In chapter 5, we dealt with what the Egyptians thought about death (*mwt*). Death and the realm of death were the opposite of life as it was longed for and the epitome of all that was abhorrent. In the Egyptian language, the word "die" had an expressly pejorative meaning, and it was mostly replaced by "to land" and other, similar, euphemisms. Here, the image of death as reversal is stood on its head and now appears as salvation, and specifically from the realm of death that existence in this world has become. In the poem "To whom can I speak today?" the "I" conjured up the image of death as isolation, presenting himself as someone who was already socially dead. To someone who belongs to the realm of death "here," "there" seems like paradise. The "I" develops this vision in his fourth and last poem:

> He who is there will be a living god
> who metes out punishment for crime on the one who commits it.
> He who is there will stand in the (sun) barque,
> distributing offerings from it to the temples.
> He who is there will be a wise man who cannot be turned away
> when he addresses the sun god, when he speaks.[28]

With these words, the "I" makes the concept of immortality his own; "there," as a "living god," he will find the connectivity that has disappeared "here." The actions of the one "who is there" are exemplary deeds of connective behavior: punishing crime, providing the temples with offerings, and, as a wise man, getting a hearing. These deeds make what is impossible "here" into a reality. It is at this point, I think, that the "I" adopts the standpoint that the *ba* represented from the very beginning, though this is only a supposition, given that the beginning of the text is lost. In a countermove, the *ba* ends by adopting the standpoint represented originally by the "I":

> Give up your complaint,
> O my neighbor, my brother!
> May you make a burnt offering,
> and cling to life as you see it.
> Love me "here" when you have set aside the West,
> but long to reach the West
> when your body touches the earth.
> I shall alight after you have grown weary.
> Then we shall dwell together.[29]

The text ends with the disputants reconciled. The "I" has come to understand what "West" and "afterlife" mean when they are viewed not in the light of continuance but in that of immortality, and the *ba* is now able to continue its association with the "I," who had advocated this association at the beginning of the dialogue.

This work of literature is from the transitional period between the First Intermediate Period and the Middle Kingdom, when the concept of the *ba*, which had previously been a purely royal concept, was now taken over into the general concept of man and thus began to extend the traditional concept of continuance in the direction of immortality.[30] With unique clarity, the text shows that in Egyptian thought, the concepts of continuance and immortality were not combined without opposition, as it has perhaps seemed to us, but rather that what became the classic conceptual complex was preceded by considerable intellectual effort and debate.

The *ba* expresses skepticism regarding the possibilities of continuance but not with regard to immortality. It derides the "resultative thought" of the "I," which believes that like someone hoarding a treasure, it can forever guarantee the assembled sum of its earthly endeavors in the form of a tomb and a mortuary cult. Nothing, however, will remain to the deceased. He will not "come back to see the sun": this does not mean that he will have no life after death but that the mortuary cult in the tomb is an illusory effort, for the deceased will not emerge through the false door to receive his offerings. These are radical views, but they are directed against the concept of continuance, not against that of immortality, which the *ba* itself personifies. Why does the *ba* debunk continuance as illusory? Because it is connected to social memory and to the solidarity of society, and because, in the historical situation in which this dialogue occurs, these bases have disappeared. The *ba* does not say this, to be sure, but the "I" says it in his first two laments, and we must imagine an introductory "you are right" in order to understand the gist of the argumentation. With these laments, the "I" gives in and surrenders to the standpoint of the *ba*. In this world from which love and memory have disappeared, hopes for a life after death can be directed only toward the world beyond and transformation into a living, that is to say, an immortal, god.

CHAPTER SEVENTEEN

Freedom from the Yoke of Transitoriness

Immortality

1. Realm of Death and Elysium: The Originally Royal Sense of This Distinction

One of the most important results of our review of the various images of death in ancient Egypt is the discovery that the Egyptians had a concept of a realm of death in which the dead were just dead, and that they depicted this state of death in the darkest colors of deprivation and reversal of all the order and beauty of life. Until now, scholars have known that there were some "heretical" voices that dared to question the wisdom of the official mortuary texts—the harpers' songs and the laments of widows—but these have been taken to be individual voices opposing the chorus of the official mortuary literature. Now, things seem quite otherwise. The concept of a realm of death belonged to the general and official picture of the world beyond, and it was no brighter or more pleasant than those of Mesopotamia, Israel, or Greece. Everyone who lived on earth had to die, even the king, the "divine seed," who in death ascended to the sky like a falcon and united with the sun, his father. Not only did the Egyptians of the Old Kingdom build mighty pyramids for this king, they made him the model for all their aspirations to immortality and salvation from death, and all their dreams of eternal life in the company of the gods. The king was believed to be above the destiny of mortals, and his special position was emphasized in the mortuary liturgies of the Pyramid Texts. We considered some of these text passages in chapter 6, in connection with the concept of death as transition; in them, the king was expressly distanced from the next-worldly destiny of ordinary morals. The king was a god. The king did not enter the earth like men, who "concealed themselves"; rather, he "flew up to the sky." He did not associate with those "whose places were hidden"; rather, he assumed rulership over them and accepted their homage. He did not belong to the subjects of Osiris, the inhabitants of the realm of death, but rather ruled over them. He escaped death and mingled with the gods.

The Story of Sinuhe begins with a description of the death of Amenemhet I, using formal expressions for the death of a king that remained in use down into the latest periods of history:

> A god ascends to his horizon,
> King Amenemhet, he distances himself to the sky
> and joins himself to the sun disk,
> the divine body mingles with its creator.[1]

Never was the death of an ordinary mortal described with such turns of expression. But to the end, a journey to the sky remained the characteristic idea of a royal death. Essentially the same terms remained in use down into Graeco-Roman times in inscriptions mentioning the death of a royal,[2] for example, Amenophis I,[3] Tuthmosis I,[4] Tuthmosis II,[5] Tuthmosis III,[6] Psammetichus II,[7] Nitocris,[8] and even Arsinoe II.[9]

This royal image sheds light on the special path trodden by Egypt, among the cultures of the ancient world, with respect to concepts of the afterlife. The grandiose visions of eternal life developed in the Egyptian mortuary texts are all connected with the image of the king and stem, in the last instance, from the political institution and theology of divine kingship. This special political choice dragged all other details in its wake, including the Egyptian concepts of afterlife and immortality. Around the end of the fourth millennium B.C.E., Egypt created the first great territorial state known to history, and the transition from prehistory to history, or from chiefdoms to the pharaonic kingdom of the "Two Lands," was synonymous with the sacralization of the office that elevated its holder into a god on earth, the embodiment of the god Horus, to which was later added his filial relationship to the sun god. The step from prehistory into history, from a phase of rival chiefdoms into history's first major state, was doubtless connected with the concept of divine kingship as a form of rulership that stood out from everything that had preceded it, as though this new realm, which in the eyes of the Egyptians stretched to the boundaries of the ordered world, transcended everything that had gone before.

The concept of "rule" now assumed a new quality of superhuman action in which divine creative power manifested itself. The person of the ruler was thus viewed as the embodiment of a god, and Egyptian imagination invested all its concepts of eternal bliss in this image of the king. In the process, the concept of the afterlife came to entail not a "heaven" and a "hell" but a "realm of death" and an "Elysium," the former a sphere in which the dead were dead and the latter a sphere in which first the king and then later all the "transfigured spirits" were saved from death and enjoyed eternal life. This Elysium was thus an originally political idea; this Elysium towered above the realm of death, just as the figure of the king towered above the rest of humanity, and just as the concept of the state in the Archaic Period and the Old Kingdom went beyond the prehistoric forms of political organization.

But for the idea of Elysium to develop into a central aspect of the Egyptian concept of the world, a second step was necessary, one that was taken a good millennium later: the demo(cra)tization of this royal image with and at the end of the Old Kingdom. Only with the extension of this exclusive postmortem destiny to (potentially) all Egyptians did the royal afterlife expand into an Elysian next-worldly space. In the process, the distinction between the realm of death and Elysium lost its political meaning (Elysium for the king, the realm of death for the rest of humankind) and became open to new interpretations. It became a question of morality and knowledge. No longer did being son of the sun save a person from the realm of the dead; rather, it was virtue and righteousness, and being provided with (or "initiated into") magical knowledge. This demotization of the royal afterlife had begun already during the Old Kingdom. In Dynasty 5, we can observe changes in tomb decoration and layout that reveal how the mortuary cult of privileged officials was carried out after the royal model. More people were involved, the lector priest made his appearance carrying his book roll, and "transfiguration spells" were chanted, spells that surely differed little, if at all, from those of the royal mortuary cult. In their inscriptions, the tomb owners of this period designated themselves as "excellent ancestral spirits who know their spell," and the concept of righteousness also came to occupy a central place. As early as Dynasty 6, we already find isolated examples of the *ba* of nonroyal individuals.[10] It was through this process—first the image of the king as a god on earth whose death was conceived as a return to his heavenly father, and then the extension of these grandiose eschatological concepts to potentially all of humankind—that the afterlife came to be divided into the realm of death and the Elysium that were characteristic of ancient Egypt.

In addition to the two roots of the Egyptian idea of the afterlife just mentioned, the image of the king and its demotization, there was a third, the concept of the sun god's journey through the netherworld, which we encounter already in the Pyramid Texts. In Pyramid Texts spell 216, the oldest, classic mortuary liturgy, which we cited in chapter 6, the king wishes to board the night barque of the sun god and to sail in it through the netherworld. In this respect, Egypt differed radically from religions that make a strict distinction between deities of the sky and of the netherworld. In Egypt, the sun god embraced both realms.

The word "Elysium," which I have been using in this work for the opposite of the realm of death, a place of immortality in which the dead were not dead but rather redeemed from death and immortally lived their eternal life, is a Greek word, not an Egyptian one. The corresponding expressions in Egyptian are "Field of Reeds" and "Field of Offerings," two terms for the same thing, as well as a series of other designations, such as "Isle of the Just," "Great City," and so forth. I use the term "Elysium" here as a concept drawn from the study of religion, preferring it to a term such as "Paradise," for "Elysium" entails no associations with primeval time and the biblical "Fall" but rather refers to the concept of an elite postmortem destiny and the regions connected with it.

Yet we may inquire as to whether the term "Elysium" is not much more closely connected to these Egyptian concepts than merely in the sense of a general category. There is reason to think that there are indications of direct cultural borrowing and perhaps even an etymological relationship between the Egyptian Field of Reeds and the Greek Elysium.[11] In the past, scholars have posited a relationship between the Egyptian word *ealu*, "reeds," in the expression "Field of Reeds" and the element *ely* of the Greek word *elysium*, for which there seems to be no Greek etymology, and also between the Egyptian expression *m^{3c}-ḥrw*, "vindicated," and the Greek word *makarios*, "blessed," which, like the Egyptian expression, refers to the status of a person saved from death and accepted into Elysium. In any event, the Greeks themselves saw the correspondences between the Egyptian Field of Reeds and their own Elysium. According to them, Orpheus, in whose mysteries these correspondences abound, brought all of it from Egypt to Greece. The early and constant equation of Osiris and Dionysos also rested on such correspondences. On this point, salvation from Hades, the realm of death, and acceptance into the Elysian Fields were rather similar to the Orphic and Dionysian mysteries.

2. *Redemption through* Unio Liturgica

We have described the mortuary literature as a supply of knowledge placed in the tomb to serve the deceased in the afterlife. This aspect of knowledge is expressly mentioned in the colophons of any number of spells in the Coffin Texts and the Book of the Dead. It is constantly stressed that one "who knows this spell" is safe from the dangers of the realm of death. The clearest indications of the redemptive function of this knowledge occur in the "Book of the Hidden Chamber," the netherworld book we usually call the Amduat, which was used in Dynasty 18 to decorate the royal tombs, especially the sarcophagus chamber. In its very title, the word *rḫ*, "to know," occurs nine times:

> Knowing the netherworldly *ba*s,
> knowing the hidden *ba*s,
> knowing the gates,
> and the paths that the Great God treads.
> Knowing what will be done,
> knowing what is in the hours, and their gods,
> knowing the course of the hours and their gods.
> Knowing the transfigurations for Re,
> knowing what he proclaims to them,
> knowing the thriving and the annihilated.

The book closes with the remark:

> The select manual, the mysterious writing of the Duat,
> which is known by none but the select.
> This representation is made in this manner
> in the hiddenness of the Duat,
> invisible, imperceptible!
> He who knows these secret images is a well-provided *akh*.
> He goes ever into and forth from the netherworld
> and ever speaks to the living.[12]

Here, it is clearly stated that the representations and texts in the tomb constitute a supply of knowledge that makes the one who knows them into a well-provided ancestral spirit endowed with freedom of movement. The Books of the Dead in the private tombs of the New Kingdom, and earlier, the Coffin Texts in the coffins of the Middle Kingdom had the same function.

The knowledge entailed here is derived from sources other than those to which we are accustomed: not from observation, measurement, and calculation but from intuition and imagination. The Egyptian Books of the Netherworld describe a reality beyond empirical experience, "invisible, imperceptible." These books arise from an imagistic form of cognition that interprets the cosmos in terms of human aspirations. They are the wish-fulfillment of the soul, not a representation of empirical reality.

Therein lies the justification of the psychological explanation of the Amduat by Andreas Schweizer and Erik Hornung.[13] These are not representations; they are an interpretation of reality, an interpretation determined by wishful fantasies.

The psychic-emotional component of the Amduat and the other Books of the Netherworld becomes clear when we ask with what justification scholars generally interpret them as mortuary literature and take them to be related to the problem of death. They are in tombs, to be sure, but this could be a secondary use. Their actual place, or *sitz im leben*, might be somewhere else altogether. I have myself taken this point of view and proposed the sun cult as the context where they were originally used. This point of view rests on a text that I continue to regard as decisive for the question of the functional context of this tradition regarding knowledge. It is not found in tombs but rather in sun temples, and it deals with the cultic role of the king as priest of the sun god.[14] Knowledge plays a central role in this text, as well, and it concerns the very matters listed in the title of the Amduat:

King N. knows
that mysterious language spoken by the eastern souls
as they sing the praises of Re
when he rises, when he appears in Light-land
when they open the door-leaves for him
at the gates of the eastern Light-land,
when he fares on the ways of the sky.

He knows their (actual, mysterious) appearance
and their embodiments,
their home (lit., "cities") in God's Land.
He knows the place where they stand
when Re begins his journey.

He knows that language
that the two crews speak when they tow the barque of He-of-the-horizon.

He knows the birthing of Re
and his transformation in the waters.
He knows that mysterious gate through which the Great God emerges,
he knows the one who is in the day barque
and the great image that is in the night barque;
he knows your landing-places in Light-land
and your steering equipment in the goddess of the sky.

Here, the verb "to know," which appears nine times in the Amduat, is repeated seven times and in reference to no fewer than thirteen things:

1. the eastern souls
      their language
      appearance
      embodiments
      home cities
      the place where they stand
2. the crews
      their language
3. the sun god
      his birthing
      his (spontaneous) origin
      the mysterious gate through which he rises
      the one in the morning barque
      the image (i.e., the moon) in the night barque
      his landing places
      his steering equipment (i.e., his course)

The king needs this knowledge, not to be saved from death as a transfigured *akh* and to be able to go forth and enter but to be able to contribute,
as a priest of the sun, to the success of the sun's course by means of his
liturgical recitations. The literature from which the king, or the solar
priests appointed by him, obtained this knowledge is preserved to us only
in small extracts. This literature would have been in the form of cosmo-
graphies like the Amduat, but it would have referred to the diurnal as well
as the nocturnal journey of the sun. The preserved fragments stem from
the Book of the Day, the cosmographical supplement to the hymns of the
wake, which constituted its liturgical part.[15]

The purpose of the liturgical recitations of the solar cult was to accompany the songs of praise addressed to the sun god by the celestial congregation of adorants—in the case of the morning prayer, the "eastern
souls." It was thus important for the sun priest to know their "language."
In the text just cited, there was the language of the eastern *ba*s, as well as
that of the two "crews." The latter were the crews of the two barques in
which the sun traveled, across the sky in the daytime and through the
netherworld at night. The oral accompaniment to the course of the sun
thus lasted all day, during his crossing of the sky as well as during his nocturnal journey through the netherworld. There is every reason to think
that on earth, the cultic accompaniment of the course of the sun began
in the evening and continued through the night, and that connected with
the nocturnal liturgies was the concept of joining in the songs of praise
of the netherworldly congregations of adorants.[16] The Amduat refers to
these next-worldly liturgies:

> Knowing the transfigurations for Re,
> knowing what he proclaims to them.

When we look at the speeches of this sort in the Amduat, we see that they play a dominating role. The liturgical, "transfigurative" element is at least as important as the descriptive element. The same is true for all the other Books of the Netherworld—especially the Litany of Re, of course, which is purely liturgical, but also the Book of Gates and the Book of Caverns.

Borrowing a formula from Peter Schäfer, a specialist in Judaism, I have called this principle *unio liturgica*.[17] This is not a matter of merging with the divine in the sense of an *unio mystica* but rather an entry into the next-worldly congregations of adorants in the sense of an *unio liturgica*. Connected with this concept of *unio liturgica* is the idea of redeeming power. One who knows how to join in the liturgy of the next-worldly beings by means of his own liturgical recitations belongs to those beings and has a share in their blessed destiny: from this, the knowledge produced and handed down in the cult of the sun god drew its transfigurative power, that is, a power to redeem from death.

The principle of *unio liturgica* doubtless referred at first to the cultic function of this knowledge; its use as royal mortuary literature was a secondary development. The solar cult rested on the concept of a temporary entry of the officiant into the next-worldly "congregations" of the eastern and western *ba*s. Thus, Queen Nedjmet states in her Book of the Dead papyrus:

> Osiris Nedjmet, vindicated, knows
> those words that the eastern souls speak;
> Osiris Nedjmet is in the midst of your tribunal,
> Osiris, and she enters into the crew of Re, every day.[18]

This becoming one with the eastern souls is also depicted in the art: for example, when the sun priest is depicted in the midst of baboons, the form the eastern souls assume when they pray to the sun god.[19] In cultic speech, the speaker enters into a context in the realm of the gods, playing the role of divine beings. He identifies himself with them, or, as it is stated in Egyptian, he "joins them":

> I have sung hymns to the sun,
> I have joined the solar apes,
> I am one of them.
> I made myself the companion of Isis and strengthened her magical power.[20]

Pronouncing a hymn to the sun, in the capacity of a priest and in the framework of prescribed cultic proceedings, an individual joined the adorants of the god in the divine realm, becoming "one of them" for the duration of the proceedings.[21]

All cultic ceremonies presupposed such a transformation. Truly great things happened. In the context of the verses cited above from Book of the Dead chapter 100, there is mention of other rituals:

> I have ferried the phoenix across to the east,
> and Osiris to Busiris.
> I have opened the vaults of Hapy
> and cleared the path of the sun.
> I have dragged Sokar on his sledge
> and empowered the Great One at the right moment. . . .
> I have knotted the rope,
> I repelled Apophis and drove him back.
> Re has extended his arms to me,
> and his crew will not drive me back.[22]

These are the words of someone who has participated in various festivals, rituals, and processions, and who could thus present himself as a member of constellations in the divine realm. Connected with the concept of membership were the motifs of initiation and secrecy:

> Re has led (the speaker) into his barque:
> he has seen the sacredness of He-in-his-*ouroboros*.
> He has beheld Re, namely, the three forms he assumes in the extension of
>   his blaze of light.
> He has prayed to him at his birth in the morning
> in his name of "Khepri,"
> he has praised him at midday
> in his name of "Re,"
> and he has soothed him in the evening
> in his name of "Atum."[23]

> How good it is to gaze with the eyes,
> how good it is to hear truth with the ears!
> . . . Osiris N. has not repeated what he has seen,
> Osiris N. has not told what he has heard in the House of the Mysteries:
> the jubilation for Re
> and the divine body of Re crossing Nun
> among those who satisfy the divine *ka* with what it desires.[24]

As represented in the texts cited, the principle of *unio liturgica*, in both the solar cult and mortuary belief, boils down to the following three points:

1. Initiation: I know the words with which the otherworldly ones praise you (knowledge).
2. Priestly activity in the cult: I praise you with these words (action).
3. Divine role: I belong to the otherworldly "congregation" (identity).

In the cult, this principle enabled communication with the realm of the gods and the integration of cultic activity into cosmic occurrences. In mortuary belief, it facilitated the deceased's entry into the realm of the gods and his transformation into a next-worldly, immortal identity in the constellations of the course of the sun. In the cult, it was a matter of keeping the cosmos in motion through ritual, while in mortuary belief, it was a matter of the individual human being, his closeness to the divine, and his immortality. Egyptian mortuary belief transformed the cultic-magical principles of cosmic influence and cooperation into the somewhat "mystical" principle of individual becoming one with the divine, the *unio liturgica*. Within this framework, knowledge of esoteric cult texts conferred divinity (belonging to the realm of the gods) and immortality. From the texts regarding the king as solar priest that we have cited above, it emerges clearly that this divinity and immortality, which rested on knowledge of the literature regarding the course of the sun, belonged to the role of the god-king and to the concept of the rule he exercised as something that kept the cosmos in motion, activity that continued, on earth, the creative work of the sun god.

Edward F. Wente has proposed a similar interpretation of the motif of knowledge in the Books of the Netherworld.[25] He wishes to interpret these books as "mystical" literature intended for the living, literature that was to make the knower one with the divine. In this connection, he refers to the remark, which occurs especially often in the Amduat, that the one who "executes" or "knows" these representations is an "image of the Great God." For Wente, the decisive factor is that the phrase "the one who knows these representations" refers not only to the dead but also to persons living "on earth":

> These (representations) are made according to this model
> in the hiddenness of the Duat.
> He who *executes* these representations
> is like the Great God himself.
> It is useful for him on earth, as proved true,
> it is very useful for him in the Duat,
> like the mystery that is written.[26]

In these remarks, certain variants sometimes replace the word *jrj*, "to do, to carry out, to execute," with *rḫ*, "to know," as, for instance, in the shorter version of the Amduat:

> These (representations) are made according to this model
> in the hiddenness of the Duat.
> He who *knows* these representations
> is like the Great God himself.
> It is useful for him on earth, as proved true,
> it is very useful for him in the Duat.[27]

There are other remarks in which the variants differ in the same way. The principal textual tradition reads:

> This is made according to this model, which is painted
> on the east side of the hidden chamber in the Duat.
> It is useful for the one who *knows* it on earth,
> in the sky, and in the earth.[28]

In the version in the tomb of the vizier User, however, we read: "It is useful for the one who *executes* it . . . "How are we to understand this "execute"? Wente thinks it is the placement of the wall decoration in the sarcophagus chamber, with the result that the artists who did the work came into the enjoyment of this usefulness. It seems rather more likely to me, though, that the reference is to the liturgical use of the texts in the solar cult, that is, while carrying out the ritual, for which the knowledge of these texts would render the sun priest competent. In any case, this is how the verb *jrj* is to be understood in the text of the seventh hour:

> This magic of Isis and of the ancient charm is *made*,
> in order to drive Apopis away from Re in the West,
> in the hiddenness of the Duat.
> It is also *executed* on earth.
> He who *executes* it is one who is in the sun barque,
> in the sky and in the earth.
> It is a little thing to know this representation!
> He who does not know it cannot drive away Neha-Her ("fearsome of
>   face").[29]

Here, the verb *jrj*, "to do," clearly refers to ritual performance and not to copying an original. In the short version, we again read: "He who *knows* it is one who is in the sun barque . . ." Here, too, mental knowledge replaces practical performance. In any case, it is important that in the remarks, it is constantly stressed that this knowledge is also important for the living. Many of these remarks confine themselves to merely affirming *akh*-effectiveness. The one who knows it is like the Great God himself, travels in the sun barque, is able to repel Neha-Her, or:

> He who knows this on earth is one
> whose water Neha-Her cannot drink up.[30]

The question is whether these explanations also refer to existence on earth or whether they are directed at life after death. Is someone already alive on earth, to whom this knowledge is recommended as effective (*akh*), to be like the Great God, to travel in the sun barque, to repel Neha-Her, and to be spared the latter's unquenchable thirst? This is how Wente understands these promises. Or will the knowing one enjoy these effects after his death, in the afterlife? It seems to me there are remarks that point in this direction, among them the following:

> Knowing the mysterious *bas*.
> He who knows their names on earth,
> he approaches the place where Osiris is,
> and he is given water in that field of his.[31]

I do not think that an *unio mystica* during life is the aim here. What this example refers to is the possibility of obtaining this redeeming knowledge while still alive on earth, a knowledge that will be beneficial later, in the afterlife. This was precisely the function of initiation in the Greek mystery cults. These initiations conveyed a knowledge that helped the living to enjoy a happy life, but above all, to enjoy a blissful destiny in the afterlife. Here, too, it was a matter of finding the right path in the world beyond, the path that led to Persephone and the Elysian fields, and of drinking from the right sources. The Amduat can also be understood in this sense. It contained a redemptive knowledge that enabled the sun priest to carry out the rituals that accompanied the course of the sun, but which also enabled all in possession of it to free themselves from the realm of death and make their way to the side of the redeemed. The question, then, is who we understand to be among the knowing ones. The Amduat supplies an interesting, but ambiguous, answer to this question:

> This is made in the hiddenness of the Duat,
> in such a way that it is sacred and hidden,
> because of the selectness of those who know it.[32]

Here, Wente thinks of secret societies, similar to the mystery cults of Greece, and he argues energetically against the connection I have drawn with the king and the sun cult, and thus against a purely cultic framework for the *unio liturgica* in question.

Similar to Wente, Reinhold Merkelbach and Maria Totti have concluded that in Egypt, living persons were inducted into knowledge about the afterlife and the course of the sun, knowledge like that codified in the Books of the Netherworld. Referring to the verses cited above from the Book of the Dead of Queen Nedjmet, they write, "When the trans-figured queen knew the language of the gods, she was inducted already during her lifetime."[33] They cite these verses to establish the Egyptian background of the Leiden *kosmopoiie* (creation story). In that text, the primeval god and creator of the cosmos is called upon "in all voices and languages," by which, exactly as in the Egyptian texts, is meant the words with which the members of the divine congregation of adorants praise their god. Just like the "king as sun priest," "the initiate of our text (that is, the Leiden text) knows those sacred words with which the gods in the sun barque have greeted the sun god as he rises," and, "An adorant of the sun god on earth joins in the song of praise that is addressed to the god in the sky, and he legitimates himself by repeating the words of the gods."[34] The ancient Egyptian understanding of the principle of *unio litur-gica* cannot be described more clearly than this. The only thing different from the Greek text is that the Egyptian priest did not have to legitimize himself. His legitimacy lay in his office and in the institution of the cult. He did not speak as N. but as a representative of the king, whose con-course with the gods was legitimated by the divinity of his office. It was a different matter, of course, when such texts were taken over into the mor-tuary literature and placed into the mouth of a deceased person, who addressed them to the god not in the exercise of a priestly office but as the deceased N., who was in need of personal closeness to the divine. Here, already within the Egyptian tradition, an individualizing reinter-pretation of the cultic words was undertaken. A further step was taken by applying it to the living N., who desired to enjoy personal closeness to the divine already during his lifetime. The Graeco-Egyptian prayers and ini-tiation ceremonies were the culmination of this step.

The concern of Merkelbach and Totti is to call attention to the gener-ally Egyptian background of the Leiden creation text. The concept of *unio liturgica*, however, designates a specific tradition. Not only is it the basic principle of Egyptian hymns, it is especially to be found where it is a matter of exclusive texts, texts that were evidently accessible only to initi-ates, texts "that are not known to any men other than the select," as we read in the Amduat. This statement has to do with the leitmotif of a cultic tradition that I have called the "mysteries" of the sun cult because of its evident exclusivity.[35] There is an obvious connection between the claim of a text to reproduce the "mysterious speech" of other-worldly adorants and its actually being kept secret.

The conditions under which the Amduat and the other Books of the Netherworld were transmitted—during the New Kingdom, they appeared almost exclusively in royal tombs—clearly confirm their highly exclusive character. In the form of mortuary literature, this store of knowledge was at the disposal only of kings. During the New Kingdom, the step from cultically legitimated king to private N. had not yet been taken, with the sole exception of the vizier Amenuser, who was allowed to use the Amduat and the Litany of Re in the decoration of his sarcophagus chamber. This need not mean that only kings belonged to those who could acquire this knowledge already "on earth," during their lifetimes.[36] But it was probably not a matter of secret societies in the sense of the Greek mysteries, societies whose beliefs people could profess and into which they could have themselves initiated. It was simply a matter of the normal, official Egyptian sun cult, which rested on the principle of identification with that which belonged to the divine realm. But with this principle, and this is the decisive point in our context, there was connected the hope of salvation from death. Whoever belonged to the congregations of adorants of the sun god would stand forever on the side of life. That was the hope that characterized the Books of the Netherworld. They "describe" the netherworld from the point of view of salvation.

The Amduat represents the netherworld in three aspects: as "realm of death," as "Elysium," and as "place of punishment." But these aspects are not distributed over separate sections or regions of the world beyond; rather, they are present in every one of the twelve hourly divisions of the night. As he passes through, the sun god wakens the deceased from the sleep of death, and by what he says to them, he endows them with Elysian conditions. But in the process, he also passes through the regions where punishment is meted out, which assume the character of a Hell.[37] The "realm of death" is not a place of punishment, it is a place where the dead are simply dead, which in the Amduat is represented as sleep. But each night, they are awakened from this sleep. From the places of punishment, however, there is no salvation. Humans could only strive for salvation from them before the fact, not after. The Amduat thus represents the netherworld as a drama of salvation and annihilation. It conveys a redemptive knowledge that can save people from the places of punishment and from remaining in the state of death.

The principle of *unio liturgica* refers not only to knowledge and language but also to action and ritual performance. We see this in the variants of the remarks in the Amduat, where instead of "knowledge," the "execution" of the original is mentioned. This practical-ritual aspect of *unio liturgica* is expressed more clearly still in the remarks of the Book of Gates, where the offering plays the same role that knowledge does in the Amduat. In the Amduat, it is the knowing one who is promised a share in the immortality of the transfigured ones, while in the Book of Gates, it is the one who makes offerings. The Book of Gates talks not of "he who knows this on earth" but of "he who offers to them (i.e., the beings who are described) on earth." As to the understanding of this stereotyped formula, which is repeated constantly in the first nine hours of the Book of Gates, I agree with Wente, who also sees this offering as a mystical act that conveys a share in the essence of those in the netherworld.[38] With this interpretation of the formula, the principle of *unio liturgica* assumes a new meaning. Just as the one who speaks joins in the words of those in the netherworld and thereby becomes one of them, so the one who makes an offering communicates with those in the netherworld and becomes one of them through his ritual action. These formulas lend expression to the longing for affiliation that underlies the image of death as isolation. What is important here is to be one of those who enjoy status and rank in the world beyond. Offering to them on earth forms a bond with them during life, a bond that is then rewarded after death by admission into the circle of those who received the offerings.

In the Book of Gates, the one who offers to the beings represented acquires a share in their salvation. Offerings are made to the transfigured spirits, not in order to save them but in order to gain a share in their salvation. Even more clearly than in the Amduat, the remarks of the Book of Gates, with their constant repetition of the phrase "on earth," stress that this information was important not just for the dead but also for the living. In the remarks that accompany the offerings, the one who makes these offerings to the described beings "on earth" is promised membership in their society. He will himself become a member of the groups to whom he makes these offerings. The mortuary cult assures membership in the society of the provisioned and the redeemed.[39]

Here as well, it seems to me that there is a straight line leading to the Hellenistic Isis mysteries, for the cult in which the initiates participated was a mortuary cult. In any case, it had to do with a communication with the world beyond that was "useful" (*akh*), at least as much so for those on earth as for those in the realm of the dead. The one who communicated with the dead did not just assure the latter's salvation in the status of a transfigured ancestral spirit: above all, he assured his own share in this salvation. Mortuary cult and mortuary concepts were ritual and spiritual exercises that had the power to confer freedom from the yoke of transitoriness. In that fact lay the importance of the mortuary cult for those who were still alive.

As described in the Books of the Netherworld, the cosmos is designed with reference to man and his longing for eternal life. These texts document not so much theoretical knowledge as an explanation of the cosmos that yields understanding. They do not deduce meaning but rather impute it, and they make use of language to confer meaning on the world. They "describe" a normative reality that the Egyptians called *maat*, a reality that is not yet realized in the given circumstances, but in whose direction the given circumstances must be steered.

In ancient Egypt, the course of the sun and the destiny of the dead, the sun cult and the mortuary cult, were the two processes whose ritual articulation and accompaniment provoked and produced many important normative descriptions. In the sun cult, these ritual words became pregnant with meaning under the designation "the elevation of *maat.*" With the recitation of solar hymns, "normative reality," the ultimate meaning behind events, was to ascend to the sun, so as to influence its course in the ways described in the hymns. In both contexts, in the hymns to the sun and in the mortuary transfiguration spells, the concern was with imparting life and with freedom from the yoke of transitoriness, not only through knowledge but also and above all through words. The sun cult and the mortuary cult consisted in the ritual enactment of the commentary, an enactment that imparted meaning and success to that which was done.

3. Salvation through Divine Grace

Did Egyptian mortuary religion entail a sort of gnosis that promised human self-salvation through understanding and knowledge? Did the mortuary literature really supply a means of freeing oneself, by dint of one's own effort, from the yoke of transitoriness and thus a means of attaining the imperishability of divine, eternal life? The innumerable prayers for salvation in the mortuary literature deny this. These prayers are concerned above all with the idea of the Judgment of the Dead, which no one could hope to survive without divine grace. The well-known chapter 17 of the Book of the Dead is a compendium of the most necessary knowledge of the world beyond; it goes back to the Coffin Texts, and it is lacking in scarcely any Book of the Dead. The second part of this chapter consists almost exclusively of such appeals for salvation in the Judgment of the Dead:

> O Re, . . . may you save N. from that god with mysterious form,
> whose eyebrows are the beam of the scale,
> on that night of reckoning with the sinner,
> (from the god) who binds the evildoer to the slaughtering block,
> (the god) who cuts up *ba*s.
>
> May you save N. from these guardians of the passageways,
> the slaughterers with skillful fingers,
> they who painfully decapitate, who are in the following of Osiris!
> They must not get hold of me,
> I must not fall into their cauldrons.
> . . .

404

> O Atum, . . .
> save N. from that god
> who robs *ba*s and devours rotted stuff,
> who lives on putrefaction,
> the companion of the dimness, the one who is in darkness,
> who is feared by the weary dead!
>
> O Khepri, . . .
> save N. from those judges
> whom the All-lord has endowed with magical power
> to guard his enemies,
> who spread disaster in the places of execution,
> from whose watch there is no escape.[40]

The concern here is to be saved from the places where punishment is meted out in the netherworld and where those condemned in the Judgment of the Dead are sent, figurations of the "second death," that is, of ultimate disappearance from the sphere of life. In the very scene of the Judgment of the Dead itself, as depicted in chapter 125, the deceased turns to his judges with pleas for salvation. He says to the forty-two members of the tribunal:

> Save me, protect me,
> institute no proceedings against me in the presence of the Great God.
> I am one with pure mouth and pure hands,
> to whom "welcome" is said by all who see him.[41]

He addresses Osiris, the Great God himself, with the words,

> May you save me from these emissaries of yours,
> who inflict bloodshed and interrogate with pain,
> whose faces betray no mercy,
> for I have done *maat* for the lord of *maat*.[42]

The deceased thus turns to each of these two authorities with a request to be saved from the other one. Egyptians placed their greatest hopes for salvation from death and oblivion on three deities: on the sun god, on Osiris, and on the mother-goddess Nut. The sun god and Osiris had redemptive power, for they themselves had undergone the fate of death, the one each night, and the other in the time of myth, *in illo tempore*. For this reason, they were called on for salvation by all the other gods, and humans also put their fate in their hands. Over both, however, there stood the mother-goddess Nut, for she represented the eternal life granted to Re and Osiris beyond the threshold of death. Re and Osiris owed their immortality not to their own power but to the fact that they were the sons of the mother- and sky-goddess Nut. This filiation constituted the sacramental explanation of placement in the coffin and in the tomb, and with that, the final goal of the burial that was accompanied by the transfiguration rituals.

Egypt and the History of Death

L ike scarcely any other religion, we may view that of ancient Egypt as the antithesis of our own cultural experience. On this point, the Bible is correct: to renounce cosmotheism and adopt monotheism, it is necessary to leave Egypt. With our belief in a single god who excludes all others and says of himself "I am who I am," we became who we are, giving up our symbiotic relationship to a deified "World." To the religious concept of monotheism, there corresponds a "monotheism" of the consciousness, of the autonomous, centered, and homogeneous Self. The "Mosaic distinction," which introduced a boundary between true and false religion and in the process created the mental space we inhabit,[1] also excluded the realm of the dead. No religion has renounced the dead and the possibility of communicating with them so thoroughly as our own, Western religion, characterized as it is by biblical monotheism. Among the boundaries and taboos that monotheism has erected against "heathendom," the most significant is that against the various ways of contacting the dead. We cannot recross this threshold in the history of consciousness, but we can at least make ourselves aware of what we have left behind, if only not to fall into the error of thinking that our view of the world is in any way natural, self-evident, or even universal. It is not; quite the contrary, it is extreme, and it results from a series of distinctions and exclusions that began with the Exodus from Egypt. If we cast our gaze backward—and to this purpose, we have the luxury of a discipline like Egyptology—it is not out of nostalgia or "longing for the origin." Rather, it is to come to grips with who and what we are and to come to a better understanding of other cultures, cultures that have not trodden this path.

From the example of Egypt, we have seen how death can be imagined and experienced in the framework of a cosmotheistic religion. There is, first of all, the "symbiotic" aspect of death, which emerges most clearly in the image of death as return. With the act of being placed in the coffin and buried, the deceased enters the womb of the Great Mother, the sky-goddess: all life comes from her, and in her body, the deceased is rejuvenated in the eternal cycle of life, on the model of the sun. In this way, death is integrated into a superordinate concept of life that finds renewal, not an end, in death. For the Egyptians, death was a passage to a continuation of life, though in an altered state. Even gods died, and this fact in no way contradicted the Egyptian concepts of divinity and immortality. Dying, they did not withdraw from the cosmic symbiosis. That even the gods could die did not mean that they were finite. Cosmic life was an interaction of the unchanging duration of Osiris and the ceaseless renewal of Re.

Second, and most important of all, stress must be placed on the "constellative" aspect of death. The Egyptian did not picture death as the end of his very self, with all the corresponding fear and angst. While still alive, he knew he was embedded in constellations that constituted him as self and person, son or daughter, husband or wife, father or mother, citizen, subject, government official, soldier, scribe, priest, songstress, and so forth, relationships in which he developed and learned, relationships that sustained him, even beyond the threshold of death, just as deceased persons were linked to him during his lifetime. In Egypt, each individual stood in a framework of reference to which both the living and the dead belonged. This might seem disconcerting to us, but the concept that after death, we live on in others, and that the dead live on in us, is not entirely foreign to us. In an address entitled "Living On in the Memory of Posterity," read before the Masonic lodge Amalia in Weimar on October 24, 1812, Christoph Martin Wieland set forth how man, to the extent that he lives for others, remains present after death in the recollection of posterity: "Does a noble-minded man not live less for himself than for others? Is not his existence more or less a perpetual self-sacrifice? For this reason, from antiquity on, has not a gradually self-consuming light been the most beautiful symbol of a noble and good man? And may we not also say with truth, that living in the recollection of posterity—for that is only the most natural consequence of a distinguished and lasting contribution—is of the same stuff as the previous, visible life among one's contemporaries, and that this recollection is regarded as a truly constant personality in itself." These impressive words touch directly on the Egyptian mystery of the "social self" and of its presence, which lasted beyond the boundary of death. The tremendous success of "systemic" psychotherapy, especially in the direction represented by Bert Hellinger, also shows that we are addressing—indeed, we are dependent on—aspects of existence that stood at the center of Egyptian culture but have faded away in our own. Hellinger works with "family teams," reconstructing the constellations in which a given client is involved in order to bring to light, through this representation of his framework of references, his hidden self, we could even say, his "social self" in the Egyptian sense.[2] Deceased family members also regularly play a central role in these "teams." In such therapeutic methods, anthropological truths return into the light, truths that in other societies, and especially in ancient Egypt, were a ritual part of the general culture.

At the outset, we made a distinction between "pieced-on death" and "life permeated by death," and we assigned Egypt to the latter category. In doing so, we took note of Kierkegaard and Heidegger, who understood life from the standpoint of death, so as to make the category of life permeated with death comprehensible in its general sense, over and above the specific example of ancient Egypt. Kierkegaard and Heidegger, however, stood firmly on the ground of Western individualism. They understand death as an individual experience, and everything else as "constellative." In this respect, existentialism represents a position that is the exact opposite of the Egyptian understanding of death.[3] The Egyptian did not love death, but for him, death was no existential drama, for his self, that is, his "social self," extended far beyond death, that is, beyond his "corporal self," which had to undergo this death. An Egyptian did not die absolutely. He died for those who stood in a relationship to him and who sustained this relationship to him beyond death; in the case of the "loving son," a whole new, intensive relationship only now began. Each death was, or at least harbored, the chance of resurrection into a new life that was lived largely in the continuity of earthly constellations.

This "symbiotic" relationship to death was not peculiar to Egyptian culture, it was a typical manifestation of early societies. What was peculiar to ancient Egypt was the massive expenditure on tomb construction. For those of the upper class, at least, who built monumental, inscribed tombs, these sums were expended on the tomb of a single individual. These persons invested in "their individual" death, or rather, in their survival of it, and they made this survival in the form of a tomb their life's goal. Must we not therefore think that in the upper class, at least, these forms of self-eternalizing through self-monumentalizing led to an individualizing of death, while the middle and lower classes, who were often buried in family tombs and in other forms of collective tombs, were less clearly focused on their individual self and its claim to immortality, or perhaps even placed no value whatsoever on it? We must first recollect that even the individual tomb, however monumental it might have been, was always embedded in the referential system of a necropolis. Among its many other functions and aspects, each tomb was also a medium of social integration. The other problem, however, remains: the enormous social inequality that is reflected in the morphology of Egyptian tombs. Are we not to think that there was a correspondingly great discrepancy in the images of death and the concepts of the afterlife? Here, we touch upon a problem of much wider scope. "Immortality is not everyone's thing," as Kurt Schwitter has said. Death, which makes all equal, provokes and produces the most extreme forms of inequality. The desire for individual immortality has always been an elite phenomenon.

This point is especially true of the Egyptian tomb culture, with its decorated tombs and inscribed coffins, Books of the Dead, stelae, offering tables, and so forth, whose texts and representations are the sources of our reconstruction of ancient Egyptian concepts of death and the afterlife. Have we not, in this book, described the conceptual world and the practice of an insignificantly small upper class? Is the thesis from which we began perhaps a purely upper class phenomenon: that man creates a cultural realm so as to be able to live with the knowledge of his finitude? These considerations impose themselves especially with a view to Egypt. The pyramids of the Old Kingdom have always raised the question of whether these monuments sprang from the prideful drive for immortality of almighty despots who enslaved an entire people in their effort to monumentalize themselves, pointing the way for their henchmen to imitate them on a smaller scale. We have described the mortuary images and rituals of such tomb owners, and we must now ask to what extent they might have been representative of what we call "Egyptian culture." This is especially true of the striking relationship between tomb ownership and authorship in Egyptian thought. Only a literate class, one that not only could write but who also viewed writing as the epitome of, and the medium of choice for, all cultural and social self-development, could have thought of parallels between tomb and book, between mortuary cult and literary communication addressed by author to reader. We must not generalize such views. In this regard, the Egyptian tomb owners stood much closer to the poets, philosophers, and artists of whom George Steiner wrote (see p. 9 above) than did the peasants of their own time and culture.

There can be no doubt about the fact that culture as a space of remembrance into which one inserts oneself through the medium of writing and representation so as to live on "virtually" is a highly elite view of things.

But the question is whether such a view existed completely independently and unexpectedly in the context of more widespread views and thus cannot be considered representative of the basic structures of Egyptian culture and of the relationship between death and culture overall. As for Egypt, I wish to point to three peculiarities of this culture in this regard.

First: It is certainly correct that only one or two percent, and in the New Kingdom, perhaps five percent, of the population could read and write.[4] Yet when we look at the representations on the walls of the tombs, which open so astonishing an insight into the world of the Egyptians, we see that scribes were everywhere. There was scarcely any area of life that did not, in some way, come in contact with writing. Only a few knew how to write, but what "writing" was, was hidden from no Egyptian. It was not an esoteric art of which most could not even dream but a cultural technology on which the entire state, with all its branches of knowledge and all its institutions, was based, and with which each person, in his own way, had something to do, even if he himself could not write. Its active mastery was perhaps highly restricted, but its influence was all-encompassing and all-penetrating, along with knowledge about writing and all that was connected with it.

Second: The Egyptians were masters of minimalization. Everything was capable of reduction. The basic form of a monumental tomb could be reduced to a tiny false door, mortuary offerings to a couple of drops of water and a prayer, embalming and mummification to a few daubs of oil and some cheap bandages. On a pars pro toto basis, some intimations could replace an entire ritual. We must thus reckon that in however minimal a form, the notions connected with these forms were spread throughout the population and reached even the lowest levels of society.

Third: The moralizing of immortality also meant its democratization. Even he who could not erect a monumental tomb perhaps had, in the framework of his circumstances, the possibility of leading a good life, holding himself to the "precepts of the Judgment of the Dead." The maxim that a (that is: a true) tomb is built by doing what is right or that virtue is the (true) monument of a man, considerably expanded access to immortality, for it made it independent of the possibility of material expenditures. Thus, continued Wieland in his address, "Perhaps many think that this sort of immortality . . . can be had by only relatively few. But such a thought can only arise from an incorrect appreciation of what it means to be of service. . . . It is not at all the case that glorious deeds, rare talents, distinguished works of art and literature, important inventions and discoveries, and the like have an exclusive right to the esteem and the gratitude of posterity; rather, virtue, a modest, quiet service demands all the more to emerge from obscurity, and a man who has served his native city (however small), of whatever sort it is, a particularly meritorious citizen, is incomparably more worthy than many a man who has stunned the world with the uproar of his deeds of having his memory held in honor by his descendants and his exemplary conduct held up to posterity, of living on beneficently among them."

Even one who was poor and needy in life could hope to find, in the afterlife, compensation for the cares and burdens of his existence on earth. The Demotic Story of Setne Khaemwese tells of this. Setne, the great priest and magus, on one occasion was witness to a state funeral.

He looked down from the bay window of his house, and he saw a rich man being taken to the desert necropolis amid loud cries of mourning, with great honors and rich burial goods. When he looked down another time, he saw a poor man being carried out of Memphis into the desert, wrapped only in a mat and with no procession whatsoever. He said, "By [Ptah, the great god, how much better off are the rich,] who are buried with loud cries of mourning and with rich burial goods, than the poor, who are carried into the desert [unaccompanied and without anything]!" But the boy Si-Osiris said to his father: "May it go with you in the realm of the dead as it will go with this poor man in the realm of the dead! May it not go with you as it will go with this rich man in the realm of the dead when you one day enter the realm of the dead!" Taken aback by these words, the father was thereupon led by his son into the realm of the dead. [In the fifth hall, they saw the rich man, "who was pleading and lamenting loudly," for "the pivot of the door was fixed in his right eye." In the sixth hall,] "Setne saw the gods of the Judgment of the Dead, who stood there according to their rank, and he saw the servants of the land of the dead standing there and making accusations." [In the seventh hall, they saw] "the form of Osiris, the great god, sitting on his throne of pure gold, bedecked with the *atef*-crown, with Anubis, the great god, on his left and the great god Thoth on his right. The gods of the Judgment of the Dead stood to his right and his left. The scale was set up in the middle before them, and bad deeds were being weighed against good ones. Thoth, the great god, was keeping a record, and Anubis was giving information to his colleague. If someone was found to have more bad deeds than good, he was handed over to the "Devouress" of the lord of the realm of the dead. His soul was annihilated, along with his body, and he could never again breathe. But if someone was found to have more good deeds than bad, he was placed among the gods of the tribunal of the lord of the realm of the dead, and his soul went to the sky along with those of the august transfigured spirits. If someone's good deeds had the same weight as the bad, he was placed among the blessed spirits who serve the god Sokar-Osiris. Then Setne saw a distinguished man, who was dressed in a garment of royal linen, near the place where Osiris was. The rank that he held was very high." [This distinguished man was none other than the poor man whose corpse Setne had seen being carried out of the city with no procession.] "His good deeds were found to be more numerous than his bad ones in relationship to his lifetime, which Thoth had assigned to him in writing at his birth, and in relationship to his luck on earth. So the command was made before Osiris that the burial equipment of the rich man be given to the poor man, and that he be placed among the august transfigured spirits as a man of god who serves Sokar-Osiris, near the place of Osiris. But that rich man was also brought to the netherworld, and his bad deeds were weighed against his good ones. His bad deeds were found to be more numerous than the good ones he had done on earth. So it was ordered to carry him away and to punish him in the realm of the dead."[5]

In this tale, the moralizing of postmortem destiny leads to a complete reversal of earthly circumstances. The first become the last, and the last become the first. But in this matter, we see that here, we are already in another world. This Demotic tale from the Hellenistic Period contains an astonishing mixture of classical Egyptian motifs and concepts derived from the Greek and early Jewish traditions. A classical Egyptian motif is the description of the Judgment of the Dead. In the Book of the Dead of Ani from the beginning of the thirteenth century B.C.E., we see, just as in the Demotic tale, symbols for "lifetime," "birth," and "luck" represented in connection with the scale, symbols that are supposed to guarantee that the judgment will turn out correctly in view of individual possibilities and circumstances.[6]

It is quite otherwise, however, with the reversal of earthly circumstances. We find nothing of this sort in texts from earlier periods. Already in Ptahhotep, we read that "the greedy one has no tomb," and thus that reckless endeavors at enrichment lead to riches on earth but not to perpetuation in the memory of posterity or to the status of a transfigured ancestral spirit. Even here, though, the essential agreement between the judgment of human society and the divine Judgment of the Dead is not placed in question. The Judgment of the Dead does not set the judgment of society on its head but rather confirms and seals it. The same *maat* that guarantees success and continuance in life is also the standard of the Judgment of the Dead and leads to immortality. Those who judge the dead see what is good and what is not good in the same way as our fellow men. What is subversively new in the Story of Setne Khaemwese and Si-Osiris is that those who judge the dead measure with a different yardstick then do men. One highly regarded on earth becomes a wretch in the afterlife, while one despised on earth attains a glorious destiny. This is precisely the point made by Jesus in the story of the poor man Lazarus, who in life lay covered with sores at the door of the rich man and now, in death, rests in the bosom of Abraham, while the rich man languishes in Hell: "what is prized by human beings is an abomination in the sight of God." With this motif, the Demotic tale takes a large and decisive step beyond the realm of classical Egyptian conceptions but in a direction that is entirely situated within the latter.

The history of the moralizing of the afterlife, from the Old Kingdom court that only met when a complaint was made, via the Judgment of the Dead of the Middle and New Kingdoms, to which every deceased person was subject, to the Judgment of the Dead as it is described in the Demotic tale of Setne Khaemwese from the Graeco-Roman Period, traces a huge developmental arc, lending a thoroughly historical line to Egyptian mortuary belief. In the introductory chapter, I stated that the history of Egyptian mortuary religion cannot be written, for too much remained constant or changed too little in decisive ways. On this one point, though, here at the end of the book, this impression can be corrected. The idea of the Judgment of the Dead had a history, and it was the history of a judging god whose verdicts became, in the course of the millennia, ever less dependent on the judgment of earthly society and of the kingship. In the beginning, the verdict of the court in the next world depended entirely on the complaint, which was brought by men, the deceased, or even the gods against a newly deceased person. Later, the Judgment of the Dead became a permanent institution, but the verdict of the god only confirmed the verdict of society, placing it on an unshakeable basis. Only in the Hellenistic Period did the verdict of the Judgment of the Dead become entirely independent of that of men, with the measuring being done according to different standards. In closing, this single leitmotif can again be stressed; it not only ran through three millennia of the history of Egyptian religion, it also continued on into Christianity.

The experience of death, together with longing for freedom from the yoke of transitoriness, were at the core of Egyptian religion. In late antiquity, therefore, Christianity, which promised the same thing, must have exerted a fascinating power on the Egyptian mind. Christian rite, with its manifold sacramental explanations with regard to death and resurrection, must have fallen on soil that had been especially fruitful for thousands of years. Here, at the end of this volume, we can only intimate these concepts.

In the religion of ancient Israel, the concepts of the immortality of the soul and reward in an eternal life had as little a place as in Mesopotamian and Greek religion. In Egypt, however, this special connection between righteousness and immortality had long been at home. In Israel, God's righteousness was fulfilled in history. Good was rewarded and evil was revenged, but in this world, not the next one. Accounts that were not worked out within the framework of a lifetime were settled in the sequence of the generations. Here, history had the place that was occupied in Egyptian thought by the afterlife. Instead of personal immortality, there was the promised everlastingness of the People of God. The individual did not live on in the afterlife but in his posterity. In this one respect, Egyptian and Old Testament religion are in agreement, while in all other distinctions, they were different answers to the same questions. The questions did not originate from a longing for immortality, for this found a solution only in Egyptian religion, not in that of the Hebrew Bible, but from a longing for justice. The finitude of human life was experienced as something painful, not only with regard to the boundedness of its time but also and especially with regard to the imperfection of its fulfillment. Too much good remained unrewarded, too much evil remained unpunished, too much suffering remained meaningless and uncompensated, for human life to seem anything other than fragmentary. Longing for meaning and justice drove these cultures to examine horizons that reached beyond the span of a lifetime, horizons in which that which was uncompensated during life found its fulfillment. In Egypt, the afterlife represented this horizon of fulfillment, while in Israel, it was history. The Egyptian concept of a horizon of fulfillment concerned the individual, his personal biography, and his equally personal destiny in the afterlife. The Israelite conception of a horizon of fulfillment had only to do with the People of God, its collective history following the Exodus from Egypt, and its future promise as a godsend to all peoples. The latter led ultimately to messianism, which in its radical expression as eschatology and apocalypticism left real history behind it and extended the horizon of fulfillment beyond the end of time into a new world and thus also advanced into a world beyond, but one that opened up not after the death of an individual but at the end of history.

The image of a judgment made a first breakthrough in the post-Exilic era, with Ezekiel. Now, under the shock of a historical catastrophe in which the people were obliged to pay for the sins of a history of blame that stretched back over more than two centuries, it was experienced as unbearable that sons had to pay for the sins of their fathers. Here, for the first time, there was talk of a "last straw." In this situation, Ezekiel promulgated a change:

> What do you mean by repeating this proverb concerning the land of Israel, "The parents have eaten sour grapes, and the children's teeth are set on edge"?
>
> As I live, says the Lord God, this proverb shall no more be used by you in Israel.
>
> Know that all lives are mine; the life of the parent as well as the life of the child is mine: it is only the person who sins that shall die. (Ezekiel 18:2–4)

Each will be judged according to his own deeds. Individual guilt thus replaces the responsibility of the collective or the generations. This was a major step in the direction of Egypt. Still, there is no talk of a reckoning in the afterlife or a hope of eternal life.[7]

It was only in the time of the Maccabean wars, around 170–160 B.C.E., that there was a further change in concepts of the afterlife, and it occurred in connection with martyrdom, which was formulated as an ideal for the first time. For the martyr, who performs the highest imaginable service by laying down his life, there can be no reward in this life. Here, the evident meaninglessness of the martyr's life is experienced as so intolerable that it absolutely calls for immediate recompense. One who wishes to maintain the righteousness of God is compelled to believe in an afterlife in which the martyr will receive his reward. From this time on, the concept that a martyr went straight to Paradise came to be accepted. In the time of Jesus, the Pharisees already believed in general immortality, while the Sadducees continued to reject such concepts. Christianity placed immortality and reward in the next life at the center of its beliefs regarding death. With his death on the cross and his descent into the realm of death, Christ overcame fear of that realm and opened the door to Elysium. With baptism, every Christian is promised a share in this immortality. At the end of time, the dead will rise and be judged. The good will go to eternal bliss, while the evil will be damned to eternal punishment in Hell. In the later history of the Christian West, there arose the idea of Purgatory. This idea led to a stronger individualizing of the concept of the Last Judgment, and time also came to play a much greater role. Each person will be judged immediately after death, so that, if necessary, he will be able to use the time until the Resurrection of the Dead paying for his sins in Purgatory. A glance at Western art shows to what an extent the Christian West was obsessed with the idea of the Judgment. Those judged guiltless went into the eternal blessedness of Paradise immediately after death, as had been believed in antiquity regarding martyrs. This Paradise had nothing to do with the realm of death of the Mesopotamian, Israelite, and Greek concepts of the netherworld, but it corresponded to the Elysium of Egyptian mortuary beliefs. It was a place where those redeemed from death enjoy eternal life, instead of leading a shadowy existence as dead people, as in the Israelite She'ol or the Greek Hades.

In Egypt, where such concepts had long been at home, these doctrines must have fallen on fertile soil indeed. The Egyptian Elysium, too, was entirely different from the She'ol of the Hebrew Bible or the Greek Hades, where the dead led only a shadowy existence. It was far more like Dante's *Paradiso*. The vindicated dead joined in the choruses that accompanied the sun god across the sky and surrounded Osiris in the netherworld, gazed on the countenance of the gods, and remained always close to them. Just this concept, that death is a threshold that brings us near to God and allows us to gaze upon Him face to face, links Christianity and Egypt, in sharp contradiction to the image of death in the Hebrew Bible, where one is close to God in life, while in death, there is no divine presence in She'ol. The prophet Isaiah says, "For Sheol cannot thank you, death cannot praise you; those who go down to the Pit cannot hope for your faithfulness" (38:18). The Psalms repeatedly state: "For in death there is no remembrance of you; in Sheol who can give you praise?" (6:5).[8] Ben Sira teaches, "Who will sing praises to the Most High in Hades in place of the living who give thanks? From the dead, as from one who does not exist, thanksgiving has ceased; those who are alive and well sing the Lord's praises" (Ecclesiasticus 17:27–28).[9] In Christianity (as otherwise also in post-Biblical Judaism and in Islam), the situation is the exact reverse: the blessed dead enter into an *unio liturgica* with the choirs of angels.

It can certainly be objected that in Egypt, there was no demand for this supply, for the native religion already made the same promises. But in late antiquity, the native religion must have been accessible only to a small number of specialists. Knowledge of the hieroglyphs was highly restricted, and religious life had become a matter for experts, played out mostly behind the high walls and closed gates of the temples. The typical Egyptian longing for salvation from death presumably no longer found fulfillment in the native tradition. With Christianity, which was in large part fashioned from the same traditions, something returned to Egypt that had already mostly dried up and fallen into oblivion there.

In Egypt, the concept of salvation from death had always been connected with the image of the king as a god incarnate who dwelled on earth. The god Osiris, whom every deceased person hoped to follow into immortality, bore the traits of a king. In Egyptian thought, kingship and the overcoming of death were a combination to which the Jewish notion of a Messiah was foreign. I shall not go so far as to say that these ideas came from Egypt—who knows how they came into Christianity?—but I shall affirm that they represented an approach—and from the point of view of the Hebrew Bible, even a return—to Egypt. No matter whence Christianity derived these ideas, they brought it closer to the world of Egypt, and this perhaps contributed to the fact that Christianity enjoyed so early and such an overwhelming success in Egypt.

If longing for immortality was an elite phenomenon that concerned only those few whose care for mere existence was fulfilled by other means, the opposite was true of the longing for justice. In its various post-Israelite expressions in Judaism, Christianity, and Islam, monotheism succeeded in combining both goals and in making the Egyptian formula of immortality through righteousness into an idea of salvation for every believer.

Notes

INTRODUCTION. DEATH AND CULTURE

1. I use the translation of E. A. Speiser, "Adapa," in J. B. Pritchard, ed., *Ancient Near Eastern Texts Relating to the Old Testament*, 2d ed. (Princeton, 1955), pp. 101–103. The oldest attestation of the text stems from the archive of cuneiform tablets at Tell el-Amarna in Egypt (fourteenth century B.C.E.). K. Deller has kindly informed me that the myth itself stems from the Old Babylonian Period. According to E. Ebeling, *Tod und Leben nach den Vorstellungen der Babylonier* (Berlin, 1931), p. 27a, *a-da-ap* is equated with "man" in an unpublished syllabary. Adapa and Adam might thus be not only mythologically but also etymologically related. See also G. Bucellati, "Adapa, Genesis and the Notion of Faith," *Ugarit-Forschung* 5 (1973): 61–66 and S. Picchioni, *Il poemetto di Adapa* (Budapest, 1981).

2. A. Heidel, *The Gilgamesh Epic and Old Testament Parallels* (Chicago, 1949); K. Oberhuber (ed.), *Das Gilgamesch-Epos*, Wege der Forschung 215 (Darmstadt, 1977).

3. Tablet IX, col. 1, 1–5; Heidel, *Gilgamesh Epic*, p. 64.

4. Heidel, *Gilgamesh Epic*, p. 70. The song of Siduri is not to be found in the twelve-tablet Neoassyrian epic; rather, it is attested only in Old Babylonian (GE Sippar, aB iii, 1–14); see A. George, *The Epic of Gilgamesh* (New York, 1999), p. 124.

5. N. Lohfink, *Kohelet*, 4th ed. (Würzburg, 1980), pp. 67–71.

6. Papyrus Harris 500, recto 6, 2–7, 3; for a hieroglyphic transcription of the text, see Michael V. Fox, *The Song of Songs and the Ancient Egyptian Love Songs* (Madison, 1985), pp. 378–380.

7. On the connections between Gilgamesh, the harpers' songs, and Ecclesiastes in ancient tradition, see S. Fischer, *Die Aufforderung zur Lebensfreude im Buch Kohelet und seine Rezeption der ägyptischen Harfnerlieder*, Wiener alttestamentliche Studien 2 (Frankfurt, 1999).

8. G. von Rad wished to explain the expression "good and evil" as a totalizing formula. Here, however, it is not a matter of "omniscience." But the formula "good and evil" is also not confined to the moral realm. See S. R. Albertz, " 'Ihr werdet sein wie Gott': Gen. 3, 1–7 auf dem Hintergrund des alttestamentlichen und des sumerisch-babylonischen Menschenbildes," *Welt des Orients* 24 (1993): 89–111; O. H. Steck, "Die Paradieserzählung: Eine Auslegung von Genesis 2, 4b–3, 24," *Biblische Studien* 60 (1970); E. Otto: "Woher weiss der Mensch um Gut und Böse: Philosophische Annäherungen der ägyptischen und biblischen Weisheit an ein Grundproblem der Ethik," in S. Beyerle, G. Mayer, and H. Strauss (eds.), *Recht und Ethos im Alten Testament* (Neurkirchen-Vluyn, 1999), pp. 207–231.

9. In the following words, which I cite from T. Macho, *Todesmetaphern: Zur Logik der Grenzerfahrung* (Frankfurt am Main, 1987), p. 108, A. Kojève summarized Hegel's insight into this matter: "Man is the only being in the world who *knows* that he must die, and, we can say, that he *is* the consciousness of his death: true human existence is an existing consciousness of death, or his self conscious death." The agreement with Heidegger "leaps," as Macho stresses, "formally to the eye."

10. Marsilio Ficino, *Lettere*, vol. 1, 149; the passage quoted here is taken from W. A. Euler, *"Pia philosophia" and "docta religio": Theologie und Religion bei Marsilio Ficino und Pico della Mirandola* (Munich, 1998), p. 50.

11. *Confessions*, book 1, 1, 1; see Augustine, *Bekenntnisse*, ed. J. Bernhart (Frankfurt am Main, 1987), pp. 12–13: *quia fecisti nos ad te et inquietum est cor nostrum, donec requiescat in te.*

12. F. Nietzsche, *The Birth of Tragedy*, in F. Golffing, trans., *The Birth of Tragedy and the Genealogy of Morals* (New York, 1956), p. 51.

13. Aeschylus, *Prometheus Bound*, verses 250–253; D. Grene and R. Lattimore, *Aeschylus, The Complete Greek Tragedies* 1 (Chicago, 1960), p. 320.

14. G. Lefebvre, *Le Tombeau de Pétosiris*, vol. 2 (Cairo, 1923), no. 127, line 5; K. Jansen-Winkeln, *Sentenzen und Maximen in den Privatinschriften der ägyptischen Spätzeit*, Achet: Schriften zur Ägyptologie, Reihe B 1 (Berlin, 1999), p. 108.

15. A. de Buck, *The Egyptian Coffin Texts*, vol. 7 (Chicago, 1961), spell 1130, 461c–464f; see E. Otto, "Zur Komposition von Coffin Texts 1130," in J. Assmann et al. (eds.), *Fragen an die altägyptische Literatur* (Wiesbaden, 1977), 1–18; J. Assmann, *The Search for God in Ancient Egypt* (Ithaca, 2001), pp. 174–177.

16. Psalm 90, 12.

17. These thoughts are anything but new, and they have most recently been succinctly and impressively developed by Z. Bauman, *Mortality, Immortality and Other Life Strategies* (Oxford, 1992).

18. G. Steiner, *In Bluebeard's Castle: Some Notes Towards the Redefinition of Culture* (New Haven, Conn., 1971), p. 89.

19. The "karmic" principle of a relationship between one's deeds and one's condition, as we find it in Hinduism and Buddhism, represents yet another possibility, one in which the horizon of accomplishment is prolonged through lifetime on earth, but not into an afterlife. In this system of belief, meaning is achieved not in the chain of generations but in that of rebirths.

20. S. Weil, *Selected Essays* (Oxford, 1970).

21. M. Heidegger, *Being and Time*, trans. J. Macquarrie and Edward Robinson (New York, 1962), pp. 274–311; the quotation is on p. 287 (emphasis Heidegger's).

22. W. Helck, *Die Lehre des Djedefhor und die Lehre eines Vaters an seinen Sohn* (Wiesbaden, 1984), pp. 6–7.; H. Brunner, *Altägyptische Weisheit* (Zurich, 1988), pp. 102–103.

23. H. Brunner, "Djedefhor in der römischen Kaiserzeit," *Studia Aegyptiaca* 1 (1974): 55–64.

24. J. F. Quack, *Die Lehren des Ani: Ein neuägyptischer Weisheitstext in seinem kulturellen Umfeld*, Orbis Biblicus et Orientalis 141 (Freiburg and Göttingen, 1995), p. 97 with n. 97, reads *bw* not as "place" but as a negation and renders, "without knowing that you cannot wait peacefully." This translation, however, defies sense. Man is not to await death peacefully, but to prepare for it actively by building a tomb.

25. Ani 17, 11–18, 4; Quack, *Ani*, pp. 96–99; Brunner, *Weisheit*, p. 202.

26. The goddess Isis says this, as though it were a commonplace, in a magical text. Metternich Stela M 50; see C. E. Sander-Hansen, *Die Texte der Metternichstele* (Copenhagen, 1956), pp. 35–36, 41; A. Klasens, *A Magical Statue Base (Socle Behague) in the Museum of Antiquities at Leiden* (Leiden, 1952), p. 10, 52; H. Sternberg, "Die Metternichstele," in O. Kaiser (ed.), *Texte aus der Umwelt des Alten Testaments*, vol. 2/3, Rituale und Beschwörungen 2 (Gütersloh, 1988), p. 376.

27. J. Baudrillard, *L'Échange symbolique et la mort* (Paris, 1976).

28. Instruction of Ani, 21, 20–22, 3; Quack, *Ani*, pp. 114–117, 182, 324–325; G. Posener, "L'Afarît dans l'ancienne Égypte," *Mitteilungen des Deutsches Archäologischen Instituts Kairo* 37 (1981): 394–401. See also chapter 5, section 3, of this volume.

29. E. Hornung, "Zur Struktur des ägyptischen Jenseitsglaubens," *Zeitschrift für ägyptische Sprache und Altertumskunde* 119 (1992): 124–130. See also chapter 9 of this volume.

30. E. Hornung, *The Ancient Egyptian Books of the Afterlife* (Ithaca, 1999).

31. On this point, see F. Borkenau, "Todesantinomie und Kulturgenerationen," in Borkenau (ed.), *Ende und Anfang: Von den Generationen der Hochkulturen und von der Entstehung des Abendlandes* (Stuttgart, 1984), pp. 83–119, and also T. Macho, "Tod und Trauer im kulturwissenschaftlichen Vergleich," in Macho (ed.), *Der Tod als Thema der*

Kulturtheorie (Frankfurt am Mainz, 2000), pp. 91–120, esp. 113–116. Borkenau distinguishes between two types of high cultures, those whose foundational myths speak to the impossibility of death, and those whose myths speak to the impossibility of immortality. Both are compelled to develop provisions that compensate for the alternatives they reject.

32. The translation here is based on that of M. Lichtheim, *Ancient Egyptian Literature: A Book of Readings*, vol. 1: *The Old and Middle Kingdoms* (Berkeley, 1973), p. 58.

33. A. J. Spencer, *Death in Ancient Egypt* (Harmondsworth, 1982).

34. See especially E. Hornung, *Tal der Könige: Die Ruhestätte der Pharaonen* (Zurich, 1982), *Das Totenbuch der Ägypter* (Zurich, 1979), and *The Ancient Egyptian Books of the Afterlife*.

35. A. Gardiner, *The Attitude of the Ancient Egyptians to Death and the Dead* (Cambridge, 1935).

36. C. E. Sander-Hansen, *Der Begriff des Todes bei den Ägyptern*, Historisk-filologiske Meddelelser 29/2 (Copenhagen, 1942).

37. P. Derchain, "De la mort ravisseuse," in *Chronique d'Égypte* 33 (1958): 29–32; Derchain, "La Mort," in Y. Bonnefoy (ed.), *Dictionnaire des mythologies* vol. 2 (Paris, 1981), pp. 124–128.

38. Especially important are S. Morenz, "Ägyptischer Totenglaube im Rahmen der Struktur ägyptischer Religion," *Eranos* 34 (1965): 399–446 and H. Altenmüller *Grab und Totenkult im Alten Ägypten* (Hamburg, 1976).

39. Especially important for our theme is the exhibition catalogue by S. D'Auria, P. Lacovara, and C. H. Roerig (eds.), *Mummies and Magic: The Funerary Arts of Egypt* (Boston, 1988).

CHAPTER 1. DEATH AS DISMEMBERMENT

1. Diodorus Siculus, *Bibliotheca historica (Library of History)* I, 11–27.

2. J. G. Griffiths, *De Iside et Osiride* (Cardiff, 1970); T. Hopfner, *Plutarch über Isis und Osiris* (Prague, 1940).

3. In all likelihood, though, the following verses of a hymn to Osiris from Dynasty 18 refer to this earthly kingdom of Osiris:

The great one, firstborn of his brothers,
eldest of the Ennead,
who establishes Maat throughout the two banks,
who places the son on the seat of his father;

praised by his father Geb,
he who is loved by his mother Nut,
great of strength when he felled the rebel,
mighty of arm when he slew his enemy;
great is the fear of him among his opponents,
he who conquers the farthest frontiers of evil,
stout of heart when he tramples his enemies.

Heir of Geb in the kingship of the Two Lands
—he (i.e., Geb) saw his ability and entrusted him with leadership over the lands,
because of the excellence of the deeds he accomplished.

This land is in his hand:
its water, its air,
its plants and all its animals,
all that flies up and alights,
its worms and its desert beasts
are made over to the son of Nut,
and the Two Lands are content with it.

He who appears on the throne of his father,
like Re when he rises in Lightland,
he has given light where there was darkness,
he has lit the air with his two plumes,
he has flooded the Two Lands like the sun in the morning,
his crown pierces the sky and mingles with the stars.

Leader of every god,
energetic in leadership, praised by the Great Ennead,
beloved of the Lesser Ennead.

Stela Louvre C 286. See A. Moret, "Légende d'Osiris," *BIFAO* 30 (1930): 725–750; G. Roeder, *Urkunden zur Religion des Alten Ägypten* (Jena, 1923), pp. 22–26; A. Erman, *The Ancient Egyptians: A Sourcebook of Their Writings* (New York, 1966), pp. 142–143; H. Kees, "Ägypten," in A. Bertholet (ed.), *Religionsgeschichtliches Lesebuch*, vol. 10 (Tübingen, 1928), pp. 28–29, no. 41 (extract); J. Assmann, *Ägyptische Hymnen und Gebete* (Zurich, 1975), no. 213.

4. E. Brunner-Traut, *Frühformen des Erkennens: Am Beispiel Altägyptens*, 2d ed. (Darmstadt, 1992).

5. Ibid., pp. 71–81; Brunner-Traut, "Der menschliche Körper—eine Gliederpuppe," *ZÄS* 115 (1988): 8–14.

6. Brunner-Traut, *Frühformen des Erkennens*, p. 72.

7. Ibid., pp. 82–84.

8. Brunner-Traut, "Wohltätigkeit und Armenfürsorge im Alten Ägypten," in G. K. Schäfer and T. Strohm (eds.), *Diakonie—biblische Grundlagen und Orientierungen* (Heidelberg, 1990), pp. 23–43; the quote is from p. 25.

9. E. Durkheim, *Über die Teilung der sozialen Arbeit* (Frankfurt, 1977); the French edition appeared in 1930.

10. Brunner-Traut, "Wohltätigkeit und Armenfürsorge im Alten Ägypten," p. 26.

11. It is, above all, Mary Douglas who has drawn attention to this relationship in her *Purity and Danger: An Analysis of the Concepts of Pollution and Taboo* (London, 1966).

12. T. Bardinet, *Les Papyrus médicaux de l'Égypte ancienne* (Paris, 1995).

13. H. Brunner, "Das Herz im ägyptischen Glauben," in *Das Herz im Umkreis des Glauben*, vol. 1 (Biberach, 1965); A. Piankoff, *Le "Coeur" dans les textes égyptiens* (Paris, 1930).

14. Instruction of Ptahhotep, 8–21; translation based on that of G. Burkard, "Ptahhotep und das Alter," *Zeitschrift für ägyptische Sprache und Altertumskunde* 115 (1988): 19–30.

15. A. de Buck, *The Egyptian Coffin Texts*, vol. 1, Oriental Institute Publications 34 (Chicago, 1935), p. 171 e–g. Cf. also K. Sethe, *Urkunden des ägyptischen Altertums*, vol. 4, reprint ed. (Berlin, 1961), p. 519.14–15 ("Lo, your heart leads you, and your limbs obey you"), with many parallels.

16. De Buck, *The Egyptian Coffin Texts*, vol. 1, p. 256 e–f. See also *The Egyptian Coffin Texts*, vol. 6, Oriental Institute Publications 81 (Chicago, 1956), 278 o–p ("My heart, raise yourself in your place, that you might recall what is in you") and *The Egyptian Coffin Texts*, vol. 6, p. 176 ("My heart forgets not its place, it remains in position. I know my name and do not forget it.")

17. Bardinet, *Les Papyrus médicaux*, pp. 68–80.

18. Brunner also understands the difference between *jb* and *ḥꜣ.tj* in the sense of a distinction between inherited and acquired characteristics; see "Das Herz im ägyptischen Glauben," p. 105.

19. See Z. I. Fabian, "Heart Chapters in the Context of the Book of the Dead," in Sylvia Schoske (ed.), *Akten des vierten Internationalen Ägyptologenkongresses, Munich, 1985*, Studien zur altägyptischen Kultur Beiheft 3 (Munich, 1988), pp. 249ff., esp. 258.

20. See H. Buchberger, *Transformation und Transformat*, Sargtextstudien 1 (Wiesbaden, 1993), chapter 5.

21. A. Hermann, "Zergliedern und Zusammenfügen: Religionsgeschichtliches zur Mumifizierung," *NUMEN* 3 (1956): 81–96; Hermann, "Einbalsamierung," in *Reallexikon für*

Antike und Christentum, vol. 4 (Stuttgart, 1959), pp. 798–802. Dismemberment as an early stage of embalming has been observed only in a few Early Dynastic tombs; see A. J. Spencer, *Death in Ancient Egypt* (Harmondsworth, 1982), 39–43.

22. G. R. H. Wright, "The Egyptian Sparagmos," *Mitteilungen des Deutschen Archäologischen Instituts Kairo* 35 (1979): 345–358.

23. See the classic essay by R. Hertz, "Contribution à l'étude sur la représentation collective de la mort," in Hertz, *Mélanges de sociologie religieuse et de folklore* (Paris, 1928), pp. 1–98.

24. K. Sethe, *Urkunden des ägyptischen Altertums,* vol. 1 (Leipzig, 1933), p.189.8–10.

25. Ibid., p.190.12–13.

26. Tomb of Ptahhotep, cited in A. Erman and H. Grapow, *Wörterbuch der aegyptischen Sprache,* reprint ed. (Berlin, 1971), vol. 2, 265.8, Belegstellen.

27. We are informed about the Egyptian processes of embalming and mummification, on the one hand, by the accounts of Herodotus and Diodorus, and on the other hand, and especially, by anthropological investigations of original mummies.

28. Liturgy NR.2. J. Assmann and M. Bommas, *Altägyptische Totenliturgien,* vol. 2 (in preparation).

29. Coffin Texts spell 229. On another coffin, we read the following invocation:

. . . Mistress of all in the mysterious place,
on whom Osiris leans his back
in this his time (= condition) of "weary of heart";
who is before the lord of Abydos,
mysterious place on the paths of the netherworld,
who surrounds her lord at the burial
in this her name of "She who surrounds her lord."
May you watch over me, I am Osiris.
May you transfigure me, may you raise my limbs! (*CT* spell 237, cf. 828)

30. Spell 761 = de Buck, *The Egyptian Coffin Texts,* vol. 6, pp. 391a–392f and spell 762 = ibid., p. 392g–p.

31. E. Hornung, *Das Buch der Anbetung des Re im Westen (Sonnenlitanei),* vol. 2, Aegyptiaca Helvetica 3 (Geneva, 1976), pp. 88–89; J. Assmann, *Liturgische Lieder an den Sonnengott: Untersuchungen zur altägyptischen Hymnik,* Münchner ägyptologische Studien 19 (Munich, 1969), p. 348.

32. The case is otherwise in the following deification of the limbs, an extract from Pyramid Texts spell 213:

Your hands are Atum,
your arms are Atum,
your belly is Atum,
your rear is Atum,
your bones are Atum,
your face is that of a jackal.

Here, a form with a human body and a jackal's head is described. It is the "cult form" of the deceased, which he is to assume when be appears in the tomb chapel to receive his food offerings.

33. Book of the Dead spell 172, translated by E. Hornung, *Das Totenbuch der Agypter* (Zurich, 1979), pp. 351–358 (extracts). O. Keel, following E. Hornung, has already pointed to the similarity of this text to the descriptive songs of the love poetry; see *Deine Blicke sind Tauben: Zur Metaphorik des Hohen Liedes* (Stuttgart, 1984), pp. 28–29.

34. On the genre of Near Eastern descriptive poems and its ancient Egyptian origin, see A. Hermann, *Altägyptische Liebesdichtung* (Wiesbaden, 1959).

35. Song of Songs, 4, 1–7:

Your eyes are doves
   behind your veil.
Your hair is like a flock of goats,
   moving down the slopes of Gilead,
Your teeth are like a flock of shorn ewes
   that have come up from the washing,
all of which bear twins,
   and not one of them is bereaved.
Your lips are like a crimson thread,
   and your mouth is lovely.
Your cheeks are like halves of a pomegranate
   behind your veil.
Your neck is like the tower of David,
   built in courses;
on it hang a thousand bucklers,
   all of them shields of warriors.
Your two breasts are like two fawns,
   twins of a gazelle,
   that feed among the lilies.
Until the day breathes
   and the shadows flee,
I will hasten to the mountain of myrrh
   and the hill of frankincense.
You are altogether beautiful, my love;
   there is no flaw in you.

Cf. Keel, *Deine Blicke sind Tauben*.
   36. Papyrus Chester Beatty I 1, 1–6; M. Lichtheim, *Ancient Egyptian Literature*, vol. 2: *The New Kingdom* (Berkeley, 1976), p. 182.

CHAPTER 2. *DEATH AS SOCIAL ISOLATION*

   1. K. Jansen-Winkeln, *Sentenzen und Maximen in den Privatinschriften der ägyptischen Spätzeit* (Berlin, 1999).
   2. E. Edel, *Die Inschriften der Grabfronten der Siut-Gräber in Mittelägypten aus der Herakleopolitenzeit: Eine Wiederherstellung nach den Zeichnungen der Description de l'Égypte*, Abhandlungen der Rheinisch-Westfälischen Akademie der Wissenschaften 71 (Opladen, 1984), fig. 7, 37–66.
   3. P. Chester Beatty IV, recto 8, 4–5 (=*Ägyptische Hymnen und Gebete* [Zurich, 1975], no. 195, 48); J. Černý and A. H. Gardiner, *Hieratic Ostraca* (Oxford, 1957), no. 89 verso (=*Ägyptische Hymnen und Gebete*, no. 190, 38 f.); Černý and Gardiner, *Hieratic Ostraca*, no. 8, 1; Leiden D 19 (G. Maspero, *Receuil de travaux relatifs à la philologie et à l'archéologie égyptiennes et assyriennes* 3 [1882]: 104).
   4. Instruction of Amenemope 1, 11.
   5. See J. Assmann, "Reden und Schweigen," in W. Helck and E. Otto (eds.), *Lexikon der Ägyptologie*, vol. 5 (Wiesbaden, 1984), cols. 195–201.
   6. In the ancient Near East and in classical antiquity, the expulsion of the sinner from the community of his group was the most fearful of punishments, for it robbed him of his identity, his personality, his security, and the basic context of his life. See G. Glotz, *La Solidarité de la famille dans le droit criminel en Grèce* (Paris, 1904).
   7. With incredible, but as it seems to me, unnecessary erudition, K. Sethe, *Übersetzung und Kommentar zu den altägyptischen Pyramidentexten*, vol. 5 (reprint ed., Hamburg, 1962), pp. 261–262, gives *nˤ* "to fare, travel," out of context, the ad hoc inferred meaning "to announce someone's death," a meaning the Arabic root *nˤ* evidently has in certain derived forms. R. O. Faulkner, *The Ancient Egyptian Pyramid Texts* (Oxford, 1969), p. 210, follows him in this.

Yet *n*ʿ*j* in its usual meaning "to fare, travel" yields excellent sense. Here, it appears in the same context as *prj* "to go up" in spell 214. The absence of the king, caused by an "ascent" (spell 214) or a "journey, passing" (for the image of death as a transition, see chapter 5), gives rise to nasty rumors, hate, and plans of rebellion.

8. Pyramid Texts spell 542, §§ 1335–1336.

9. From the Dialogue of a Man with His *Ba*, P. Berlin 3024; see chapter 16, section 3 of this volume.

10. Pyramid Texts spell 600, §§ 1652–1653.

11. K. Sethe, *Dramatische Texte zu altägyptischen Mysterienspielen*, Untersuchungen zur Geschichte und Altertumskunde Ägyptens 10 (Leipzig, 1928), pp. 76–77.

12. A. de Buck, *The Egyptian Coffin Texts*, vol. 1, Oriental Institute Publications 34 (Chicago, 1935), p. 81a–e. Cf. the offering spell in Theban Tomb 100 (spell for bringing the heart), N. de G. Davies, *The Tomb of Rekh-mi-Re*, (reprint ed. [New York, 1973], pp. 70–72 and pl. 76). For parallel texts, see Ritual for Amenophis I, Turin XVII, 8–10; Fragment Cairo (C), cols. 11–21, published by G. Daressy, *Annales du Service des Antiquités de l'Égypte* 16 (1916): 58–59; beginning: Pyramid Texts spell 595, § 1640; fragment: offering table of *Tꜣwj*, published by J. J. Clère, *Bulletin de l'Institut Français d'Archéologie Orientale* 81 (1981): 224; Tomb of Pay in Saqqara, published by Schneider et al., *The Tomb Complex of Pay and Raʿja* (Leiden, 1995), pp. 13–31 (J. van Dijk). See also S. Schott, *Bücher und Bibliotheken im Alten Ägypten* (Wiesbaden, 1990), p. 131, no. 299:

> Be silent, you gods,
> hear, Ennead,
> heed this command that Horus has made
> for his father Osiris,
> that he may become great through it, that he may become strong through it, that he
> may become Foremost of the Westerners through it.

13. For translations, see E. Hornung, *Das Totenbuch der Ägypter* (Zürich, 1979), pp. 157–164 and H. Brunner, *Zeitschrift der Deutschen Morgenländischen Gesellschaft* 111 (1961): 439–445.

14. R. Grieshammer, *Das Jenseitsgericht in den Sargtexten*, Ägyptologische Abhandlungen 20 (Wiesbaden, 1970), pp. 25–29; Grieshammer, "Zur Formgeschichte der Sprüche 38–41 der Sargtexte," *Orientalia Lovaniensia Periodica* 6/7 (1975/76): 231–235; A. de Jong, "Coffin Texts Spell 38: The Case of the Father and the Son," *Studien zur altägyptischen Kultur* 21 (1994): 141–157.

15. De Buck, *The Egyptian Coffin Texts*, vol. 1, 157–176.

16. Pyramid Texts spell 422, §§ 759–760. On the motif of the division of the kingship between father and son, see also J. Assmann, in M. Bommas (ed.), *Altägyptische Totenliturgien*, vol. 3 (in preparation).

17. See chapter 17, section 2 of this volume.

18. Hornung, *Das Totenbuch*, pp. 358–362.

19. S. Schott, "Der Denkstein Sethos' I. für die Kapelle Ramses' I," in *Abydos*, Nachrichten der Akademie der Wissenschaften in Göttingen 1964 (Göttingen, 1964); K. A. Kitchen, *Ramesside Inscriptions: Historical and Biographical*, vol. 1 (Oxford, 1975), pp. 110–114.

20. Schott renders "Die Majestät . . . zog aus"; the form is *prj*, however, not (*jw*) *pr.n*, evidently in a balanced sentence with the following *trj* = *f* "he will honor."

21. The proposed restoration is Schott's.

22. Schott's proposed restoration seems rather certain.

23. *Ḏrjw* actually means "strong, hard"; what is meant is probably the sound physical condition in which the deceased hears the transfiguration spells, or into which he is transformed by them.

24. This is Schott's translation of the verb *jp*, which actually means "to count"; it is often used in connection with the heart.

25. Kitchen, *Ramesside Inscriptions*, vol. 2 (Oxford, 1979), p. 327.5–10; J. Assmann, *Stein und Zeit: Mensch und Gesellschaft im alten Ägypten* (Munich, 1991), p. 123.

26. Kitchen, *Ramesside Inscriptions*, vol. 2, pp. 334.14–15; 335.4–5; 335.16–336.2; 336.4–5.

27. The Egyptian word *nḏ*, which is usually translated as "to protect" or "to avenge," encompasses the entire spectrum of the son's activities.

28. G. Posener, *L'Enseignement Loyaliste: Sagesse Égyptienne du Moyen Empire* (Geneva, 1976), § 12.

29. Only in manuscripts L2 and C: "let my son take my place!"

30. Only in L2 and C: "before you go to rest."

31. H. Brunner, *Altägyptische Weisheit* (Zurich, 1988), pp. 110–111. L2 is the conventional designation of P. British Museum 10409, while C is Carnarvon tablet I, otherwise known as Cairo Museum 41790.

32. In the case of the two instructions addressed to a king (Merikare and Amenemhet I), the father is deceased and speaks from the afterlife. On the testamentary character of such texts, see J. Bergman, "Discours d'adieu—testament—discours postume: Testaments juifs et enseignements égyptiens," in *Sagesse et religion: Colloque de Strasbourg, octobre 1976* (Paris, 1979) and "Gedanken zum Thema 'Lehre—Testament—Grab—Name,'" in E. Hornung and O. Keel (eds.), *Studien zu altägyptischen Lebenslehren*, Orbis Biblicus et Orientalis 28 (Freiburg and Göttingen, 1979), pp. 73–104.

33. In one magical text, the goddess Isis invokes this maxim as though it were a commonplace: Metternich Stela M 50; see C. E. Sander-Hansen, *Die Texte der Metternichstele*, Analecta Aegyptiaca 7 (Copenhagen, 1956), pp. 35–36, 41; A. Klasens, *A Magical Statue Base (Socle Behague) in the Museum of Antiquities at Leiden*, Oudheidkundige mededelingen uit het Rijksmuseum van Oudheden te Leiden 33 (Leiden, 1952), p. 10, 52; H. Sternberg, "Die Metternichstele," in O. Kaiser (ed.), *Texte aus der Umwelt des Alten Testaments*, vol. 2.3: *Rituale und Beschwörungen*, vol. 2 (Gütersloh, 1988), p. 376.

34. A maxim attested in a wisdom text points in the same direction: "A man comes into being (only) if he is surrounded by men. He is greeted with reverence for the sake of his children"; Instruction of Ani, Louvre version, see J. F. Quack, *Die Lehren des Ani: Ein neuägyptischer Weisheitstext in seinem kulturellen Umfeld*, Orbis Biblicus et Orientalis 141 (Freiburg and Göttingen, 1995), p. 285.

35. Ptahhotep 575–587, P. Prisse 17, 4–9; Z. Žába, *Les Maximes de Ptahhotep* (Prague, 1956), pp. 60–61. My translation mostly follows the masterful treatment of the passage by P. Seibert, *Die Charakteristik: Untersuchungen zu einer ägyptischen Sprechsitte und ihren Ausprägungen in Folklore und Literatur*, Ägyptologische Abhandlungen 17 (Wiesbaden, 1967), pp. 78–84.

36. H. Brunner, "Das Hörende Herz," *Theologische Literaturzeitung* (1954): 697–700.

37. Ptahhotep 398–315; H. Brunner, *Altägyptische Weisheit*, pp. 119–120, verses 237–251; see also the penetrating analysis of Seibert, *Die Charakteristik*, pp. 78–84.

38. Stela University College London 14333, published by H. Goedicke, "Stela London UC 14333," *Journal of Egyptian Archaeology* 48 (1962): 26; see also W. Schenkel, "Eine neue Weisheitslehre?" *Journal of Egyptian Archaeology* 50 (1964): 11–12.

39. T. Sundermeier, *Nur gemeinsam können wir leben: Das Menschenbild schwarzafrikanischer Religionen* (Gütersloh, 1988).

40. See the masterful study by Seibert, *Die Charakteristik*.

41. Pyramid Texts spell 257, § 304.

42. Pyramid Texts spell 273, §§ 393–394.

43. Coffins S 1 C and S 2 C.

44. Spell 609; in Faulkner's translation, *The Ancient Egyptian Coffin Texts*, vol. 2 (Warminster, 1977), pp. 197–198, it is entirely misunderstood.

45. Theban Tomb 183 (unpublished, after my own copy).

46. See J. Assmann, *Ägyptische Hymnen und Gebete* (Zurich, 1975), no. 131.

47. B. Gunn, "The Decree of Amonrasonther for Neskhons," *Journal of Egyptian Archaeology* 41 (1955): 83–95.

48. E. Otto, "Götterdekret," in W. Helck and E. Otto (eds.), *Lexikon der Ägyptologie*, vol. 2 (Wiesbaden, 1976), cols. 675–677; J. Quaegebeur, "Lettres de Thoth et décrets pour Osiris," in H. Kamstra, H. Milde, and K. Wagtendonk (eds.), *Funerary Symbols and Religion: Essays Dedicated to Professor M. S. H. G. Heerma van Voss on the Occasion of His Retirement from the Chair*

of the History of Ancient Religions at the University of Amsterdam (Kampen, 1988), pp. 105–126; L. Kákosy, "Three Decrees of Gods from Theban Tomb 32," *Orientalia Lovaniensia Periodica* 23 (1992): 311–328; S. Schott, *Bücher und Bibliotheken: Verzeichnis der Buch- und Spruchtitel und der Termini technici* (Wiesbaden, 1990), pp. 64–65 (111).

49. J. Assmann, *Das Grab der Mutirdis*, Archäologische Veröffentlichungen 13 (Mainz, 1977), p. 123.

50. Ibid., p. 13.

51. Ibid., text 11, p. 31.

52. J. Assmann, *Das Grab des Basa (Nr. 389) in der thebanischen Nekropole* (Mainz, 1973), text 21, p. 64.

53. Ibid., text 14, p. 61.

54. Mortuary liturgy SZ.1, spell 7; see J. Assmann and M. Bommas, *Altägyptische Totenliturgien*, vol. 3 (in preparation).

CHAPTER 3. DEATH AS ENEMY

1. In his dissertation entitled *Death as an Enemy* (Leiden, 1960), Jan Zandee put together a collection of phraseology referring to beings and actions against which the deceased sought to protect themselves in the afterlife. This image of death, however, refers to the "second death" that threatened the one who was already dead, and thus in the world beyond, with a definitive annihilation, while here, I am concerned with death as enemy in reference to the first and (in our sense) actual, biological death. But with regard to the second death, we must note a distinction that eluded Zandee. The danger to the deceased came either from Seth and his minions, and thus personifications of the first death, who were resolved to attack yet again and could be held at bay only through the most drastic of defensive measures, or—and this was the more typical and common instance—it came from the defensive measures themselves, and from their protagonists, who could always turn against the deceased. The deceased appears in the role of a citizen caught up in the "underworld," who must beware not only of the "gangsters," but also of the "police" he has called upon to protect him from the gangsters.

2. T. Macho, *Todesmetaphern: Zur Logik der Grenzenerfahrens* (Frankfurt, 1987), p. 47.

3. On this spell, see J. Zeidler, "Zur Frage der Spätentstehung des Mythos in Ägypten," *Göttinger Miszellen* 132 (1993): 85–109, esp. 101–104.

4. Coffin Texts spell 837 = spell 23 of mortuary liturgy CT.3; see J. Assmann and M. Bommas, *Altägyptische Totenliturgien*, vol. 1 (Heidelberg, 2002).

5. Spell 24 of mortuary liturgy CT.3; see J. Assmann and M. Bommas, *Altägyptische Totenliturgien*, vol. 3 (in preparation).

6. In section 3 c) of chapter 13 of this volume, we shall deal with a ritual slaughter in the framework of the Opening of the Mouth ritual, which also refers to this scene in which Seth appears before the divine tribunal. Here, a bull is slaughtered, and Isis speaks "in his ear":

Recitation in his ear by the "Great Kite" (i.e., Isis as mourning woman):
"It is your lips that have done this to you through the cleverness of your mouth!"

With what he said in the House of the Prince in Heliopolis, Seth evidently pronounced his own doom.

7. On this point, see J. Assmann, *Ma'at: Gerechtigkeit und Unsterblichkeit in Alten Ägypten* (Munich, 1990), chapter 6.

8. H. Roeder, *Mit dem Auge sehen: Studien zur Semantik der Herrschaft in den Toten- und Kulttexten* (Heidelberg, 1996), pp. 23–45.

9. See J. Spiegel, *Die Idee vom Totengericht in der ägyptischen Religion*, Leipziger Ägyptologische Studien 2 (Glückstadt, 1935); J. Yoyotte, "Le Jugement des morts dans l'Égypte anci-

enne," in *Le Jugement des morts*, Sources orientales 4 (Paris, 1961); S. G. F. Brandon, *The Judgment of the Dead: An Historical and Comparative Study of the Idea of a Post-mortem Judgment in the Major Religions* (London, 1967); J. Vergote, "Immortalité conditionnée de l'âme ou survie inconditionelle dans l'Égypte ancienne," in A. Théodoridès, P. Nasater, and J. Ries (eds.), *Vie et survie dans les civilisations orientales*, Acta Orientalia Belgica 3 (Leuven, 1993), 65–74; M. Lichtheim, *Ma'at in Egyptian Autobiographies and Related Studies*, Orbis Biblicus et Orientalis 120 (Freiburg and Göttingen, 1992); J. G. Griffiths, *The Divine Verdict: A Study of Divine Judgement in the Ancient Religions*, Studies in the History of Religions 52 (Leiden, 1991); Assmann, *Ma'at*, chapter 5; Assmann, *The Mind of Egypt: History and Meaning in the Time of the Pharaohs* (New York, 2002), chapter 3, section 5; J. Assmann, B. Janowski, and M. Welker (eds.), *Gerechtigkeit: Richten und Retten in der abendländischen Tradition und ihren altorientalischen Ursprüngen* (Munich, 1998), "Introduction."

10. Instruction for Merikare, P 53–57, see J. F. Quack, *Studien zur Lehre für Merikare*, Göttinger Orientforschungen 23 (Wiesbaden, 1992), pp. 34–35. I largely follow the beautiful metric translation of G. Fecht, *Der Vorwurf an Gott in den "Mahnworten des Ipu-wer,"* Abhandlungen der Heidelberger Akademie der Wissenschaften, Philosophisch-historische Klasse 1972/1 (Heidelberg, 1972), p. 147, with "Nachträge," pp. 222, 228–229.

11. For a more detailed discussion, see chapters 11 and 12 of this volume.

12. G. Lefebvre, *Le Tombeau de Petosiris*, vol. 2 (Cairo, 1923), p. 54, no. 81.

13. See V. W. Turner, *The Forest of Symbols: Aspects of Ndembu Ritual* (Ithaca, 1967), pp. 93–111; Turner, *The Ritual Process: Structure and Anti-Structure* (Ithaca, 1969), pp. 94–130; Turner, "Liminality and the Performative Genres," in J. MacAloon (ed.), *Cultural Frames and Reflexions* (San Francisco, 1981); Turner, *Rite, Arama, Festival, Spectacle: Rehearsals Toward a Theory of Cultural Performance* (Philadelphia, 1984), pp. 19–41.

14. On the iconography of the Judgment of the Dead, see C. Seeber, *Untersuchungen zur Darstellung des Totengerichts im Alten Ägypten*, Münchner ägyptologische Studien 35 (Munich, 1976).

15. Song 3; see R. Hari, *La Tombe thébaine du père divin Neferhotp (TT 50)* (Geneva, 1958), pl. 4. See also J. Assmann, "Fest des Augenblicks—Verheissung der Dauer: Die Kontroverse der ägyptischen Harfnerlieder," in J. Assmann, E. Feucht, and R. Grieshammer (eds.), *Fragen an die altägyptischer Literatur* (Wiesbaden, 1977), p. 69 and E. Hornung, "Altägyptische Wurzeln der Isismysterien," in C. Berget, G. Clerc, and N. Grimal (eds.), *Hommages à Jean Leclant*, Bibliothèque d'Étude 106 (Cairo, 1994), p. 289.

16. On the fate of those damned in the Judgment of the Dead, see E. Hornung, *Ägyptische Höllenvorstellungen*, Abhandlungen der Sächsischen Akademie der Wissenschaften zu Leipzig, Philologisch-historische Klasse 59/3 (Berlin, 1968).

17. See Assmann, *Ma'at*, chapter 5.

18. See S. Morenz, *Egyptian Religion* (Ithaca, 1973), pp. 126–135.

19. There follows a large strophe of 2 × 6 verses, in which Baki tells of his success in the royal service and stresses that it was "my character that advanced my rank and distinguished me before millions of men."

20. Turin stela 156, published by Varille, *Bulletin de l'Institut Français d'Archéologie Orientale* 54 (1954): 129–135. See Assmann, *Ma'at*, pp. 134–136 and M. Lichtheim, *Ma'at in Egyptian Autobiographies*, pp. 103–105 and 127–133.

21. R. Merkelbach, "Priestereid," *Zeitschrift für Papyrologie und Epigraphik* 2 (1968): 7–30; Merkelbach, "Priestereid und Totenbuch," in *Religions en Égypte hellénistique et romaine* (Paris, 1969), pp. 69–73; R. Grieshammer, "Zum 'Sitz im Leben' des negativen Sündenbekenntnisses," *XVIII. Deutscher Orientalistentagung*, Zeitschrift der Deutschen morgenländischen Gesellschaft Supplement 2 (Wiesbaden, 1974), pp. 19–25.

22. Merkelbach, *Unschuldserklärungen und Beichten im ägyptischen Totenbuch, in der romischen Elegie und im antiken Roman*, Kurzberichte aus den Papyrus-Sammlungen 43 (Giessen, 1987), pp. 15–16.

23. For the time being, see J. F. Quack, "Das Buch vom Tempel und verwandte Texte: Ein Vorbericht," *Archiv für Religionsgeschichte* 2/1 (2000): 1–20.

24. Porphyry, *De abstinentia* 4, 10.3–5; G. Clark (trans.), *Porphyry: On Abstinence from Killing Animals* (Ithaca, 2000), p. 108.

25. Porphyry, *De abstinentia* 4, 10 is cited as "funebris Aegyptiorum Apologia," for example, by J. Marsham, *Canon Chronicus Aegyptiacus, Ebraicus, Graecus* (Leipzig, 1676), pp. 156–157.

26. Diodorus Siculus, *Bibliotheca historica* (*Library of History*) 1, 91–93; see R. Merkelbach, "Diodor über das Totengericht der Ägypter," *Zeitschrift für agyptische Sprache und Altertumskunde* 120 (1993): 71–84.

27. See B. Gessler-Löhr, "Totenfeier im Garten," in J. Assmann (ed.), *Das Grab des Amenemope*, Theben 3 (Mainz, 1991), pp. 162–183.

28. R. Merkelbach, "Diodor über das Totengericht der Ägypter," pp. 71–84.

29. I have made use of the English-language edition by O. Ranum and E. Forster: J.-B. Bossuet, *Discourse on Universal History* (Chicago, 1976), pp. 308–309.

30. [Jean Terrasson,] *Séthos: Histoire ou Vie, tirée des monuments: Anecdotes de l'ancienne Égypte*, rev. ed. (Paris, 1767), pp. 38–48.

31. V. Herrmann, *Die Motivation des Helfens in der altägyptischen Religion und in der urchristlichen Religion: Ein Vergleich anhand von Totenbuch Kap. 125/Texten der idealen Selbstbiographie und Mt. 25, 31–46* (Heidelberg, 1990/91).

32. W. Warburton, *The divine legation of Moses demonstrated on the principles of a religious deist, from the omission of the doctrine of a future state of reward and punishment in the Jewish dispensation* (London, 1738–1741).

CHAPTER 4. DEATH AS DISSOCIATION

1. T. G. Allen, "Additions to the Egyptian Book of the Dead," *Journal of Near Eastern Studies* 11 (1952): 177–186; J.-C. Goyon, "La véritable attribution des soi-disant chapitres 191 et 192 du Livre des Morts," in *Studia Aegyptiaca*, vol. 1 (Budapest, 1974), pp. 117–127.

2. N. de G. Davies and A. H. Gardiner, *The Tomb of Amenemhet*, Theban Tomb Series 1 (London, 1915).

3. Ibid., pl. 19, text above the procession of offering bearers.

4. Ibid., pl. 23.

5. See J. Assmann, "Harfnerlied und Horussöhne," *Journal of Egyptian Archaeology* 65 (1979): 54–77. The Theban variants are Theban Tombs 163, 157, and 373. On Theban Tomb 373, see K. J. Seyfried, *Das Grab des Amonmose (TT 373)*, Theben 4 (Mainz, 1990), pp. 55–57.

6. G. Lefebvre, *Le Tombeau de Petosiris*, vol. 2 (Cairo, 1923), p. 61, and vol. 3 (Cairo, 1924), pl. 29.

7. L. Kákosy, "Probleme der ägyptischen Jenseitsvorstellungen in der Ptolemäer- und Kaiserzeit," in P. Derchain (ed.), *Religions en Égypte hellénistique et romaine* (Paris, 1969), pp. 65–68.

8. Theban Tomb 163 has Imset playing this role, and the remainder, Hapy.

9. Theban Tomb 163 has Hapy, and the remainder, Duamutef.

10. Theban Tomb 163 has Duamutef, and the remainder, Imset.

11. S. Cauville, *Dendara*, vol. 10 (Cairo, 1997), p. 82. On this ritual, which has to do with the assembling of Osiris' body, and at the same time Egypt (in the form of its nome capitals), see chapter 15, section 3 of this volume.

12. P. Berlin 3024, lines 43–49.

13. On this spell, see chapter 13 of this volume.

14. L. V. Žabkar, *A Study of the Ba-Concept in Ancient Egyptian Texts*, Studies in Ancient Oriental Civilization 34 (Chicago, 1968), p. 111, n. 139, with reference to K. Sethe, *Urkunden des ägyptischen Altertums*, vol. 4 (reprint ed., Berlin, 1961), pp. 481 and 484.14 and A. Erman and H. Grapow, *Wörterbuch der aegyptische Sprache* (reprint ed., Berlin, 1971), Belegstellen to vol. 5, p. 415.8.

15. For a collection of representative text passages, see J. Assmann and M. Bommas, *Altägyptische Totenliturgien*, vol. 2, chapter 1, paragraph 28 (in preparation).

16. S. Sauneron, *Rituel de l'Embaumement* (Cairo, 1952), 7.18. Similarly, 10.20:

Your *ba* is seen in the sky,
your corpse in the netherworld,
your statues in the temples.

Similarly Cairo Catalogue général 42224, published by Legrain, *Statues et statuettes des rois et des particuliers*, vol. 3 (Cairo, 1914), p. 57:

Your *ba* to the sky,
your corpse to the netherworld,
your statues among the praised ones.

There is a reference to a temple statue in the text of the stela of Ptahmose in Moscow, published by S. Hodjash and O. D. Berlev, *The Egyptian Reliefs and Stelae in the Pushkin Museum of Fine Arts, Moscow* (Leningrad, 1982), no. 71:

ba to the sky,
corpse to the netherworld,
statues hidden in Egypt.
May he circle the walls on the day of the Sokar festival,
like the following of Horus.
May onions be placed around his neck
on the morning of provisioning.

17. Embalming Ritual 2, 12; Sauneron, *Rituel de l'Embaumement*, p. 4.
18. A. de Buck, *The Egyptian Coffin Texts*, vol. 2, Oriental Institute Publications 49 (Chicago, 1938), p. 185 a–b.
19. The concept that the corpse of the sun god rests in Heliopolis is also to be found in the Books of the Netherworld and the solar hymns of the New Kingdom. See J. Assmann, *Sonnenhymnen in thebanischen Gräbern*, Theben 1 (Mainz, 1983), pp. 213–214, note (n) to text 158, 39, "Re goes to rest in Heliopolis." We may also cite A. de Buck, *The Egyptian Coffin Texts*, vol. 4, Oriental Institute Publications 67 (Chicago, 1951), p. 64 c–d (*d.t*); vol. 6, Oriental Institute Publications 81 (Chicago, 1956), p. 376 e; and vol. 7, Oriental Institute Publications 87 (Chicago, 1961), p. 19 h–i, where the corpse is also said to be in Heliopolis. Perhaps we are to imagine that the sun temple of Heliopolis included a crypt, like that of Osiris at Abydos and in the edifice of Taharqa by the sacred lake at Karnak. D. Raue has convincingly demonstrated that the necropolis of the Mnevis bulls (Mnevis was the sacred animal of the sun god) was considered to be the tomb of the sun god; see *Heliopolis und das Haus des Re: Eine Prosopographie und ein Toponym im Neuen Reich*, Abhandlungen des Deutschen Archäologischen Instituts 16 (Berlin, 1999), pp. 107–108.
20. J. E. Quibell and A. G. K. Hayter, *Teti Pyramid North Side* (Cairo, 1927), pp. 32–33 and pl. 9.
21. E. Hornung, *Das Amduat: Die Schrift des verborgenen Raumes*, Ägyptologische Abhandlungen 7 (Wiesbaden, 1963), vol. 1, pp. 195–196 and vol. 2, p. 187. Similarly:

My *ba* belongs to the sky, that I may rest there,
my corpse belongs to the earth among the gods.

Hornung, *Das Buch der Anbetung des Re im Westen (Sonnenlitanei)*, Aegyptiaca Helvetica 3 (Geneva, 1976), vol. 2, p. 96, and

Your *ba* belongs to the sky, O lord of the Horizon,
your shadow it is, that crosses through the *shetit*.
Your corpse belongs to the earth, O you who are in the sky!
Give it (i.e., the sky) to us, O Re!
You breathe when you occupy your corpse, which is in the Duat.

Hornung, *Das Buch von den Pforten des Jenseits*, Aegyptiaca Helvetica 7–8 (Geneva, 1979–1980), vol. 1, pp. 227–228 and vol. 2, pp. 163–164 and Hornung, *Ägyptische Unterweltsbücher*, 2d ed. (Zurich, 1984), p. 246; and

> Acclamation in the sky for the *ba* of Re,
> adoration in the earth for his corpse!
> Your *ba* belongs to the sky,
> your corpse belongs to the earth,
> O you who have determined (your) own size!

Hornung, *Das Buch von den Pforten*, vol. 1, p. 374 and vol. 2, p. 265; Hornung, *Ägyptische Unterweltsbücher*, p. 294. In the concluding text of the third hour of the Amduat, the mysterious gods say to the sun god:

> The sky belongs to your *ba*,
> the earth to your corpse!

Hornung, *Amduat*, vol. 1, p. 60, top and vol. 2, p. 74. In his response, the sun god expresses the same wish with regard to Osiris:

> Your *ba* to the sky, Osiris!
> your corpse to the earth, O foremost one of the realm of the dead!

Hornung, *Amduat*, vol. 1, p. 60, top and vol. 2, p. 74.

22. De Buck, *The Egyptian Coffin Texts*, vol. 1, Oriental Institute Publications 34 (Chicago, 1935), p. 56 a–f. The later version of this spell in Book of the Dead chapter 169 changes the statement about the *ba* and the corpse into the usual New Kingdom assigning of the two to the sky and the netherworld:

> Your *ba* to the sky,
> your corpse underground.

The earlier version makes more sense.

23. In the variant B1Ca.

24. In all these text passages, the preposition *m* "with" is used instrumentally. The *ba* is not the partner but rather the medium or instrument of Osiris' intended sexual enjoyment. W. Barta misunderstood this point in his commentary on the Dialogue of a Man with His *Ba*, where he rendered this very passage as "the gods have commanded that it (the *ba*) copulate with him (Osiris)" (*Das Gespräch eines Mannes mit seinem Ba* [*Papyrus Berlin 3024*], Münchner ägyptologische Studien 18 [Berlin, 1969], p. 72). The actual meaning is, "that he (Osiris) copulate by means of it (the *ba*)." R. O. Faulkner also seems to have misunderstood this passage: "I am the great soul of Osiris with whom the gods commanded him to copulate" (*The Ancient Egyptian Coffin Texts*, vol. 1 [Warminster, 1973], p. 94). "By means of whom/which" would be the correct rendering.

25. De Buck, *The Egyptian Coffin Texts*, vol. 3, Oriental Institute Publications 64 (Chicago, 1947), p. 296 i–l.

26. De Buck, *The Egyptian Coffin Texts*, vol. 1, p. 182 b–g.

27. See J. Assmann, "Muttergottheit," in W. Helck and E. Otto (eds.), *Lexikon der Ägyptologie*, vol. 4 (Wiesbaden, 1982), col. 267. See now also E. Hermsen, "Regressus ad uterum: Die embryonale Jenseitssymbolik Altägyptens und die prä- und perinatale Psychologie," in *International Journal for Prenatal and Perinatal Medicine* 5 (1993): 361–382.

28. J. Assmann and M. Bommas, *Altägyptische Totenliturgien*, vol. 3 (in preparation), chapter 1 (liturgy Z.1), spell 10, section 6b.

29. Coffin Texts spell 45 = *The Egyptian Coffin Texts*, vol. 1, pp. 197g–198c.

30. Žabkar, *A Study of the Ba-Concept*, pp. 108–109, devotes special attention to this text passage, which, in his estimation, "more clearly than any quoted thus far emphasizes the interdependence of the Ba and the corpse."

31. Coffin Texts spell 333 = de Buck, *The Egyptian Coffin Texts*, vol. 4, p. 178m–n.

32. See chapter 14, section 3 of this volume.

33. S. Cauville, *Le Temple de Dendara*, vol. 10 (Cairo, 1999); S. Cauville, *Dendara: Chapelles osiriennes, transcription et traduction* (Cairo, 1997), p. 38; commentaire, p. 27. In a late Osirian liturgy, it is stated that the ceremony is to be carried out during the "night of the diadem," which "his *ba* appears in the *wḏꜣ.t*-eye (i.e., the moon; variant, "in the temple of Sokar") in order to be over his corpse (*r ḫpr ḥr ḥꜣ.t=f*); see Papyrus Metropolitan Museum of Art 35.9.21, I, 2, published by J.-C. Goyon, *Le Papyrus d'Imouthès, fils de Psintaes au Metropolitan Museum of Art de New-York* (New York, 1999), p. 27.

34. For a survey of the history of research on this topic, see A. J. Bolshakov, *Man and his Double: The Ka in Egyptian Ideology of the Old Kingdom*, Ägypten und Altes Testament 37 (Wiesbaden, 1970), pp. 123–132.

35. Papyrus Westcar 7, 23–26.

36. See R. O. Faulkner, *The Ancient Egyptian Pyramid Texts* (Oxford, 1969), pp. 148–149. Pyramid Texts spell 450 is a variant of this one.

37. Coffin Texts spell 821, preserved only in the version T1Be.

38. See R. Cooley, "Gathered to his People: A Study of a Dothan Family Tomb," in M. Inch et al. (eds.), *The Living and the Active Word of God* (Winona Lake, Ind., 1983), pp. 47–58.

39. K. Sethe, *Urkunden des ägyptischen Altertums*, vol. 1 (Leipzig, 1932–1933), p. 189.12–15 (Ptahhotep) and 190.10; see U. Schweitzer, *Das Wesen des Ka im Diesseits und Jenseits der Alten Ägypter*, Ägyptologische Forschungen 19 (Glückstadt, 1956), p. 84, and K. J. Seyfried, "Generationeneinbindung," in J. Assmann, E. Dziobek, H. Guksch, and F. Kampp (eds.), *Thebanische Beamtennekropolen: Neue Perspektiven archäologischer Forschung*, Studien zur Archäologie und Geschichte Altägyptens 12 (Heidelberg, 1995), pp. 228–229.

40. Erman and Grapow, *Wörterbuch*, vol. 3, p. 430.1–2 and vol. 5, p. 87.7.

41. V. Loret, *La Tombe de Khâ-m-hâ*, Mémoires publiés part les membres de la Mission Archéologique Française au Caire 1 (Cairo, 1884), p. 130, liturgy NR.5.2.2; cf. also liturgy NR.7.2 § 17.

42. S. Schott, *Kanais: Der Tempel Sethos' I. im Wadi Mia*, Nachrichten der Akademie der Wissenschaften in Göttingen 1961 (Göttingen, 1961), pl. 19, text C, lines 14–15 and p. 155 with n. 9 (referring to Erman and Grapow, *Wörterbuch*, vol. 3, 430).

43. Sethe, *Urkunden der ägyptischen Altertums*, vol. 4, 1800, 6.

44. Liturgy NR.7 XIII; see Assmann and Bommas, *Altägyptische Totenliturgien*, vol. 2 (in preparation), chapter 7.

45. See ibid., chapter 3, § 2.

46. In the Coffin Texts, this motif is also attested in reference to the *ba*. In the role of the air god Shu, the deceased states:

I have created my *ba* around me,
in order to cause that it know what I knew.

De Buck, *The Egyptian Coffin Texts*, vol. 1, p. 362 a–b; cf. also p. 394 b–c and 395 a. See G. Wirz, *Tod und Vergänglichkeit: Ein Beitrag zur Geisteshaltung der Ägypter von Ptahhotep bis Antef* (Sankt Augustin, 1982), p. 42.

47. Important studies of the *ka* include Schweitzer, *Das Wesen des Ka*; L. Greven, *Der Ka in Theologie und Königskult des Alten Reiches*, Ägyptologische Forschungen 17 (Glückstadt, 1952); P. Kaplony, "Ka," in Helck and Otto (eds.), *Lexikon der Ägyptologie*, vol. 3 (Wiesbaden, 1978), cols. 275–282; and Bolshakov, *Man and His Double*.

48. On the embrace of the *ka*, see Assmann and Bommas, *Altägyptische Totenliturgien*, vol. 2, chapter 7, § 17.

49. On this royal aspect of the *ka*, see especially L. Bell, "Le Temple de Louqsor et le culte du Ka royal," in *Dossiers histoire et archéologie* 101 (1986): 57–59 and H. Jacobsohn, *Die dogmatische Stellung des Königs in der Theologie der alten Ägypter*, Ägyptologische Forschungen 8 (Glückstadt, 1939), p. 58. According to Schweitzer, *Das Wesen des Ka*, p. 36, the father was "the bearer of the sexually potent *ka*, to which he himself owed his life, and which he passed

along to the son, so that he might live and reproduce himself, and so forth, in an endless sequence of generations."

50. See H. P. Hasenfratz, "Tod und Seele im alten Ägypten," in G. Binder and B. Effe (eds.), *Tod und Jenseits im Altertum* (Trier, 1991), pp. 88–102, and my discussion in chapter 3 of this volume.

51. See the excellent observations of H. P. Hasenfratz, "Zur 'Seelenvorstellung' der alten Ägypter," *Zeitschrift für Religions- und Geistesgeschichte* 42 (1990): 193–216.

52. Coffin Cairo Catalogue générale 41057 = H. Gauthier, *Cerceuils anthropoïdes des prêtres de Montou* (Cairo, 1913), p. 300; similarly, Catalogue générale 41046 = ibid., p. 86, Catalogue générale 41053 = ibid., p. 224, and Catalogue générale 41056 = ibid., p. 271.

53. H. Beinlich and M. Saleh, *Corpus der hieroglyphischen Inschriften aus dem Grab des Tutanchamun* (Oxford, 1989), p. 92. In the Leiden Book of the Dead of the "merchant" Qenna, in spell 151, which deals with embalming, the speech of Anubis is enhanced by the following:

You enter the house of *jb*-hearts
and the place full of *ḥ₃.tj*-hearts.
You take your own and set it in its place.
You do not lose your hand,
you do not lose your foot for going,
you do not go upside down,
you go upright.

See J. van Dijk, "Entering the House of Hearts: An Addition to Chapter 151 in the Book of the Dead of Qenna," in *Oudheidkundige Mededelingen uit het Rijksmuseum van Oudheden te Leiden* 75 (1995), pp. 7–11. This "house full of hearts," which the deceased is to enter in search of his own heart, is often mentioned in mortuary spells:

May you enter the house full of *jb*-hearts,
the building full of *ḥ₃.tj*-hearts.
May you take your own and put it in its place.

Papyrus British Museum 10819, 3.4–6 (unpublished); similarly, Theban Tomb 100, N. de G. Davies, *The Tomb of Rekh-mi-Rēʿ at Thebes*, Publications of the Metropolitan Museum of Art Egyptian Expedition 11 (New York, 1943), pl. 86; Book of the Dead chapter 26, see L. Kákosy, "Beiträge zum Totenkult der heiligen Tiere," *Zeitschrift für ägyptische Sprache und Altertumskunde* 96 (1970): 110, n. 4; Theban Tomb 298, K. Kitchen, *Ramesside Inscriptions: Historical and Biographical*, vol. 1 (Oxford, 1975), pp. 370–371; Papyrus Louvre 3279, J.-C. Goyon, *Papyrus du Louvre N 3279* (Paris, 1966), p. 32 and p. 35 with n. 8. In a Theban tomb of the Ramesside Period, we find the following prayer:

A mortuary offering for Hathor, the chieftainess of the western desert,
and Isis, the great one, the god's mother,
mistress of the sky and ruler of the Two Lands;
may they grant the *jb*-heart in the house of *jb*-hearts
and your *ḥ₃.tj*-heart in the house of *ḥ₃.tj*-hearts.
May you take your own and set it in its place,
may you not go without it.

Theban Tomb 298; B. Bruyère, *Rapport sur les fouilles de Deir el-Médineh (1927)* (Cairo, 1928), p. 92.

54. Book of the Dead spell 30A; E. Hornung, *Das Totenbuch der Ägypter* (Zurich, 1979), pp. 95–96.

55. Spell 30B; ibid., p. 96.

56. Spell 30B; ibid., p. 96. The rendering here differs slightly from Hornung's.
57. The text reads:

My heart quickly scurries away
when I think of your love.
It does not let me act like a (normal) person—
it has leapt (out) of its place.

Papyrus Chester Beatty I, C 2, 9—C 3, 1; the translation is that of M. V. Fox, *The Song of Songs and the Ancient Egyptian Love Songs* (Madison, Wisc., 1985), p. 53; see also S. Schott, *Altägyptische Liebeslieder* (Zurich, 1950), p. 41.
58. We read:

I am awake, but my heart sleeps,
my heart is not in my body.
All my limbs are seized by evil,
my eyes too weak to see,
my ear, it hears not,
my voice is hoarse, all my words are garbled.

Papyrus Anastasi IV, 4, 11–5, 5. A. H. Gardiner, *Late-Egyptian Miscellanies*, Bibliotheca Aegyptiaca 7 (Brussels, 1937), p. 39; R. A. Caminos, *Late-Egyptian Miscellanies*, Brown Egyptological Studies 1 (London, 1954), pp. 150–152; Schott, *Liebeslieder*, p. 116; J. Assmann, *Ägyptische Hymnen und Gebete* (Zurich, 1975), no. 184.
59. The text states:

It is I, I!
but the child was too weak to answer.
My breasts were full, his body was empty,
(his) mouth longed for his nourishment.
The wells overflowed, but the child was thirsty,
my heart leapt from its place in great fear.

A. Klasens, *A Magical Statue Base (Socle Behague) in the Museum of Antiquities at Leiden*, Oudheidkundige Mededelingen uit het Rijksmuseum van Oudheden te Leiden 33 (Leiden, 1952), p. 23. The crucial passage is usually translated, "I wished to protect him," but we are to read *jb=j rwj.w ḥr mk.t=f* "my heart leapt (from) upon its place."
60. Sinuhe B 252–256; A. M. Blackman, *Middle Egyptian Stories*, Bibliotheca Aegyptiaca 2 (Brussels, 1932), p. 37; R. Koch, *Die Erzählung des Sinuhe*, Bibliotheca Aegyptiaca 17 (Brussels, 1990), p. 74.
61. For the expression *sḥm m ḏ.t*, see Assmann and Bommas, *Altägyptische* Totenliturgien, vol. 3, liturgy SZ.2 spell 19, verses 4 and 18; liturgy SZ.1 spell 10, verse 58.
62. Coffin Texts spell 517 = liturgy SZ.2, spell 3.
63. For example, Pyramid Texts spell 468, § 894:

A great one shall awaken with his *ka*,
but this great one is asleep with his *ka*;
this N. shall awaken with his *ka*,
but this N. is asleep with his *ka*.
Awaken, O this great one, awaken, O N.!

64. T. Macho, "Tod und Trauer im kulturwissenschaftlichen Vergleich," in J. Assmann (ed.), *Der Tod als Thema der Kulturtheorie* (Frankfurt, 2000), p. 99. See also the brilliant essay by C. Ginzburg, "Repräsentation: Das Wort, die Vorstellung, der Gegenstand," in Ginzburg (ed.), *Holzaugen: Über Nähe und Distanz* (Berlin, 1999), pp. 100–119; Ginzburg treats the problem of representation as a connecting theme of the mortuary rituals.

65. H. Belting, "Aus dem Schatten des Todes: Bild und Körper in den Anfängen," in C. von Barloewen (ed.), *Der Tod in den Weltkulturen und Weltreligionen* (Munich, 1996), p. 94. In its struggle against idolatry, Judaism also viewed the experience of death as the origin of the making of images:

> For a father, consumed with grief at an untimely bereavement, made an image of his child, who had been suddenly taken from him; and he now honored as a god what was once a dead human being, and handed on to his dependents secret rites and initiations. Then the ungodly custom, grown strong with time, was kept as a law.

Wisdom of Solomon 14.15–16.

66. See N. Tacke, "Die Entwicklung der Mumienmaske im Alten Reich," *Mitteilungen des Deutschen Archäologischen Instituts Kairo* 52 (1996): 307–336.

67. See K. Lehmann, "Der Serdab in den Privatgräbern des Alten Reiches," dissertation, Heidelberg University, 2000; Bolshakov, *Man and His Double*, pp. 106–110.

68. The statue seems to be connected with the social self and the *ka*, rather than with the physical self and the *ba*. The common expression "*ka*-statue" is an Egyptological, not an Egyptian one, though it has not been created out of thin air. At Giza, in a frieze inscription in the mastaba of Rewer I, the *serdab* is referred to as a "*ka*-house (*ḥw.t-k3*); see H. Junker, *Giza*, vol. 3 (Vienna, 1938), pp. 118–120. It is possible, however, that this inscription refers to the entire cult area of the tomb. More telling is the designation *pr tw.t* "statue house" in the inscription of *Ppj-ʿnḫḤnjj-km* from Meir, on which see Lehmann, "Der Serdab." The clearest indication of the social aspect of the statue is in the Opening of the Mouth ritual, whose closing rites, after the second slaughter of a bull, are to be explained as an "investiture." The statue is anointed, dressed, and crowned, and thus invested as bearer of the status and honor of the deceased; see chapter 13 of this volume.

69. See Assmann and Bommas, *Altägyptische Totenliturgien*, vol. 3, liturgy SZ.1, spell 6.

70. Hornung, *Das Totenbuch*, pp. 318–323.

71. Hornung thinks that these verses address Anubis; a reference to the mask itself, which has already been addressed in the preceding, seems more plausible.

72. See Beinlich and Saleh, *Corpus der hieroglyphischen Inschriften*, pp. 82–83; B. Lüscher, *Untersuchungen zu Totenbuch 151*, Studien zum altägyptischen Totenbuch 2 (Wiesbaden, 1998), pp. 132–152 and 244–250.

73. See Ginzburg, "Repräsentation."

74. D. Arnold, *Der Tempel des Mentuhotep von Deir el Bahari*, vol. 1: *Architektur und Deutung*, Archäologische Veröffentlichungen 8 (Mainz, 1974), pp. 51–53.

75. The tomb of Rewer II at Giza had 25 *serdabs* containing more than a hundred statues; see Bolshakov, *Man and His Double*, pp. 107–108.

76. M. Eaton-Krauss, "Pseudo-Groups," in *Kunst des Alten Reichs*, Sonderschrift des Deutschen Archäologischen Instituts Kairo 28 (Mainz, 1995), pp. 57–74; S. Rzepka, "The Pseudo-groups of the Old Kingdom," in *Studien zur Altägyptischen Kultur* 23 (1996): 335–347.

77. *Shabty* is the older Egyptian term for these statuettes, and *ushabty* a later one, first attested in the Late Period.

78. The only text to hint at a negative valuation of this obligatory labor is in the tomb of Djehutiemheb, Theban Tomb 194 (liturgy NR.8.2.9):

> The *shabty*s there work in my name,
> when I am summoned to the work of a praised one.
> Penpen brings me offerings,
> that I may receive *snw*-bread as offering.
> It does not happen that I must carry sand from west to east.

Theban Tomb 194, plate 32, text 111, lines 63–64. But even here, the work as such is positively evaluated, for it is designated the "work of a praised one." Penpen is a special god, attested only in Theban tombs of the Ramesside Period, whose task was to keep a list of those who received mortuary offerings. Here, these mortuary offerings are explained as a stipend that the deceased receives for the work that he, that is to say, the *shabty*s who act in his name, perform in the afterlife. But when Djehutiemheb protects himself from having to carry sand from west to east, he distances himself either from his *shabty*s, who carry out this task as his substitutes, or from certain forms of work that he considers to be beneath his dignity. More generally, however, we must assume that the *shabty*s were to participate in this work, which was evidently conceived of as a structured form of meaningful existence, one that was ordained by and pleasing to the gods.

79. See H. Schneider, *Shabtis*, 3 vols. (Leiden, 1977).

80. Papyrus British Museum 10819, verso, lines 102–104.

81. A spell for the deceased from a Dynasty 18 tomb contains the following wish on his behalf:

> If one calls, your *shabty* will answer
> and say: "Yes, I shall do it!"

From the lost Theban Tomb C1 (reign of Amenophis III); see A. Hermann, *Die Stelen der thebanischen Felsgräber der 18. Dynastie* (Glückstadt, 1940), pp. 47*–49*, after Loret, *Tombe de Khâ-m-hâ*, p. 25.

82. *Shabty* chest no. 912 (2430; 107), Turin Museum. Probably from Thebes. See H. Brugsch, *Thesaurus inscriptionum aegyptiacarum*, part 1, reprint ed. (Graz, 1968), p. 248; A. Febretti, F. Rossi, and R. V. Lanzone, *Regio Museo di Torino, Catalogo Generale dei Musei di Antichita* (Turin, 1882), pp. 342–343.

83. In the old royal necropolis of Abydos, where the tomb of Osiris was localized from the Middle Kingdom on, during excavations in the vicinity of the tomb of King Den of Dynasty 1, archaeologists came upon two small pits containing a sort of model burial that consisted of two wooden sarcophagi about 16.3 and 15.5 inches in length and a series of *shabty*-figures that must originally have been about 11.8 inches tall and were destroyed by robbers out of fear of the vengeance of the deceased. See F. Pumpenmeier, *Eine Gunstgabe von seiten des Königs: Ein extrasepulkrales Schabtidepot Qen-Amuns in Abydos* (Heidelberg, 1998).

84. It emerges from Frauke Pumpenmeier's research on extrasepulchral *shabty* deposits that the figurines were supposed to represent the deceased in particular on major festival occasions, to serve as a medium for his participation. A large deposit of *shabty*s of the same Qenamun has been found at Zawyet Abu Mesallam, south of Giza.

85. M. Idel, *Golem: Jewish Magical and Mystical Traditions on the Artificial Anthropoid* (Albany, N.Y., 1990). On pp. 3–4, he makes reference to the case of Egyptian *shabty*-figures.

86. E. Brunner-Traut, "Der Magier Merirê und sein Golem," *Fabula* 31 (1990): 11–16; Brunner-Traut, "Ein Golem in der ägyptischen Literatur," *Studien zur altägyptischen Kultur* 16 (1989): 21–26.

87. Sethe, *Urkunden des ägyptischen Altertums*, vol. 1, pp. 146–147.

88. On the cemeteries and the tomb architecture of the Old Kingdom, see N. Alexanian, "Die provinziellen Mastabagräber und die Friedhöfe im Alten Reich," dissertation, Heidelberg University, 2000. On the Theban cemetery of the New Kingdom and the location and typology of the tombs, see B. Engelmann-von Carnap, *Die Struktur des thebanischen Beamtenfriedhofs in der erster Hälfte der 18. Dynastie: Analyse von Position, Grundrissgestattung und Bildprogramm in der Gräber*, Abhandlungen des Deutschen Archäologischen Instituts 15 (Berlin, 1999) and F. Kampp-Seyfried, *Die thebanische Nekropole: Zum Wandel des Grabgedankens von der XVIII. biz xur XX. Dynastie*, 2 vols., Theben 13 (Mainz, 1996).

CHAPTER 5. *DEATH AS SEPARATION AND REVERSAL*

1. E. Lüddeckens, *Untersuchungen über religiösen Gehalt, Sprache und Form der ägyptischen Totenklagen, Mitteilungen des Deutschen Archäologischen Instituts Kairo* 11 (1943): 24; Ptahhotep, end of Dynasty 5 (?).

2. Ibid., p. 25; tomb of Idu, Dynasty 6.

3. Ibid., pp. 33–34; tomb of Reneni, early Dynasty 18.

4. Ibid., no. 21, pp. 55–57; tombs of Paheri, Theban Tombs 82 and 100. J. Settgast, *Untersuchungen zu Altägyptischen Bestattungsdarstellungen*, Abhandlungen des Deutschen Archäologischen Instituts Kairo (Glückstadt, 1963), p. 37, n. 4 adds ostracon 51 from Theban Tomb 71; see also W. C. Hayes, *Ostraca and Name Stones from the Tomb of Sen-Mut (no. 71) at Thebes* (New York, 1942), pl. 10, with examples from Theban Tombs 224 and 55.

5. Lüddeckens, *Untersuchungen über religiösen Gehalt*, pp. 109–110 and pl. 24; Theban Tomb 49.

6. *Nḥm=k*.

7. Lüddeckens, *Untersuchungen über religiösen Gehalt*, pp. 111–113.

8. J. Osing, *Das Grab des Nefersecheru in Zawiyet Sultan*, Archäologische Veröffentlichungen des Deutschen Archäologischen Instituts Kairo (Mainz, 1992), pp. 54–55.

9. Papyrus Berlin 3008, 2, 1–13, published by R. O. Faulkner, "The Lamentations of Isis and Nephthys," in *Mélanges Maspero*, Mémoires publiées par les membres de l'Institut Français d'Archéologie Orientale du Caire 66/1 (Cairo, 1935–1938), p. 339. See also S. Schott, *Altägyptische Liebeslieder* (Zurich, 1950), no. 129.

10. Papyrus Bremner-Rhind (Papyrus British Museum 10188), 6.24–7.13; Papyrus Nesbanebdjed I, published by G. Burkard, *Spätzeitliche Osirisliturgien im Corpus der Asasif-Papyri: Übersetzung, Kommentar, formale und inhaltliche analyse*, Ägypten und Altes Testament 31 (Wiesbaden, 1995), pp. 140–141; Schott, *Liebeslieder*, no. 130.

11. Papyrus New York Metropolitan Museum of Art 35.9.21, 5.8–9, published by J.-C. Goyon, *Le Papyrus d'Imouths, Fils de Psinthaês au Metropolitan Museum of Art de New-York (Papyrus MMA 35.9.21)* (New York, 1999), p. 31.

12. Papyrus Bremner-Rhind, 12.9–12 = Nesbanebdjed I, 12.9–12.

13. Papyrus New York Metropolitan Museum of Art 35.9.21, 5.4–6, Goyon, *Papyrus d'Imouthès*, p. 31; Schott, *Liebeslieder*, p. 135.

14. Papyrus New York Metropolitan Museum of Art 35.9.21, 5.11–13, Goyon, *Papyrus d'Imouthès*, pp. 31–32; Schott, *Liebeslieder*, p. 136.

15. Papyrus New York Metropolitan Museum of Art 35.9.21, 7.1–4, Goyon, *Papyrus d'Imouthès*, p. 33; Schott, *Liebeslieder*, p. 137.

16. *ꜥ.t*—read *ꜣ.t*?

17. Lüddeckens, *Untersuchungen über religiösen Gehalt*, pp. 162–164. On his mortuary stela, a child laments about the loneliness of death with similar words:

I died as a small child.
The dead spirits of this tomb keep all men from me,
before the time of being alone has come;
my heart is pleased by the sight of many.

Leiden V F; Lüddeckens, *Untersuchungen über religiösen Gehalt*, p. 163.

18. Theban Tomb 50, see R. Hari, *La Tombe Thébaine du Père Divin Neferhotep (TT 50)* (Geneva, 1985), pl. 4, second song; M. Lichtheim, "The Songs of the Harpers," *Journal of Near Eastern Studies* 4 (1945): 197–198, "Neferhotep II"; Lichtheim, *Ancient Egyptian Literature*, vol. 2 (Berkeley, 1978), pp. 115–116; Schott, *Liebeslieder*, p. 137, no. 101. The second and third songs from the tomb of Neferhotep have a parallel in Theban Tomb 32; see L. Kákosy and Z. I. Fábián, "Harper's Song in the Tomb of Djehutimes (TT 32)," *Studien zur Altägyptischen Kultur* 22 (1995): 211–225 and L. Kákosy, *Dzsehutimesz Sírja Thébában* (Budapest, 1989), pp. 94–95. As the text differs in many respects, it is not copied from Theban Tomb 50 but rather rests on an independent tradition. Here, it is the song of a lute player, not a harper. On the comparison of life to a dream, see also the ostracon published by J. Černý and A. H. Gardiner, *Hieratic Ostraca*, vol. 1 (Oxford, 1957), pl. 39 = J. Assmann, *Ägyptische Hymnen und Gebete* (Zurich, 1975), no. 186:

How short is a lifetime! It passes away.
Let our destiny be fulfilled in Thebes.
This life is something we saw in a dream.
You who remain in the land, do not let us have to stray far from you!

Here, in the age of personal piety, the afterlife no longer draws its luminosity, whose reality outshines that of this world, from the idea of stoniness but from the concept of a closeness to the divine that was possible only in the next life. This concept that postmortem closeness to and knowledge of the divine makes life seem like a sleep from which one wakes in death plays a central role in Islam; see A. Schimmel, "Träume im Islam," in G. Benedetti and E. Hornung (eds.), *Die Wahrheit der Träume* (Munich, 1997), pp. 39–83.

19. The other harpers' songs appear in tombs as captions to the depiction of a harper (less often a lute player), just as described in the caption to the papyrus version. On this text genre, see J. Assmann, "Harfnerlieder," in W. Helck and E. Otto, *Lexikon der Ägyptologie*, vol. 2 (Wiesbaden, 1977), cols. 972–982.

20. On this text, see M. Lichtheim, *Journal of Near Eastern Studies* 4 (1945): 192–193; Lichtheim, *Ancient Egyptian Literature*, vol. 1 (Berkeley, 1973), pp. 195–197; J. Assmann, "Fest des Augenblicks," in J. Assmann, E. Feucht, and R. Grieshammer (eds.), *Fragen an die ägyptische Literatur* (Wiesbaden, 1977), pp. 55–57; and especially M. V. Fox, "A Study of Antef," *Orientalia* 46 (1977): 393–423; and Fox, "The 'Entertainment Song' Genre in Egyptian Literature," *Scripta Hierosolymitana* 28 (1982): 268–316.

21. See the illustration in K. Lange and M. Hirmer, *Ägypten*, 2d ed. (Munich, 1957), pl. 196.

22. Papyrus British Museum 10060 (Papyrus Harris 500), recto 6.2–7.3.

23. Later songs, such as Paser, lines 6–7, Neferhotep 1, lines 5–6, and Theban Tomb 395, lines 3–4 have "come" instead of "stay," which is without doubt better; see also W. Helck, *Urkunden des ägyptischen Altertums*, vol. 4 (Berlin, 1955), p. 2114.

24. The translation is that of Lichtheim, *Ancient Egyptian Literature*, vol. 1, pp. 196–197.

25. A. Heidel, *The Gilgamesh Epic and Old Testament Parallels* (Chicago, 1949), p. 70.

26. K. Jansen-Winkeln, *Ägyptische Biographien der 22. und 23. Dynastie*, Ägypten und Altes Testament 8 (Wiesbaden, 1985), pp. 26–27.

27. A. de Buck, "Een Egyptische Versie van Achilles' klacht (Od. XI, 489–491)," in *Jaarboek der Koninklijke Nederlandse Akademie der Wissenschaften, 1957/58* (1958): 74–96.

28. Literally, "heart-fish." The expression is otherwise unattested.

29. Jansen-Winkeln, *Ägyptische Biographien der 22. und 23. Dynastien*, p. 122. See also S. L. Burkes, *Death in Qoheleth and Egyptian Biographies of the Late Period*, Society of Biblical Literature Dissertation Series 170 (Atlanta, 1997).

30. Cf. Leiden V 55: *jb.kwj jw mw r-gs = j.*

31. Stela of Taimhotep, reign of Cleopatra VII; after Brugsch, *Thesaurus Inscriptionum egyptiacarum* (reprint ed., Graz, 1968), pp. 926–927 and E. Otto, *Die biographischen Inschriften der ägyptischen Spätzeit*, Probleme der Ägyptologie 2 (Leiden, 1954), no. 57.

32. M. Lichtheim, "Songs of the Harpers," p. 203, pl. 11.

33. Papyrus Sallier I, 8; Assmann, *Ägyptische Hymnen und Gebete*, no. 182, 8–12.

34. Ostracon Cairo, published by Černý and Gardiner, *Hieratic Ostraca*, vol. 1, pl. 5.1. Cf. Theban Tomb 111, ceiling text, middle (= liturgy NR.2, no. 15), ceiling, western portion, south. After my own hand copy and that of K. Sethe, *Wörterbuch* Zettel ⟨1701⟩⟨1703⟩:

> (You) are vindicated before that court
> on that day of "Come, then!"
> You are at the forefront of the living,
> as though you were (still) on earth,
> O Osiris N.

35. Cf. also the day on which the gods say "bring him" (A. de Buck, *The Egyptian Coffin Texts*, vol. 1, Oriental Institute Publications 34 [Chicago, 1935], p. 24), by which the day of the Judgment of the Dead is unequivocally meant. Perhaps it is a matter of the day of "summons" in all the text passages.

36. Assmann, *Ägyptische Hymnen und Gebete*, no. 219. This hymn to Osiris is preserved on three stelae: (a) Louvre C 218; P. Pierret, *Receuil d'inscriptions inédites du Musée égyptien du Louvre*, Études Égyptologiques 8 (reprint ed., Hildesheim, 1978), p. 135; E. A. W. Budge, *Transactions of the Society for Biblical Archaeology* 8 (1885), pp. 336–338; S. Sharpe, *Egyptian Inscriptions from the British Museum and Other Sources* (London, 1837), pl. 97; H. Kees, *Reli-*

gionsgeschichtliches Lesebuch, 2d ed. (Tübingen, 1928), p. 17; (b) British Museum 164; T. G. H. James, *Hieroglyphic Texts from Egyptian Stelae, etc.*, vol. 9 (London, 1970), pl. 21, contains verses 1–2, 18–19, and 26–42; and (c) British Museum 142 (fragment, beginning with verse 32); K. A. Kitchen, *Ramesside Inscriptions: Historical and Biographical*, vol. 3 (Oxford, 1980), pp. 218–219. Additionally, the Book of the Dead of Ani, Papyrus British Museum 10470, contains verses 1–2, 18–19, and 26–35; E. A. W. Budge, *The Papyrus of Ani* (London, 1913).

37. The same formula occurs in the second harper's song from Theban Tomb 50, cited above.

38. E. Hornung, *Das Totenbuch der Ägypter* (Zurich, 1979), pp. 62–64.

39. Ankhnesneferibre, lines 310–326.

40. Hornung, *Das Totenbuch*, p. 123 = Coffin Texts spell 199, beginning.

41. On this word, see *Recueil de travaux* 29 (1907): 151.

42. Here probably as the protective tree of the tomb of Osiris.

43. Coffin Texts spell 173 = A. de Buck, *The Egyptian Coffin Texts*, vol. 3, Oriental Institute Publications 64 (Chicago, 1947), 50b–51e.

44. Hornung, *Das Totenbuch*, p. 144, verses 21–28.

45. Metaphor for the aroma of a deity, see A. Erman and H. Grapow, *Wörterbuch der aegyptischen Sprache*, reprint ed. (Berlin, 1971) vol. 1, p. 36.5.

46. See Coffin Texts spell 187.

47. Mortuary liturgy SZ.1, spell 10.

48. Coffin Texts spell 190 = de Buck, *The Egyptian Coffin Texts*, vol. 3, 98 j–m ("Spell for not eating excrement in the realm of the dead"). Similarly, Coffin Texts spell 208 = de Buck, *The Egyptian Coffin Texts*, vol. 3, pp. 130 f–131 b (in version S1C, the title is "not eating excrement, not walking upside down"):

I fly up as a swallow,
I gabble as a goose.
I swoop down on the sycamore
that nourishes the one who endows it in the midst of the flood.
I have been granted an alighting
on the leaves of the *hes-neferet*-tree
on the isle of the flood.
I have been granted an alighting
on the beautiful sycamore on the hill
of the two sycamores of the two floods.

Also, spell 205, de Buck, *The Egyptian Coffin Texts*, vol. 3, pp. 143 f–145 b (in version B2Bo, the title is "not walking upside down"; in version B1Bo, the title is written at the end: "not eating excrement in the realm of the dead"):

I have risen to the place where *maat* is,
I have flown up as a swallow, like Thoth,
I have cried out to them as a goose, like Shesemu,
I have flown up as a *gebga*-goose on that great shore.
I stand on it, I appear as a god.
The one they espy, he does not "land."

49. Note also a text in the tomb of Puyemre, published by N. de G. Davies, *The Tomb of Puyemrê at Thebes*, Publications of the Metropolitan Museum of Art Egyptian Expedition 2 (New York, 1922), pl. 6:

May you have disposal of bread,
may you have a surfeit of beer,
may you enjoy yourself like the goose on the shore.

50. A. de Buck, *The Egyptian Coffin Texts*, vol. 6, Oriental Institute Publications 81 (Chicago, 1956), pp. 196–198.

51. Book of the Dead chapter 153A; see Hornung, *Das Totenbuch*, p. 325, lines 16–27; de Buck, *The Egyptian Coffin Texts*, vol. 6, pp. 18–19, spell 474.

52. See A. de Buck, *The Egyptian Coffin Texts*, vol. 4, Oriental Institute Publications 67 (Chicago, 1951), pp. 23 d and 38 j.

53. After Papyrus Nu (British Museum 10477, col. 9), E. A. W. Budge, *The Book of Coming Forth by Day or the Theban Recension of the Book of the Dead* (London, 1910), vol. 2, pp. 63–64.

54. Coffin Texts spell 397 = de Buck, *The Egyptian Coffin Texts*, vol. 3, pp. 85–89; translated by R. O. Faulkner, *The Ancient Egyptian Coffin Texts*, vol. 2 (Warminster, 1977), p. 25; P. Barguet, *Les Textes des sarcophages égyptiens du Moyen Empire*, Littératures anciennes du Proche-Orient 12 (Paris, 1986), p. 347. Book of the Dead chapter 99, see Hornung, *Das Totenbuch*, p. 191.

55. De Buck, *The Egyptian Coffin Texts*, vol. 2, Oriental Institute Publications 49 (Chicago, 1938), pp. 48–57; Barguet, *Les Textes des sarcophages*, pp. 358–362; D. Mueller, "An Early Egyptian Guide to the Hereafter," *Journal of Egyptian Archaeology* 58 (1972): 99–125; Hornung, *Das Totenbuch*, pp. 210–212.

56. Hornung, *Das Totenbuch*, p. 194.

57. Ibid., p. 195.

58. In an important essay, E. Otto has tracked down these verses in a Coffin Texts spell for offering food, and he has indicated the possibility that the entire text extract stems from the Middle Kingdom; see "Zwei Paralleltexte zu TB 175," *Chronique d'Égypte* 37 (1962): 249–256.

59. These verses are cited in another Coffin Text (spell 1130), as well as in a hymn to Osiris from the Ptolemaic Period; see Otto, "Zwei Paralleltexte zu TB 175."

60. I have somewhat changed the text as it has come down to us. The actual sequence, which seems less meaningful to me, is: (1) the prayer of the deceased to Osiris (Hornung, *Das Totenbuch*, verses 51–62; (2) the praise in Herakleopolis (verses 63–68); and (3) the concluding speech of Osiris to Re(-Atum) (verses 69–77). I have rendered the text in the sequence (3)-(2)-(1).

61. P. Seibert, *Die Charakteristik: Untersuchungen zu einer altägyptischen Sprechsitte und ihren Ausprägungen in Folklore und Literatur,* Ägyptologische Abhandlungen 17 (Wiesbaden, 1967), pp. 20–25. See also W. Schenkel, "Sonst–Jetzt: Variationen eines literarischen Formelements," *Welt des Orients* 15 (1984): 51–61. Unlike Seibert, Schenkel derives the "once–now" literary convention not from laments but from legal complaints.

62. Prophecy of Neferti, 54.

63. Admonitions of Ipuwer, 7, 12.

64. Admonitions, 7, 8.

65. Admonitions, 8, 5.

66. Admonitions, 7, 14.

67. Admonitions, 7, 11.

68. Admonitions, 8, 2.

69. Bertolt Brecht, *The Caucasian Chalk Circle*, translated by Eric Bentley (New York, 1966), pp. 108–109.

70. A. Erman, *Die Literatur der Ägypter* (Leipzig, 1923), pp. 130–148, esp. 133–135.

71. The expression *ḥr.t-nṯr* is perhaps better translated as "realm of death" here.

72. Neferti, 54–56; W. Helck, *Die Prophezeihurg Les Nfr.tj* (Wiesbaden, 1970), pp. 46–47.

CHAPTER 6. DEATH AS TRANSITION

1. N. de G. Davies, *The Tomb of Antefoqer* (London, 1920), pl. 21.

2. K. Sethe's edition of the Pyramid Texts gives only the version in the pyramid of Wenis, creating the impression that the liturgy does not occur in the later pyramids. More recent research by J. Leclant and his team has revealed that the liturgy was carved in all the pyramids of the Old Kingdom. The lengthy list of texts cited in T. G. Allen, *Occurrences of Pyramid Texts with Cross Indexes of These and Other Mortuary Texts*, Studies in Ancient Oriental Civilizations 27 (Chicago, 1950), pp. 68–69 informs us of how widespread this liturgy became

in later eras, down to the Saite Period (Theban Tomb 33, published by J. Dümichen, *Der Grabpalast des Patuamenap in der thebanischen Nekropolis*, 3 vols. [Leipzig, 1884–1894], vol. 2, pls. 16–20).

3. On this expression, see J. Popielska-Grzybowska, "Some Preliminary Remarks on Atum and Jackal in the Pyramid Texts," *Göttinger Miszellen* 173 (1999): 143–153, 148 (i). She refers to § 1641b, "who are mysterious in their tombs, their seats." In § § 665d, 747a, 873b, 900d, 1641b, 1995c, and 2023a, the king also belongs to those with mysterious seats.

4. Pyramid Texts spell 213.

5. Pyramid Texts § § 1930c–1933b, according to R. O. Faulkner; cf. J. P. Allen, *The Inflection of the Verb in the Pyramid Texts*, Bibliotheca Aegyptia 2 (Malibu, 1984), pp. 691–692.

6. Cf. Pyramid Texts 136a, 872d, 885, 1752c.

7. Coffin Texts spell 67 = A. de Buck, *The Egyptian Coffin Texts*, vol. 1, Oriental Institute Publications 34 (Chicago, 1935), pp. 284e–285a.

8. *B3-pf*, "that *ba*," was a god with priests of his own; see L. Kuchman, "The Titles of Queenship," part 1: "The Evidence from the Old Kingdom," *The Newsletter of the Society for the Study of Egyptian Antiquities* 7.3 (1977): 10–12 and pl. 2. This is presumably a designation of a god of the dead, such as Osiris or Kherti; the deceased king does not wish to stray into his territory, yet he wants to capture his throne. In Pyramid Texts spell 262, we learn that the deceased did not come on his own initiative but at the summons of the god:

> N. has passed by the house of that *ba*,
> the rage of the great lake has missed him.
> The fare for the great ferry was not taken (from him).
> The palace of the white mace of the great ones has not rebuffed him.
> See, N. has reached the celestial heights.

9. In one Coffin Text, it is stated, "You have not died dead": de Buck, *The Egyptian Coffin Texts*, vol. 1, p. 287a. Only version Sq3C adds, "and I shall not command that you die the death."

10. See Pyramid Texts spell 262, § 333 (Teti version):

> See, N. has come, see, N. has come!
> But he has not come of his own volition ("of himself"):
> it is your messengers who have brought him,
> the word of a god has caused him to ascend.

And Pyramid Texts spell 262 (Pepy and Neferkare versions):

> See, N. has come, see, N. has come!
> But he has not come of his own volition:
> The message of a god came to him,
> the word of a god caused him to go up.

11. Pyramid Texts spell 214.

12. Pyramid Texts spell 578, § § 1531a–1534a. Here, the deceased is warned off from the east and sent to the west, but the opposite directions also occur:

> Go not on those western roads,
> those who fare on them do not return.
> Go, O N., on those eastern roads
> among the followers of Re, who swings his arm in the east.

Pyramid Texts spell 697, § 2175a–d.

13. Pyramid Texts spell 302, § 459a.

14. Pyramid Texts spell 665, § 1904c. Cf. the following passages:

> I have claimed him from the hand of Kherti
> and shall never give him over to Osiris.

Pyramid Texts spell 667A, § 1945.

He has saved him from the hand of Inuti.
he will not be given over to Kherti.

Pyramid Texts spell 556, § 1386b–c.
In a mortuary liturgy of the Middle Kingdom, we read:

You will not be delivered to Kherti,
you will not be given over to "the reservation of the hunters,"
you will not row the *Jss*-barque,
you will not bail out the *h̲ȝ-sj͗r.t*-barque.

A. de Buck, *The Egyptian Coffin Texts*, vol. 4, Oriental Institute Publications 67 [Chicago, 1951], spell 12 (Theban Tomb 353)
   15. See E. Hornung, *Das Totenbuch der Ägypter* (Zurich, 1979), p. 150.
   16. In the version on coffin S1C/S2C:

To be recited. Commanding that the West pleasantly welcome so-and-so; commanding that the West rejoice over so-and-so with all that is done for him on that New Year's in the realm of the dead.
To be recited on all the annual festivals and on that special day at that special time.

   17. J. J. Tylor, *Wall Drawings and Monuments of El Kab: The Tomb of Renni* (London, 1900), pl. 12/13; E. Lüddeckens, *Untersuchungen über religiösen Gehalt, Sprache und Form der ägyptischen Totenklagen, Mitteilungen des Deutschen archäologischen Instituts Kairo* 11 (Cairo, 1943), pp. 35–36.
   18. On this goddess, see H. Refai, *Die Göttin des Westens in den thebanischen Gräbern des Neuen Reichs* (Cairo, 1995).
   19. It is also possible to translate ". . . with what it did not know," but the meaning is less suitable. The sense is that in the form of the deceased, something entirely new, heretofore unheard of, enters into the earth. In the Pyramid Text, we read, "He has opened (broken up?) the earth with what he knows."
   20. B4L, B12C, B13C, and B16C insert:

Behold, his sweat of life and lastingness
is upon his posterity, who I am, while he lives.
I am his living *ba* on earth.

   21. What is meant is unclear. Perhaps there is an allusion to *fd.t* "sweat, scent."
   22. Or, "after you have dispelled his grief over his family on earth"?
   23. This is presumably an allusion to an enumeration, as in de Buck, *The Egyptian Coffin Texts*, vol. 1, p. 9: "your male enemies and your female enemies, who act against you, who hate you, and who bring legal action against you."
   24. A. H. Gardiner and K. Sethe, *Egyptian Letters to the Dead, Mainly from the Old and Middle Kingdoms* (London, 1928); see also the book review by B. Gunn, *Journal of Egyptian Archaeology* 16 (1930): 147–155; A. H. Gardiner, "A New Letter to the Dead," *Journal of Egyptian Archaeology* 16 (1930): 19–22; A. Piankoff and J. J. Clère, "Letter to the Dead on a Bowl in the Louvre," in *Journal of Egyptian Archaeology* 20 (1934): 157–169; W. K. Simpson, "The Letter to the Dead from the Tomb of Meru (N 3737) at Naga ed-Deir," *Journal of Egyptian Archaeology* 52 (1966), 39–52; Simpson, "A Late Old Kingdom Letter to the Dead from Naga ed-Deir N 3500," *Journal of Egyptian Archaeology* 56 (1970): 58–64; R. Grieshammer, "Briefe an Tote," in W. Helck and E. Otto (eds.), *Lexikon der Ägyptologie*, vol. 1 (1974), cols. 864–870; E. F. Wente, "A Misplaced Letter to the Dead," *Orientalia Lovanensia Analecta* 6/7 (1975/76): 595–600; W. K. Simpson, "The Memphite Epistolary Formula on a Jar Stand of the First Intermediate Period from Naga ed-Deir," in W. K. Simpson and W. M. Davies (eds.), *Studies in Ancient Egypt, the Aegean, and the Sudan* (Boston, 1981), pp. 173–179; M. Bommas, "Zur

Datierung einiger Briefe an die Toten," *Göttinger Miszellen* 173 (1999): 53–60; D. Czerwik, "Some Remarks on the Letters to the Dead from the FIP," *Göttinger Miszellen* 173 (1999): 61–65.

25. An epistolary formula with which the writer of the letter refers to himself.

26. G. Fecht, "Der Totenbrief von Naga ed-Deir," *Mitteilungen des Deutschen Archäologischen Instituts Kairo* 24 (1969): 105–128.

27. The inducing of visions in dreams was one of the magical practices of ancient Egypt. J. Gee explains Coffin Texts spells 89 and 99–104 as a ritual for sending out the *ba* to appear before someone else ("that man"), evidently in a dream (communication to the Eighth International Congress of Orientalists in Cairo, March 31, 2000). The spells were to be recited over a figure of clay inscribed with the name of the man.

28. Gardiner and Sethe, *Letters to the Dead*, pp. 1–2 and 13–16, plate 1 ("Cairo text on linen," Journal d'entrée 25975).

29. Bowl Cairo Catalogue Générale 25375; Gardiner and Sethe, *Letters to the Dead*, pp. 7–8 and 22. Translation based on that of M. Bommas.

30. H.-W. Fischer Elfert, *Literarische Ostraka der Ramessidenzeit in Übersetzung* (Wiesbaden, 1986), pp. 74–77. The text contains another two strophes.

31. Read *srḫw*?

32. Papyrus Boulaq 4, 22, 1–3; F. J. Quack, *Die Lehren des Ani*, Orbis Biblicus et Orientalis 141 (Freiburg and Göttingen, 1994), pp. 114–117.

CHAPTER 7. DEATH AS RETURN

1. I have published this inscription in two essays: "Die Inschrift auf dem äusseren Sarkophagdeckel des Merenptah," *Mitteilungen des Deutschen Archäologischen Instituts Kairo* 28/1 (1972): 47–73 and "Neith spricht als Mutter und Sarg," *Mitteilungen des Deutschen Archäologischen Instituts Kairo* 28/2 (1973): 115–139.

2. Note the reversal of the normal order, in which the sun is born in the morning and impregnates in the evening by entering the womb of the sky goddess.

3. Actually, "those who dwell in Nut."

4. The four torches of chapter 137 of the Book of the Dead. On the text passages cited in *Mitteilungen des Deutschen Archäologischen Instituts Kairo* 28/1 (1972): 63, see also J. Quaegebeur, *Le Dieu égyptien Shai dans la religion et l'onomastique*, Orientalia Lovaniensia Analecta 2 (Louvain, 1975), pp. 157–158 and I. E. S. Edwards, *Oracular Amuletic Decrees of the Late New Kingdom*, Hieratic Papyri in the British Museum, 4th series (London, 1960), pp. 96–97, n. 38.

5. Cf. A. de Buck, *The Egyptian Coffin Texts*, vol. 1, Oriental Institute Publications 34 (Chicago, 1935), § 25.

6. Coffin Cairo Catalogue générale 29305; G. Maspero, *Sarcophages des époques persane et ptolémaique*, vol. 1 (Cairo, 1919), p. 217.

7. Coffin board; R. Lepsius, *Denkmäler aus Aegypten und Aethiopien*, part 3, reprint ed. (Osnabrück, 1972), pl. 271d.

8. Papyrus Louvre 3148, 11, 9–11; S. Schott, "Nut spricht als Mutter und Sarg," *Revue d'Égyptologie* 17 (1965): 81–87.

9. On the goddess of the sky as Great Mother, see also A. Weiss, *Die Madonna Platytera* (Königstein i.Ts., 1985).

10. Papyrus Rhind 11, 5.

11. *Št3.t št3.t iwty rḫ sj, jj nṯr.t wr.t nn sfḫ.tw qrjs = s.*

12. Papyrus Louvre 3148, 3, 4–6; see note 8 above.

13. H. Refai, *Die Göttin des Westens in den thebanischen Gräbern des Neuen Reiches: Darstellung, Bedeutung und Funktion*, Abhandlungen des Deutschen Archäologischen Instituts Kairo 12 (Berlin, 1996).

14. J. Assmann, "Eine Traumoffenbarung der Göttin Hathor: Zeugnisse 'Persönlicher Frömmigkeit' in thebanischen Privatgräbern der Ramessidenzeit," *Revue d'Égyptologie* 30 (1979): 34–36.

15. Admittedly, this could be a secondary meaning. W. Westendorf, "Die *njnj*-Begrüssung," in U. Verhoeven and E. Graefe (eds.), *Religion und Philosophie im Alten Ägypten*, Orientalia Lovanensia Analecta 39 (Louvain, 1991), pp. 351–362, infers a verb *njnj* with the meaning "to spread (the fingers)." He points to the close relationship between the *njnj* greeting and the embrace, and he explains the *njnj* greeting as a "gesture of welcome" that indicates the "marriage of the celestial mother to her son as he returns to her (in her womb)."

16. Westendorf, "Die *njnj*-Begrüssung," pp. 39–40. Refai, *Die Göttin des Westens*, p. 47 mentions seven tombs in which the goddess of the West is represented making the *njnj*-gesture: Valley of the Kings 8 and Theban Tombs 23, 41, 51, 189, 195, and 259 (his "Darstellungstypus F").

17. For the time being, see Assmann "Traumoffenbarung," p. 38, and K. J. Seyfried, "'Generationeneinbindung'" in J. Assmann et al. (eds.), *Thebanische Beamtennekropolen: Neue Perspektiven archäologischer Forschung*, Studien zur Archäologie und Geschichte Altägyptens 12 (Heidelberg, 1995), pp. 219–231. The tomb will be published by the Institute of Egyptology of Heidelberg University.

18. C. G. Jung, *Symbole der Wandlung der Libido*, 4th ed. (Zurich, 1952), pp. 346–348 and 378–380; see also H. Frankfort and G. Bing, "The Archetype in Analytical Psychology and the History of Religion," *Journal of the Warburg and Courtauld Institutes* 21 (1958): 166–178, esp. pp. 174–175. On the interpretation of burial as *regressus ad uterum*, see J. Assmann, "Tod und Initiation im altägyptischen Totenglauben," in H. P. Duerr (ed.), *Sehnsucht nach dem Ursprung: zu Mircea Eliade* (Frankfurt, 1983), pp. 336–359, esp. pp. 340–341, "Sarglegung als regressus ad uterum"; and Assmann, "Muttergottheit," in W. Helck and E. Otto (eds.), *Lexikon der Ägyptologie*, vol. 4 (1982), cols. 266–271. See also E. Hermsen, "Regressus ad uterum: Die embryonale Jenseitssymbolik Altägyptens und die prä- und perinatale Psychologie," *International Journal of Prenatal and Perinatal Psychology and Medicine* 5 (1993): 361–382.

19. J. Assmann, *Liturgische Lieder an den Sonnengott*, Münchner ägyptologische Studien 19 (Munich, 1969), text 113, pp. 229 and 236–237:

Descending into the body
of his mother Nut.

J. Assmann, *Ägyptische Hymnen und Gebete* (Zurich, 1975), no. 23, lines 15–16:

You set as Atum.
You embrace your mother, your mother embraces you.

J. Assmann, *Ägyptische Hymnen und Gebete*, no. 130, lines 70–72:

Msqt receives you, your mother embraces you,
the western Light-land opens up to you,
its arms are outstretched to receive you.

In the Book of Caverns, which is a description of the netherworld, the sun god constantly says:

I enter the earth from which I emerged,
I settle down on the place of my first birth.

See *Liturgische Lieder an den Sonnengott*, p. 98 (text 12).

20. J. Assmann, *Ägyptische Hymnen und Gebete*, no. 129:

The one who is carried in pregnancy during the night and is born in the morning,
when it becomes light, he is at his place of yesterday.
The one who enters the mouth and emerges from the thighs,
. . . rising without wearying,

that he may shine upon the lands and the islands,
runner who courses forever,
who does not cease shining daily.

21. J. Assmann, *Ägyptische Hymnen und Gebete*, no. 225.
22. Cf. an inscription in the tomb of Kheruef (Theban Tomb 192), to which K. J. Seyfried has drawn attention. In the entrance from the court to the transverse chamber of the tomb, there is a ceiling inscription that compares this entrance into the interior of the tomb with the entrance to the netherworld:

To be spoken by N.:
O first gate of Imhet, (called)
"She allows coming in, her abomination is going out"!

See K. J. Seyfried, ""Kammern, Nischen und Passagen in Felsgräbern des Neuen Reiches," in H. Guksch and D. Polz (eds.), *Stationen: Beiträge zur Kulturgeschichte Ägyptens, Rainer Stadelmann gewidmet* (Mainz, 1998), p. 389.
23. Book of the Dead papyrus Dublin no. 4; Pierret, *Études égyptiens*, vol. 1 (Paris, 1873), pp. 83-84. In the concluding words, the deceased commends himself to the mother goddess with the same words he utters before Osiris, his judge and ruler:

I come to you bearing *maat*,
I did no wrong on earth.
I have done that which pleases the king and that with which the gods are content.

24. K. Sethe, *Urkunden des ägyptischen Altertums*, vol. 4 (reprint ed., Berlin, 1961), p. 965.
25. In many variants of this appeal, burial and return are intimately connected, as, for example, in the inscription of one Sebekhotep:

As you wish that your city gods praise you,
that you endure in your place (i.e., tomb),
that your children inherit your offices,
that you return in peace,
and that your wife can recount your campaigns.

Inscription of Sebekhotep; K. Sethe, *Ägyptische Lesestücke zum Gebrauch im akademischen Unterricht* (Leipzig, 1924), pp. 88-89, § 28g.
26. E. Brunner-Traut, "Die Lehre des Djedefhor," *Zeitschrift für ägyptische Sprache und Altertumskunde* 76 (1940): 3-9; G. Posener, "Le Début de l'Enseignement de Hardjedef," *Revue d'Égyptologie* 9 (1952): 109-117; Posener, "Quatre tablettes scolaires de Basse Époque," *Revue d'Égyptologie* 18 (1966): 62-65.
27. Papyrus Leiden I 350, 6, 9-10 = J. Assmann, *Ägyptische Hymnen und Gebete*, no. 142 and Assmann, *The Search for God in Ancient Egypt* (Ithaca, 2001), p. 21.
28. G. Lefebvre, *Le Tombeau de Petosiris*, vol. 2 (Cairo, 1923), p. 83, no. 116 = Assmann, *Search for God*, pp. 21-22.
29. Shipwrecked Sailor (Papyrus Leningrad 1115), lines 119-123; A. M. Blackman, *Middle-Egyptian Stories*, Bibliotheca Aegyptiaca 2 (Brussels, 1932), p. 45.
30. Shipwrecked Sailor, lines 167-169; Blackman, *Middle-Egyptian Stories*, p. 47.
31. Story of Sinuhe R, lines 5-8; Blackman, *Middle-Egyptian Stories*, p. 3.
32. Story of Sinuhe B, lines 156-160 and 167-173; Blackman, *Middle-Egyptian Stories*, pp. 29-30. Cf. the translations of E. Blumenthal, *Altägyptische Reiseberichte* (Leipzig, 1982), p. 14 and R. Koch (ed.), *Die Erzählung des Sinuhe*, Bibliotheca Aegyptiaca 17 (Brussels, 1990), pp. 57-58.
33. There follows a description of the burial rites:

The sky is above you, while you lie on the bier.
Oxen draw you, singers precede you.

The dance of the weary ones is danced at the entrance to your tomb.
The offering list is recited for you.
Sacrifice is made at the door of your offering stone.
Your pillars are built of white limestone
in the vicinity of the (tombs of the) royal children.

34. Sinuhe B, lines 188–199; Blackman, *Middle-Egyptian Stories*, p. 32.

35. Papyrus Leiden I 384, 5, 14–21; F. de Cénival, *Le Mythe de l'oeil du soleil: Translittération et traduction avec commentaire philologique*, Demotische Studien 9 (Sommerhausen, 1988), pp. 12–13; E. Brunner-Traut, *Altägyptische Märchen*, 8th ed. (Munich, 1989), pp. 155–157, no. 17, 314–315. Parallel Demotic texts: papyrus Tebtunis Tait 8 and papyrus Lille unnumbered; see M. Smith, "Sonnenauge," in W. Helck and E. Otto (eds.), *Lexikon der Ägyptologie*, vol. 5 (Wiesbaden, 1984), cols. 1982–1987.

36. Coffin Texts spell 1130; de Buck, *The Egyptian Coffin Texts*, vol. 7, Oriental Institute Publications 87 (Chicago, 1961), p. 464 d–e.

37. P. Leiden I 384, 5, 14–21; F. de Cénival, *Le Mythe de l'oeil du soleil*, pp. 12–13.

38. H. Junker, *Die Stundenwachen in den Osirismysterien* (Vienna, 1910), p. 87; spell accompanying the libation in the third hour of the night.

39. Sinuhe B 57, in E. Blumenthal's translation, "Nicht kommt zum Ziel, wer ihm den Rücken kehrt" ("he who turns his back on him does not reach his goal").

40. Loyalist Instruction § 6, lines 3–4; G. Posener, *L'Enseignement loyaliste: Sagesse égyptienne du Moyen Empire* (Geneva, 1976), p. 93.

41. Loyalist Instruction § 7, 1–5; Posener, *L'Enseignement loyaliste*, pp. 32–33 and 97–99.

42. G. Posener, "L'Anachoresis dans l'Égypte pharaonique," in J. Bingen et al. (eds.), *Le Monde grec: Hommages à Claire Préaux* (Brussels, n.d.), pp. 663–669.

43. "*Tous anthropous phesin Aklmaion dia touto apollysthai, hoti ou dynantai ten archen to telei proshapsai.*" Fragment 2, cited by Aristotle, *Problems*, 17.3 s.; H. Diels and W. Kranz (eds.), *Die Fragmente der Vorsokratiker*, vol. 1 (Berlin, 1964), p. 215.

44. E. Hornung, "Zeitliches Jenseits im Alten Ägypten," *Eranos Jahrbuch* 1978: 269–307; cf. Hornung, "Verfall und Regeneration der Schöpfung," *Eranos Jahrbuch* 1977: 411–449.

45. Cf. also the verses in the speech of Neith on the coffin of Merneptah:

I am pregnant with you in the morning
and bear you as Re in the evening.

This motif has been investigated by W. B. Kristensen in his work *Het Leven uit den dood: Studien over egyptische en oud-griekse godsdienst*, 2d ed. (Haarlem, 1926); see also P. Derchain, "Perpetuum mobile," *Orientalia Lovanensia Periodica* 6/7 (1976): 153–161.

46. Papyrus Chester Beatty IV, recto, 11, 8–9; see J. Assmann, *Ägyptische Hymnen und Gebete*, no. 195, verses 274–278; O. Kaiser (ed.), *Texte aus der Umwelt des Alten Testaments*, vol. 2/6 (Gütersloh, 1991), p. 891.

47. Papyrus Berlin 3024, lines 130–142.

CHAPTER 8. DEATH AS MYSTERY

1. This is the Egyptian term for a mortuary or memorial temple; see G. Haeny, *Basilikale Anlagen in der Baukunst des Neuen Reiches*, Beiträge zur ägyptischen Bauforschungen und Altertumskunde 9 (Wiesbaden, 1970); D. Arnold, "Vom Pyramidenbezirk zum Millionenjahrhaus," *Mitteilungen des Deutschen Archäologischen Instituts Kairo* 34 (1978): 1–8; Haeny, "La Fonction religieuse des 'chateaux de millions d'années,'" in *L'Égyptologie en 1979: Axes prioritaires des recherches*, vol. 1 (Paris, 1982), pp. 111–116; Arnold, *Die Tempel Ägyptens: Götterwohnungen, Baudenkmäler, Kultstätten* (Zurich, 1992), pp. 34–35.

2. On this point, see E. Hornung, *Tal der Könige: Die Ruhestätte der Pharaonen* (Zurich, 1982).

3. E. Hornung, *Die Nachtfahrt der Sonne: Eine altägyptische Beschreibung des Jenseits* (Zurich, 1991).

4. R. O. Faulkner, in E. von Dassow (ed.), *The Egyptian Book of the Dead: The Book of Going Forth by Day* (San Francisco, 1994), pl. 7:

> To me belongs yesterday, I know tomorrow.
> *What does it mean?* As for yesterday, that is Osiris. As for tomorrow, that is Re on that day in which the foes of the Lord of All were destroyed and his son Horus was made to rule.

5. Book of the Dead chapter 15g, after the mortuary papyrus of Gatseshni; see J. Assmann, *Liturgische Lieder an den Sonnengott*, Münchner ägyptologische Studien 19 (Munich, 1969), pp. 93 and 101–105. Similar turns of expression occur often in hymns to the night sun. In the Litany of Re, a hymn recorded only in royal tombs, we read:

> Jubilation rings out in the mystery:
> It is Re, who rests in Osiris, and vice versa.

Hornung, *Das Buch der Anbetung des Re im Westen (Sonnenlitanei)*, vol. 1, Aegyptiaca Helvetica 2 (Geneva, 1975), p. 178 and vol. 2, Aegyptiaca Helvetica 3 (Geneva, 1976), pp. 83 and 137–138 (text 406).

6. See Assmann, *Liturgische Lieder*, p. 102, n. 65; Hornung, *Conceptions of God in Ancient Egypt: The One and the Many* (Ithaca, 1982), pp. 93–94; Hornung, *Das Buch der Anbetung*, vol. 2, pp. 53–54.

7. A. Piankoff, *Mythological Papyri*, Egyptian Religious Texts and Representations 3, Bollingen Series 40 (Princeton, 1957), pp. 89 and 90.

8. Papyrus Salt 825, 18, 1–2; see P. Derchain, *Le Papyrus Salt 825: Rituel pour la conservation de la vie en Égypte* (Brussels, 1965), vol. 1, pp. 163–165 and vol. 2, p. 19.

9. Assmann, *Liturgische Lieder*, pp. 84–86.

10. Ibid.

11. Book of Gates, scene 38. See E. Hornung, *Das Buch von den Pforten des Jenseits*, 2 vols., Aegyptiaca Helvetica 7–8 (Geneva, 1979–1984), vol. 2, pp. 162–163; Hornung, *Ägyptische Unterweltsbücher*, 2d ed. (Zurich, 1984), p. 246. Cf. also ibid., p. 247:

> It is you who surround my mystery,
> who are the protection of my mystery, which is in the House of the *Benben*.

Further, innumerable examples of this usage could be adduced. In particular, the uniting of Re and Osiris is described as the sun god resting in his mystery:

> You are Re when you lower yourself onto your corpse,
> you are mighty in your mystery.

Litany of Re, Hornung, *Das Buch der Anbetung*, vol. 1, p. 157 and vol. 3, pp. 81 and 134–135 (text 371).

> You lower yourself, O Re, onto your mystery.

Book of Gates, published by C. Maystre and A. Piankoff, *Le Livre des portes*, 3 vols. (Cairo, 1939–1962), vol. 2, p. 183.

> The god has come to his corpse,
> the god has been drawn to his shadow.
> You occupy your body (*d.t*) and you are drawn,
> you who are hale in your mystery.

Book of Gates, scene 65; Hornung, *Das Buch von den Pforten*, pp. 233–234.

12. H. Junker, *Das Götterdekret über das Abaton*, Denkschriften der Österreichischen Akademie der Wissenschaften (Vienna, 1913).

13. Diodorus Siculus, *Library of History*, book 1, chapter 21.

14. D. Meeks, "Oiseaux des carrières et des cavernes," in U. Verhoeven and E. Graefe (eds.), *Religion und Philosophie im Alten Ägypten: Festgabe für Philippe Derchain zu seinem 65. Geburtstag am 24. Juli 1991*, Orientalia Lovaniensia Analecta 39 (Louvain, 1991), pp. 233–241.

15. Papyrus Westcar 7, 23–26.

16. Cf. Coffin Texts spell 901.

17. E. B. Pusch, *Das Senet-Brettspiel in alten Ägypten*, Münchner ägyptologische Studien 38 (Munich, 1979). For a playable reconstruction of the game, see T. Kendall, *Passing through the Netherworld* (Belmont, 1978). The final moves of the game had to do with provisioning ("bread in the house of bread, cool water in the house of cool water") and vindication ("You are vindicated!" says he, namely Mehen, to me").

18. Theban Tomb 1; Pusch, *Das Senet-Brettspiel*, pl. 28.

19. J. Assmann, "Le Temple égyptien et la distinction entre le dedans et le dehors," in *Le Temple, lieu du conflit: Actes du colloque de Cartigny 1988*, Les Cahiers du CEPOA 7 (Louvain, 1995), pp. 13–34, esp. pp. 23–24. On two-dimensional representations of this temple concept, see Françoise Le Corsu, "Stèles-portes égyptiennes à éléments emboîtés d'époque gréco-romaine," *Revue d'Égyptologie* 20 (1968): 109–125.

20. E. Hornung, *Das Totenbuch der Ägypter* (Zurich, 1979), p. 389, fig. 90.

21. Cf. the translation of Faulkner, *The Egyptian Book of the Dead*, p. 133.

22. B. Lüscher, *Untersuchungen zu Totenbuch Spruch 151*, Studien zum altägyptischen Totenbuch 2 (Wiesbaden, 1998), pp. 237–240.

23. On this point, see T. DuQuesne, "Anubis Master of Secrets (*ḥry-sštʒ*) and the Egyptian Conception of Mysteries," in A. Assmann and J. Assmann (eds.), *Schleier und Schwelle, Archäologie der literarischen Kommunikation 5*, part 2: *Geheimnis und Offenbarung* (Munich, 1998), pp. 105–121.

24. On this chamber, see the exhibit catalogue *Sen-nefer: Die Grabkammer des Bürgermeisters von Theben* (Mainz, 1986). In this uniquely decorated burial chamber, we find scenes from thematic area (3), such as the funeral and the Opening of the Mouth, along with the tomb owner in the company of the tree goddess (here called Isis) and in adoration of Osiris, as well as representations of Anubis over the entrance, all of which belong to (4). The scenes in which Sennefer's wife presents him with strips of cloth and jeweled collars also belong to the area of next-worldly life (4) and not to the mortuary cult in the tomb (2).

25. The tomb will be published by L. Kákosy et al. For the time being, see Kákosy, *Dsehutimesz Sírja Thébában* (Budapest, 1989), jacket photo.

26. See pp. 119 above and 202–203 below, both cited from versions in Theban Tomb 50.

27. A. Hermann, *Die Stelen der thebanischen Felsgräber der 18. Dynastie*, Ägyptologische Forschungen 11 (Glückstadt, 1940), pp. 46–47, type III.

28. Ibid., pp. 47–48, type IV.

29. J. Assmann, *Das Grab des Amenemope (Nr. 41) in der thebanischen Nekropole*, Theben 3 (Mainz, 1991).

30. K. J. Seyfried, "Entwicklung in der Grabarchitektur des Neuen Reichs als eine weitere Quelle für theologische Konzeptionen der Ramessidenzeit," in J. Assmann, G. Burkard, and V. Davies (eds.), *Problems and Priorities of Egyptian Archaeology* (London, 1987), 219–254; F. Kampp-Seyfried, *Die thebanische Nekropole: Zum Wandel des Grabgedankens von der XVIII. bis zur XX. Dynastie*, 2 vols., Theben 13 (Mainz, 1996); on the development of the forecourt, see pp. 58–81; on pyramids, see pp. 95–109.

31. R. Hari, *La Tombe thébaine du Père Divin Neferhotep (T50)* (Geneva, 1985), pl. 4, third song.

32. This in any event remained a rarity; see Kampp-Seyfried, *Nekropole*, p. 51.

33. J. Assmann, "Eine Traumoffenbarung der Göttin Hathor: Zeugnisse 'Persönlicher Frömmigkeit' in thebanischen Privatgräbern der Ramessidenzeit," *Revue d'Égyptologie* 30 (1978): 22–50.

34. E.g., chapters 15 B III; 148; 190; 130; 134; 137 A and B.

35. Book of the Dead chapter 137 A, rubric (Nu, 25, 31–33 and 39–40).

36. Book of the Dead chapter 137 (Nebseni, 24, 18–19).

37. Litany of Re, published by E. Naville, *La Litanie du Soleil: Inscriptions receueillis dans les tombeaux des rois à Thèbes* (Leipzig, 1875), XII, 13; A. Piankoff, *The Litany of Re*, Egyptian Texts and Representations 4, Bollingen Series 40 (New York, 1964), p. 36.

38. J. Assmann, *Liturgische Lieder an den Sonnengott* (Berlin, 1969), no. 19 (Book of the Dead 15 B III); E. Hornung, *Das Totenbuch der Ägypter*, p. 406 (Book of the Dead 190).

39. Assmann, *Liturgische Lieder*, p. 31.

40. E. Hornung, *The Secret Lore of Egypt: Its Impact on the West* (Ithaca, 2001).

41. R. Hari, *La Tombe thébaine du Père Divin Neferhotep*, pl. 4, third song; M. Lichtheim, "The Songs of the Harpers," *Journal of Near Eastern Studies* 4 (1945): 178–212, see "Neferhotep III," pp. 198–199. Neferhotep II and III have a parallel in Theban Tomb 32, see L. Kákosy and Z. I. Fábián, "Harper's Song in the Tomb of Djehutimes (TT 32)," *Studien zur altägyptische Kultur* 22 (1995): 211–225. This is the song of a lutist, not a harper; see Kákosy, *Dzsehutimesz*, pp. 94–95. Since the latter text displays a number of differences, it was not copied from Theban Tomb 50 but rather rests on an independent tradition. The parallel to Neferhotep III begins in line 17.

42. Lichtheim: "Beginning of song: Remember, o heart, that day of death"; so also Hari. For my own part, I take the entire section as the title of the text and understand it as a deliberate inversion of the usual *ḥsw r smḫ jb*, "song to make the heart forget." Titles that begin with *ḥ3.t-ᶜ* are usually more elaborate than this one is, according to Lichtheim's understanding.

43. So also in the hymn to Osiris Louvre C 218 (*Ägyptische Hymnen und Gebete*, no. 219, verses 40–41; above, chapter 6, section 1b): "Whether one fares upstream or downstream in the course of a lifetime—morning after morning, your majesty is there as Re, and all that is and is not yet follows you." The Neferhotep II variant in Theban Tomb 32 closes with the words: *ḥd ḫnt m ḫnw n ᶜḥᶜw ḥr n zj nb r[=f]* "whether one fares downstream or upstream in life, all faces are turned to him."

44. So in the case of Theban Tomb 32. Theban Tomb 50 reverts to the second person here, probably erroneously.

45. That is, outside the door of the place of embalming.

46. Book of the Dead Chapters 108, 109, and 112–116, on which see K. Sethe et al., "Die Sprüche zum Kennen der Seelen der heiligen Orte," *Zeitschrift für ägyptische Sprache und Altertumskunde* 59 (1924): 1–99.

47. Hornung:

"I am a *wab*-priest in Busiris,
an elevated one who is in the primeval hill (?)."

48. A. Erman and H. Grapow, *Wörterbuch der ägyptische Sprache*, reprint ed. (Berlin, 1971), vol. 5, p. 330.9, stating that the word is used in reference to the dismemberment of Osiris on the Sokar festival, and referring to A. Mariette, *Dendéra; Description générale du temple de cette ville*, vol. 4 (Paris, 1875), p. 38, lines 88–89.

49. Hornung: "I have opened the vaults to wash the Weary of Heart."

50. Hornung: "in order to hide the mysteries in Rasetau."

51. Hornung: "right."

52. Hornung: "as a flame."

53. Hornung: "when offerings were made to Re." "Re" is lacking in the version on the papyrus of Ani.

54. On this spell, see B. Lüscher, *Totenbuch Spruch 1, nach Quellen des Neuen Reichs* (Wiesbaden, 1986).

55. See, in particular, R. Merkelbach, *Isis-Regina, Zeus-Sarapis* (Stuttgart, 1995), chapter 23, pp. 266–303; J. G. Griffiths, *Apuleius of Madauros: The Isis-Book (Metamorphoses, Book XI)* (Leiden, 1975), pp. 296–308; J. Bergman, "Per omnia vectus elementa remeavi," in U. Bianchi and M. J. Vermaseren (eds.), *La Soterologia degli culti orientali nell'impero romano* (Leiden, 1982), pp. 671–702; E. Hornung, "Altägyptische Wurzeln der Isismysterien," in C. Berger, G. Clerc, and N. Grimal (eds.), *Hommages à Jean Leclant*, Bibliothèque d'Étude 106 (Cairo, 1994), pp. 287–293; F. Dunand, *Isis, mère des dieux* (Paris, 2000), pp. 127–140.

56. On this point, see especially the essay by Hornung, "Altägyptische Wurzeln der Isismysterien."

57. C. Riedweg, "Initiation—Tod—Unterwelt: Beobachtungen zur Kommumikationssituation und narrativen Technik der orphisch-bakchischen Goldplättchen," in *Ansichten griechischer Rituale* (Stuttgart und Leipzig, 1998), pp. 359–398.

58. See E. Bresciani, *Il Volto di Osiri: Telle funerarie dipinte nell'Egitto romano / The Face of Osiris: Painted Funerary Shrouds in Roman Egypt* (Lucca, 1996).

59. S. Morenz, "Das Werden zu Osiris: Die Darstellungen auf einem Leinentuch der römischen Kaiserzeit (Berlin 11 651) und verwandten Stücken," *Staatliche Museen zu Berlin, Forschungen und Berichte* 1 (1957): 52–70 = *Religion und Geschichte des alten Ägypten* (Weimar, 1975), pp. 231–247; Morenz, "Das Problem des Werdens zu Osiris in der griechisch-römischen Zeit," in *Religions en Égypte hellénistique et romaine* (Vendôme, 1969), pp. 75–91 = *Religion und Geschichte des alten Ägypten*, pp. 248–262; C. Römer, "Das Werden zu Osiris im römischen Ägypten," *Archiv für Religionsgeschichte* 2/2 (2000): 141–161.

60. K. Parlasca, *Mumienportraits und verwandte Denkmäler* (Wiesbaden, 1966); Parlasca, *Repertorio d'arte dell'Egitto greco-romano* (Palermo, 1961).

61. See A. Schweizer, *Seelenführer durch den verborgenen Raum: Das ägyptische Unterweltsbuch Amduat* (Munich, 1994) and G. Schoeller, *Isis: Auf der Suche nach dem göttlichen Geheimnis* (Munich, 1991). See also chapter 17, section 2a.

CHAPTER 9. GOING FORTH BY DAY

1. K. Brandt, "Scheintüren und Entablaturen in den Privatgräbern der 18. Dynastie." Ph.D. dissertation, Heidelberg University, 2000.

2. W. Barta, *Aufbau und Bedeutung der altägyptischen Opferformel*, Ägyptologische Forschungen 24 (Glückstadt, 1968), p. 66, wish 92; H. O. Lange and H. Schäfer, *Grab- und Denksteine des Mittleren Reiches im Museum von Kairo*, vol. 2 (Berlin, 1908), p. 73.

3. Barta, *Opferformel*, p. 79, wish no. 92 (a); H. O. Lange and H. Schäfer, *Grab- und Denksteine*, vol. 1 (Berlin, 1902), p. 15.

4. Wish 92 (b); J. Capart, *Receuil des monuments égyptiens* (Brussels, 1902), pl. 32.

5. Lange and Schäfer, *Grab- und Denksteine*, vol. 2, p. 192.

6. Barta, *Opferformel*, p. 118; C. Boreux, *La Statue du serviteur royal Nofirronpit* (Paris, 1933), pp. 12–13.

7. Barta, *Opferformel*, p. 119; Theban Tomb 912, A. Fakhry, *Annales du Service des Antiquités de l'Égypte* 42 (1943): 501.

8. I. G. Botti, in *Studi in memoria di Ippolito Rosellini nel primo centenario della morte (4 giugno 1843)*, vol. 1 (Pisa, 1949), pl. 2.

9. O. Koefoed-Petersen, *Receuil des inscriptions hiéroglyphiques de la Glyptothèque Ny Carlsberg*, Bibliotheca Aegyptiaca 6 (Brussels, 1936), p. 6.

10. B. Bruyère, *Rapport sur les fouilles de Deir el-Médineh (1935–40)*, Fouilles de l'Institut Français d'Archéologie Orientale 22, fascicle 1 (Cairo, 1948), p. 6.

11. As the determinative of the word in the parallel passage in A. de Buck, *The Egyptian Coffin Texts*, vol. 5, Oriental Institute Publications 73 (Chicago, 1954), p. 209n makes clear, the reference is to sexual pleasure.

12. *Coffin Texts* spell 697. J.-E. Gautier and G. Jéquier, *Mémoire sur les fouilles de Licht*, Mémoires publiés par les membres de l'Institut Français d'Archéologie Orientale du Caire 6 (Cairo, 1902) pl. 20; H. Kees, *Totenglauben und Jenseitsvorstellungen der alten Ägypter*, 2d ed. (Berlin, 1956), p. 264, translates:

> . . . dass NN in sein Haus eintrete, dass er seine Sprösslinge zähle,
> dass er Lust ausübe und Zuneigung empfange,
> zusammen mit denen auf Erden in alle Ewigkeit,
> dass er alle Gestalten annehme, die er wünscht,
> dass ihm die Alterswürde des ehrwürdigen Gottes in seinem Grabe zuteil werde,
> dass er Luft atme am Tage der grossen Prüfung.

13. R. O. Faulkner, *The Ancient Egyptian Coffin Texts*, vol. 2 (Warminster, 1977), pp. 56–57; see D. Mueller, "An Early Egyptian Guide to the Hereafter," *Journal of Egyptian Archaeology* 58 (1972): 104–105 and W. Westendorf, "Bemerkungen zur Kammer der Wiedergeburt im Tutanchamungrab," *Zeitschrift für ägyptische Sprache und Altertumskunde* 94 (1967): 146–147.

14. Variant:

The one who knows this spell, who goes out by day,
will not be kept away from any gateway in the realm of the dead.
He transforms into a swallow—
a genuine remedy, proved millions of times.

15. De Buck, *The Egyptian Coffin Texts*, vol. 4, Oriental Institute Publications 67 (Chicago, 1951), spell 340 = Book of the Dead chapter 121 (= 13) and 122 (= 58); see Kees, *Totenglauben*, p. 279.

16. J. Assmann and M. Bommas, *Altägyptische Totenliturgien*, vol. 2 (in press), no. 5.2.3.

17. The parallel text 8.3.1 reads, *ȝḥ n bȝ = k* "may it be well with your *ba*."

18. Assmann and Bommas, *Altägyptische Totenliturgien*, vol. 2, no. 8.3.4 (Theban Tomb 23).

19. There was such a book in the solar cult, the Book of the Transformations of Re. It contained 24 different forms assumed by the sun god during the 24 hours of the day and the night; see A. Gasse, "La Litanie des douze noms de Re-Horakhty," *Bulletin de l'Institut Français d'Archéologie Orientale* 84 (1984): 189–227. The twelve transformations of the deceased might be related to the twelve hours of the day. As early as 1867, H. Brugsch drew attention to a coffin in Cairo whose decoration combines the hourly forms of the sun god and the vignettes of the transformation spells; see H. Brugsch, *Zeitschrift für ägyptische Sprache und Altertumskunde* 5 (1867): 21–26 and E. Hornung, *Das Totenbuch der Ägypter* (Zurich, 1979), p. 461.

20. Assmann and Bommas, *Altägyptische Totenliturgien*, vol. 2, no. 4.1.1.1 (Theban Tomb 110).

21. Theban Tomb 24.

22. Theban Tomb 83; *Wörterbuch der ägyptischen Sprache* Zettel <701>.

23. Unpublished; from N. de G. Davies notebook 1/74.

24. S. Schott, *Das schöne Fest vom Wüstental: Festbräuche einer Totenstadt*, Abhandlungen der Akademie der Wissenschaften und der Literatur Mainz, Geistes- und sozialwissenschaftlichen Klasse, Jahrgang 1952/11 (Mainz, 1953), wished to interpret all these scenes as representaitons of the "Beautiful Festival of the Valley"; this is true of a number of these scenes, but on the whole, he went too far.

25. E. Hornung, "Zur Struktur des ägyptischen Jenseitsglaubens," *Zeitschrift für ägyptische Sprache und Altertumskunde* 119 (1992): 124–130; see also J. Assmann, "Totenglauben," in W. Helck and E. Otto (eds.), *Lexikon der Ägyptologie*, vol. 6 (Wiesbaden, 1986), col. 670.

26. Hornung, *Akhenaten and the Religion of Light* (Ithaca: Cornell University Press, 1999).

27. Ibid., p. 102; see also L. V. Žabkar, *A Study of the Ba-Concept in Ancient Egyptian Texts*, Studies in Ancient Oriental Civilizations 34 (Chicago, 1968), pp. 156–159.

28. M. Sandman, *Texts from the Time of Akhenaten*, Bibliotheca Aegyptiaca 8 (Brussels, 1938), p. 49.

29. Sandman, *Texts from the Time of Akhenaten*, p. 34; the text occurs in the tombs of Huya and Pentu.

30. Assmann and Bommas, *Altägyptische Totenliturgien*, vol. 2, no. 3, lines 59–60.

31. A. Brack and A. Brack-Hug, *Das Grab des Tjanuni*, Archäologische Veröffentlichungen 19 (Mainz, 1977), p. 25, fig. 2. In another inscription from the same tomb, this wish is expressed again in similar terms;

Going out as a living *ba*,
without being turned away at the gates of the *Duat*.
Visiting his house of the living,
in the manner of his existence on earth. (Ibid., p. 53, text 60)

32. *Rwy.t.* Defined otherwise by A. Erman and H. Grapow (eds.),*Wörterbuch der aegyptischen Sprache*, reprint ed. (Berlin, 1971), vol. 2, p. 407.13.

33. Assmann and Bommas, *Altägyptische Totenliturgien*, vol. 2, no. 5.1.3, from Theban Tomb 82 (text 431).

34. *ḥꜣ.t tꜣ.wj*, an otherwise unknown festival.

35. Brussels E 4295, J. Capart, *Recueil de travaux relatifs à la philologie et à l'archéologie égyptiennes et assyriennes* 22 (1900): 107; D. Meeks, "Oiseaux des carrières et des cavernes," in U. Verhoeven and E. Graefe (eds.), *Religion und Philosophie des Alten Ägypten* (Louvain, 1991), p. 241.

36. Assmann and Bommas, *Altägyptische Totenliturgien*, vol. 2, no. 8.2.13 = G. T. Martin, *The Tomb-Chapels of Paser and Ra'ia at Saqqâra* (London, 1985), pl. 10. On the opposite side of the entrance, a corresponding inscription reads:

> May you go in and out where you will,
> without your *ba* being confined.
> When you are called, may you come immediately,
> May you visit your house on earth.

Similarly a harper's song, Assmann and Bommas, *Altägyptische Totenliturgien*, vol. 2, no. 8.5.2: "May you [he]ar the requests of the children of your house." The deceased continues to care for his family, who can turn to him with requests; see further chapter 5, section 3 of this volume.

37. N. de G. Davies, *The Town House in Ancient Egypt*, Metropolitan Museum of Art Studies 1/2 (New York, 1929).

38. After the copy by Sethe, *Wörterbuch der ägyptischen Sprache* Zetteln <1575> and <1576> and the copy by Davies, mss. 11.7.

39. Assmann and Bommas, *Altägyptische Totenliturgien*, vol. 2, no. 8.1.8: Theban Tomb 106, south stela, with parallels in Theban Tomb 23 (16) and Theban Tomb 222; all of these are unpublished.

40. The tomb will be published by Heike Guksch, whom I thank for sharing her text collation.

41. Barta, *Opferformel*, wish no. 179.

42. Barta, *Opferformel*, wish no. 160. Text: tomb of Haremhab, E. de Rougé, *Inscriptions hiéroglyphiques copiés en Égypte pendant la mission scientifique de M. le vicomte Emmanuel de Rougé* (Paris, 1877), p. 105. Similarly, Turin 100, published by G. Maspero, *Recueil de travaux relatifs à la philologie et à l'archéologie égyptiennes et assyriennes* 4 (1873): 135–136, no. XXV (no. 100).

43. Louvre C 55, K. Piehl, *Inscriptions hiéroglyphiques recueillies en Europe et en Égypte*, 3 vols. (Leipzig, 1886–1903), inscription xv = Stockholm, stela 55; stela text of Menkheper, W. Helck, *Urkunden des ägyptischen Altertums*, vol. 4 (Berlin, 1956), pp. 1525–1527; J.-C. Hugonot, *Le Jardin dans l'Égypte ancienne* (Frankfurt, 1989), p. 170; H. Guksch, *Die Gräber des Nacht-Min und des Men-cheper-Raseneb*, Archäologische Veröffentlichungen 34 (Mainz, 1995), p. 152.

44. The reference is to the water table, which fills the fountain of the garden.

45. Theban Tomb 82, Assmann and Bommas, *Altägyptische Totenliturgien*, vol. 2, no. 5.1.4; 432. N. de G. Davies and A. H. Gardiner, *The Tomb of Amenemhet (No. 82)*, Theban Tomb Series 1 (London, 1915), p. 102 and pl. 27; Helck, *Urkunden*, vol. 4, p. 1064; Hugonot, *Le Jardin*, p. 166.

46. Theban Tomb 99 = Theban Tomb 91 (from my own hand copy) = Theban Tomb 110, A. Hermann, *Die Stelen der thebanischen Felsgräber der 18. Dynastie*, Ägyptologische Forschungen 11 (Glückstadt, 1940), pp. 31*–32*; N. de G. Davies, "Tehuti, Owner of Tomb 110 at Thebes," in S. R. K. Glanville (ed.), *Studies Presented to F. Ll. Griffiths* (Milford, 1932), pls. 37 and 40.

47. B. Gessler-Löhr, *Die heiligen Seen ägyptischer Tempel*, Hildesheimer ägyptologische Beiträge 21 (Hildesheim, 1983), pp. 101–108.

48. The reference is to the tomb. On *sꜣḥ* as the necropolis district, see J. Assmann, *Grab des Basa (nr. 389) in der thebanischen Nekropole*, Archäologische Veröffentlichungen 6 (Mainz, 1973), p. 70 (c).

49. This "sitting at the pond" reminds us of representations of fishing in a seated position: see Hugonot, *Le Jardin*, fig. 113 (Hatiai); M. Eaton-Krauss and E. Graefe, *The Small Golden Shrine from the Tomb of Tutankhamun* (Oxford, 1985), and K. Seele, *The Tomb of Tjanefer at Thebes*, Oriental Institute Publications 86 (Chicago, 1959), pl. 36 (Theban Tomb 158). See also D. Kessler, "Zu den Jagdszenen auf dem kleinen goldenen Tutanchamun-schrein," *Göttinger Miszellen* 90 (1986): 35–43 and Kessler, "Zur Bedeutung der Szenen des täglichen Lebens in den Privatgräbern, I: Die Szenen des Schiffbaues und der Schiffahrt," *Zeitschrift für ägyptische Sprache und Altertumskunde* 114 (1987): 59–61.

50. Assmann and Bommas, *Altägyptische Totenliturgien*, vol. 2, no. 8.2.11 (466) = Theban Tomb 373, transverse chamber, east wall, published by K.-J. Seyfried, *Das Grab des Amonmose (TT 373)*, Theben 4 (Mainz, 1990), p. 50, text 22; the tomb is dated to regnal years 20–40 of Ramesses II.

51. B. Gessler-Löhr, "Die Totenfeier im Garten," in Assmann, *Das Grab des Amenemope (TT 41)*, Theben 3 (Mainz, 1991), pp. 162–183.

52. In the same sense, see also E. Feucht, "Fishing and Fowling with the Spear and the Throw-stick Reconsidered," in U. Luft (ed.), *The Intellectual Heritage of Egypt*, Studia Aegyptiaca 14 (Budapest, 1992), pp. 157–169.

53. G. Lapp, *Die Opferformel des Alten Reichs* (Mainz, 1986), p. 141.

54. Assmann and Bommas, *Altägyptische Totenliturgien*, vol. 2, no. 1.7.

55. See, e.g., Coffin Texts spell 203, A. de Buck, *The Egyptian Coffin Texts*, vol. 3, Oriental Institute Publications 64 (Chicago, 1947), p. 130 and Coffin Texts spell 723, de Buck, *The Egyptian Coffin Texts*, vol. 6, Oriental Institute Publications 81 (Chicago, 1956), p. 353. Cf. also already Pyramid Texts spell 470, § 916.

56. E. Otto, "Die beiden vogelgestaltigen Seelenvorstellungen der Ägypter," *Zeitschrift für ägyptische Sprache und Altertumskunde* 77 (1942), p. 81, n. 1; L. Žabkar, *A Study of the Ba-Concept*, p. 138; A. Hermann, *Stelen*, p. 52*, 6–16, and cf. p. 22*, 11–13. On the tree goddess, see the splendid study by O. Keel, "Ägyptische Baumgöttinnen der 18.–21. Dynastie: Bild und Wort, Wort und Bild," in Keel (ed.), *Das Recht der Bilder, gesehen zu werden: Drei Fallstudien zur Methode der Interpetation altorientalischer Bilder*, Orbis Biblicus et Orientalis 122 (1992), pp. 61–138.

57. Theban Tomb 99, etc.; see n. 46.

58. Louvre C 55, Piehl, *Inscriptions*. 125 = Stockholm Stela no. 55; stela text of Menkheper, Helck, *Urkunden*, vol. 4, pp. 1525–1527. See Hugonot, *Le Jardin*, p. 170. Interestingly, the association of the *ba*-bird and the sycamore is not attested iconographically until after the Amarna Period, as Erik Hornung has noted (cited by O. Keel, "Ägyptische Baumgöttinnen," pp. 74–75). Similarly Theban Tomb 99, etc., see n. 46:

Transforming into a living *ba*,
ah, may he alight upon his grove,
may he enjoy the shade of his sycamores.

Assmann and Bommas, *Altägyptische Totenliturgien*, vol. 2, no. 6.2.6 (479); sun hymn from the tomb of Haremhab in Saqqara, published by de Rougé, *Inscriptions*, pls. 104–106 and G. T. Martin, *The Memphite Tomb of Ḥoremḥeb, Commander-in-Chief of Tut'ankhamun*, 2 vols., Egypt Exploration Society Excavation Memoir 55 (London, 1989–1996), pls. 24–25 and pp. 33–35:

May I stroll on the shore of my pond
daily, without cease,
may my *ba* alight on the branches of my palms.

Theban Tomb 82, published by Davies and Gardiner, *The Tomb of Amenemhet*, pl. 27; Sethe, *Urkunden*, vol. 4, p. 1082; and Hugonot, *Le Jardin*, p. 166:

May your heart take joy in your grove,
and may you be refreshed under your sycamores.

The topic of visiting the garden is also mentioned in captions that accompany depictions, on pillars and doorway thicknesses of the tomb owner striding out of the tomb, e.g., in Theban Tomb 85 (published by H. Guksch), Theban Tomb 95 (edited by A. Gnirs), and Theban Tomb 76 (published by U. Bouriant, *Recueil de travaux relatifs à la philologie et à l'archéologie égyptiennes et assyriennes* 11 [1889]: 158).

59. Theban Tomb 106, south stela text; there are parallel texts in Theban Tomb 23 (16) and Theban Tomb 222.

60. Such a garden is also archaeologically attested in tomb 106, in the form of a miniature pond with plants.

61. Theban Tomb 106 (unpublished); cf. Theban Tomb 41, Assmann, *Das Grab des Amenemope (TT 41)*, Theben 3 (Mainz, 1991), p. 37, text 18.

62. Ibid., pp. 37–38, text 19.

63. See Assmann, "Das ägyptische Prozessionsfest," in J. Assmann and T. Sundermeier (eds.), *Das Fest und das Heilige* (Gütersloh, 1991), pp. 105–122.

64. On the "Abydos mysteries," see most recently M. Lavier, "Les Mystères d'Osiris d'après les stèles du Moyen Empire et du Nouvel Empire," in S. Schoske (ed.), *Akten des 4. Internationalen Ägyptologen-Kongresses München 1985*, vol. 3, Studien zur altägyptische Kultur Beiheft 3 (Hamburg, 1989), pp. 289–295.

65. Lange and Schäfer, *Grab- und Denksteine*, vol. 1, p. 27.

66. Lange and Schäfer, *Grab- und Denksteine*, vol. 2, p. 192.

67. P. Vernus, "La Stèle C 3 du Louvre," *Revue d'Égyptologie* 25 (1973): 226–227; M. Lichtheim, *Ancient Egyptian Autobiographies, Chiefly of the Middle Kingdom*, Orbis Biblicus et Orientalis 84 (Freiburg and Göttingen, 1988), pp. 86–88.

68. The term *meskhenet*, an *m*-formation from the verb *sekhen* "to lower oneself" with the meaning "place of seating oneself," refers to the two bricks upon which an Egyptian woman sat during childbirth with support from both sides and from a midwife. Here, the reference is clearly to a rebirth of the deceased in the realm of the gods. The deities Khnum and Heqet (see the following note) belong to this birth scene.

69. On Khnum and Heqet, see J. Spiegel *Die Götter von Abydos*, Göttinger Orientforschungen 1 (Wiesbaden, 1973), pp. 82–88. The two deities were worshiped together at Antinoe in the Hermopolitan nome, and they appear together in the ritual of the birth of the divine king (in the New Kingdom) or of the god (in the Greco-Roman Period). Spiegel rightly presumes that their collaboration in the Abydene transfiguration ritual points to an equation of birth and embalming (transfiguration). Khnum and Heqet also occur together in offering formulas; see ibid., pp. 85–86 and index, pp. 171–172 s.v. Khnum and Heqet (nineteen occurrences).

70. On a stela from Edfu, a short version of this spell also occurs as an address in the second person (C. Kuentz, "Deux Stèles d'Edfou," *Bulletin de l'Institut Français d'Archéologie Orientale* 21 [1923]: 109–111):

> May you travel on the lake of the sky
> and move on the horizon.
> May you be provided with things that are in superabundance
> and with what they give in the District of Offerings.
> May the great ones of Busiris transfigure you,
> the royal seat of the lord of Abydos.
> May you open the ways that you strive for
> in peace to the District of Offerings.
> May "welcome!" be said to you
> (by the) gods in the necropolis.
> (May) arms (be extended to you in the) *neshmet*-barque (in the) horizon
> of [. . .]. May you ply the rudder in the night-barque
> and sail in the day-barque.

71. See also E. Otto, *Osiris und Amun: Kult und Heiligen Stätten* (Munich, 1966); I am largely in agreement with his interpretation of Ikhernofret's inscription.

72. Stela of Ikhernofret, Berlin 1204; K. Sethe, *Ägyptische Lesestücke zum Gebrauch im akademischen Unterricht* (Leipzig, 1928), p. 71, lines 11–13.

73. Scholars have pictured the beating back of rebels as a ritual drama, referring to Herodotus, who describes a ritual mock battle in Papremis. This seems unthinkable, however, for earlier periods in Egyptian history.

74. Sethe, *Ägyptische Lesestücke*, p. 71, lines 13–16.

75. British Museum, *Hieroglyphic Texts from Egyptian Stelae, &c., in the British Museum*, vol. 2 (London, 1912), pl. 45; Lange and Schäfer, *Grab- und Denksteine*, vol. 1, p. 27; Barta, *Opferformel*, p. 64, wish no. 73 = text (500).

76. Sethe, *Ägyptische Lesestücke*, p. 71, lines 17–18.

77. Theban Tomb 192 (4).

78. Text published by W. Spiegelberg, "Varia," *Recueil de travaux relatifs à la philologie et à l'archéologie égyptiennes et assyriennes* 19 (1897): 97–98.

79. Assmann and Bommas, *Altägyptische Totenliturgien*, vol. 2, no. 7, 11.

80. On this topic, see chapter 11 of this volume.

81. See chapter 12 of this volume.

82. J. Dümichen, *Altägyptische Kalenderinschriften in den Jahren 1863–1865 an Ort und Stelle gesammelt und mit erläuternden Text herausgegeben* (Leipzig, 1866), pl. 43, line 14; cf. Lichtheim, *Ancient Egyptian Autobiographies*, pp. 85–88 and Spiegel, *Die Götter von Abydos*, p. 147. Spiegel renders *Ḥr šn* as "der streitbare Horus" (valiant Horus), while Lichtheim translates it "Horus the fighter." BM 567, line 11 and 573, line 9; Louvre C3, line 14; Munich Glyptothek WAF 35, line 14; see Lavier, "Les Mystères d'Osiris," p. 291.

83. Sethe, *Ägyptische Lesestücke*, p. 71, lines 18–23.

84. The stela of a lady from the Middle Kingdom depicts her participation in the festival at Abydos in the following terms:

May she go to Abydos
on that day which is not spoken of.
May she enter the chapel and behold the mysteries,
may she go up into the *neshmet*-barque
and cross the river in the god's ship.
May N. come out from the field of Re
with *ankh-imi* plants at her eyes, her nose, and her ears,
and *znw* plants on her body.
After Tait has clothed her,
after the clothing of the eldest Horus has been given to her
on that day when he took the *wrrt* crown.
Your nose belongs to you, your eyes belong to you, O N.!

See M. Lichtheim, "The Stela of Taniy," *Studien zur altägyptischen Kultur* 16 (1989): 211.

85. Spiegel, *Die Götter von Abydos*, pp. 115–169, esp. pp. 138–140.

86. Instead of embalming, there was now the preparation of a grain mummy, with the canonical number of seventy days reduced to seven. On the first day of the festival, the eighteenth day of Khoiak, the grain mummy was begun by planting moistened barley seeds in a mummy-shaped bed. It took the seeds seven days to sprout. On the twenty-second day of Khoiak, in the middle of the seven-day period, there was the Festival of Hacking the Earth. This festival had an obviously agricultural meaning: the earth was hacked up so as to receive seeds. Nevertheless, the explanation the festival receives in the texts associated with it goes in an entirely different direction, interpreting it as a battle and victory of Osiris over his enemies.

87. See G. A. Gaballa and K. A. Kitchen, "The Festival of Sokar," in *Orientalia* 38 (1969): 1–76.

88. Schott, *Das schöne Fest vom Wüstental: Festbräuche einer Totenstadt.*

89. C. Graindorge-Héreil, *Le Dieu Sokar à Thèbes au Nouvel Empire*, Göttinger Orientforschungen 28 (Wiesbaden, 1994).

90. See Assmann, "Das ägyptische Prozessionsfest," in Assmann (ed.), *Das Fest und das Heilige* (Gütersloh, 1981), pp. 105–122, esp. pp. 117–119, "Amarna als Antifest."

91. Tomb of Aya, M. Sandman, *Texts from the Time of Akhenaten*, Bibliotheca Aegyptiaca 8 (Brussels, 1938), p. 92.

92. N. de G. Davies, *The Tomb of Neferhotep at Thebes*, Publications of the Metropolitan Museum of Art 9 (New York, 1933), pl. 34 and p. 49. A shawabti inscription from the reign of Amenophis III also speaks of the "night of the dinner" during the Wag festival and participation in the offerings; see H. D. Schneider, *Shabtis: An Introduction to the History of Ancient Egyptian Funerary Statuettes*, Collections of the National Museum of Antiquities at Leiden 2 (Leiden, 1977), vol. 1, pp. 270–272. Similarly, in a ceiling text from Theban Tomb 49, published by Davies, *Neferhotep*, pl. 58–59, we read:

> Following Wennefer in Rasetau
> during his festival of the *neshmet*-barque;
> playing the helmsman in the god's boat
> on the day of the procession to Busiris;
> I am given a bunch of *hsjjt*-plants
> on the morning of the Neheb-kau festival;
> taking the faïence necklace during the festival of Sakhmet,
> and a garment of red material.

In Theban Tomb 158, pl. 4, there is mention of a "*thnw*-pendant on your breast" in connection with the festival of Sokar and a garland of onions.

93. Assmann and Bommas, *Altägyptische Totenliturgien*, vol. 2, no. 8.1.7.

94. Theban Tomb 106, south stela text; there are parallels in Theban Tomb 23 (16) and Theban Tomb 222. Similarly, Theban Tomb 106 (1):

> May I follow Wennefer to U-poqe
> on the beautiful day of the *neshmet*-barque.
> May I receive [. . .]
> on the day of Rasetau.
> May I follow the *henu*-barque with onions around my neck
> like all the living,
> and may I eat a cake from the *khesit*-plant
> on the morning of the Neheb-kau festival.
> May I wear a faïence pendant and clothing of red material
> on the festival of Sakhmet.
> May I receive offering meals at the beginning of the inundation, on the morning of
>   the New Year festival.
> May my name be called out and found
> on the day of erecting the *djed*-pillar.

95. Paper read in Leipzig (new research), June 1998.

96. Paper read at the Eighth International Congress of Egyptologists in Cairo, March–April 2000.

97. See S. Wiebach, "Die Begegnung von Lebenden und Verstorbenen im Rahmen des thebanischen Talfestes," *Studien zur Altägyptischen Kultur* 13 (1986): 274–291.

98. *Odyssey* 24.1–2; see R. L. Eickhoff (trans.), *Homer: The Odyssey* (New York, 2001), p. 359.

99. See R. Merkelbach, *Isis regina—Zeus Sarapis: Die Griechisch-ägyptische Religion nach den Quellen dargestellt* (Stuttgart, 1995), pp. 232–233.

CHAPTER 10. MORTUARY LITURGIES AND MORTUARY LITERATURE

1. J. L. Austin, *How to Do Things with Words* (Oxford, 1962).

2. J. R. Searle, *Speech Acts: An Essay in the Philosophy of Language* (Cambridge, 1969).

3. K. Sethe (ed.), *Die altägyptischen Pyramidentexte*, 4 vols. (Leipzig, 1908–1922); English translation by R. O. Faulkner, *The Ancient Egyptian Pyramid Texts*, 2 vols. (Oxford, 1969).

4. A. de Buck, *The Egyptian Coffin Texts,* 7 vols. (Chicago, 1935–1961); English translation by R. O. Faulkner, *The Ancient Egyptian Coffin Texts,* 3 vols. (Warminster, 1973–1978).

5. German translation by E. Hornung, *Das Totenbuch der Ägypter* (Zurich, 1979), with bibliographical details regarding editions and other translations; English translation by R. O. Faulkner in E. von Dassow (ed.), *The Egyptian Book of the Dead: The Book of Going Forth by Day* (San Francisco, 1994), with interpretive essays by O. Goelet.

6. See, e.g., G. Zuntz, *Persephone: Three Essays on Religion and Thought in Magna Graecia* (Oxford, 1971), pp. 275–393; C. Riedweg, "Initiation—Tod—Unterwelt: Beobachtungen zur Kommunikationssituation und narrativen Technik der orphisch-bakchischen Goldplättchen," in F. Graf (ed.), *Ansichten griechischer Rituale* (Stuttgart and Leipzig, 1998), pp. 359–398; W. Burkert, "Der geheime Reiz des Verborgenen: Antike Mysterienkulte," in H. G. Kippenberg and G. Stroumsa (eds.), *Secrecy and Concealment: Studies in the History of Mediterranean and Near Eastern Religions* (Leiden, 1995), pp. 79–100, esp. 95–97; and R. Merkelbach, "Die goldenen Totenpässe: Ägyptisch, Orphisch, Bakchisch," *Zeitschrift für Papyrologie und Epigraphik* 128 (1999): 1–13.

7. This is the number counted by Faulkner in *The Ancient Egyptian Pyramid Texts.*

8. See the preface to E. Hornung, *The Ancient Egyptian Books of the Afterlife* (Ithaca, 1999).

9. On the discussion that follows, see J. Osing, "Zur Disposition der Pyramidentexte des Unas," *Mitteilungen des Deutschen Archäologischen Instituts Kairo* 42 (1986): 131–144.

10. On these spells, see chapter 6 of this volume.

11. See chapter 9 of this volume.

12. On this text, see chapter 14, section 3 of this volume.

13. Cf. chapter 14, section 3 of this volume.

14. The following excerpt is from a solar hymn of the New Kingdom:

Your sphinx-standard fells your enemy.
Rejoice, O you who are in your barque!
Your crew is in harmony.
The day barque has joined you, your heart is broad.

O lord of the gods you created,
they give you praise.
Nut shines lapis-lazuli colors at your side,
you have penetrated the primeval water with your rays.
Shine on me, that I may gaze upon your beauty:
I am one who was hale on earth.
I give praise to your beautiful visage
(when) you ascend in the Light-land of the sky.
I praise the sun disk when it descends
over that mountain of Sankh-Tawi.

Transfigurations thus could also be characterized as "hymns to the dead."

15. E. Erman and H. Grapow, *Wörterbuch der aegyptischen Sprache,* reprint ed. (Leipzig, 1971), vol. 2, p. 471.4 lists a few late occurrences in which the visitor to the tomb is addressed with *ḥ3.*

16. Erman and Grapow, *Wörterbuch,* vol. 2, p. 471.3; occurrences that refer to Osiris and the nocturnal sun god are of course transfiguring speeches.

17. P. Wegener, *Untersuchungen über die Grundfragen des Sprachlebens* (Halle, 1885).

18. A. H. Gardiner, *The Theory of Speech and Language* (Oxford, 1932, 2nd ed. 1951), p. 7.

19. B. Dominicus, *Gesten und Gebärden in Darstellungen des Alten und Mittleren Reichs,* Studien zur Archäologie und Geschichte Altägyptens 10 (Heidelberg, 1994), pp. 61–65 and 85.

20. See J. Assmann, *Liturgische Lieder an den Sonnengott* (Berlin, 1969), p. 45.

21. G. Möller, *Über die im einem späthieratischen Papyrus des Berliner Museums enthaltenen Pyramidentexte* (Berlin, 1900).

22. See F. Junge, "Sprachstufen und Sprachgeschichte," *Zeitschrift der deutschen Morgenländischen Gesellschaft,* Supplement 6/22 (Stuttgart, 1985), pp. 17–34.

23. See the apposite remarks of H. te Velde, "Some Remarks on the Mysterious Language of the Baboons," in J. H. Kamstra, H. Milde, and K. Wagtendonk (eds.), *Funerary Symbols and Religion: Essays Dedicated to Professor Heerma van Voss on the Occasion of His Retirement from the Chair of the History of Ancient Religions at the University of Amsterdam* (Kampen, 1988), pp. 129–136, esp. pp. 134–135.

24. On *descensio* and *translatio* as the basic principles of the Egyptian cult in the sense of an earthly reflection of celestial events, see the *Corpus Hermeticum*, "Asclepius," lines, 23–25, and the comments on this passage by J. Assmann, *The Search for God in Ancient Egypt* (Ithaca, 2001), pp. 40–52.

25. Iamblichus, *De mysteriis Aegyptiorum*, ed. E. des Places (Paris, 1989). The title of the work stems from the Renaissance. Iamblichus stylized his text as a letter written by an Egyptian priest named Abammon in response to a letter written by the philosopher Porphyry to a priest named Anebo, a letter that contained questions critical of Egyptian religion.

26. Iamblichus, *De mysteriis Aegyptiorum* I 12; T. Taylor, *Iamblichus on the Mysteries of the Egyptians, Chaldeans, and Assyrians* (San Diego, 1984), p. 56.

27. Iamblichus, *De mysteriis Aegyptiorum* IV 3; translation based on that of T. Hopfner, *Über die ägyptischen Geheimlehren: Die Mysterien der Ägypter, Chaldäer, und Assyrer* (Leipzig, 1922), pp. 121–122.

28. Iamblichus, *De mysteriis Aegyptiorum* VI 6; Taylor, *Iamblichus*, p. 281.

29. Stela of Sethos I for Ramesses I, see chapter 2 of this volume.

30. Less often, such mortuary texts are also found on the walls of the sarcophagus chambers. Especially instructive is the sarcophagus chamber of a man named Senwosretankh in the Residence cemetery of Lisht from the reign of Senwosret I. Not only do the inscriptions in this chamber consist solely of Pyramid Texts but also they mostly follow the order and the arrangement of the texts in the pyramid of Wenis. Only in the area of the entrance and in the northeast corner of the chamber are there spells that did not yet occur in the pyramid of Wenis. These are spells 364, 677, 365, and the beginning of 373 (entrance) and spells 593, the beginning of 356, the end of 357, the beginning words of 364, the end of 373, and Coffin Texts spell 516 (northeast corner). These spells are from another mortuary liturgy well attested from Middle Kingdom coffins down to tombs and papyri of the Late Period:

P. BM 10081 SZ.21	PT spells	Sq4C lines	B9C lines	B10C1 lines	B10C2 lines	PzmTk lines
XXIII: spell 8a	593	157–169	291–297	256–260	395–399	102–113
8b–c	356–357	169–177	297–302	260–263	399–402	113–125
8d	364	177–198	302–312	263–269	402–408	125–131
XXIV: 9	677	198–212	312–319	269–274	408–413	142–150
XXV: 10	365 + 373	212–229	319–325	274–279	413–418	150–157

This liturgy corresponds to H. Altenmüller's sequence of spells D, which he established on the basis of a comparison of coffins B9C, B10C1, and B10C2 (all belonging to the nomarch Amenemhet from el-Bersha), Sq4C, Sq5Sq, and Sq13C with the mastaba of Senwosretankh; see H. Altenmüdller, *Die Texte zum Begräbnisritual in den Pyramiden des Alten Reiches* (Wiesbaden, 1972), pp. 34 and 49–50. This has, as we shall see, a ritual reference entirely different from the liturgy of spells 213–219 and 220–222.

31. On the Book of the Dead, see the survey of editions and translations by E. Hornung, *Altägyptische Jenseitsführer: Ein einführender Überblick* (Darmstadt, 1997), pp. 22–23.

32. On the Saite Period as the time when the Book of the Dead was canonized, see U. Verhoeven, *Untersuchungen zur späthieratischer Buchschrift* (Wiesbaden, 2001).

33. The relationship of image to magic is discussed by P. Eschweiler, *Bildzauber im alten Ägypten: Die Verwendung von Bildern und Gegenständen in magischen Handlungen nach den Texten des Mittleren und Neuen Reichs*, Orbis Biblicus et Orientalis 137 (Freiburg and Göttingen, 1994) and Eschweiler, *Das Ägyptische Totenbuch: Vom Ritual zum Bild* (Frankfurt, 1999).

34. L. Borchardt, "Das Dienstgebäude des auswärtigen Amtes unter den Ramessiden," *Zeitschrift für ägyptischen Sprache und Altertumskunde* 44 (1907–1908): 59–61.

35. See above, p. 220. On p. 231, it is confirmed that Tjay is the owner of Theban Tomb 23.

36. P. Westcar 7.17–19.

37. P. Westcar 7.23–26.

38. See H. Grapow, *Wie die alten Ägypter sich anredeten, wie sie sich grüssten, und wie sie miteinander sprachen*, 2d ed. (Berlin, 1960), pp. 105–107.

39. P. Anastasi I; see H. W. Fischer-Elfert, *Die literarische Streitschrift des Papyrus Anastasi I*, 2 vols. (Wiesbaden, 1983–1986).

40. The same is also true of the corresponding wish formulas in the Moscow literary letter of P. Pushkin 127, which are, if anything, even more elaborate. See R. A. Caminos, *A Tale of Woe from a Hieratic Papyrus in the A. S. Pushkin Museum of Fine Arts in Moscow* (Oxford, 1977).

41. According to Gardiner, the hieroglyph for lips was erroneously inserted and should be omitted.

42. *Ntj nb=s{st}*; the entire group seems superfluous and is perhaps to be omitted.

43. *M ḫnw*, literally "within."

44. Written with the divine determinative.

45. *Šbn.k bꜣ.w iqr.w*, Gardiner, after P. Anastasi I, 3.5.

46. *Šms*, written *šmj*, emended by Gardiner.

47. So after Ostracon Gardiner 28.

48. Or, "more than the pointer (of a scale)," though both translations yield no meaning. Gardiner proposes changing *nṯrj* to *mtr*, which better suits "pointer," but not *bꜣ*: "may your *ba* be more accurate than the pointer."

49. A. H. Gardiner, *Late-Egyptian Miscellanies*, Bibliotheca Aegyptiaca 7 (Brussels, 1937), pp. 38–39, no. 6; R. A. Caminos, *Late-Egyptian Miscellanies*, Brown Egyptological Studies 1 (Oxford, 1952), pp. 143–144.

50. J. Osing, *Das Grab des Nefersecheru in Zawyet Sultan*, Archäologische Veröffentlichungen des Deutschen Archäologischen Instituts Kairo 88 (Mainz, 1992), pl. 43 and pp. 75–78.

51. For other addresses to the living embedded in mortuary spells, see J. Assmann and M. Bommas, *Altägyptische Totenliturgien*, vol. 2 (in press), no. 4.1.6.

52. On the deceased's wish to transform into a heron, see Coffin Texts spells 624 and 703, and Book of the Dead spell 84.

53. The reference is to the *bas* of those already dead, into whose company the deceased will be accepted.

54. In the "mortuary spells of unusual form," this connection is expressed explicitly; see H. Grapow, "Ägyptische Jenseitswünsche in Sprüchen ungewöhnlicher Fassung aus dem Neuen Reich," *Zeitschrift für ägyptische Sprache und Altertumskunde* 77 (1942): 57–91.

55. Stela of Neferhotep, Cairo Catalogue générale 34057, from Gurna, time of Thuthmosis III/Amenophis II; P. Lacau, *Stèles du Nouvel Empire* (Cairo, 1909), pp. 101–103 and pl. 34.

CHAPTER 11. IN THE SIGN OF THE ENEMY

1. Stela of *Jnj-jtj = f*, son of *Mjjt*, British Museum 1164; J. J. Clère and J. Vandier, *Textes de la Première Période Intermédiaire et de la 8. Dynastie*, Bibliotheca Aegyptiaca 10 (Brussels, 1948), § 33; *Hieroglyphic Texts from Egyptian Stelae, &c., in the British Museum*, vol. 1 (London, 1911), p. 55; H. O. Lange, *Eine neue Inschrift aus Hermonthis*, Sitzungsberichte der (Kgl.) Preussischen Akademie der Wissenschaften 38 (Berlin, 1914), pl. 4; W. Schenkel, *Memphis—Herakleopolis—Theben: Die epigraphischen Zeugnisse der 7.–11. Dynastie Ägyptens*, Ägyptologische Abhandlungen 12 (Wiesbaden, 1965), p. 235, no. 379.

2. G. Lapp, *Die Opferformel des Alten Reiches, unter Berücksichtigung einiger späteren Formen*, Sonderschriften des Deutschen Archäologischen Instituts Kairo 21 (Mainz, 1986), § 329, no. 2.

3. Sinuhe B 191–192; R. Koch, *Die Erzählung des Sinuhe*, Bibliotheca Aegyptiaca 17 (Brussels, 1990), p. 61.

4. A. de Buck, *The Egyptian Coffin Texts*, vol. 1, Oriental Institute Publications 34 (Chicago, 1938), pp. 216b–217b.

5. So with B10C^c, B13C, and B16C. B10C^b has *jn Jnp.w* "by Anubis." B12C has only *Jnp.w.* "Anubis has come in peace."

6. The word "your" is superfluous and is missing in B10C^c.

7. So with B10C^b and B10C^c. B12C has *nhz.w n^{c}w.w* "who guard the serpents."

8. H. Junker, *Die Stundenwachen in den Osirismysterien*, Denkschriften der Kaiserlichen Akademie der Wissenschaften in Wien, Philosophisch-historische Klasse 54 (Vienna, 1910).

9. Papyrus British Museum 10081 (unpublished); see J. Assmann and M. Bommas, *Altägyptische Totenliturgien*, vol. 3 (in preparation), liturgy SZ.3.

10. On the coffin of Panehemisis in Vienna, they appear as a group of eight seated gods with knives in their hands and sun disks on their head. The text reads:

To be recited:
O you gods with piercing eyes in the following of Osiris,
whom Re has assigned to protect Osiris,
for he did not want Seth to see him.
Keep watch, O you who are in your hours,
Be attentive, O you who are in the darkness,
oh, may you keep watch over the $^c h^c$-serpent,
this vindicated high priest,
see, he is one of you!

E. V. Bergmann, *Der Sarkophag des Panehemisis* (Vienna, 1883), pp. 5–7.

11. Cairo Catalogue générale 29301, published by G. Maspero, *Sarcophages des époques persane et ptolémaique*, vol. 1 (Cairo, 1919), pp. 34–36.

12. M. de Rochemonteix, *Le Temple d'Edfou*, vol. 1, Mémoire publiés par les membres de la Mission Archéologique Française au Caire 10 (Cairo, 1897) p. 189; S. Cauville, *La Théologie d'Osiris à Edfou* (Cairo, 1983), p. 23.

13. De Buck, *Coffin Texts*, vol. 4, Oriental Institute Publications 67 (Chicago, 1951), pp. 69c–70b; E. Hornung, *Das Totenbuch der Ägypter* (Zurich, 1979), p. 157.

14. In fact, the list cited above in the text names only six of the "seven *akh*-spirits." Missing is the fourth, *^{c}q ḥr jmj wnw.t=f*, "He with attentive face in his hour-service."

15. De Buck, *Coffin Texts*, vol. 1, p. 242f.

16. Ibid., p. 250b.

17. The barque is towed by the gods. A word *mty* "rope," however, is not attested. Perhaps the word *mty* "bolt" is meant; see A. Erman and H. Grapow (eds.), *Wörterbuch der aegyptischen Sprache*, reprint ed. (Berlin, 1971), vol. 2, p. 167.14. In that case, the statement refers to the door bolt of the hall of embalming, which is pulled open.

18. On these priestly titles, see chapter 13 of this volume.

19. See M. Kamal, "The Stela of *ShtpjbR^c* in the Egyptian Museum," *Annales du Service des Antiquités de l'Égypte* 38 (1938): 278–280; J. G. Griffiths, "Hakerfest," in W. Helck and E. Otto (eds.), *Lexikon der Ägyptologie*, vol. 2 (Wiesbaden, 1976), cols. 929–931; M.-C. Lavier, "Les Mystères d'Osiris d'après les stèles du Moyen Empire et du Nouvel Empire," in S. Schoske (ed.), *Akten des 4. Internationalen Ägyptololen-Kongresses München 1985*, Studien zur altägyptiscnhe Kultur Beiheft 3 (Hamburg, 1989), pp. 289–295.

20. See chapter 9, n. 75 of this volume.

21. E. A. W. Budge, *The Chapters of Coming Forth by Day or the Theban Recension of the Book of the Dead*, vol. 1 (London, 1910), p. 100 (papyrus of Ani). Cf. de Buck, *The Egyptian Coffin Texts*, vol. 4, pp. 336e (spell 338) and 338g (spell 339).

22. J.-C. Goyon, *Le Papyrus d'Imouthès fils de Psinthaês au Metropolitan Museum of Art de New York (Papyrus MMA 35.9.21)* (New York, 1999).

23. Ibid., p. 27 and pl. 1, col. 1, lines 1–5.

24. Ibid., p. 27 and pl. 1, col. 1, lines 6–7.

25. Ibid., p. 30 and pl. 3, col. 4, lines 8–13.

26. Ibid., pp. 30–34 and pls. 3–6, cols. 4, 14–7, 15.

27. Ibid., p. 32 and pl. 5, col. 6, lines 1–16.

28. Ibid., p. 34 and pl. 6, col. 7, line 15.

29. Ibid., pp. 44–45 and pl. 14, col. 15, lines 11–15.

30. In the Coffin Texts, the word *ʾft.t* is often attested with the meaning "afterlife." In Coffin Texts spell 302 = de Buck, *The Egyptian Coffin Texts*, vol. 4, pp. 54d and 59a, *ʾft.t* is a variant of *ʾfd.t*, which is known from Papyrus Westcar as a word for "afterlife": *rḫ bȝ=k wȝ.wt ʾfd.t r sbḫ.t n.t ḥbs-bȝg*, "may your *ba* know the ways of the *ʾfd.t*, which lead to the portal of *ḥbs-bȝg*. The "ways of the *ʾft.t*" are mentioned in Coffin Texts spell 47 = de Buck, *Coffin Texts*, vol. 1, p. 208c. Coffin Texts spell 243 = de Buck, *Coffin Texts*, vol. 3, Oriental Institute Publications 64 (Chicago, 1947), p. 329b has to do with equipping the *ʾft.t* of the *ḥr.t-nṯr*.

31. Goyon, *Le Papyrus d'Imouthès*, p. 46 and pls. 15–16, cols. 16, lines 16–17, line 4.

32. So with R. O. Faulkner, *The Ancient Egyptian Coffin Texts*, vol. 1 (Warminster, 1973), p. 58.

33. Erman and Grapow, *Wörterbuch der aegyptischen Sprache*, vol. 3, p. 283.5. To the attestations, add K. Sethe, *Urkunden des ägyptischen Altertums*, vol. 4, reprint ed. (Berlin, 1961), p. 1237.8.

34. See chapter 7, section 1 of this volume.

35. See, for example, the passages cited in chapter 4, section 3 of this volume.

36. In chapter 1, we cited some passages that had to do with this connection between heart and recollection.

37. The motif of recollection also occurs in the text of the Greek gold tablets that were placed in the graves of Bacchic mystics. Therein, it is said to the deceased that in the next world, they will arrive at two sources:

> In the house of Hades, you will find on the right a source, near which there is a white cypress. There breathe the souls of the dead, which are descending. You shall not approach this source! Furthermore, you will find the cool water that flows out of the pond of Mnemosyne (recollection).

The deceased are to drink of this water, but only after successfully undergoing an interrogation by the guardians, exactly as in Egypt; see R. Merkelbach, "Die goldenen Totenpässe: ägyptisch, orphisch, bakchisch," *Zeitschrift für Papyrologie und Epigraphik* 128 (1999): 1–14, esp. pp. 2–5.

38. Coffin Texts spell 467; de Buck, *The Egyptian Coffin Texts*, vol. 5, Oriental Institute Publications 73 (Chicago, 1954), p. 364. Book of the Dead spell 110; Budge, *The Chapters of Coming Forth by Day*, vol. 2, p. 96, lines 21–22 (Nebseni); Hornung, *Das Totenbuch der Ägypter*, p. 213.

39. Book of the Dead spell 100, version B; Budge, *The Chapters of Coming Forth by Day*, vol. 2, p. 102 (Yuya); Hornung, *Das Totenbuch der Ägypter*, p. 214.

40. On *ṯbw.tj*, cf., in a similar (if not entirely clear) context, the Tale of the Eloquent Peasant, B 231 (old 200):

> Crossing the river "on the back of sandals,"
> is that a good crossing? No!

41. With this translation, I follow F. Vogelsang, *Kommentar zu den Klagen des Bauern*, Untersuchungen zur Geschichte und Altertumskunde Ägyptens 6 (Leipzig, 1913), pp. 155–157 and M. Lichtheim, *Ancient Egyptian Literature: A Book of Readings*, vol. 1: *The Old and Middle Kingdoms* (Berkeley, 1973), p. 177. On *nn*, see P. Vernus, "Études de philologie et de linguistique (IV.)," *Revue d'Égyptologie* 36 (1985): 153.

42. The Greek word "phoenix" is a rendering of the Coptic word BOINE, which for its part goes back to *bnw*, which designates a kind of heron. See R. T. Rundle Clark, "The Origin of the Phoenix," *University of Birmingham Historical Journal* 2 (1949/50): 1–29 and 105–140.

43. See J. Assmann, *Re und Amun: Die Krise des polytheistischen Weltbilds im Ägypten der 18.–20. Dynastie*, Orbis Biblicus et Orientalis 51 (Freiburg and Göttingen, 1983), pp. 71–82.

44. A. de Buck, *The Egyptian Coffin Texts*, vol. 1, p. 43 b.

45. Ibid., pp. 19 c–d/20 a.

46. Though *šdj* clearly means "to dig" here, I understand the word in verse 27 of our text to be *šdj* "to recite." In my opinion, "a hacking of the earth is dug for you" yields no sense, and if this were the meaning, the text would have *ḥbs n=k t3* "the earth is hacked up for you"; see Pyramid Texts spell 458 = § 863a; Pyramid Texts spell 441 = § 817a; Pyramid Texts spell 719 = § 2234d; Pyramid Texts spell 720 = §2238c. Similarly, Pyramid Texts spell 510 = § 1138a; Pyramid Texts spell 509 = § 1120c; Pyramid Texts spell 539 = § 1323c and 1326a; Pyramid Texts spell 560 = § 1394a; and Pyramid Texts 582 = § 1561c:

ḥbs n=k t3   The earth is hacked up for you,
sqr n=k wdn.t   an offering is consecrated ("smitten") for you

I thus conclude that *šdj* "to read, recite" is meant, a word that is used in connection with the carrying out of transfigurations, by which I mean the rite called *šdj s3ḥ.w* *'š3.w* "reciting many transfigurations" in the mortuary cult; cf. also Theban Tomb 110, "transfiguration spells are recited for you," N. de G. Davies, "Tehuti, Owner of Tomb 110 at Thebes," in S. R. K. Glanville (ed.), *Studies Presented to F. Ll. Griffith* (London, 1932), pls. 37 and 40.

47. On the details, see J. Assmann and M. Bommas, *Altägyptische Totenliturgien*, vol. 1, Supplemente zu den Schriften der Heidelberger Akademie der Wissenschaften, Philosophisch-historische Klasse 14 (Heidelberg, 2002).

48. H. Grapow, "Die Vogeljagd mit dem Wurfholz," *Zeitschrift für Ägyptische Sprache und Altertumskunde* 47 (1910): 132–134; E. Feucht, "Fishing and Fowling with the Spear and the Throw-Stick Reconsidered," in U. Luft (ed.), *The Intellectual Heritage of Egypt: Studies Presented to Laszló Kákosy by Friends and Colleagues on the Occasion of his 60. Birthday*, Studia Aegyptiaca 14 (Budapest, 1992), pp. 157–169.

49. This point was already made around the turn of the twentieth century by the sociologist Thorstein Veblen in his classic work, *The Theory of the Leisure Class* (New York, 1899).

50. *M jr h3w hr mdd.wt* (Pr), var. *m jr h3w hr mdw=k* (L²). G. Burkard, "Die Lehre des Ptahhotep," in O. Kaiser (ed.), *Texte aus der Umwelt des Alten Testaments*, vol. 3.2 (Gütersloh, 1991), p. 203 translates "das, was verlangt wurde (that which was required)." There is a word *mdw.w* "word, speech," that, like Hebrew *dbarim*, also means "matter, thing," and from there, "concerns." "That which was required" assumes the concept of vertical dependence, which does not suit so expressly aristocratic a context.

51. I adopt Burkard's translation, which presumably suits the intended meaning, although it is difficult to bring it into line with the formulation *m ngb zp hr.t-hrww*.

52. Instruction of Ptahhotep, verses 186–193, Papyrus Prisse 7.9–10. Burkard's translation "if one is sluggish" evidently rests on the emendation of *jw sf3=f* to *wsf=f*. But the notion of "sluggishness" does not well suit the context of a warning against undue assiduousness. I connect the suffix *.f* with *jb* "heart" and hold to *sf3* "to hate," here in the intransitive meaning "to be full of hate."

53. There is also something supernatural and magical about the hunting scene edited by R. A. Caminos under the title "The Pleasures of Fishing and Fowling" in *Literary Fragments in the Hieratic Script* (Oxford, 1956), pp. 1–21. In section A, page 2, line 6 (pl. 1 and p. 8), it states, "We shall trap birds by the thousands," and in section B, page 2, lines 7–8, we read, "I kill at every thrust, there is no stop for [my] shaft" (pl. 2 and p. 10).

Perhaps the hunting scenes on the shrine of Tutankhamun are also to be understood in the sense of this sort of supernatural ease. The king hunts birds while seated, which in the real world is every bit as impossible as what is described in the Coffin Text. On these scenes, see M. Eaton-Krauss and E. Graefe, *The Small Golden Shrine from the Tomb of Tutankhamun* (Oxford, 1985). In The Pleasures of Fishing and Fowling, the protagonist also seems to be seated as he thrusts his spear at fish.

54. Cairo Catalogue général 42231; see K. Jansen-Winkeln, *Ägyptische Biographien der 22. und 23. Dynastie* (Wiesbaden, 1985), p. 196. Similarly, the description of a pleasure trip on the "Lake of *Maat*" in the Tale of the Eloquent Peasant is also to be understood metaphorically:

When you go down to the Lake of *Maat,*
may you voyage on it in a fair wind.
. . .
Then may the shy fish come to you,
and you shall encounter fatted fowl.

R. B. Parkinson, *The Tale of the Eloquent Peasant* (Oxford, 1991), B1 85–86 and 91–93 = R 14.3 and 15.2–3.

55. So also in Papyrus British Museum 10819, 2.11–3.9.

56. Cf. the wish "to take the faïence pendants on the festival of Sakhmet and a garment of red fabric" in Theban Tomb 49, ceiling text, N. de G. Davies, *The Tomb of Neferhotep at Thebes,* Publications of the Metropolitan Museum of Art 9 (New York, 1933), pls. 58–59, and "May I wear a faïence pendant and clothing of red fabric on the festival of Sakhmet," Theban Tomb 106 (1), with parallels in Theban Tombs 222 and 23. In Theban Tomb 158, there is mention of a "*ṯḥnw*-pendant on your breast" in connection with the Sokar festival and the garland of onions; see K. C. Seele, *The Tomb of Tjanefer at Thebes,* Oriental Institute Publications 86 (Chicago, 1959), pl. 4.

57. E.g.: Pyramid Texts § 390a, § 472a–b, § 479a, § 542b, § 971a, § 1253a, §1431c, § 1474b, § 1763a, § 2079b, § 2082b.

58. See H. Altenmüller, "'Messersee,' 'gewundener Wasserlauf' und 'Flammensee,'" *Zeitschrift für ägyptische Sprache und Altertumskunde* 92 (1966): 86–95 and R. Krauss, *Astronomische Konzepte und Jenseitsvorstellungen in den Pyramidentexten,* Ägyptologische Abhandlungen 59 (Wiesbaden, 1997), pp. 14–66. Krauss identifies the "Winding Canal" with the "ecliptic."

59. See J. Assmann, *Liturgische Lieder an den Sonnengott,* Münchner ägyptologische Studien 19 (Berlin, 1969), pp. 134 and 137–138 (3); Assmann, *Sonnenhymnen in thebanischen Gräbern,* Theben 1 (Mainz, 1983), no. 47a = no. 163, 40; no. 230, 15; no. 244, 8; no. 267, 6. "Ropes of bronze" occur in Pyramid Texts spell 214, § 138.

CHAPTER 12. THE NIGHT OF VINDICATION

1. Papyrus Metropolitan Museum of Art 35.9.21, cols. 18.14–19.7, published by J.-C. Goyon, *Le Papyrus d'Imouthès, fils de Psinthaês au Metropolitan Museum of Art de New York (Papyrus MMA 35.9.21)* (New York, 1999), p. 52 and pls. 17–18; papyrus Louvre 3079, 110, 12–19, published by Goyon, "Le Cérémonial des glorifications d'Osiris du papyrus du Louvre," *Bulletin de l'Institut Français d'Archéologie Orientale* 65 (1965): 96–97; papyrus British Museum 10208, 13–20, published by F. M. H. Haikal, *Two Hieratic Funerary Papyri of Nesmin,* Bibliotheca Aegyptiaca 14, vol. 1 (Brussels, 1970), pp. 50–53.

2. H. Willems, "Anubis as a Judge," in W. Clarysse et al. (eds.), *Egyptian Religion, The Last Thousand Years: Studies Dedicated to the Memory of J. Quaegebeur* (Louvain, 1998), vol. 1, pp. 721–734.

3. Pyramid Texts spell 441, § 817a (beginning of the spell); spell 458, § *863a (restored text). Similarly, spell 720, § 2238c (Faulkner); spell 509, § 1120c; spell 510, § 1138a; spell 560, § 1394a–b; spell 582, § 1561c; spell 719, § 2234e–f (Faulkner); and spell 720, § 2238c (Faulkner):

May the earth be hacked up and an offering brought to you,
may the arms be extended to you and the dance go down to you.

4. *De errore profanarum religionum,* 2, 3, after T. Hopfner, *Fontes historiae religionis Aegyptiacae,* vol. 4 (Bonn, 1924), p. 519.

5. Papyrus Insinger 17.22. See J. J. Thissen, "Die Lehre des P. Insinger," in O. Kaiser (ed.), *Texte aus der Umwelt des Alten Testaments,* vol. 3, part 2: *Weisheitstexte* 2 (Gütersloh, 1991), pp. 280–319, esp. p. 300.

6. J. Assmann, "Die Inschrift auf dem äusseren Sarkophagdeckel des Merenptah," *Mitteilungen des Deutschen Archäologischen Instituts Kairo* 28 (1972): 54–55.

7. E 56–57; J. F. Quack, *Studien zur Lehre für Merikare* (Wiesbaden, 1992), pp. 36–37.

8. This court is also mentioned in spell 62:

May you be vindicated on the day of judgment
in the tribunal of the lord of sighs.

9. On *sšm ʿnḫ*, "to lead life," see E. Otto, *Gott und Mensch nach den Tempelinschriften der griechisch-römischen Zeit* (Heidelberg, 1964), pp. 55 and 152–153.

10. See H. Kees, *Totenglauben und Jenseitsvorstellungen der alten Ägypter*, 2d ed. (Berlin, 1956), pp. 180–181.

11. Stela of Qemnen-Sebeknakht, K. Piehl, *Inscriptions hiéroglyphiques recueillis en Europe et en Égypte*, vol. 2 (Leipzig, 1892); similarly, the stela of Tjeti, M. Lichtheim, *Ancient Egyptian Autobiographies, Chiefly of the Middle Kingdom*, Orbis Biblicus et Orientalis 84 (Freiburg, 1988), p. 48, and that of Henenu, ibid., p. 60.

12. In the well-attested mortuary spell that we have already cited as an example of the "art of the wish," vindication and provisioning by means of a plot of land are also juxtaposed:

May you enter the hall of the Two Truths,
may the god who is in it greet you.
May you take possession of your dwelling place within the netherworld
and stride freely out in the city of the inundation.
May you take pleasure in your plowing
on your plot of land in the Field of Reeds.
May your provisioning turn out well with what you have created.
May the harvest come to you as a plenitude of grain.

K. Sethe, *Urkunden des ägyptischen Altertums*, vol. 4, reprint ed. (Berlin, 1961), pp. 115–117; see G. Fecht, "Die Form der altägyptischen Literatur: Metrische und stilistische Analyse (Schluss)," *Zeitschrift fur ägyptische Sprache und Altertumskunde* 92 (1965): 22–23.

13. So B1P and B6C; T9C, T1L, and BH5C have "the god."

14. E. A. W. Budge, *The Chapters of Coming Forth by Day or the Theban Recension of the Book of the Dead* (London, 1910), vol. 1, pp. 15–16, "the speech of the gods." See also E. Dondelinger, *Das Totenbuch des Schreibers Ani* (Graz, 1987), pl. 3.

15. See J. Assmann, "Ein Wiener Kanopentext und die Stundenwachen in der Balsamierungshalle," in J. van Dijk (ed.), *Essays on Ancient Egypt in Honour of Herman te Velde* (Groningen, 1997), pp. 1–8.

16. This is also the idiosyncratic form in which Hecataeus of Abdera, as cited by Diodorus Siculus, reports the conducting of the Judgment of the Dead as part of the funeral ritual.

CHAPTER 13. *RITUALS OF TRANSITION FROM HOME TO TOMB*

1. In his article "Bestattungsritual," in W. Helck and E. Otto (eds.), *Lexikon der Ägyptologie*, vol. 1 (Wiesbaden, 1975), cols. 745–765, H. Altenmüller lists no fewer than 102 representations from Dynasty 1 to the beginning of the Ptolemaic Period. The most important literature on the funeral ritual is J. Settgast, *Untersuchungen zu altägyptischen Bestattungsdarstellungen*, Abhandlungen des Deutschen Archäologischen Instituts Kairo 3 (Glückstadt, 1963); H. Altenmüller, *Die Texte zum Begräbnisritual in den Pyramiden des Alten Reichs*, Ägyptologische Abhandlungen 24 (Wiesbaden, 1972), though with over-reaching hypotheses regarding the ritual reference of the Pyramid Texts; and J. Barthelmess, *Der Übergang ins Jenseits in den thebanischen Beamtengräbern der Ramessidenzeit*, Studien zur Archäologie und Geschichte Altägyptens 2 (Heidelberg, 1992).

2. J. Assmann, *Das Grab des Amenemope (TT 41) in der thebanischen Nekropole*, Theben 3 (Mainz, 1991). This especially rich representation of the funeral rituals is not included in Altenmüller's list.

3. Ibid., vol. 2, pl. 40 and vol. 1, pp. 92–100.

4. In this interpretation of the *tekenu*, I am in accord with E. Hornung, *Idea into Image: Essays on Ancient Egyptian Thought* (New York, 1992), p. 169. So also Barthelmess, *Der Übergang ins Jenseits,*, pp. 56–57 and J. Taylor, *Death and Afterlife in Ancient Egypt* (London, 2000), pp. 63 and 190.

5. See Settgast, *Untersuchungen zu altägyptischen Bestattungsdarstellungen*, p. 43.

6. K. Piehl, *Inscriptions hiéroglyphiques receuellies en Europe et en Égypte*, vol. 1 (Leipzig, 1886), p. 44 = J. Berlandini, "La Stèle de Paraherounemyef, Varia Memphitica VI," *Bulletin de l'Institut Français d'Archéologie Orientale* 85 (1985): 46–47.

7. Piehl, *Inscriptions hiéroglyphiques*, vol. 1, p. 73 = Cairo catalogue générale 22054; M. Kamal, *Stèles ptolémaiques et romaines*, vol. 1 (Cairo, 1904), p. 53.15 and pl. 17.

8. On the motif of opening the way with milk, Barthelmess refers to K. Sethe, *Urkunden des ägyptischen Altertums*, vol. 4, reprint ed. (Berlin, 1961), p. 1084.

9. This verse is a citation from a work of literature, the Loyalist Instruction; see G. Posener, *L'Enseignement loyaliste: Sagesse égyptienne du Moyen Empire* (Geneva, 1976), §7.1.

10. N. de G. Davies, "Tehuti, Owner of Tomb 110 at Thebes," in S. R. K. Glanville (ed.), *Studies Presented to F. Ll. Griffiths* (Milford, 1932), p. 288 and pls. 37 and 40; A. Hermann, *Die Stelen der thebanischen Felsgräber der 18. Dynastie*, Ägyptologische Forschungen 11 (Glückstadt, 1940), pp. 31*–32* and 38*–39*; Barthelmess, *Der Übergang ins Jenseits*, pp. 172–173.

11. No. 8.3.3. Unpublished inscription in the court, after my own copy. This list is largely consistent with the list of personnel who participated in the Opening of the Mouth ritual in the tomb of Petamenophis (Theban Tomb 33); see E. Otto, *Das ägyptische Mundöffnungsritual* (Wiesbaden, 1960), vol. 2, p. 15.

12. After Barthelmess, *Der Übergang ins Jenseits*, p. 19.

13. After ibid., pp. 20–21.

14. After Settgast, *Untersuchungen zu altägyptischen Bestattungsdarstellungen*, pp. 101–102.

15. B. Gessler-Löhr, "Die Totenfeier im Garten" in Assmann, *Das Grab des Amenemope*, pp. 162–183.

16. Theban Tomb 41, text 50; see Assmann, *Das Grab des Amenemope*, pp. 55–58; text 194, pp. 134–136.

17. R. F. Herbin, *Le Livre de parcourir l'éternité* (Louvain, 1994), p. 99; cf. Book of the Dead chapter 18.

18. R. Hari, *La Tombe thébaine du Père Divin Neferhotep (TT 50)* (Geneva, 1985), pp. 41–42 and pls. 27–30.

19. Parallel text in Theban Tomb 100, N. de G. Davies, *The Tomb of Rekh-Mi-Re at Thebes* (New York, 1943), pl. 94 (middle register, left, caption to the journey to Abydos).

20. A. M. Blackman, "The Funerary Papyrus of Enkhenefkhons," *Journal of Egyptian Archaeology* 4 (1918): pl. 26, lines 3–4.

21. This *tekenu* might also be a reminiscence from prehistory, when bodies were buried in a crouching position in animal skins; see H. Kees, *Totenglauben und Jenseitsvorstellungen der alten Ägypter*, 2nd ed. (Berlin, 1956), p. 251.

22. Ibid.; in this interpretation, the *tekenu* was a symbol of distancing and thus connected with the image of "death as enemy." In the mortuary texts, we occasionally find mention of a being with the similar designation *nu-tekenu*, of which it is said that the deceased is not to be left to its devices or is to be freed of it; see chapter 5, section 1, end, as well as J. Zandee, *Death as an Enemy According to Ancient Egyptian Conceptions*, Studies in the History of Religions 5 (Leiden, 1960), p. 207.

23. Settgast, *Untersuchungen zu altägyptischen Bestattungsdarstellungen*, pp. 38–39.

24. Theban Tomb 224, Settgast, *Untersuchungen zu altägyptischen Bestattungsdarstellungen*, p. 38.

25. For instance, the "Trauerrelief" in the Berlin Museum.

26. A. Radwan, "Der Trauergestus als Datierungsmittel," *Mitteilungen des Deutschen Archäologischen Instituts Kairo* 30 (1974):115–129.

27. See the *Frankfurter Allgemeine Zeitung*, 25 February 2000.

28. Often, as in Theban Tomb 44, the mummy is held upright by Anubis or "by a priest dressed as Anubis" (Barthelmess). For attestations, see Barthelmess, *Der Übergang ins Jenseits*, p. 100, n. 565.

29. The ritual has been published and studied by E. Otto, *Das ägyptische Mundöff-nungsritual*, 2 vols., Ägyptologische Abhandlungen 3 (Wiesbaden, 1960).

30. Papyrus London British Museum 1008, col. 18 (unpublished).

31. Theban Tombs 178 and 259, after Barthelmess, *Der Übergang ins Jenseits*, pp. 100–101.

32. Theban Tomb 255, after Barthelmess, *Der Übergang ins Jenseits*, p. 102. Similarly, Theban Tomb 409, Barthelmess, *Der Übergang ins Jenseits*, p. 105:

Carrying out the Opening of the Mouth for N., vindicated.
His face is (oriented) southwards on the desert sand,
he being bathed in light on the earth
on the day of being clothed.

So, too, the Book of the Dead papyrus of Hunefer (British Museum 9901):

Spell for carrying out the Opening of the Mouth
for the statue of the Osiris, the royal scribe Hunefer,
its face oriented southwards on the desert sand behind it;
to be recited by the chief lector priest
while the *sem*-priest circles it four times.

33. Hermann, *Die Stelen der thebanischen Felsgräber*, pp. 99–100; J. Assmann, "Neith spricht als Mutter und Sarg," *Mitteilungen des Deutschen Archäologishen Instituts Kairo* 28/2 (1972): 126–127.

34. Third harper's song, published by Hari, *La Tombe thébaine du Père Divin Neferhotep*, pl. 26, line 15. The passage is usually interpreted quite differently, cf. Hari: "On dresse vos (!) momies devant Re, tandis que vos (!) gens sont dans l'affliction. (On ne fait pas) . . . quand vient la Moissoneuse(!—the restoration *Rnn.t* goes back to a proposal by Maspero) à son heur et que le Destin compte compte (*sic*) ses jours."

35. Theban Tomb 224 (1); similarly Theban Tomb 106 (1); cf. no. 8.1.8.

36. Theban Tomb 178 (12); E. Hoffman, *Das Grab des Neferrenpet, genannt Kenro (TT 178)* (Mainz, 1993), p. 62, text 116. See also the statue in Turin (unnumbered, Dynasty 20) cited by Hermann, *Die Stelen der thebanischen Felsgräber*, p. 99, n. 447: "Your mummy will be set up before Re in the *wsḫ.t* of your tomb." Similarly, A. Piankoff, *Mythological Papyri*, Egyptian Religious Texts and Representations 3, Bollingen Series 40 (New York, 1957): "My mummy will be set up before Re in the *wsḫ.t* of the entrance to my tomb."

37. No. 7.2 (Theban Tomb 23); parallel text in Theban Tomb 35, *Wörterbuch* slip <1533>.

38. On the development of Theban tomb courts, see F. Kampp-Seyfried, *Die thebanische Nekropole: Zum Wandel des Grabgedankens von der XVIII. bis zur XX. Dynastie*, vol. 1, Theben 13 (Mainz, 1996), pp. 58–81.

39. Theban Tomb 44, after Barthelmess, *Der Übergang ins Jenseits*, pp. 103–104; Theban Tomb 23, ibid., p. 110.

40. Bologna KS 1922; E. Bresciani, *Le Stele egiziani del Museo Civico Archaeologico di Bologna* (Bologna, 1985), no. 23, pl. 30. See also A. Schulman, "The Iconographic Theme 'Opening the Mouth' on Stelae," *Journal of the American Center of Research in Egypt* 21 (1984): 191 (document 22).

41. See J. Assmann, *Sonnenhymnen in thebanischen Gräbern*, Theben 1 (Mainz, 1983), pp. xv–xvii.

42. Schulman, "The Iconographic Theme 'Opening the Mouth'"; Kampp-Seyfried, *Die thebanische Nekropole*, pp. 76–77.

43. Assmann, *Das Grab des Amenemope*, pl. 25.

44. Written *Ndr*.

45. This version omits Pyramid Texts § 200c: "He has come to you, O *Pnḏn*, he has come to you, his father."

46. The version in the Pyramid Texts has "seize the sky and take possession of the horizon."

47. Also incomprehensible in the Pyramid Texts.

48. The Pyramid Texts version has "become dark."

49. Again, the Pyramid Texts version has "become dark."

50. The Pyramid Texts version has "may you be born for Horus, may you be carried in pregnancy for Seth."

51. P. Dorman, *The Tombs of Senenmut: The Architecture and Decoration of Tombs 71 and 353* (New York, 1991), § 13. This text differs in significant ways from the version in Pyramid Texts spell 222. The name of the god Seth is regularly replaced by other divine names: in 204a and 205b by that of Horus (24 and 30), and in 211b by that of Thoth (62). Rare words such as *snk* "to grow dark" are replaced by better-known terms such as *sʿq* "to gather." The eight gods of the litany are reduced to seven by the omission of *Pnḏn*. The text was thus modernized to adapt it to the New Kingdom horizon of understanding. In this form, it can be considered a text of the New Kingdom and thus as an example not of an age-old tradition but of a still-living one.

52. See J. Assmann, *The Search for God in Ancient Egypt* (Ithaca, 2001), pp. 44–45; Assmann, "Neith spricht als Mutter und Sarg," pp. 126–127; Assmann, *Das Grab des Amenemope*, p. 7 with n. 20; W. Waitkus, *Die Texte in den unteren Krypten des Hathortempels von Dendera*, Münchner ägyptologische Studien 47 (Mainz, 1995), pp. 68–69.

53. Text 115 in Theban Tomb 178 also begins with this verse; see Hofmann, *Das Grab des Neferrenpet*, p. 62.

54. *Md.t nṯr*, entirely clear in both variants. The word *wʿb* "to purify" is otherwise never used in the figurative sense "to transfigure, sanctify." *Md.t nṯr* means "hieroglyphs" and refers to the sacred text of the ritual, which was read at the funeral. In tombs of the Ramesside Period, this point is also stressed iconographically by the oft-attested representation of the lector priest, who functions along with the *sem*-priest and reads from a half-unrolled book roll; see Barthelmess, *Der Übergang ins Jenseits*, pp. 97–98. In Theban Tomb 44, on the unrolled portion of papyrus, we can read the words *jr.t wp.t rꜣ n wsjr Jmn-m-ḥꜣb* "carrying out the Opening of the Mouth ritual for Osiris Amenemheb"; see L. Collins, "The Private Tombs of Thebes: Excavations by Sir Robert Mond 1905 and 1906," *Journal of Egyptian Archaeology* 62 (1976): 24.

55. I. Collins, "The Private Tombs of Thebes: Excavations by Sir Robert Mond 1905 and 1906," *Journal of Egyptian Archaeology* 62 (1976): 24, has *mdꜣ.wt ḥdb*. *Ḥdb* means "to kill," which is disconcerting in this context. The word *mdꜣ.t* is not determined unequivocally as "chisel" in either variant. Theban Tomb 23 has a loop, and the scribe was evidently thinking of *mdꜣ.t* "book roll," which is also suggested by the "divine words" mentioned in what precedes. Theban Tomb 44 has a book roll and plural strokes. See also verses 14–15.

56. Barthelmess, *Der Übergang ins Jenseits*, reads *bd špss* "august natron." The reference is probably to the implements used in the Opening of the Mouth ritual, which are also mentioned in verse 17.

57. See n. 54 above.

58. Usually pictured as a tray bearing the implements of the Opening of the Mouth ritual; see Barthelmess, *Der Übergang ins Jenseits*, p. 98, n. 548.

59. This is the title of a priest in the purification ritual; see Otto, *Das ägyptische Mundöffnungsritual*, vol. 1, pp. 31 and 34.

60. On this motif, see Coffin Texts liturgy 1, § 26 and no. 1.7, § 26.

61. A. Erman and H. Grapow, *Wörterbuch der aegyptischen Sprache*, reprint ed. (Berlin, 1971), vol. 2, p. 377.5.

62. Barthelmess, *Der Übergang ins Jenseits*, reads *rwj* and translates "may you distance yourself," but this verb is written with neither the lion hieroglyph nor the *mꜣ*-sickle.

63. Theban Tombs 218 and 360, after Barthelmess, *Der Übergang ins Jenseits*, p. 89.

64. Otto, *Das ägyptische Mundöffnungsritual*, vol. 2, pp. 73–87 and 102–108. Scehe 46 is followed by a censing.

65. The text reads:

Think of it, Seth . . . ,
when you said, "I did not do it,"
. . . as you said, Seth:
"It was he who provoked me,"
. . . when you said, Seth:
"It was he who came (too) close to me."

Speaking such words, Seth brought the punishment down on himself.

66. During the Khoiak rituals of the Osiris chapels at Dendara, one of the two mourning women also says to the animal being offered:

Your mouth, it is your mouth,
your lips, it is your lips,
it is your mouth that has done it to you,
it is your lips that have done it to you!

S. Cauville, *Le Temple de Dendara: Les Chapelles osiriennes, transcription et traduction* (Cairo, 1997), p. 51. On page 53, the slaughterer himself speaks. The scene corresponds exactly to scenes 23–24 of the Opening of the Mouth ritual.

67. Erman and Grapow, *Wörterbuch*, vol. 3, p. 472: "run quickly, hasten." Otto translates, "approach with them" and thus misses the crucial point of the scene.

68. This reference has not been previously recognized, because the formula *ḥw-sw n mw.t=f* was taken as a reference to the son and translated "He who smites for his mother, who bewails him." Otto, *Das ägyptische Mundöffnungsritual*, vol. 2, pp. 78–79 renders, following K. Sethe, "Der sich mit seiner Mutter vereinigt, die ihn beweint, der sich mit seiner Gesellin vereinigt."

69. No. 8.3.14 (485) = stela of Pareherwenemef from Saqqara, now in Cairo, published by A. Mariette, *Monuments divers recueillis en Égypte et en Nubie* (Paris, 1872), p. 20 and pl. 61; and J. Berlandini, "La Stèle de Paraherounemyef," pp. 41–62.

70. Offering spell (4335), Theban Tomb 100, pl. 86: *rꜣ n jr.t iḫ.t* "spell for the offering ritual" = spell 5 in Papyrus British Museum 10819, 2.11–3.9 (unpublished).

71. No. 8.1.4.

72. Otto, *Das ägyptische Mundöffnungsritual*, scene 71 (excerpts), see vol. 1, pp. 186–194 and vol. 2, pp. 158–161.

73. Ibid., vol. 1, pp. 200–203 and vol. 2, pp. 165–167.

74. In the tomb of Rekhmire, a brief version of this spell serves as a caption:

To be recited: O sons of Horus, hurry
with your father, Osiris N.
Do not let him be far from you!
Bring what is his to the earth.
Carrying by the nine friends:
The god is coming, beware, O earth!

N. de G. Davies, *The Tomb of Rekh-Mi-Re at Thebes*, pl. 89.

75. Cauville, *Le Temple de Dendara*, p. 426.

76. N. de G. Davies and A. H. Gardiner, *The Tomb of Amenemhet* (London, 1915), pl. 10.

77. Davies, *The Tomb of Rekh-Mi-Re*, pl. 93, where the scene is displaced to the cultic drama in the sacred temenos.

78. This is the interpretation of the scene by Kees, *Totenglauben und Jenseitsvorstellungen*, p. 250 and Settgast, *Untersuchungen zu altägyptischen Bestattungsdarstellungen*, p. 110.

CHAPTER 14. PROVISIONING THE DEAD

1. J.-J. Clère, "Le Fonctionnement grammatical de l'expression *prj ḫrw* en ancien égyptien," in *Mélanges Maspero*, vol. 1, Mémoires publiés par les membres de l'Institut Français d'Archéologie Orientale du Caire 66 (Cairo, 1935), p. 755, n. 2.

2. On the rite of *wꜣḥ jḫ.t*, see the excellent study by C. Favard-Meeks, *Le Temple de Behbeit el Hagara: Essai de reconstitution et d'interprétation*, Studien zur altägyptischen Kultur Beiheft 6 (Hamburg, 1991), pp. 401–433. On the relationship between the terms *wꜣḥ jḫ.t* and *prj ḫrw*, cf. the following mortuary wish from the Old Kingdom: *wꜣḥ n=f jḫ.t nb.t ḏ.t m jz=f m bw nb n pr.t ḫrw*, "may offerings be made for him forever in his tomb and in every place of mortuary offerings": mastaba of Akhethotep, S. Hassan, *Excavations at Giza*, vol. 1 (Cairo, 1929),

fig. 136 and Favard-Meeks, *Le Temple de Behbeit el Hagara*, pp. 404–405. In the tomb of Debehni, the great inaugural offering on the roof of the mastaba at the end of the funeral procession is called *wꜣḥ jḥ.t*; see E. Edel, *Das Akazienhaus und seine Rolle in den Begräbnisriten des alten Ägyptens*, Münchner ägyptologische Studien 24 (Munich, 1970), pp. 9–11, p. 14, nn. 8, 22 and 32, and fig. 1; and Favard-Meeks, *Le Temple de Behbeit el Hagara*, pp. 402–403. In other mastabas, *wꜣḥ jḥ.t* occurs in connection with the offering list; see Favard-Meeks, *Le Temple de Behbeit el Hagara*, p. 403 and G. Lapp, *Die Opferformel des Alten Reiches unter Berücksichtigung einiger späterer Formen*, Deutsches Archäologisches Institut Kairo Sonderschrift 21 (Mainz, 1986), p. 174. In the Middle Kingdom, *wꜣḥ jḥ.t* makes its first appearance among the wishes expressed in the offering formula: "may offerings be made for him on the *wag*-festival, on the Thoth-festival, on the New Year's festival, and on all the goodly festivals, consisting of 1000 of bread and beer, 1000 *sr*-geese and *z.t*-ducks, 1000 doves, and 1000 antelopes and gazelles, for the unique friend *Ḥmgw*; see W. Schenkel, *Memphis—Herakleopolis—Theben: Die epigraphischen Zeugnisse der 8.–11. Dynastie*, Ägyptologische Abhandlungen 12 (Wiesbaden, 1965), pp. 65–66, no. 45. The festival calendar in the New Kingdom tomb of Neferehotep (Theban Tomb 50, no. 6.2.4) also provides for a *wꜣḥ jḥ.t* for Osiris on the *wag*-festival and various other festivals; see Favard-Meeks, *Le Temple de Behbeit el Hagara*, pp. 406–407.

3. Favard-Meeks, *Le Temple de Behbeit el Hagara*, p. 404 with nn. 834 and 836, including a reference to S. Sauneron, *Bulletin de l'Institut Français d'Archéologie Orientale du Caire* 63 (1965): 83–84. Favard-Meeks interprets the *wꜣḥ jḥ.t* as the opening rite of the mortuary offering, which was followed by the list of individual offering items (*ḥtp-dj-njswt*) and, finally, the "recitation of many transfigurations"; see *Le Temple de Behbeit el Hagara*, p. 405. There is a harper's song in which a mention of making offerings seems to be connected with a day of festival:

> May your *ba* rest in it (i.e., in the West)
> when you are called by the chief lector priest on the day of *wꜣḥ jḥ.t*.

The text is published by W. K. Simpson, "A Short Harper's Song from the New Kingdom in the Yale University Art Gallery," *Journal of the American Research Center in Egypt* 8 (1969–70): 49–50.

4. Many examples are cited by Favard-Meeks, *Le Temple de Behbeit el Hagara*, pp. 407–409. She does not, however, sufficiently investigate the corresponding formulas for the emergence of the *ba* in connection with other words for the mortuary offering. In her opinion, *wꜣḥ jḥ.t* was a specific rite whose purpose was to cause the *ba* to "emerge." See also no. 6, § 2 (calling out the name) and no. 8.5.2, § 17 (calling out the mortuary offering).

5. Theban Tomb 277; J. Vandier d'Abbadie, *Deux tombes ramessides à Gournet-Mourrai* (Cairo, 1954), pl. 4. Similarly,

> May my *ba* live in the presence of the lord of eternity.
> May the doorkeepers not turn it away,
> they who guard the gates of the netherworld.
> May it emerge at the calling out of the offering
> in my tomb of the necropolis.
> May it enjoy bread
> and have an abundance of beer,
> and may it drink water at the drinking-place by the river.

Theban Tomb 111; K. Sethe, *Urkunden des ägyptischen Altertums*, vol. 4, reprint ed. (Berlin, 1961), p. 430, text 762. For further examples, see no. 8.5.2, § 17.

6. See J. Assmann and M. Bommas, *Altägyptische Totenliturgien*, vol. 3: *Totenliturgien in Papyri der Spätzeit* (in preparation), liturgy SZ2; W. Runge, *Totenliturgien in den Pyramidentexten* (in preparation).

7. Pyramid Texts spell 413, §§ 735b–736c.

8. On the motif of food that does not spoil, cf. CT.3, § 15 and SZ.1, spell 9, verses 92–93. T. G. Allen, *Occurrences of Pyramid Texts with Cross Indexes of These and Other Mortuary Texts,*

Studies in Ancient Oriental Civilizations 27 (Chicago, 1950), p. 81, points to parallels in Pyramid Texts spell 457, § 859a–b; Pyramid Texts spell 521, § 1226a–b; and Coffin Texts spell 327, A. de Buck, *The Egyptian Coffin Texts*, vol. 4, Oriental Institute Publications 67 (Chicago, 1951), p. 163 g–h.

9. Pyramid Texts spell 457, §§ 858a–859b.

10. Pyramid Texts spell 612, §§ 1731b–1733a.

11. Allen, *Occurrences of Pyramid Texts*, spell 665B = R. O. Faulkner, *The Ancient Egyptian Pyramid Texts* (Oxford, 1969), spell 665A, § 1908.

12. Allen, *Occurrences of Pyramid Texts*, spell 667B = Faulkner, *The Ancient Egyptian Pyramid Texts*, spell 667A, § 1947.

13. Pyramid Texts spell 463, §§876a–b clearly has to do with the celestial gate:

The door-leaves of the sky open up for you,
the door-leaves of the "cool place," which keep away the subjects, open up for you.

14. De Buck, *The Egyptian Coffin Texts*, vol. 1, Oriental Institute Publications 34 (Chicago, 1935), pp. 289d–290b = CT.e, spell 8; see J. Assmann and M. Bommas, *Altägyptische Totenliturgien*, vol. 1, Supplemente zu den Schriften der Heidelberger Akademie der Wissenschaften, Philosophisch-historische Klasse 14 (Heidelberg, 2002), § 26 for further parallels.

15. Cf. Pyramid Texts §§ 285a and 1719e.

16. Cf. Pyramid Texts §§ 923a–b, 977b–c, 1264b–c, 1696a–b, and 2076a–b.

17. *Dj ꜥ.wj r* "to extend the arms to someone," cf. Pyramid Texts § 555b.

18. Cf. Pyramid Texts §§ 1901, 1945c, 1947a, and 744b.

19. PT 665C, § *1916c–d (according to the numbering of Allen).

20. There are already three different versions of this spell in the Coffin Texts, and it then remained one of the most common offering recitations down into the later stages of Egyptian history, both in the cult of the dead and in that of the gods.

21. The title occurs in the tomb of Rekhmire from the reigns of Tuthmosis III and Amenophis II.

22. A variant reads *ḥnfy.wt* "rejoicing ones," "praising ones."

23. A verb *wṯb* with the meaning "to prepare" or the like is not attested in A. Erman and H. Grapow, *Wörterbuch der aegyptischen Sprache*, reprint ed. (Berlin, 1971), vol. 1. On the parallel passage in de Buck, *The Egyptian Coffin Texts*, vol. 6, Oriental Institute Publications 81 (Chicago, 1956), p. 106e, see the commentary.

24. See J. Assmann, "Das Bild des Vaters im alten Ägypten," in J. Assmann (ed.), *Stein und Zeit: Mensch und Gesellschaft im Alten Ägypten* (Munich, 1991), pp. 115–138. On the meaning of *ꜣḫ*, see K. Jansen-Winkeln, "'Horizont' und 'Verklärtheit': Zur Bedeutung der Wurzel *ꜣḫ*," *Studien zur altägyptischen Kultur* 23 (1996): 201–215.

25. A. M. Moussa and F. Junge, *Two Tombs of Craftsmen*, Archäologische Veröffentlichungen 9 (Mainz, 1975), pl. 4a, lines 24–25.

26. The first tomb of Senenmut, Theban Tomb 353, § 29; see P. Dorman, *The Tombs of Senenmut*, Publications of the Metropolitan Museum of Art Egyptian Expedition 24 (New York, 1991), pp. 110–111 and pl. 79.

27. Erman and Grapow, *Wörterbuch der aegyptischen Sprache*, vol. 3, p. 469.3–4, attested only in the Pyramid Texts "as something that precedes *gm*, 'to find.'"

28. Ibid., p. 469.5–8.

29. Ibid., pp. 468.14–15 and 469.1–2.

30. *Sḫm=k m ḏ.t=k.*

31. Pyramid Texts 537, § 1300c: *sḫm=k m ḏ.t=k wnḥ.t ḏ.t=k.*

32. *Dd-mdw zp 4 wnḥ d.t=k jw.t.k ḥr=sn.*

33. In a late liturgy consisting of ten mortuary offering spells, our spell begins each of the presentations:

Spell for presenting offerings.
O Osiris N.,
If you are in the sky, come to your *bꜣ*!

If you are in the earth, come to your *ꜣḫ*!
If you are in the south, the north,
the west, or the east,
come, may you be satisfied and strong in your *ḏ.t*-body!
May you emerge from there, you being *bꜣ* and *ꜣḫ*,
mighty like Re,
perfect like a god.
Come to this bread of yours and this beer of yours,
to this draught of yours, that you may have disposal of all good things.

Papyrus British Museum 10209, 1, lines 13–18, published by Goyon, "La Fête de Sokaris à Edfou à la lumière d'un texte liturgique remontant au Nouvel Empire," *Bulletin de l'Institut Français d'Archéologie Orientale* 78 (1978). In this version, which is attested elsewhere as well, the deceased is to come not "as" but "to" his *ba* and *akh*. This is difficult to comprehend. But there is also mention of the *ḏ.t*-body in which the deceased is to emerge "from there," that is, from the sky or the earth or one of the four cardinal points, and come to his tomb.

34. No. 2.

35. Instruction for Merikare, pp. 53–57; see J. F. Quack, *Studien zur Lehre für Merikare* (Wiesbaden, 1992), pp. 34–35. These lines from Merikare occur in a description of the Judgment of the Dead, and our text thus alludes to this Judgment and to a freedom of movement that is accorded only to the vindicated. It is possible, of course, that the Instruction for Merikare cites the mortuary spell, which under this assumption would have to go back to the Middle Kingdom.

36. J. Assmann, *Liturgische Lieder an den Sonnengott*, Münchner ägyptologische Studien 19 (Berlin, 1969), p. 188, text II 2, verses 5–19; pp. 191–192, comment 4 on Papyrus Berlin 3050; and p. 192, n. 6 on Papyrus Berlin 3055, 12, line 10 (a censing spell).

37. Regarding Nepri, Louvre C 66 states:

May Nepri give his food offerings
from the grain of the Field of Reeds.

38. She also appears in this role in the wishes expressed in the literary letter that we cited in chapter 10:

May the god of grain give you bread, and Hathor beer,
may you nurse at the breast of the milk goddess.

H.-W. Fischer-Elfert, *Die satirische Streitschrift des Papyrus Anastasi I: Textzusammenstellung* (Wiesbaden, 1983), pp. 52–53; Fischer-Elfert, *Die satirische Streitschrift des Papyrus Anastasi I: Übersetzung und Kommentar* (Wiesbaden, 1986), p. 37.

39. In a scene in the Osiris chapels at Dendara, we see a quintet of deities presenting nourishment: Hapy (water), Nepyt (bread), Hathor (beer), Seshat-Hor (milk), and Renenutet (wine); see S. Cauville, *Le Temple de Dendara: Les Chapelles osiriennes, transcription and traduction* (Cairo, 1997), p. 34.

40. Such wishes occur often in mortuary liturgies, e.g., Coffin Texts spell 61, de Buck, *The Egyptian Coffin Texts*, vol. 1, p. 262f:

May bars of silver be brought for you,
to the bowl with the turquoise rim.

See further Book of the Dead chapter 172, lines 41–42:

May you wash your feet on a bar of silver
and on the rim of the bowl of the divine lake.

E. A. W. Budge, *The Chapters of Coming Forth by Day or the Theban Recension of the Book of the Dead* (London, 1898), vol. 3, p. 60.

May you walk on silver ground
and a floor of gold.
May you wash yourself on a bar of silver
and on a floor of gold.
May you be embalmed on a *ḥr.t* of turquoise.

S. Sauneron, *Le Rituel de l'embaumement* (Cairo, 1952), p. 43. On washing the feet as a ritual, see S. Schott, *Die Reinigung Pharaohs in einem memphitischen Tempel*, Nachrichten der Akademie der Wissenschaften in Göttingen, Philologisch-historische Klasse 1957/3 (Göttingen, 1957), pp. 71–75; our text is discussed on p. 73.

41. Theban Tomb 100; N. de G. Davies, *The Tomb of Rekh-Mi-Re at Thebes*, Publications of the Metropolitan Museum of Art Egyptian Expedition 11 (New York, 1943), pl. 76.

42. Ptah otherwise appears often as a god of weaving who is responsible for the garments of the deceased, as, for instance, in an offering spell in Theban Tomb 100:

May you put on the garments that Ptah gives you
as (?) something discarded by Hathor.

Similarly, de Buck, *The Egyptian Coffin Texts*, vol. 1, p. 285f:

May you put on a pure garment of Ptah
and a discarded garment of Hathor.

A. Piankoff, *Les Chapelles de Tut-ankh-amon*, Mémoires publiés par les membres de l'Institut Français d'Archéologie Orientale du Caire 72 (Cairo, 1951), pl. 24:

(may you put on) a pure garment as (read "of"?) Ptah,
you being clad by the hands of the goddess of weaving.

In a mortuary spell on the sarcophagus of Princess Ankhnesneferibre of Dynasty 26, we read:

Re has caused that the fabric for your clothing be woven of gold
as the work of Ptah, the beautiful of face.

43. E. Hornung, "Vom Sinn der Mumifizierung," *Welt des Orients* 14 (1983): 167–175.

44. E. Hornung, A. Brodbeck, and E. Staehelin, *Das Buch von den Pforten des Jenseits*, vol. 1 (Geneva, 1979), pp. 235–239. Translation: Hornung, *Ägyptische Unterweltsbücher* (Zurich, 1982), pp. 195–308.

45. The meaning of this motif is stressed by Hornung in the introduction to his *Ägyptische Unterweltsbücher*, pp. 38–42.

46. "Lord of the rituals" is a frequent title of the Egyptian king. I do not know this wish otherwise in Egyptian mortuary texts, but the general concept that the deceased is to approach the god carrying out priestly functions characterized the decorative program of tombs from the end of Dynasty 18 on.

47. In the wishes expressed in the literary letter, there are similar turns of expression regarding sunlight and the Nile flood:

May you see the light of the sun in the netherworld, when it passes over you,
may Nun overflow in your house and flood your path,
may it flow seven cubits high beside your tomb.

Papyrus Anastasi I, 3, lines 7–8; Fischer-Elfert, *Die satirische Streitschrift des Papyrus Anastasi I: Textzusammenstellungen*, p. 51; ibid., *Übersetzung und Kommentar*, p. 37 with note ai.

48. Lower part of a scribal statue of Amenmose (Theban Tomb 373) in Vienna, Kunsthistorisches Museum, Ägyptische Sammlung 5749, Corpus Antiquitatum Aegyptiarum, Wien 6, pp. 101–103.

49. On this point, note also Louvre C 66: "May Hapy grant you fresh water from the august libation vessel that Ptah has fashioned of gold."

50. Davies, *Two Ramesside Tombs at Thebes*, Publications of the Metropolitan Museum of Art Egyptian Expedition 5 (New York, 1927), pl. 19.

CHAPTER 15. SACRAMENTAL EXPLANATION

1. S. Schott, *Mythe und Mythenbildung im Alten Ägypten*, Untersuchungen zur Geschichte und Altertumskunde Ägyptens 15 (Leipzig, 1945), pp. 33–34.

2. See J. Assmann, "Altägyptische Kultkommentare," in J. Assmann and B. Gladigow (eds.), *Text und Kommentar*, Archäologie der literarischen Kommunikation 4 (Munich, 1995), pp. 93–110.

3. K. Sethe, *Dramatische Texte zu altägyptischen Mysterienspielen*, Untersuchungen zur Geschichte und Altertumskunde Ägyptens (Leipzig, 1928), pp. 81–83.

4. Ibid., pp. 211–213; cf. J. Assmann, "Die Verborgenheit des Mythos in Ägypten," *Göttinger Miszellen* 25 (1977): 16–18, and R. B. Parkinson, *Voices from Ancient Egypt: An Anthology of Middle Kingdom Writings*, Oklahoma Series in Classical Culture 9 (London, 1991), pp. 124–125, no. 45.

5. Sethe, *Dramatische Texte*, p. 256.

6. I have attempted to reconstruct the "implicit linguistic theory" of Egyptian cult recitations in *The Search for God in Ancient Egypt* (Ithaca, 2001), pp. 83–110.

7. Pyramid Texts spell 366, § 627; see Assmann, *The Search for God in Ancient Egypt*, p. 85.

8. The problem of the primacy of ritual, to which myth was added only secondarily, will have to be elaborated in a future study. In the meantime, see E. Otto, *Das Verhältnis von Rite und Mythus im Ägyptischen*, Sitzungsberichte der Heidelberger Akademie der Wissenschaften, Philosophisch-historische Klasse, Jahrgang 1958/1 (Heidelberg, 1958) and W. Helck, "Rituale," in W. Helck and E. Otto (eds.), *Lexikon der Ägyptologie*, vol. 5 (Wiesbaden, 1984), cols. 271–285.

9. See Assmann, "Altägyptische Kultkommentare."

10. Dino Bidoli dealt with the spells having to do with the net and with the ferryman text in his dissertation. With the help of parallels from Islamic and European guild systems, he was able to reconstruct a highly convincing *sitz im leben* for these examinations. The ferryboat text, for instance, could in fact go back to a ceremony in an Old Kingdom shipyard, presumably when a new member was inducted into the professional association of the ship builders, a ceremony in which individuals played the various roles. If so, we have here an ancient Egyptian example of initiation into the "secrets" of a profession, in the typical form of stock verbal exchanges, as they are often to be encountered in the customs of artisans in various periods and cultures, and especially, at least occasionally, in the guilds of modern Egypt at a relatively recent date. Such examinations were not essentially a matter of proving one's technical knowledge. Rather, in order to justify one's acceptance into the group, it was a matter of demonstrating knowledge of an allegorical form of speaking. The members of the guilds in question generally kept this knowledge secret, and it mostly consisted of a symbolic or mythic description of the most important parts of the object to be produced (in our case, the boat designated "ferry") and of the tools and equipment used in making it. See D. Bidoli, *Die Sprüche der Fangnetze in den altägyptischen Sargtexten*, Abhandlungen des Deutschen Archäologischen Instituts Kairo 9 (Glückstadt, 1976), pp. 30–31.

11. Ibid., p. 28.

12. See E. Hornung, *Das Totenbuch der Ägypter* (Zürich, 1979), pp. 241–242.

13. J. Vandier, *Le Papyrus Jumilhac* (Paris, 1960); H. Beinlich, *Das Buch vom Fayum: Zum religiösen Eigenverständnis einer ägyptischen Landschaft*, Ägyptologische Abhandlungen 51 (Wiesbaden, 1991).

14. J. G. Griffiths, *Plutarch De Iside et Osiride* (Cardiff, 1970), pp. 172–174 and 436–438. On the various explanations of water and the discharges during the mummification process, see especially J. Kettel, "Canopes, *rdw.w* d'Osiris et Osiris-Canope," in *Hommages à Jean Leclant*, vol. 3: *Études Isiaques*, Bibliothèque d'Étude 106/3 (Cairo, 1994), pp. 315–330, with rich bibliographical references. On the water-cult of the Isis-Serapis religion, see R. A. Wild,

Water in the Cultic Worship of Isis and Sarapis, Études préliminaries aux religions orientales dans l'empire romain 87 (Leiden, 1981).

15. F. M. H. Haikal, *Two Hieratic Funerary Papyri of Nesmin*, 2 vols., Bibliotheca Aegyptiaca 14 (Brussels, 1970–1972).

16. Excerpt from (*jnj r*) the Book of the Festival of the Valley (*sšd n ḥȝb jn.t*).

Making offerings (*wȝḥ jḥ.t*) by the king himself,
of beer, water,
wine, and milk.
Spell that the lector priest recites.

17. See especially B. Altenmüller-Kesting, "Reinigungsriten im ägyptischen Kult," Ph.D. dissertation, Hamburg, 1968.

18. See S. P. Vleeming and P. W. Pestman (eds.), *Hundred-Gated Thebes: Acts of a Colloquium on Thebes in the Graeco-Roman Period*, Papyrologica Lugduno-Batava 27 (Leiden, 1995).

19. Papyrus Berlin 3115. On the cultic association of the choachytes and the Theban decade festival, see F. de Cenival, *Les Associations religieuses en Égypte d'après les documents démotiques*, Bibliothèque d'Étude 46 (Cairo, 1972), pp. 103–105, and K. Parlasca, "Bemerkungen zum ägyptischen Gräberwesen der griechisch-römischen Zeit," in *Ägypten, Dauer und Wandel: Symposium anlässlich des 75jährigen Bestehens des Deutschen Archäologischen Instituts Kairo am 10. und 11. Oktober 1982*, Deutsches Archäologisches Institut Kairo Sonderschrift 18 (Mainz, 1987), pp. 97–103.

20. F. R. Herbin, *Le Livre de parcourir l'éternité*, Orientalia Lovaniensia Analecta 58 (Louvain, 1994), pp. 142–145.

21. In the Book of Traversing Eternity, Osiris at *Tȝmw.t* is also connected with the Festival of the Valley; see ibid., p. 139 on A II, 26 and II, 27.

22. Pyramid Texts spell 436, §§ 788–789.

23. Pyramid Texts spell 33, §§ 24–25.

24. Situla of the high priest *Wsjr-wr* in the Louvre; P. Pierret, *Recueil d'inscriptions inédites du Musée égyptien du Louvre*, Études égyptologiques, vol. 2, reprint ed. (Hildesheim, 1978), pp. 113–115.

25. A. Mariette, *Dendéra: Description générale du temple de cette ville*, vol. 1 (Paris, 1870), pl. 10.

26. See H. Beinlich, *Die Osirisreliquien: Zum Motiv der Körperzergliederung in der altägyptischen Religion*, Ägyptologische Abhandlungen 42 (Wiesbaden, 1984). For further literature, see Kettel, "Canopes," p. 315, n. 1; and cf. especially L. Pantalacci, *Recherches sur Osiris démembré*, Paris, 1981 (unpublished).

27. H. Junker, *Die Stundenwachen in den Osirismysterien*, Denkschriften der Kaiserlichen Akademie der Wissenschaften in Wien, Philosophisch-historische Klasse 54 (Vienna, 1910), p. 79.

28. S. Schott, *Die Reinigung Pharaos in einem memphitischen Tempel*, Nachrichten der Akademie der Wissenschaften in Göttingen, Philologisch-historische Klasse 1957/3 (Göttingen, 1957), p. 55.

29. Papyrus Jumilhac 3.19–4.38 and 5, vignette, right; Vandier, *Le Papyrus Jumilhac*, pp. 99–100, 135–138, and 224–239.

30. Beinlich, *Die Osirisreliquien*; L. Pantalacci, "Une Conception originale de la survie osirienne d'après les textes de Basse Époque," *Göttinger Miszellen* 52 (1981): 57–66; Pantalacci, "Sur quelques termes d'anatomie sacrée dans les listes ptolémaïques de reliques osiriennes," *Göttinger Miszellen* 58 (1982): 65–72; Pantalacci, "Sur les méthodes de travail des décorateurs tentyrites," *Bulletin de l'Institut Français d'Archéologie Orientale* 86 (1986): 267–275; Pantalacci, "Décor de la 2e chapelle osirienne de l'est (sud) sur le toit du temple de Dendara," in Sylvia Schoske (ed.), *Akten des vierten internationalen Ägyptologenkongresses, München 1985*, vol. 3, Studien zur Altägyptischen Kultur Beiheft 3 (Hamburg, 1989), pp. 327–337; J.-C. Goyon, "Momification et recomposition du corps divin: Anubis et les canopes," in J. H. Kampstra, H. Milde, and K. Wagtendonk (eds.), *Funerary Symbols and Religion: Essays Dedicated to Professor M. S. H. G. Heerma van Voss on the Occasion of His Retirement from the Chair of the History of Ancient Religions at the University of Amsterdam* (Kampen, 1988),

34–44; S. Cauville *Dendara: Les Chapelles osiriennes*, vol. 2: *Commentaire* (Cairo, 1997), pp. 33–45.

31. Cauville, *Dendara: Les Chapelles osiriennes*, vol. 1 (Cairo, 1997), pp. 40–51.

32. Kettel, "Canopes," pp. 315–330.

33. Beinlich, *Die Osirisreliquien*, p. 89; Cauville, *Dendara*, vol. 10 (Cairo, 1997), pp. 71–72; Cauville, *Dendara: Les Chapelles osiriennes*, vol. 1, p. 40.

34. Beinlich, *Die Osirisreliquien*, p. 147; Cauville, *Dendara*, vol. 10, p. 82; Cauville, *Dendara: Les Chapelles osiriennes*, vol. 1, p. 46.

35. Beinlich, *Die Osirisreliquien*, p. 149; Cauville, *Dendara*, vol. 10, p. 82; Cauville, *Dendara: Les Chapelles osiriennes*, vol. 1, p. 46.

36. Beinlich, *Die Osirisreliquien*, p. 153; Cauville, *Dendara*, vol. 10, p. 83; Cauville, *Dendara: Les Chapelles osiriennes*, vol. 1, p. 46.

37. A. Egberts, *In Quest of Meaning: A Study of the Ancient Egyptian Rites of Consecrating the Meret-Chests and Driving the Calves*, 2 vols., Egyptologische Uitgaven 8 (Leiden, 1995).

38. Ibid., pp. 173–199.

39. Ibid., pp. 153–154; similarly, p. 131.

40. Ibid., p. 96.

41. Ibid., pp. 107–108.

42. Ibid., p. 179.

43. Ibid., 153–154; text from Dendara, reign of Ptolemy XII.

44. D. B. Redford, *Pharaonic King-Lists, Annals and Day-Books: A Contribution to the Study of the Egyptian Sense of History*, Society for the Study of Egyptian Antiquities Publication 4 (Mississauga, 1986), pp. 277–281.

CHAPTER 16. FREEDOM FROM THE YOKE OF TRANSITORINESS:
RESULTATIVITY AND CONTINUANCE

1. M. Walser, *Ein springender Brunnen* (Frankfurt, 1998), p. 9. I owe this reference to Aleida Assmann.

2. See the third text studied in chapter 13 of this volume.

3. E. Dziobek, *Die Denkmäler des Vezirs User-Amun*, Studien zur Archäologie und Geschichte Ägyptens 18 (Heidelberg, 1998), pp. 78–79.

4. See G. Posener, "Le Début de l'Enseignement de Hardjedof," *Revue d'Égyptologie* 9 (1952): 109–110.

5. H. Brunner, "Djedefhor in der römischen Kaiserzeit," in *Studia Aegyptiaca*, vol. 1 (1974), pp. 55–64, reprinted in Brunner, *Das Hörende Herze: Kleine Schriften zur Religions- und Geistesgeschichte Ägyptens*, Orbis Biblicus et Orientalis 80 (Freiburg and Göttingen, 1988); pp. 49–58; Braunner, "Zitate aus Lebenslehren," in E. Hornung and O. Keel (eds.), *Studien zu altägyptischen Lebenslehren*, Orbis Biblicus et Orientalis 28 (Freiburg and Göttingen, 1979), pp. 113–114 and 121–122.

6. H. Brunner, *Altägyptische Weisheit: Lehren für das Leben* (Zurich, 1988), p. 103.

7. Ibid., p. 103, verses 32–37.

8. Merikare P 127–128; see G. Posener, *Annuaire du Collège de France 1966/67* (Paris, 1967), p. 343 and G. Fecht, *Der Habgierige und die Ma'at in der Lehre des Ptahhotep (5. und 19. Maxime)*, Abhandlungen des Deutschen Archäologischen Instituts Kairo 1 (Glückstadt, 1958), pp. 50–51.

9. Hecataeus of Abdera, cited by Diodorus Siculus, *Bibliotheca Historiae* (*Library of History*), book 1, chapter 51; Edwin Murphy, *Diodorus on Egypt* (Jefferson, N.C., 1985), pp. 67–68.

10. Papyrus Chester Beatty IV, verso 2.5–3.11; see Brunner, *Altägyptische Weisheit*, pp. 224–226 and J. Assmann, *Stein und Zeit: Mensch und Gesellschaft im Alten Ägypten* (Munich, 1991), pp. 173–175.

11. A. Assmann, *Erinnerungsräume: Formen und Wandlungen des kulturellen Gedächtnis* (Munich, 1999) and J. Assmann, *Religion und kulturelles Gedächtnis* (Munich, 2000).

12. Cited after Z. Bauman, *Mortality, Immortality and Other Life Strategies* (Cambridge, 1992), p. 65.

13. Ibid., chapter 2, "Bidding for Immortality."

14. K. Ehlich, "Text und sprachliches Handels: Die Entstehung von Texten aus dem Bedürfnis nach Überlieferung," in A. Assmann, J. Assmann, and C. Hardmeier (eds.), *Schrift und Gedächtnis* (Munich, 1983), pp. 24–43.

15. See W. Westendorf, "Eine auf die Ma'at anspielende Form," *Mitteilungen des Instituts für Orientforschung* 2 (1954): 165–182; the thought is that in the time of Osiris, *maat* was in fact destroyed (through the murder of the god by the hand of his brother Seth); see A. de Buck, *The Egyptian Coffin Texts*, vol. 6, Oriental Institute Publications 81 (Chicago, 1956), p. 278d, where it is said of the enemies of Osiris: "They have said that they will destroy *maat*."

16. Ptahhotep, Devéria lines 84–98; Z. Žába, *Les Maximes de Ptahhotep*, p. 24; G. Fecht, *Der Habgierige und die Ma'at*, pp. 34–47. In Fecht's opinion, the last verse is displaced from maxim 6.

17. *R nmt.t=f,* cf. the Decree of Haremhab, W. Helck, *Zeitschrift für ägyptische Sprache und Altertumskunde* 80 (1955): 127 ("gemäss seiner Bestimmung").

18. Žába, *Les Maximes de Ptahhotep*, pp. 39–40, 85–86, and 141–142; G. Fecht, *Der Habgierige und die Ma'at*, pp. 34–47; P. Seibert, *Die Charakteristik: Untersuchungen zu einer altägyptischen Sprechsitte und ihren Ausprägungen in Folklore und Literatur*, Ägyptologische Abhandlungen 17 (Wiesbaden, 1967), pp. 72–77.

19. F. Nietzsche, *On the Genealogy of Morals* (New York, 1967); S. Freud, *Civilization and Its Discontents* (New York, 1961) and *Totem and Taboo: Some Points of Agreement Between the Mental Lives of Savages and Neurotics* (New York, 1950).

20. K. Sethe, *Urkunden des ägyptischen Altertums*, vol. 1, 2d ed. (Leipzig, 1903), pp. 203–204; A. Roccati, *La Littérature historique sous l'Ancien Empire égyptien* (Paris, 1982), § 119. See also the inscription of Ikhekhi, ibid., § 156.

21. M. Lichtheim, *Maat in Egyptian Autobiographies and Related Studies*, Orbis Biblicus et Orientalis 120 (Freiburg and Gättingen, 1992); Lichtheim, *Moral Values in Ancient Egypt*, Orbis Biblicus et Orientalis 155 (Freiburg and Göttingen, 1997).

22. Lichtheim, *Maat in Egyptian Autobiographies*, pp. 103–105 and esp. 128–130, no. 22.

23. This is a citation from the Instruction for Merikare; see chapter 4 of this volume.

24. Stela Turin 156, published by A. Varille, "*La Stèle du mystique Béky* (no. 156 du Musée de Turin)," *Bulletin de l'Institut Français d'Archéologie Orientale* 54 (1954): 129–135.

25. W. Barta, *Das Gespräch eines Mannes mit seinem Ba (Papyrus Berlin 3024)* (Mainz, 1969); H. Goedicke, *The Report about the Dispute of a Man with his Ba* (Baltimore, 1970); O. Renaud, *Le Dialogue du désespéré avec son âme* (Geneva, 1991); K. Lehmann, "Das Gespräch eines Mannes mit seinem Ba," *Studien zur altägyptischen Kultur* 25 (1998): 207–236.

26. Papyrus Berlin 3024, lines 56–68.

27. Papyrus Berlin 3024, lines 130–142.

28. Papyrus Berlin 3024, lines 142–147; Barta, *Das Gespräch eines Mannes*, pp. 18, 28, and 47; Goedicke, *The Report about the Dispute*, pp. 178–182. On the last two verses, cf. a coffin text from Kom el-Hisn, cited by A. Loprieno, *Topos und Mimesis: Zum Ausländer in der ägyptischen Literatur*, Ägyptologische Abhandlungen 48 (Wiesbaden, 1988), p. 97:

May you sit at the side of Re,
may he hear your speech.

29. Papyrus Berlin 3024, lines. 147–154.

30. Lehmann, "Das Gespräch eines Mannes," pp. 207–236, has argued for a dating to the New Kingdom, given that laments and harpers' songs criticizing the afterlife first appear in the textual tradition in the Amarna and Ramesside Periods. This dating founders, however, on the palaeography of Papyrus Berlin 3024, which belongs, entirely and unequivocally, to the Middle Kingdom.

CHAPTER 17. FREEDOM FROM THE YOKE OF TRANSITORINESS: IMMORTALITY

1. Sinuhe R 6–7; see R. Koch, *Die Erzählung des Sinuhe*, Bibliotheca Aegyptiaca 17 (Brussels, 1990), p. 4.

2. See L. V. Žabkar, *A Study of the* Ba-*Concept in Ancient Egyptian Texts*, Studies in Ancient Oriental Civilization 34 (Chicago, 1968), pp. 73–74; G. Lefebvre, *Romans et contes égyptiens*, reprint ed. (Paris, 1976), p. 5, n. 5; p. 9, n. 27; p. 47, n. 77; and p. 158, n. 83.

3. Biography of Ineni, Theban Tomb 81, Sethe, *Urkunden des ägyptischen Altertums*, vol. 4, reprint ed. (Berlin, 1961), p. 54; J. H. Breasted, *Ancient Records of Egypt*, reprint ed. (New York, 1962), vol. 2, § 46.

4. Biography of Ineni, Sethe, *Urkunden*, vol. 4, p. 58; Breasted, *Ancient Records*, vol. 2, § 108.

5. Biography of Ineni, Sethe, *Urkunden*, vol. 4, p. 59; Breasted, *Ancient Records*, vol. 2, § 118.

6. Biography of Amenemheb, Theban Tomb 85, Sethe, *Urkunden*, vol. 4, p. 1896; Breasted, *Ancient Records*, vol. 2, §592.

7. Breasted, *Ancient Records of Egypt*, reprint ed. (New York, 1962), vol. 4, § 988 E.

8. Ibid., § 988 G.

9. Sethe, *Urkunden des ägyptischen Altertums*, vol. 2 (Zeipzig, 1916), p. 80.8–10; cf. S. Sauneron, "Un Document relatif à la divinisation de la reine Arsinoé II," *Bulletin de l'Institut Français d'Archéologie Orientale* 60 (1960): 96.

10. In *A Study of the* Ba-*Concept*, pp. 61, with n. 53, Žabkar mentions the unpublished inscription of a man named Harmeru from Saqqara: "May he reach the land (i.e., be buried), may he traverse the firmament, may he ascend to the great god, may his Ka be preeminent with the king, may his Ba endure with the god, may his certificate be accepted (or, "may his hand be taken") by the god at the pure places."

11. P. Chantraine, *Dictionnaire étymologique de la langue grècque: Histoire des mots*, vol. 2 (Paris, 1970), s.v. Elysium.

12. Amduat, short version, lines 297–300.

13. A. Schweizer, *Seelenführer durch den verborgenen Raum: Das ägyptische Unterweltsbuch Amduat* (Munich, 1994). The Zurich psychotherapist A. Schweizer reads the Amduat as the expression of "collective unconsciousness" in the sense of a "deep psychological level that developed over the course of millennia." We cannot agree with this interpretation, for it ignores the cultural boundaries of this tradition, appealing instead to general human experience, and it all too radically psychologizes the content of the Egyptian Books of the Netherworld. Undeniable, though, is the psycho-imaginative, as opposed to the ratio-cognitive, aspect of these compositions.

14. J. Assmann, *Der König als Sonnenpriester: Ein kosmographischer Begleittext zur kultischen Sonnenhymnik in thebanishen Tempeln und Gräbern*, Abhandlungen des Deutschen Archäologischen Instituts Kairo 7 (Glückstadt, 1970).

15. See Assmann, *Liturgische Lieder an den Sonnengott*, Münchner ägyptologische Studien 19 (Mainz, 1969), pp. 113–164.

16. To the text concerning the morning role of the king as solar priest, there is also a companion piece for praying to the sun god in the evening; see M. C. Betrò, *I Testi solari del Portale di Pascerientaisu (BN 2)* (Pisa, 1990).

17. J. Assmann, "Unio Liturgica: Die kultische Einstimmung in götterweltlichen Lobpreis als Grundmotiv 'esoterischere' Überlieferung im alten Ägypten," in H. G. Kippenber and G. Stroumsa (eds.), *Secrecy and Concealment: Studies in the History of Mediterranean and Near Eastern Religions*, Studies in the History of Religions 65 (Leiden, 1995), pp. 37–60.

18. J. Assmann, *Re und Amun: Die Krise des polytheistischen Weltbilds im Ägypten der 18.–20. Dynastie*, Orbis Biblicus and Orientalis 51 (Freiburg and Göttingen, 1983), p. 52.

19. See J. Assmann, "Das Dekorationsprogramm der königlichen Sonnenheiligtümer des Neuen Reichs nach einer Fassung der Spätzeit," *Zeitschrift für ägyptische Sprache und Altertumskunde* 110 (1983): 91–98.

20. Book of the Dead chapter 100; E. Hornung, *Das Totenbuch der Ägypter* (Zurich, 1979), pp. 198–199; H. te Velde, "Some Remarks on the Mysterious Language of the Baboons," in J. H. Kamstra (ed.), *Funerary Symbols and Religion: Essays Dedicated to Prof. Heerma van Voss on the Occasion of His Retirement from the Chair of the History of Ancient Religions at the University of Amsterdam* (Kampen, 1988), p. 129.

21. Cf. Book of the Dead chapter 81B, Hornung, *Das Totenbuch der Ägypter*, p. 168:

I know the spell of those who are with these gods, the lords of the realm of the dead,
I am one of you.
Let me gaze upon the gods who lead the netherworld,
grant me a place in the realm of the dead!

22. Hornung, *Das Totenbuch der Ägypter*, pp. 198–199.
23. Book of the Dead papyrus Louvre 3292; G. Nagel, "Un Papyrus funéraire de la fin du Nouvel Empire (Louvre 3292 [Inv.])," *Bulletin de l'Institut Français d'Archéologie Orientale* 29 (1929): 47.
24. Book of the Dead chapter 133, lines 14–15 (papyrus of Nu).
25. E. Wente "Mysticism in Pharaonic Egypt?" *Journal of Near Eastern Studies* 41 (1982): 161–179.
26. Hornung, *Ägyptische Unterweltsbücher* (Zurich, 1982), p. 69 (first hour, concluding text).
27. Amduat, short version, lines 12–16.
28. Hornung, *Ägyptische Unterweltsbücher*, p. 183 (twelfth hour, introduction).
29. Ibid., p. 134 (seventh hour, middle register).
30. E. Hornung, *Das Amduat: Die Schrift der verborgenen Kammer*, vol. 1, Ägyptologische Abhandlungen 7/1 (Wiesbaden, 1963). p. 125.6 (seventh hour).
31. Hornung, *Das Amduat*, vol. 1, p. 45.4–5 (third hour, introduction).
32. Hornung, *Das Amduat*, vol. 2, Ägyptologische Abhandlungen 7/2 (Wiesbaden, 1963), p. 24 and S. Schott, *Die Schrift der Verborgenen Kammer in den Königsgräbern des Neuen Reichs*, Nachrichten der Akademie der Wissenschaften in Göttingen, Philologisch-historische Klasse 1958/5 (Göttingen, 1958), p. 349–350. For the translation of *ꜥnḏ* as "select," Hornung makes reference to the discussion of S. Morenz, *Egyptian Religion* (Ithaca, 1973), pp. 225–226, on the esoteric character of the mortuary literature.
33. R. Merkelbach and M. Totti, *Abrasax: Ausgewählte Papyri religiösen und magischen Inhalt*, vol. 3, Abhandlungen der rheinisch-westfälischen Akademie der Wissenschaften, Sonderreihe Papyrologica Coloniensia 17 (Opladen, 1992), p. 52.
34. Ibid., pp. 51–52.
35. Assmann, *Re und Amun*, chapter 1.
36. Wente thinks of a small circle of persons to whom this knowledge and action was disclosed through "initiation." The king thus (originally) had nothing to do with it. But it remains puzzling why the corresponding texts then constitute an exclusively royal tomb decoration. I see no reason to exclude the king from this circle of the "select"; rather, I maintain that here, we again have to do with "demotized" elements of the image of the king.
37. On this aspect of the netherworld, see E. Hornung, *Altägyptische Höllenvorstellungen*, Abhandlungen der Sachsischen Akademie der Wissenschaften zu Leipzig, Philologisch-historische Klasse 59/3 (Berlin, 1968).
38. Wente, "Mysticism," pp. 167–175.
39. Ibid., pp. 174–175.
40. Book of the Dead chapter 17, lines 209–327; see Hornung, *Das Totenbuch der Ägypter*, pp. 69–74.
41. Book of the Dead chapter 125, lines 132–135; see Hornung, *Das Totenbuch der Ägypter*, p. 240.
42. Book of the Dead chapter 125, lines 146–149; Hornung, *Das Totenbuch der Ägypter*, p. 241.

AFTERWORD

1. See J. Assmann, *Moses the Egyptian: The Memory of Egypt in Western Monotheism* (Cambridge, Mass., 1997) and *Die mosaische Unterscheidung oder Der Preis des Monotheismus* (Munich, 2003).
2. Of the innumerable books by and about B. Hellinger, I note here only *Religion, Psychotherapie, Seelsorge* (Munich, 2000) and *Was in Familien krank macht und heilt* (Heidelberg, 2000).

3. Reiner Marten, in particular, has called attention to this issue in his book *Der menschliche Tod: Eine philosophische Revision* (Paderborn, 1987).

4. On this point, see J. Baines and C. Eyre, "Four Notes on Literacy," *Göttinger Miszellen* 61 (1983): 65–96.

5. The translation here is based on that of E. Brunner-Traut, *Altägyptische Märchen*, 8th ed. (Munich, 1989), pp. 244–246.

6. See J. Assmann, "Das Herz auf der Waage: Schuld und Sünde im Alten Ägypten," in T. Schabert and D. Clemans (eds.), *Schuld, Eranos*, n.s. 7 (Munich, 1999): 99–147, esp. pp. 120–124.

7. In Ezekiel, there is already the vision of a sort of resurrection: he beholds the graves opening and the bones of the dead rising up from them (37:13–14). But this is a vision only of resurrection, and the afterlife is not mentioned. The dead return to the land of Israel. Messianic time occurs here, and it concerns the house of Israel, the People of God.

8. Cf., similarly, "What profit is there in my death, if I go down to the Pit? Will the dust praise you? Will it tell of your faithfulness?" (Psalms 30:9); "Do you work wonders for the dead? Do the shades rise up to praise you? Is your steadfast love declared in the grave, or your faithfulness in Abaddon? Are your wonders known in the darkness, or your saving help in the land of forgetfulness?" (88:10–12); "The dead do not praise the Lord, nor do any that go down into silence" (115:17).

9. Similarly, Baruch 2.17–18: ". . . for the dead who are in Hades, whose spirit has been taken from their bodies, will not ascribe glory or justice to the Lord, but the person who is deeply grieved, who walks bowed and feeble, with failing eyes and famished soul, will declare your glory and righteousness, O Lord."

Index

Abaton, 190

Abydos, 48–51, 111, 190, 206, 287; festival at, 61, 212, 225–30, 266–67, 453 n. 70, 454 n. 84; journey to, 305–8

Achilles, 122

Adam and Eve, myth of, 5

Adapa, 3

Admonitions of Ipuwer, 138–39

Afterlife, 10–11; and Amarna Period, 15–16, 217–18; Christian view of, 10, 86, 115–16, 414, 416–17; demotization of, 147–48, 391, 411–14, 476 n. 10; Greek concept of, 232–33, 392; kings' ascent to, 144–47, 149–50, 183, 272, 277, 334–37, 389–91; leisure activities in, 275–77, 461 nn. 53, 54; monsters in, 148–49, 191, 295; moralization of, 75–76, 83, 85–86, 147–49, 379–84, 391, 411–14 (*See also* Judgment of the Dead); nourishment in, 58–59, 128–30, 153, 223, 233, 337 (*See also* Offerings; Provisioning spells); Old Testament view of, 11, 86, 414–17, 478 nn. 7, 8, 9; as ordered world, 162; social connectivity in, 58–63; summons to, 124–25, 144–47, 437 n. 34, 440 nn. 8, 10, 12; as termination, 119–24; water crossing to, 32–33, 130–34, 143–44, 273–74, 304–5. *See also* Elysium; Going forth by day; Immortality; Realm of Death; Salvation

Akh, 15, 42, 88; as mutual effectiveness, 47–48, 52, 296, 339–40. *See also* Transfiguration spells

Akhenaten (Amenophis IV), 15–16, 217, 310

Alcmaeon of Croton, 182–83

Amarna Period, 15–16, 198, 204; art during, 251, 303, 310; and expression of grief, 114, 119, 310; and going forth by day, 211, 217–18, 224, 230; harpers' songs during, 120–21

Amduat, the, 16, 183, 393–96, 398–400, 401–2, 476 n. 13

Amenemheb, tomb of, 221

Amenemhet (grain assessor), tomb of, 88–89, 328

Amenemhet I, King, 178, 182, 390

Amenemhet (nomarch), coffin of, 270, 279. *See also* Coffin Texts, spell 62

Amenemope (domain administrator), tomb of, 197–98, 225, 299–300, 319, 320

Amenhotep (son of Hapu), mortuary temple of, 222

Amenophis (high steward), 99

Amenophis II, King, 111

Amenophis III, King, 320

Amenophis IV, King (Akhenaten), 15–16, 217, 310

Amenuser (vizier), tomb of, 372, 402

Amun, 60–61; of Luxor, 355

Anachoresis, 181–82

Ani, Book of the Dead of, 296–97, 413

Animals, 17, 109; slaughter of, 68–69, 92, 314–15, 324–29, 426 n. 6, 466 n. 65, 467 n. 66

Ankhhapy, coffin of, 263

Ankhnesneferibre (princess), sarcophagus of, 471 n. 42

Ankhpakhrod, coffin of, 118–19

Antefoqer (vizier), tomb of, 141–42

Antef Song, 120–21

Anubis, 102, 103, 207, 211, 268; as master of the scale, 76, 282; mystery of, 192–94; priests portraying, 303, 310

Apologia funebris, 84–85. *See also* Judgment of the Dead

Apopis, 69–70, 137, 187

Apuia, tomb of, 92–93

Apuleius, 205–6

and festivals, 212, 217, 225–32, 453
n.70, 454n.84, 455nn.92, 94; to the
garden, 221–25, 452n.58; to home,
218–21, 450n.31, 451n.36;
transformation for, 213–16, 450n.14
Golden Ass, The (Apuleius), 205–6
Golems, 111
Grace, 404–6
Graeco-Roman Period, 204–5, 207–8,
355–56, 363, 367, 413–14
Grain mummies, 96, 109, 284, 363
Great City, 287
"(Great) Hacking up of the Earth,"
274–75, 278, 281–84, 363–67, 462n.3.
See also Liturgy A
Great Staircase, 287
"Great *Tjeheb* Comes, The," 275, 278
Greed, 54–55, 380, 413
Greek mystery cults, 201, 205–6, 207,
231–33, 400, 403, 460n.37
Greetings, 252–55; in mortuary spells,
255–59
Grief. *See* Mourning
Grieshammer, Reinhard, 81
Guilt: Egyptian concept of, 76, 77–78,
285–86; Old Testament view of, 415. *See
also* Judgment of the Dead

"Hacking up of the Earth." *See* "(Great)
Hacking up of the Earth"; Liturgy A
Hades, 10, 144, 207, 392, 416
Hadrian, 205
Haker festival, 226, 228–29, 230, 266–67
Hapy, 223, 345, 348. *See also* Nile
inundation
Harmeru, inscription of, 476n.10
Harpers' songs, 119–21, 201–3, 436n.18
Hathor, 153, 171, 198–99, 345, 348, 470
n.38
Heart, 28–30, 433n.57; and *ba* and *ka*,
88, 89, 92, 100, 112; following the,
275–76; restoration of, 34, 102–4, 271,
272–73, 432n.53; sacrificial offering of,
92, 314–15, 324–26, 466n.65; and
social connectivity, 49, 52, 54; weighing
of, 30, 75–76, 78, 102–3, 149, 282
Hecataeus of Abdera, 374–75, 378
Heidegger, Martin, 2, 12, 409
Heliopolis, 59, 92, 100, 204, 306, 429
n.19
Hellenistic Period. *See* Graeco-Roman
Period
Hellinger, Bert, 409
Heni, 159–60
Heqmaatrenakht, tomb of, 231
Herodotus, 189–90
Hesat, 345, 348

Hieroglyphs, 375–76; for corpse, 106; for
ka, 44. *See also* Writing
Histories (Herodotus), 189–90
History, and immortality, 11, 414–16
Hnw-gesture, 243
Home, deceased's visits to, 218–21, 450
n.31, 451n.36
Homeland, burial in, 176–82, 444nn.25,
33
Homer, 233
Horace, 376–77
Hornung, Erik, 20, 183–84, 201, 208,
217, 218, 247, 345–46, 394
Horus, 23–25, 103, 169, 203–4, 345;
deceased as, 145–46, 155; Edfu festival
of, 367; and Judgment of the Dead,
76–77; kingship of, 64–65, 135–36; and
mourning, 115; Osiris' social
rehabilitation by, 38, 41–48, 424n.12;
sem-priest as, 303; and Seth's
punishment, 64–69; and wakes, 270,
272–74, 279; and Wepwawet
procession, 227–28
"Horus texts," 42–48, 424n.12
House of Life, 188
Hunefer, Book of the Dead of, 465n.32
Hymns, 242–43, 456n.14

Iamblichus, 245–46
Ikhernofret, stela of, 227–29
Illustrations, book, 250–51
Immortality: *vs.* continuance, 369,
384–88; and cultural memory, 375–79;
and cyclical time, 173–76, 371–72;
desire for, 6, 7–9; through history, 11,
414–16. *See also* Afterlife
Imperfective aspect, 370
*In Bluebeard's Castle: Some Notes Towards the
Redefinition of Culture* (Steiner), 9
Individual self, 14
Initiation, 156, 200–208, 397–98; in
Graeco-Roman Period, 201, 205–6,
207–8
Initiatory examinations, 131–33, 352–55,
472n.10
Instructional texts, 53
Instruction for King Merikare, 55, 73–74,
288, 344, 373–74, 379, 383
Instruction of Any, 13, 15, 163
Instruction of Hardjedef, 13, 17–18, 176,
372–74
Instruction of Ptahhotep, 28, 53, 54–55,
275–76, 381
Inversion: death as, 128–30, 138–40; *vs.*
renewal, 183
Inyotefoqer, tomb of, 328
Isaiah, Book of, 417